Transportation Engineering and Planning

Second Edition

C. S. Papacostas
P. D. Prevedouros
University of Hawaii at Manoa
Honolulu, Hawaii

PRENTICE HALL Englewood Cliffs, NJ 07632

Library of Congress Cataloging-in-Publication Data

Papacostas, C. S.
    Transportation engineering and planning / C.S. Papacostas, P.D.
  Prevedouros.
        p.   cm.
    Rev. ed. of: Fundamentals of transportation engineering. c1987.
    Includes bibliographical references and index.
    ISBN 0-13-958075-1
    1. Transportation engineering.   I. Prevedouros, P. D. (Panos D.),
  1961-   . II. Title.
  TA1145.P33 1993
  388--dc20   92-4428
                                                           CIP

Acquisitions Editor: Doug Humphrey
Production Editor: Joe Scordato
Copy Editor: Barbara Zeiders
Cover Designer: Bruce Kenselaar
Prepress Buyer: Linda Behrens
Manufacturing Buyer: Dave Dickey
Supplements Editor: Alice Dworkin
Editorial Assistant: Jaime Zampino

 © 1993, 1987 by Prentice-Hall, Inc.
A Simon & Schuster Company
Englewood Cliffs, New Jersey 07632

Printed in the United States of America

10 9

ISBN 0-13-958075-1

PRENTICE-HALL INTERNATIONAL (UK) LIMITED, *London*
PRENTICE-HALL OF AUSTRALIA PTY. LIMITED, *Sydney*
PRENTICE-HALL CANADA INC., *Toronto*
PRENTICE-HALL HISPANOAMERICANA, S.A., *Mexico*
PRENTICE-HALL OF INDIA PRIVATE LIMITED, *New Delhi*
PRENTICE-HALL OF JAPAN, INC., *Tokyo*
SIMON & SCHUSTER ASIA PTE. LTD., *Singapore*
EDITORA PRENTICE-HALL DO BRASIL, LTDA., *Rio de Janeiro*

To our parents

Symeon and Loulla Papacostas
Dimitrios and Toula Prevedouros

ABOUT THE AUTHORS

CONSTANTINOS S. PAPACOSTAS

Professor of Civil Engineering, and Graduate Program Chair at the University of Hawaii at Manoa, B.S. 1969, Youngstown State University (Magna Cum Laude), M.S. 1971, Ph.D. 1974, Carnegie-Mellon University (Civil/Transportation). Teaches undergraduate courses in traffic engineering and urban and regional transportation planning, and graduate courses in applications of advanced computer-based techniques to transportation planning and traffic systems simulation. Research work includes transportation planning, air quality, bus operations, traffic safety, driver behavior, and population, energy, and infrastructure systems. Author of numerous articles published in professional journals. Author of the first edition of *Fundamentals of Transportation Engineering* (1987). Awarded the Hawaii ASCE 1990 Outstanding Faculty Award. 1991 President-elect of the Hawaii Chapter of ASCE, and adviser to the UMTA (now FTA), the Oahu MPO, and other local and state agencies. Reviewer for the *Transportation Research Record, Transportation Research*, and *Transportation Quarterly*. Member of AAAS, ASCE, APA, ITE, and TRB. Member of Sigma Tau, Sigma Chi, and Phi Kappa Phi honor societies.

PANOS D. PREVEDOUROS

Assistant Professor of Civil Engineering at the University of Hawaii at Manoa, B.S. 1984, Aristotle University, Greece, M.S. 1987, Ph.D. 1990 Northwestern University (Civil/Transportation). Teaches undergraduate courses in fundamentals of transportation (modes, urban transportation, geometric design, and vehicular flow models), and traffic engineering (systems capacity analysis, traffic impact, and parking studies), and graduate courses in advanced transport demand modeling, and in evaluation of transportation alternatives. Research projects in the area of transport behavior, traffic/transportation modeling, traffic safety, transportation noise, airport operations, and transport-related marketing analysis. Publishes extensively in professional journals. Member of ITE's committee on IVHS, member of several TRB committees, member of Oahu MPO's technical committees, member of the Manoa Writing Program Faculty Board of the University of Hawaii, reviewer for the *Transportation Research Record, Transportation Research*, and *Transportation*, and representative of TRB to the University of Hawaii. Member of ASCE, ASEE, IATB, ITE, and TRB.

Contents

Contents

Preface

The scope of transportation engineering is enormous. Clearly, the tremendous impact that transportation-related decisions have on society cannot be addressed in a single book or in a single course of study. This book provides a solid introduction to the field by covering its major topical areas in a well-organized manner. It is intended to be a learning tool for the novice student of civil engineering or transportation planning. Hence, its pedagogical strategy emphasizes subject continuity and smooth transition. The book begins with what is most familiar to the student and gradually introduces new concepts. These are clearly developed and illustrated by carefully chosen examples, most of which are accompanied by discussions and interpretations of the results. Policy issues, questions relating to management, and the theoretical treatment of methodological subtleties remain in the background.

Great effort has been devoted to enriching and updating the first edition of this most successful transportation engineering book to produce this second edition. New changes were introduced and state-of-the-art tables, figures, and discussions were added. In this edition we present one chapter exclusively on transportation modes, another on urban transportation, and a third on traffic impact and parking studies along with a presentation of traffic simulation and transportation planning software packages. The chapter on flow interruptions (traffic intersections) was greatly expanded to include signalization technologies, signal timings, traffic survey methods, and principles of the analysis of unsignalized intersections. Chapter 2 was enriched with a new section on pavement structures, and Chapter 8 now includes a detailed presentation on transport behavior and modeling. Several organizational changes were also made. Hypothesis and model testing was added to regression modeling and the whole placed in Appendix C.

The theoretical chapter on probability, queuing, and simulation models (Chapter 6 of the first edition) was placed in Appendix D.

We are most appreciative of the dozens of instructors and departments that have chosen to use this book for their transportation classes since it was first published in 1987. We believe that this edition will be even more helpful in providing comprehensive, unbiased, state-of-the-art knowledge on transportation engineering. We are looking forward to your continued support, and as always, your comments and suggestions for improvements are most welcome.

C. S. Papacostas wishes to acknowledge the influence that Joseph S. Drake, his unofficial mentor at Carnegie-Mellon University, has had on his professional development. He is also grateful to Michael Demetsky, professor of civil engineering at the University of Virginia, for reviewing the entire manuscript of the first edition. P. D. Prevedouros wishes to acknowledge the unending support of Northwestern University professors Joseph L. Schofer and Frank S. Koppelman.

We would like to express our gratitude to Ms. Cathy L. Chang, senior associate at Barton-Aschman Associates (Evanston, Illinois) for her careful review of Chapter 9 on traffic impact and parking studies; Mr. William A. Davidson, vice-president at Barton-Aschman Associates (San Jose, California) for supplying us with an educational version of EMME/2; Dr. Alan J. Horowitz, president, AJH Associates (Milwaukee, Wisconsin) for the complimentary copy and updates of QRS II; and Mr. Steven K. L. Fong, president of CCPI (Honolulu, Hawaii) for his most useful remarks on the section on pavement structures. Also, "mahalo" to the hundreds of our students through whom the manuscript was tested and refined over the years.

Finally, we wish to acknowledge the Transportation Research Board for providing the means and accessibility to the ever-expanding and changing body of transportation information and knowledge.

Honolulu, Hawaii   *C. S. Papacostas*
                                                                                             P. D. Prevedouros

Introduction

THE TRANSPORTATION SYSTEM

Definition and Scope

A transportation system may be defined as consisting of the *fixed facilities*, the *flow entities*, and the *control system* that permit *people and goods* to overcome the friction of geographical space *efficiently* in order to *participate* in a *timely* manner in some *desired activity.*

At first glance, this definition may appear to be either trivial or pretentious. After all, "overcoming the friction of geographic space" is a very awkward way of saying "to move from point *A* to point *B*"! However, this definition helps you to appreciate the breadth of transportation engineering and to delineate the purpose and scope of this introductory text. It identifies the functional components of a transportation system (the fixed facilities, the flow entities, and the control system) and encapsulates the fact that transportation provides the connectivity that facilitates other societal interactions.

Fixed Facilities

Fixed facilities are the physical components of the system that are fixed in space and constitute the *network* of *links* (e.g., roadway segments, railway track, pipes) and *nodes* (e.g., intersections, interchanges, transit terminals, harbors, and airports) of the transportation system. Their design, which has traditionally been

1

within the realm of civil engineering, includes soil and foundation engineering, structural design, the design of drainage systems, and *geometric design*, which is concerned with the physical proportioning of the elements of fixed facilities. Although related, geometric design is different from other aspects of design (e.g., structural design, which is concerned with the strength of structures to withstand efficiently the expected forces or loads), which are covered elsewhere in the typical civil engineering curriculum.

Flow Entities and Technology

Flow entities are the units that traverse the fixed facilities. They include vehicles, container units, railroad cars, and so on. In the case of the highway system, the fixed facilities are expected to accommodate a wide variety of vehicle types, ranging from bicycles to large tractor–trailer combinations. For the purposes of geometric design, the American Association of State Highway and Transportation Officials (AASHTO) has specified a set of *design vehicles*, each describing a typical class of highway vehicles [1].

In this book, flow entities are considered only in terms of their generic characteristics (such as size, weight, and acceleration and deceleration capabilities) rather than in terms of their specific technological design, which is normally undertaken by mechanical and electrical engineers. Thus vehicular motion and vehicle flow equations are expressed as general relationships between the generic variables and can be applied to many vehicle technologies once their specific attributes are determined.

Control System

The *control system* consists of *vehicular control* and *flow control*. Vehicular control refers to the technological way in which individual vehicles are guided on the fixed facilities. Such control can be manual or automated. The proper geometric design of the fixed facilities must incorporate, in addition to the characteristics of the vehicle, the characteristics of the vehicular control system. In the case of highway facilities, where the vehicles are manually controlled, these include driver characteristics, such as the time a driver takes to perceive and react to various stimuli; examples of such *human factors* are included in this book. In the case of automated systems, similar but more precisely definable response times exist as well.

The flow control system consists of the means that permit the efficient and smooth operation of streams of vehicles and the reduction of conflicts between vehicles. This system includes various types of signing, marking, and signal systems and the underlying rules of operation. Traffic signal control is discussed in Chapter 5.

Transportation Demand

The definition of a transportation system given earlier addresses another consideration that is of concern to transportation specialists: Transportation systems are constructed neither as pure expressions of engineering ingenuity nor as monuments of purely aesthetic quality. They are built to serve people in undertaking their economic, social, and cultural activities. In the jargon of the economist, the demand for transportation is *derived*, or *indirect*, meaning that people do not normally travel or move their possessions for the sake of movement but to fulfill certain needs, for example, to go to school, to work, to shop, or to visit with friends. By the same token, workers do not place themselves in the middle of the morning and evening rush hours because they enjoy traffic congestion but because their work schedules require it. Transportation engineers are among the professionals concerned with accommodating these societal activities by providing efficient ways to satisfy the population's needs for mobility. As used in the foregoing definition of a transportation system, the word *efficient* stands for the balancing of a variety of often conflicting requirements that society in general considers to be important. These requirements include, but are not limited to, cost considerations, convenience, protection of environmental quality, and protection of individual rights, which may have a variable priority, depending on the issue. To be responsive to these needs, transportation engineers often cooperate with other professionals, including economists, planners, and social scientists.

Quantification versus Valuation

Suppose that the following question was posed to a classical physicist and to an Aristotelian philosopher:

> An object is let go from a height of 20 feet directly above the head of a person. What will the value of the object's velocity be at the instant when it comes in contact with the person's head?

It would not be surprising if after mentally applying the appropriate equation, the classical physicist were to reply: "Well . . . the object's velocity will be about 36 feet per second." However, an engineering student may be somewhat surprised at the philosopher's response along this line: "I believe that, to the person, the object's velocity at that instant will be of no value whatsoever."

The difference between the two answers lies in the meaning that each of the respondents attached to the term "value." The philosopher's use of the word is related to the quality of a thing being useful or desirable to someone or perhaps how much desirable or undesirable. Clearly, the assignment of such value is subjective: It depends on the *value system* of the person making the assessment. On the other hand, the physicist's response involved an attempt to objectively *quantify* the state of the object's velocity, which is independent of the person who attempts to assess it. Of course, the physicist could have given the wrong answer either by using the wrong equation (i.e., not understanding how gravity works) or by making a calculation error when using the right equation.

Engineers often encounter both meanings of value in their work. For example, suppose that an engineer is asked to estimate the reduction in carbon monoxide emissions that would result from a public policy that aims to encourage people to form car pools. Using the best available mathematical formulation of the problem, the engineer would produce an estimate in essentially the same way as the physicist.

Now, consider that the implementation of the public policy requires the expenditure of a certain level of funding and that an estimate of this level has been obtained as objectively as the current understanding of the subject allows. Having quantified these estimates does not in itself reveal whether or not implementation of the policy is desirable. Before such a decision can be made, it is necessary to place relative values on the costs associated with the implementation of the policy and on the benefits that will be derived from it. Simply stated, to make this ''apples-and-oranges'' decision, someone or some group must assess whether reducing pollutant emissions (by x parts per million) is worth the expenditure of y dollars.

In the private sector of the economy, people frequently make such judgments based on their own value systems. By contrast, decisions made in the public sector generally involve compromises between the often-conflicting values of the groups that constitute the community (e.g., those in the construction industry versus environmentalists vis-à-vis the construction of a freeway).

This book emphasizes the basic methods and techniques that are presently available to the practitioner for the purpose of *quantifying* the impacts or consequences of transportation-related proposals. The chapter on *evaluation* includes some techniques that are often used to aid in the selection of the most suitable course of action from a set of alternatives. The real-world application of these evaluative techniques, however, *presupposes* the existence of a value system. Analysts tend to valuate the consequences of transportation proposals based on their analyses of the economic choices of consumers, or other philosophical perspectives. One of the fundamental purposes of government is to provide the mechanism for the resolution of such differences.

TRANSPORTATION SYSTEM CLASSIFICATION

Classification Schemes

Transportation systems can be categorized in several ways. For example, they may be classified according to the types of technology they employ, according to the function or type of service they provide, according to who owns or is responsible for their implementation and operation, and so forth. Each of these diverse typologies views transportation systems from a different perspective and is useful in making distinctions that are relevant to different types of transportation-related decisions.

The definition of the transportation system given earlier makes a distinction between *passenger* and *freight* transportation. Both are needed to satisfy human needs and both constitute a significant portion of the U.S. gross national product (GNP). During the past few decades, the total U.S. expenditures for personal and freight transportation have fluctuated, respectively, around 12% and 8% of the GNP [2].

The transportation system is further categorized into four major subsystems according to the medium on which the flow elements are supported. These subsystems are commonly referred to as *modes*, but it should be understood that this term is also used to make finer distinctions between the various means of travel. For example, driving alone and forming car pools are sometimes considered to be different modes. The four major subsystems are:

1. Land transportation
   a. Highway
   b. Rail
2. Air transportation
   a. Domestic
   b. International
3. Water transportation
   a. Inland
   b. Coastal
   c. Ocean
4. Pipelines
   a. Oil
   b. Gas
   c. Other

Transportation services are also classified as either *for-hire* or *not-for-hire* services. These categories are also known, respectively, as *public* and *private* transportation, but these terms refer to their availability to the general public and to private parties, respectively, not to their ownership. For example, a city bus system may be owned either privately or publicly. In either case, the service provided is public transportation because the system is available for use by the general public. For-hire systems are further classified into *contract carriers* and *common carriers*. The former stand ready to provide service to the public under individual contractual arrangements. Common carriers, on the other hand, generally offer scheduled service and are open to all members of the public willing to pay the posted fare. The terms *mass transportation* or *mass transit* usually refer to the common carriage of passengers. Taxis, car rentals, and certain other individually arranged services belong to the category of contract public transportation. All modes of transportation are presented in detail in Chapter 1.

Urban Transportation Systems

The *intracity* or *urban* distribution of freight is predominantly accomplished by the highway subsystem using vans and trucks of various sizes. The major movements within urban areas are related to the travel undertaken by people. Water-based urban transportation is found in only a few cities, and air transportation is largely unsuited for urban travel. Thus the means of travel available for urban passenger transportation are mainly land-based and include private transportation (walking and private motor vehicles) and various public transportation services, of which some are highway-based (i.e., regular city buses), others are not (e.g., urban rail transit systems). The latter operate on an *exclusive right-of-way* unrestricted from the interference caused by highway vehicles; however, systems that are commonly thought to use *shared right-of-ways*, such as buses, can also operate on exclusive facilities, thus improving their service quality to levels that rival those of certain other exclusive pathway systems. The following brief history of urban transportation is presented to aid the understanding of contemporary terminology.

   Initially, modern-era cities were pedestrian-oriented. Even after the development of mechanized long-distance transportation systems such as railroads, the size of most cities was sufficiently small for people to walk to most places. Private transportation in the form of horseback and animal-drawn carriages was sufficient for longer distances. Public transportation in the form of *sedan chairs* in European cities and *jinrikisha* (rickshaw) in Japan was the exception rather than the rule. The first public transportation service per se has been attributed to the French mathematician Pascal, who in 1662 began to offer a horse-drawn service in Paris. However, horse- and mule-drawn *omnibuses* (derived from "omnis," meaning "all," i.e., offering services to the general public) did not come into their own until the mid-nineteenth century. These services spread widely in Europe and America and remained a major mode of urban public transportation until early in the twentieth century. In 1832, the first horse-drawn rail streetcar began service in Harlem, New York, and portended the eventual replacement of the omnibus (which was driven on cobblestone pavements) by rail-supported *horse-drawn streetcars* that offered a much more comfortable ride. They operated along designated routes in mixed traffic at relatively low speeds and made frequent stops to take on and discharge passengers. Since propulsive power was the greatest limitation of horse-drawn streetcars, alternate power sources were sought. An early contender was the *cable car*, in which the vehicle is propelled by attaching it to a continuously moving cable. The cable is kept in motion by a stationary source of power. One of the most famous cable car systems opened in San Francisco in 1873, and a few cable car systems are extant to this day, mostly at special locations such as steep inclines and ore mines. Experimentation with the steam engine also occurred, but the major power-supply breakthrough came late in the nineteenth century in the form of rail-supported *electric streetcars*, which received their power from overhead wires. At about the same time, intercity railroads began to extend their lines into a few major central cities like London and Boston. These urban extensions are known as *commuter railroads*, since their urban service is confined to moving commuters between suburban areas and the city during the morning and evening peak hours. Unlike the typical streetcar lines, these heavy rail systems offered limited express service without many intermediate stops and operated on their own rights-of-way. The superior service of these exclusive pathway lines encouraged the development of heavy rail *rapid-transit systems* that were capable of moving large numbers of passengers quickly within the elsewhere congested city. The first underground steam engine rapid-transit line opened in London in 1863, and the first elevated urban railroad line, also using steam, was inaugurated in New York City 5 years later. Both cities subsequently converted their systems to electricity. Many large, high-density cities followed suit. Most other cities relied exclusively on electric streetcar lines.

The next chapter in the evolution of transportation in general and public transportation in particular belongs to the adaptation of the internal combustion engine to motorized transportation. In the area of urban public transportation, the *motor bus* began to make inroads into the electric-streetcar market around 1920. Coupled with an increasing willingness of government to support the construction of streets and highways and with comparatively low fuel costs, the city bus emerged victorious over the electric streetcar, in some instances after a transition to the hybrid *trolley bus*, which operated on rubber tires but gathered its power from overhead wires. The conversion to city buses occurred despite a courageous attempt by the Electric Railways Presidents Conference Committee (PCC) in the 1930s to systematically develop a superior streetcar, the marvelous PCC car. The same technology that replaced the electric streetcar also marked the beginning of the demise of its successor, the city bus, and public transportation in general. The source of this demise was the private automobile, which attracted patronage from public-transportation systems. To add insult to injury, a few entrepreneurs even began to use their automobiles to offer competing for-hire services by seeking customers at transit stops. These *jitney* services are undoubtedly the precursors of the modern *taxi*, which now operates in a regulated environment.

During the 1960s, several societal changes encouraged a reevaluation of the automobile-based urban system and led to a revision of the hencetofore highway-oriented federal transportation policy to include support for the improvement, research, and development of public-transportation systems. The following are terms found in this technical literature in this connection.*

Rapid transit: refers to all exclusive right-of-way systems. To clarify other technological differences, modifiers such as heavy rail, light rail, fixed guideway,

---

* Further discussion of specific technologies that belong to these overlapping categories may be found in the technical literature (e.g., [3–12]).

personal, and bus are prefixed to "rapid transit." Light rail transit and buses can be operated in mixed traffic and as rapid-transit modes. *Personal rapid transit* (PRT) refers to systems that operate on exclusive pathways employing small vehicles to allow for frequent service and scheduling flexibility; they may be described as "horizontal elevators."

Fixed-guideway transit: systems in which the vehicles are affixed to a guideway and include *dual-rail* systems, *monorail* systems of various types, rubber-tired systems that are attached to the guideway either on the side of the vehicle or on a third rail, and so forth. *Automated guideway transit* (AGT) refers to fixed-guideway systems that operate without the intervention of an on-board operator; they may or may not be PRT systems.

Articulated systems: systems in which flow units can be connected to form trains. An *articulated bus* is a long bus that consists of two sections connected by a flexible joint, also known as a *bandy bus* from the German word for tapeworm (bandwurm).

Dual-mode systems: systems in which vehicles can operate on the street under manual control and on automated guideways. Two types of automated operation have been proposed. The first employs a guideway consisting of moving pallets on which vehicles of various types may be carried, and the second uses vehicles with a secondary electric motor that may be attached to the power source of the automated guideway. *Automated highways* have also been proposed.

Demand-responsive systems: systems that enjoy flexibility in route or time scheduling or both to respond to the actual demand placed on them. These systems represent an attempt to rival the flexibility of the private automobile, in contrast to the traditional *fixed route–fixed schedule* transit systems. Taxis are naturally demand responsive but other systems have also been developed, including *dial-a-ride* and prescheduled systems that allow for the dispatching and rerouting of common carriers to serve temporally changing demands. These types of *paratransit* systems have found applicability as specialized services for elderly and handicapped person.

The characteristics of urban transportation systems are presented in detail in Chapter 6.

THE ROLE OF GOVERNMENT

Governmental Participation

A characteristic of human social organizations is the establishment of a "government," which—in an impartial sense—may be defined as consisting of the rules of conduct, the collective decision-making processes, and the means of enforcing the rules that attempt to impart social and economic order and to maintain the cohesiveness of a society.

A transportation system provides the necessary connectivity that enhances the interaction between people. It is a historical fact that, by facilitating the movement of peoples and the spreading of ideas, advances in transportation technology have been closely related to the evolution of civilization as we know it. Since ancient times, cities have developed in locations that took advantage of the availability of transportation connections such as rivers and protected harbors. The Roman Empire was held together by a very elaborate system of roadways, some of which (e.g., the Appian Way) remain to the present day. Catanese and Snyder [13] state that in eighteenth-century England,

> transportation was the key to industrialization. Unless raw materials could be brought to the factories and finished products distributed to market areas, the industrial revolution could not happen.

Similarly, the westward expansion in nineteenth-century America would not have been possible without the construction of the transcontinental railroads; many modern American cities have had their origins at the junctures of railroad lines. Because of the profound role that transportation plays in society, governments have always become involved in the provision, operation, and regulation of transportation systems through the enactment of laws and through the establishment of public planning processes.

The specific actions that a government takes at any given time as well as the method by which it chooses to implement those actions reflect the contemporary value system of the society it represents. Conceptually, there exists a continuum of governmental forms ranging from anarchy (i.e., complete lack of governmental intervention in the affairs of people) to totalitarianism (i.e., complete control by government). Actual governmental structures lie somewhere between the two extremes.

The U.S. governmental structure places a high value on individual freedom and civil rights. Individuals and groups are permitted to pursue what they consider to be in their best interests. They are also afforded relatively greater opportunities to vie with others in persuading the government to take actions favoring what they value. Citizen participation is, in fact, a requirement of public planning law [14]. Dissent and difference of opinion are tolerated and permitted to find expression in the political arena.

Instruments of Governmental Involvement

In rough outline, the typical ways by which the government intervenes in the market place to accomplish objectives that, in its representational role, it finds to be in the public interest include *soft promotion, regulation,* and *investment.* Incidentally, at any given time, the meaning of the term *public interest* is largely implicit in the specific actions that the government takes and thus is itself in a state of flux. Also, differences of opinion as to what is in the public interest frequently arise.

Soft promotion refers to attempts by the government to encourage or to discourage certain situations without legally requiring them. An advertising campaign favoring carpooling aimed at reducing rush-hour congestion and obviating the need for costly highway construction or as a strategy to reduce energy consumption is an example of soft promotion.

Regulation refers to those government actions that place legal requirements on individuals and firms to satisfy the public interest. Transportation-related examples of regulation include the establishment of automobile bumper standards to reduce fatalities, automobile air-pollution-emission standards to improve environmental quality, and engine-efficiency standards to conserve energy. Other examples include the regulation of airline route structures to ensure the availability of service to all and the regulation of the rates that trucking companies can charge their customers.

Investment involves the financial support, public financing, or even public ownership of various systems or services. Subsidies to privately owned bus companies to ensure service to mobility-disadvantaged groups, public ownership of highways to maintain a comprehensive level of accessibility, and participation in the construction of airports and harbors are but a few examples of investment actions.

TOOLS AND APPLICATIONS

The typical program of study leading to the first course in transportation engineering includes the basic sciences, mathematics, and computer programming. The subject matter of those courses of study stresses the basic tools needed for work in the field of engineering. The latter differs from the pure sciences in that it is more concerned with the *application* of scientific knowledge. When seeking solutions to real-world problems, attendant questions of economy and other considerations prescribe a need to employ appropriate simplifying assumptions. In order to be useful, such simplifications must render a problem amenable to efficient solution while retaining the essential aspects of the postulated situation. The importance of making judicious assumptions that are based on a clear understanding of the problem at hand cannot be overemphasized. These assumptions are based on the current state of the art and are themselves subject to change as our understanding of systems is enhanced through additional experience and research. The student should always be attentive to the fundamental assumptions that are involved in a particular situation and the extent to which these assumptions can affect the results.

Mathematical Models

Transportation engineers and planners employ models to study and analyze the systems of concern. A *model* may be defined as the representation of a part of reality. Figure 1 shows that models may be classified as *physical* or *mathematical* on one hand and as *static* or *dynamic* on the other [15]. Static models represent the structure of a system, whereas dynamic models also incorporate a representation of the system's process, that is, the way in which it changes over time. The familiar models of molecular structures are examples of physical static models. Physical dynamic models include wind tunnels, where facsimiles of systems based on the laws of similitude are tested before implementation. Such models also include models relying on analogy, such as those representing the vibration of a mechanism via an equivalent electrical circuit (see Fig. 2). *Analog computers* are well suited for this type of modeling. It is interesting to recognize that the two diagrams shown in Fig. 2 are, in fact, static representations of a mechanical and an electrical system. When constructed, the electrical circuit can be used as a physical dynamic model of the mechanical system.

A mathematical model employs one or more equations to represent a system and its behavior. Thus Newton's second law and Bernoulli's equation are examples of mathematical models. In addition to being either static or dynamic, mathematical models may be classified according to the method of solution employed, for example, analytical or numerical. Numerical models have proliferated in recent years because they are amenable to solution by *digital computers*.

All models are abstractions of the systems they represent. In other words, a system and its model are not identical in all respects: The model is a simplified

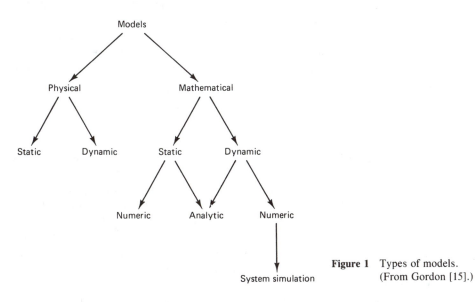

Figure 1 Types of models. (From Gordon [15].)

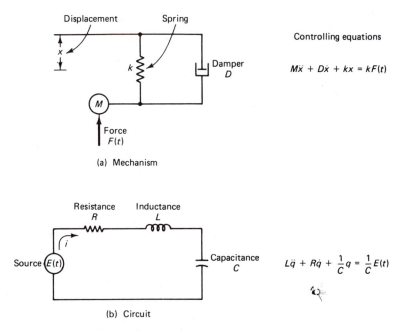

Figure 2   Model analogy. (From Gordon [15].)

representation of the system. Consequently, a number of different models can be used to describe the same system. The appropriate model to a particular endeavor should be selected in such a way as to strike a balance between ease of application on one hand and realistic representation of the subject system on the other. For example, Newton's theory is sufficiently accurate for the cases examined in engineering mechanics to be given preference over the more complicated theory of relativity. The same is not true, however, for the study of interplanetary motion.

Components of Mathematical Models

A mathematical model can have one of an infinite number of mathematical forms. It can be linear, nonlinear, exponential, differential and so forth. Most of the mathematical models with which the student is conversant have been simply presented to the student and, therefore, the fact that someone (usually the person whose name is associated with the model) had to *postulate* its mathematical form possibly remains obtuse. Researchers are constantly faced with the problem of model postulation, and in many situations, including certain areas of transportation engineering, analysts are also required to select the mathematical forms of their models.

Selecting a mathematical form, however, is not the same as having a useful model. Consider, for example, the following mathematical form relating four variables, X, Y, Z, and W:

$$Y = a\,X^b Z^c W^d \tag{1}$$

In this equation, variable Y is a function of the other three. In other words, Y can be computed if the numerical values of X, Z, and W are known. For this reason Y is called the *dependent*, or *explained*, variable and the other three are called the *independent*, or *explanatory*, variables. The model also contains four constants, a, b, c, and d, that must also be known. These constants are referred to as the *parameters* of the model.

Model calibration is the process by which the numerical values of the parameters of a postulated model are determined. It is usually accomplished through the use of statistical methods and is based on *experimental* knowledge of the dependent and independent variables. This means that, once the nature of the variables is identified, a series of experiments are conducted to obtain a set of N simultaneous observations on the dependent and independent variables, in our case, Y_i, X_i, Z_i, W_i, with i varying from 1 to N. These observations are then employed to estimate the numerical values of the model parameters that render the postulated model capable of reproducing the experimental data. To avoid misspecification of the mathematical form that relates the variables, alternative functions may be postulated and calibrated. After several goodness-of-fit tests, the one that best describes the experimental data can then be selected. In this manner, it is ensured that the selected model is realistic.

Model validation refers to the testing of a calibrated model using empirical data other than those used to calibrate the model in the first place. This is how scientific theories (models) are tested, modified, or replaced. An improved model must be able to explain everything that the old model can plus something that the old model cannot. As mentioned earlier, the old model may still be a useful tool as long as the scope of its applicability is understood.

To comprehend the importance of the modeling steps above, consider that X and Z in Eq. 1 stand for the masses M_1 and M_2 of two bodies, W stands for the distance R separating them, and the dependent variable Y represents their mutual attraction force F. Moreover, assume that the calibration of this postulate vis-à-vis experimental observations has resulted in the following numerical values of the model's parameters:

$$a = K = 3.442(10^{-8})\,\frac{\text{ft}^4}{\text{lb-s}^4}$$

$$b = c = 1 \quad \text{and} \quad d = -2$$

Equation 1 becomes

$$F = \frac{KM_1M_2}{R^2} \tag{2}$$

which is Newton's law of gravitation.

Transportation Models

The study of many engineering subjects, most appropriately, tends to concentrate on systems of physical objects under the influence of forces. Stripped to its essentials, the transportation system involves a physical phenomenon, the motion of flow entities on the fixed facilities. Hence mathematical *models of the physical system* are required, including the equations of motion.

Additionally, transportation engineering must explicitly incorporate the human dimension, which consists of *human factors* and *human behavior*. As used in this book, the term "human factors" refers to those measurable characteristics of human beings that are relatively difficult to modify, such as sensory, perceptual, and kinesthetic characteristics. A driver's perception-reaction time that elapses between the instant when a stimulus is first displayed (e.g., the onset of the amber phase of a traffic signal) and the instant when a driver reacts to the stimulus (e.g., applying the brakes) is a specific example of a human factor that can be measured either in the field or in the laboratory. *Human-factor models* are needed in addition to models of the physical transportation system.

The line of demarcation between human factors and human behavior is not very clear. Nevertheless, the use of the term *human behavior* in this book will generally refer to the way in which people act, the types of choices they make, and so forth. Specifically, this book is concerned with *travel behavior*, which includes the way people decide whether and when to travel, where to go, how to get there, and the like. The transportation analyst's arsenal of mathematical models includes *models of human behavior*. Human behavior is in a continuous state of flux and is affected by technological changes: The behavioral patterns of the ancient Greeks were very different from those of modern Americans, but the range of visual perception of the two populations has remained about the same. In fact, no universally applicable calibrated model of travel behavior exists. Even when using the same mathematical form, transportation studies for different cities must calibrate the forms to conform to local conditions.

SUMMARY

In this introduction we have defined a transportation system in terms of its fixed facilities, flow entities, and control system and identified its general function as that of providing the necessary connectivity that facilitates other societal activities. A brief outline of several transportation classification schemes for intercity and urban systems followed. The means by which government participates in the transportation sector (i.e., promotion, regulation, and investment) were presented to place transportation engineering within its larger societal context. The fundamental concepts of mathematical modeling (i.e., model postulation, calibration, and validation) were presented and the three categories of quantitative models used by transportation engineers (i.e., models of the physical system, human factor models, and travel behavior models) were explained. A distinction between quantification and valuation was also drawn.

REFERENCES

1 AMERICAN ASSOCIATION OF STATE HIGHWAY AND TRANSPORTATION OFFICIALS, *A Policy on Geometric Design of Highways and Streets*, AASHTO, Washington, D.C., 1984.

2 TRANSPORTATION POLICY ASSOCIATES, *Transportation in America, A Statistical Analysis of Transportation in the United States*, 2nd ed., TPA, Washington, D.C., 1984.

3 VUCHIC, VUKAN R., *Urban Public Transportation Systems and Technology*, Prentice Hall, Englewood Cliffs, N.J., 1981.

4 WATKINS, R. A., et al., *Urban Transportation Planning System Lexicon*, Report UMTA-UPM20-81-1, prepared by Rock Creek Associates for the U.S. Department of Transportation: Urban Mass Transportation Administration, Washington, D.C., 1981.

5 HIGHWAY RESEARCH BOARD, *Demand-Actuated Transportation Systems*, Special Report 124, National Research Council, Washington, D.C., 1971.

6 IRVING, JACK H., ed. and principal author, *Fundamentals of Personal Rapid Transit*, Lexington Books, Lexington, Mass., 1978.

7 TRANSPORTATION RESEARCH BOARD, *Dual Mode Transportation*, Special Report 170, National Research Council, Washington, D.C., 1976.

8 ———, *Light Rail Transit*, Special Report 161, National Research Council, Washington, D.C., 1975.

9 ———, *Light Rail Transit: Planning and Technology*, Special Report 182, National Research Council, Washington, D.C., 1978.

10 ———, *Light Rail Transit: Policy, Design, and Implementation*, Special Report 195, National Research Council, Washington, D.C., 1982.

11 ———, *Paratransit*, Special Report 164, National Research Council, Washington, D.C., 1976.

12 ———, *Better Use of Existing Transportation Facilities*, Special Report 153, National Research Council, Washington, D.C., 1975.

13 CATANESE, A. J., and J. C. SNYDER, eds., *Introduction to Urban Planning*, McGraw-Hill, New York, 1979

14 TRANSPORTATION RESEARCH BOARD, *Citizen Participation in Transportation Planning*, Special Report 142, National Research Council, Washington, D.C., 1973.

15 GORDON, G., *System Simulation*, 2nd ed., Prentice Hall, Englewood Cliffs, N.J., 1978.

1

Transportation Modes

1.1 INTRODUCTION

In this chapter we provide an overview of the basic characteristics of major transportation modes, some of which are illustrated in Fig. 1.1.1. The presentation is focused on the transportation industry in the United States. Motor carriers (trucking industry), railroads, pipelines, domestic and international water carriers, air carriers, and forwarders are presented, followed by intercity passenger transportation providers. Basic service and cost characteristics are discussed for each carrier or industry, along with their respective advantages and disadvantages.

Certain definitions are presented below to facilitate the reader of this chapter. The total cost of owning and operating a company, including transportation companies, is usually broken into fixed and variable costs. Fixed costs do not relate to production or utilization of equipment. Aircraft, trucks, trains, computers, and offices cost a fixed amount of money (purchase or lease price) no matter what the degree of utilization (i.e., from idle to around-the-clock utilization, the fixed cost remains the same). Variable costs, on the other hand, tend to be proportional to the degree of utilization. The more the equipment is utilized, the more labor that is necessary to operate them, the more fuel that is necessary to produce propulsion, and the more maintenance that is required, due to the increased wear and tear. All costs tend to become variable in the long term (5 years or more) as corporations expand or reduce their activities (increase or decrease of fixed facilities, equipment, and operations).

The absolute magnitude of the fixed cost and the magnitude of the variable

Figure 1.1.1 Major transportation modes.

cost relative to the fixed cost determine the existence of economies of scale. In simple terms, when economies of scale are present, production increases lower the cost per unit and increase the profit per unit. Economies of scale exist when first, the fixed cost is high (thus the more the units over which it is spread, the lower the cost per unit), and second, the variable cost is small compared with the fixed cost. The existence of economies of scale (EOS) is depicted in Fig. 1.1.2.

When EOS are not present, the cost per unit does not change substantially

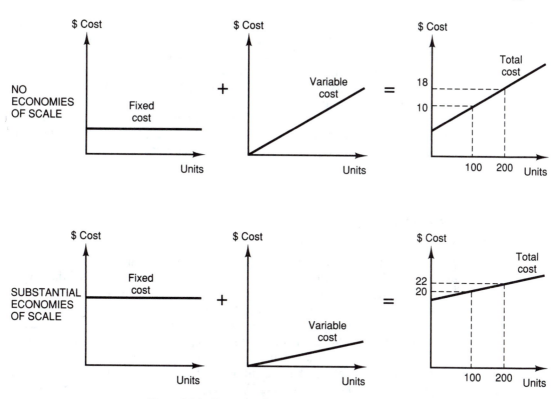

Figure 1.1.2   Example of the principles of economies of scale.

as the number of units produced (or transported) increases:

$$\text{100 units transported:}\quad \frac{10}{100} = \$0.10 \text{ cost per unit}$$

$$\text{200 units transported:}\quad \frac{18}{200} = \$0.09 \text{ cost per unit}$$

A 10% decrease in the cost per unit is observed.

In contrast, when EOS are present, the cost per unit decreases substantially as the number of units produced (or transported) increases:

$$\text{100 units transported:}\quad \frac{20}{100} = \$0.20 \text{ cost per unit}$$

$$\text{200 units transported:}\quad \frac{22}{200} = \$0.11 \text{ cost per unit}$$

A 45% decrease in the cost per unit is observed.

Transportation carriers can be private or for-hire. Private carriers are usually the transportation subsidiary of a large manufacturing industry. They carry only materials and goods of a specific manufacturer. For-hire carriers are further categorized into common and contract. Common carriers serve the general public, often on a first-come, first-served basis. Contract carriers provide services to the public on a contract basis only. For-hire carriers can be either regulated or exempt from economic regulation, depending on the types of products they carry. Transportation of agricultural commodities is exempt from regulation by the Interstate Commerce Commission (ICC), which supervises and regulates the trade among states.

1.2 MOTOR CARRIERS

Motor carriers (trucking industry) constitute the most ubiquitous mode of freight transportation. The extensive roadway network is the major cause of the popularity and efficiency of this mode (Fig. 1.2.1). Motor carriers have the major advantage of being able to provide door-to-door service to both the shipper and the receiver or consignee. The truck is the most common local delivery mode.

The structure of this industry is rather complex. There are for-hire and private carriers. For-hire carriers may be licensed to operate locally or regionally (intercity), each of which can be exempt or regulated. Intercity-regulated carriers can be common or contract carriers. The common carriers may serve regular or irregular routes and transport general or special commodities, depending on the type of operating certificate they posses. Examples of national motor carriers are Yellow Freight, Consolidated Freightways, North American Van Lines, and Roadway.

Motor carriers transport a variety of goods and provide a multitude of services, such as armored truck service, agricultural commodities, building materials,

Figure 1.2.1 Trucks are a small volume, low weight, fast and flexible mode of transportation.

dump trucking, forest products, hazardous materials, heavy machinery, household goods, moving services, petroleum products, refrigerated goods, rental services, retail store items, and vehicles. In 1989, the industry accounted for 25.4% of the total intercity freight tonnage but 60.5% of the respective revenues [1.1]. The average intercity haul is approximately 300 mi.

The major advantages of this mode of transportation are high speed and high accessibility. Limitations in volume and weight are the principal disadvantages, and the rates charged are less competitive compared with the railroads, particularly for heavy hauls over 1000 mi or more. Truck transportation is certainly faster than railroad transportation, and in many cases it is faster than air transportation for hauls up to 1000 mi, due to the limited flight schedule and the pickup and delivery times incurred by air cargo carriers. Additional advantages are the relatively smooth ride and timely delivery, which makes this type of transportation appropriate for delicate or high-value products (i.e., produce, electronic equipment). The high level of integration of motor carriers with all other modes of transportation is another advantage of this industry. Motor carriers link transportation terminals (i.e., ports and docks, airports, railroad yards) with shippers or receivers.

This industry is characterized by low fixed (management, overhead, vehicle fleet) and high variable costs (drivers, fuel, maintenance, insurance, tires, licenses, fleet depreciation). There are no economies of scale in this industry as there are for railroads and pipelines (Sections 1.3 and 1.4). There are, however, economies of utilization (i.e., large companies tend to utilize terminals and management specialists at a higher rate), as well as economies of equipment (i.e., volume discounts for the purchase of vehicles, parts, tires, and insurance).

Competition in this industry is strong, as evidenced by the large number of companies in existence (569,000 in 1983 [1.2]). This is due largely to the fact that the cost of entering the industry is low; financed purchase of a truck is sufficient, with the right-of-way, roads, and highway infrastructure provided by the general public. Motor carriers remit only a user fee. Many argue that motor carriers do not pay their fair share of the bill for the maintenance and repairs of roadway facilities, because heavy vehicles may cause most of the damage to pavement and bridges. This issue is explained in Section 2.5.

Some details of motor carrier operations, specifically truck loadings, terminals, and types of equipment, are noteworthy. Two common truck loading schemes are truckload (TL) and less-than-truckload (LTL). In the former, one shipment or part of one shipment occupies all cargo capacity, while in the latter, either smaller shipments are consolidated to the truck's capacity at a terminal, or small shipments are picked up on the way until the truck's capacity is reached.

Three main types of terminals facilitate the movement of freight by trucks: (1) consolidation terminals, where shipments are sorted and consolidated to form truck loads to specific destinations; (2) break-bulk, where large shipments are partitioned for distribution; and (3) relay terminals, where drivers are relieved, while the trucks continue with other drivers, given the existing regulation, which requires 8 h of rest following every 10 h of duty.

Various vehicle and cargo space configurations are available. The general vehicle form varies from a regular two-axle truck (35 to 50 ft long) to twin trailers (70 to 110 ft long), while the cargo space can be configured as dry van (all sides enclosed), open top, flatbed, tank, refrigerated container, or other cargo-tailored configurations.

1.3 RAILROADS

In the United States, railroads (railroad corporations) are mostly common carriers. There are a handful of private railroads and there is only one intercity passenger railroad, Amtrak, the operation of which is subsidized by the federal government. Amtrak was formed in 1971 with purchases of failing passenger services of railroad companies. Commuter railroads and rail rapid transit serving urban areas are presented in Chapter 6.

Until 1830, settlements and developments in the United States occurred mostly along coastal and waterway regions.† Railroads are responsible for opening the horizon to the western United States. Railroads reached their golden era between 1850 and 1880. Since then, they have experienced continuous decline. There were 186 major (class I) railroads in 1920, and only 31 in 1984 [1.3]. A similar trend was observed for the total miles of line in use, which declined from 235,000 mi in 1939 to 165,000 mi in 1982 [1.4]. The railroad industry, however, still plays a vital role in the nation's transportation supply: in 1982 it accounted for 37.3% of the total intercity freight traffic and 25.1% of the respective revenues [1.1]. In 1982, based on annual revenue figures, the five largest railroads in the nation were Norfolk Southern/Santa Fe, CSX, Burlington Northern, Union Pacific, and Conrail [1.5].

The railroad industry serves all the contiguous U.S. states, but individual railroad companies serve specific regions. Interregional shipments are switched among railroads at interchange points. This service characteristic tends to create rate discontinuities as well as delays in delivery. The large geographic coverage and carrying capacity of railroads as well as the low cost of transportation charged are the major advantages of this mode. Another advantage of railroads is that they are more energy efficient and friendlier to the environment in terms of energy used and pollution emitted per ton-mile carried, compared with their arch-rival, the motor carriers.

Railroads are more suited to transport large-volume or high-weight and low-value commodities such as coal, grain, oil and chemical products, pulp and paper

---

† A comprehensive historical background of railroads is presented in Section 7.2.3.

products, forest products, and manufactured products such as vehicles, machinery, parts, and equipment (Fig. 1.3.1). The average haul is 660 mi [1.1].

Various types of railcars are used for transportation: boxcars for general commodities, tankers for liquids and gases, hoppers for bulk materials, and flat cars. Flat cars are used for the transportation of containers (COFC: container on flat car) and trailers (TOFC: trailer on flat car). COFCs and TOFCs have increased the integration between the railroad and the motor carrier industry to provide intermodal transportation; railroads transport over the long haul, while trucks provide pickup and delivery service between the clients and the railroad line exchange points (terminals). The railroads' ownership of a fixed right-of-way (ROW) poses a service constraint that makes door-to-door service infeasible unless both shipper and receiver have side rail lines or rail yards along the railroad mainline.

The railroad industry is characterized by high fixed costs since they own and maintain their ROW (trackage, bridges, tunnels, switches), terminals (switching yards, interchanges, maintenance and storage facilities), and rolling stock (locomotives, cars, repair machinery). Their variable costs are relatively low; they include labor, fuel, electricity, insurance, taxes, depreciation, and equipment maintenance and upgrading. Consequently, substantial economies of scale are present in this industry since increases in volume carried are accompanied by relatively low increases in costs.

Worsening financial status as well as benefits from economies of scale fueled the tendency for consolidations and mergers. As a result, by 1984 the 10 largest railroads transported 94% of the total freight carried by the entire railroad industry. Also, automation and computerization has helped this industry overcome major problems of car availability and distribution (i.e., having the right number and type of cars wherever needed) as well as empty backhaul (i.e., cars become available after being transported empty from somewhere else, which is an inefficient operation) [1.6].

Figure 1.3.1   Railroads are a large volume and high weight mode of transportation. (From *1987 Annual Report*, CSX Corporation.)

1.4 PIPELINES

Pipelines provide mainly an underground form of transportation; they are often referred to as the hidden giants of the freight transportation industry (Fig. 1.4.1) This is because pipelines are both largely unknown to the general public, and they transport a large share of the intercity freight traffic (i.e., 21.3% of the total ton-miles in 1989 but only 6.1% of the respective revenues [1.1]).

Pipelines have certain unique characteristics. First they transport a very limited variety of commodities which must be in liquid form; second, they have a limited geographic coverage; and third, they have no backhaul movement (i.e., one-way transportation only). Pipeline corporations are mostly for-hire common carriers, although there are a few private carriers. They operate through a network of trunk (large diameter, long haul) and gathering (smaller diameter, distribution) lines. Trunk lines are laid underground, while gathering lines are often laid on the surface of the ground.

Typical products carried by pipelines are natural gas, crude oil, petroleum products, liquid chemical products, and coal slurry (crushed coal mixed with water). The average haul is approximately 610 mi [1.1]. Usually, a minimum of 500 barrels (1 barrel equals 42 U.S. gallons) is required for shipment, and rates are on a per barrel basis. Pipeline rates are extremely low; for example, in 1983, 1 gallon of crude oil could be sent from Texas to New York for 1.8 cents [1.7]. Only ocean supertankers can match the cost per barrel charged by pipelines.

The number of pipeline companies is limited largely because of the high capital costs required for establishing a pipeline service. These costs include the purchase or lease of land, construction of the pipeline(s) and pumping stations, control infrastructure, and terminal facilities. On the other hand, variable costs, which include mostly labor, administration, and insurance, are relatively low. For example, the Transalaskan Pipeline, which is among the few federally owned and operated pipelines, was built between 1974 and 1977 at a cost exceeding $9 billion, yet a labor force of 450 is sufficient to operate it [1.8].

Figure 1.4.1 Pipelines are a liquids only, very large volume but one-way only mode of transportation. (From *1987 Annual Report*, CSX Corporation.)

The high fixed and low variable costs result in strong economies of scale for this industry. Financial interests tend to consolidate and start with a large initial investment, which tends to yield higher payoffs, partly because of economies of scale and partly because of inherent performance characteristics (i.e., a 12-in. pipe operating at capacity transports three times the liquid transported by an 8-in. pipe [1.2]). A typical trunk-line diameter is 30 in.

Sophisticated monitoring of facilities with computers as well as insignificant influence by the elements result in minimal loss and damage (i.e., quick detection of leaks) and in highly reliable delivery schedules. The only negative characteristic is the slow service, which actually has positive implications: The high accuracy and reliability of forecasted delivery times diminish the need for safety stock at the receiving end, while in essence pipelines offer free storage for as long as the order is on the way to delivery.

1.5 WATER TRANSPORTATION

Water transportation is the oldest form of mass freight transportation over seas or long distances (Fig. 1.5.1). Traditionally, vibrant economic and industrial centers as well as population settlements were developed around ports, harbors, lakes, and navigable rivers. At present, water transportation is an important mode for shipping raw materials, crude oil, and manufactured products among domestic and international points of trade.

Inland and coastal water transportation accounted for 15.7% of the total intercity ton-miles of freight in 1984, and only 0.9% of the respective revenues [1.1]. Barges are the primary vessels of inland water transportation. Due to the growth of multinational firms, foreign investment, reduced trade barriers and sales opportunities, ocean-borne trade has been steadily increasing over the past two decades. Deep-sea water transportation includes shipments across the seas and

Figure 1.5.1 Water transportation is a very large volume and tonnage mode of transportation. (From *1987 Annual Report*, CSX Corporation.)

between coastal areas. Common vessels used are liners (containers and break-bulk shipments), nonliners (bulk bottom), and tankers. International water carriers originate from or are destined to a port outside the United States.

The structure of the domestic water carrier industry is similar to that of the motor carrier industry. Domestic water carriers are either for-hire or private. The former can be either regulated or exempt—carrying bulk commodities. For-hire, regulated water carriers are either common or contract. Domestic water carriers operate in three distinct areas: (1) inland navigable waterways, mostly rivers and canals; (2) great lakes; and (3) coastal ports. Waterway and lake service is occasionally affected by ice formation and drought.

Water transportation offers in general low-cost but slow service. Domestically operating carriers transport at a speed of approximately 5 mi/h upstream and 10 mi/h downstream along the Mississippi river and its tributaries. Both the shipper and the receiver need to have access to the waterway or port; otherwise, connections with railroads or motor carriers are necessary. Since the capacity of vessels exceeds the capacity of rail cars and trucks by far, warehousing must be provided for storage. Specifically, the capacity of one 1500-ton barge is equivalent to 15 jumbo hopper rail cars or 60 semitrailer trucks, while the equivalent of the capacity of a 22,500-ton vessel is 225 railcars or 900 semitrailer trucks [1.9].

Typical products carried by domestic water carriers are coal, coke, iron, steel, grains, lumber, sand, gravel, stone, chemicals, petroleum products, paper, and waste and scrap material. Ocean vessels transport beverages, coffee, grain and foods, oil, petroleum products and chemicals, machinery, automobiles, and consumer products. Usually, freight is subjected to multiple handlings and to rough waters; therefore, expensive protective packaging is necessary for certain types of shipments.

The domestic waterway transportation industry is characterized by low fixed and high variable costs. Casualty and insurance is a substantial part of the variable costs; they are necessary to cover loss and damage from the elements of nature. Part of the reason for the low fixed cost is that water carriers operate in free (deep-sea operations) or publicly financed (waterways, ports) media. Often, private firms handling large amounts of commodities or special shipments invest in building docks and terminals.

By contrast, the fixed costs of deep-sea operations are substantially higher than those of inland water operations, and strong economies of ship utilization persist. Given that a ship generates revenue only when it travels with a load, empty backhauls and long docking times become costly. This is part of the reason that containerization and mechanization of port operations became popular: Dock times for loading and unloading of 3 days or more have been reduced to less than half a day with the use of containers.

Water transportation is second least labor intensive. The respective million ton-miles per employee for 1989 in the industries we examined are as follows: 0.47 for motor carriers, 3.55 for railroads, 5.37 for water carriers, and 17.1 for pipelines [1.1].

Domestic water carriers compete with railroads for the shipment of dry, bulk commodities and with pipelines for the shipment of liquid commodities. The rates of international water carriers, primarily ocean liners, are set by cartel-like bodies called steamship conferences. This arrangement hinders competition but offers stability with respect to fluctuating international currencies, which is an issue of paramount importance in international trading. Tariffs (charges) are usually made on a weight or measure (W/M) basis; the shipment is charged according to the largest between the weight ton and the cubic ton (40 ft^3).

Due to benefits in taxes, labor, and safety requirements, ships are registered in countries that provide such shelters and economic benefits to shipowners. Liberia and Panama provide the so-called "flags of convenience."

Three noteworthy types of ocean vessels are the following: (1) liners, which follow fixed routes and schedules and charge according to published tariffs, a special type of liner being the RORO ship (roll on, roll off), which carries vehicles and rolling equipment (i.e., construction equipment) much like a ferryboat; (2) tramp ships, which can be hired, rented, or leased on a short-term basis, much like a taxi or a rental car; and (3) private ships that are owned or leased on a long-term basis, tankers being prime examples.

Ports and docks are usually owned and operated by port authorities, the largest of which is PANYNJ (Port Authority of New York and New Jersey). These authorities provide comprehensive planning and development through their ability to make substantial investments as well as to promote trade, political support, and integration of industrial and shipping activities.

1.6 AIR CARRIERS

Historically, air travel is the latest developed mode of transportation. After the inauguration of the first commercial flight, air travel has been growing steadily. The worldwide expected growth in air travel from 1989 to 1998 will be as high as 5.6% per annum [1.10]. The major explanation of this growth is the speed and convenience provided by this mode: The farthest points on earth are accessible in a matter of hours (Fig. 1.6.1).

The structure of this industry is simple. Air carriers are either private or for-hire. For-hire carriers are classified according to their size or according to the type of service they provide. Size is determined by the annual revenues; three types are recognized (examples in parentheses): majors (American, United), nationals (Aloha, Southwest), and regionals (Aspen, Sierra Pacific). Service describes the type of service offered: cargo only; air taxi, which offers passenger service on demand; commuter, which offers passenger service based on published timetables; charter, for which the route and schedule are negotiated in a contract; and international.

The advantages of this mode are fast terminal-to-terminal transportation,

Figure 1.6.1 Air transportation provides the fastest mode of transportation for people and high-value goods. (From the Boeing Company [1.20].)

reliable service (except under extremely poor weather conditions), and attention to the customer (in flight services and entertainment). Limited frequency of flights, capacity restrictions, and poor service of small cities are disadvantages. Also, long travel times to and from airports, which are traditionally located at the out-skirts of urban areas, as well as often long wait times—check-in, boarding, taxiing, baggage claim—increase the overall travel time (see further discussion in Section 1.8).

Air cargo is a fast-growing mode of transportation: 420 million freight ton-miles in 1970, 1050 million in 1988, worldwide [1.10]. In 1989 air cargo accounted for only 0.3% of the total domestic ton-miles of freight but for 7.4% of the re-spective revenues [1.1]. The average cargo haul is approximately 1200 mi.

Advantages of air cargo are the smooth ride along with the automated and efficient handling facilities, while the high cost and the limited capacity are dis-advantages. In general, high-value, emergency, and low-weight items are shipped via air carriers. Such items are mail and documents, photography equipment, parts and electric components or devices, perishables such as flowers and news-papers, medical components, and human organs. Airlines contract motor carriers to overcome customer-accessibility problems.

The airline industry is characterized by low fixed and high variable costs. Fixed costs include the aircraft fleet and maintenance facilities, computer reser-vation systems (CRS), management, logistics, airport counters, gates, and bag-gage-handling facilities, as well as offices in cities. Several of these may be leased, including aircraft, which makes them semivariable in nature. Variable costs in-clude landing fees [which cover the use of local, state, or federal facilities (airport facilities, roadway access networks, aircraft traffic controls)], labor and fuel (which combined account for 65% of the total variable costs [1.11]), maintenance, and commissions to travel agents. Passengers pay the same price for the tickets regardless of the source of purchase, but part of the profit of tickets booked through travel agents goes to the travel agent (commission).

There are economies of scale in the form of aircraft size utilization. Table 1.6.1 presents approximate total cost per seat-mile updated for 1990 for four widely

TABLE 1.6.1   COST PER SEAT-MILE

Aircraft	Seats	Cost
Boeing 747	450	$0.043
Douglas DC-10	270	0.050
Boeing 727	150	0.056
Douglas DC-9	80	0.072

used commercial jet aircraft [1.12]. Aircraft seating configurations (number of total seats as well as number of seats per class) vary widely and so does the price of fuel. Thus the illustrated values should not be used for practical applications. The figures in this table suggest that use of larger aircraft may result in higher profit margins, provided that there is enough demand to fill the seats.

Large aircraft are also part of the solution for the increasingly important problem of airport congestion. Airport congestion is observed when the number of arriving and departing aircraft reaches or exceeds the capacity of a field. The capacity of an airfield is defined by a maximum number of landing and takeoff slots. At congested airports, arriving aircraft are placed on a holding pattern (usually, spirals in the airspace near the airport) and departing aircraft are queued on taxiways. Larger aircraft require longer but fewer landing and takeoff slots for serving a fixed number of passengers. For example, the 450 passengers served by one 747, which requires one landing slot and one gate, can be served by three 727 flights or six DC-9 flights, with respective requirements for landing slots and gates. Therefore, consolidation of flights and use of larger aircraft less frequently may offer some relief to congested airports by decreasing the required number of operations per passenger served.

There is strong competition among airlines for the acquisition of rights over high-volume routes (airport and trade constraints determine the maximum number of flights allowed) as well as for passengers, through pricing (fare wars). A consequence of the former is that low-density routes tend to be abandoned; therefore, the service offered to small cities deteriorates. This is one of a few major drawbacks caused by the airline deregulation act of 1978 [1.13].

Deregulation also fostered the development of hub and spoke networks (see Fig. 1.6.2), where in essence travelers are consolidated at hub airports such as Atlanta, Chicago, and Denver, and then flown to their destinations.

The fare wars materialize through supersaver fares aimed at filling up empty seats. These fares are accompanied by several restrictions which tend to dis-

Figure 1.6.2 1988 routes of a regional U.S. commercial air carrier; the hub and spoke structure is clear.

courage customers who can afford to pay the full fare price: primarily, business travelers. In addition, frequent flier programs were developed to enforce customer loyalty to a particular airline. Travelers still have the freedom to select the lowest-fare airline serving their destination, but by doing so they may forgo the advantage of free trips after a sufficient number of miles has been accumulated in their account.

The analysis of airline operations is complex. One part concerns pricing of fares and seat allocation per flight. The primary issue is to allocate the proper number of seats in each fare class so that the flight will be full, while the maximum revenue will be collected by securing seat availability for all passengers who would fly at full fare price. This process is called yield management. Another part concerns airline operations. First, flights, departure times, and connections are developed. Then aircraft and crews need to be assigned to each flight. The problem becomes complex because of the variable sizes and capabilities of each aircraft, the crews (which are able to fly only specific types of aircraft), the preferences and seniority of crews, while the demand for each origin and destination pair needs to be satisfied. For example, in 1989 United Airlines had 1700 daily flights served with 429 aircraft operated by 19,800 flight crew (cockpit crew and flight attendants) [1.14]. Of course, the selection of aircraft and crews is limited to those available to each company. Scheduled aircraft maintenance and maximum crew hours of service are additional constraints.

The federal government through the Federal Aviation Administration (FAA) provides control of runway, taxiway, and flight operations with a dense network of air traffic control (ATC) facilities. It is important to realize that commercial aircraft are not equipped so that the control crew knows about the traffic in the area where they fly. Visual identification of neighboring aircraft is hardly feasible given the speeds realized. Only ATC operators have the ability to channel and separate air traffic—both vertically and horizontally—so that operations take place safely. Given the large volumes of passengers carried daily and the disastrous outcomes of an accident, the role of air traffic controllers is of insurmountable importance to air traffic operations.

1.7 COURIERS

Couriers are essentially a form of privately owned and operated mail service, which serves businesses much as the regular mail service serves the general public. The best known U.S. couriers are Federal Express and United Parcel Service (UPS). The former concentrates on express shipment of documents and small packages (overnight delivery), while the latter concentrates on fast transportation of larger packages (up to 70 lb). Both couriers, as well as smaller or international competitors (i.e., DHL), expanded tremendously in the 1980s, in both domestic and international markets. This growth is due largely to the speed, efficiency, and reliability of service provided (Fig. 1.7.1).

Figure 1.7.1 Advanced applications of electronics for optimal routing and package tracking are common in couriers. (From *1989 Annual Report*, United Parcel Service.)

The equipment utilized by couriers includes a large number of sorting terminals, trucks, vans, and all-cargo aircraft. Vans are used for pickup and delivery; packages and documents are sorted at the terminals and then shipped via trucks or aircraft for the long haul. Presently, UPS ships more than twice the number of packages shipped via regular mail (e.g., in 1989, UPS surpassed 1 million regular daily pickup and delivery points), and it is expanding in express transportation of documents. As of 1989, UPS served 80 countries by utilizing a fleet of 116,000 trucks and vans and 100 owned and approximately 250 leased aircraft; 238,000 employees manage an annual volume of 2778 million packages [1.15]. Couriers typically charge higher rates than those of the federally subsidized mail service. However, their dependability has made them the fastest and most reliable mode for shipping business documents and parcels.

1.8 INTERCITY TRAVEL INDUSTRY

The basic purposes of generating intercity transportation are business, vacation, and personal reasons (i.e., visit family or friends, medical emergency). The full array of travel modes available to serve intercity travelers includes air travel via scheduled airlines, chartered flights (tourist groups), or private aircraft. Travel by bus is provided by two privately owned and operated national carriers, Greyhound and Trailways. Bus transportation is the most extensive in terms of geographic coverage; most cities with a population of 1000 or more residents are served.

Rail service is provided by Amtrak along a series of corridors connecting large urban areas. The most heavily utilized corridor is the one between Boston and Washington, D.C., which also includes the cities of New York and Philadelphia. Upgraded lines on which trains operate at speeds between 90 and 120 mi/h have been established between Boston and Washington, D.C., and between Chicago and New York.

Cruising on passenger ocean liners has regained its popularity for vacation travel since the early 1980s. Cruise ships offer all types of entertainment. Favored cruise regions are the caribbean islands, the coasts and islands of the Mediterranean sea, the Hawaiian islands, and the coasts of Alaska.

Automobile—private or rented—is the most readily available mode. This mode is among the slowest for long-distance trips. Part of the reason for the large volume of intercity travel by autos is the convenience of its use as well as the people's misperception of true costs. People tend to recognize out-of-pocket costs such as gasoline, tolls, and parking, and ignore other important costs, such as insurance, maintenance, and depreciation [1.16].

The choice of mode for long distance is heavily dependent on the sensitivity of the traveler with respect to time and cost. By and large, business travel is time sensitive, vacation travel is price sensitive, and travel for personal reasons may be either time or price sensitive, or both. The basic attributes of each mode are schedule, speed, cost, service offered, and perceptions regarding the service offered.

Schedule and speed prescribe the ability of the mode to serve passengers at the times they want and at the speed (or travel time) they require; for example, a same-day round trip from Chicago to New York can be accomplished by air travel only. Cost is a major consideration for most passengers. Rail and bus are least expensive, with private or rented car following, and air travel coming last as the most expensive means of travel. Advance purchase of supersaver fares may reduce the air transportation cost substantially. For example, in January 1992, the supersaver Honolulu–Washington, D.C. round-trip fare was around $800, the full economy class fare was around $1,800, and the first class was around $3,600. The destination point may restrict the mode-choice set, or it may require the use of more than one long-distance transportation mode (i.e., air and bus). In the Honolulu-to-Washington, D.C., example, the only practical way to travel is by air.

Service is an important factor as well. Travel by private or rented car offers the convenience of having a car available at all times. This may be of great importance to some travelers (i.e., traveling salespeople). Bus or rail offer few amenities on board, while airlines offer a wide variety of services on board (cocktails, meals, minimart, multichannel music, and screen entertainment). Perceptions of passengers regarding the overall service offered by a mode compared with other modes (comparison between modes, e.g., auto versus bus or rail), or among providers of the same mode (i.e., American versus United Airlines, Avis versus Hertz Car Rental) affect the choice of modes and providers.

Setting costs aside, the competitiveness of modes can be judged by their ability to provide fast service from origin to destination on a door-to-door basis (i.e., from the office in town A to the meeting place in town B, or from the house in town X to the hotel room in town Y). All modes except private auto and rented or company car provide terminal-to-terminal service. There are several time-consuming components before and after the main haul as well as in the terminals.

For rail transportation these time components are listed below along with the assumed time durations, which are based on experiences in large urban areas:

- Access origin terminal = 20 min
- Wait for train and board = 15 min
  . . . trip (terminal-to-terminal main haul) . . .
- Leave train and walk to exit from terminal = 5 min
- Access destination point = 20 min

Hence the total nontrip time by rail is about 1 h long; it is similar by bus.

The respective time components by air are as follows:

- Access origin terminal = 30 min
- Check-in, walk to gate, and wait = 30 min
- Board and time until plane leaves gate = 15 min
- Taxiing and stops until takeoff = 10 min
  . . . trip (terminal-to-terminal main haul) . . .
- Landing and taxiing to gate = 5 min
- Permit to open doors, exit, and walk to baggage claim = 15 min
- Wait for luggage = 10 min
- Walk to exit terminal = 5 min
- Access destination point = 30 min

Hence the total nontrip time by air is about $2\frac{1}{2}$ h long. These time estimates are variable; they depend on origin and destination locations, transportation systems congestion levels, weather and equipment condition, terminal size and efficiency, and so forth. It is normal to expect, however, that a 2-h trip (terminal to terminal) by airplane should take at least 4 h from origin to destination (door to door). Considering the door-to-door time frame, it is likely that several modes may offer competitive service. This is analyzed below.

Figure 1.8.1 compares four alternative modes of intercity transportation. The following average main haul speeds were assumed: auto, 60 mi/h; regular rail, 75 mi/h; high-speed rail, 200 mi/h; subsonic jet aircraft, 500 mi/h. Zero access and wait times were assumed for private and rented auto because this mode is, in most cases, readily available. One hour of access and wait times was assumed for rail (note the value of the corresponding y-axis intercept), and $2\frac{1}{2}$ h were assumed for air travel, based on the earlier derivations of these times.

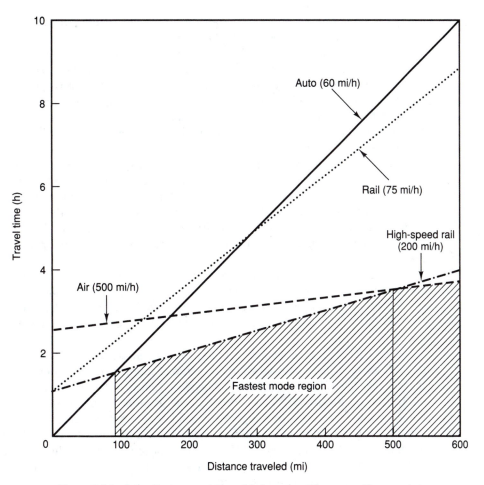

Figure 1.8.1 Intercity transportation: Mode competitiveness with respect to travel time.

   Auto results as the fastest mode for trips up to 100 mi long, high-speed rail is most competitive for distances between 100 and 500 mi, and air transportation is fastest for all trips exceeding 500 mi. Regular rail and bus (not shown) are not competitive for any trip distance with respect to minimum travel time. In the domestic U.S. market, the average trip length for bus is 127 mi, for rail is 265 mi, and for air travel is 786 mi [1.1]. A number of institutions or industries complement the various intercity transportation modes: travel agents, taxi and limousine service companies, mass transit authorities, airport and terminal authorities, car rental companies, local sightseeing services, hotels and restaurants, and the entertainment industry.

Future advances in intercity transportation are expected to come in the form of high-speed trains capable of reaching or exceeding 300 mi/h, and second-generation supersonic (the Anglo–French Concord aircraft constitutes the first generation) and/or suborbital aircraft capable of traveling from New York to Tokyo in less than 4 h. Thus the major objective of advanced intercity transportation technologies is the substantial reduction of travel times through high cruising speeds. Additional objectives are the reduction of fuel consumption, pollution, and noise. Most of the research and applications are concentrated in passenger rail and air transportation.

Two major approaches have emerged in high-speed rail transportation: conventional (steel wheels on steel rails) systems and magnetic levitation systems. The former has been fully operational for some years in Japan (Shinkansen or Bullet train) and France (TGV or Train à Grand Vitesse). Presently, these systems operate at cruising speeds of 150 to 170 mi/h with an impeccable time and safety performance record. Upgraded versions are developed that will cruise at 220 to 300 mi/h [1.17].

German (Fig. 1.8.2) and Japanese industrial consortia experiment with real-world, full-scale magnetic levitation trains; at least one consortium from each of these two countries markets an implementation-ready system. Urban transit as well as intercity versions cruising at speeds in excess of 300 mi/h have been developed.

MAGLEV (prevalent abbreviation for "magnetic levitation") trains essentially float on a magnetic cushion. Superconducting magnets interact with aluminum coils fixed on the guideway. Magnetic repulsion on the vertical plane lifts the train 1 to 5 in. from the guideway. Lateral magnetic repulsion on the horizontal plane enables the train to snuggle the guideway, thereby averting derailment. Finally, longitudinal magnetic attraction and repulsion generate forward and backward propulsion [1.18]. Major advantages of these systems are little energy consumption, no emissions, practically noiseless operation, and minimal wear and tear due to the frictionless operation.

Similarly, in air transportation there are two dominant new technologies: one fully applied, the other at a purely conceptual level. The former is the fly-by-wire technology commercially introduced by the European aircraft manufac-

Figure 1.8.2 The German version of MAGLEV intercity rail, TRANSRAPID model 06. (From TRANSRAPID brochure.)

turing consortium Airbus (model A320). The technology utilizes electronic signals to command mechanisms that adjust control surfaces (i.e., flaps), whereas in conventional aircraft the pilot moves the control surfaces directly by operating levers or other mechanical devices [1.10].

Multiple on-board computers inspect flying conditions and pilot commands, and suggest optimal actions or warn about potentially erroneous judgments. Fewer, improved technology engines are necessary to propel the aircraft, while emissions, noise, and consumption continue to decline. Extensive use of composite materials further reduces aircraft weight. All these developments on conventional commercial jet aircraft make air travel more efficient, safer, and less harmful to the environment.

As mentioned in Section 1.6, airport congestion can be partly alleviated by using larger aircraft. Existing airports, however, have a limited number of wide gates which can handle large aircraft, while most airports have little room for expansion. This is taken into account in the design of the new Boeing 777, expected to enter service in the late 1990s. This aircraft will be equipped with folding wings which will enable it to park in narrow airport gates.

Fast growth of world markets and international business travel necessitates the substantial reduction of air travel times. International trade centers such as Chicago, Frankfurt, Hong Kong, Los Angeles, London, Moscow, New York, Paris, Seoul, Singapore, Sydney, and Tokyo require long flight times; the travel times for all transcontinental trips between the cities above exceed 10 h. As a result, at least two business days are lost in travel, while often passengers arrive in poor shape, all of which are detrimental to business.

A conceptual suborbital supersonic aircraft cruising at 5 Mach per hour could reduce travel times substantially (e.g., 2.5 h would be needed for a 13-h trip with a Boeing 747). The potential travel-time savings are substantial. Such an aircraft could overcome airport curfews, while it may also enable same-day arrival and departure, thereby expediting business transactions and efficiency. Existing runway facilities are expected to be sufficient, but due to residual skin temperature, people and baggage handling as well as refueling will require special procedures. The potentially large negative effect of such aircraft on the ozone layer is a major concern.

A vastly smaller fleet of transcontinental aircraft will be needed. Where in one day a commercial aircraft can travel, for example, Los Angeles–Tokyo–Los Angeles at best, the suborbital aircraft may be able to travel on the following hypothetical itinerary, which includes the necessary ground times: Tokyo–Los Angeles–Tokyo–New York–London–New York–Tokyo, which serves complete round trips between Los Angeles–Tokyo, New York–London, and New York–Tokyo [1.19].

Short-haul intercity air transportation and airport operations could be benefitted from tilt-rotor aircraft technology. The advantage of tilt-rotor aircraft is that they can take off and land vertically, thus saving runway landing slots and delays for taxiing, and cruise as regular propelled aircraft (ie., the engine and fan group gradually tilts from a vertical position to a horizontal position). The Boeing-Bell tilt-rotor aircraft, fully tested by the military, can carry 8 to 75 passengers in various commercial configurations and travel at speeds up to 500 mi/h [1.20].

1.9 SUMMARY

In this chapter we presented a multiperspective overview of major transportation modes. Historical, present, and future developments as well as basic economic issues for each mode of transportation were discussed. Motor carriers are ubiquitous and provide door-to-door service. Railroads are best suited for transporting bulky products in large quantities. For liquid commodities, pipelines offer fast reliable and inexpensive transportation. Intercontinental transportation of freight is made almost exclusively by ocean liners and tankers. Air carriers carry little freight, mostly mail. Air carriers facilitate the fast transportation of people over long distances. Couriers offer fast and guaranteed-delivery mail and package shipping service. Air carriers, intercity buses, Amtrak, rental cars, cruising ships, and private automobiles are the modes servicing intercity travelers and vacationers along with a myriad of other service industries, such as travel agencies, hotels, taxi companies, urban transportation authorities, and the entertainment industry.

1.10 EXERCISES

1. The Concrete Products Corporation (CPC) is considering the purchase of a transportation company to facilitate the distribution of their products. Their options are (1) a trucking company with fixed assets of $3 million, variable costs of 6.2 cents per ton-mile, and annual fixed costs of $0.25 million; and (2) a small railroad company with fixed assets of $21 million, variable costs of 3.3 cents per ton-mile, and annual fixed costs of $0.6 million. Given that CPC will be shipping 32,000 tons of products over an 800-mi corridor each year for the next 10 years, which transportation company should CPC purchase, and what other factors of motor carrier and railroad transportation do they have to consider before the purchase? Costs are expected to be increasing by 5% and shipments by 8% per annum. Assume that assets remain constant over the time period considered. (*Note*: To estimate the present size of quantities increasing for the next n years, consult Appendix B.)

2. The cost function of a large railroad corporation is $Y = 10^9 + 0.5u$, where Y is the total cost of shipping in U.S. dollars and u is the number of units (tons) shipped. Last year, the company charged on average $19.5 for each ton of freight transported. Their annual shipments totaled 48 million tons. This year they are considering geographical expansion through the purchase of a smaller railroad corporation which last year shipped a total of 21 million tons. Economists estimated that the total cost function

(for the merged corporations) will be $Y = 13.5^8 + 0.32u$, while 10% more freight shipments should be expected due to the better geographic coverage. (a) Show that the large and the merged railroad realize substantial economies of scale. Which railroad realizes greater EOS? Use a numerical example or a graphic for proof. (b) Did the large railroad make or lose money last year? (c) Should the large railroad merge with the smaller one?

3. Coal Distributors Corporation (CDCorp) is considering adding one coal slurry pipeline between their main facility and a location M. The length of the line is 125 mi. The cost of placing a pipeline varies by size:

    Gathering line: $250,000 per mile (throughput: 25 gal/s)

    Trunk line: $400,000 per mile (throughput: 90 gal/s)

    A third option of CDCorp is to lease trucks at a cost of 35 cents per mile-s at full truckload. One truckload is equivalent to throughput of 10 gal/s. Only full truckload shipments will be made. The demand for the first 5 years is estimated at 40 gal/s; it is expected to drop to 20 gal/s after that point, and diminish after another 5 years. If the operating cost is 1 cent and 0.7 cents per gal for the trunk and the gathering pipeline, respectively, and if CDCorp charges a flat rate of 4 cents per gallon, which option should they choose?

4. Atlantic Containers Corporation (ACC) operates container ships between New York and Liverpool. Due to uneven demand, the rates and utilization are: New York to Liverpool: $800 per container, 40% capacity utilization; Liverpool to New York: $3000 per container, 100% capacity utilization. The capacity of ACC is several hundred containers per month. A current client of ACC has approached them with the following proposal: ship containers either way at a fixed rate of $1600 per container and guarantee to pay for at least 100 containers from New York to Liverpool, regardless of the fact that there may be months when fewer than 100 or even no containers are shipped. ACC's database of past shipments shows that the client's shipments from New York to Liverpool are as follows: 10% no shipment, 50% 60 containers, 40% 120 containers, and 300 containers per month are shipped from Liverpool to New York, on the average. Should ACC accept the deal?

5. Safeway motor carrier has a contract with Byte Computer Company which corresponds to 160 million pounds of freight per annum. Safeway operates a fleet of trucks with 45-ft trailers, each providing a capacity of 2900 ft^3. The total cost per mile for each tractor–trailer unit is $2.00. Safeway charges Byte $2.50 per mile per 20,000 lb of freight. The average shipment from Byte is full truckload transported over 300 mi. Recently Byte requested a rate decrease from $2.50 to $2.25. Safeway has agreed to lower the rate. Given that the freight density of Byte's shipments is 8 lb/ft^3, should Safeway keep their current fleet or upgrade to a fleet of 48-ft trailers with a capacity of 3300 ft^3 each and a total cost per mile equal to $2.10 (which includes the cost of upgrade)?

6. Researchers from Boeing Corporation, the aircraft manufacturer, suggest that the risk of accident during a commercial airliner flight is as follows: 36% during takeoff and climb, 5% during cruise, and 56% during descent, approach, and landing. The remaining 3% risk is during loading, unloading, and taxiing; this component should be ignored in this exercise. These risk findings reflect empirical conditions derived from

airline accident statistics. Considering the commercial jet aircraft data supplied below and assuming that on average 80% of the seating capacity is utilized and that the average trip is two-thirds of the maximum range, calculate the risk factor for each aircraft for every 1 billion passenger-miles. Then set the highest risk estimate equal to 100 and scale the other three estimates. Interpret the results based on the scaled estimates.

Aircraft	Passenger capacity	Maximum range (mi)	Takeoff, climb distance (mi)	Descent, approach, land distance (mi)
B747	350	5100	60	40
DC-10	235	4700	60	40
A310	200	850	30	20
B737	110	1100	30	20

(*Hint:* Estimate the flights required to serve 1 billion passenger-miles and estimate the risk for each trip segment, according to its length.)

7. An airline serving the Hawaiian islands is planning to introduce service between Honolulu (Oahu) and Kahului (Maui). The airline wants to choose the right size of aircraft for a particular set of new flights. Two types of aircraft are available for scheduling:

   MacDonnel Douglas DC-9 with 100 seats and $50 cost per seat

   MacDonnel Douglas DC-10 with 235 seats and $35 cost per seat

   The cost per seat is specific to the one-way trip between the two cities considered. Given the following set of four flights and the expected passenger demand, which aircraft or combination of aircraft should the airline select to minimize the actual cost per seat?

	Expected number of passengers for flight:			
	1	2	3	4
Honolulu–Kahului	120	150	175	130
Kahului–Honolulu	130	140	185	120

   Flights cannot be combined. Passengers who cannot get in a flight are lost to competitors.

8. A Chicago-based international air carrier plans to purchase a jumbo-class aircraft to serve the Chicago–London city pair. Restrictions in landing slots at Heathrow airport in London allowed the purchase of five landing/takeoff slots, one per weekday. The carrier does not intend to offer weekend service. The following table presents passenger demand estimates and fares charged by competitors:

Trip	Five-weekday demand	Fare
Chicago–London–Chicago	975	$800
Chicago–London	230	680
London–Chicago–London	880	950
London–Chicago	400	775

The round trip Chicago–London–Chicago is 7900 mi, and the aircraft choices and the respective costs are as follows:

Aircraft	Seating capacity	Operating cost per seat-mile (cents)	Annual fixed cost
B747	350	6.34	$33.8 million
DC-10	235	6.55	20.8 million

Should the airline enact service, and which aircraft should be chosen? Round-trips are preferred to one-way trips.

9. The OTR bus company must replace or rebuild their fleet of 100 buses because they have reached their useful life. Three options are available: (A) purchase new standard bus; (B) purchase new superbus, which is more costly but lasts longer; and (C) rebuild available buses. The costs of these options are as follows:

Option	Capital cost	Life (years)	Annual O&M cost[a]	Overhaul cost	Overhaul year
A	$175,000	12	$50,000	$50,000	5th
B	250,000	20	37,500	25,000	5th, 10th, 15th
C	100,000	5	50,000	None	None

[a] O&M, operating and maintenance.

Which bus is preferred at a 10% discount rate? If the available budget is $20 million, which option is preferred? (*Hint:* Annualize and sum up the capital, operating, and overhaul costs, and compare the options. Consult Appendix B for the appropriate formulas.)

10. A businessman residing in Chicago considers his options for a trip to Detroit. His options are private car, rental car, bus, and airplane. Given the following data, suggest the best mode for his travel.

Distance between cities (one way): 270 mi
Estimated access travel at origin and destination: 30 mi at each city
Costs: (1) private auto, 25 cents per mile (all types of costs combined), no access

mode required; (2) rental car (2 days), $40 per day plus $8 insurance per day, 25 mi per gallon fuel efficiency, $1.25 per gallon of gasoline, no access mode required; (3) bus, round-trip fare $45, access mode required; (4) air, round-trip fare $80, access mode required

Access modes and costs: in Chicago taxis charge $1.40 per mile, buses charge $1.00 per ride (assume two rides); in Detroit taxis charge $0.90 per mile, buses charge $0.80 per ride (assume four rides).

The door-to-door travel times by mode are as follows:

	Private auto	Rental car	Bus	Air
Best	4.5	5.0	6.0	1.5
Worst	6.0[a]	6.5[a]	8.0[b]	3.0[b]

[a] Accounts for potentially congested conditions.

[b] Use of bus for access.

To make his selection, the businessman assumed a disutility function (a measure of "discomfort" due to the cost and travel time encountered):

$$\text{disutility} = (\text{total trip cost})/5 + 8(\text{one-way travel time})$$

The lower the disutility, the better the mode. Thus the businessman plans to select the mode with the lowest disutility.

1.11 REFERENCES

1.1 Eno Foundation for Transportation, *Transporation in America: A Statistical Analysis of Transportation in the United States*, 8th ed, EFT, Washington, D.C., 1990.

1.2 Coyle, J. J., E. J. Bardi, and J. L. Cavinato, *Transportation*, 2nd ed., West Publishing Company, St. Paul, Minn., 1986.

1.3 Association of American Railroads, *The ABZs of the Railroad Industry*, AAR, Washington, D.C. 1984.

1.4 ———, *Railroad Facts*, AAR, Washington, D.C. 1984.

1.5 Harper, D. V., *Transportation in America: Users Carriers, Government*, Prentice Hall, Englewood Cliffs, N.J., 1978.

1.6 Haghani, A. E., and M. S. Daskin, "A Combined Model of Train Routing, Makeup and Empty Car Distribution," *The Logistics and Transportation Review*, 23, 2 (1987): 173–188.

1.7 Amoco Educational Services, *Oil on the Move*, Amoco, Chicago, 1983.

1.8 Wood, D., and J. Johnson, *Contemporary Transportation*, Petroleum Publishing, Tulsa, Okla., 1975.

1.9 Chatterjee, A., G. P. Fisher, and R. A. Staley, eds., *Goods Transportation in Urban Areas*, American Society of Civil Engineers, New York, 1989.

1.10 AIRBUS INDUSTRIE, *Market Perspectives for Civil Jet Aircraft*, AI, Toulouse, France, 1990.

1.11 AIR TRANSPORT ASSOCIATION OF AMERICA, *Air Transport 1983*, ATTA, Washington, D.C., 1983.

1.12 CIVIL AERONAUTICS BOARD, *Aircraft Operating Cost and Performance Report*, CAB, Washington, D.C., 1984.

1.13 TRANSPORTATION CENTER, NORTHWESTERN UNIVERSITY, "Transportation Deregulation and Safety," *Conference Proceedings*, 1987.

1.14 UAL CORPORATION, *United Airlines: 1989 Annual Report*, UAL, Chicago, 1989.

1.15 UPS *1989 Annual Report to Shareholders*, United Parcel Service of America Incorporated, Greenwich, Conn., 1989.

1.16 METCALF, A., "The 'Misperception' of Car Running Costs and Its Impact on the Demand for Energy in the Transport Sector," *Proceedings of the World Conference on Transport Research*, London, 1980:1583–1603.

1.17 TRANSPORTATION RESEARCH BOARD, *Toward a European High-Speed Rail Network*, *TR News* 145 (1989).

1.18 HEIRICH, K., and R. KRETZSCMAR, *Transrapid MagLev System*, Hestra-Verlag, Darmstadt, Germany, 1989.

1.19 LIGHTFOOT, B. H., "A Market for the Orient Express," presented at the *66th Annual Meeting of the Transportation Research Board*, 1987.

1.20 THE BOEING COMPANY, *Products and Programs*, Boeing, Seattle, Washington, 1988.

2 Vehicle Motion, Human Factors, Geometric and Pavement Design

2.1 INTRODUCTION

Stripped to its barest essentials, a transportation system involves the motion of vehicles. It is, therefore, important to review the basic *kinematic* and *kinetic* equations of motion. These two branches of dynamics are related: *Kinematics* is the study of motion irrespective of the forces that cause it, whereas *kinetics* accounts for these forces. The motion of a body can be *rectilinear* or *curvilinear* and can be investigated in relation to a fixed coordinate system (i.e., *absolute* motion) or in relation to a moving coordinate system (i.e., *relative* motion). In this chapter, the basic equations of motion of a single vehicle are cast in the form in which they are used for the purposes of design. Three examples of human-factor models are then introduced to illustrate how human characteristics can be incorporated in design. The important differences between the *maximum* technological capabilities of vehicles on one hand and the *practical* design levels necessitated by considerations of passenger *safety* and *comfort* are explained. Finally, the methods of *geometric design* are presented for the horizontal and vertical alignment of highways and railways and for the channelization of intersections and interchanges. Geometric design is concerned only with the size, shape, and geometry of transportation facilities. Other aspects of engineering design are also needed for the successful implementation of these facilities, including the proper selection of pavement and structural materials, geotechnical design, and the structural design of various components such as bridges. In addition, complex decisions related to whether a new facility is needed, or whether an existing facility should be improved must necessarily precede the design phase.

2.2 EQUATIONS OF MOTION

2.2.1 Rectilinear Motion

The rectilinear *position x* of a particle is measured from a reference point and has units of length. The displacement of the particle is the difference in its position between two instants.

   Velocity v is the displacement of the particle divided by the time over which the displacement occurs. In the limit, the instantaneous value of velocity is given by the first derivative of displacement with respect to time:

$$v = \frac{dx}{dt} \tag{2.2.1}$$

Speed is a scalar quantity and is equal to the magnitude of velocity, which is a vector. However, the two terms are used interchangeably in this book when the meaning is clear from the context.

   Acceleration a is the rate of change of velocity with respect to time:

$$a = \frac{dv}{dt} \tag{2.2.2}$$

It can be positive, zero, or negative. Negative acceleration (i.e., *deceleration*) is often denoted by *d*, and its magnitude is given in the positive. Thus a deceleration of 16 ft/s^2 is the same as an acceleration of -16 ft/s^2.

   Applying the chain rule yields

$$a = \frac{dv}{dx}\left(\frac{dx}{dt}\right)$$

or

$$a = \left(\frac{dv}{dx}\right)v$$

which leads to

$$v\,dv = a\,dx \tag{2.2.3}$$

   Often, the given variables are expressed as functions of time or of each other [e.g., $a = f(v)$], and the specific relationships between pairs of variables are derived through the application of the calculus. These relationships are often plotted to aid the visualization of the particle's motion.

   The simplest case of rectilinear motion is the case of *constant acceleration*, where

$$\frac{dv}{dt} = a = \text{constant}$$

Separating variables and integrating over the limits $t = 0$ to t gives

$$\int_{v_0}^{v} dv = \int_0^t a \, dt$$

$$v = at + v_0 \tag{2.2.4}$$

The velocity of the particle can also be expressed as a function of distance by integrating Eq. 2.2.3 over the appropriate limits of integration to yield

$$\tfrac{1}{2}(v^2 - v_0^2) = a(x - x_0) \tag{2.2.5}$$

which, upon the rearrangement of terms, becomes

$$x - x_0 = \frac{v^2 - v_0^2}{2a} \tag{2.2.6}$$

This expression is useful for computing the distance traveled by a vehicle at constant acceleration (or deceleration) from an initial velocity v_0 to a final velocity v.

In view of Eq. 2.2.1, Eq. 2.2.4 may be integrated to express x as a function of time:

$$x = \tfrac{1}{2} at^2 + v_0 t + x_0 \tag{2.2.7}$$

Example 2.1: Constant Acceleration

A vehicle approaches an intersection at 30 mi/h. At time $t = 0$ it begins to decelerate at $d = 16$ ft/s^2. Calculate the time it would take the vehicle to stop. Given that at the beginning of deceleration the vehicle was located 55 ft away from the stopping line, determine whether it was able to stop legally (i.e., behind the stopping line). Plot the relationships of acceleration, velocity, and position as functions of time and the relationship between velocity and position.

Solution   Set the positive x-axis in the direction of motion, with the origin at the initial position of the vehicle. Thus at $t = 0$, $x = 0$, $v = 44$ ft/s, and $a = -16$ ft/s^2. This is the case of constant acceleration. The time it took the vehicle to stop from an initial velocity of 44 ft/s is given by Eq. 2.2.4:

$$0 = -16t + 44 \quad \text{or} \quad t = 2.75 \text{ s}$$

The distance covered during deceleration may be computed either from Eq. 2.2.6 or from Eq. 2.2.7:

$$x = 60.5 \text{ ft}$$

Since this is greater than the available distance of 55 ft, the vehicle was not able to stop before reaching the stopping line. The required plots are shown in Fig. 2.2.1.

Discussion   Since acceleration is the derivative of velocity with respect to time, the slope of the v–t diagram is equal to the acceleration at time t. In this example, the slope of the v–t diagram is negative, constant, and equal to -16 ft/s^2. Similarly, the particle's velocity is equal to the slope of the x–t diagram. Thus, when

Figure 2.2.1 Examples of rectilinear motion relationships.

velocity is equal to zero, the x–t diagram attains a critical point, in this case, a maximum. The plots of the mathematical functions derived earlier extend beyond the instant when the vehicle comes to a complete stop (see dashed lines). This range is not applicable in this situation because the subject vehicle will not continue to decelerate at 16 ft/s² beyond that instant—that is, reverse its direction by backing up! The assumption of an "average" constant deceleration is an idealized but often acceptable approximation.

Example 2.2: Acceleration as a Function of Velocity

The acceleration of a vehicle from an initial speed v_0 is given by the relationship

$$a = \frac{dv}{dt} = A - Bv \tag{2.2.8}$$

where A and B are constant [2.1]. Derive and plot the x–t, a–t, and v–t relationships assuming that, at $t = 0$, $x = 0$.

Solution   This is a case of variable acceleration. Consequently, the equations employed in Example 2.1 do not apply. Separating the variables of Eq. 2.2.8 and integrating over the appropriate limits, we obtain

$$\int_{v_0}^{v} \frac{dv}{A - Bv} = \int_{0}^{t} dt$$

or

$$\frac{-1}{B} \ln(A - Bv) \Big|_{v_0}^{v} = t$$

and

$$\frac{A - Bv}{A - Bv_0} = e^{-Bt}$$

Solving for v as a function of t yields

$$v = \frac{A}{B}(1 - e^{-Bt}) + v_0 e^{-Bt}$$

Substitution of this expression into Eq. 2.2.8 results in the needed relationship of acceleration as a function of time:

$$a = (A - Bv_0)e^{-Bt}$$

Finally, substituting $v = dx/dt$ into the v–t equation and integrating leads to the following x–t relationship:

$$x = \left(\frac{A}{B}\right)t - \frac{A}{B^2}(1 - e^{-Bt}) + \frac{v_0}{B}(1 - e^{-Bt})$$

The required plots are shown in Fig. 2.2.2.

Discussion   Equation 2.2.8 closely approximates the situation where a vehicle traveling at an initial speed v_0 attempts to accelerate as quickly as possible to its maximum speed ("pressing the accelerator to the floor"). Examination of the value of acceleration at $t = 0$ shows that the initial value of acceleration depends on the initial speed. Moreover, A has the dimensions of acceleration and is the maximum acceleration that the vehicle can attain starting from rest (i.e., $v_0 = 0$). Theoretically, the maximum speed attainable by the vehicle is A/B. This can be verified by examining the v–t curve in the limit. The values of the constants A and B depend on the technological design of the subject vehicle and can be measured experimentally. Dimensional consistency requires B to have the units of 1/time. The equations developed so far are based on kinematics. They are used in the study of kinetics where the relationship between force, mass, and acceleration is of prime concern. Newton's second law provides the fundamental equation relating the three variables:

$$F = ma \qquad (2.2.9)$$

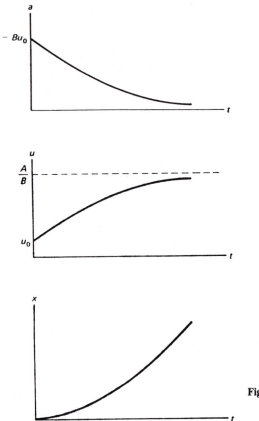

Figure 2.2.2   Acceleration, speed and distance as a function of time.

2.2.2 Braking Distance

A very common case of rectilinear motion is the case of a vehicle braking on a grade, that is, while moving either uphill or downhill. Figure 2.2.3 shows the major forces acting on a vehicle as it climbs uphill. Ignoring all resistances except friction and grade resistance, the free-body diagram of the vehicle becomes as shown in Fig. 2.2.4.

It is customary to designate the *braking distance* D_b in the horizontal direction rather than along the incline, which is taken as the x-axis. For small incline angles α, the difference between the two distances is very small, as their relationship verifies:

$$D_b = x \cos \alpha \qquad (2.2.10)$$

where both x and D_b are measured from the point at which braking commences.

The condition of static equilibrium is satisfied in the y-direction with the y-component of the vehicle's weight counteracted by the normal force $N = W \cos$

Figure 2.2.3 Forces acting on a moving vehicle.

Figure 2.2.4 Vehicle braking.

α. Equation 2.2.9 in the x-direction yields

$$\left(\frac{W}{g}\right)a + Wf\cos\alpha + W\sin\alpha = 0 \tag{2.2.11}$$

Substituting Eq. 2.2.10 into Eq. 2.2.6 and solving for acceleration, we have

$$a = (v^2 - v_0^2)\frac{\cos\alpha}{2D_b} \tag{2.2.12}$$

Substituting Eq. 2.2.12 in Eq. 2.2.11, dividing by $W\cos\alpha$, and solving for D_b gives

$$D_b = \frac{v_0^2 - v^2}{2g(f + G)} \tag{2.2.13}$$

where $G = \tan\alpha$, or the *percent grade* divided by 100.

Repeating the solution above for the case when a vehicle is braking while traveling downhill yields an equation identical to Eq. 2.2.13 except for a reversal of the sign of G in the denominator. Equation 2.2.13 is often expressed to cover both situations as

$$D_b = \frac{v_0^2 - v^2}{2g(f \pm G)} \tag{2.2.14}$$

where the plus and minus signs correspond to *uphill* and *downhill* braking, respectively. It is easy to remember the proper sign by remembering that the uphill braking distance is shorter than the downhill braking distance because of the effect of gravity.

To compute the total braking distance from an initial speed v_0 to a complete stop, simply substitute $v = 0$. For level paths, the gradient G is equal to zero. The fact that Eq. 2.2.6 was used in the development of the above model implies that the acceleration rate is assumed to be constant. This assumption is reflected in the value of the coefficient of friction f, which is considered to represent the average effect of friction during the entire braking maneuver. The coefficient of friction, of course, depends on the characteristics of the contacting surfaces, that is, the vehicle's tires and the pavement. Because of a wide range of possible pavement–tire combinations and conditions, the coefficient of friction is often calculated experimentally as follows: At the location of interest where G is known, the braking distance needed to stop a vehicle from a known speed is measured. These values are then substituted in Eq. 2.2.13 to obtain the value of f. For the purposes of statistical reliability, the test is repeated a number of times. As a rule of thumb, f is approximately equal to 0.6 when the pavement is dry and about 0.3 when the pavement is wet. On ice, of course, f is much lower. The coefficient of friction has also been found to decrease somewhat with increasing initial speed [2.2]. Engineering design is normally based on wet rather than dry conditions.

Equation 2.2.14 can also aid in the estimation of initial speed v_0 at which a vehicle was traveling prior to a collision based on the length of the skid marks left on the pavement. However, the speed at impact v must also be estimated. This is accomplished by considering the kinetic energy dissipated for the damage or deformation sustained by the vehicle(s) involved in the collision.

Example 2.3: Braking Distance

A driver of a car applied the brakes and barely avoided hitting an obstacle on the roadway. The vehicle left skid marks of 88 ft. Assuming that $f = 0.6$, determine whether the driver was in violation of the 45-mi/h speed limit at that location if she was traveling (a) uphill on a 3° incline; (b) downhill on a 2.3° incline; (c) on a level roadway. Also compute the average deceleration developed in each case.

Solution   The stopping distance D_b is computed from the length of the skid marks using Eq. 2.2.10, and the initial velocity is calculated by Eq. 2.2.14, since the final velocity is zero in all three cases. The kinematic relationship of Eq. 2.2.6 can then be solved to compute the corresponding deceleration.

Case	G	D_b (ft)	v_0 (ft/s)	d (ft/s^2)
(a)	0.05	87.88	60.65	20.90
(b)	0.04	87.93	56.30	18.03
(c)	0.00	88.00	58.31	19.32

Since the speed limit was 45 mi/h, or 66 ft/s, the driver was not speeding in any of the three cases.

Discussion The kinematic equation 2.2.6 and the kinetic equation 2.2.14 describe the same phenomenon. Comparison of these equations shows that the deceleration of the braking vehicle can be expressed in terms of two components: The first is due to the friction developed between the tires and the pavement and the second is due to the effect of grade. The difference between D_b and the distance traveled along the incline x is very small for typical highway grades. Finally, the coefficient of friction given in this problem implies a dry pavement.

2.2.3 Curvilinear Motion

Vehicles do not traverse straight paths exclusively but must also negotiate curved paths, as illustrated by Fig. 2.2.5(a). The figure shows the direction of velocity is always tangent to the path. The vehicle's acceleration may be resolved into

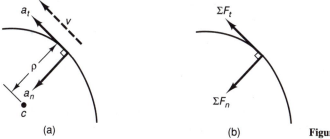

(a)   (b)   **Figure 2.2.5** Curvilinear motion.

two components in the tangential and normal directions, respectively. The magnitude of the tangential component is

$$a_t = \frac{dv}{dt} \tag{2.2.15}$$

The normal component of the acceleration acts toward the center of curvature and has a magnitude of

$$a_n = \frac{v^2}{\rho} \tag{2.2.16}$$

where ρ is the radius of curvature of the path. For a constant velocity v, the tangential component of the acceleration vanishes, but the normal component remains. For circular paths, the radius of curvature is constant and equal to the radius of the circular path R.

Figure 2.2.5(b) shows the tangential and normal components of the forces acting on a vehicle as it traverses a curved path. Applying Newton's second law to the two directions, we have

$$\sum F_t = m\left(\frac{dv}{dt}\right) \tag{2.2.17}$$

and

$$\sum F_n = \frac{mv^2}{\rho} \tag{2.2.18}$$

For a horizontal roadway cross section AA, as shown in Fig. 2.2.6(b), the only force in the normal direction is due to the *side friction* between the vehicle's tires

(a)   (b)   (c)

Figure 2.2.6 Lateral effect.

and the pavement, which resists the tendency of the vehicle to slide. To minimize this tendency, highway design provides for the banking, or *superelevation*, of the cross section of the roadway, as shown in Fig. 2.2.6(c): The cross section is tilted by an angle β so that the component of the vehicle's weight along the tilted pavement surface also resists the sliding tendency of the vehicle. This effect is extremely pronounced in the design of car-racing tracks because of the large normal accelerations developed at racing speeds. The slope to which a highway cross section is tilted is known as the *rate of superelevation*. It is denoted by the letter *e* and equals the tangent of the angle β. The banking angle β should not be confused with the grade angle α discussed in Section 2.2.2.

Figure 2.2.7 shows the free-body diagram of the vehicle as it travels along

Figure 2.2.7 Free-body diagram of turning vehicle.

a circular path at the verge of sliding. In the y-direction perpendicular to the surface of the pavement, static equilibrium is satisfied, as the y-component of the vehicle's weight is counteracted by the normal force. Writing Newton's second law for the x-direction gives

$$W \sin \beta + f_s W \cos \beta = m a_n \cos \beta$$

$$= \frac{W}{g}\left(\frac{v^2}{R}\right)\cos \beta$$

Dividing both sides by $W \cos \beta$ yields

$$e + f_s = \frac{v^2}{gR} \tag{2.2.19}$$

where $e = \tan \beta$ and f_s is the *coefficient of side friction*.

Example 2.4: Curvilinear Motion

A 2000-lb vehicle is traveling along a horizontal circular path of radius $R = 500$ ft. At the instant of interest, the vehicle is traveling at 88 ft/s while decelerating at 8 ft/s². Determine the total horizontal force acting on the vehicle.

Solution   As Fig. 2.2.5(b) illustrates, the total force can be resolved into a tangential and a normal component as follows:

$$F_t = m a_t = \frac{2000}{32.2}(-8) = -497 \text{ lb}$$

and

$$F_n = m a_n = m\left(\frac{v^2}{R}\right) = \frac{2000}{32.2}\left(\frac{88^2}{500}\right) = 962 \text{ lb}$$

The total horizontal force F is 1083 lb, as shown in Fig. 2.2.8.

Figure 2.2.8   Resultant force.

Discussion   The direction of the tangential force in this case is in the negative direction, because the vehicle is decelerating. The normal force, however, is still in the direction toward the center of curvature. The total force, of course, is given by the vector addition of the two components.

Example 2.5: Superelevation

A vehicle is traveling along a horizontal circular curve of radius $R = 1000$ ft at the legal speed limit of 60 mi/h. Given that the coefficient of side friction is 0.2, determine the angle β at which the pavement should be banked to avoid outward sliding.

Solution From Eq. 2.2.19,

$$e = \frac{v^2}{gR} - f_s = 0.04 \text{ ft/ft}$$

Hence $\tan \beta = e = 0.04$ and $\beta = 2.3°$.

Discussion The friction developed between the tires and the pavement is aided by gravity so that the curve can be safely negotiated at 60 mi/h, or 88 ft/s. Solving Eq. 2.2.19 for v with $e = 0$ shows that without superelevating the pavement cross section, the maximum safe speed would be 80 ft/s, or about 55 mi/h.

When the center of gravity of the vehicle is high above the pavement, there exists the danger of overturning; Fig. 2.2.9 is used to examine this situation. Note

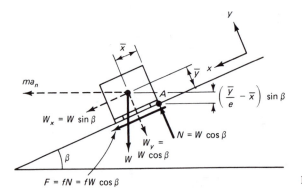

$$F = fN = fW \cos \beta$$

Figure 2.2.9 Case of overturning.

that at the instant when overturning or tipping is imminent, the normal force is acting on the outside wheel idealized by point A. The location of the center of gravity of the vehicle is given by X and Y in relation to point A. Taking moments about point A gives

$$XW \cos \beta + YW \sin \beta = \left(\frac{Y}{e} - X \right)(\sin \beta)ma_n$$

Dividing both sides by $W \cos \beta$ and rearranging terms, we have

$$\frac{v^2}{gR} = \frac{X + Ye}{Y - Xe} \qquad (2.2.20)$$

Example 2.6: Slipping and Overturning

A truck with a center of gravity at $X = 4$ ft and $Y = 5$ ft is traveling on a circular path of radius $R = 600$ ft and superelevation $e = 0.05$. Determine the maximum safe speed to avoid both slipping and overturning, assuming that the coefficient of side friction is 0.2.

Solution   Equation 2.2.19 applies to slipping. The maximum speed to avoid slipping is

$$v^2 = gR(e + f) \qquad \text{or} \qquad v = 69.5 \text{ ft/s}$$

The maximum speed to avoid overturning is given by Eq. 2.2.20:

$$v = 130.8 \text{ ft/s}$$

The maximum safe speed is 69.5 ft/s, the smaller of the two.

Discussion   The proper design of highways involves the selection of a design speed, the radius of curvature, and the superelevation rate. Determining the chance of overturning requires knowledge of the dimensions of the vehicles using the roadway. If the dimensions of vehicles change subsequent to the construction of the roadway, the highway engineer is left with a number of choices, including roadway reconstruction, changing the speed limit, or prohibiting certain vehicles from using the roadway.

2.2.4 Relative Motion

It is often practical to examine the motion of one particle in relation to another. For example, the motion of vehicles on a highway may be studied from the point of view of the driver of a moving vehicle. The simplest case of *relative motion* involves the motion of one particle B relative to a coordinate system (x,y,z) that is *translating* but not rotating with respect to a fixed coordinate system (X,Y,Z), as shown by Fig. 2.2.10.

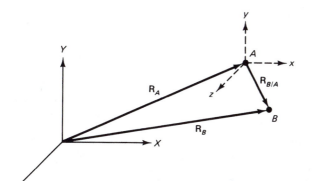

Figure 2.2.10   Relative position of two particles.

The relationship between the position vectors of the two particles in relation to the fixed system, $\mathbf{r}_A$ and $\mathbf{r}_B$, and the position vector $\mathbf{r}_{B/A}$ of B with respect to the moving particle A is

$$\mathbf{r}_B = \mathbf{r}_A + \mathbf{r}_{B/A} \tag{2.2.21a}$$

Differentiating with respect to time gives

$$\mathbf{v}_B = \mathbf{v}_A + \mathbf{v}_{B/A} \tag{2.2.21b}$$

and

$$\mathbf{a}_B = \mathbf{a}_A + \mathbf{a}_{B/A} \tag{2.2.21c}$$

Example 2.7: Relative Motion

A police car, A, equipped with a radar capable of measuring the relative speed and the relative acceleration between it and another vehicle, B, is following a suspected speeding vehicle in a 40-mi/h straight roadway (Fig. 2.2.11). At the instant of interest,

Figure 2.2.11   Relative speeds of vehicles.

the police car is accelerating at 8 ft/s² from a speed of 50 mi/h. The radar reads $v_{B/A} = -5$ mi/h and $a_{B/A} = -16$ ft/s². Determine the absolute speed and acceleration of the vehicle B.

Solution

$$v_{B/A} = v_B - v_A$$

or

$$-5 = v_B - 50 \quad \text{and} \quad v_B = 45 \text{ mi/h}$$

Similarly,

$$a_{B/A} = a_B - a_A$$

or

$$-16 = a_B - 8 \quad \text{and} \quad a_B = -8 \text{ ft/s}^2$$

Discussion   The driver, B, was going 5 mi/h above the speed limit and was decelerating at 8 ft/s², perhaps to minimize the consequences of the transgression.

Example 2.8: Polar Coordinates

Car A is traveling at $v = 88$ ft/s. At the instant shown in Fig. 2.2.12 $dr/dt = -25.4\mathbf{n}_r$ and $d\theta/dt = 1.47\mathbf{n}_\theta$ rad/s, where $\mathbf{n}_r$ and $\mathbf{n}_\theta$ are unit vectors in the r- and θ-directions, respectively. Determine the absolute velocity of car B.

Figure 2.2.12   Polar coordinates r and θ.

Solution 1   The relative velocity expressed in the r- and θ-directions is

$$\mathbf{v}_{B/A} = \left(\frac{dr}{dt}\right)\mathbf{n}_r + \left(\frac{r\,d\theta}{dt}\right)\mathbf{n}_\theta$$

or

$$\mathbf{v}_{B/A} = -25.4\mathbf{n}_r + (100)(0.147)\mathbf{n}_\theta$$

Since

$$\mathbf{n}_r = \cos 30°\mathbf{i} + \sin 30°\mathbf{j} = 0.866\mathbf{i} + 0.500\mathbf{j}$$

and

$$\mathbf{n}_\theta - -\sin 30°\mathbf{i} + \cos 30°\mathbf{j} = -0.500\mathbf{i} + 0.866\mathbf{j}$$

where $\mathbf{i}$ and $\mathbf{j}$ are unit vectors in the x- and y-directions,

$$\mathbf{v}_{B/A} = -25.4(0.866\mathbf{i} + 0.500\mathbf{j}) + 14.7(0.500\mathbf{i} + 0.866\mathbf{j})$$

$$= -29.3\mathbf{i}$$

Hence

$$\mathbf{v}_B = \mathbf{v}_A - \mathbf{v}_{B/A} = 88\mathbf{i} - 29.3\mathbf{i} = 58.7\mathbf{i}$$

Solution 2

$$\mathbf{r}_{B/A} = r(\cos \theta)\mathbf{i} + r(\sin \theta)\mathbf{j}$$

Recalling that for a purely translating frame, $d\mathbf{i}/dt = d\mathbf{j}/dt = 0$,

$$\mathbf{v}_{B/A} = \frac{d\mathbf{r}_{B/A}}{dt}$$

$$= (-r \sin \theta\theta' + r' \cos \theta)\mathbf{i} + (-r \cos \theta\theta' + r' \sin \theta)\mathbf{j}$$

$$= 29.3\mathbf{i}$$

as before.

2.3 HUMAN FACTORS

2.3.1 Perception-Reaction

The equations developed so far are based purely on the equations of motion without taking into account the effect of driver performance on the motion described. For example, Eq. 2.2.14 gives the braking distance for a vehicle from the moment when the brakes take effect to the moment when the vehicle reaches its final speed. Normally, a driver undertakes such a maneuver in response to a stimulus such as avoiding an object on the roadway. When a stimulus appears, a driver requires a certain amount of time to perceive and comprehend it, to decide on the appropriate response, and to react accordingly. The vehicle *braking* distance or time constitutes only a portion of the overall *stopping* distance or time. In many applications the overall maneuver may be divided into two parts: *perception-reaction*, which includes the occurrences up to the beginning of the vehicular response, and braking, which is described by the equations of motion developed in the previous section. If a driver takes 1.5 s to perceive and react to a hazard in the vehicle's path, at a speed of 60 mi/h (88 ft/s) the vehicle would cover 132 ft before the braking phase begins.

Figure 2.3.1 presents the findings of a study conducted by Johannson and Rumar [2.3] regarding driver response times to anticipated braking. The continuous curve at the low end of the histogram represents the reaction time of the person who took the measurements and which was accounted for in computing the driver data shown. Johannson and Rumar also found that the response times were longer than those shown when the drivers were surprised. The figure illustrates the presence of a great deal of variability between individuals. In order to enhance safety, engineering designs that incorporate driver characteristics are typically based on values in the 85th to 95th percentile range.

Driver response is related to driver characteristics and conditions such as age, medical condition, alcohol and drug use, fatigue, sleep deprivation, and emotional condition. It also depends on the complexity of the stimulus and the complexity of the required response. Good traffic engineering designs attempt to minimize the stimuli and driving tasks to which the driver must attend at the same time. This is the "one task at a time" rule, which, due to the complexity of the driving environment, is not always possible.

Figure 2.3.2 offers two useful insights. The first is that the time to react to unexpected information is clearly longer than the time to react to expected information (e.g., since the traffic signal ahead turned red, the vehicles ahead are expected to slow down and stop). The other insight is that the complexity of the given information has a positive relationship with reaction time (and conceivably a positive relationship with accident risk). Thus the larger the quantity and the

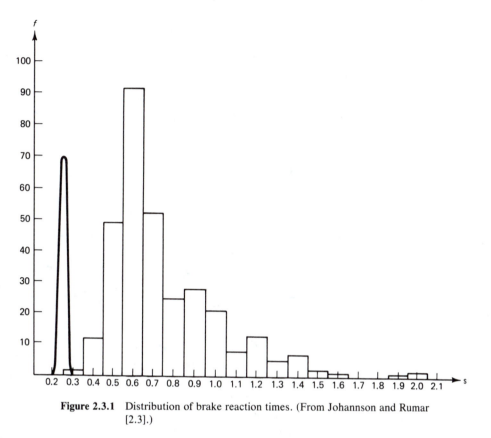

Figure 2.3.1   Distribution of brake reaction times. (From Johannson and Rumar [2.3].)

more complex the information is, the longer it will take drivers to comprehend it and react accordingly. This principle is useful to remember when placing regulatory or information traffic signs: They should be clear and properly spaced to avoid giving drivers too much information at a time (this is euphemistically called the *information pollution* phenomenon).

Example 2.9

Using the data of Example 2.3, determine the stopping distances horizontally (D_s) and along the pavement (X_s) in each of the three cases, given that the driver's perception-reaction time was $\delta = 1.5$ s.

Solution   The distance traveled during the perception-reaction time must be added to the braking distance to compute the total stopping distance. *Assuming* that the

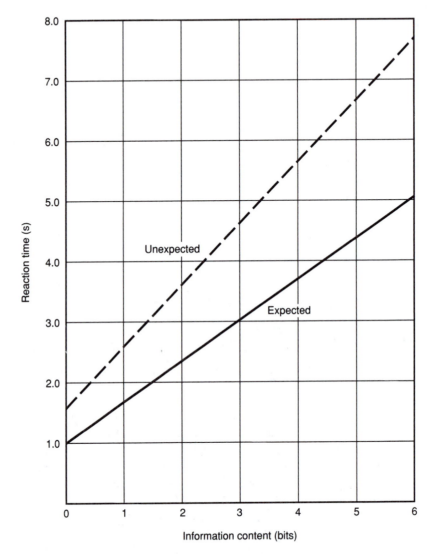

Figure 2.3.2 Eighty-fifth percentile driver reaction time to expected and unexpected information. (From American Association of State and Highway Officials, "A Policy on Geometric Design of Highways and Streets" [2.2], (Fig. 11-19, p. 48). Copyright 1990. Used with permission.)

vehicle was not accelerating during the time interval δ, the distances traveled during δ were $X_r = \delta v_0$ along the pavement and $D_r = X_r \cos \alpha$ horizontally.

Case	D_s (ft)	X_s
(a)	178.73	178.98
(b)	172.31	172.45
(c)	175.47	175.47

Discussion   The difference between the two distances D_s and X_s is insignificant considering typical highway grades. The reason computed stopping distances are longer for steeper grades is because of differences in the initial speeds required to stop within the 88 ft specified *in this case*. The assumption of constant speed prior to the stopping maneuver has an effect on the results.

2.3.2 Dilemma Zones

Most probably, the reader has encountered the situation of approaching a signalized intersection just when the traffic signal turned amber (yellow) and has faced the decision of whether to apply the brakes in order to stop for the red signal or to attempt to clear the intersection on yellow. On occasion, the reader may have felt that it was impossible to safely execute either maneuver. The duration of the amber phase of the traffic signal, τ, is related to this situation. A properly selected amber duration that incorporates the motion of the vehicle during the driver's perception-reaction time can eliminate this problem, and a design formula has been developed by Gazis et al. [2.4] as follows.

Figure 2.3.3 shows a vehicle approaching a signalized intersection at a speed v_0. When the signal turns yellow, the vehicle is located at a distance x from the stop line. The driver must then decide whether to stop or go. The stopping maneuver requires that the vehicle can travel no more than the distance x to the stop line. Clearing the intersection, on the other hand, requires that the vehicle must

Figure 2.3.3 Vehicle approaching a signalized intersection. (From Gazis et al. [2.4].)

travel a distance of at least $(x + w + L)$, where w is the width of the intersection and L is the length of the vehicle. Moreover, this distance must be covered prior to the onset of red (i.e., during yellow). Employing the subscripts 1 and 2 to represent the clearing and the stopping maneuvers, respectively, we obtain

$$x - v_0\delta_2 \geq \frac{v_0^2}{2a_2} \tag{2.3.1}$$

is necessary for a successful stopping maneuver.

The left side of this inequality is the difference between the total distance to the stopping line minus the distance traveled during perception-reaction at the approach speed v_0, and it therefore specifies the maximum braking distance available to the vehicle. For a successful stopping maneuver, this distance should be equal to or greater than the braking distance required by the vehicle at a deceleration a_2. The smallest deceleration rate to accomplish the task is given by the solution of Eq. 2.3.1 as

$$a_2 = \frac{v_0^2}{2(x - v_0\delta_2)} \tag{2.3.2}$$

Considering v_0 and δ_2 to be known, the relationship between x and a_2 is plotted on Fig. 2.3.4. It is a rectangular parabola with an asymptote at $x = v_0\delta_2$, or the perception-reaction distance. This is reasonable because, if the vehicle was closer to the stop line at the onset of amber, it would enter the intersection before the commencement of braking. The mathematical relationship shows the deceleration a_2 to be unbounded. However, there exists a practical upper limit $a_2(\text{max})$ to the deceleration that a real vehicle can develop. Furthermore, this limit is often higher than the deceleration rate that the drive and passengers of the vehicle would

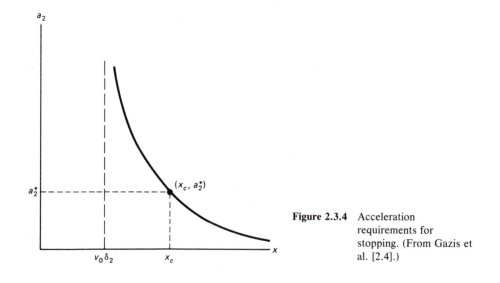

Figure 2.3.4 Acceleration requirements for stopping. (From Gazis et al. [2.4].)

consider comfortable. The comfortable deceleration rate a_2^* is normally in the vicinity of 8 to 10 ft/s^2 when passengers are seated and around 4 or 5 ft/s^2 when passengers are standing, as in a transit vehicle. The distinction between the *maximum attainable level* and a *desired lower level* must always be kept in mind. The corresponding distance x_c represents the minimum distance for which the vehicle can be stopped comfortably. For shorter distances it would be uncomfortable, unsafe, or impossible to stop. This critical distance is

$$x_c = v_0\delta_2 + \frac{v_0^2}{2a_2^*} \tag{2.3.3}$$

A successful clearing maneuver is represented by

$$x + w + L - v_0\delta_1 \leq v_0(\tau - \delta_1) + \tfrac{1}{2}a_1(\tau - \delta_1)^2 \tag{2.3.4}$$

The right side of Eq. 2.3.4 represents the distance traveled from an initial speed v_0 at constant acceleration a_1 during the time interval $(\tau - \delta_1)$, that is, subsequent to the perception-reaction time and before the onset of the red. The left side of Eq. 2.3.4 represents the distance available for the clearing maneuver. The acceleration needed just to clear the intersection is

$$a_1 = \frac{2x}{(\tau - \delta_1)^2} + \frac{2(w + L - v_0\tau)}{(\tau - \delta_1)^2} \tag{2.3.5}$$

which, for known values if W, L, v_0, and δ_1, represents a straight line, as shown in Figure 2.3.5. The distance x_a corresponds to the maximum comfortable acceleration rate a_1^*, and the x-intercept specifies the maximum distance between the vehicle and the stop line from which the vehicle can clear the intersection without accelerating.

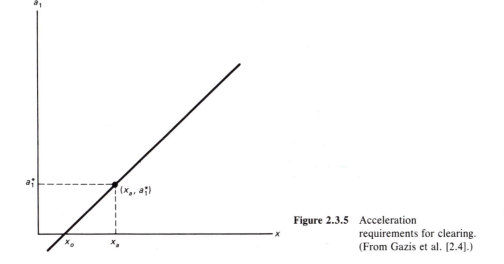

Figure 2.3.5 Acceleration requirements for clearing. (From Gazis et al. [2.4].)

The distance

$$x_o = v_0 \, \tau - (w + L) \qquad (2.3.6)$$

is relevant to this analysis because a vehicle that approaches the intersection at the speed limit should not be required to accelerate in order to clear the intersection and thus break the law. The distance x_o defines a point beyond which a vehicle traveling at the speed limit would not be able to safely or legally clear the intersection on yellow.

For a particular site, the relative magnitudes of the two critical distances x_o and x_c determine whether a vehicle can or cannot safely execute either or both maneuvers, as illustrated by Figure 2.3.6. In part (a), $x_c < x_o$ and the driver can

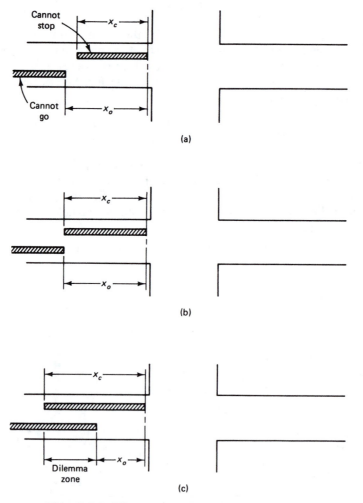

(a)

(b)

(c)

Figure 2.3.6   Dilemma zone. (From Gazis et al. [2.4].)

execute either maneuver no matter where the vehicle is located at the onset of amber. The limiting case is represented by part (b). A problem becomes apparent when $x_c > x_o$, when a *dilemma zone* of length $x_c - x_o$ exists: A vehicle approaching the intersection at the legal speed limit can execute neither of the two maneuvers safely, legally, and comfortably if it happens to be located within the dilemma zone at the onset of amber.

The dilemma zone may be eliminated either by changing the speed limit which in certain locations may be undesirable or by selecting an appropriate minimum duration for the amber signal phase that results in $x_c = x_o$. In this case Eqs. 2.3.3 and 2.3.6 yield

$$\tau_{min} = \delta_2 + \frac{v_0}{2a_2^*} + \frac{w + L}{v_0} \tag{2.3.7}$$

Thus properly selected values of a vehicle length, human factors (i.e., comfortable deceleration and sufficient perception-reaction time), and speed limit v_0 specify the *minimum* amber duration, which, barring *driver error*, ensures that if the vehicle cannot stop, it can clear the intersection. Exercise 7 at the end of this chapter, however, shows that vehicles traveling at other speeds may still experience a dilemma zone problem, depending on their position at the onset of amber.

Example 2.10

A driver traveling at the speed limit of 30 mi/h was cited for crossing an intersection on red. He claimed that he was innocent because the duration of the amber display was improper and, consequently, a dilemma zone existed at that location. Using the following data, determine whether the driver's claim was correct.

$$\text{amber duration} = 4.5 \text{ s}$$

$$\text{perception-reaction time} = 1.5 \text{ s}$$

$$\text{comfortable deceleration} = 10 \text{ ft/s}^2$$

$$\text{car length} = 15 \text{ ft}$$

$$\text{intersection width} = 50 \text{ ft}$$

Solution   The required minimum duration of the amber phase is

$$\tau_{min} = 1.5 + \frac{44}{20} + \frac{65}{44} = 5.18 \text{ s}$$

Since the actual duration was 4.5 s, the driver's claim cannot be dismissed. There was a dilemma zone, the length of which was

$$x_c - x_o = v_0 \delta_2 - v_0 \tau + \frac{v_0^2}{2a_2^*} + w + L$$

$$= 29.8 \text{ ft}$$

Whether the vehicle was within the dilemma zone at the onset of amber and whether the driver was not speeding cannot be proven.

Example 2.11

A car stalled 50 ft from the stopping line at an approach to a signalized intersection of $w = 40$ ft. The driver managed to start it again at the moment the traffic signal turned yellow and decided to clear the intersection. Given that the car accelerated according to

$$a = 4.8 - 0.06v \text{ ft/s}^2$$

and that $\tau = 4.5$ s and $\delta_1 = 1.0$ s, determine whether the driver was able to clear the intersection on yellow.

Solution   Of the available 4.5 s of yellow, 1 s elapsed during perception-reaction. According to Example 2.2, during the remaining 3.5 s, the vehicle covered a distance of

$$x = \frac{4.8}{0.06}(3.5) - \frac{4.8}{0.06^2}[1 - e^{-(0.06)(3.5)}] + 0 = 27.45 \text{ ft}$$

Since $27.45 < (50 + L)$, the driver was unable to clear the intersection on yellow.

Discussion   In this case, the given acceleration was a function of speed and implicitly of time. Therefore, the distance traveled had to be computed accordingly. The design in Eq. 2.3.7 is based on a vehicle approaching at the speed limit and either decelerating at an average rate or clearing the intersection without having to accelerate.

2.3.3 Visual Acuity

A driver visually perceives the actions of other vehicles, the location of objects, traffic-control devices, and the general traffic environment. *Visual acuity* refers to the sharpness with which a person can see an object [2.1, 2.5, 2.6]. One measurement of visual acuity is the *recognition acuity* obtained by the use of the standard Snellen chart familiar to anyone who has visited an ophthalmologist for an eye examination: The person is asked to read letters of different heights from a specified distance. The result of the test is specified in relation to a subject of normal vision. Normal vision is taken to mean that in a well-lit environment, a person can recognize a letter of about $\frac{1}{3}$ in. in height at a distance of 20 ft; the visual acuity of this person is given as 20/20. A person with worse vision must be closer to the display in order to recognize the same letter. This relative visual acuity is designated by a ratio such as 20/40, meaning that the person can clearly see an object at a distance of 20 ft when a distance of 40 ft is sufficient for a person with normal vision. Alternatively, the person with 20/40 vision requires an object twice as large as the one that a person with normal vision can clearly discern from the same distance.

Visual acuity is affected by factors such as the contrast and brightness of the object, the level of illumination, and the relative motion between the observer and the object. Visual acuity is termed *static* in the absence of relative motion and *dynamic* when relative motion exists. Night driving requires artificial illumination of signs either by permanent fixtures or by reliance on the vehicle's headlights. In addition, acuity decreases with increasing visual angles, as illustrated by Figure 2.3.7. The most clear vision occurs within a cone of vision in

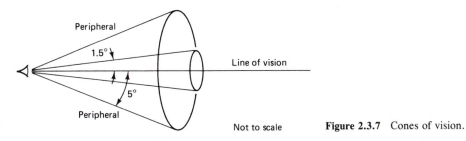

Figure 2.3.7   Cones of vision.

the vicinity of 3°. The clarity of vision is fairly good up to approximately 10°, beyond which lies the region of peripheral vision, which may extend up to 160°. For practical design, traffic signs should be placed within the 10° cone and at locations permitting ample distance for perception-reaction and maneuver execution.

Example 2.12

A driver with 20/20 vision can read a sign from a distance of 90 ft. If the letter size is 2 in., how close would a person with 20/50 vision have to be to be able to read the same sign? For the given definition of normal vision, calculate the height of the lettering that a driver with 20/60 vision can read from a distance of (a) 90 ft and (b) 36 ft.

Solution   The distance x from the location of the sign can be computed by simple proportions as follows:

$$x = (90 \text{ ft})(20/50) = 36 \text{ ft}$$

Similarly, the required letter heights can be obtained by proportioning as:

(a) $h = (2 \text{ in.})\frac{60}{20} = 6$ in.

(b) $h = (2 \text{ in.})\frac{60}{50} = 2.4$ in.

Example 2.13

Assume that a driver with normal vision can read a sign from a distance of 50 ft. for each inch of letter height and that the "design driver" has a 20/40 vision. Determine how far away from an exit ramp a directional sign should be located to allow a safe reduction of speed from 60 mi/h to 30 mi/h, given a perception-reaction time of 1.5 s, a coefficient of friction of 0.30, a letter size of 8 in., and a level freeway.

Solution   As specified, a driver with normal vision can recognize the sign from a distance of 50 × 8 = 400 ft. A driver with 20/40 vision must be no more than 200 ft away. Including perception-reaction, the distance traveled to decelerate from 60 mi/h to 30 mi/h is

$$x = v_0 t + \frac{v_0^2 - v^2}{2g \, (f + G)} = (88)(1.5) + \frac{88^2 - 44^2}{2(32.2)(0.30)} = 433 \text{ ft}$$

Hence the sign must be located at least $433 - 200 = 233$ ft, or about 250 ft, in advance of the exit ramp (Fig. 2.3.8).

Figure 2.3.8 Determination of sign location for good visibility.

Discussion   The solution to this problem brings to bear the perception-reaction phenomenon discussed in Section 2.3.1 and the braking distance covered in Section 2.2.2. Moreover, the "design driver" does not represent the best performer, and the design conditions assume a wet pavement (i.e., $f = 0.30$).

2.3.4 Lateral Displacement

When approaching an object located near their paths, as shown by Figure 2.3.9, drivers show a tendency to displace laterally away from the object even though it may not be on their direct path. Taragin [2.7] reported a set of experiments, which measured this tendency: Various objects were placed at different lateral

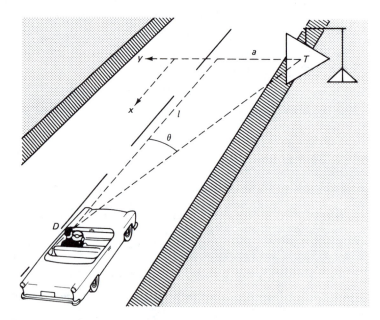

Figure 2.3.9   Geometry of lateral clearance. (From Michaels and Gozan [2.8], with slight modification.)

distances on two-lane and multilane highways of various pavement widths, and the effects of these objects were compared to cases where no object was present. The measured effects consisted of speed adjustments, the longitudinal distance l at which vehicles were seen to displace laterally, and the magnitude of the observed lateral displacement.

The major results of the experiments included the following: The narrower the pavement and the closer the object to the pavement edge, the greater the magnitude of lateral displacement. When the object was placed at the edge of pavement, the lateral displacement was found to be 3.3 ft in the case of two-lane highways with 8-ft lanes and 1.8 ft for 12-ft lanes. In certain cases, speed reductions became apparent.

Subsequent research by Michaels and Gozan [2.8] compared two mathematical models of this phenomenon and concluded that ''a model of lateral displacement based on the rate of change of visual angle accounts best for the obtained results.'' Mathematically, this model can be derived as follows.

The relationship between the longitudinal distance l, the lateral placement of the object a, and the visual angle θ is

$$l = a \cot \theta \qquad (2.3.8)$$

$$\frac{dl}{dt} = -a \csc^2\theta \, \frac{d\theta}{dt} \qquad (2.3.9)$$

Since $dl/dt = -v$, the vehicle's velocity and $\csc^2\theta = (a^2 + l^2)/a^2$,

$$\frac{d\theta}{dt} = \frac{va}{a^2 + l^2} \qquad (2.3.10)$$

Thus given the vehicle's speed, the longitudinal distance l, and the rate of change of the visual angle, the driver can estimate the lateral placement of the object to judge whether it lies in the vehicle's path or not. If the object lies directly in the vehicle's path (i.e., $a = 0$), the driver cannot detect any angular change. According to this human factor model, each driver has a subjective *critical rate of change in visual angle*, below which the driver presumes that the vehicle is in a collision path and displaces away from the object in the lateral direction.

Michaels and Gozan pointed out that this model explains Taragin's findings with regard to speed adjustments, and they provide additional information regarding other factors affecting both the magnitude of lateral displacement, including the size, shape, and brightness of the object. This model can be extended to situations where the object is another moving vehicle on the roadway, in which case the equations of relative motion must be employed [2.1].

The understanding of the driver characteristic described in this section can aid in controlling vehicular speeds in highway construction zones through the proper placement of cones or barricades and in design decisions relating to the placement of objects (signs, bridge abutments, and raised medians) along highways.

Example 2.14

A vehicle traveling at 40 mi/h was observed to displace laterally when it was located 300 ft away from a bridge abutment placed 6 ft to the right of its path. At what longitudinal distance from the same abutment would you expect the same driver to displace laterally when traveling at 60 mi/h?

Solution   By Eq. 2.3.10, the critical rate of change in visual angle for this driver is

$$\left(\frac{d\theta}{dt}\right)_{cr} = 0.0039 \text{ rad/s}$$

For the case of $v = 60$ mi/h $= 88$ ft/s,

$$0.0039 = \frac{(88)(6)}{6^2 + l^2}$$

and

$$l = 368 \text{ ft}$$

2.4 GEOMETRIC DESIGN OF HIGHWAYS

2.4.1 Introduction

Geometric design refers to the physical proportioning of facilities, as distinguished from other aspects of design, such as structural design. In this section we address the basic components of geometric design, with the emphasis placed on highway facilities. The five elements examined are the cross section, horizontal alignment, superelevation, vertical alignment, and channelization. A brief discussion on pavement design is included.

2.4.2 Functional Classification of Highways

In the United States, highways are classified according to the function they serve (*functional classification*) and with respect to the entity (private, municipal, state, or federal) responsible for their construction, maintenance, and operation (*jurisdictional classification*). Of the two, the functional classification is more relevant to geometric design. Table 2.4.1 lists the major functional categories of highways in the United States [2.2, 2.5, 2.9]. Figure 2.4.1 is a conceptual description of the relative emphasis that each highway category places on the functions of providing "mobility" (i.e., continuous travel) on one hand and "accessibility" (i.e., direct access to abutting property) on the other: Local streets are predominantly designed for accessibility rather than mobility, whereas high-level facilities such as expressways and freeways are predominantly designed for high-speed continuous

TABLE 2.4.1 HIGHWAY FUNCTIONAL CLASSIFICATION

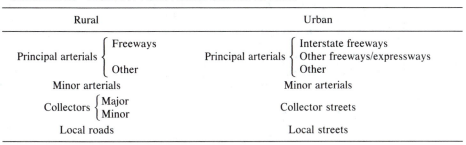

Rural	Urban
Principal arterials { Freeways / Other	Principal arterials { Interstate freeways / Other freeways/expressways / Other
Minor arterials	Minor arterials
Collectors { Major / Minor	Collector streets
Local roads	Local streets

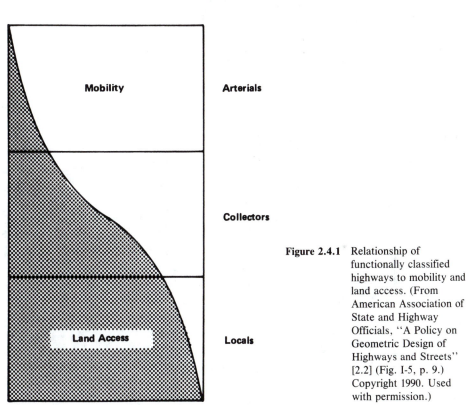

Mobility — Arterials

Collectors

Land Access — Locals

Figure 2.4.1 Relationship of functionally classified highways to mobility and land access. (From American Association of State and Highway Officials, "A Policy on Geometric Design of Highways and Streets" [2.2] (Fig. I-5, p. 9.) Copyright 1990. Used with permission.)

movement. The technical difference between freeways and expressways is that the former are characterized by *full control of access*, meaning that access to and egress from these facilities are permitted only at controlled locations such as entrance and exit ramps, whereas the latter have *partial control of access*, meaning that access or egress may also be permitted directly from or to abutting property or via a limited number of at-grade intersections. The functional hierarchies of rural and urban highways are schematically illustrated by Fig. 2.4.2.

Figure 2.4.2 Illustration of functionally classified highways. (From American Association of State and Highway Officials, "A Policy on Geometric Design of Highways and Streets" [2.2] (Figs. I-3 and I-4, pp. 7–8.) Copyright 1990. Used with permission.)

Generally, the design requirements for the various highway types follow the functions served. At one extreme, local roads and streets are designed primarily for light, low-speed traffic to gain access to residences and other land uses; they are closely spaced and are often designed to discourage through traffic. At the other extreme, freeways are designed for high traffic levels at high speeds; they are sparsely spaced and are designed to facilitate continuous travel between major activity centers. Urban and rural principal arterials are interconnected to serve continuous intercity and interstate movements.

2.4.3 Cross-Section Design

Cross-section design refers to the profile of the facility perpendicular to the centerline and extending to the limits of the right-of-way within which the facility is constructed. Figure 2.4.3 illustrates the cross section of a typical *undivided* two-

Figure 2.4.3   Cross section of a two-lane rural highway. (From American Association of State and Highway Officials, "A Policy on Geometric Design of Highways and Streets" [2.2] (Fig. VII-1, p. 501.) Copyright 1990. Used with permission.)

lane rural highway with a lane in each direction of travel. Lane separation is designated by longitudinal *pavement markings*. A *normal crown*, that is, a mild slope in the pavement on either side of the centerline, is provided to facilitate the removal of water. Depending on drainage requirements, crowns in the range of $\frac{1}{8}$ to about $\frac{1}{4}$ in./ft of width are typical. Paved or unpaved *shoulders* are provided at either end of the *travel-way* pavement for emergency situations. Beyond the shoulders, drainage ditches are provided with cut or filled side slopes at appropriate angles to ensure slope stability. Figure 2.4.4 shows typical types of *divided* multilane rural highways. The separation of the two directions of travel may be accomplished by constructing independent roadways and by utilizing raised or depressed *medians*. Various types of *barriers* (including guardrails and concrete barriers) may be used along the median and at the end of the *clear zone* beyond the shoulders. Depending on their function, urban facilities may also be either undivided or divided. Urban roadways often incorporate drainage ditches or gut-

INDEPENDENT ROADWAY

– A –

TYPICAL

– B –

RESTRICTED

– C –

Figure 2.4.4 Cross sections of four-lane rural highways. (From American Association of State and Highway Officials, "A Policy on Geometric Design of Highways and Streets" [2.2] (Fig. VIII-48, p. 662.) Copyright 1990. Used with permission.)

ters and raised curbs. Urban arterials can be at ground level (i.e., *at grade*), *elevated*, or *depressed*; they may also contain special bus lanes and rail transit-ways within their rights-of-way.

2.4.4 Horizontal Alignment

The *horizontal alignment* of a highway, railway, or transit guideway represents the projection of the facility on a horizontal plane. It generally consists of straight-line segments (*tangents*) connected by *circular curves* either directly (*simple curves*) or via intermediate *transition curves*. Figure 2.4.5 illustrates these two

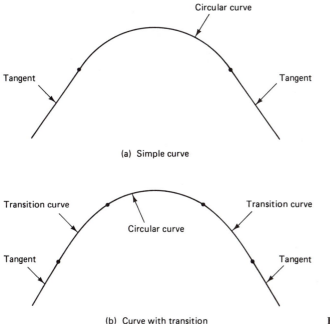

(a) Simple curve

(b) Curve with transition

Figure 2.4.5 Typical horizontal curves.

common geometric arrangements. The length of the facility is measured along the horizontal alignment of a control line (such as the centerline of a highway) and is usually expressed in terms of 100-ft *stations* from a reference point. Thus a point on the alignment designated as *sta. 14* is located at a distance of 14 stations (i.e., 14 × 100 = 1400 ft) from the reference point. Similarly, a point identified as *sta. 14 + 56.70* is located at a distance of 1456.70 ft from the reference point.

Figure 2.4.6 shows the horizontal alignment of the centerline of a simple curve. A simple circular curve connects two tangents, which—when projected—meet at a *point of intersection*, or PI. Proceeding in the direction of increasing station values, point A is designated as the *point of curvature* (PC), that is, the point where the curve begins. Point B, or the end of the curve, is denoted as the *point of tangency*, or PT. At these two points, of course, the radii of the circular curve are perpendicular to the tangents. The length of the curve AB equals

$$L = 2\pi R\left(\frac{\Delta}{360}\right) \qquad\qquad (2.4.1)$$

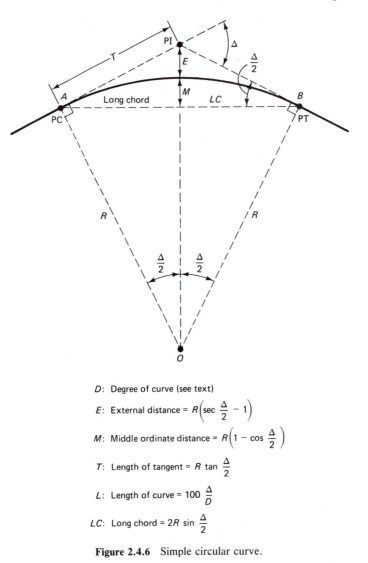

D: Degree of curve (see text)

E: External distance = $R\left(\sec \dfrac{\Delta}{2} - 1\right)$

M: Middle ordinate distance = $R\left(1 - \cos \dfrac{\Delta}{2}\right)$

T: Length of tangent = $R \tan \dfrac{\Delta}{2}$

L: Length of curve = $100 \dfrac{\Delta}{D}$

LC: Long chord = $2R \sin \dfrac{\Delta}{2}$

Figure 2.4.6 Simple circular curve.

where R is the curve radius. Other important distances and equations are shown in Fig. 2.4.6.

Two straight lines intersecting at the PI can be connected by an infinite number of circular curves. Each of these curves may be defined by its radius R or by its *degree of curve D*, for which two alternative definitions are encountered in practice. The *arc definition* is preferred by highway engineers and is equal to the central angle (in degrees) subtended by an arc of 100 ft. In this case, the radius of the curve and the degree of curve are related by the following proportion:

$$\frac{100}{2\pi R} = \frac{D}{360}$$

or   (2.4.2)

$$D = \left(\frac{5729.58}{R}\right)^{\circ}$$

Railway design, on the other hand, uses the *chord definition* for the degree of curve, which is equal to the angle subtended by a chord of 100 ft, in which case the relationship between the radius and the degree of curve is

$$\sin\left(\frac{D}{2}\right) = \frac{50}{R}$$ (2.4.3)

Figure 2.4.7 illustrates the two definitions of the degree of curve. In either case, specifying the degree of curve is equivalent to specifying the radius. The

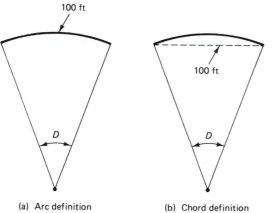

(a) Arc definition   (b) Chord definition   **Figure 2.4.7** Degree of curve.

degree of curve D must not be confused with the *external angle* of deflection (Δ) between the tangents, which is equal to the total *central angle* subtended by the entire length of the curve AB. Using the arc definition for the degree of curve, the following relationship between the length of the curve L, the degree of curve D, and the external angle Δ becomes apparent:

$$L = \frac{100\Delta}{D}$$ (2.4.4)

2.4.5 Determination of Design Radius

The requirement for lateral banking or *superelevating* of the cross section of curved paths (discussed in Section 2.2.3) imposes a constraint on the *minimum radius* that the curve may have. Equation 2.2.19 (reproduced as Eq. 2.4.5) expresses the relationship between the superelevation rate e, the design speed v, the coefficient of side friction f_s, and the curve radius R:

$$e + f_s = \frac{v^2}{gR} \qquad (2.4.5)$$

An alternative specification of this formula found in U.S. design manuals is the following mixed-unit equation:

$$e + f_s = \frac{v^2}{15R} \qquad (2.4.6)$$

where the design speed has units of miles per hour and the radius is specified in feet.

The maximum allowable design value for e [2.2] is 0.12 ft/ft and the suggested maximum is set at 0.10, but special conditions may override these values. For example, a maximum superelevation rate of 0.08 ft/ft may be more appropriate at localities where snow and ice conditions occur. The maximum *design* values for the coefficient of side friction depend on design speed and range from about 0.17 at 20 mi/h to 0.10 at 70 mi/h. According to Eq. 2.4.5, the *minimum radius* for the selected design speed is

$$R_{min} = \frac{v^2}{g(e_{max} + f_{max})} \qquad (2.4.7)$$

and the corresponding *maximum degree of curve* is given by Eq. 2.4.2.

From the perspective of the driver, the longer the radius the better. Thus the minimum radius does not represent the desired design radius. Where conditions permit the selection of a design radius that is longer than the minimum, the design value of e can be computed by

$$e_{des} = \frac{v^2}{gR} - f_s \qquad \text{for } R > R_{min} \qquad (2.4.8)$$

Example 2.15

Calculate the maximum degree of curve and the minimum radius of a simple circular curve with an external angle of 100°. The design speed is 50 mi/h, the corresponding value of f_{max} is 0.14, and the maximum design value for e is 0.10. Also calculate the design value for e for a curve that has a radius of 800 ft.

Solution   By either Eq. 2.4.5 or 2.4.6,

$$R = 695 \text{ ft}$$

and by Eq. 2.4.2,

$$D = \frac{5729.58}{695} = 8.24°$$

The external angle does not enter these calculations.
For a radius of 800 ft, Eq. 2.4.8 yields

$$e_{\text{des}} = 0.21 - 0.14 = 0.07 \text{ ft/ft}$$

2.4.6 Superelevation Design

Banking of the cross section is needed on the curved portion of the facility but is not necessary along the tangent segments of the horizontal alignment. Consequently, a transition of the cross section from the normal crown on the tangent to a fully superelevated pavement on the curve must be developed.

As an illustration of superelevation design, consider a simple circular curve for the two-lane highway of Fig. 2.4.8. The cross section is at the normal crown at point A and fully superelevated at point E. Point B represents the intermediate condition, where the outside edge of the travel way has been rotated to the level of the centerline; point C represents the condition where the outside edge, the centerline, and the inside edge are aligned at a slope equal to the normal crown. Since the normal crown is milder than the design superelevation rate, the cross section must be further rotated until it reaches full superelevation at point E with an intermediate slope at the PC (i.e., point D). The distances AB and BE along the horizontal alignment are called the *tangent runout* and the *superelevation runoff*, respectively. The length of the superelevation runoff depends on the rate at which the cross section is rotated.

The selection of the length of superelevation runoff is not an exact science. Table 2.4.2 presents minimum lengths for *two-lane* rural highways having either 10- or 12-ft lanes. The superelevation runoff lengths for three-, four-, and six-lane highways should be 1.2, 1.5, and 2.0 times those calculated for two-lane highways.

On simple curves, about two-thirds of the superelevation runoff is typically placed on the tangent and the rest of the curve. When transition curves are used, the superelevation runoff is developed on them. Transition curves (see Fig. 2.4.5) are usually introduced on high-speed curves. Most often, they are appropriate lengths of spirals with end radii of curvature that are consistent with those of the tangent (i.e., infinite at the TS and the ST) and the circular curve (i.e., R at the SC and the CS); TS is tangent to spiral, CS is curve to spiral, etc.

Figure 2.4.9 illustrates four common methods of developing the transition to full superelevation. For ease of presentation, the curved alignment is shown to be stretched out into a straight line. The first method rotates the pavement about the centerline, the second about the inside edge, and the third about the outside edge. The fourth method applies to pavements that begin with a straight cross-section slope and are revolved about the outside edge. This type of cross

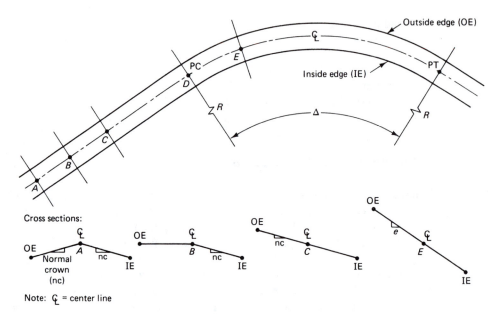

Figure 2.4.8 Development of superelevation.

TABLE 2.4.2 REQUIRED LENGTH OF SUPERELEVATION RUNOFF FOR TWO-LANE ROADS

Superelevation rate, e	Length of runoff (ft), L, for design speed (mi/h) of:							
	20	30	40	50	55	60	65	70
12-ft lanes								
0.02	50	100	125	150	160	175	190	200
0.04	60	100	125	150	160	175	190	200
0.06	95	110	125	150	160	175	190	200
0.08	125	145	170	190	205	215	230	240
0.10	160	180	210	240	255	270	290	300
0.12	195	215	250	290	305	320	350	360
10-ft lanes								
0.02	50	100	125	150	160	175	190	200
0.04	50	100	125	150	160	175	190	200
0.06	80	100	125	150	160	175	190	200
0.08	105	120	140	160	170	180	190	200
0.10	130	150	175	200	215	225	240	250
0.12	160	180	210	240	255	270	290	300

Source: American Association of State and Highway Officials, "A Policy on Geometric Design of Highways and Streets" [2.2] (Table III-15, p. 178.) Copyright 1990. Used with permission.

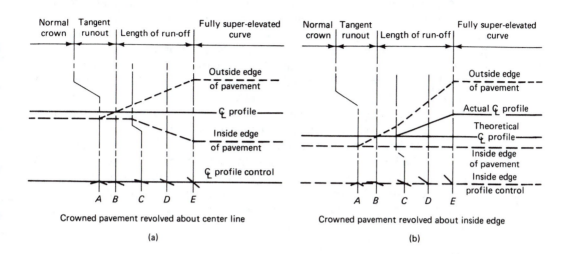

Crowned pavement revolved about center line

(a)

Crowned pavement revolved about inside edge

(b)

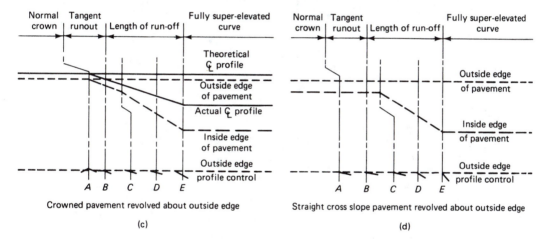

Crowned pavement revolved about outside edge

(c)

Straight cross slope pavement revolved about outside edge

(d)

Note: Angular breaks to be appropriately
rounded as shown by dotted line.

Figure 2.4.9 Methods of attaining full superelevation. (From American Association of State
and Highway Officials, "A Policy on Geometric Design of Highways and
Streets" [2.2] (Fig. III-16, p. 183.) Copyright 1990. Used with permission.)

slope may be found on the separate roadways that make up a divided multilane facility (see Fig. 2.4.4). The longitudinal profile of the pavement along the length of the highway corresponding to each of the four methods of obtaining full superelevation is shown in Fig. 2.4.9. In (a), the location of the inside edge, the centerline, and the outside edge are shown relative to the elevation of the centerline. In (b) and (c), the edge and centerline profiles are shown relative to the unrotated centerline, that is, the "theoretical centerline profile." At point A of the first three diagrams, the outside edge is as far below the centerline as the inside edge, the difference in elevation being equal to the normal crown times the pavement width in each travel direction. At point B, the outside edge has reached the level of the centerline, and at point C the outside edge is located as far above as the inside edge is below the centerline. Finally, at point E the cross section is fully superelevated. The reverse of these profiles is found at the other end of the circular curve. As the note at the bottom of Fig. 2.4.9 suggests, the angular breaks should be rounded by smooth curves.

Example 2.16

Draw the longitudinal profile of the curve of Example 2.15 using the minimum radius for a two-lane rural highway given a normal crown of $\frac{1}{4}$ in./ft and a lane width $W = 12$ ft.

Figure 2.4.10   Cross sectional drawing of superelevation along a curve. Caution: x and y scales are different.

Solution   With the calculated radius of 695 ft and an external angle of 100°, Eq. 2.4.1 gives a curve length of

$$L = 1213 \text{ ft}$$

For $e = 0.10$, a design speed $v = 50$ mi/h, and 12-ft lanes, the suggested minimum length of superelevation runoff (Table 2.4.2) is 240 ft. Place two-thirds (or 160 ft) of the runoff on each tangent at either end and the rest (80 ft) on the curve. This leaves $1213 - 2 \times 80 = 1053$ ft of the curve's length at full superelevation. Rotation about the centerlines means that, at full superelevation, the inside and outside edges are offset by $W \times e = 12 \times 0.10 = 1.2$ ft from the centerline. At the normal cross section, the two edges are $12 \times 0.25 = 3$ in. or 0.25 ft, below the centerline. Simple calculations lead to a longitudinal profile, as shown in Fig. 2.4.10.

2.4.7 Vertical Alignment

The vertical alignment of highways and railways consists of *grade tangents* connected with *parabolic vertical curves*. The desirable maximum design grades and gradient change depend on facility type and on vehicular characteristics. For highways, the desirable maximum grades range from about 2% for freeways to about 6% for local streets. Higher grades may be unavoidable at locations of difficult topography, and the combined effect of gradient and the length over which it is sustained (i.e., the *length of grade*) must also be considered, especially at locations frequently used by heavy vehicles with limited climbing capability. Railroad design tolerates much smaller maximum grades, with about 4% representing the limit corresponding to the worst topography. The maximum grades for fixed-guideway transit systems are a function of the tract and wheel combinations employed. Steel-wheel on steel-rail systems are similar to railroads, whereas rubber-tire systems approach the highway case. Some systems are specifically designed for very steep inclines.

The *length of a vertical curve is measured along the horizontal alignment*, and a point on the curve is specified by its station location on the horizontal alignment and its elevation from a datum. The beginning and end of a vertical curve are denoted, respectively, as the *vertical point of curvature* (VPC) and the *vertical point of tangency* (VPT), and the point where the grade lines intersect is known as the *vertical point of intersection* (VPI). Figure 2.4.11 describes a *symmetrical* vertical curve for which the grade tangents are equal; asymmetrical vertical curves are used only in places of unusual constraints. The figure applies to both *crest* curves, as shown, and *sag* curves, the latter being merely a reflection of the former with the curve lying above the VPI. In the case of symmetrical curves, a vertical line passing through the VPI bisects the length of the curve, but the high (or low) point of the curve does not necessarily lie directly below (or above) the VPI. For convenience, the horizontal alignment is shown as a straight line, but in reality it may be prescribing a curved path. Moreover, there

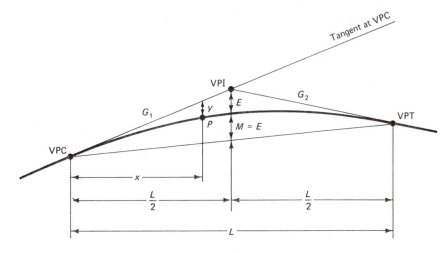

Figure 2.4.11   Symmetric vertical curve.

is no necessary coincidence between the VPC, the VPI, and the VPT on one hand and the PC, the PI, and the PT on the other.

Denoting the *percent grade* at the VPC as G_1 and the percent grade at the VPT as G_2, the total change in grade

$$A = G_2 - G_1 \text{ percent} \tag{2.4.9}$$

is negative in the case of crest curves and positive in the case of sag curves. The ratio of the curve's length to the absolute value of the change in grade

$$K = \frac{L}{|A|} \tag{2.4.10}$$

specifies the *vertical curvature* of the curve. Special attention to drainage design is warranted when K is greater than 167. The *external distance E* from the VPI to the middle of the curve is

$$E = \frac{AL}{800} \text{ ft} \tag{2.4.11}$$

where L is the length of the curve in feet. Note that E is positive in the case of sag curves and negative in the case of crest curves, indicating that the midpoint of the curve lies above and below the VPI, respectively.

Other vertical *offsets y* between the grade tangent passing through the VPC and the vertical curve are calculated by

$$y = 4E\left(\frac{x}{L}\right)^2 \tag{2.4.12}$$

where x is the distance along the horizontal alignment from the VPC to the point of interest. The high (or low) point is located at a distance

$$X = \frac{LG_1}{G_1 - G_2} \qquad X \geq 0 \tag{2.4.13}$$

from the VPC. The *curve elevation* of any point P is computed by

$$\text{elevation of } P = \left[\text{elevation of VPC} + \left(\frac{G_1}{100}\right)x \right] + y \tag{2.4.14}$$

where the term in brackets represents the *tangent elevation* on the vertical tangent passing through the VPC. In practice, curve elevations are computed at 25- or 50-ft intervals. In addition, the elevations are calculated for critical points such as the high or low point, and points where necessary clearances below the pavement (e.g., drainage facilities such as culverts) or above the pavement (e.g., overpasses) are present.

Example 2.17

A 600-ft vertical curve connects a $+4\%$ grade to a -2% grade at station $25 + 60.55$ and elevation 648.64 ft. Calculate the location and elevation of the VPC, the middle of the curve, the VPT, and the curve elevation at stations $24 + 00$ and $27 + 00$.

Solution   The curve is a crest with $A = -2 - (+4) = -6\%$ and $K = 600/6 = 100$. The middle distance is $E = -4.5$ ft. The middle point of the curve is 4.5 ft below the VPI at sta. $25 + 60.55$. The VPC and the VPT are located at either side of the VPI at distances of $L/2 = 300$ ft, or 3 stations. Hence the VPC is $3 \times 4 = 12$ ft below the VPI at sta. $22 + 60.55$, and the VPT is $3 \times 2 = 6$ ft below the VPI at sta. $28 + 60.55$. The high point is located at a distance $X = 400$ ft, or 4 stations from the VPC (i.e., at sta. $26 + 60.55$). The following table illustrates the use of Eqs. 2.4.12 and 2.4.14 to calculate the required curve elevations.

Point P (sta.)	x (ft)	Tangent elevation	Offset y (ft)	Curve elevation
$22 + 60.55$ (VPC)	000.00	636.64	0.00	636.64
$24 + 00.00$	139.45	642.22	-0.97	641.25
$25 + 60.55$	300.00	648.64	-4.50	644.14
$26 + 60.55$ (high)	400.00	652.64	-8.00	644.64
$27 + 00.00$	439.45	654.22	-9.66	644.56
$28 + 60.55$ (VPT)	600.00	660.64	-18.00	642.64

Discussion   Figure 2.4.12 shows the vertical curve. Offsets are measured in relation to the tangent at the VPC irrespective of whether the subject point P is to the right or to the left of the VPI. The negative sign of the offsets indicates that the curve elevations are below the tangent elevations. The application of Eq. 2.4.12 in the given table resulted in the same curve elevations for the middle point and for the VPT as those obtained by the calculations preceding the table. All the tabulated results could have been obtained by viewing the curve from the VPT. In that case,

Figure 2.4.12   Example of vertical curve connection.

G_1 and G_2 would be $+2\%$ and -4%, respectively, the distance x would be measured to the left of the VPT, and the offsets would be measured from the tangent at the VPT.

2.4.8 Stopping and Passing Sight Distance

The design of a facility must ensure that drivers are provided with adequate *sight distances* to perceive dangerous situations ahead and to take preventive action. If an object is present in the vehicle's path, warranting that the vehicle be stopped to avoid a mishap, the object must be visible to the driver from a distance at least equal to a minimum *stopping sight distance*, S_s. Table 2.4.3 presents the design values suggested by AASHTO [2.2], which incorporate several practical approximations.

To overtake another vehicle safely on two-lane highways (i.e., one lane in each direction), a driver must consider the relative speeds and positions of the driver's own vehicle, the vehicle to be overtaken, and an oncoming vehicle in the opposite direction. A successful passing maneuver involves the elements shown in Fig. 2.4.13. The minimum *passing sight distances* suggested by AASHTO for various design speeds are also shown. Safe stopping sight distances must be adhered to at all points along the alignment and where adequate passing distances are not possible, no-passing zones must be established. Reducing the speed limit to assure adequate sight distances is also a possibility, but frequent speed limit changes should be avoided.

2.4.9 Geometrics of Sight Distance

On the horizontal plane, the available sight distance is affected by the presence of objects, embankments, and other restrictions, as shown by Fig. 2.4.14. The

TABLE 2.4.3 STOPPING SIGHT DISTANCE

Design Speed (mi/h)	Assumed speed for condition (mi/h)	Brake reaction Time (s)	Brake reaction Distance (ft)	Coefficient of friction f	Braking distance on level[a] (ft)	Stopping sight distance Computed[a] (ft)	Stopping sight distance Rounded for design (ft)
20	20–20	2.5	73.3– 73.3	0.40	33.3– 33.3	106.7–106.7	125–125
25	24–25	2.5	88.0– 91.7	0.38	50.5– 54.8	138.5–146.5	150–150
30	28–30	2.5	102.7–110.0	0.35	74.7– 85.7	177.3–195.7	200–200
35	32–35	2.5	117.3–128.3	0.34	100.4–120.1	217.7–248.4	225–250
40	36–40	2.5	132.0–146.7	0.32	135.0–166.7	267.0–313.3	275–325
45	40–45	2.5	146.7–165.0	0.31	172.0–217.7	318.7–382.7	325–400
50	44–50	2.5	161.3–183.3	0.30	215.1–277.8	376.4–461.1	400–475
55	48–55	2.5	176.0–201.7	0.30	256.0–336.1	432.0–537.8	450–550
60	52–60	2.5	190.7–220.0	0.29	310.8–413.8	501.5–633.8	525–650
65	55–65	2.5	201.7–238.3	0.29	347.7–485.6	549.4–724.0	550–725
70	58–70	2.5	212.7–256.7	0.28	400.5–583.3	613.1–840.0	625–850

[a]Different values for the same speed result from using unequal coefficients of friction.
Source: American Association of State and Highway Officials, "A Policy on Geometric Design of Highways and Streets" [2.2] (Table III-1, p. 120.) Copyright 1990. Used with permission.

effect of curvature (i.e., either R or D) is captured by the inserted equations. This figure corresponds to the low range of stopping sight distance shown in Table 2.4.3.

On crests, the vertical curvature of the facility itself causes sight restrictions, as illustrated by Fig. 2.4.15(a), which shows the line of sight between the driver's eyes (located at a distance h_1 above the pavement) and the top of an object of height h_2. For many years, the design specifications promulgated by AASHTO [2.10] provided for an eye height of 3.75 ft, an object height of 6 in. for the computation of stopping sight distance, and an object height of 4.5 ft for the computation of passing sight distance. The rationale for these values was that an object of less than 6 in. in height is lower than the undercarriage height of the vast majority of vehicles on the roadway, and a height of 4.5 ft represents the height of oncoming vehicles that are relevant to the passing maneuver. Because of changing vehicular dimensions, subsequent research has recommended a modification of these values. In 1984, AASHTO lowered the values for the driver's eye height and the height of oncoming vehicles to 3.50 and 4.25 ft, respectively. The 6-in. object height involved in the calculation of stopping sight distances has been retained. On sag curves the worst situation occurs at night when the line of sight is limited within the area of headlight illumination [Figure 2.4.15(b)].

In either case, the sight distance may be shorter, equal to, or longer than the length of the curve. The following equations can be used to calculate the minimum length of curve that satisfies a given sight-distance requirement:

Figure 2.4.13   Passing sight distance. (From American Association of State and Highway Officials, "A Policy on Geometric Design of Highways and Streets" [2.2] (Fig. III-2, p. 130.) Copyright 1990. Used with permission.)

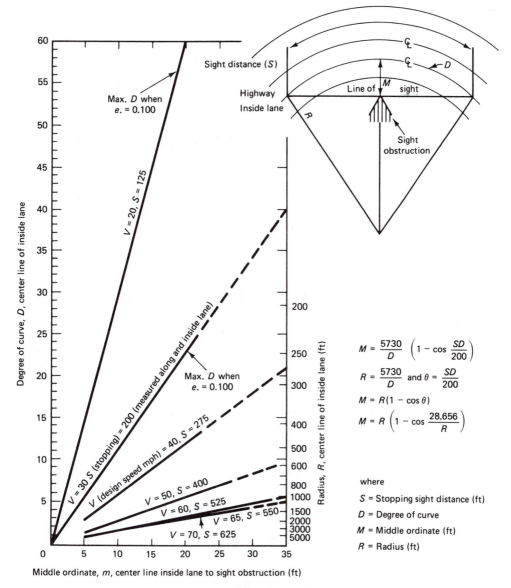

The figure contains the following labels and equations:

Sight distance (S)

Max. D when $e. = 0.100$

Highway
Inside lane

Line of M sight

Sight obstruction

$V = 20, S = 125$

R

$V = 30\ S\ (stopping) = 200\ (measured\ along\ and\ inside\ lane)$

Max. D when $e. = 0.100$

$V\ (design\ speed\ mph) = 40, S = 275$

$V = 50, S = 400$

$V = 60, S = 525$

$V = 65, S = 550$

$V = 70, S = 625$

Degree of curve, D, center line of inside lane

Radius, R, center line of inside lane (ft)

Middle ordinate, m, center line inside lane to sight obstruction (ft)

$$M = \frac{5730}{D}\left(1 - \cos\frac{SD}{200}\right)$$

$$R = \frac{5730}{D} \quad \text{and} \quad \theta = \frac{SD}{200}$$

$$M = R(1 - \cos\theta)$$

$$M = R\left(1 - \cos\frac{28.656}{R}\right)$$

where

S = Stopping sight distance (ft)
D = Degree of curve
M = Middle ordinate (ft)
R = Radius (ft)

Figure 2.4.14   Geometry of horizontal sight distance. (From American Association of State and Highway Officials, ''A Policy on Geometric Design of Highways and Streets'' [2.2] (Fig. III-26A, p. 222.) Copyright 1990. Used with permission.)

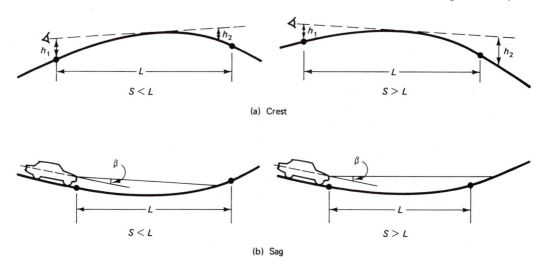

Figure 2.4.15   Geometry of vertical sight distance.

Crest vertical curves:

$$L = \frac{|A|S^2}{200(\sqrt{h_1} + \sqrt{h_2})^2} \qquad \text{for } S \leq L \qquad (2.4.15a)$$

$$L = 2S - \frac{200(\sqrt{h_1} + \sqrt{h_2})^2}{|A|} \qquad \text{for } S \geq L \qquad (2.4.15b)$$

Sag vertical curves:

$$L = \frac{|A|S^2}{200(h + S \tan \beta)} \qquad \text{for } S \leq L \qquad (2.4.16a)$$

$$L = 2S - \frac{200(h + S \tan \beta)}{|A|} \qquad \text{for } S \geq L \qquad (2.4.16b)$$

where

L = length of curve, in feet

S = sight distance, in feet

$|A|$ = $|G_2 - G_1|$, in percent

h_1 = height of driver's eyes, in feet

h_2 = height of object, in feet

h = headlight height: approximately 2 ft

β = beam angle: approximately 1°

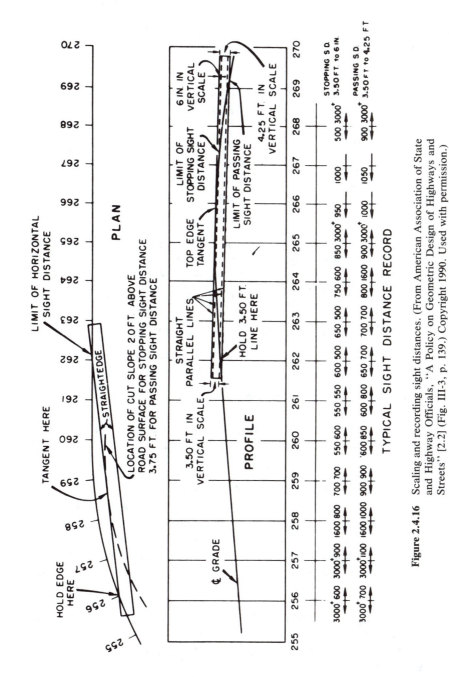

Figure 2.4.16 Scaling and recording sight distances. (From American Association of State and Highway Officials, "A Policy on Geometric Design of Highways and Streets" [2.2] (Fig. III-3, p. 139.) Copyright 1990. Used with permission.)

93

Figure 2.4.16 illustrates that stopping and passing distances may be measured directly on scaled horizontal and vertical profiles.

Example 2.18

> For a design speed of 50 mi/h, determine the minimum length of a crest vertical curve with $A = -4\%$ that meets the post-1984 AASHTO criteria for (a) stopping and (b) passing.
>
> **Solution**   (a) Since A is negative, the curve is a crest. Conservatively, a minimum stopping sight distance of 475 ft is obtained from Table 2.4.3 and substituted in Eqs. 2.4.15 along with the AASHTO recommended heights of $h_1 = 3.50$ and $h_2 = 0.5$ ft:

$$\text{For } S \leqslant L: \quad L = 679 \text{ ft}$$

$$\text{For } S \geqslant L: \quad L = 618 \text{ ft}$$

The first answer is selected because it satisfies the constraint, that is, $475 < 679$.

   (b) The minimum recommended passing sight distance of about 1700 ft is obtained from Fig. 2.4.11 for a design speed of 50 mi/h. With $h_1 = 3.50$ and $h_2 = 4.25$ ft, the crest equations yield

$$\text{For } S \leqslant L: \quad L = 3738 \text{ ft}$$

$$\text{For } S \geqslant L: \quad L = 2627 \text{ ft}$$

Since the first satisfies the condition $S \leqslant L$, it gives the proper answer.

2.4.10 Discussion of Alignment Design

So far, the basic elements of the horizontal and vertical design have been discussed separately. These two aspects of the three-dimensional control line must be integrated and drawn to a suitable scale to aid in the eventual layout and construction of the facility. Figure 2.4.17 illustrates the standard plan and profile drawings of the center line of a two-lane highway.

   On the horizontal plane, the highway segment prescribes a circular curve to which 400-ft transition spirals have been introduced. The station locations of important points are clearly marked, and the characteristics of the curves are specified. The location of the PI is fixed and referenced to local monuments, and other surveying benchmarks are included. The property lines that are crossed by the highway and existing structures are also identified.

   The "stretched-out" vertical profile of the center line is shown on the lower portion of the figure: It consists of a crest curve connecting a $+4\%$ grade and a -4% grade, followed by a sag curve between the -4% grade and a $+5.02\%$ grade. The irregular solid line represents the existing ground elevation to which the vertical alignment or grade line conforms as much as possible. Fitting the grade line to the existing ground, however, must meet maximum grade and adequate sight-distance criteria as explained earlier. Another major consideration in grade control is related to the amounts of earthwork required. Economic con-

Figure 2.4.17   Typical plan and profile of a highway. (From T. F. Hickerson, *Route Surveys and Design*, 4th ed., McGraw-Hill, New York, 1959. Reproduced with permission of the publisher.)

siderations warrant that *cut* and *fill* should be balanced within the limits of the construction area as much as possible to avoid the cost of bringing extra material (*borrow*) to the site and the cost of removing excess excavated quantities to locations that lie outside the site (*overhaul*).

The process of selecting, designing, and locating the final alignment of a facility connecting two points is a highly complex undertaking. It begins with a determination that such a facility is, in fact, needed. Given that the need for a facility has been established, a sequence of interrelated steps follows. These entail the collection and study of the necessary information, including topographic maps, the conducting of photogrammetric reconnaissance surveys, the identification of alternative alignments, the preliminary selection of the preferred alignment, the surveying and mapping of the corridor through which the preferred alignment passes, and the design of the final alignment [2.11]. These activities take place within a variety of economic, legal, and environmental constraints. For example, federal legislation requires that proposed facilities should have a minimum impact on environmentally sensitive areas, natural habitats of endangered species, and sites of historical and archaeological significance. Only after these and other socioeconomic requirements have been met in a satisfactory manner would the phases of detailed surveying and route layout, and finally, construction, proceed.

Elements of pavement widening

SU design vehicle

(1) $w = W_c - W_n$

(2) $W_c = N(U + C) + (N - 1)F_A + Z$

    N = number of lanes

    w = widening for pavement on curve, ft

    W_c = width of pavement on curve, ft

(3) $U = u + R - \sqrt{R^2 - L^2}$

(4) $FA = \sqrt{R^2 + A(2L + A)} - R$

(5) $Z = V/\sqrt{R}$

W_n = width of pavement on tangent, ft
U = track width of vehicle (out-to-out tires), ft
C = lateral clearance per vehicle; assumed 2, 2.5 and
    3 ft for W_n of 20, 22 and 24 ft, respectively
F_A = width of front overhang, ft
Z = extra width allowance for difficulty of driving
    on curves, ft
u = track width on tangent (out-to-out) 8.5 ft
R = radius on centerline of two-lane pavement, ft
L = wheelbase
A = front overhang
V = design speed of highway, mi/h

Figure 2.4.18 Curve widening. (From American Association of State and Highway Officials, "A Policy on Geometric Design of Highways and Streets" [2.2] (Fig. III-25, p. 215.) Copyright 1990. Used with permission.)

2.4.11 Delineation of Vehicular Paths

In addition to the design of the horizontal and vertical alignment of a highway, geometric design includes the delineation of vehicular paths within the travel way to conform to the physical (space) requirements of vehicles and to the steering tendencies of drivers. Figure 2.4.18 illustrates the practice of *curve widening* that is recommended for sharp curves to allow for the fact that the vehicle's front and rear wheels do not track exactly the same trajectories and in response to a tendency on the part of drivers to steer away from the pavement's edge.

The proper delineation of vehicular paths is accomplished by a number of devices, including longitudinal and transverse pavement markings, raised medians and islands, curbing, guardrails, and the like. These devices are accompanied by appropriate directional signs and other pavement markings, such as painted turning arrows [2.12].

The most common pavement markings in the direction of travel are *yellow* and *white lines*, the former separating paths in opposing directions and the latter delineating paths in the same direction. In either case, *solid lines* designate segments where path changes for the purpose of either passing or lane changing are prohibited. *Broken lines* permit the execution of such maneuvers.

At intersection and interchange areas where conflicting paths are found, special design efforts are necessary either to minimize the number of conflicting movements or to reduce their severity. Figure 2.4.19 shows the major types of freeway interchanges, where, by introducing special directional roadways, the more severe *crossing conflicts* are eliminated in favor of the less severe *merging* and *diverging conflicts*. This practice often necessitates the construction of *grade-separated* facilities (i.e., underpasses and overpasses). Additionally, *auxiliary lanes*, such as acceleration and deceleration lanes, permit safe speed changes and reduce the speed differences between conflicting vehicles. The conflicts in the area of *at-grade* intersections are typically reduced by the spatial separation of paths (*channelization*) and by the temporal separation of conflicting movements (e.g., by *signal control*).

2.4.12 Design Vehicles

Whether designing special roadways at an interchange or channelizing an at-grade intersection, it is important to consider the turning characteristics of the vehicles that are expected to use the facility. For purposes of design consistency, the weights, dimensions, and operating characteristics of ten types of vehicles have been selected to represent the wide variety of vehicular types that normally use the highway system. Table 2.4.4 summarizes the dimensions of these design vehicles, and Fig. 2.4.20 shows the space requirements for a W-60 design vehicle when executing turns between 30 and 180° at the minimum turning radius for that vehicle that correspond to low speeds. The selection of the proper design vehicle

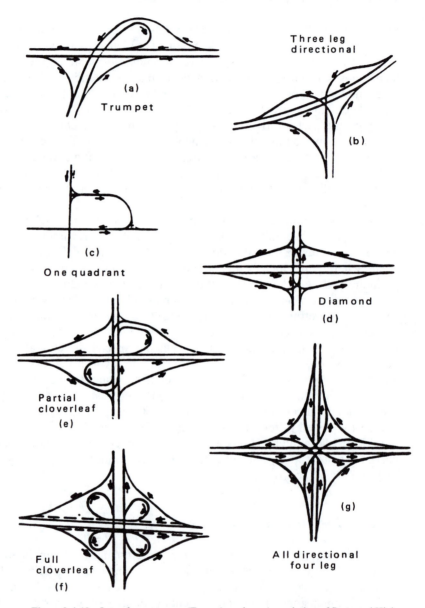

Figure 2.4.19   Interchange types. (From American Association of State and High-way Officials, "A Policy on Geometric Design of Highways and Streets" [2.2] (Fig. X-1, p. 854.) Copyright 1990. Used with permission.)

TABLE 2.4.4 SPECIFICATIONS OF DESIGN VEHICLES

Design vehicle type	Symbol	Overall			Overhang		Dimension[a] (ft)					
		Height	Width	Length	Front	Rear	WB$_1$	WB$_2$	S	T	WB$_3$	WB$_4$
Passenger car	P	4.25	7	19	3	5	11					
Single-unit truck	SU	13.5	8.5	30	4	6	20					
Single-unit bus	BUS	13.5	8.5	40	7	8	25					
Articulated bus	A-BUS	10.5	8.5	60	8.5	9.5	18		4[b]	20[b]		
Combination trucks												
Intermediate semitrailer	WB-40	13.5	8.5	50	4	6	13	27				
Large semitrailer	WB-50	13.5	8.5	55	3	2	20	30				
"Doublebottom" semitrailer–full trailer	WB-60	13.5	8.5	65	2	3	9.7	20	4[c]	5.4[c]	20.9	
Interstate semitrailer	WB-62[d]	13.5	8.5	69	3	3	20	40–42				
	WB-67[e]	13.5	8.5	74	3	3	20	45–47				
Triple semitrailer	WB-96	13.5	8.5	102	2.5	3.3	13.5	20.7	3.3[f]	6[f]	21.7	21.7
Turnpike double semitrailer	WB-114	13.5	8.5	118	2	2	22	40	2[g]	6[g]	44	
Recreation vehicles												
Motor home	MH		8	30	4	6	20					
Car and camper trailer	P/T		8	49	3	10	11	18	5			
Car and boat trailer	P/B		8	42	3	8	11	15	5			
Motor home and boat trailer	MH/B		8	53	4	8	20	21	6			

[a] WB$_1$, WB$_2$, WB$_3$, WB$_4$, are effective vehicle wheelbases. S is the distance from the rear effective axle to the hitch point. T is the distance from the hitch point to the lead effective axle of the following unit.

[b] Combined dimension 24, split is estimated.

[c] Combined dimension 9.4, split is estimated.

[d] Design vehicle with 48-ft trailer as adopted in 1982 STAA (Surface Transportation Assistance Act).

[e] Design vehicle with 53-ft trailer as grandfathered in 1982 STAA (Surface Transportation Assistance Act).

[f] Combined dimension 9.3, split is estimated.

[g] Combined dimension 8, split is estimated.

Source: American Association of State and Highway Officials, "A Policy on Geometric Design of Highways and Streets" [2.2], (Table II-1, p. 21). Copyright 1990. Used with permission.

Figure 2.4.20   Minimum turning paths for W-60 design vehicle. (From American Association of State and Highway Officials, "A Policy on Geometric Design of Highways and Streets" [2.2] (Fig. II-7, p. 31.) Copyright 1990. Used with permission.)

for a particular application must allow for the great majority of the vehicles that are expected to use the facility. For example, while the BUS design vehicle may be adequate for downtown streets, the largest WB-60 vehicle is appropriate for the design of truck routes. Table 2.4.5 shows the minimum turning radii of design vehicles.

TABLE 2.4.5   MINIMUM TURNING RADII OF DESIGN VEHICLES

Design vehicle type	Symbol	Minimum design turning radius (ft)	Minimum inside radius (ft)
Passenger car	P	24	13.8
Single-unit truck	SU	42	27.8
Single-unit bus	BUS	42	24.4
Articulated bus	A-BUS	38	14.0
Semitrailer, intermediate	WB-40	40	18.9
Semitrailer combination, large	WB-50	45	19.2
Semitrailer–full trailer combination	WB-60	45	22.2
Interstate semitrailer	WB-62[a]	45	9.1
Interstate semitrailer	WB-67[b]	45	00
Triple semitrailer	WB-96	50	20.7
Turnpike double semitrailer	WB-114	60	17
Motor home	MH	40	26.0
Passenger car with travel trailer	P/T	24	2.0
Passenger car with boat and trailer	P/B	24	6.5
Motor home and boat trailer	MH/B	50	35

[a] Design vehicle with 48-ft trailer as adopted in 1982 STAA (Surface Transportation Assistance Act).

[b] Design vehicle with 53-ft trailer as grandfathered in 1982 STAA (Surface Transportation Assistance Act).

Source: American Association of State and Highway Officials, "A Policy on Geometric Design of Highways and Streets" [2.2], (Table II-2, p. 22). Copyright 1990. Used with permission.

2.4.13 Channelization of At-Grade Intersections

Channelization has been defined as "the separation or regulation of conflicting traffic movements into definite paths by means of traffic islands or pavement markings to facilitate the safe and orderly movements of both vehicles and pedestrians" [2.13].

At-grade intersections are classified into Y-, T-, four-leg, multileg, and rotary intersections. Within each category, a very large number of variations is possible and, in fact, no two intersections are exactly the same. Consequently, each intersection must be treated individually as a separate design problem. Each design consists of the placement of combinations of triangular and elongated islands, the latter including medians and median treatments, edge-of-pavement treatments, pavement markings, and associated signing and traffic controls.

The channelization devices must be of sufficient number and size to command the attention of motorists, but cluttered designs containing too many small islands and signs must be avoided. The design should provide natural and well-defined paths to minimize vehicle wander. It must enhance the confidence and convenience of drivers by affording them adequate sight distances, by clearly guiding them into the proper channels of movements, and by preventing the choice of prohibited paths. The possibility of multiple paths between the same two points must be eliminated, and drivers should not be required to make many decisions at the same time.

Whenever possible, especially at high-speed locations, auxiliary storage lanes should be provided for turning vehicles that are required either to slow down

Figure 2.4.21   Example of channelization. (From American Association of State and Highway Officials, "A Policy on Geometric Design of Highways and Streets" [2.2] (Fig. IX-7, p. 682.) Copyright 1990. Used with permission.)

or to stop. Moreover, the angles and areas of conflict must be controlled. The length over which merging and diverging movements are accommodated must be of adequate length, and these movements must be confined to low angles. Crossing paths should minimize the area of conflict and, hence, be as close to right angles as possible.

Among the channelization concepts illustrated by Fig. 2.4.21 are the rounded or bullet-shaped median openings and the corner curb radii that are designed to fit the paths of vehicles as closely as possible. The corners of islands are also rounded, and the island edges on the approach side are slightly offset to guide, or "catch," the vehicle into the proper channel. Figure 2.4.22 illustrates this requirement.

AASHTO [2.2] provides specific guidelines for adherence to channelization principles and for the design of appropriate treatments. In addition, the Transportation Research Board issued a report [2.14] in which nine principles of channelization and proven techniques for the cost-effective design of channelized intersections are described. Table 2.4.6 summarizes how various design elements may be implemented to address the nine principles of channelization. Figure 2.4.23 illustrates how approach alignment and physical channelization devices can be used to clearly define proper vehicle paths. The dashed lines shown delineate the space requirements of design vehicles. Figure 2.4.24 shows how the proper place-

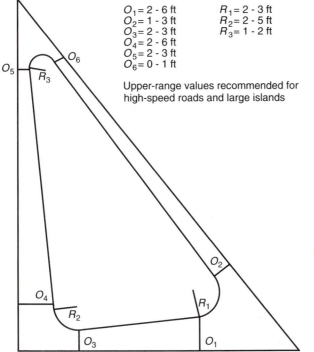

$O_1 = 2 - 6$ ft $R_1 = 2 - 3$ ft
$O_2 = 1 - 3$ ft $R_2 = 2 - 5$ ft
$O_3 = 2 - 3$ ft $R_3 = 1 - 2$ ft
$O_4 = 2 - 6$ ft
$O_5 = 2 - 3$ ft
$O_6 = 0 - 1$ ft

Upper-range values recommended for
high-speed roads and large islands

Figure 2.4.22   Radii and offsets of traffic islands. Offsets measured from the geometric island fitting the channelization specifications. (From Transportation Research Board [2.14].)

TABLE 2.4.6 OBJECTIVES OF CHANNELIZATION AND DESIGN ELEMENTS TO ACHIEVE THEM

Design Elements	Prohibitions of movements	Definition of vehicle paths	Promotion of safe speeds	Separation of conflicts	Angles of cross and merge	Facilitation of high priority movements	Facilitation of traffic control	Accommodation of slow or decelerating vehicles	Safe refuge for pedestrians
Traffic lanes						•	•	•	
Traffic islands	•	•		•	•		•		•
Median dividers	•	•		•	•		•		•
Corner radii	•	•	•			•			•
Approach geometry	•	•	•	•	•	•			
Pavement tapers or transitions		•	•		•			•	
Traffic control devices	•			•		•	•		•

Source: Transportation Research Board [2.14].

Figure 2.4.23 Design of all median elements must consider the natural paths of design vehicles. (From Transportation Research Board [2.14].)

Raised medians block left turns to and from minor streets or driveways. Such treatment may be appropriate at locations where left turns are dangerous or cause congestion.

Placement of median channelization and design of corner radii can effectively discourage dangerous wrong-way movements onto freeway ramps without hindering other intended movements.

Alignment of the approach and design of corner radii can encourage right-turn-only movements and discourage undesirable left turns.

Raised traffic islands can block through movements or undesirable turning movements without hindering other intersection movements.

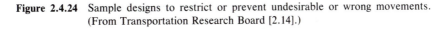

Figure 2.4.24   Sample designs to restrict or prevent undesirable or wrong movements. (From Transportation Research Board [2.14].)

ment of channelization devices may be used to discourage undesirable or wrong-way movements (shown by dashed lines). Figure 2.4.25 shows an application of physical channelization and pavement markings at an intersection involving a double-left-turn movement. The pavement markings shown are consistent with the provisions of the *Manual on Uniform Traffic Control Devices* [2.15].

Figure 2.4.25 Sample design and application of channelization and pavement markings at a complex intersection. (From Transportation Research Board [2.14].)

2.5 PAVEMENT STRUCTURES

2.5.1 Introduction

Pavements serve a structural, a functional, and a safety purpose. They are necessary not only for roadways but also for parking lots, airports (runways, taxiways, aprons, and service roads), industrial sites, ports, and so forth. The structural performance of a pavement is aimed at distributing the loads under the wheels of vehicles over larger areas to prevent stressing, beyond its load-bearing capacity, the native soil (or subgrade) on which the pavement system is constructed. Figure 2.5.1 illustrates this situation: The load at the interface between the wheel and

Figure 2.5.1   Distribution of weight of wheel from the contact area to the native soil.

the pavement surface is applied over a relatively small area, causing high stresses at that point, but these stresses decrease with depth as the load is spread over larger areas. The degree of load distribution decreases from the top to the bottom of the pavement structure.

The functional performance of pavements is related to the users' requirement for smooth and comfortable riding conditions. The quality of riding comfort is typically measured by the Present Serviceability Index (PSI) which was developed in 1957 by the American Association of Highway Officials (AASHO). The PSI is based primarily on measurements of pavement roughness. This is accomplished by a variety of available equipment that essentially measure the profile of the pavement along the traveled way [2.16]. The PSI deteriorates with usage and pavement age and is one of several criteria employed to aid decisions relating to maintenance, rehabilitation, or reconstruction of the pavement. Typical symptoms of pavement distresses are longitudinal and transverse cracking, breaking, swelling, and heaving. They affect the structural integrity of a pavement and the level of service to the users.

The safety performance of pavements is mainly related to the skid resistance developed at the tire–pavement interface. This friction or skid resistance can be enhanced by the choice of materials and by various treatments, such as texturing the pavement surface [2.17]. Another characteristic that is related to safety is the light reflectance of the pavement surface [2.18].

2.5.2 Pavement Materials and Types

Throughout the ages, compaction of the native soil by repetitive use was the common way in which roadbeds were maintained. Some exceptions were the heavy stone roadways constructed by some advanced ancient civilizations, including the Romans, whose famous Apian Way is extant to the present day. Any attempt to replicate the works of these ancient societies given today's material and labor costs would be prohibitively expensive. A derivative of this method of roadbuilding, known as the French method, was used into the nineteenth century, and the practice of overlaying a prepared roadbed with natural or artificial stones (e.g., cobblestones) continued until fairly recently. Other roadbed treatments include artificial compaction and stabilization of unpaved roads, typically found in rural areas, on farms, and at construction sites; surface treatments of the native soil; the use of asphalt-based pavements; and the construction of portland-cement concrete pavements. The last two are the most common types of pavements in use today.

The Asphalt Institute [2.19] describes asphalt as a "strong cement, readily adhesive, highly waterproof, and durable. It is a plastic substance which imparts controllable flexibility to mixtures of mineral aggregates with which it is usually combined. Although a solid or semisolid at ordinary atmospheric temperatures, asphalt may be readily liquefied by the application of heat." Asphalt is classified as a "bituminous" cement, a term which refers to the fact that it consists of hydrocarbons.

The combination of asphalt with graded mineral aggregates is known as asphalt concrete. It is in this manner that asphalt is usually applied to pavement design. Asphalt concrete mixtures are sometimes discussed in terms of the gradation of their component mineral aggregates and fillers into categories such as open-graded, coarse-graded, or fine-graded. Open-graded aggregate contains little mineral filler material and, consequently, is characterized by relatively large void areas between aggregate particles in a compacted mix. Coarse-graded aggregates exhibit a continuous grading of sizes but show a predominance of coarse sizes, whereas fine-graded aggregates have a predominance of fine sizes (i.e., those passing the No. 8 sieve). A coarse aggregate of uniform size, known as a macadam aggregate, received its name from the Scottish engineer John McAdam, who first used it in an asphalt mix. Sheet asphalt refers to a special type a mix that contains a well-controlled combination of asphalt, sand (i.e., fine aggregate), and mineral filler.

When the asphalt concrete is placed, spread, and compacted at atmospheric temperature, it is referred to as a cold-laid mixture, in contrast to hot-laid mixtures, which involve elevated temperatures. The combinations of material characteristics and proportions on one hand and mixing and placing conditions on the other can lead to asphalt concretes of differing characteristics in terms of their stability, durability, and flexibility to suit a variety of application requirements [2.17, 2.19].

It is interesting to note that natural deposits of asphalt exist. For example, skeletons of prehistoric animals have been preserved in such deposits at the La Brea pit near Los Angeles, California. Asphalt material was used in Mesopotamia for roadway construction and for waterproofing purposes. According to the Asphalt Institute [2.19], imported rock asphalt was used in Philadelphia, Pennsylvania in 1838, and the first asphalt pavement was built in Newark, New Jersey in 1870. Today, asphalt is recovered from petroleum in the process of separation and refinement of constituents.

Portland cement is mainly a calcium aluminum silicate which is produced by fusing limestone and clay in a rotary kiln to form a clinker material which is then ground into a fine powder. First used by an Englishman, Joseph Aspdin, who patented the substance in 1824, it derives its name from its ability to react with water and, through hydration, produce an artificial stone that resembles the limestone deposits found on the Isle of Portland in England. It is a "nonbituminous" cement and is classified as a "hydraulic" cement because it solidifies under water. In various combinations with water, graded mineral aggregates, and other admixtures and additives, portland cement is used to produce numerous construction materials, such as grout, plaster, mortar, and portland-cement concrete. By controlling the combinations of the constituents of the mix, a wide variety of desirable characteristics (e.g., strength, durability, workability) can be obtained to suit particular applications. The most notable characteristic of portland-cement concrete is its compressive strength: It far exceeds its tensile strength, which is only about 10% of its compressive strength. For this reason, portland-cement concrete pavements are typically designed to resist compressive forces only. The first reported use of portland-cement concrete for pavement construction in the United States occurred in 1891 in Bellefontaine, Ohio.

In case prominent tensile forces are present under particularly heave loads, continuous reinforcement with steel bars is applied to withstand the applied tension. Also, prestressing the structural element is another way for taking full advantage of the compressive strength. This involves the application, via tendons embedded in the concrete, of a compressive load on the structure prior to applying the service loads. The compressive prestress counterbalances tensile stress produced by the loads in such a way that the concrete remains under compression. Continuously reinforced or prestressed concrete pavements are commonly used for airport runways and aprons.

A fundamental difference between asphalt and portland-cement concrete pavements lies in the fact that the former is characterized by flexibility, whereas the latter provides rigidity. For this reason the two types of pavement are classified, respectively, as flexible and rigid pavements. Following are the corresponding AASHTO definitions [2.16].

Flexible pavement: a pavement structure which maintains intimate contact with and distributes loads to the subgrade and depends on aggregate interlock, particle friction, and cohesion for stability.
Rigid pavement: a pavement structure which distributes loads to the subgrade, having as one course a portland cement concrete slab of relatively high bending resistance.

Rigid pavements are further subdivided according to the method of reinforcement into plain (unreinforced) with or without dowels, conventionally rein-

Form of pavement structure
in the absence of traffic

Form of pavement after loading
from traffic (exaggerated)

Figure 2.5.2   States of pavement structure with and without traffic load.

forced, continuously reinforced, and prestressed. Dowels are steel rods that connect individual pavement slabs to facilitate the transfer of loads between them. In the case of continuously reinforced portland-cement concrete pavements, the reinforcing steel serves this function.

Both types of pavement tend to deform under the applied loads as illustrated in Fig. 2.5.2, with the top fibers of the pavement in compression and the bottom fibers in tension. Because of the rigidity and stiffness expected from portland-cement concrete pavements, they require special structural engineering attention. This includes the provision of contraction joints at recurrent intervals to control transverse cracking, expansion joints, load transfer devices, and joint sealants to prevent water and incompressible debris from entering the joint reservoirs. Figure 2.5.3 shows an undoweled and a doweled contraction joint as well as an example of doweled contraction joints and transverse joints with distributed steel.

Composite pavements consisting of an asphalt surface overlay on a portland-

Figure 2.5.3   Basic types of jointing for portland-cement concrete pavement slabs.

cement concrete slab are common. Moreover, a recent practice of overlaying a portland-cement concrete layer on old asphalt pavements, called "whitetopping" [2.20], appears to be gaining in popularity.

2.5.3 Pavement Structure

A pavement structure consists of a series of layers beginning with the native soil that constitutes the prepared roadbed (or subgrade), which is typically overlaid by the subbase and base layers. The strength of these layers increases from the bottom up to conform with the increasing requirements of stress and load distribution (Fig. 2.5.1). This practice contributes to economical and efficient use of materials by avoiding "overdesigning" the lower layers. Some of these layers may be omitted, depending on the strength of native soil and material availability. An asphalt pavement that is placed directly on the subgrade is known as a full-depth asphalt pavement. In this case, the thickness of the base and subbase is simply replaced by appropriate "layers" of asphalt concrete to form a thicker layer than would otherwise be required. In the case of rigid pavements, the wheel loads are distributed over larger areas than in the case of asphalt pavements, and this reduces the strength requirements of the base and subbase. Figure 2.5.4 presents examples of flexible and rigid pavements. A flexible pavement may include the following five layers (from bottom up): (1) prepared roadbed; (2) subbase course, typically from compacted granular material; (3) base course, which provides structural support to the pavement, made from aggregates such as crushed gravel, which may be treated with fly ash, cement, or asphalt; (4) drainage layer, which is part of the base made with select aggregates or fabrics with sufficient permeability so that water can be quickly removed from the structure; and (5) surface course mix of bituminous materials and aggregates. The proportion of bituminous material and aggregates as well as the gradation, strength, abrasion, and other characteristics of the aggregates determine the resistance to cracking and the supplied skid resistance. The surface mix must be properly compacted.

The rigid pavements usually consist of four major layers. (1) prepared roadbed (as for flexible pavements); (2) subbase course, with characteristics similar to those for flexible pavements with the exception that often, lean concrete (econocrete) subbases are constructed to reduce erosion of the bottom side of the slabs, the joints between slabs, and the edges of the slabs; (3) base course, which may contain a drainage layer (often the base and subbase are combined into one supportive layer, with or without a drainage layer); and (4) pavement slab, which is a concrete mix with portland cement, aggregates, and various optional admixtures. The interlocking of aggregates provides the mechanism with which loads are transferred in portland-cement concrete pavements (aggregate interlock).

The proportion of portland cement and aggregates as well as the gradation, strength, abrasion, and other characteristics of the aggregates determine the resistance to cracking and the supplied skid resistance. The slabs may be reinforced

Figure 2.5.4 Cross-section examples of flexible and rigid pavements.

with steel; they may have steel reinforced joints (for the proper transfer of loads between slabs; see Fig. 2.5.3), and joint sealants. Continuously reinforced concrete pavements consist of one continuous slab without joints.

Drainage is a paramount element and the rule of thumb is avoidance of "bathtub" design, whereby rainfall or groundwater accumulates in the layers of the pavement structure. The drainage of water should be rapid; thus certain gradations of materials which supply a high proportion of voids and no fines as well as careful design should be implemented (Fig. 2.5.4). The incorporation of drainage in the pavement structure (which is often neglected) increases the initial construction cost, but it can prolong the life of the structure substantially, thereby offsetting the higher initial cost.

2.5.4 Pavement Design

Pavement design includes, among other elements, selection of a pavement type (flexible, rigid, or composite), the design of the concrete mix (asphalt or portland cement, gradation of aggregates, admixtures, etc.), the selection of materials for the soil layers below the pavement, and the thickness of the soil and pavement layers. This process is complex and hard to define unequivocally because of the multiplicity of engineering and nonengineering factors involved. According to AASHTO [2.16], "currently, the most realistic pavement type selection process can result by obtaining five to ten most nearly optimal cost solutions for each pavement type being considered and examining these options qualitatively in the light of [these] factors." For this reason, AASHTO recommends designing pavements with the use of computers (e.g., [2.19–2.21]). Another reason is that manual application based on tables and nomographs is bound to result in multiple approximations that may compromise final accuracy. Major factors affecting pavement design include: (1) traffic load, (2) soils, (3) environment, and (4) reliability. These are discussed below.

Traffic load is the most important factor in pavement design because it largely determines the thickness of the pavement structure. The measurement of traffic load varies according to the method utilized. In general, pavements are designed according to the heavy vehicle traffic they are expected to receive. The AASHTO [2.16] method utilizes 18-kip ESALs (equivalent single-axle load). All traffic is transformed in equivalent 18,000-lb single-axle loads. Large loaded trucks with trailers are estimated to cause loads the equivalent of which exceeds 1000 passenger cars. For example, the ESAL factor for passenger cars is 0.0008 and for tractor–semitrailers with five or more axles it is 2.3719 [2.16].

Other methods utilize the annual average daily traffic (AADT) and the percentage of heavy vehicles per category (i.e., single truck, semitrailer, etc.) in the AADT [2.20]. The major difficulty with regard to traffic loads is that they need to be forecast over the design life of the roadway (i.e., 30 years). Forecast data are partly based on a time series of highway traffic data and truck weight station logs. Then, growth rates are estimated or assumed to derive the future expected traffic.

Soils on which the roadway structure will be founded are of critical importance. Weak and/or unstable soil beds may require extensive soil improvement efforts before placement of the pavement structure. Expansive and frost-heave susceptible soils are most problematic for the placement of a pavement structure. The major load-bearing property of the soilbed considered is the resilient modulus. The resilient modulus of the compacted roadbed soil represents the amount of the recoverable deformation at given stress levels. Standardized tests are conducted to determine this property [2.16, 2.20].

Environment affects pavements mainly through rainfall and temperature. Rainfall penetrating the structure alters the properties of layers and makes the pavement vulnerable to loads. Temperature also affects the properties of pavements by generating stresses, contraction, and expansion. The combined effect of the presence of water in the pavement layers and low temperatures (i.e., below the freezing point) creates frost heaving (expansion), and in thawing periods the bearing capacity of a pavement may be greatly reduced (e.g., several rural roads in northern states limit the weight per axle during spring to avoid excessive pavement damage). Even with good drainage, thawing from the surface downward is most destructive since water from melted ice is trapped by the frozen layers underneath. Soils containing fine particles are most susceptible to frost heaving. Thus selection of properly graded soils and aggregates can ameliorate most of the frost heaving problem.

Reliability analysis of pavement structures accounts for a number of uncertainties over time. A pavement structure designed with average values has a 50% probability of fulfilling its required performance life. Thus the uncertainty in major design factors such as pavement structure factors, which include traffic loads, roadbed soil factors, climatic factors, and pavement condition (serviceability) factors, must be accounted for. Proper adjustments can be made to the design factors to achieve a desired reliability level (i.e., 80 to 99% for most major streets and highways).

2.5.5 Design Methods

All or most of the aforementioned factors are incorporated in the two major pavement thickness analysis methodologies which apply to both flexible and rigid pavements: the traditional experimental/statistical method of AASHTO [2.16] and the emerging, although not new, mechanistic/empirical method advocated by the Asphalt Institute [2.19] and the Portland Cement Association [2.20]. The former is based on the two-year extensive real-world pavement testings conducted in the late 1950s by AASHO (the then acronym of AASHTO) in Ottawa, Illinois and the continuous collection of pavement performance data from the nationwide highway system. The method is a statistical modeling of the behavior of a large variety of pavements given their specifications (construction characteristics such as type, materials, thickness, base and subbase, and so forth), the number of loadings until observable failure, and soil and environmental factors. The latter method is based on theory (i.e., it assumes that the pavement is a multilayered elastic structure on an elastic foundation) and calibrated to conform to empirical observations of performance for a variety of prevailing conditions.

There are several other methods for pavement design. All share several analysis elements with the aforementioned methods. Some of these methods are the National Crushed Stone Association method [2.21], the U.S. Army Corps of Engineers method [2.22], the Shell Petroleum Corporation method [2.23], and the Concrete Reinforcing Steel Institute method [2.24].

The selection of the type of pavement (rigid or flexible) is decided on the basis of a number of factors, such as economic (i.e., initial and life-cycle costs, availability of funds, etc.), local supply and availability of materials, past experience with various pavement types, construction considerations, continuity of pavement type, recycling opportunities, safety considerations (i.e., friction, contrast, reflectance), competition among industries, and local government preference.

Most pavement design methods are available in software form (i.e., [2.25] to [2.27]) for computer application, which decreases calculation time and allows for investigation of alternative scenarios. All methods consider the life-cycle costs of pavement structures. Life-cycle analysis is discussed in the following section.

2.5.6 Life-Cycle Economic Analysis

Life-cycle costs analysis accounts for several cost components, their time of occurrence, the design life of the structure, and its salvage value at the end of its design life. The main cost components are (1) initial cost, which includes the land acquisition and all construction costs; (2) annual maintenance costs; (3) designed rehabilitation cost (i.e., resurfacing at the tenth and twentieth years of a pavement with a design life of 30 years); and (4) user costs, which include vehicle operating costs (i.e., fuel consumption, tire wear, maintenance, etc., depend partly on the type and condition of the pavement), user travel-time cost (this becomes a major component during rehabilitation stages when lanes or a segment of a roadway facility is closed to traffic), and traffic accident cost (i.e., accidents attributed to the pavement's condition, or during construction and rehabilitation periods). User costs are often ignored in economic evaluations partly because of the difficulty of their assessment. Some argue that this is disadvantageous to rigid (portland-cement based) pavements because their reduced need for rehabilitation and the lower generated fuel consumption compared with flexible (asphalt based) pavements are not accounted for in the evaluation and choice [2.28, 2.29].

There are two widely used evaluation methods that aid in the choice of pavement design alternatives: the equivalent uniform annual cost method, and the present worth method. In the former method all costs are translated into an equivalent annual cost for each year of the life of the structure. Thus annual costs remain unchanged and fixed costs are spread over the life of the structure. In the latter method all costs are collapsed to present time, thereby reflecting the total present time worth of the structure given its design life. Appendix B presents various evaluation methods in detail.

The critical element that allows either allocation of costs (uniform spread over all time points or collapse at a single time point) is the discount rate, which is the difference between the prime interest rate and the prevailing inflation rate. In other words, the discount rate reflects the true cost of borrowing money. The fluctuations of interest and inflation rates tend to counterbalance each other. As a result, the discount rate tends to remain fairly stable [2.20]. Consider the following example.

Paving a road with portland cement or asphalt concrete is estimated to cost the following amounts per mile:

- *Portland-cement concrete:* initial cost = $400,000, annual maintenance = $500, 30-year life
- *Asphalt concrete:* initial cost = $325,000, resurfacing at the fifteenth year = $100,000 (present time value), annual maintenance = $1000, 30-year life

If the prime interest and the inflation rate are 7% and 4%, respectively, the corresponding present time cost per mile is: portland cement = $410,235 and asphalt = $412,627 (i.e., first inflate by 4% and then discount by 7%). If the prime interest and the inflation rate is 14% and 11%, respectively, the corresponding present time cost per mile is: portland cement = $410,134 and asphalt = $414,627. (*Note:* The present worth formulas are given in Appendix B.)

Thus despite the large difference between the interest and inflation rates in the hypothetical examples, the stable (3%) discount rate resulted in nearly identical cost estimates. The salvage (remaining) value of the road at the end of its design life (i.e., worth as recyclable material or as a secondary facility) should be subtracted from the total cost estimates.

2.5.7 Pavement Management Systems

With nearly all of the interstate highway and roadway system complete in the United States, the emphasis is being switched from construction to maintenance. The development of a pavement management system originated near the turn of the century has grown steadily, due to the increased need for pavement maintenance.

A pavement management system incorporates the coordination of activities associated with the design, planning, construction, maintenance, research, and evaluation of pavements. Most of these activities are focused on existing pavements. The system consists of three essential elements: (1) surveys related to pavement condition and serviceability and compilation of a continuously updated data base; (2) prioritization of needs, alternative repair options, evaluation, and decision for action; and (3) implementation procedures [2.30].

The condition and serviceability of a pavement as perceived by the user is represented by its roughness, which is a measure of the irregularities in the pavement surface, which cause discomfort to the users. Longitudinal, transverse, and horizontal components of roughness affect the comfort and safety of users. Roughness is assessed with various mechanical devices called profilometers. Advanced techniques utilize video imaging, radar, sonics, and infrared technologies for assessing surface and structural pavement damage [2.31].

The Federal Highway Administration as well as state agencies are largely responsible for the development of strategies for the prioritization of needs, evaluation, and decision for action. Implementation involves the so-called 4R procedures (resurfacing, restoration, rehabilitation, reconstruction). *Resurfacing* is self-explanatory; both asphalt layer on a rigid pavement or portland-cement layer on a flexible pavement are feasible resurfacing options, in addition to asphalt on asphalt and portland cement on portland cement. When resurfacing asphalt concrete pavements, a layer 1 to 3 in. thick is usually removed before the new surface layer is applied. *Restoration* includes the removal and replacement of portland-cement slabs, the patching of potholes, the sealing of cracks, the retrofitting of edge support, and various other localized repairs. *Rehabilitation* is large-scale restoration. It includes elements such as replacement of bridge decks, resurfacing of a substantial segment of a roadway facility, recycling of materials, and minor subgrade work incidental to other repairs. *Reconstruction* is the complete removal of the pavement structure to the base layer and the replacement with virgin or recycled materials. Recycling includes the removal and crushing of portland-cement slabs and the use of the product as coarse aggregates or stockpile material for bases. In the case of flexible pavements, removed asphalt material is used as base material or it is recycled at a hot-mix plant. The overall network priorities and scheduling for 4R constitute a major part of pavement management systems [2.32].

2.6 SUMMARY

In this chapter we reviewed the fundamental kinematic and kinetic equations of particle motion and developed the formulas that govern the rectilinear and curvilinear motion of single vehicles. Basic models of human factors were then introduced to illustrate how driver responses to stimuli in the driving environment can be incorporated in highway design. The factors examined included driver perception-reaction, visual acuity, and responses to laterally placed objects. Perception-reaction was shown to affect the total distance covered by a stopping vehicle and the presence of "dilemma zones" at signalized intersections; laterally located objects create a tendency for the driver to slow down and to steer the vehicle away from them even when the vehicle is not on a collision course with the objects.

The basic aspects of geometric design, that is, the proportioning of the visible elements of fixed facilities, were covered next. The elements described included cross-section design, horizontal alignment, superelevation, vertical alignment, and channelization. To ensure safe operation, driver needs were shown to be met through the provision of adequate stopping and passing sight distances, and by the proper selection and placement of channelization treatments, including pavement markings, elongated and triangular islands, and medians. Vehicle characteristics are reflected in the selection of appropriate design vehicles. Human and design factors are summarized in Table 2.6.1.

Fundamental principles of pavement structures and design as well as elements of economic analysis for flexible and rigid pavements were presented.

TABLE 2.6.1 SUMMARY OF HUMAN AND DESIGN FACTORS

Human factors		
Cause/fact	Effect	Elements of interest
Perception and reaction time	Useful time is lost in critical situations	Delayed undertaking of corrective action
Ambiguity in decision making	Driver in dilemma zone	Any action will compromise safety (proper selection of duration of amber)
Acuity of vision	Potential inability to perceive conditions correctly	May result in poor judgment (wrong information fed to brain)
Instinctive fear or insecurity	Reduction of speed or positioning at a longer distance from hazard or vehicle ahead	Lateral displacement; car-following behavior
Fatigue, intoxication, or other impairment	Inability to perceive conditions correctly and react in a timely manner	May result in poor judgment (body or brain incapable of functioning properly)

Design factors			
Cause/fact	Effect	Element of interest	Critical unit
Must stop	Discomfort if abrupt or danger if not successful	Stopping distance	Bus with standing passengers plus wet conditions
Must be able to see ahead	Safe navigation of vehicle	Sight distance	Sight distance ≥ stopping distance
Driver and vehicle must be able to follow roadway comfortably	Vehicle under driver's control; comfortable and safe ride when speed limits are observed	Maximum slopes; minimum radii; superelevation; design speed; speed limit	Heavy vehicle; wet conditions; conservative height of eyes and headlights
Lack of proper channelization	Confusion and failure to follow proper paths	Inefficient service process; accident occurrence	Potential conflicts; volumes; available space and resources

2.7 EXERCISES

1. Given the acceleration pattern shown in Fig. E2.1, (a) derive and plot the relationship between speed and time and (b) calculate the total distance traveled during the 20-s interval. At $t = 0$ the vehicle was traveling at 12 mi/h.

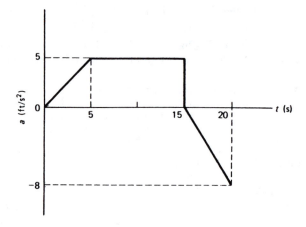

Figure E2.1

2. The driver of a car traveling up a 2% grade at an initial speed V_0 applied the brakes abruptly and the vehicle slid to a complete stop at an average deceleration of 8 ft/s². Was the pavement wet or dry?

3. At time $t = 0$ two persons entered the elevator of the tower shown in Fig. E2.3. The first person rode to the restaurant level. The second person went to the observation

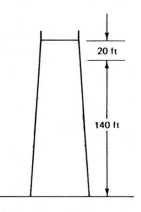

Figure E2.3

deck. Plot the time–elevation and the velocity–elevation diagrams for each of the two persons considering that the elevator started up 3 s after they entered, made no intermediate stops between the ground and the restaurant levels, and stayed for 6 s at the restaurant level. The elevator manufacturer's brochure provides the following technological specifications: acceleration = 5 ft/s²; deceleration = 4 ft/s²; and maximum cruising velocity = 20 ft/s.

4. A rapid-transit system uses a tubular guideway in which a close-fitting vehicle is propelled by a pressure difference between the front and rear cross-sectional areas [Fig.

E2.4(a)]. At departure time t_0, the pressure difference $P_2 - P_1$ is instantaneously raised from zero to some initial level and the vehicle accelerates forward. The pressure difference is then decreased until it reaches zero and the vehicle attains its cruising

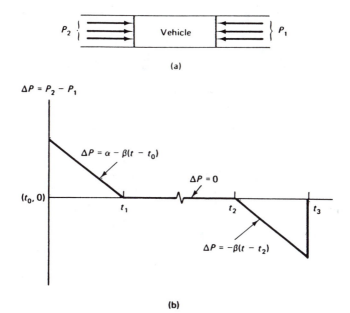

(b)

Figure E2.4

velocity, which is sustained until the vehicle begins its deceleration toward the next station [Fig. E2.4(b)]. Neglecting friction, (a) express acceleration, velocity, and distance traveled as functions of time, and (b) sketch the relationship between velocity and time for the movement between two stations 1 mi apart. Use the following data.

A = cross-sectional area of the vehicle = 100 ft^2

W = vehicle weight = 40,000 lb

α = 100 lb/ft^2

β = 3.33 lb/ft^2-s

5. A car collided with a telephone pole and left 20-ft skid marks on the dry pavement. Based on the damages sustained, an engineer estimated that the speed at collision was 15 mi/h. If the roadway had a +3% grade, calculate the speed of the car at the onset of skidding.

6. A large rock became visible to a driver at a distance of 175 ft. Assuming a perception-reaction time of 0.8 s, an initial speed of 42 mi/h, a coefficient of friction equal to 0.5, and a level roadway, calculate the speed at impact.

7. Plot the relationship between the approach speed v and the length of the dilemma zone for the following data: $a_2 = 0.5\ g$, $\delta_2 = 1.0$ s, $w = 65$ ft, $L = 15$ ft, and $\tau = 4.5$ s.

To help you interpret this plot, draw another diagram in which the v versus x_c and the v versus x_0 relationships are superposed.

8. Assuming a comfortable deceleration of 8 ft/s^2, an intersection width of 42 ft, a perception-reaction time of 0.9 s, and a vehicle length of 18 ft, plot τ_{min} versus approach speed v_0. At what speed does τ_{min} attain a minimum? What is that minimum?

9. Prepare a computer program for the general case of Exercise 8. Run your program several times and plot the results.

10. A driver with 20/40 vision and a sixth-grade education needs 2 s to read a directional sign. The letter size is such that the sign can be read by a person with 20/20 vision from a distance of 200 ft. Does the subject driver have enough time to read the sign at a speed of 30 mi/h?

11. The street name signs at a certain location can be discerned by a person with 20/40 vision from a distance of 300 ft. How much larger should they be in order to be legible to a person with 20/50 vision from a distance of 450 ft?

12. A witness with 20/60 vision supplied to the investigating officer the license plate number of a vehicle involved in a hit-and-run accident. If, under the conditions that prevailed at the time of the accident, a license plate can be read by a person with 20/20 vision from a distance of 180 ft, what is the maximum distance for which the witness's testimony can be relied upon?

13. Vehicles A and B are traveling toward each other in the opposing lanes on a straight segment of a two-lane highway at 35 and 40 mi/h, respectively. If the critical rates of angular change of the two drivers are 0.0065 and 0.0055 rad/s, determine (a) which driver will be the first to displace laterally and (b) the longitudinal distance between vehicles when the displacement will occur. Assume that the lateral separation between the two vehicles is 6 ft.

14. Inside a tunnel, the distance between the drivers and the curb is 10 ft. Assuming that the drivers fix their eyes on the curb at an angle of 2°, calculate the appropriate speed limit for a critical angular rate of change of 0.005 rad/s.

15. How far to the side of the drivers of Exercise 14 should the curb be to allow a speed of 45 mi/h?

16. What is the maximum allowable degree of curve (arc definition) for a two-lane highway if $e_{max} = 0.08$, $f_{max} = 0.12$, and the design speed is 50 mi/h?

17. A simple highway curve is planned to connect two horizontal tangents that intersect at sta. 2500 + 00.0 at an external angle of 52°. For a design speed of 60 mi/h and a curve radius of about 1.25 times the minimum allowable, calculate (a) the design rate of superelevation and (b) the required length of superelevation runoff. Assume a four-lane undivided highway and 10-ft lanes. Clearly state any other assumptions you think are needed.

18. Sketch the plan view and the longitudinal profile of your curve design (Exercise 17) assuming a normal crown of 0.02 ft/ft and pavement rotation about the centerline.

19. A sight obstruction is located at a distance of 20 ft from the center of the inside lane of a highway that prescribes a circular curve (Fig. 2.4.14). If the degree of curve for the centerline of the inside lane is 15°, calculate (a) the curve's radius and (b) the available horizontal sight distance. Does the computed sight distance meet the AASHTO stopping criterion for a speed of 35 mi/h?

20. A 2000-ft vertical curve connects a $+3\%$ grade to a -5% grade. If the vertical tangents intersect at sta. 52 + 60.55 and elevation 877.62 ft, calculate the elevations at the VPC, VPT, high point, and sta. 54 + 00.

21. A -4% grade and a 0% grade meeting at sta. 24 + 40 and elevation 2421.54 ft are joined by an 800-ft vertical curve. The curve passes under an overpass at sta. 25 + 00. If the lowest elevation of the overpass is 2439.93 ft, calculate the available clearance.

22. A $+2\%$ grade meets a $+6\%$ grade at sta. 10 + 30 and elevation 168.21 ft. For a design speed of 55 mi/h, find the minimum length of vertical curve that satisfies the 1984 AASHTO stopping sight-distance criterion. Also calculate the elevation of the middle point of this curve.

23. Calculate the available passing sight distance on a 2000-ft vertical curve with $G_1 = +5\%$ and $G_2 = -2\%$ for (a) the pre-1984 and (b) the post-1984 oncoming vehicle and driver eye heights.

24. Prepare a computer program that, given the station location and elevation of the intersection of two vertical grades and the required sight distance, calculates (a) the minimum length of vertical curve, (b) the station location and elevation of the VPC and the VPT, and (c) the curve elevation of any specified intermediate point.

2.8 REFERENCES

2.1 DREW, DONALD R., *Traffic Flow Theory and Control*, McGraw-Hill, New York, 1968.

2.2 AMERICAN ASSOCIATION OF STATE HIGHWAY AND TRANSPORTATION OFFICIALS, *A Policy on Geometric Design of Highways and Streets*, AASHTO, Washington, D.C., 1990.

2.3 JOHANNSON, GUNNAR and KÄRE RUMAR, "Drivers' Brake Reaction Times," *Human Factors*, 13, 1 (1971): 23–27.

2.4 GAZIS, DENOS, ROBERT HERMAN, and ALEXEI MARADUDIN, "The Problem of the Amber Signal in Traffic Flow," *Operations Research*, 8 (1960): 112–132.

2.5 INSTITUTE OF TRANSPORTATION ENGINEERS, *Transportation and Traffic Engineering Handbook*, Prentice Hall, Englewood Cliffs, N.J., 1976.

2.6 KANTOWITZ, BARRY H. and ROBERT D. SORKIN, *Human Factors: Understanding People–System Relationships*, Wiley, New York, 1983.

2.7 TARAGIN, A., "Driver Behavior as Affected by Objects on Highway Shoulders," *Highway Research Board Proceedings*, 34 (1955): 453–472.

2.8 MICHAELS, R. M., and L. W. GOZAN, *Perceptual and Field Factors Causing Lateral Displacement*, Highway Research Record 25, Highway Research Board, National Research Council, Washington, D.C., 1963.

2.9 FEDERAL HIGHWAY ADMINISTRATION, *Highway Functional Classification: Concepts, Criteria and Procedures*, U.S. Department of Transportation, Washington, D.C., 1974.

2.10 AMERICAN ASSOCIATION OF STATE HIGHWAY OFFICIALS, *A Policy on Geometric Design of Rural Highways*, AASHO, Washington, D.C., 1965.

2.11 HICKERSON, THOMAS F., *Route Surveys and Design*, 4th ed. McGraw-Hill, New York, 1959.

2.12 FEDERAL HIGHWAY ADMINISTRATION, *Manual on Uniform Traffic Control Devices for Streets and Highways*, U.S. Department of Transportation, Washington, D.C., 1971.

2.13 AMERICAN ASSOCIATION OF STATE HIGHWAY AND TRANSPORTATION OFFICIALS, *A Policy on Design of Urban Highways and Arterial Streets*, AASHTO, Washington, D.C., 1973.

2.14 TRANSPORTATION RESEARCH BOARD, *Intersection Channelization Design Guide*, National Cooperative Highway Research Program Report 279, National Research Council, Washington, D.C., 1985.

2.15 FEDERAL HIGHWAY ADMINISTRATION, *Manual on Uniform Traffic Control Devices*, U.S. Department of Transportation, Washington, D.C., 1991.

2.16 AMERICAN ASSOCIATION OF STATE HIGHWAY AND TRANSPORTATION OFFICIALS, *AASHTO Guide for Design of Pavement Structures 1986*, AASHTO, Washington, D.C., 1986.

2.17 RACIBORSKI, R., K. K. TAM, and D. F. LYNCH, "Friction Courses for Moderate Traffic Highways," *Transportation Research Record 1259*, Transportation Research Board, National Research Council, Washington, D.C., 1990.

2.18 STARK, R. E., "Road Surface's Reflectance Influences Lighting Design," *Lighting Design + Application* (Apr. 1986).

2.19 THE ASPHALT INSTITUTE, *Thickness Design: Asphalt Pavements for Highways and Streets*, Manual Series No. 1, AI, 1981.

2.20 PORTLAND CEMENT ASSOCIATION, *Thickness Design for Concrete Highway and Street Pavements*, PCA, Skokie, Ill., 1984.

2.21 NATIONAL CRUSHED STONE ASSOCIATION, *Flexible Pavement Design Guide of Highways*, NCSA, Washington, D.C., 1972.

2.22 U.S. ARMY CORPS OF ENGINEERS, *Roads, Streets, Walks and Open Storage Areas, Flexible Pavement Design*, U.S. Army Technical Manual TM-5-822-5, 1980.

2.23 SHELL INTERNATIONAL PETROLEUM COMPANY, *Shell Pavement Design Manual*, Shell, 1978.

2.24 CONCRETE REINFORCING STEEL INSTITUTE, *Design of Continuously Reinforced Concrete for Highways*, CRSI, Schaumburg, Ill., 1981.

2.25 AMERICAN CONCRETE PAVEMENT ASSOCIATION, *Simplified Guide for the Design of Concrete Pavements Based on the 1986 AASHTO Guide for the Design of Pavement Structures*, Personal Computer Software, ACPA, Arlington Heights, Ill., 1988.

2.26 PORTLAND CEMENT ASSOCIATION, *PCAPAV: Thickness Design of Highway and Street Pavements*, Personal Computer Software, PCA, Skokie, Ill., 1990.

2.27 ———, *AIRPORT: Concrete Thickness Design for Airport and Industrial Pavements*, Personal Computer Software, PCA, Skokie, Ill., 1989.

2.28 KHER, R., W. A. PHANG, and R. C. G. HAAS, *Economic Analysis Elements in Pavement Design*, Highway Research Board Record 572, Highway Research Board, National Research Council, Washington, D.C., 1976.

2.29 ZANIEWSKI, J. P., *Effect of Pavement Surface Type on Fuel Consumption*, Portland Cement Association, Skokie, Ill., 1989.

2.30 KERR, W. O., and B. A. RYAN, *Avoiding the Pitfalls of Life-Cycle Costs Analysis*, Washington Economic Research Consultants, Washington, D.C., 1987.

2.31 BOMAR, L. C., W. F. HORNE, D. R. BROWN, and J. L. SMART, *Determining Deteriorated Areas in Portland Cement Concrete Pavements Using Radar and Video Imaging*, National Cooperative Highway Research Program Report 304, Transportation Research Board, National Research Council, Washington, D.C., 1988.

2.32 VOIGHT, G. F., and M. J. KNUTSON, *Development and Selection of the Preferred 4R Strategy*, American Concrete Pavement Association, Arlington Heights, Ill., 1989.

3   Vehicular Flow Models

3.1   INTRODUCTION

Chapter 2 was concerned primarily with the motion of a single vehicle. From the resulting equations of motion, the basic geometric design formulas for highways were derived and their application was illustrated. Occasionally, single vehicles traverse the transportation facilities without significant interference from other vehicles. But the same facilities also experience simultaneous usage by streams of vehicles. The resulting traffic conditions range from almost free flow when only a few relatively unconstrained vehicles occupy a roadway to highly congested conditions when the roadway is jammed with slow-moving vehicles. In this chapter we examine the consequences of vehicular interactions. The equations developed in Chapter 2 are used to formulate a general model of a vehicular stream for the simple case of identically scheduled vehicles on an exclusive right of way. This model is then extended to the case of highway traffic, where a great amount of variability prevails. The determinant of these traffic flow models is the car-following rule adopted by drivers in an attempt to maximize their speeds while maintaining an acceptable level of safety. They accomplish this by adjusting the distance between vehicles, depending on their speed. The basic variables that describe the prevailing conditions within a vehicular stream (flow, concentration, and mean speed) are introduced, and the fundamental relationship between the three stream variables is postulated and applied to several traffic phenomena, including the propagation of shock waves in traffic.

3.2 VEHICULAR STREAM MODELS

3.2.1 Vehicular Following

Consider the case of vehicles following each other on a long stretch of roadway or guideway. Furthermore, assume that these vehicles are not required to interrupt their motion for reasons that are external to the traffic stream, such as traffic lights, transit stations, and the like. In this case of *uninterrupted flow*, the only interference that a single vehicle experiences is caused by other vehicles on the roadway. Figure 3.2.1 shows two typical stream vehicles traveling at a speed v and a *spacing s* between the front of the leading vehicle to the front of the following vehicle. As a general rule, the spacing between vehicles should be such that if a sudden deceleration becomes necessary for a leading vehicle, the following vehicle has ample time and distance to perceive the situation, react to it, and be able to decelerate safely without colliding with the stopping, leading vehicle. A similar rule was applied in Chapter 2 to compute the necessary safe stopping distance that served as a criterion for the proper geometric design of roadways.

Figure 3.2.1(a) shows the locations of the leading and following vehicles described above at the moment when the leading vehicle begins to decelerate, and Fig. 3.2.1(b) shows the limiting acceptable conditions at the end of the stopping maneuver of the following vehicle. Parenthetically, the term *vehicle* may be taken to mean a vehicular train consisting of a number of articulated vehicles rather than a single vehicle. Using the following notation, a relationship between

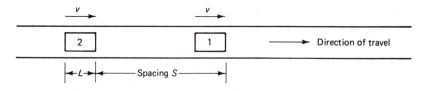

(a) Location of two vehicles at the beginning of the leading vehicle's deceleration

(b) Distances traveled

Figure 3.2.1 Vehicle following concept.

spacing, speed, and deceleration (assumed constant) can be developed:

v = initial speed of the two vehicles

d_l = deceleration rate of the leading vehicle

d_f = deceleration rate of the following vehicle

δ = perception-reaction time of the following vehicle

x_o = safety margin after stop

L = length of vehicle

N = number of vehicles in a train (if applicable)

Under constant deceleration, the braking distance of the leading vehicle is

$$x_l = \frac{v^2}{2d_l} \tag{3.2.1}$$

Including perception-reaction, the total distance that would be covered by the responding following vehicle is

$$x_f = v\delta + \frac{v^2}{2d_f} \tag{3.2.2}$$

In terms of the initial spacing s, the length of the vehicular unit (NL), and the safety margin x_o,

$$x_f = s + x_l - NL - x_o \tag{3.2.3}$$

Substituting Eqs. 3.2.1 and 3.2.2 in Eq. 3.2.3 and solving for s gives

$$s = v\delta + \frac{v^2}{2d_f} - \frac{v^2}{2d_l} + NL + x_o \tag{3.2.4}$$

Thus, given the speed of normal operation of the system and the other performance parameters, it is possible to compute the necessary spacing so that the following vehicle will just be able to avoid a collision by anticipating a potential stopping maneuver by the vehicle ahead. The application of this equation to a specific system requires the specification of the *anticipated* deceleration of the leading vehicle and the *desired* deceleration of the following vehicle. The combined choice of particular values for these variables has some important implications with respect to the level of safety provided by the system's operation.

3.2.2 Safety Considerations

Three particular values of deceleration are relevant to the operation's safety level [3.1]:

d_n = normal or comfortable deceleration

d_e = emergency deceleration

∞ = "instantaneous" or "stonewall" stop

Normal deceleration is related to passenger comfort as discussed in Chapter 2. The instantaneous stop condition may arise when an accident or a stalled vehicle or other obstruction suddenly comes within the perception field of the subject vehicle.

The safest level of operation occurs when the spacing between vehicles is such that the following vehicle can safely stop by applying *normal* deceleration even when the leading vehicle comes to a stonewall stop. A lower level of safety results when the spacing is selected so that the following vehicle would have to apply an *emergency* brake rather than normal deceleration in order to avoid a collision. The combinations of leading and following vehicle decelerations that designate various *safety regimes* are shown in Table 3.2.1.

Figure 3.2.2 plots spacing versus speed (Eq. 3.2.4) for the four safety regimes corresponding to the values inserted in the figure. Also included in Fig. 3.2.2 is the limiting case of a hypothetical continuous train, which is assumed to operate at any constant speed without ever having to decelerate [3.1]. The figure clearly

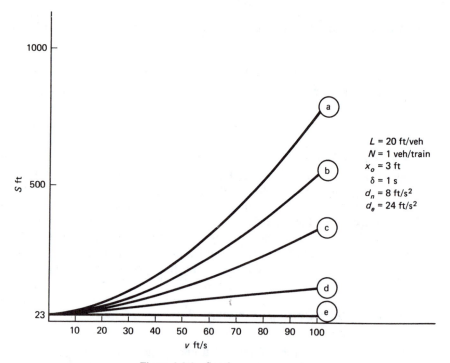

Figure 3.2.2 Spacing versus speed.

TABLE 3.2.1 SAFETY REGIME DEFINITIONS

Regime	Deceleration of leading vehicle	Deceleration of following vehicle
a	∞	d_n
b	d_e	d_n
c	∞	d_e
d	$d_1 = d_f$	
e	(no braking)	

Note: For $d_e < 2d_n$, regime c is safer than regime b.
Source: Vuchic [3.1].

shows that the higher the level of safety, the higher the required spacing just to avoid a collision. On this basis alone it would seem reasonable to choose the safest level of operation. However, by increasing the level of safety, the capacity of the system (i.e., the maximum number of vehicles or passengers that can be accommodated during a given period of time) suffers. Consequently, a *trade-off* between safety and capacity exists.

3.3 STREAM VARIABLES

3.3.1 Spacing and Concentration

Consider the uniform operation described in the preceding section and assume that a single photograph of a roadway segment is taken at an instant of time. The photograph would show a number of equally spaced vehicles along the roadway segment. The ratio of the number of vehicles appearing on the photograph to the length of the roadway segment is defined as the *concentration k* of the vehicular stream. This is an instantaneous measurement taken at the instant when the photograph was taken. Since the operation of the system described here is uniform (i.e., constant spacing and operating speed), the numerical value of concentration obtained at any instant of time on any segment of roadway will be the same. However, if the spacings and speeds of the vehicles that make up the stream are not equal, as is the case with the typical operation of highways, the value of concentration can vary with time and can also differ from one location to another at the same time. The dimensions of concentration (which is sometimes referred to as *density*) are given in terms of vehicles per length of roadway, for example, vehicles per mile (or veh/mi). The relationship between spacing (or average spacing when not constant) and concentration is

$$s = \frac{1}{k} \tag{3.3.1}$$

3.3.2 Headway and Flow

Consider a stationary observer next to the roadway. Vehicles pass the observer's location one after another at intervals of time defined as the *headways* between vehicles and denoted by the letter h. In the simple example described above, the headway between vehicles is constant and can be computed by dividing the constant spacing by the constant speed of system operation. It is not too difficult, however, to imagine a situation, such as highway traffic, where the measured headway between subsequent vehicles varies. In either case, during a period of observation T, the observer would count a number of headways, each corresponding to an individual vehicle in relation to its leader, the sum of which equals the total time of observation T. The number of vehicles counted at the point of observation divided by the total observation time is defined as the stream *flow* q—sometimes referred to as *volume V*—and measured in vehicles per unit time, for example, vehicles per hour (veh/h). Flow is a *measurement at a point* on the roadway over time. The relationship between headway (or average headway when variable) and flow is

$$h = \frac{1}{q} \tag{3.3.2}$$

3.3.3 Average or Mean Speed

The third basic measurement of traffic is that of *average*, or *mean, speed*. In the case of the uniform vehicular stream described above, all vehicles were assumed to operate at the same speed v. Therefore the average speed of any group of vehicles in the stream is also equal to v. This is not always the case, however. In a typical highway situation, for example, vehicles are traveling at different speeds, which they adjust as they traverse the highway. The problem of when, where, and how to take speed measurements that are representative of the traffic stream is not trivial [3.2]. For example, the speeds of successive vehicles may be taken at a single point of the roadway over a long period of time. These speeds are also known as *spot speeds*. Alternatively, the speeds of all the vehicles occupying a length of highway may be taken at the same instant. Also, by taking two aerial photographs of the highway separated by a small interval of time, the speed of each vehicle may be calculated by dividing the distance traveled by that time interval. The method by which the speed measurements are taken and the way in which their average is computed affect the results and interpretation of this quantity. Two common ways of computing the average, or mean, speed are the *time mean speed* and the *space mean speed*. The time mean speed U_t is the *arithmetic average* of the spot speeds just defined, that is,

$$U_t = \frac{1}{N} \sum_1^N U_i \tag{3.3.3}$$

where N is the number of observed vehicles and U_i is the spot speed of the ith vehicle.

The space mean speed is calculated on the basis of the average travel time it takes N vehicles to travese a length of roadway D. The ith vehicle traveling at speed U_i will take

$$t_i = \frac{D}{U_i} \tag{3.3.4}$$

seconds to cover the distance D. Thus the average travel time for N vehicles will be

$$t_{\text{ave}} = \frac{1}{N} \sum_1^N \frac{D}{U_i} \tag{3.3.5}$$

and the average speed based on the average travel time (i.e., the space mean speed) is the *harmonic average* of the spot speeds, or

$$U_s = \frac{1}{\dfrac{1}{N} \sum\limits_1^N \dfrac{1}{U_i}} \tag{3.3.6}$$

The two average speeds may be calculated alternatively by

$$U_t = \frac{\sum\limits_1^N \Delta x_i}{N \, \Delta t} \tag{3.3.7}$$

and

$$U_s = \frac{N \, \Delta x}{\sum\limits_1^N \Delta t_i} \tag{3.3.8}$$

where Δx_i is the distance traveled by the ith vehicle during a fixed time interval Δt and Δt_i is the time taken by the ith vehicle to cover a fixed distance Δx [3.3, 3.4].

There are, of course, many other ways to take speed measurements and averages. However, for the purposes of this book it suffices to state that the space mean speed (and not the time mean speed) is the proper stream speed average needed in this chapter's mathematical models.

Example 3.1

The spot speeds of four vehicles were observed to be 30, 40, 50, and 60 ft/s, respectively. Compute the time mean speed and the space mean speed.

Solution   The time mean speed is the arithmetic average of the spot speeds, or

$$\frac{30 + 40 + 50 + 60}{4} = 45 \text{ ft/s}$$

On the other hand, the space mean speed is the harmonic average. Equation 3.3.6 yields

$$U_s = 42.1 \text{ ft/s}$$

Discussion   The same results may be obtained by applying Eq. 3.3.7 (with, say, Δt = 1 s) and Eq. 3.3.8 (with Δx = 1 ft). The time mean speed is greater than the space mean speed. This is always the case because of the relative contribution to each average of slow- and fast-moving vehicles.

3.3.4 Time–Distance Diagrams of Flow

The vehicular variables (spacing, headway, vehicle speed) and stream variables (flow, concentration, mean speed) just described can be clearly illustrated via a *time–distance diagram* of the trajectories of the vehicles constituting a traffic stream. Figure 3.3.1 is such a diagram for the simple case of uniformly operated

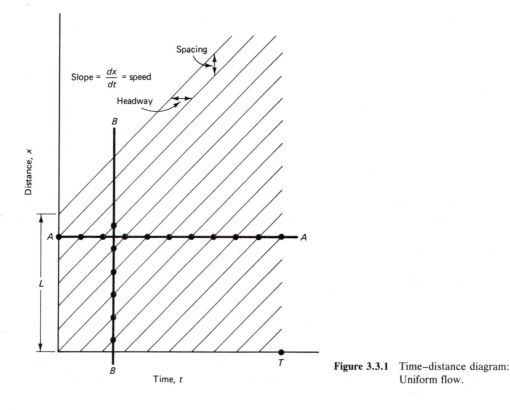

Figure 3.3.1   Time–distance diagram: Uniform flow.

vehicles represented as particles. Since in this case the speed of the vehicles is constant, the time–distance plot for each vehicle is simply a straight line, the slope of which, dx/dt, equals the speed, v. A point on a plot represents the location of the subject vehicle at the corresponding instant of time. A horizontal line (line AA, for example) intersects a number of time–distance lines and the (time) difference between pairs of vehicles along the horizontal line is the headway between those vehicles. Also, this horizontal line represents a stationary observer whose location does not change with time. The number of vehicles that the observer would be able to count over a period of observation T is equal to the number of times the horizontal line AA intersects a vehicle time–distance line: The higher the number of vehicles counted during time T, the higher the stream flow.

A vertical line (BB) represents the conditions prevailing at a given instant. The difference between subsequent vehicles is the spacing between vehicles. Also, line BB represents an aerial photograph of the stream at that instant: The number of time–distance lines that are intersected by line BB corresponds to the number of vehicles that would appear on a photograph of the roadway segment shown. The smaller the number of such vehicles, the lower the stream concentration.

The problem of determining a representative measure of mean speed becomes clearer when viewing the time–distance diagram of the stream. One way to average the speeds of vehicles in the stream is to measure their speeds as they pass a given location (i.e., the slopes of the time–distance lines as they cross line AA), the speeds of all vehicles in the stream at an instant (i.e. the slopes of time–distance lines as they cross line BB), the speeds computed for a small interval of time (Δt) over the length of the highway, the speeds computed for a small interval of distance (Δx) over a long period of time, or even by computing the average speed for each vehicle over the entire length of roadway and averaging that. This may seem irrelevant in the case of uniformly scheduled vehicles shown on Fig. 3.3.1, since all the vehicles are assumed to maintain the same speed throughout their movement. But in cases of nonuniform operations, the problem becomes clear. The reader is encouraged to consider the differences obtained by computing the alternate speed averages just described for the typical highway traffic time–distance diagram illustrated by Fig. 3.3.2, which represents a stream of vehicles on the curb lane of a highway in Columbus, Ohio [3.5]. The data shown were collected by aerial photogrammetry from a helicopter flying above the highway. The extent of any vertical line BB on the diagram is the range within the view of the camera at the corresponding instant. Any such line shows a great amount of variability in spacings at and between instants and at various locations. The slopes of the vehicle time-distance diagrams change, indicating speed changes, and the concentration of vehicles is seen to exhibit great variability, higher when and where the lines are densely packed and lower when and where they are sparsely packed. It is interesting to note that concentration is highest at points where the speeds are lowest. This phenomenon is eminently reasonable: When the speeds are low, the safe spacing selected by individual drivers is shorter leading to higher concentrations. The effect of this relationship on stream flow is not as obvious.

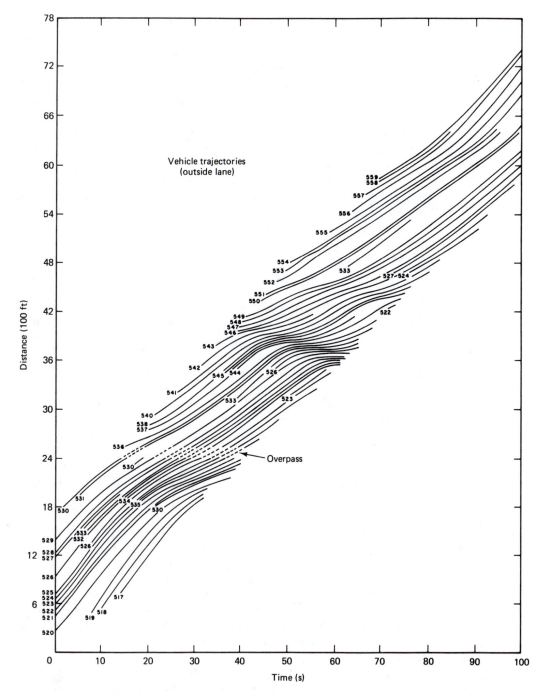

Figure 3.3.2   Highway flow. (From Rockwell and Treiterer [3.5].)

3.4 *VEHICULAR STREAM EQUATIONS AND DIAGRAMS*

3.4.1 *The Fundamental Equation of a Vehicular Stream*

If two vehicles are traveling at a spacing s and speed u, the headway between them is simply $h = s/u$. Substituting Eqs. 3.3.1 and 3.3.2 in this relationship leads to the fundamental equation describing a traffic stream:

$$q = uk \qquad (3.4.1)$$

Note that the units balance to vehicles per hour on both sides of this equation, which represents a three-dimensional relationship between the basic vehicular stream variables: flow, mean speed, and concentration. It is of the utmost importance to realize that the three variables vary simultaneously. Consequently, it would generally be incorrect to attempt to compute the value of one of the three variables by varying another while holding the third constant. As it was shown earlier, when speed is increased, the safe spacing between vehicles also increases, causing the concentration to decrease. According to Eq. 3.4.1, the resulting flow is given by the product of a *higher speed* times a *lower concentration*. Hence, the flow may increase, decrease, or remain the same, depending on the relative magnitudes of these two opposing effects.

To gain a clearer understanding of this phenomenon, consider the two-dimensional *projections* of Eq. 3.4.1 on the u–k, u–q, and q–k planes, first for the simple case of uniform flow and then for the more complex case of highway traffic.

3.4.2 *The Case of Uniform Flow*

Substituting Eq. 3.3.1 into Eq. 3.2.4, solving for k in terms of u, and adjusting the units of concentration to vehicles per mile leads to

$$k = f(u) = \frac{1}{u\delta + \dfrac{u^2}{2d_f} - \dfrac{u^2}{2d_l} + NL + x_o} \qquad (3.4.2)$$

This equation is plotted in Fig. 3.4.1 with k on the abscissa and u on the ordinate for the values that are inserted in the figure and for four of the five safety regimens discussed earlier, including the limiting case of the hypothetical continuous train. Excepting the hypothetical case, the relationship between speed and concentration is seen to be monotonically decreasing as should be expected: the higher the speed, the longer the required spacing and, consequently, the lower the concentration. The conditions around very low concentration and very high speed are referred to as the *free-flow conditions* and the maximum speed at zero concentration is known as the *free-flow speed* u_f. Although Eq. 3.4.2 shows speed to

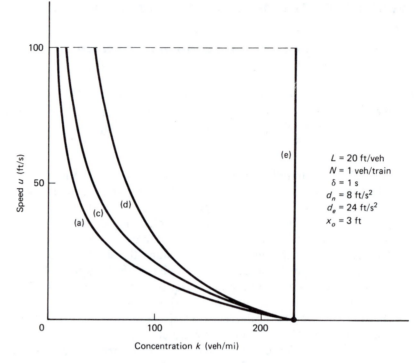

Figure 3.4.1 Speed–concentration curves.

approach infinity asymptotically as concentration approaches zero, for all practical purposes there exists a maximum speed (see dashed line), which depends on the technological characteristics of the system.

In view of Eq. 3.4.1, multiplication of both sides of Eq. 3.4.2 by the mean speed u leads to

$$q = \frac{u}{u\delta + \dfrac{u^2}{2d_f} - \dfrac{u^2}{2d_l} + NL + x_o} \tag{3.4.3}$$

Figure 3.4.2 shows the plots of this relationship for each of the four safety regimes. The units of q have been converted to vehicles per hour. For each value of u, each of the curves shown represents the flow that is attainable if the spacing is kept *just long enough* to avoid a collision in accordance with the corresponding safety regime. Stream operations between the curves, that is, at safety levels along the continuum from one safety regime cutoff point to another, are quite possible. In other words, if viewed alone, each of the four curves outlines an area of operation in terms of q and u that offers a level of safety *equal to or better* than the safety regime represented.

Each curve indicates zero flow at zero speed, meaning that, since no vehicle

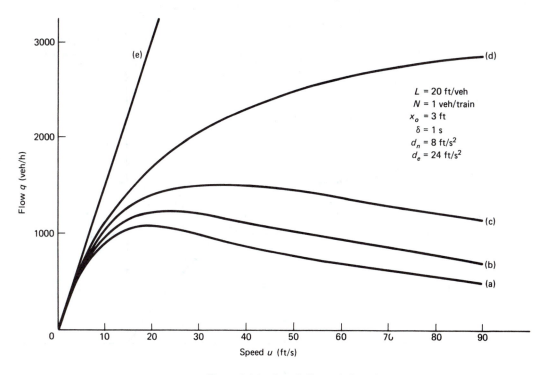

Figure 3.4.2   Speed–flow relationships.

is moving, zero vehicles *per unit time* flow by a point on the facility. At the high-speed end, the flow exhibits a decline because of the increasingly longer spacing requirements for safe operation. The *maximum flow* (q_{max}) shown on each curve is the *capacity* of the roadway or guideway at the specified safety regime. The units of capacity are the same as the units of flow, that is, vehicles per unit time and *not* simply vehicles. Capacity occurs at an intermediate speed u_m and not at maximum (i.e., free) flow: Up to u_m, increasing speed corresponds to increasing flow; beyond u_m, increasing speed is associated with decreasing flow. Hence, in this range, a trade-off exists between speed and flow: Higher speeds can be attained only by sacrificing the throughput capability of the highway or guideway.

Finally, the relationship between flow and concentration can be examined by solving Eq. 3.4.2 for u in terms of k and multiplying both sides by k to obtain

$$q = ku(k) \tag{3.4.4}$$

Figure 3.4.3 shows a typical plot of this relationship for safety regime *b* as described before and, for the sake of discussion, the hypothetical train as well. The free-flow end of Fig. 3.4.3 (i.e., low flow and low concentration) corresponds to the high-speed end of Figs. 3.4.1 and 3.4.2. At the other end of the diagram, concentration attains its maximum value, flow is zero, and speed is also zero. In

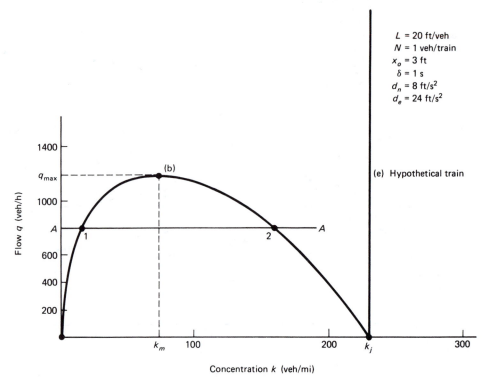

L = 20 ft/veh
N = 1 veh/train
x_o = 3 ft
δ = 1 s
d_n = 8 ft/s^2
d_e = 24 ft/s^2

(e) Hypothetical train

Figure 3.4.3　Flow–concentration curve.

other words, the roadway or guideway is occupied by as many vehicles as it can hold, but no vehicle is moving. Hence no flow is developed. These conditions correspond to a traffic jam, where maximum "packing" of stationary vehicles occurs. The value of concentration at that end is denoted by the *jam concentration* k_j. Again, maximum flow or capacity occurs at intermediate values of speed u_m and concentration k_m.

The horizontal line AA in Fig. 3.4.3 intersects the q–k curve at *two* points. Although the flow is the same at these points, the concentration is different. Also, the speeds corresponding to these two points are different (see Figs. 3.4.1 and 3.4.2). Point 1 represents conditions that are closer to free-flow, whereas point 2 represents conditions that are more congested. If a straight line is drawn from the origin to a point on the q–k curve, the *slope* of this line is simply equal to q/k, which—according to Eq. 3.4.1—is equal to the mean speed u. Therefore, it is possible to specify the numerical values of the three basic stream variables (q, k, and u) by using only one of the three diagrams. It is customary (especially in highway traffic analysis) to use the q–k diagram for this purpose.

Figure 3.4.4 shows a q–k curve for some safety regime, say b. As discussed earlier, operating conditions that do not lie exactly on the curve are quite possible.

Figure 3.4.4   Flow interpretations.

For example, all points associated with safety regime d lie above the regime b curve shown. Thus, it is the desired level of safety that fixes the q, k, and u points on a particular curve and not the physical capabilities of the system. Consider, for example, the limiting hypothetical case of a continuous train that operates on a closed loop at a constant speed u and that is never required to decelerate [3.1]. In this case, considerations of safe stopping are not relevant. Theoretically, the concentration of the continuous train can be kept at jammed conditions on the track. Point C represents a stationary train at jam concentration, zero flow, and zero speed. If the train is operated at some constant speed u, its concentration remains at jam concentration, but the flow becomes finite (see point D, Fig. 3.4.4). If the operating speed is higher, as exemplified by the slope of line BE, the conditions associated with point E result. Thus the vertical line at jam concentration represents this hypothetical case. Clearly, it is physically impossible to operate the system at any of the conditions shown to the right of this line.

Now consider line AB. The slope of this line represents a high speed. This line would represent situations where the same high speed can be maintained at all values of concentration, a situation that is approached in the case of car racing: Irrespective of concentration, the speeds that race-track drivers sustain are very high. Of course, in the case of car racing the predominant consideration is not safety but speed.

Points below this race-track line are also attainable. Thus, for a given transportation technology, triangle ABC encloses the area on the q–k plane within which it is physically possible to operate the system. Within this triangle, the conditions described by points below as well as above the q–k curve shown are physically possible. Even points lying on the k-axis may be given a physical interpretation. For example, point H may represent a sparsely occupied parking lane at concentration below jammed conditions, zero speed, and zero flow. But in this case, speed (i.e., getting to a destination as quickly as possible) is not important!

What gives rise to the q–k curve shown within the region ABC in a typical travel situation is the trade-off between a desire to get to one's destination as quickly as possible (i.e., maximize speed) on one hand and getting there safely (as reflected by the preferred safety regime) on the other.

3.4.3 The Case of Highway Traffic Flow

The case of uniform flow considered above approximates the operation of a uniformly scheduled transit service on an exclusive right of way, where the decisions relating to the trade-off between safety and speed that give rise to the typical q–k diagram (see Fig. 3.4.3) are made explicitly by the operator of the system. In the case of highway traffic, drivers make their own decisions regarding this trade-off. Some drivers keep close to the car in front of them and try to increase their speeds when possible, whereas others keep unusually long spacings by stressing safety more than speed [3.6]. In addition, highway vehicles are not identical but exhibit a great amount of variability in size and technological attributes. The upshot of all these individual differences is a statistical *clustering* of points representing the stream conditions around a curve similar in shape to that shown on Fig. 3.4.3, and the stream diagrams and equations are typically estimated by statistical methods. This difference not withstanding, the flow diagrams of highway traffic exhibit the same general form and are subject to the same kind of interpretation as those developed for the simple case of uniformly scheduled rapid transit.

Figure 3.4.5 illustrates the general form of the u–k, u–q, and q–k diagrams corresponding to highway flow. The u–k relationship is monotonically decreasing, reflecting the rule that drivers follow on the average as they follow one another. The rule of the road suggested by many city traffic ordinances of keeping a distance of one car-length for each 10-mi/h increment of speed is but one such *car-following rule*. The q–u and q–k relationships are "backward bending" as before, with

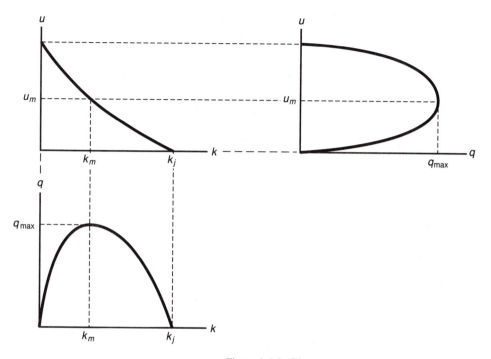

Figure 3.4.5 Flow curves.

maximum flow occurring at an intermediate speed u_m and concentration k_m. Typically, given the u–k relationship, it is possible to estimate the other two relationships by following the procedure that was applied earlier for the case of uniformly scheduled transit.

Example 3.2

Assume that drivers in fact follow the rule of the road of keeping a gap of one car-length (L) for each 10-mi/h increment of speed. Assuming a car-length of 20 ft, develop the equations of stream flow and draw the u–k, q–u, and q–k diagrams.

Solution According to the rule of the road, the safe spacing is a function of speed, or

$$s = L + \left(\frac{u}{10}\right)L = \frac{20 + 2u}{5280} \text{ mi/veh}$$

Applying Eq. 3.3.1 to find the implied k–u relationship yields

$$k = \frac{1}{s} = \frac{2640}{10 + u} \text{ veh/mi}$$

or

$$10k + uk = 2640$$

But according to Eq. 3.4.1, $q = uk$. Thus the relationship between q and k becomes

$$q = 2640 - 10k \text{ veh/h}$$

Finally, expressing this equation in terms of u rather than k yields

$$q = 2640 - \frac{26{,}400}{10 + u}$$

The three diagrams of flow are shown in Fig. 3.4.6.

Figure 3.4.6   Numerical example of flow curves.

Discussion   The u–k diagram has the expected general shape, showing a monotonically decreasing function. Note that the shaded area equals the product $q = uk$. The q–u and q–k diagrams, however, seem to deviate from the expected "backward bending" shape illustrated by the dashed line on the q–k diagram. In view of the observed conditions on actual facilities, this implies that the rule of the road becomes unrealistic for low concentrations and high speeds. In fact, the equations just developed allow vehicles to travel at very high speeds, which is unrealistic. In other words, if the dashed line represents realistic conditions, it may be said that the rule of the road is a linear approximation of the stream conditions at the upper range of concentration. Moreover, the capacity of the roadway is not to be found at zero concentration, as the extrapolating of the straight line beyond its proper range would indicate.

Example 3.3

Given that the relationship between speed and concentration obtained from actual data is $u = 54.5 - 0.24k$, repeat the steps of Example 3.2 to estimate q_{max}, u_m, and k_j.

Solution   To find the relationship between q and k, multiply both sides of the given u–k relationship by k and substitute the fundamental Eq. 3.4.1 in the result:

$$q = uk = 54.5k - 0.24k^2$$

To find the q–u relationship, solve the given equation for k and multiply both sides of the result by u:

$$k = 227 - 4.17u$$

and

$$q = uk = 227u - 4.17u^2$$

The plots of the three flow relationships are shown in Fig. 3.4.7.

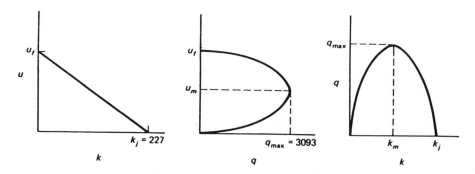

Figure 3.4.7   Derivation of flow properties from flow curves.

To find k_j, the given equation is evaluated at $u = 0$. Thus $k_j = 227$ veh/mi. The free-flow speed u_f occurs at $k = 0$ and equals 54.5 mi/h. The capacity of the highway is $q_{max} = u_m k_m = 3093$ veh/h. The reader is asked to verify these results by applying the calculus to maximize q using either the q–k or the q–u relationship.

Discussion   The results above indicate that the general mathematical form of a *linear* u–k relationship is

$$u = u_f\left(1 - \frac{k}{k_j}\right)$$

This relationship was first postulated by Greenshields [3.7]. If the u–k relationship is linear, the q–u and q–k relationships are both parabolic. In that case, capacity, or q_{max}, occurs at $u_m = u_f/2$ and $k_m = k_j/2$.

3.5 STREAM MEASUREMENTS: THE MOVING-OBSERVER METHOD

3.5.1 Introduction

As shown in Appendix C, the method of least squares can be used to determine the relationship between two or more variables based on a set of experimental observations. Examples of calibrating u–k relationships are also presented. The data used in curve fitting are obtained from an appropriate experiment or experimental observation session. Many vehicular stream-measurement techniques are available for collecting the necessary data [3.2]. Because flow, speed, and concentration are interrelated, a proper measurement technique must take simultaneous measurements on two of the three variables; the third variable can be computed by applying Eq. 3.4.1. Taking measurements of only one of the three variables cannot describe the prevailing vehicular stream conditions. For example, the stream flow can be measured as the ratio of the number of vehicles crossing a pneumatic tube recorder that is stretched across a highway at a given location divided by the total time of measurement. Recall, however, that the same value of q is found at two points on the q–k diagram (Fig. 3.4.3), one closer to free-flow and the other toward the jammed-flow end of the diagram. This means that, in order to distinguish between these two conditions, the values of k and u must also be known.

3.5.2 The Moving-Observer Method

The moving-observer method of traffic stream measurement has been developed to provide simultaneous measurements of stream variables. It involves an observer, who is taking certain measurements while moving in relation to the traffic stream being measured. Referring to the two-way street operation illustrated by Fig. 3.5.1, consider the problem of measuring the stream conditions prevailing in the northbound direction. To develop the appropriate equation of the moving-observer method, consider two cases, corresponding to the *relative motion* between the observer and the vehicular stream being measured.

The first case considers the traffic stream relative to the observer, that is, it assumes a stationary observer and a moving vehicular stream. If N_o vehicles overtake the observer during a period of observation T, the observed flow is simply equal to

$$q = \frac{N_o}{T} \quad \text{or} \quad N_o = qT \qquad (3.5.1)$$

The second case (i.e., the movement of the observer relative to the stream) assumes that only the observer is moving and the rest of the traffic is stationary. By traveling a distance L, the observer would overtake a number of vehicles N_p. Thus the concentration of the stream being measured may be computed as

$$k = \frac{N_p}{L} \quad \text{or} \quad N_p = kVT \qquad (3.5.2)$$

where V is the observer's speed and T is the time it takes the observer to traverse the distance L.

Now, consider that the observer is actually moving within the traffic stream being measured. In that case, some vehicles M_o will overtake the observer, and

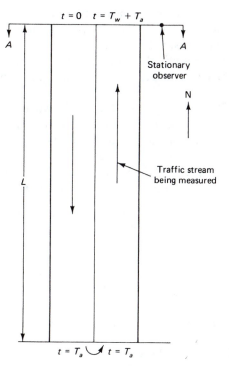

Figure 3.5.1 Moving observer method.

some vehicles M_p will be overtaken by the observer in a test vehicle. The magnitudes of the two counts will depend on the relative speeds between the test vehicle and the rest of the traffic: If the test vehicle is traveling faster than average, it will overtake more vehicles than will overtake it, and vice versa. This case is the combined effect of the "relative" counts described for the two cases of the previous paragraph. Denoting the difference between the two counts as M gives us

$$M = M_o - M_p = qT - kVT \tag{3.5.3}$$

and dividing both sides of Eq. 3.5.3 by T yields

$$\frac{M}{T} = q = ku \tag{3.5.4}$$

This is the basic equation of the moving-observer method, which relates the stream variables q and k to the counts M, T, and V that can be obtained by the test vehicle. The test vehicle's speed V should not be confused with the unknown mean speed u of the stream.

The values of M, T, and V taken on any particular test run are substituted in Eq. 3.5.4, leaving the two unknown stream variables q and k. To solve for these unknowns, two independent equations are needed, and a second test run,

at a different test vehicle speed to ensure independence, can provide the second
equation. Normally, one test run is performed *with traffic* (i.e., moving in the
direction of the stream being measured) and the other is performed *against traffic*
(i.e., moving in the opposite direction). In both cases, however, the test vehicle
counts the M_o and M_p vehicles in the vehicular stream whose conditions are being
measured.

When the test vehicle is moving against traffic, it will only be overtaken (in
a relative sense) be vehicles in the stream; it will overtake no vehicles. In this
case, then, M is simply equal to the number of vehicles in the northbound stream
that the test vehicle encounters while traveling south.

Substituting the measurements taken during the two test runs into Eq. 3.5.4
and using subscripts w and a to refer to the test runs "with" and "against" traffic,
respectively, we obtain

$$\frac{M_w}{T_w} = q - kV_w \qquad (3.5.5a)$$

$$\frac{M_a}{t_a} = q + kV_a \qquad (3.5.5b)$$

The plus sign in the second equation reflects the fact that the test vehicle travels
in the negative direction.

The simultaneous solution of these equations yields

$$q = \frac{M_w + M_a}{T_w + T_a} \qquad (3.5.6)$$

The units of q are vehicles per unit time, which is consistent with the definition
of stream flow. However, whether this value is in fact the unknown stream flow
is a legitimate question. Recalling that flow is a point measurement, the answer
to this question would be affirmative if a point along the roadway length L can
be found where a flow measurement during the total observation time $(T_w + T_a)$
yields the stream flow obtained by Eq. 3.5.6. Point A on Fig. 3.5.1 is such a point.

To prove this claim, consider the following situation: Assume that the test
vehicle begins its run against traffic at time zero. At the same time, an independent
observer located at point A begins to count the vehicles passing that point and
continues to do so until the test vehicle crosses the same point going north. The
test vehicle reaches the end of the run against traffic T_a units of time after the
start of the test. It then turns around instantaneously and begins the test run with
traffic, which takes T_w units of time. The total number of vehicles that would
cross line A during the total time $(T_a + T_w)$ is equal to the number of vehicles
M_a that the test vehicle encounters during its run against traffic *plus* the number
of vehicles that overtake the test vehicle during its run with traffic *minus* any
vehicles that the test vehicle overtakes during its run with traffic. The difference
between the latter two counts taken during the run in the direction of the stream

is simply equal to M_w, as defined before. The sum of M_a and M_w is exactly the number of vehicles that the independent observer at point A will be able to count during the time $(T_w + T_a)$. Consequently, the computation of Eq. 3.5.6 yields the required stream flow q.

To calculate the space mean speed u for the vehicular stream, Eq. 3.5.5a is rewritten as

$$\frac{M_w}{T_w} = q - \frac{q}{u}\left(\frac{L}{T_w}\right) \tag{3.5.7}$$

The quantity (L/u) is the time T it takes the average vehicle in the stream to traverse the length L. This average time can be computed from Eq. 3.5.7:

$$T = T_w - \frac{M_w}{q} \tag{3.5.8}$$

where T_w is the travel time of the test vehicle in the direction of the stream being measured, M_w is the count taken during that run, and q is the flow computed by Eq. 3.5.6.

Equation 3.5.8 relates the travel time of the test vehicle to the average travel time of the vehicles in the stream. If the test vehicle is traveling faster than average, it will overtake more vehicles than will overtake it, and M_w will be negative. Consequently, the average stream travel time will be greater than the test vehicle's travel time. If the test vehicle is slower than the rest of the traffic, M_w will be positive, and the average stream travel time (Eq. 3.5.8) will be less than the test vehicle's. Finally, if the test vehicle is traveling at the average stream speed, it will (on the average) overtake as many vehicles as will overtake it, and Eq. 3.5.8 will reflect this fact. Once the average stream travel time is computed from Eq. 3.5.8, the average stream speed can be obtained from

$$u = \frac{L}{T} \tag{3.5.9}$$

This speed is the *space mean speed* because it is computed on the basis of travel time as described in Section 3.3. The calculation of the stream concentration is a matter of substitution of the flow computed from Eq. 3.5.6 and the mean speed computed from Eq. 3.5.9 into Eq. 3.4.1.

To ensure statistical reliability, the test is run a number of times (usually, five or six) and the average results are employed in the final calculations.

Example 3.4

A bicycle racer practices every day at different times. Her route includes a ride along a 0.5-mi bikeway and back, as shown in Fig. 3.5.2. Since she is a traffic engineer, she has made it a habit to count the number of cars in lane A that she meets while riding southward (M_s), the number of cars in lane A that overtake her while riding northward (M_o), and the number of cars in lane A that she overtakes while riding

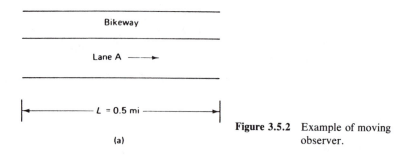

Figure 3.5.2 Example of moving
observer.

northward (M_p). The table summarizes the average measurements that she obtained
for each period of the day.

Time of day	M_s	M_o	M_p
8:00–9:00 A.M.	107	10	74
9:00–10:00	113	25	41
10:00–11:00	30	15	5
11:00–12:00	79	18	9

Given that the bicyclist travels at a constant speed of 20 mi/h, (a) find the traffic
stream conditions for each period of the day, (b) calibrate $u = a + bk$ and plot the
q–k relationship, and (c) estimate the capacity of lane A.

Solution   (a) It takes the bicyclist (0.5 mi/20 mi/h = 0.025 h to traverse the half-
mile distance. Hence $T_a = T_w = 0.025$ h. For each period of the day, the flow,
average travel time, mean speed, and concentration of lane A are computed as illustrated for the 8:00–9:00 A.M. period:

$$q_1 = \frac{107 + 10 - 74}{0.025 + 0.025} = 860 \text{ veh/h}$$

$$u_1 = \frac{0.5}{0.025 - \dfrac{10 - 74}{860}} = 5 \text{ mi/h}$$

$$k_1 = q_1/u_1 = 172 \text{ veh/mi}$$

The results for the other periods of the day are

$$q_2 = 1940 \qquad q_3 = 800 \qquad q_4 = 1760$$
$$u_2 = 15 \qquad u_3 = 40 \qquad u_4 = 25$$
$$k_2 = 129 \qquad k_3 = 20 \qquad k_4 = 70$$

(b) To find the speed–concentration relationship of the form $u = a + bk$, apply
simple linear regression to the pairs (k,u), with u as the dependent variable. The
result is

$$u = 42.76 - 0.22k$$

Multiply both sides of this equation by k and substitute $q = uk$:

$$q = 42.76k - 0.22k^2$$

which is a parabola similar to that of Example 3.3. The plots of the last two equations are shown in Fig. 3.5.3, along with the original data points.

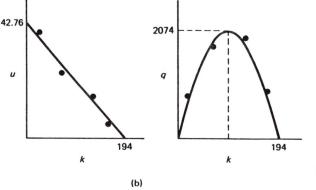

(b)

Figure 3.5.3 Flow curves from moving observer data.

(c) As in Example 3.3, q_{max} occurs at $u_m = u_f/2$ and $k_m = k_j/2$. Moreover, $u_f = 42.76$ mi/h at $k = 0$, and $k_j = 194$ veh/mi at $u = 0$. Hence

$$q_{max} = 2074 \text{ veh/h}$$

Discussion This example illustrates the use of the moving-observer method to take traffic stream measurements, it applies the method of least squares to calibrate the relationship between u and k, and it applies the fundamental characteristics of traffic streams to find the q–k curve.

The first step assumed that the traffic conditions prevailing during each period of the day remain relatively stable from day to day, since the observations were averaged by time of day. The results show that during the morning peak hour between 8:00 and 9:00 A.M. lane A is very congested with very low speed ($u = 5$ mi/h) and high concentration ($k = 172$ veh/mi). Between 9:00 and 10:00 A.M., the traffic eases and the prevailing conditions move closer to free flow. Finally, between 11:00 A.M. and 12:00 noon, concentration increases and speed decreases once more, perhaps due to the lunchtime crowd.

3.6 SHOCK WAVES IN TRAFFIC

3.6.1 Introduction

Suppose that a traffic stream is moving on a roadway at a given flow, speed, and concentration as illustrated by point 1 on the q–k diagram of Figure 3.6.1. Based on the calibrated diagram shown, point 1 corresponds to a flow of 1000 veh/h, a

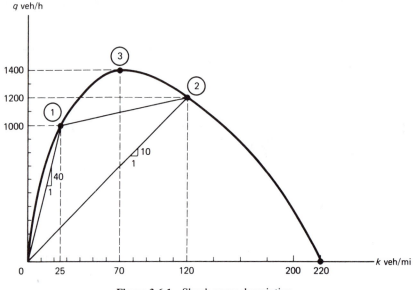

Figure 3.6.1 Shock wave description.

concentration of 25 veh/mi, and a mean speed (i.e., the slope of chord 0-1) of 40 mi/h. The spacing between vehicles may be computed by Eq. 3.3.1 to be about 212 ft. Now, assume that a truck in the stream decides to slow down to 10 mi/h. If passing is not permitted, the following vehicles will also have to slow down to match the truck's speed. With time, a moving platoon of vehicles traveling at 10 mi/h will grow behind the truck. At any instant, the last vehicle to join the platoon will be traveling at 10 mi/h, but farther upstream vehicles would continue to approach the platoon at the original conditions. Since the vehicles within the platoon are traveling slower than before they joined, they will tend to adjust their spacing to a shorter safe spacing than before. The resulting stream conditions for vehicles within the platoon are represented by point 2 on Figure 3.6.1, where the slope of chord 0–2 is the platoon speed. In this example, the values of platoon flow and concentration are shown to be 1200 veh/h and 120 veh/mi, respectively.

Thus at any time after the truck slowed down, a stationary observer will see a platoon defined by the truck at its front and the last vehicle to join at its rear. The platoon, consisting of slow-moving vehicles at relatively high concentrations, is moving with a speed of 10 mi/h and grows in length as more vehicles join it. After some time, the traffic conditions in front of the truck are at free flow (i.e., zero concentration). Behind the last vehicle to join the platoon the stream conditions are at 40 mi/h and a concentration of 25 veh/mi. Figure 3.6.2 illustrates the dynamics of platoon formation described above: At time $t = 0$, the vehicles in the stream are shown to travel at the average stream conditions corresponding to point 1 of Fig. 3.6.1. The truck slows down to 10 mi/h at this instant. A short time later, the truck has displaced somewhat and a following vehicle is shown to

Figure 3.6.2 Platoon formation.

have matched its speed. The platoon now contains two vehicles [Fig. 3.6.2(b)]. Later on, additional vehicles join the moving platoon, as illustrated. Fig. 3.6.2(d) shows a clear roadway in front of the truck, the high-concentration platoon behind the truck, and approaching vehicles at the original stream conditions farther upstream. The same situation is described by the time–distance diagram of Fig. 3.6.3.

Using a hydrodynamic analogy [3.8], a *shock wave* is said to exist whenever traffic streams of varying stream conditions meet. In the above example, there are two such lines of demarcation, or shock waves. One is seen between the platoon conditions and the free-flow conditions in front of the platoon (line *AA*, Fig. 3.6.2). The other is seen between the approach conditions and the platoon conditions (line *BB*, Fig. 3.6.2). The shock wave at the front of the platoon is defined by the truck, whereas the shock wave at the rear of the platoon is defined by the last vehicle to join the platoon. Figures 3.6.2 and 3.6.3 show that the shock waves *AA* and *BB* displace with time in relation to the roadway. The rate at which the platoon grows is related to the relative speeds of the two shock waves *AA* and *BB*. Moreover, given the platoon concentration (120 veh/mi in this case) and the length of the platoon, the number of vehicles within the platoon can easily be computed.

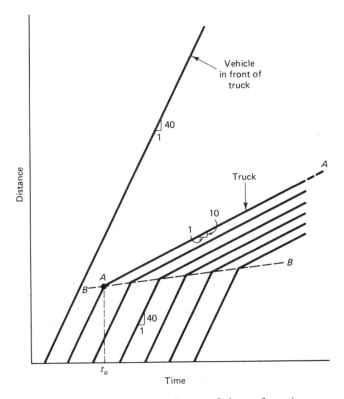

Figure 3.6.3 Time–distance diagram of platoon formation.

If, after a time, the truck driver decides either to accelerate or to exit the highway, the vehicles stuck behind the truck will be free to increase their speeds, and another shock wave will begin between the release conditions and the platoon conditions. The next section shows that the fundamental diagram of stream flow can be used to explain the shock wave phenomenon.

3.6.2 The Shock Wave Equation

It has been shown [3.8] that the speed of a traffic stream shock wave is given by the slope of the chord connecting the two stream conditions that define the shock wave (e.g., points 1 and 2, Figure 3.6.1). Labeling the two conditions as *a* and *b* *in the direction of traffic movement*, the *magnitude and direction* of the speed of the shock wave between the two conditions are given by

$$U_{sw} = \frac{q_b - q_a}{k_b - k_a} \qquad (3.6.1)$$

If the sign of the shock wave speed is positive, the shock wave is traveling in the direction of stream flow; if it is zero, the shock wave is stationary with respect to the roadway; if it is negative, the shock wave moves in the upstream direction. The example illustrated by Figs. 3.6.2 and 3.6.3 shows two shock waves both traveling in the direction of the stream of vehicles. Situations arise where the shock wave travels in the opposite direction. For example, consider the case where a vehicular stream is interrupted by a traffic signal. Vehicles stopped by the red light are packed at jam concentration (i.e., zero speed and flow). Upstream of the stationary platoon, vehicles approach the platoon at the approach conditions. The shock wave between the approaching vehicles and the jammed vehicles defined by the last vehicle to be stopped is, in fact, moving in the negative (i.e., upstream) direction.

Example 3.5

For the illustration of Fig. 3.6.1, determine the magnitude and direction of the speeds of the two shock waves AA and BB and determine the rate at which the platoon is growing behind the truck.

Solution   The conditions that define the shock wave at the front of the platoon are (1) the platoon conditions (i.e., q_a = 1200 veh/h and k_a = 120 veh/mi) and (2) the free-flow conditions in front of the truck (i.e., q_b = 0 and k_b = 0). Equation 3.6.1 yields the speed of the shock wave AA:

$$U_{sw}(AA) = \frac{0 - 1200}{0 - 120} = +10 \text{ mi/h}$$

which happens to be the speed of the truck, as expected in this situation. The speed of the shock wave at the rear of the platoon defined by (1) the approach conditions (i.e., q_a = 1000 veh/h and k_a = 25 veh/mi) and (2) the platoon conditions is

$$U_{sw}(BB) = \frac{1200 - 1000}{120 - 25} = +2.1 \text{ mi/h}$$

The front of the platoon moves at 10 mi/h forward relative to the roadway and the rear of the platoon travels at 2.1 mi/h in the same direction. The rate of growth of the platoon is given by the relative speed between the two, or 10.0 − 2.1 = 7.9 mi/h. The platoon grows at this rate as it travels forward.

Discussion   The speed of the front of the platoon is the same as the speed of the truck only because the conditions in front of the truck are at free flow (see Fig. 3.6.3). In the general case, however, the speed of the shock wave should not be confused with the speed of any of the vehicles in the stream, as the speed of shock wave BB in this example clarifies. Platoon vehicles are traveling at 10 mi/h, approaching vehicles are traveling at 40 mi/h (see slope of line 0-1, Fig. 3.6.1), but the shock wave between the two travels at 2.1 mi/h. It is of interest to note that although the truck forced the traffic to slow down, the flow increased from 1000 to 1200 veh/h, a situation of which the frustrated drivers would be unaware. In certain cases, slowing the traffic via the traffic-control system may be a good way of increasing the flow. But this consequence goes totally unnoticed by the drivers.

Example 3.6

For Example 3.5, assume that the truck exited the traffic stream 10 min after slowing down. Vehicles at the front of the platoon were then released to a speed of 20 mi/h and a concentration of 70 veh/mi. Compute the amount of time it took the 10-mi/h platoon to disappear.

Solution   The release conditions imply a flow of (20 mi/h)(70 veh/mi) = 1400 veh/h (i.e., point 3 on Fig. 3.6.1). At the end of 10 min (or $\frac{1}{6}$ h) the platoon had grown to a length of

$$L = (7.9 \text{ mi/h})(\tfrac{1}{6} \text{ h}) = 1.3 \text{ mi}$$

Incidentally, at that instant the 120-veh/mi platoon contained (1.3)(120) = 156 vehicles. After the truck exited the traffic stream, a shock wave between (1) the platoon conditions and (2) the release conditions developed. The speed of this shock wave is

$$U_{sw} = \frac{1400 - 1200}{70 - 120} = -4.0 \text{ mi/h}$$

relative to the roadway. Thus the shock wave at the front of the platoon moved upstream at 4.0 mi/h, whereas the shock wave at the rear of the platoon continued to move downstream at 2.1 mi/h. The relative speed of the two waves was 4.0 + 2.1 = 6.1 mi/h. Since the platoon was 1.3 mi long to begin with, it took (1.3)/(6.1) = 0.21 h or 12.6 min after the truck's departure for the platoon to dissipate totally.

Discussion   The time–distance diagram in Fig. 3.6.4 plots the location of the front and the rear of the platoon from the moment the truck slowed down to the moment when the last vehicle caught in the platoon was released. At any instant, the dif-

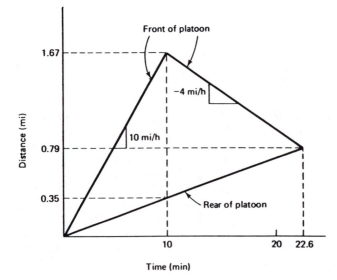

Figure 3.6.4   Time–distance diagram of platoon positions.

ference between the two represents the length of the platoon, which is seen to grow from 0 to 1.3 mi during the first 10 min and then to shrink back to 0 approximately 12.6 min after the truck's exit. During this second phase, the front and rear of the platoon were defined by different vehicles at different times as vehicles at the front were sequentially released and additional vehicles joined at the rear.

The point where the platoon disappeared was 0.79 mi from the initial point, even though the front of the platoon had been as far as 1.67 mi ahead of the location where the truck slowed down.

Typically, the congestion relief time is longer than the duration of the flow disruption (i.e., 10 and 12.6 min in this example). This is why freeway accidents during peak periods tend to create long-lasting jams.

Example 3.7

For Example 3.6, determine the speed of the shock wave that commenced at the instant when the 10-mi/h platoon was totally eliminated.

Solution   After the last platoon vehicle was released, a shock wave commenced between (1) the approach conditions behind this last vehicle and (2) the release conditions in front of it. The speed of this new shock wave was

$$U_{sw} = \frac{1400 - 1000}{70 - 25} = +8.9 \text{ mi/h forward}$$

Discussion   The appearance of this, perhaps unexpected, shock wave illustrates the complexity of the dynamics of traffic flow. These accordionlike movements occur back and forth as vehicles slow down and accelerate in response to various stimuli, including other vehicles, traffic controls, sight-distance restrictions, sharp horizontal curves, and so forth. The 8.9 mi/h shock wave presumably continued as long as the approach and release conditions were sustained. In reality, these conditions change over time, as a comparison between the traffic at midnight vis-à-vis the morning rush hour would attest. Moreover, even under identical *average* conditions, there is enough variability in individual vehicle conditions to cause the continuous commencement and dissipation of such shock waves.

3.7 SUMMARY

In this chapter we extended the equations of single-vehicle motion to vehicular interactions. A general relationship between safe spacing and speed was developed and shown to affect the capacity of highways and transitways. Based on the single-vehicle variables of speed, spacing, and headway, the fundamental variables of vehicular streams (average speed, concentration, and flow) were defined, and the fundamental relationship between the stream variables was examined. A method of measuring stream conditions (the moving-observer method) was also presented. Finally, the phenomenon of shock waves in traffic streams was illustrated.

3.8 EXERCISES

1. A rapid-transit system employing single vehicles is scheduled at constant headways. For safety regime b (Table 3.2.1) plot the relationship between spacing in feet and speed in feet per second using the following data: perception-reaction time = 1.5 s, normal deceleration = 8 ft/s², emergency deceleration = 32 ft/s², vehicle length = 40 ft, and safety clearance x_o = 4 ft.

2. Repeat the solution to Exercise 1 for safety regime a.

3. For Exercises 1 and 2, calculate the maximum flows in vehicles per hour and the corresponding speeds.

4. Given $s = 0.30/(60 - u)$, where s is the spacing in miles and u is the speed in miles per hour, derive the relationships u–k, u–q, and q–k. Also estimate the capacity (i.e., q_{max}) of the roadway.

5. For the data of Exercise 4, plot spacing in feet versus headway in seconds.

6. Prepare a computer program, which, given the necessary inputs and a particular safety regime, calculates the spacing for increasing values of speed.

7. A study of the traffic using a tunnel showed that the following speed–concentration relationship applies:

$$u = 17.2 \ln(228/k) \text{ mi/h}$$

Find (a) the capacity of the tunnel, (b) the values of speed and concentration at capacity, and (c) the jam concentration.

8. The u–k relationship for a particular freeway lane was found to be

$$u + 2.6 = 0.001(k - 240)^2$$

Given that the speed is in miles per hour and the concentration is in vehicles per mile, find (a) the free-flow speed, (b) the jam concentration, (c) the lane capacity, and (d) the speed at capacity.

9. The following relationship applies to a particular urban highway:

$$q = 273u - 70u \ln u$$

Calculate q_{max}, u_m, k_m, and u_f.

10. According to the General Motors Research Laboratory, the fuel consumption rate of passenger cars is of the form

$$F = K_1 + \frac{K_2}{V}$$

where F is the fuel consumption in gallons per mile, V is the space mean speed, and K_1 and K_2 are calibration parameters. The following data were obtained by an experiment using a typical mix of passenger cars.

F	0.40	0.10	0.12	0.07	0.06
V	2.50	10.20	14.08	25.12	52.00

Calibrate, sketch, and interpret this model.

11. The following data were taken on a highway:

$$
\begin{array}{llllll}
u & 52. & 34 & 36 & 22 & 21 & \text{mi/h} \\
k & 8 & 41 & 48 & 70 & 105 & \text{veh/mi}
\end{array}
$$

(a) Estimate the free-flow speed assuming that $q = AkB^k$. (b) Calculate the capacity of the highway. (c) Find u_m and k_m.

12. A moving observer conducted two test runs on a 5-mi stretch of roadway. Both tests were in the direction of traffic. Given the following measurements, calculate the flow, concentration, space mean speed, average spacing, and average headway of the traffic stream.

Test run	Test vehicle speed (mi/h)	$M_o - M_p$ vehicles
1	10	100
2	20	−150

13. While taking measurements by the moving-observer method, a test vehicle covered a 1-mi section in 1.5 min going against traffic and 2.5 min going with traffic. Given that the traffic flow was 800 veh/h and that the test vehicle passed 10 more vehicles than passed it when going with traffic, find (a) the number of vehicles encountered by the test vehicle while moving against traffic, (b) the speed of the traffice being measured, (c) the concentration of the traffic stream, and (d) whether on its run with traffic, the test vehicle was traveling faster or slower than the traffic stream.

14. Given the following u–k relationship,

$$
u = 30 \ln \left(\frac{300}{k} \right) \text{ mi/h}
$$

find the jam concentration, the capacity of the roadway, and the speed of the shock wave between conditions $u_a = 60$ mi/h and $u_b = 40$ mi/h.

15. A line of traffic moving at a speed of 30 mi/h and a concentration of 50 veh/mi is stopped for 30 s at a red light. Calculate (a) the velocity and direction of the stopping wave, (b) the length of the line of cars stopped during the 30 s of red, and (c) the number of cars stopped during the 30 s of red. Assume a jam concentration of 250 veh/mi.

16. A vehicular stream at $q_a = 1200$ veh/h and $k_a = 100$ veh/mi is interrupted by a flag-person for 5 min beginning at time $t = t_0$. At time $t = t_0 + 5$ minutes, vehicles at the front of the stationary platoon begin to be released at $q_b = 1600$ veh/h and $u_b = 20$ mi/h. Assuming that $k_j = 240$ veh/mi, (a) plot the location of the front of the platoon versus time and the location of the rear of the platoon versus time and (b) plot the length of the growing platoon versus time.

17. A 15-mi/h school zone is in effect from 7:30 to 9:00 A.M. Traffic measurements taken on October 10, 1985, showed that at precisely 9:00 A.M., the conditions presented in Fig. E3.17 prevailed. How long did it take for the 3-mi platoon to disappear, and what was the speed of the shock wave that commenced at the moment when the platoon dissipated completely?

Figure E3.17

18. You were the driver of the *sixth* car to be stopped by a red light. *Ten* seconds elapsed after the onset of the following green before you were able to get going again. Given that the release flow was 1200 veh/h, calculate the release concentration and the release mean speed. Assume an average car length $L = 18$ ft and a safety margin $x_o = 2$ ft.

19. Prepare a computer program that calculates the speed of the shock wave between two conditions specified by input values for k_a and k_b. Assume that $u = C - Dk$, where C and D are parametric values to be specified by the user of your program. Your program should be constrained by

$$40 \leqslant u_f \leqslant 70 \text{ mi/h}$$

$$200 \leqslant k_j \leqslant 300 \text{ veh/mi}$$

Run your program several times and interpret the results.

3.9 REFERENCES

3.1 VUCHIC, VUKAN R., *Urban Public Transportation Systems and Technology*, Prentice Hall, Englewood Cliffs, N.J., 1981.

3.2 GERLOUGH, DANIEL L., and MATTHEW J. HUBER, *Traffice Flow Theory, A Monograph*, Special Report 165, Transportation Research Board, National Research Council, Washington, D.C., 1975.

3.3 DICKEY, JOHN W., *Metropolitan Transportation Planning*, Scripta Book Company (McGraw-Hill), New York, 1975.

3.4 INSTITUTE OF TRANSPORTATION ENGINEERS, *Transportation and Traffic Engineering Handbook*, Prentice Hall, Englewood Cliffs, N.J., 1976.

3.5 ROCKWELL, THOMAS H., and JOSEPH TREITERER, *Sensing and Communication between Vehicles*, National Cooperative Highway Research Program Report 51, Highway Research Board, National Research Council, Washington, D.C., 1968.

3.6 SYNODINOS, N. E., and C. S. PAPACOSTAS, "Driving Habits and Behaviour Patterns of Unviersity Students," *International Review of Applied Psychology*, 34 (1985): 241–257.

3.7 GREENSHIELDS, B. D., "A Study of Traffic Capacity," *Highway Research Board Proceedings*, 14 (1935): 448–477.

3.8 LIGHTHILL, M. J., and G. B. WHITMAN, "On Kinematic Waves: II. A Theory of Traffic Flow on Long Crowded Roads," *Proceedings of the Royal Society* (London), Series A, 229, 1178 (1955): 317–345.

4

Capacity Analysis

4.1 INTRODUCTION

This chapter is concerned with the stream characteristics of actual transportation systems. The flow relationships and the capacities of selected urban mass-transportation systems operating on exclusive pathways and a model that can be used to estimate the fleet size required to provide a desired flow are followed by a practical method of examining the capacity and level of service of high-level highway facilities (i.e., freeways and expressways). The described highway capacity method can be used either to determine the number of highway lanes required to satisfy a desired level of service, or to estimate the level of service prevailing on a highway given its geometric design and the actual flow conditions. Finally, calibrated pedestrian flow models are presented and discussed, and the fundamental similarity between vehicular and pedestrian flow models is illustrated.

4.2 URBAN MASS-TRANSPORTATION SYSTEMS

4.2.1 Introduction

In the introduction to this book a historical note about the evolution of public transportation systems was presented to clarify the nomenclature associated with these systems. Among the categories discussed were the following:

Light rail transit (LRT) is essentially a modernized electric streetcar with possibilities of articulation and capable of being operated both in mixed traffic and on exclusive rights of way. The PCC car is a very successful electric streetcar design that resulted from the cooperative efforts of the Electric Railway Presidents' Conference Committee during the 1930s.

Personal rapid transit (PRT) refers to system designs that generally employ small vehicles operating on a network of exclusive pathways and characterized by route and scheduling flexibility.

Automated guideway transit (AGT) is designed to operate on exclusive guideways without intervention from an onboard driver in an attempt to minimize labor costs and to increase productivity; it may or may not be a PRT system.

Rail rapid transit (RRT) generally refers to high-performance, electrically-propelled, multicar systems that operate on grade-separated rail facilities with few stops.

Regional rail (RGR) [4.1] or commuter rail (CR) [4.2] denotes multicar diesel or electric trains with very few stops that had its origins as an extension of intercity railroads.

An articulated bus is a long urban motor bus consisting of two sections, which are connected by a flexible joint to allow for short turning radii and increased passenger-holding capacity vis-à-vis the standard 40-ft urban bus.

TABLE 4.2.1 CHARACTERISTICS OF TYPICAL TRANSIT SYSTEMS[a]

Item[b]	Unit	Standard bus	Articu-lated bus	Single four-axle LRT vehicle	Personal rapid transit	Two-car AGT	Two-car articu-lated LRT	Eight-car AGT	Six-car RRT	Ten-car RRT/RGR
n	veh/TU	1	1	1	1	2	2	8	6	10
l'	m	12.0	17.0	14.0	2.3	6.5	24.0	10.7	18.0	21.0
C_v	sps/veh	53[c]	73[c]	110	4[c]	40	189	70	145	175
S_0	m	1	1	2	1	1	2	1	2	2
t_r	s	1	1	1	0	0	1	0	0	0
b_n	m/s^2	1.4	1.4	1.2	1.6	1.4	1.2	1.4	1.1	1.1
b_e	m/s^2	4.0	4.0	3.0	5.0	4.0	3.0	4.0	1.8	1.8
V_{max}	km/h	90	80	80	70	50	90	80	100	120
v_{max}	m/s	25.0	22.2	22.2	19.4	13.9	25.0	22.2	27.7	33.3
Operating safety regime		c	c	b	a	a	a	a	a	a
Typical model		GMC's "New Look"	M.A.N.	PCC	Aramis	Airtrans	DÜWAG U-2	Skybus	Munich U-Bahn	San Francisco BART

[a] Data given are typical for the selected models. They are taken from the models given, with the exception of a few rounded or modified values to eliminate nontypical features (e.g., BART's A and C cars have different lengths; Airtrans' V_{max} = 27 km/h). Acceleration rate $a = 0.8$ m/s^2 and station standing time $t_s = 20$ s are assumed for all modes.

[b] TU, transit unit (train); l', effective vehicle length; C_v, passenger spaces/vehicle; t_r, perception-reaction time; b_n, normal deceleration; b_e, emergency deceleration.

[c] Assumes seating only.

Source: Vuchic [4.1].

Table 4.2.1 lists the attributes of the typical designs listed in the last row from each of these categories.

4.2.2 Uninterrupted Speed–Flow Relationships

Figures 4.2.1 and 4.2.2 present the q–u relationships derived by Vuchic [4.1] and specify the typical operational safety regimes of the technological systems listed in Table 4.2.1. Vuchic uses the term *way capacity* to refer to the flow on the curve corresponding to a specific safety regime. This is to capture the fact that each q–u curve represents the maximum flow possible for a given speed and a specific safety regime. Note, however, that for each curve, there exists a speed for which the flow (or way capacity) is maximum. This is what, in this book, is referred to as the capacity of the system, q_{max}.

Figure 4.2.1 Actual system speed flow: Vehicles per hour. (From Vuchic [4.1].)

Figure 4.2.2 Actual system speed flow: Spaces per hour. (From Vuchic [4.1].)

Figure 4.2.1 presents flow in terms of *vehicles per hour*. Also note that certain of the systems plotted permit *transit units* (TU) or trains, each consisting of a number of such vehicles. Each train may be thought of as a series of vehicles having a jam spacing in contrast to the much longer spacing between transit units. Thus the coupling of vehicles into transit units in effect organizes the stream into a series of small spacings (and headways) followed by a larger spacing (and headway). This arrangement results in a higher vehicular flow than if single vehicles were scheduled individually at the constant spacing required by the same safety regime.

Figure 4.2.2 presents the flow characteristics of the same technological systems, not in terms of vehicles per hour but in terms of what Vuchic calls *spaces per hour*. Consequently, these curves represent the passenger-carrying capability of each system.

Two important points relating to Figs. 4.2.1 and 4.2.2 must be stressed here. First, system comparisons of passenger flow on one hand and vehicular flow and capacity on the other do not lead to the same conclusion with respect to dominance of one system over another. It should also be noted that just because a system is capable of carrying a certain flow of passengers, it does not necessarily mean that it actually carries that maximum. To illustrate this point consider the private automobile: The passenger-holding capacity of a typical automobile is about five to six passengers. But actual usage shows an average loading of 1.5 to 2.0 passengers per automobile, depending on the time of day, the trip purpose, and other factors.

The second point worthy of mention in connection with Figs. 4.2.1 and 4.2.2 is the fact that irrespective of how flow is considered (i.e., passenger or vehicular), there are ranges where one system dominates another, but there are also ranges where the reverse is true. Thus, in many cases, it is not possible to state unequivocally that one system is always superior to another. Differences in safety regime, capital and operating costs, and system flexibility are among the variables that enter the calculus of choosing between systems.

4.2.3 Fleet Size

The *number* of vehicles needed to sustain a transit line *flow* of q vehicles per hour for a time period T is affected by the fact that some vehicles may be able to traverse the line more than one time during T. A vehicular count over the time period T will yield

$$N = qT \quad \text{vehicles} \tag{4.2.1}$$

some of which will be counted more than one time. Assuming that the round-trip time of a single vehicle is T_{rt}, this vehicle will, on the average, traverse the line approximately T/T_{rt} times. Hence, to provide N vehicle departures during T, a fleet F of

$$F = N\left(\frac{T_{rt}}{T}\right) = qT_{rt} \tag{4.2.2}$$

is needed.

The average round-trip travel time is the sum of the average travel times between stops plus the average dwell time at each stop multiplied by the number of stops. The dwell time varies between 20 and 90 s, depending on the geometry of the access gates (number, width of doors, existence of steps, etc.), the number and split of passengers processed (boarding and alighting), and the degree of passenger "packing."

Example 4.1

A transit line employing nonarticulated vehicles is expected to carry 10,000 passengers during the 2-h morning peak period. Given a round-trip time of 30 min and an average vehicle occupancy of 75 passengers, calculate the hourly flow q and the number of vehicles F required to provide this flow.

Solution   The number of vehicular departures needed to carry the given demand is

$$N = \frac{10,000}{75} = 133.3 \quad \text{or} \quad 134 \text{ departures in 2 h}$$

The hourly flow is

$$q = \frac{134}{2} = 67 \text{ veh/h}$$

Assuming that this flow is attainable, the number of vehicles needed is

$$F = (67 \text{ veh/h})(0.5 \text{ h}) = 33.5 \quad \text{or} \quad 34 \text{ vehicles}$$

4.2.4 Transit Network Fleet Size

In the preceding subsection we developed a simple formula that can be used to estimate the number of vehicles needed to accommodate a known passenger demand on a single line. The calculation of the fleet size needed to provide services on a large transit network consisting of many transit lines is complicated by the fact that the travel desires of people vary by time of day and by spatial orientation. Moreover, the selection of appropriate transit lines is a difficult task, which frequently results in overlapping lines and transferring between lines. As a simple illustration of line overlapping, consider the two-line network of Fig. 4.2.3.

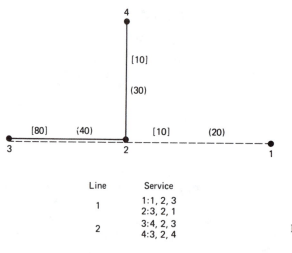

Line	Service
1	1:1, 2, 3 2:3, 2, 1
2	3:4, 2, 3 4:3, 2, 4

Figure 4.2.3   Transit line overlap. (From Papacostas [4.3].)

The vehicle flow requirements for each link of the network are shown in parentheses for the inbound movement (i.e., toward node 3) and in brackets for the outbound movement (i.e., away from node 3). The two transit lines shown overlap on the link 2-3; hence passengers on this link can choose either line. To accommodate the known demand, the line requirements must satisfy the following conditions:

$$N_{\mathrm{I}} \geqslant 30 \text{ departures} \qquad (4.2.3a)$$

$$N_{\mathrm{II}} \geqslant 20 \qquad (4.2.3b)$$

and

$$N_{\mathrm{I}} + N_{\mathrm{II}} \geqslant 80^a \qquad (4.2.3c)$$

The problem then is to distribute the extra flow on link 2–3 (i.e., $80 - 30 - 20 = 30$) between the two lines. This may be accomplished by minimizing the fleet size, for example,

$$\min F = \sum \left(\frac{N_i T_{rt,\,i}}{T} \right) \qquad (4.2.4)$$

or since the minimization above would generally favor shorter lines, by some other rule, such as distributing the extra flow to the overlapping lines in proportion to the minimum needs according to constraints 4.2.3a and 4.2.3b [4.3]. Another option involves the introduction of a shuttle line between points 2 and 3. Computer-based methods of transit network analysis are available in the technical literature [4.4].

The level of service (LOS) definition for mass transit is complex. It incorporates a multitude of factors, such as geographic coverage, on-time performance, scheduling and frequency of service, speed, comfort, safety, and security. The 1985 *Highway Capacity Manual* [4.5] includes several tables on mass transit LOS. The approach of the manual is much simplified since LOS is determined only on

TABLE 4.2.2 EXAMPLES OF MASS TRANSIT LEVEL OF SERVICE ASSESSMENT

Peak-hour level of service	Passengers	Approx. ft²/pass.	Pass./seat (approx.)
A	0–26	13.1 or more	0.00–0.50
B	27–40	13.0–8.5	0.51–0.75
C	41–53	8.4–6.4	0.76–1.00
D	54–66	6.3–5.2	1.01–1.25
E (maximum scheduled load)	67–80	5.1–4.3	1.26–1.50
F (crush load)	81–85	<4.3	1.51–1.60

Peak-hour level of service	Approx. ft²/pass.	Approx. pass./seat
A	15.4 or more	0.00–0.65
B	15.2–10.0	0.66–1.00
C	9.9–7.5	1.01–1.50
D	6.6–5.0	1.51–2.00
E-1	4.9–4.0	2.01–2.50
E-2 (maximum scheduled load)	3.9–3.3	2.51–3.00
F (crush load)	3.2–2.6[a]	3.01–3.80

[a] The maximum crush load can be realized in a single car but not in every car on the train.

Source: Transportation Research Board [4.5].

the basis of square footage available per passenger. Table 4.2.2 presents two such tables from HCM.

4.3 HIGHWAY CAPACITY AND LEVEL OF SERVICE

4.3.1 Introduction

The general relationships among highway flow, concentration, and speed were derived and interpreted in Chapter 3, which also illustrated the moving-observer method of measuring these variables.

From the practical point of view, it is often difficult to devote the resources needed for data collection and curve fitting for each specific highway segment under investigation. Moreover, it is impossible to take measurements on a facility that is under design, that is, before it is actually built. Yet the designer must anticipate the operational characteristics of the facility in order to make prudent geometric design decisions. Such estimates are based on observations of existing facilities of similar types, and practical methods of analysis and design that utilize these estimates have evolved and been codified over the years [4.5–4.9]. This section summarizes the basic method by which the capacity of long segments of highway facilities that are removed from the influence of external interruptions (i.e., at-grade intersections or entrance and exit ramps) can be assessed. The concept of *level of service* is first introduced, and a method of estimating the capacity and operating conditions of freeway segments is presented.

4.3.2 Level of Service

The earlier discussion of the fundamental diagrams of vehicular streams pointed out that each diagram, q–k or u–q, encloses a region that subtends the stream conditions meeting a certain safety level. It was also shown that the counteracting incentives of safety versus speed tend to cause actual stream conditions to cluster around the curve. Moreover, since the q–k and u–q curves were "backward bending," each level of flow q was shown to correspond to two distinct stream conditions on either side of capacity: one closer to free-flow and the other toward traffic jam conditions. To capture this difference, the 1965 *Highway Capacity Manual* [4.7] uses the concept of *level of service*, as illustrated by Fig. 4.3.1. The overall shape of this conceptualized relationship is the familiar u–q curve, except that the abscissa plots the normalized flow (or volume), that is, flow divided by the capacity of the roadway. The resulting volume-to-capacity (v/c) ratio ranges from 0 to 1. The area encompassed by the normalized u–q curve is divided into six subareas denoted by the letters A to F, each designating a specific level of service.

Figure 4.3.1 Levels of service. (From Highway Research Board [4.7].)

The qualitative descriptions of the conditions that correspond to each level of service found in the 1965 *Highway Capacity Manual* [4.7] have been superseded by new definitions, which appear in the 1985 *Highway Capacity Manual* as follows:

> *Level-of-service A* represents free flow. Individual users are virtually unaffected by the presence of others in the traffic stream. Freedom to select desired speeds and to maneuver within the traffic stream is extremely high. The general level of comfort and convenience provided to the motorist, passenger, or pedestrian is excellent.
>
> *Level-of-service B* is in the range of stable flow, but the presence of other users in the traffic stream begins to be noticeable. Freedom to select desired speeds is relatively unaffected, but there is a slight decline in the freedom to maneuver within the traffic stream from LOS A. The level of comfort and convenience provided is somewhat less than LOS A, because the presence of others in the traffic stream begins to affect individual behavior.
>
> *Level-of-service C* is in the range of stable flow, but marks the beginning of the range of flow in which the operation of individual users becomes significantly affected by the presence of others, and maneuvering within the traffic stream requires substantial vigilance on the part of the user. The general level of comfort and convenience declines noticeably at this level.
>
> *Level-of-service D* represents high-density, but stable, flow. Speed and freedom to maneuver are severely restricted, and the driver or pedestrian experiences a generally poor level of comfort and convenience. Small increases in traffic flow will generally cause operational problems at this level.

Level-of-service E represents operating conditions at or near the capacity level. All speeds are reduced to a low, but relatively uniform value. Freedom to maneuver within the traffic stream is extremely difficult, and it is generally accomplished by forcing a vehicle or pedestrian to "give way" to accommodate such maneuvers. Comfort and convenience levels are extremely poor, and driver or pedestrian frustration is generally high. Operations at this level are usually unstable, because small increases in flow or minor perturbations within the traffic stream will cause breakdowns.

Level-of-service F is used to define forced or breakdown flow. This condition exists whenever the amount of traffic approaching a point exceeds the amount which can traverse the point. Queues form behind such locations. Operations within the queue are characterized by stop-and-go waves, and they are extremely unstable. Vehicles may progress at reasonable speeds for several hundred feet or more, then be required to stop in a cyclic fashion. Level-of-service F is used to describe the operating conditions within the queue, as well as at the point of breakdown. It should be noted, however, that in many cases operating conditions of vehicles or pedestrians discharged from the queue may be quite good. Nevertheless, it is the point at which arrival flow exceeds discharge flow which causes the queue to form, and level of service F is an appropriate designation for such points ([4.5], pp. 1-3 and 1-4).

The foregoing description of the six levels of service reveals several interesting facts. First, level-of-service E around maximum flow or capacity does not correspond to acceptably comfortable and convenient conditions from the point of view of the driver. Second, as the description of level-of-service A implies, the specific u–q curve and the actual capacity of a roadway depend on its physical and operating characteristics. The former include items such as grades and sight distances, as described in Chapter 2, and the latter include factors such as posted speed limits and vehicle mix. Third, along the u–q curve, each level of service constitutes a range of speeds and flows demarcated by upper and lower limits in the values of concentration, as illustrated by Fig. 4.3.2.

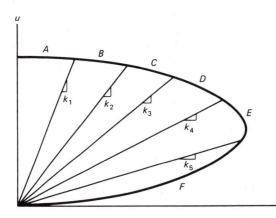

Figure 4.3.2 Level of service, speed, flow, and concentration.

4.3.3 "Ideal" Freeway Conditions

This subsection introduces the procedure recommended by the *1985 Highway Capacity Manual* [4.5] for the calculation of the capacity and level of service of a geometrically uniform section of a freeway that is removed from the vicinity of external interruptions. The procedure estimates the capacity of a freeway in terms of passenger-car equivalents under the following "ideal conditions," and then modifies this estimate to capture the effect of any deviations from the ideal conditions that are present at the freeway section under study.

Lane width and lateral clearance.   Ideal conditions require that lanes be at least 12 ft wide and that obstructions such as bridge abutments be located at a lateral distance of at least 6 ft from the edge of pavement. The typical driver responses to lateral restrictions were presented in Section 2.3.

Trucks, buses, and grades.   Ideal conditions represent level roadways and a vehicular stream that consists entirely of passenger cars. Larger and slower vehicles such as buses and trucks tend to have an adverse effect on the vehicular flow that the freeway can accommodate, especially at locations characterized by long stretches of vertical grades.

Uniformity of demand.   Within statistically acceptable limits, the flow conditions are assumed to be uniform throughout the period of analysis. Peaking of the demand within the period of analysis would cause disruptions and shock waves, which, as Chapter 3 explained, would take some time to dissipate completely. The typical period of analysis is 1 h. To quantify the degree to which the demand is peaked, a very important distinction is made between the term *volume* V, on one hand, and *rate of flow q* on the other. Volume is defined as

> the number of vehicles passing a point on a highway or highway lane during one hour, expressed as vehicles per hour [4.8].

whereas rate of flow is defined as

> the number of vehicles passing a point on a highway or highway lane during some period of time *less* than one hour, expressed as *an equivalent rate* in vehicles per hour [4.8] (emphasis added by the authors).

Thus if 100 vehicles were counted during a 5-min period, the rate of flow would be 100 vehicles per 5-min period *times* twelve 5-min periods per hour *equals* 1200 veh/h. The actual volume V counted during the entire hour to which the above 5-min period belongs may or may not equal 1200 veh/h. The consecutive 60 min (1-h period) of the day when a highway experiences the highest volume as just defined is known as the *peak hour*. The ratio of the peak-hour volume to the *maximum* rate of flow computed on the basis of an interval *t* within the peak hour is known as the *peak-hour factor* (PHF). Thus, given a volume V and a maximum rate of flow q based on a set interval t less than 1 h (e.g., 5 min), the peak-hour factor is

$$\text{PHF} = \frac{V}{q} = \frac{V}{N_t(60/t)} \qquad (4.3.1)$$

where N_t is the maximum number of vehicles counted during any interval t within the hour. For the purpose of highway capacity analysis, t is taken to be around 5 min. The analysis of intersections (see Chapter 5) uses a t of 15 min. In either case, the PHF is a measure of demand uniformity or demand peaking, as the following examples illustrate.

Example 4.2: Uniform Demand

Assume that 50 vehicles were counted during each of all possible 5-min intervals during the peak hour. Compute the PHF.

Solution   The total number of vehicles that were counted during the entire hour was 600 vehicles. Thus

$$V = 600 \text{ veh/h}$$

The rate of flow based on the maximum number of vehicles observed during *any* 5-min period was, according to the denominator of Eq. 4.3.1,

$$q = 50\left(\frac{60}{5}\right) = 600 \text{ veh/h}$$

Hence the PHF is

$$\text{PHF} = \frac{600}{600} = 1.00$$

Example 4.3: Extremely Peaked Demand

Consider the extreme case where 150 vehicles were counted during a 5-min interval and no vehicles were observed during the rest of the hour.

Solution   The counted volume was 150 veh/h. On the other hand, the rate of flow based on the 5-min interval was

$$q = 150\left(\frac{60}{5}\right) = 1800 \text{ veh/h}$$

Hence the PHF is

$$\text{PHF} = \frac{150}{1800} = 0.083$$

Discussion   The two examples calculated the PHF for two (unrealistically) extreme conditions and found that, for an absolutely uniform demand, the PHF is equal to unity, whereas for an absolutely peaked demand (i.e., the entire hourly volume observed during a 5-min period), it was 0.083. In realistic conditions, the PHF would lie between these limits: The closer it is to unity, the more uniform the demand and, conversely, the closer the PHF is to 0, the more peaked the demand. It can easily be shown that the theoretical lower bound of the PHF is 0.25 when t is taken to be 15 min. In the discussion that follows, the term *flow* denotes the rate of flow. Consequently, when hourly volumes are given, they must be converted to flows by

$$q = \frac{V}{\text{PHF}}$$

4.3.4 Freeway Capacity and Level of Service

The technical literature contains highly refined procedures for incorporating the above (and other) factors in the study of freeway segments. Only a rough outline of these procedures is included here to familiarize the reader with the rationale of the method. For the sake of clarity, the notation used in the following paragraphs is partly the authors'.

Figure 4.3.3 presents the speed–flow relationship per freeway lane for sev-

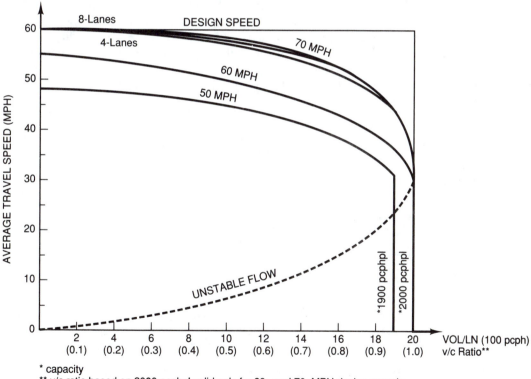

Figure 4.3.3   Speed–flow relationship under ideal conditions. (From Transportation Research Board [4.5].)

eral freeway designs, defined by the design speed and the number of lanes available, under ideal conditions. The design speed is designated as the *average highway speed* (AHS) to allow for the computation of a single value for the entire highway segment under investigation when it consists of subsections that have different design speeds: The AHS is the average of these design speeds weighted by the length of each subsection. Moreover, the design speed is the speed used to design the facility (see Chapter 3) and not the posted speed limit. The figure shows that under ideal conditions, the capacity of a freeway lane is about 2000 passenger cars per hour (pc/h) for designs speeds of 60 and 70 mi/h and about 1900 pc/h for design speeds of 50 min/h.

Table 4.3.1 summarizes the speed, flow, and concentration ranges corresponding to the six levels of service for the same freeway designs. In each case, capacity corresponds to the limiting flow for level-of-service E. The table shows that for a 70-mi/h design speed, level-of-service C corresponds to speeds between 54 and 57 mi/h, concentrations (i.e., densities) between 20 and 30 passenger cars per mile (pc/mi) per lane, a single-lane flow between 1100 and 1500 pc/h/lane, and a v/c ratio between 0.54 and 0.77. With appropriate adjustments, the values found in the table can be used either to analyze the conditions prevailing on a particular facility—that is, to determine the operating level of service when the number of lanes and the actual freeway volume are known—or to design a facility—that is, to determine the number of lanes needed to accommodate a given volume under a desired level of service.

The column of Table 4.3.1 that is labeled *maximum service flow* (MSF) was derived by the following equation:

$$MSF_i = q_{max}\left(\frac{v}{c}\right)_i \text{ pcphpl and ideal conditions} \qquad (4.3.2)$$

TABLE 4.3.1   LEVEL OF SERVICE FOR BASIC FREEWAY SECTIONS

LOS	Density (pc/mi/lane)	70 mi/h design speed			60 mi/h design speed			50 mi/h design speed		
		Speed[a] (mi/h)	v/c	MSF[b] (pc/h/lane)	Speed[a] (mi/h)	v/c	MSF[b] (pc/h/lane)	Speed[a] (mi/h)	v/c	MSF[b] (pc/h/lane)
A	≤12	≥60	0.35	700	—	—	—	—	—	—
B	≤20	≥57	0.54	1100	≥50	0.49	1000	—	—	—
C	≤30	≥54	0.77	1550	≥47	0.69	1400	≥43	0.67	1300
D	≤42	≥46	0.93	1850	≥42	0.84	1700	≥40	0.83	1600
E	≤67	≥30	1.00	2000	≥30	1.00	2000	≥28	1.00	1900
F	>67	<30	c	c	<30	c	c	<28	c	c

[a] Average travel speed.

[b] Maximum service flow rate per lane under ideal conditions.

[c] Highly variable, unstable.

Note: All values of *MSF* rounded to the nearest 50 pc/h.

Source: Transportation Research Board [4.5].

where MSF$_i$ is the maximum service volume corresponding to level-of-service i that can be accommodated by a freeway lane under ideal conditions, q_{max} is the capacity of a freeway lane (i.e., the MSF at level-of-service E), and $(v/c)_i$ is the maximum volume-to-capacity ratio corresponding to level-of-service i. The table entries for the MSF have been rounded to the nearest 50 pc/h/lane.

The following equation converts an *ideal lane flow* q^*, expressed in passenger cars per hour per lane, to the *service flow* q, expressed in vehicles per hour, for a freeway consisting of N lanes, under the prevailing conditions:

$$q = q^* N f_w \, f_{hv} \qquad (4.3.3)$$

where

q = prevailing (service) flow, in veh/h

q^* = ideal flow, in pc/h/lane

N = number of freeway lanes

f_w = adjustment for the combined effect of lane widths other than 12 ft and for lateral obstructions closer to 6 ft

f_{hv} = adjustment factor for the presence of heavy vehicles

The adjustment factor f_w, obtained from Table 4.3.2, depends on the number of lanes provided by the freeway, the lane width, the lateral distance from the traveled way to objects such as bridge abutments, and on whether the laterally placed objects are found on one or on both sides of the roadway. When objects are present on both sides but are located at different distances, the average distance is used in the table.

The following equation represents an approximation of the adjustment for heavy vehicles:

$$f_{hv} = \frac{1}{1 + P_T(E_T - 1) + P_R(E_R - 1) + P_B(E_B - 1)} \qquad (4.3.4)$$

where P_T, P_R, and P_B correspond to the proportions of trucks, recreational vehicles, and buses, respectively, in the traffic stream, and E_T, E_R, and E_B are the passenger car equivalents for trucks, recreational vehicles, and buses. The latter depend on the general terrain of the highway and are given in Table 4.3.3.

Example 4.4: Design

A freeway that is being designed is expected to carry a volume of 3000 veh/h. Trucks and buses are estimated to constitute 12% and 5% of the traffic, respectively, and no recreational vehicles are anticipated. Determine the minimum number of lanes required to provide level-of-service C, given a peak hour factor of 0.80, a rolling terrain, a design speed of 70 mi/h, 12-ft lanes, and adequate lateral clearances.

TABLE 4.3.2 ADJUSTMENT FACTORS FOR RESTRICTED LANE WIDTH
AND LATERAL CLEARANCE

Distance from traveled pavement[a] (ft)	Adjustment factor, f_w							
	Obstructions on one side of the roadway				Obstructions on both sides of the roadway			
	Lane width (ft)							
	12	11	10	9	12	11	10	9
	Four-lane freeway (2 lanes each direction)							
≥6	1.00	0.97	0.91	0.81	1.00	0.97	0.91	0.81
5	0.99	0.96	0.90	0.80	0.99	0.96	0.90	0.80
4	0.99	0.96	0.90	0.80	0.98	0.95	0.89	0.79
3	0.98	0.95	0.89	0.79	0.96	0.93	0.87	0.77
2	0.97	0.94	0.88	0.79	0.94	0.91	0.86	0.76
1	0.93	0.90	0.85	0.76	0.87	0.85	0.80	0.71
0	0.90	0.87	0.82	0.73	0.81	0.79	0.74	0.66
	Six- or eight-lane freeway (3 or 4 lanes each direction)							
≥6	1.00	0.96	0.89	0.78	1.00	0.96	0.89	0.78
5	0.99	0.95	0.88	0.77	0.99	0.95	0.88	0.77
4	0.99	0.95	0.88	0.77	0.98	0.94	0.87	0.77
3	0.98	0.94	0.87	0.76	0.97	0.93	0.86	0.76
2	0.97	0.93	0.87	0.76	0.96	0.92	0.85	0.75
1	0.95	0.92	0.86	0.75	0.93	0.89	0.83	0.72
0	0.94	0.91	0.85	0.74	0.91	0.87	0.81	0.70

[a] Certain types of obstruction, high-type median barriers in particular, do not cause any deleterious effect on traffic flow. Judgment should be exercised in applying these factors.

Source: Transportation Research Board [4.5].

TABLE 4.3.3 PASSENGER-CAR EQUIVALENTS ON EXTENDED GENERAL FREEWAY
SEGMENTS

Factor	Type of terrain		
	Level	Rolling	Mountainous
E_T for trucks	1.7	4.0	8.0
E_B for buses	1.5	3.0	5.0
E_R for RVs	1.6	3.0	4.0

Source: Transportation Research Board [4.5].

Solution   The service flow is

$$SF = q = \frac{V}{PHF} = \frac{3000}{0.80} = 3750 \text{ veh/h}$$

From Table 4.3.1 the ideal lane flow for level-of-service C is

$$MSF_C = 1550 \text{ pc/h/lane}$$

From Table 4.3.2, the adjustment factor f_w is equal to 1.00, and from Eq. 4.3.4

$$f_{hv} = \frac{1}{1 + 0.12(4 - 1) + 0.05(3 - 1)} = 0.68$$

Solving Eq. 4.3.3 for the number of lanes, N, gives

$$N = \frac{3750}{1550(1.00)(0.68)} = 3.56 \text{ or 4 lanes}$$

Example 4.5: Analysis

A freeway on a level terrain carries a volume $V = 4500$ veh/h on four 11-foot lanes in one direction. The vehicle mix consists of 75% passenger cars, 10% trucks, 10% buses, and 5% recreational vehicles. Lateral obstructions are located at a distance of 5 ft on the right side and 3 ft on the left side of the roadway. Given that the design speed is 60 mi/h and the peak hour factor is 0.75, calculate the level of service provided and the v/c ratio.

Solution   The service flow is

$$SF = q = \frac{V}{PHF} = \frac{4500}{0.75} = 6000 \text{ veh/h}$$

For level terrain and the given percentages of heavy vehicles, Eq. 4.3.4 yields

$$f_{hv} = \frac{1}{1 + (0.10)(0.7) + (0.05)(0.6) + (0.10)(0.5)} = 0.87$$

With an average lateral clearance on both sides of $(5 + 3)/2 = 4$ ft, a lane width of 11 ft, and an 8-lane freeway (4 lanes in each direction), Table 4.3.2 yields

$$f_w = 0.94$$

Solving Eq. 4.3.3 for q^*, we obtain

$$q^* = \frac{6000}{4(0.94)(0.87)} = 1834 \text{ pc/h/lane}$$

Consulting Table 4.3.1 for a design speed of 60 mi/h, the computed ideal lane flow falls within the range of level-of-service E. The corresponding v/c ratio is

$$\frac{v}{c} = \frac{1834}{2000} = 0.92$$

4.3.5 Capacity Restrictions

The preceding subsection dealt with the uninterrupted flow of vehicles on long freeway sections. Under these circumstances, variations in flow conditions and stoppages are possible as a result of *nonrecurring* random events or incidents such as accidents, spilled loads, disabled and slow-moving vehicles, and other extraordinary events. In addition, geometric restrictions give rise to high concentrations, or congestion, along the stream channel. These include reductions of capacity at lane drops (i.e., at points where the number of lanes decreases), at points of abrupt alignment changes, and at locations where two streams come together, such as merging areas. When the approaching volume (i.e., the demand) exceeds the capacity of these locations, conditions of high concentration begin to appear upstream, and shock waves develop between these conditions and the approaching flow farther upstream. The duration and the severity of the congested flow depend on the degree of capacity reduction and on the pattern of demand over time. The high-concentration platoon may spill into similar conditions at adjacent capacity restrictions. Because such restrictions are permanent in space and the demand for travel exhibits a daily regularity, these effects are *recurring* events that take place during the regular periods of high demand [4.10].

4.4 PEDESTRIAN FLOW

4.4.1 Introduction

Pedestrian-flow models have been developed that bear a close resemblance to the concepts discussed in connection with vehicular streams. The speed of a pedestrian regime is, naturally, measured in units of distance divided by time, for example, feet per second. Flow is given in terms of pedestrians per unit width of a walkway per unit time. It is thus a point measurement in the same way as highway flow, where the point at which flow is observed stretches across a number of lanes. Pedestrians, of course, are not normally obliged to follow strictly any type of lane assignment, but pedestrian flow per linear foot of walkway width is a tangible measure. Concentration or density is specified as the number of pedestrians per unit area, for example, pedestrians per square foot. The reciprocal of pedestrian concentration is called *space* and has units of surface area per pedestrian (e.g., square feet per pedestrian). Its vehicular stream equivalent is spacing. The fundamental relationship $q = uk$ has been found to apply in the case of pedestrians under generally uninterrupted conditions.

4.4.2 Pedestrian-Flow Models

Figure 4.4.1 presents the calibrated pedestrian speed–density relationships obtained by three researchers. These diagrams conform to the general shape observed in the case of vehicular flow, that is, they are monotonically decreasing

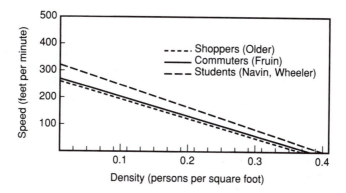

Figure 4.4.1 Pedestrian speed and density. (From Transportation Research Board [4.5].)

from free-flow speed at zero concentration to zero speed at jammed concentration. Figure 4.4.2 presents the speed–flow relationships corresponding to the aforementioned calibrated *u–k* curves. Obviously, the vehicular stream parallel extends to this diagram as well: The maximum pedestrian flow (i.e., capacity) occurs at

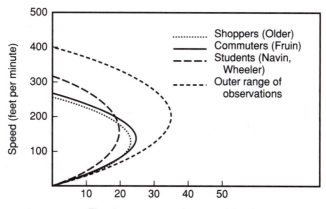

Figure 4.4.2 Pedestrian speed and flow. (From Transportation Research Board [4.5].)

an intermediate point between free-flow and jammed conditions. Figure 4.4.3 plots the flow versus space, and Figure 4.4.4 plots the relationship between speed and space.

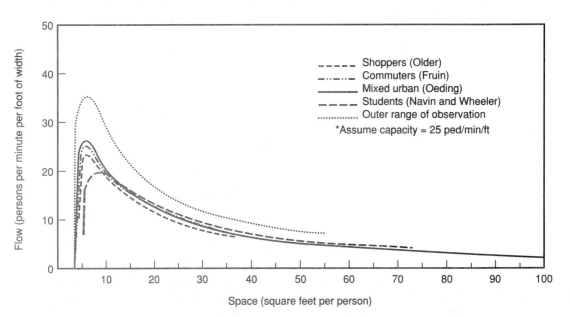

Figure 4.4.3   Pedestrian flow and space. (From Transportation Research Board [4.5].)

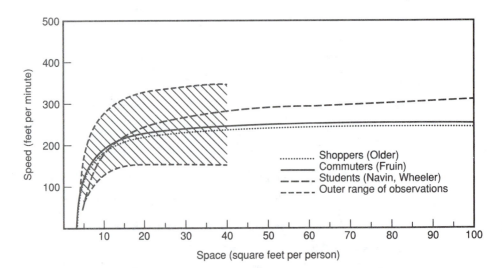

Figure 4.4.4   Pedestrian speed and space. (From Transportation Research Board [4.5].)

LEVEL OF SERVICE A

Pedestrian Space: ≥ 130 sq ft/ped   Flow Rate: ≤ 2 ped/min/ft

At walkway LOS A, pedestrians basically move in desired paths without altering
their movements in response to other pedestrians. Walking speeds are freely
selected, and conflicts between pedestrians are unlikely.

LEVEL OF SERVICE B

Pedestrian Space: ≥ 40 sq ft/ped   Flow Rate: ≤ 7 ped/min/ft

At LOS B, sufficient area is provided to allow pedestrians to freely select
walking speeds, to bypass other pedestrians, and to avoid crossing conflicts with
others. At this level, pedestrians begin to be aware of other pedestrians, and to
respond to their presence in the selection of walking path.

LEVEL OF SERVICE C

Pedestrian Space: ≥ 24 sq ft/ped   Flow Rate: ≤ 10 ped/min/ft

At LOS C, sufficient space is available to select normal walking speeds, and to
bypass other pedestrians in primarily unidirectional streams. Where reverse-
direction or crossing movements exist, minor conflicts will occur, and speeds
and volume will be somewhat lower.

LEVEL OF SERVICE D

Pedestrian Space: ≥ 15 sq ft/ped   Flow Rate: ≤ 15 ped/min/ft

At LOS D, freedom to select individual walking speed and to bypass other
pedestrians is restricted. Where crossing or reverse-flow movements exist, the
probability of conflict is high, and its avoidance requires frequent changes in
speed and position. The LOS provides reasonably fluid flow; however,
considerable friction and interaction between pedestrians is likely to occur.

LEVEL OF SERVICE E

Pedestrian Space: ≥ 6 sq ft/ped   Flow Rate: ≤ 25 ped/min/ft

At LOS E, virtually all pedestrians would have their normal walking speed
restricted, requiring frequent adjustment of gait. At the lower range of this LOS,
forward movement is possible only by "shuffling." Insufficient space is provided
for passing of slower pedestrians. Cross- or reverse-flow movements are
possible only with extreme difficulties. Design volumes approach the limit of
walkway capacity, with resulting stoppages and interruptions to flow.

LEVEL OF SERVICE F

Pedestrian Space: ≤ 6 sq ft/ped   Flow Rate: variable

At LOS F, all walking speeds are severely restricted, and forward progress is
made only by "shuffling." There is frequent, unavoidable contact with other
pedestrians. Cross- and reverse-flow movements are virtually impossible. Flow is
sporadic and unstable. Space is more characteristic of queued pedestrians than
of moving pedestrian streams.

Figure 4.4.5 Levels of service on walkways. (From Transportation Research Board [4.5].)

4.4.3 Pedestrian Level of Service

Table 4.4.1 presents the recommended ranges of pedestrian levels of service in terms of the space (and, implicitly, concentration), speed, and flow. The delimiting values of the v/c ratio are also shown. Figure 4.4.5 illustrates the typical levels

TABLE 4.4.1 PEDESTRIAN LEVELS OF SERVICE ON WALKWAYS

Level of service	Space (ft²/ped)	Expected flows and speeds[a]		
		Ave. speed, S (ft/min)	Flow rate, v (ped/min/ft)	Vol./capacity ratio, v/c
A	≥130	≥260	≤ 2	≤0.08
B	≥ 40	≥250	≤ 7	≤0.28
C	≥ 24	≥240	≤10	≤0.40
D	≥ 15	≥225	≤15	≤0.60
E	≥ 6	≥150	≤25	≤1.00
F	< 6	<150	Variable	

[a] Average conditions for 15 min.

Source: Transportation Research Board [4.5].

of concentration that are encountered within each level of service. Pedestrian capacity is found to be the "maximum service flow" for level-of-service E. It corresponds to about 25 pedestrians per minute per foot of walkway width. Forced flow (i.e., level-of-service F) includes the "backward-bending" portion of the u–k and q–k diagrams.

4.5 SUMMARY

In this chapter we presented the flow and capacity characteristics of selected transportation systems. The flow–speed relationships of typical urban mass transportation systems that have been derived by Vuchic [4.1] were presented and discussed, and a brief discussion of the fleet size required to provide a desirable transit vehicle flow followed. The concept of highway level of service was introduced next, and the 1985 *Highway Capacity Manual* [4.5] method for analyzing and designing freeway sections that are removed from external interruptions was presented. Finally, the applicability of the flow relationships of Chapter 3 to pedestrian flow was illustrated.

4.6 EXERCISES

1. A rapid-transit system employs vehicles that can be connected into transit units. To investigate the effect of vehicular articulation, calculate the capacity (veh/h) and the speed at capacity (ft/s) by varying the number of vehicles per train from $N = 1$ to $N = 5$. Assume a perception-reaction time of 1.5 s, a vehicular length of 40 ft, a normal deceleration of 5 ft/s^2, a clearance length x_o of 4 ft, and a safety regime a (Table 3.2.1).

2. Repeat Exercise 1 for safety regime b, assuming an emergency deceleration of 15 ft/s^2.

3. Computerize your solution procedure to Exercises 1 and 2.

4. For the system of Example 4.1, calculate the effect of a 5-min decrease in the round-trip time on the fleet size. Also calculate the before and after headways between vehicles.

5. For the system of Exercise 4, calculate the average headway that would result if the original 34 vehicles were still used.

6. The peak-hour volumes at two locations were counted and found to be equal. However, the PHFs were 0.85 at the first location and 0.60 at the second. Describe the difference between the two locations.

7. The following 12 consecutive 5-min vehicle counts were taken on a highway:

$$60 \quad 50 \quad 40 \quad 60 \quad 90 \quad 80 \quad 100 \quad 120 \quad 140 \quad 95 \quad 60 \quad 30$$

(a) Plot the histogram of these counts and the histogram of the flow rates computed on the basis of the counts above, and (b) calculate the hourly volume and the PHF.

8. Show that for $t = 15$ min, the PHF can theoretically range from 0.25 to 1.00.

9. Obstructions are located at the edge of the pavement on one side of a six-lane highway. Estimate the percent increase in the highway's capacity that may result from relocating the obstructions to a distance of 6 ft. Assume 10-ft lanes.

10. A six-lane freeway accommodates 3500 veh/h in the peak direction. This volume includes 10% trucks, no buses and no recreational vehicles. The freeway is in rolling terrain, is designed for 60 mi/h, and otherwise conforms to the ideal conditions. Given that the peak 5-min traffic count is 350 vehicles, estimate (a) the capacity of the freeway in one direction, (b) the prevailing level of service, and (c) the prevailing speed.

11. For the freeway of Exercise 10, calculate the range of volumes at the same PHF for which the prevailing level of service would be C.

12. For the freeway of Exercise 10, find the number of lanes needed in one direction to ensure a level-of-service C or better.

13. Estimate the one-way capacity of a highway section that is removed from any major interruptions given four 11-ft lanes in each direction, a uniform demand, obstructions at both sides at 3 ft from the edge of pavement, 5% buses, 20% trucks, mountainous terrain, and a 50 mi/h design speed.

14. Derive Eq. 4.3.4.

15. An airport corridor is 50 ft wide. Given a peak demand of 600 pedestrians per minute, calculate (a) the prevailing level of service, (b) the approximate concentration, and (c) the approximate average speed.

4.7 REFERENCES

4.1 VUCHIC, VUKAN R., *Urban Public Transportation Systems and Technology*, Prentice Hall, Englewood Cliffs, N.J., 1981, pp. 550–552.

4.2 WATKINS, R. A., et al., *Urban Transportation Planning System Lexicon*, Report UMTA-UPM20-81-1, prepared by Rock Creek Associates for the U.S. Department of Transportation: Urban Mass Transportation Administration, Washington, D.C., 1981.

4.3 PAPACOSTAS, C. S., *Energy and Pollution Implications of Bus-Automobile Alternatives*, Ph.D. dissertation, Carnegie-Mellon University, Pittsburgh, Pa., 1974.

4.4 DIAL, ROBERT B., SCOTT G. RUTHERFORD, and LAWRENCE QUILLIAN, *Transit Network Analysis: INET,* Report UMTA-UPM-20-79-3, U.S. Department of Transportation, Urban Mass Transportation Administration, Washington, D.C., 1979.

4.5 Transportation Research Board, *Highway Capacity Manual*, Special Report 209, National Research Council, Washington, D.C., 1985.

4.6 Bureau of Public Roads, *Highway Capacity Manual*, U.S. Government Printing Office, Washington, D.C., 1950.

4.7 Highway Research Board, *Highway Capacity Manual*, Special Report 87, National Research Council, Washington, D.C., 1965.

4.8 TRANSPORTATION RESEARCH BOARD, *Interim Materials on Highway Capacity*, Circular 212, National Research Council, Washington, D.C., 1980.

4.9 ———, *Proposed Chapters for the 1985 Highway Capacity Manual*, Circulars 281 and 284, National Research Council, Washington, D.C., 1984.

4.10 CAPELLE, DONALD G., *Freeway Traffic Management*, National Cooperative Highway Research Program, Project 20-3D, Final Report, Sept. 1979.

5 Flow Interruptions

5.1 INTRODUCTION

Traffic streams are often subject to intended interruptions: Transit vehicles are stopped at transit stations to discharge and take on passengers; highway traffic is interrupted at street intersections to permit the use of the same space by several vehicular streams. With regard to at-grade street intersections, the *1965 Highway Capacity Manual* [5.1] states that

> intersections not only control, to a large extent, the capability of major and secondary arterial streets to accommodate the flow of vehicles and pedestrians, but they also may seriously affect or limit the ability of nearby freeways to perform at maximum efficiency.

With respect to transit stations, Vuchic [5.2] states that

> station capacity governs the capacity of a transit line in a vast majority of cases.

This chapter is concerned with stream-flow interruptions. The case of scheduled rapid-transit vehicles is examined first, and a model of transit station capacity is developed. The operation of signalized street intersections is covered next. Following some basic definitions, the technique of coordinating signal systems in order to minimize the effect of interruptions is described, a detailed presentation of principles of signalization is given, and methods for assessing the capacity and level of service of at-grade signalized and unsignalized intersections are presented.

Techniques for data collection for intersection capacity analysis are presented as well.

5.2 TRANSIT INTERRUPTIONS

5.2.1 Introduction

The movement of a transit vehicle *between* stations can be described by the equations of motion covered in Chapter 2. A typical vehicle or train leaving a station will accelerate to a *cruising speed* and maintain that speed until the point when it must begin to decelerate to a complete stop at the next station. The distance and time over which the cruising speed is maintained depend on the distance between the two stations, that is, the *station spacing*. Following a *dwelling time* at a station, the vehicle again enters its acceleration phase.

Figure 5.2.1 illustrates the time–distance diagram of uniformly scheduled arrivals and departures at a typical station. For simplicity, individual transit units are shown as points. The identical decelerating, dwelling, and accelerating phases of two consecutive units are shown in Fig. 5.2.1(a) for the situation where only one unit is permitted to occupy the station at any time. The headway between two units, measured horizontally, is constant as long as it is measured between points when the two vehicles are, respectively, in the same state (e.g., entering the station, leaving the station, halfway in their dwelling phase). On the other hand, the spacing between units, measured vertically, varies with time. Figure 5.2.1(b) shows two consecutive units that are permitted to dwell at the station simultaneously. The time period shown begins during the dwelling phase of unit 1 and ends with the departure of unit 3. Unit 4 is shown to have arrived prior to the departure of unit 3. The way in which headway and spacing are measured in this situation is identical to that of Fig. 5.2.1(a).

The minimum headway at which units enter and exit a station is affected by the combined effect of the dwelling time and the number of units that can be accommodated at the station simultaneously. This minimum station-headway is most often longer than the minimum headway that is technologically attainable under uninterrupted conditions.

5.2.2 Transit Stations

The basic element of a transit station is the *platform*, where vehicles or trains stop to take on and drop off passengers. Although differing in geometric design and also in the terminology employed, all passenger-serving stations, including simple bus stops, rapid-transit stations, harbors, and airport terminals, share this basic element. A *terminal* is a large station that accommodates high volumes of

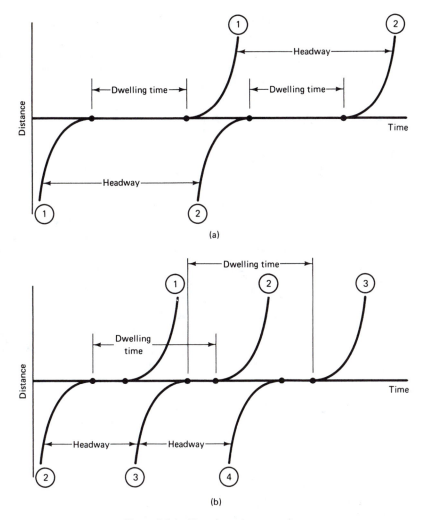

Figure 5.2.1 Transit station operations.

entering, leaving, and transferring passengers or freight. The physical facilities preceding and following the platform, on which vehicles decelerate and accelerate, respectively, can be considered to be a part of the station. In addition, some station designs include vehicle holding areas on either side of the platform to be occupied by vehicles awaiting clearance to enter or exit the station.

The maximum number of vehicles (and passengers) that a station can process in a given period of time, that is, the station's capacity, depends on the number and type of platforms available, the desired level of safety, and related rules of operation. The length of each platform limits the maximum number of vehicles that can be accommodated simultaneously either singly or in trains.

Station platforms can be either *off-line* or *on-line*. Off-line platforms branch out of the main line so that when a local vehicle or train is at the station, another unit not scheduled to serve that station can proceed on the main line. Because overtaking is not possible at on-line platform locations, vehicles that are not scheduled to serve a station may be delayed behind local vehicles serving the station.

5.2.3 Single-Platform Capacity

The simplest type of transit station consists of a single on-line platform capable of accommodating a train of N vehicles of length L and allowing only one train to occupy the platform at any given time. Figure 5.2.2 shows the operation of two consecutive trains of length (NL) from the moment when the first begins its deceleration into the station to the moment when the second comes to a complete stop at the station, the location of which is shown on the distance axis. Each train is represented by the two parallel trajectories of its front and rear. The headway between the two trains consists of three parts: the dwelling time, the time it takes the first train to clear the platform, and a "safety" clearance interval. A clearance interval of zero represents the limiting situation when the second train reaches the front of the platform at the moment when the first vehicle clears it. The length of the clearance interval is related to the level of safety associated with the operation. The technical literature (e.g., [5.2, 5.3]) discusses the details of safety-regime analysis of station operations for various technologies. For the purposes of this book, the minimum headway under uninterrupted conditions for a desired

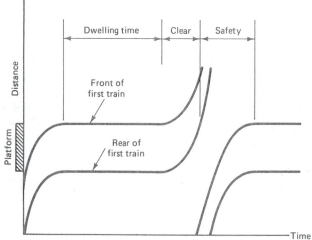

Figure 5.2.2   Transit station times.

safety regime (given by the reciprocal of Eq. 3.4.3) is used as an approximation for the length of the clearance interval. The minimum station headway then becomes

$$h_s(\text{min}) = T_{\text{dwell}} + \left(\frac{2NL}{a_n}\right)^{1/2} + \left(\delta + \frac{u}{2d_f} - \frac{u}{2d_1} + \frac{NL + x_o}{u}\right) \qquad (5.2.1)$$

where the second term represents the time it takes a train of N vehicles to clear the platform while accelerating at normal acceleration a_n and the third to last terms give the minimum headway under uninterrupted conditions.

Example 5.1

Plot the relationship between cruising speed and station vehicle flow for the system described in connection with Fig. 3.4.2 for safety regime a. Assume a dwelling time of 10 s and a normal acceleration of 8 ft/s^2.

Solution   For safety regime a, the following vehicle maintains a spacing such that it can stop at normal deceleration in the eventuality that the leading vehicles stops "instantaneously." Substituting in Eq. 5.2.1 gives

$$h_s(\text{min}) = 10 + (5.0)^{1/2} + 1 + \frac{u}{16} - 0 + \frac{20 + 3}{u}$$

$$= 13.24 + \frac{u}{16} + \frac{23}{u}$$

$$q = (3600)\left(13.24 + \frac{u}{16} + \frac{23}{u}\right)^{-1} \text{ veh/h}$$

This equation is plotted in Fig. 5.2.3.

Discussion   The maximum flow for safety regime a occurs at $u = 19.18$ ft/s and equals 230 veh/h, which is significantly below the capacity corresponding to uninterrupted conditions (see Fig. 3.4.2).

Figure 5.2.3   Transit vehicle flow and speed.

5.2.4 Other Designs

The capacity of a station can be enhanced by providing multiple parallel platforms, simultaneous dwelling, off-line platforms, and possible combinations of the three. Figure 5.2.4 illustrates two possibilities. The first involves on-line stimultaneous dwelling by platoons of three units, whereas the second shows the case of n parallel platforms. It is noteworthy that the pattern of headways becomes more complex; in the case depicted by Fig. 5.2.4(a), the headways within platoons are much shorter than the headways between platoons.

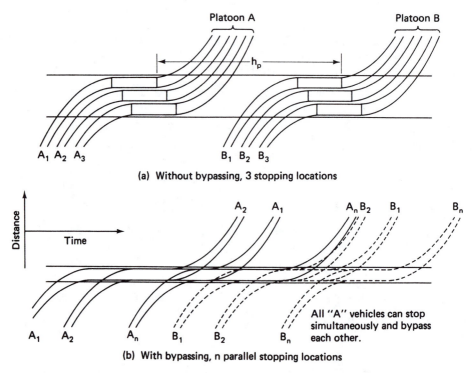

(a) Without bypassing, 3 stopping locations

(b) With bypassing, n parallel stopping locations

Figure 5.2.4   Operation of stations with simultaneous standing. (From Vuchic [5.2].)

5.3 HIGHWAY INTERRUPTIONS

5.3.1 Introduction

The most common interruption of highway flow, especially in urban areas, is the at-grade intersection where a common space is shared by several traffic streams. The conflicts between streams may be reduced either by separating them in space (i.e., by constructing overpasses), or by separating them in time (i.e., by interrupting each stream via signal controls). To maintain a smooth progression of traffic through intersectional areas, the geometric design of intersections frequently includes the addition of regular and special turning lanes.

5.3.2 Types of Signals

The typical traffic signal controlling an intersection provides a sequential display of the green, amber, red, and special indications, such as single or combined turning arrows, to each approach. One complete sequence of the signal displays constitutes the signal cycle, the duration, or *length*, of which is equal to the sum of the durations of its components.

Traffic signals can be *pretimed* or *demand-actuated* [5.3, 5.4]. Pretimed signals repeat a preset constant cycle. Demand-actuated signals have the capability to respond to the presence of vehicles or pedestrians at the intersection. They are augmented by detectors and the necessary control logic to respond to the demands placed on them. Ensuring a proper clearance interval between the green and the red phases (see Section 2.3.2) is part of this logic. *Semiactuated* signals are implemented at intersections of a major and a minor street, with the detectors placed only on the minor-street approaches to the intersection. The heavily used major street is given a green display, which is interrupted only when either vehicles are detected on the lightly used minor street or when a predetermined maximum green duration for the major street is reached. A maximum length of green is specified in order to rectify problems arising from a failure of the minor-street detectors to recognize the presence of vehicles. *Fully actuated* signals employ detectors on all legs of the intersection and are applicable to intersections of streets that carry about equal but fluctuating flows. *Volume-density* or *flow-concentration* controllers are capable of sensing detailed demand information and of responding to it by revising the cycle lengths and the phasing pattern of the signal. A complex extension of this is a signal-control system that employs a central computer to control the flows on large highway networks. Special types of demand-actuated signals recognize and give priority to particular classes of vehicles, such as city buses or emergency vehicles.

5.3.3 Signal Controllers

In 1976, the National Electrical Manufacturers Association (NEMA) promulgated a Standards Publication relating to the various components of traffic control equipment and functional specifications. A revised NEMA standard, issued in 1983 [5.5], covers vehicle detector systems, basic and advanced signal controller units, interface (i.e., input and output) standards, solid-state flashers, and other signalization devices.

The most common type of vehicle detector used in the United States is the inductive loop detector, which employs a wire sensor loop embedded in the road-way pavement. Figure 5.3.1 illustrates two such loops, one for each of two traffic lanes. A vehicle within the detection zone of the sensor affects the magnetic field of the loop by causing a decrease in its inductance. A loop detector unit, which energizes and monitors the loop, responds to a preset decrease in inductance and sends an output signal to the controller unit. The sensitivity of the sensor can be adjusted by selecting the magnitude of the inductance drop caused by a vehicle that would generate an output signal indicating the presence or the passage of a vehicle. NEMA specifications require a sensitivity to detect small and large mo-torcycles and automobiles causing a signal reduction of 0.13%, 0.32%, and 3.2%, respectively. Thus vehicles occupying the detection zone may be classified ac-cording to the magnitude of inductance drop they cause.

Figure 5.3.1 Example of inductive loop detectors.

Vehicle detectors can be used to accomplish several functions, the two most basic being passage detection and presence detection. Passage detection is ac-complished with a small loop that is occupied only briefly by a moving vehicle. In this case a short-duration pulse is generated to signal the vehicle's passage. Presence detection is accomplished via a long loop or a series of interconnected short loops as shown in Fig. 5.3.2. The figure also shows that a combination of short loops spaced at an appropriate distance apart may be used to detect vehicle speeds.

NEMA [5.5] uses the term "detector mode" to describe the duration and the conditions of the channel output of a detector. In the case of presence detectors four modes are specified: *Pulse mode* refers to the case when the detector pro-duces a short-duration pulse when vehicle detection occurs; *controlled output* refers to the case when a set-duration pulse is produced, irrespective of the length of time over which a vehicle occupies the detection zone; *continuous-presence mode* refers to the operation when the detector output continues as long as at least one vehicle occupies the zone of detection; and *limited-presence mode* cor-responds to the operation when the output continues for some limited period if

Figure 5.3.2 Examples of forms and uses of loop detectors. 1, two sets of loops, 60 ft apart for 30- to 35-mi/h speeds; 2, two 6 × 8 ft loops to detect driveway activity; 3, long loop for presence detection; 4, four 6 × 6 ft loops over 54-ft length for presence detection; 5, two sets of loops 80 ft apart for 40-mi/h speeds; 6, two 6 × 6 ft loops for pulse operation; 7, diamond loops for presence detection; 8, 9, pedestrian and bike crossing button.

vehicles remain within the detection zone. Among the many features of a standard NEMA detector system is the ability, when selected, to delay its output for a certain period of time and to inhibit the output if the actuating vehicle leaves before this time expires. This feature is useful in situations where right turns on red are permitted because it helps avoid the situation of changing or extending a signal phase for a vehicle that has already departed. A feature allowing the extension of the detector output for a set time after the vehicle's departure is useful in permitting sluggish vehicles (e.g., slow trucks) to clear the intersection prior to a signal phase change.

The controller unit is the "brain" of a traffic controller system: It receives "calls" from the detectors and interfaces with the signal display equipment to provide for the sequencing and timing of the traffic signal displays. NEMA provides physical and functional standards for basic and advanced units to ensure compatibility between the products of various manufacturers. Some manufacturers, however, offer certain features beyond the NEMA standard. In addition to the most common NEMA controller assembly, a system known as Type 170 was developed jointly by the states of California and New York. This and an updated version (Type 179) involve the specifications for a general-purpose microprocessor controller [5.6]. The functionality of the system is implemented through software rather than through the specific switch-setting options provided by the NEMA controller. Both types of controller units are capable of implementing a variety of phasing and timing strategies, including pretimed (fixed) and complex actuated control schemes.

Two fundamental concepts that aid the understanding of the operation of traffic signal controllers are the definition of the terms "phase" and "ring." A *phase* is defined as consisting of the green interval, the amber (yellow) interval, and where applicable, the subsequent short red (clearance) interval that are associated with a combination of movements which are always given the right-of-way simultaneously. As will be explained later, modern actuated controllers are capable of displaying two phases at the same time. It is thus easy for a casual observer of a traffic signal to think of the two simultaneously displayed phases as a single phase, even though under alternate traffic demand conditions the controller has the ability to display the two phases independent of each other. A phase is said to be active if any of its three component parts is being displayed; otherwise, the phase is inactive (red).

A *ring* is defined as a sequence of phases in the order in which they would be displayed if demand existed for all of them. A single ring may contain from two to four such phases. By convention, the phases in a ring are designated by the Greek capital letter phi (for phase) followed by a phase number (e.g., $\Phi 1$). Figure 5.3.3 illustrates the phase designations for a two-, three-, and four-phase ring. The wraparound arrow shows the direction of the phase sequence. If the signal were to operate in a fixed timing pattern, each phase would be displayed in sequence and would be of the pretimed duration. If the signal were to operate in the actuated mode, the duration of each phase would depend on the traffic demand placed on it (see below). For each of the three rings shown in Fig. 5.3.3, a typical phasing example is presented. Each phase shows its associated movements. In the case of the left-turning movements, a solid arrow indicates a protected turn (i.e., a turn that does not face opposing through flows); a dashed arrow designates a permitted left-turn movement (i.e., a movement that must yield to opposing traffic). The dashed straight-line segments that appear in connection with some of the illustrated phases indicate the pedestrian movements that are allowed during each of those phases.

For more complex phasing patterns, dual-ring controllers are used. These consist of two parallel four-phase rings as shown in Fig. 5.3.4, so that a maximum of eight phases can be defined. The two rings allow for the possibility of displaying two phases concurrently, one from each ring. However, the two rings are interlocked at two reference points (also known as *barriers*). The two rings are forced to cross these barriers simultaneously. In other words, phases 2 and 6 on one hand, and 4 and 8 on the other must terminate concurrently. This is required to avoid conflicting movements that are typically found on opposite sides of the barriers.

Obviously, it is critical when defining the movements associated with the various phases to avoid conflicting movements between the phases defined for

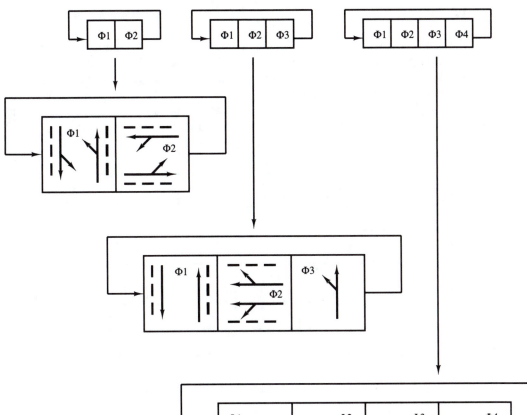

Figure 5.3.3 Examples of single-ring operation.

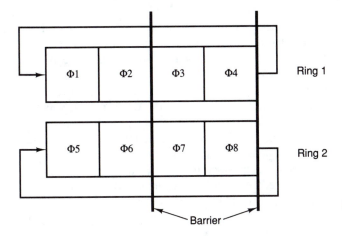

Figure 5.3.4 Example of double-ring operation.

the two rings that lie on the same side of a barrier. Figure 5.3.5 illustrates a typical two-ring phasing scheme known as "quad left" operation. A mode of operation which requires that one phase from each ring must always be active is known as the dual-entry mode of operation. By contrast, a single-entry mode allows for only a phase belonging to one ring to be active while all phases of the other ring could be inactive in the absence of calls for phases in the other ring.

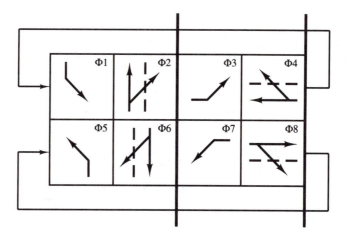

Figure 5.3.5   Example of eight-phase "quad-left" operation.

Figure 5.3.6 illustrates the possible phase combinations that would result under dual-entry operations. Of note is the fact that based on the traffic demand placed on the various phases on the same side of a barrier, alternate phase display combinations are possible. For example, if the demand for left-turn phase 5 is larger than for phase 1, phase 5 would continue to be active in combination with phase 2 after the termination of phase 1. If, on the other hand, the demand for phase 1 is greater than for phase 5, phase 1 will be displayed concurrently with phase 6 after the termination of phase 5. Finally, if the demand for phases 1 and 5 is equal, the next combination to be displayed would consist of phases 2 and 6. In this arrangement, phases 2 and 6 must terminate concurrently irrespective of their relative demands because of the barrier constraint; otherwise, unacceptable conflicting phases (such as 2 and 7 or 6 and 3) could result. A useful way of visualizing the relationship between the dual-ring phasing diagram (such as Fig. 5.3.5) and the resulting phasing combinations has been suggested by McShane and Roess [5.7] as illustrated by Fig. 5.3.7. In that figure the "length" of each phase is proportioned according to a possible demand pattern subject to the barrier constraints; the corresponding phase display combinations are clearly seen.

   In the preceding discussion, reference has been made to the ability of actuated controllers to adjust the duration of phases based on the corresponding traffic demand. An exhaustive coverage of how this is accomplished is beyond

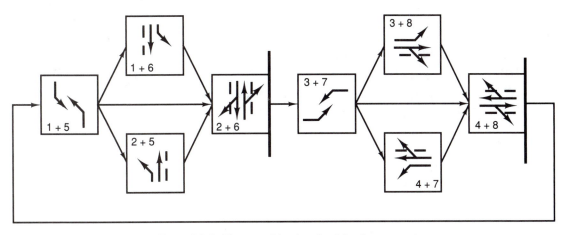

Figure 5.3.6 Phase combinations in eight-phase operation.

the scope of this book and only the basic principles are presented next. In the simplest case, the duration of the green component of a given phase may be thought of as consisting of a minimum green and an extensible portion as illustrated in Fig. 5.3.8. When the phase becomes active, the preset minimum green is displayed, and depending on the gaps between detector actuations for that phase, green is extended by the passage time, also known as the vehicle extension. This is illustrated in Fig. 5.3.8, where the abscissa represents time and the bullets

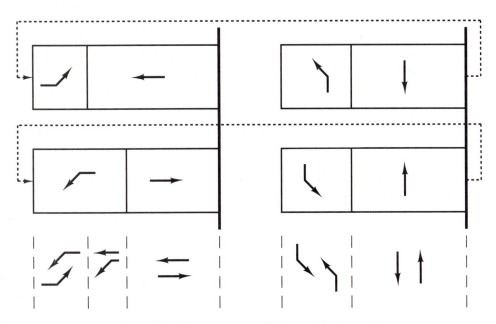

Figure 5.3.7 Ring concept applied to an eight-phase roller.

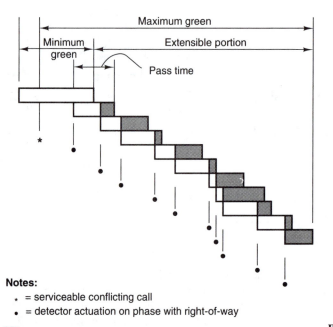

Notes:

* = serviceable conflicting call
• = detector actuation on phase with right-of-way
▓ = unexpired portions of vehicle intervals

Figure 5.3.8   Example of basic timing of actuated green times.

designate the times of vehicle detection. The maximum green limits the length of the extensible portion. In the case of NEMA controllers, the maximum green begins to time when a serviceable conflicting call is received rather than from the onset of green. In the case shown, continuous demand is present and the green "maxes out." If any one of the extensible portions were to expire without a vehicle actuation, the phase would have "gapped out." In the case just described, the minimum green was assumed to be fixed at a preset duration. NEMA, however, provides for a more complex possibility where the initial green (prior to the extensible portions) is variable and consists of a minimum initial interval plus an additional interval which depends on the number of vehicles that are queued prior to the onset of green.

Another advanced feature of NEMA controllers is known as the gap-reduction function. In the case illustrated by Fig. 5.3.8 the duration of the gap between vehicles that would cause a gap-out is fixed. By contrast, the gap-reduction feature provides for a reduced gap between vehicle actuations. At the start of a green phase, the gap that can trigger a gap-out is set at its maximum value. After a specified delay following a call for a conflicting phase, this gap begins to decrease with time (see Fig. 5.3.9). The gap is not allowed to decrease below a minimum value. Depending on vehicle demand, a gap-out can occur at the maximum, the minimum, or any of the intermediate levels.

Other controller functions include the provision for pedestrian "walk" and

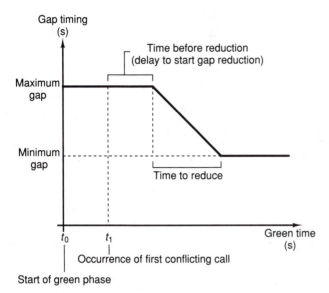

Figure 5.3.9 Example of timing with gap reduction.

clearance (i.e., flashing "don't walk") displays and several options relating to storing and recalling information relating to detector calls for future use. This feature is known as detector (or locking) memory.

5.3.4 Signal Timings

Signal timings describe the set of parameters defining the operation of a signalized intersection (i.e., the sequence and duration of the signal indications for each intersection approach). From an analytical perspective it involves the identification of the sequence by which the various movements at an intersection are served as well as the time duration of service (i.e., green time) for each movement.

The process of identifying the sequence of service is called phasing and it precedes all other signal timing steps. Then the cycle length is estimated and green times are allocated to each phase according to the relative magnitude of traffic flows served in each phase. The latter part also includes the allocation of phase change intervals (amber and all red). Certain constraints must be checked to ensure the safe and efficient processing of vehicles and pedestrians at an intersection.

Signal phasing.   Phasing is the sequence by which the various movements of both vehicles and pedestrians are being served at a signalized intersection. In traffic engineering, the definition of phasing is slightly different from the one encountered in the discussion of signal controllers in the previous section. For example, the equivalent of the eight-phase operation in Fig. 5.3.6 is a four-phase operation in traffic engineering (Fig. 5.3.11), because controller phases (usually denoted by numbers, e.g., $\Phi 1$, $\Phi 2$, etc.) which are executed simultaneously are taken as one phase (usually denoted by letters, e.g., ΦA, ΦB, etc.) in traffic analysis. This difference should be better understood after reading the rest of this section.

The objective of phasing is the minimization of the potential hazards arising from the conflicts of vehicular and pedestrian movements, while maintaining the efficiency of flow through the intersection. A large number of phases may be required if all conflicts are to be eliminated. Typical conflicts are (1) left-turning vehicles conflict with opposing through traffic as well as with pedestrians, and (2) right-turning vehicles conflict with pedestrians [see Fig. 5.3.10(a)]. Increasing the number of phases promotes safety but hinders efficiency because it results in increasing delays. Delays increase because (1) startup lost times increase (i.e., the time between the display of green and the discharge of the first vehicle in queue), (2) phase change intervals increase (i.e., the number of amber intervals required for transition from one phase to the next increase), and (3) minimum phase duration requirements have to be met. These requirements are based on minimum pedestrian crossing times; they are discussed later in this section.

Three common phasing schemes are presented in Fig. 5.3.10. The simplest phasing scheme is a two-phase operation [Fig. 5.3.10(a)]. This operation is appropriate at intersections with low pedestrian volumes, low-to-moderate turning volumes, and vehicle arrivals with an adequate number of sufficiently long gaps that permit left-turning vehicles to be served within the green time allotted to the phase. Right-turning vehicles conflict with pedestrians, whereas left-turning vehicles conflict both with opposing through traffic and pedestrians.

A three-phase operation is appropriate when one of the conditions under a two-phase operation is violated:

1. *High volume of pedestrians* [Fig. 5.3.10(b), case 1]. In this case, pedestrians are prohibited to cross when vehicles are served (phases A and B), and an exclusive phase is allotted to serve pedestrians (phase C). Phase C is called the all-red phase because all vehicle approaches have a red signal indication.

2. *High left-turning volume on one of the two intersecting streets* [Fig. 5.3.10(b), case 2]. In this case a specific phase (phase B) is allocated to serve left turns on one of the two streets. The left turns served in this fashion are protected (*protected movement*) since they have no conflicts with either vehicles or pedestrians. Left turns may be allowed or disallowed in the next phase (phase C). If they are allowed, they are a *permitted movement*; they can be served only if conditions permit (i.e., if there are long enough gaps in the opposing vehicular and pedestrian flow). The case where left turns are not allowed (after the end of the phase serving the left turns) is usually implemented with an exclusive set of traffic signals with arrows pointing to the left and a sign notifying that "left turn on arrow only" is allowed. High left-turning volumes varying by time (i.e., different directional left-turn overloads during morning and evening peak periods) can be treated with leading

Notes on *protected* and *permitted* movements:
- Left-turn movement in phases A and C is protected
- Left-turn movement in phase B is permitted
- Left-turn movement in phase D is prohibited

Phase A

Phase B

Phase C

Phase D

(c)

Pedestrians
Vehicles

Phase A

Phase B

(a)

Case 2: heavy left-turn volume on major street

Phase A

Phase B

Phase C

(b)

Case 1: heavy pedestrian flow

Phase A

Phase B

Phase C

All red

Figure 5.3.10 Examples of (a) two-, (b) three-, and (c) four-phase signal operation. (From Berry [5.8].)

203

or lagging left-turn-green allocations. Their discussion is beyond the scope of this document.

If heavy left-turning volumes are present on both intersecting streets, a four-phase operation is preferred [Fig. 5.3.10(c)]. This signalization scheme is most effective when coupled with left-turning bays or exclusive left-turn lanes and with actuated signal controllers. Left-turn bays or exclusive lanes make the operation of the intersection more efficient by reducing interference with the through movements in each approach. The traffic-actuated controller gives the ability to skip or elongate left-turning phases depending on the presence of low or high demand for left turns in each approach.

Figure 5.3.11 illustrates the operation of a four-phase scheme under actuated control. In the beginning of a new cycle, the controller assesses the demand for left turns. If there is sufficient demand in both the east and westbound directions, it selects the top box for phase A. If there is only eastbound left-turning demand, it selects the box second from the top. Thus, along with the eastbound left turns, it releases the through and right-turning eastbound movements. If there is only west-bound left-turning demand, it selects the box second from the bottom. If there is no left-turning demand, the controller skips phase A altogether and proceeds to phase B. Similar decisions are made for the north–south left-turning traffic (phase C). Comparison of Figs. 5.3.6 and 5.3.11 reveals that ΦA is $\Phi 1 + \Phi 5$ or $\Phi 1 + \Phi 6$ or $\Phi 2 + \Phi 5$, ΦB is $\Phi 2 + \Phi 6$, and so on.

Actuated controllers are also able to modify the cycle length as well as the durations of green to better serve the actual demand. In light traffic, a short cycle length is selected and green durations are kept to a minimum. The opposite happens when traffic is heavy. Minimum and maximum cycle lengths and green durations are prespecified by the traffic analyst prior to implementation. Minimum greens are required for safe processing of pedestrians. Maximum greens are required so that the movements which receive correspondingly long reds will not accumulate more vehicles than the length of the block can handle (i.e., queue backups spilling over to adjacent intersections). The flexibility of these systems results in more efficient service of traffic and in the minimization of delays. Actuated controllers perform best at isolated locations (i.e., intersection not a part of a coordinated signal network system) and during off peak times (i.e., drastic reduction of unnecessary delays).

Cycle-length selection.   Cycle length is a complete sequence of signal indications; it is the duration of time in which the whole set of phases at a signalized intersection takes place once. The length of cycle should not be set arbitrarily. Unnecessarily long cycle lengths cause substantial delays, while too short cycle lengths may cause congestion or endanger the processing of pedestrians through an intersection.

The appropriate cycle length can be estimated by Webster's formula; it results in the optimal cycle length:

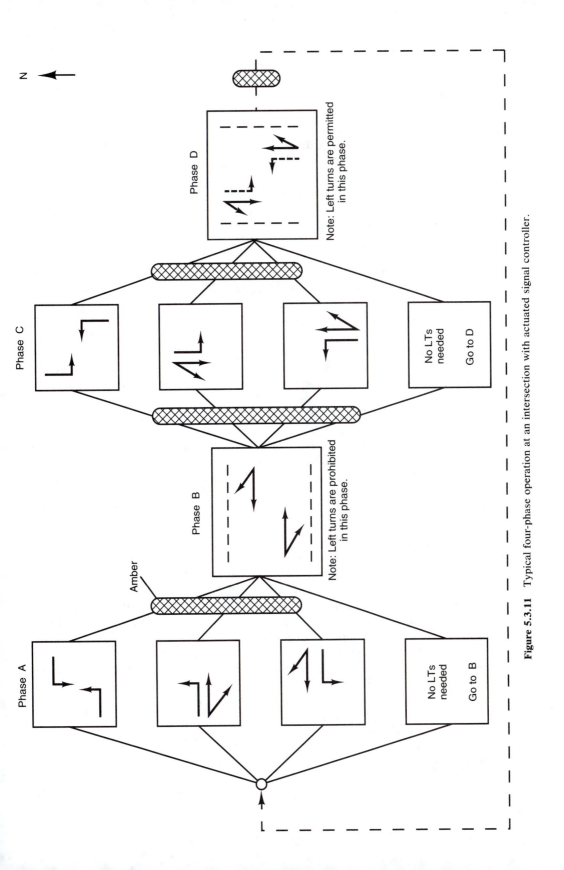

Figure 5.3.11 Typical four-phase operation at an intersection with actuated signal controller.

$$C_o = \frac{1.5L + 5}{1 - Y} \qquad (5.3.1)$$

where,

C_o = optimal cycle length, in seconds

L = total lost time during a cycle, which consists of the startup delay minus the portion of amber utilized by drivers (see Fig. 5.4.3); 3 to 4 s per phase is a good approximation

Y = sum of the flow ratios of critical movements (discussion follows)

Before estimating the cycle length, the phasing at the intersection must be set. There is no technique or computer algorithm that can produce an optimal phasing scheme. Reliance on common sense, experience, and trial and error are the only tools for identifying a phasing scheme. Ultimately, the best phasing scheme is the one that coupled with an optimal cycle length results in the shortest delays for the vehicles using the intersection.

Flow ratio is the demand over the servicing rate, or in traffic engineering terminology, the volume over the saturation flow (flow ratio = v/s). The saturation flow is discussed in detail in Section 5.4.2. Meanwhile, it will be treated as a given property.

Critical movements are discussed in the following example of signal timings estimation. Figure 5.3.12 displays an intersection that is assumed to be unsignalized. Due to the high peak-hour volumes, signalized control is warranted. The north–south direction is one way (southbound only). It has four lanes. The rightmost and leftmost lanes operate in a shared-use fashion (i.e., through as well as turning traffic share the use of those lanes). The east–west traffic can go both ways. This is a small street with only one lane per direction and low traffic volumes. All lanes are 12 ft wide.

First, the phasing scheme is established; a two-phase operation seems appropriate; dashed lines represent the simultaneous serving of pedestrians. Then the critical movement in each phase is identified. It corresponds to the lane or groups of lanes with the highest flow ratio. For phase A the critical movement is the westbound traffic, while for phase B the critical movement is the through-southbound movement (both lanes are combined since they serve the same movement). Factor Y results by simply adding up the maximum flow ratios. For a two-phase operation, two maximum flow ratios should be identified and added up (one per phase). For a three-phase operation, three maximum flow ratios should be identified and added up, and so forth.

The cycle length is estimated to be equal to 50 s. Empirical results show that cycle lengths within a ±30% from the optimal cycle-length estimate from Webster's formula are still performing nearly optimally [5.8, 5.9]. Therefore, all cycle lengths between 35 and 65 s are likely to perform satisfactorily at the ex-

Selection of maximum flow ratios for each phase:

Phase A: $\max \left\{ \dfrac{250}{1700}, \dfrac{335}{1650} \right\} = \max \{0.15, 0.20\} = 0.20$

Phase B: $\max \left\{ \dfrac{765}{1700}, \dfrac{850 + 820}{2 * 1800}, \dfrac{725}{1650} \right\} = \max \{0.45, 0.46, 0.44\} = 0.46$

Then, $Y = 0.46 + 0.20 = 0.66$

Lost time:
Assuming 4 s per phase lost time, the total lost time per cycle is $L = 2(4) = 8$ s

Optimal cycle length (Webster's formula)

$$C_0 = \frac{1.5\,(8) + 5}{1 - 0.66} = 50 \text{ s}$$

Figure 5.3.12   Estimation of optimal cycle length.

amined intersection. Cycle lengths between 45 and 180 s are used in the field. All cycle lengths typically end in 0 or 5; thus, if the cycle length estimate is 52 s, a cycle equal to 50 or 55 s should be selected.

Green allocation.   After the cycle length has been estimated, green and amber times must be allocated to each phase. The proper way to identify the duration of amber is to go through the dilemma zone calculations (Section 2.3.2). The dilemma zone analysis may indicate that different approaches may require different durations of amber due to higher speeds or different crossing lengths (i.e., in the intersection examined, the east–west traffic needs to cross four lanes to clear the intersection, while the southbound traffic needs to cross only two lanes). Variable amber durations can easily be accommodated in the green allocation procedure. An additional safety buffer between phases is a short (e.g., 1 or 2 s) all-red interval which is called the *clearance interval* (sometimes it is also called the all-red or phase-change interval).

The top table in Fig. 5.3.13 presents the green time allocation. Green time is allocated proportionally to the critical flow ratios for each phase. Note that the total amber duration is subtracted from the cycle length for the allocation. The total of green times and amber times should be equal to the cycle length.

Before accepting these timings as final, a check of whether pedestrians can

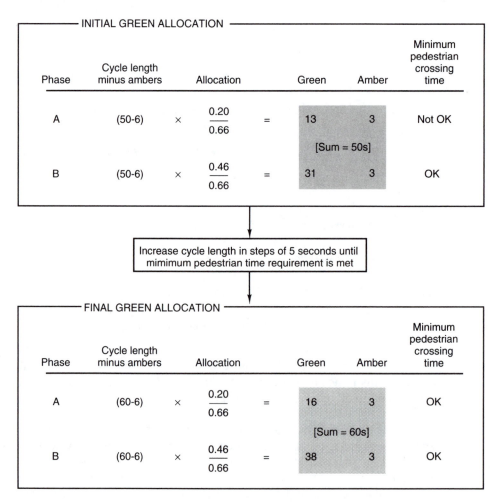

Figure 5.3.13 Green time allocation.

be safely served by the allotted times is necessary. Pedestrians served during phase *A* must cross four lanes. The minimum time required is

$$C_p = 7 + \frac{W}{4} - Y' = 7 + \frac{4 \times 12}{4} - 3 = 16 \text{ s} \qquad (5.3.2)$$

where

W = width of the crossing, in feet

Y' = total change interval time (amber plus all red, if exists)

The green time allotted to phase *A* cannot pass the minimum pedestrian time requirement, while the green time allotted to phase *B* is sufficient for safe pedestrian crossing: A minimum of 10 s is needed and 31 s are available.

Increasing the cycle length to 55 s still results in phase *A* green time shorter than required for safe pedestrian crossing. Further increase of the cycle length to 60 s (which is still in the near-optimal cycle length range) results in the green time allocation presented in the bottom table of (Fig. 5.3.13). The final green times are now acceptable.

Figure 5.3.14 presents the signalization stripes corresponding to this example application. One-second clearance intervals have been added to illustrate their position. Note that 1s has been subtracted from each final green estimated in Fig. 5.3.13 to accommodate the clearance intervals.

Another constraint imposed on cycle length selection is the network-wide cycle length. If the studied intersection is ½ mi away from the nearest signalized intersection, it may be considered to be isolated (not in a network); therefore, the aforementioned constraint does not apply. If the distance between neighboring intersections is shorter that ½ mi, the studied intersection belongs to a network, and for efficiency reasons, progression of platoons of vehicles should be maintained (arterial progression is discussed in Section 5.3.6). Effective progression cannot be achieved unless all intersections in the network operate under the same cycle length. This may impose a severe constraint in selecting an optimal cycle length for a specific intersection. Some flexibility exists, however. Progression can be achieved if some intersections operate in half-cycle or double-cycle. Thus if the network cycle length is 80 s, some intersections may operate in a 40- or 160-s cycle length.

Network analysis packages such as TRANSYT [5.9] can help identify an optimal network-wide cycle length given the phasing, traffic loads, and saturation flows at each intersection as well as other network characteristics such as distances between intersections and speeds. TRANSYT, which is presented in detail in Section 9.3.1, estimates the network-wide amount of delays for each cycle length selected. Alternative runs probing a number of cycle lengths results in a U-shaped curve (plot of delays versus the cycle length). The best cycle length for the network is the one that results in the lowest delays.

A previously unsignalized intersection may have been intimidating (per-

Figure 5.3.14 Examples of signalization stripes for vehicular and pedestrian traffic.

Note (*): The indicated intervals must be equal to or greater than the corresponding minimum pedestrian crossing times so that a pedestrian who started crossing at the end of WALK can clear the roadway safely: 16 seconds required in phase A and 12 seconds in phase B.

ceived as unsafe) or inconvenient (long delays incurred) for some drivers. The emplacement of signals may alter these perceptions, and therefore new traffic may divert to the newly signalized facility. Hence a few months after the installation, new traffic counts must be obtained and new timings should be estimated if the net volumes or the directional distribution of flows has changed. This may not be necessary if actuated signalization has been installed because it instantly adapts and serves existing demand.

5.3.5 Time–Distance Diagram of Interrupted Flow

Figure 5.3.15 shows an idealized time–distance diagram for an interrupted traffic stream. The signal is stationary and its display changes over time. A total of 12 vehicles are shown. At time $t = 0$ vehicle 1 is already stopped by the red light. Vehicles 2 to 8 consecutively join the stopped platoon. Line AB represents the shock wave between the approach conditions and the stationary-platoon conditions (see Section 3.6). After an *initial* (or *startup*) *delay* due mostly to the first driver's perception-reaction following the onset of green, the platoon leader moves

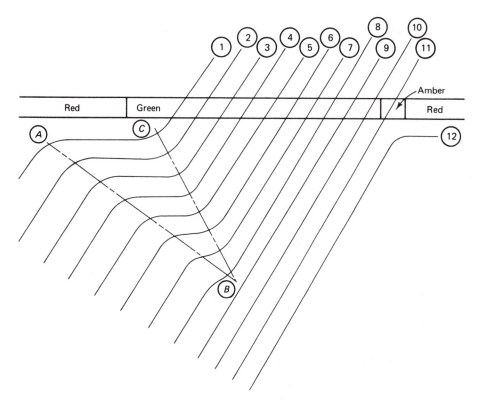

Figure 5.3.15   Traffic interruption.

through the intersection. Subsequent vehicles follow at a shorter release headway. Line *CB* represents the shock wave at the front of the platoon between the jam and the release conditions. When the two shock waves meet, the stationary platoon is totally dissipated. In the case shown, this event occurs before the onset of the following red, so that vehicles 9, 10, and 11 are able to clear the intersection without interruption. Finally, vehicle 12 is obliged to stop for the next red display. As explained in Chapter 3, a third shock wave between the approach and the release conditions may begin when the stationary platoon disappears, but for simplicity, this shock wave is not shown in Fig. 5.3.15.

5.3.6 Pretimed Signal Coordination

The fact that certain vehicles can avoid stopping at an intersection presents the opportunity to coordinate a series of pretimed signals to allow platoons of vehicles to clear all the signals without interruption [5.4]. This scheme works when the signals being coordinated have the same cycle length but not necessarily the same distribution of green, amber, and red within the common cycle. Figure 5.3.16

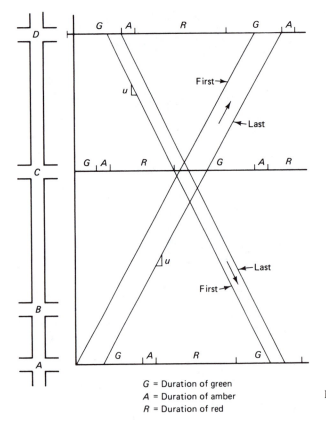

G = Duration of green
A = Duration of amber
R = Duration of red

Figure 5.3.16 Pretimed signal coordination.

shows a system of four intersections, three of which are signalized. The relative timing of each signal is specified by its *offset*, which is the time difference between a reference time and the beginning of the *first complete* green phase thereafter. The two pairs of parallel lines drawn on the figure represent the constant-speed trajectories of the first and last vehicles in each direction that can clear all intersections without stopping. The time difference between the parallel trajectories in each direction of movement is known as the *through band* for the direction. Dividing the through band by the average vehicular headway gives the number of vehicles constituting the uninterrupted platoon. The *width of the through band*, measured in seconds, may be adjusted by "sliding" each signal diagram horizontally. A *balanced design* refers to the case when the through bands in the two directions of travel are equal. A balanced design, however, does not always represent the best design. For instance, a *preferential design* may be more appropriate during the morning or evening peak periods on streets with unbalanced directional flows.

The solution to a signal-coordination problem may be accomplished graphically, analytically, or by computer, using several simple equations. For example, the time it takes a vehicle to travel between intersections at a constant speed equals the distance traveled divided by the speed. Also, the following equation may be used to discern the status of a signal at any time $t = T$ after the reference time $t = 0$:

$$\text{time into cycle} = \{T - \text{offset}\} \text{ modulo } C \qquad (5.3.3)$$

Knowledge of the duration of the green, amber, and red displays can pinpoint the exact status of the signal at $t = T$.

Example 5.2

> A signal has an offset of 10 s, a green, $G = 50$ s, an amber, $Y = 5$ s, and a red, $R = 65$ s. Find the status of the signal at times (a) $t = 45$ s, (b) 150 s, (c) 720 s, and (d) 782 s.
>
> **Solution** The signal cycle $C = (G + Y + R) = 120$ s. Apply Eq. 5.3.1.
>   (a) For $t = 45$: $(45 - 10)/120 = 0$ remainder 35; 35 s into the $(0 + 1)$ (i.e., first) cycle. Since $35 < G$, the display is green.
>   (b) For $t = 150$: $(150 - 10)/120 = 1$ remainder 20; 20 s into the second cycle. Since $20 < G$, the display is also green.
>   (c) For $t = 720$: $(720 - 10)/120 = 5$ remainder 110: 110 s into sixth cycle. Since $(G + Y) < 110 < C$, the display is red.
>   (d) For $t = 782$: $(782 - 10)/120 = 6$ remainder 52; 52 s into the seventh cycle. Since $G < 52 < (G + Y)$, the display is amber.

Example 5.3

> The signals at the intersections of the one-way street have been pretimed and coordinated as follows:

Intersection	Green	Amber	Red	Offset	Distance from A
A	40 s	5 s	35 s	0 s	—
B	50 s	5 s	25 s	40 s	2000 ft
C	35 s	5 s	40 s	10 s	5000 ft

Given a design speed of 30 mi/h, determine the width of the resulting through band.

Solution   The three signals have equal cycles of 80 s. Therefore signal coordination is possible. A vehicle clearing intersection A at time $t = 0$ will arrive at B (2000 ft)/ (44 ft/s) = 45.5 s later. At this instant, the display at B is 5.5 s into the first green display. Hence the vehicle can proceed toward C without interruption. It will reach C at $t = 45.5 + (3000/44) = 113.7$ s. At this time, the signal at C is 23.7 s into the second cycle and is green. Therefore, this vehicle can clear all three intersections.

To find the last vehicle that can do the same, the remaining green duration after the passage of the first vehicle is calculated (see Fig. 5.3.17):

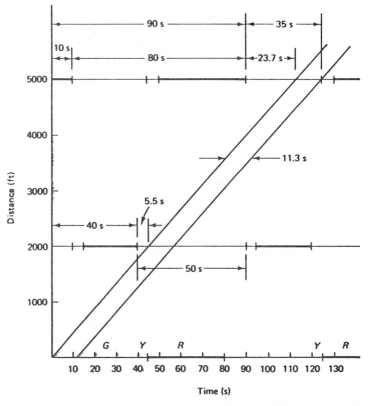

Figure 5.3.17   Example of bandwidth derivation.

At A: $40 - 0 = 40$ s

At B: $90 - 45.5 = 44.5$ s, or $50 - 5.5 = 44.5$ s

At C: $125 - 113.7 = 11.3$ s, or $35 - 23.7 = 11.3$ s

The minimum of these values defines the width of the through band (i.e., 11.3 s) and fixes the trajectory of the last vehicle as shown in the figure.

Discussion   Often, the width of the through band is taken to include the amber, that is, the last vehicle is allowed to clear an intersection on yellow. In this event, the width of the through band would be reported as 16.3 s. Note that in this example the width of the through band can be increased by increasing the offset of intersection C. As a general rule, allowing a few seconds of green to elapse before the first vehicle in the main platoon reaches a signal is considered good practice because it allows any main- or side-street vehicles caught by the preceding red phase to clear the way before the platoon's arrival.

5.4 CAPACITY OF SIGNALIZED INTERSECTIONS

5.4.1 Introduction

Under uninterrupted conditions, the definition of flow is simply the number of vehicles that pass a point during a specified time interval. At intersections, a unique point where flow measurements can be taken does not exist. Figure 5.4.1 shows the variety of movement desires that a typical four-leg intersection is ex-

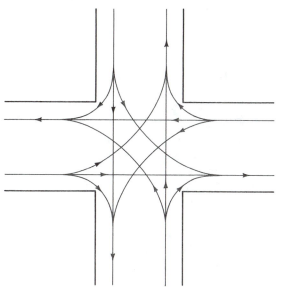

Figure 5.4.1   Intersection movement desires.

pected to accommodate and the resulting points of conflict between these movements. The ability of a signalized intersection to process the approaching flows is affected by the magnitudes and vehicular composition of these volumes, their movement desires, the geometric design of the intersection, and the characteristics of the signal. The presence of bus stops in the immediate vicinity of the intersection also affects its operating conditions. Several practical methods of signalized intersection analysis are found in the technical literature. Most of these methods are empirical and approximate. Hence their ability to explain the many subtleties encountered at intersections is, accordingly, limited. Nevertheless, their usefulness for practical analysis cannot be denied.

5.4.2 Capacity and Performance Analysis

The operating characteristics of signalized intersections can be estimated and evaluated with a procedure of capacity and performance analysis. The capacity of an intersection represents the throughput of the facility (i.e., the maximum number of vehicles that can be served in 1 h). An important outcome of the capacity analysis is the volume-to-capacity ratio (v/c ratio), which is also called the degree of saturation (X). This ratio indicates the proportion of the capacity (supply) utilized by the existing traffic volume (demand).

The performance of an intersection is based on estimates of average delay for each vehicle utilizing the facility. Short delays result in a good level of service (LOS), whereas long delays result in poor LOS (e.g., average delay equal to 5 s per vehicle corresponds to LOS A, while 30 s per vehicle corresponds to LOS D). Facilities performing at D or worse may need to be upgraded (i.e., improvements in signal timings and progression, rechannelization or widening of the road space). Intersection performance is discussed in detail toward the end of this section.

The 1985 *Highway Capacity Manual* (HCM) [5.10] procedures for analysis of signalized intersections are widely accepted in traffic engineering practice. Its predecessors (HCM-1965 and TRB Circular 212 [5.11]) are still used by some. Among other differences, the older procedures do not require the estimation of delays. Levels of service are derived directly from v/c ratios.

A summary of the 1985 HCM procedures for analysis of signalized intersections is presented next. A substantial number of inputs is required for the application of these procedures. The inputs may be classified in five categories: (1) traffic characteristics, such as volumes by direction (i.e., through, right and left for each intersection approach); (2) traffic composition, such as proportion of heavy vehicles in traffic by lane or approach; (3) geometric characteristics, such as number of lanes, lane widths, approach grades; (4) signal timing characteristics, such as type of control—pretimed, actuated, cycle length, duration of greens, phase-change intervals; and (5) other operating characteristics, such as arterial progression, existence of parking and frequency of parking maneuvers, and bus stop blockage.

After all inputs have been gathered, *traffic volumes are adjusted* to reflect peak period conditions. This is done by multiplying peak hourly volumes by the peak-hour factor (PHF), which is defined as follows:

$$\text{PHF} = \frac{\text{peak-hour volume}}{4(\text{peak 15-min volume})} \tag{5.4.1}$$

Usually, traffic volumes are recorded every 15 min. Based on the counts, first the peak hour is identified: for example, traffic volume counts taken between 4:00 and 6:00 P.M. indicate that the peak hour is between 4:30 and 5:30; this is the peak-hour volume to be used in Eq. 5.4.1. Then the highest peak 15-min count is selected from the peak hour; this is the peak 15-min volume to be used in Eq. 5.4.1.

The two, three, four, or more intersection approaches may have different peak characteristics (i.e., they may reach their peaks at a different time of day). The 1985 HCM procedure brings all these peaks together (i.e., artificial over-loading). Thus the resulting estimates tend to be conservative.

The final step in the adjustment of volumes is the grouping of directional flows in lane groups based on the utilization of each lane (i.e., types of movements utilizing a lane) and the phasing scheme. For example, a two-lane approach on a two- by two-way street intersection (Fig. 5.4.2) may be analyzed in one of three possible ways: (1) one-lane group serving all three movements (usually selected when turning flows are low); (2) two-lane groups: one serving left-turning and through movements and the other serving right-turning and through movements (usually selected when moderately high turning volumes prevail); and (3) two-lane groups: one lane serving the left-turn movement only, and one serving the through and right-turning movements; this happens when left-turn volume is high, so that left-turning traffic essentially occupies the left lane at all times or when there exists an exclusive left-turn phase in the signalization plan.

The second step in the analysis is the *estimation of prevailing saturation flows* for each lane group. The saturation flow describes the (behavioral) way of driver discharge from an intersection stop-line. The saturation flow is essentially the service rate: It represents the maximum number of vehicles that can be served in 1 h, assuming a continuous display of green and a continuous queue of vehicles. The saturation flow is expressed in vphg (vehicles per hour of green).

Figure 5.4.3 presents the concept of saturation flow. Assume an intersection approach with one lane which has an infinite number of cars waiting in queue. An x–y plot is employed to represent the discharge pattern of drivers. The signal is red. At time t_0 green is displayed. There is a typical reaction and action time delay (i.e., react to signal and then shift into gear and press the gas pedal), and at time t_1 the first car in queue crosses the stop-line. Each car crossing the stop-line is considered discharged.

Approximately after the fourth car, the discharge rate becomes rapid and fairly uniform: Cars pass by at a fairly constant rate and the headways between them are almost equal. The saturation point has been reached. This saturation

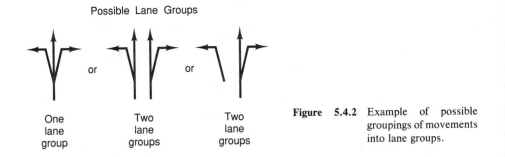

Possible Lane Groups

One lane group   or   Two lane groups   or   Two lane groups

Figure 5.4.2 Example of possible groupings of movements into lane groups.

discharge rate is the highest attainable under normal conditions; this is the saturation flow. Normally, the discharge process may not be as uniform, but the plot in Fig. 5.4.3 depicts reality reasonably well.

At the end of green, amber is displayed (at time t_3). Some drivers proceed to clear the intersection and others stop. There are occasions when t_3 falls after t_4, which denotes the beginning of red. This means that some drivers utilized a small part of the red phase, often mistakenly. These drivers are called "sneakers" in traffic engineering jargon. Substantial presence of sneakers calls for both enforcement of traffic laws and reevaluation of the duration of amber (dilemma zone problem).

The major determinant of the saturation flow is the average headway be-

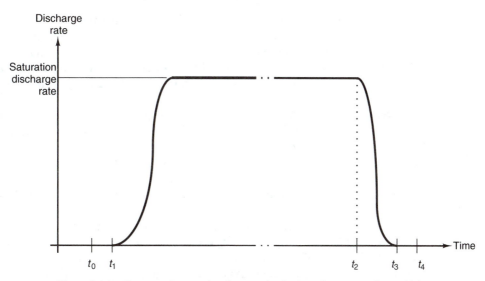

Figure 5.4.3   Concept of saturation flow. t_0, beginning of green; t_1, first vehicle crosses stop-line; t_1–t_0, startup delay; t_2, beginning of amber (end of green); t_3, last vehicle to discharge during this cycle; t_3–t_2, amber utilization; t_4, end of amber (beginning of red); t_2–t_1, signal green time; t_3–t_1, effective green time.

tween vehicles discharging from an intersection. The saturation flow (s) is defined as

$$s = \frac{3600}{h} \tag{5.4.2}$$

where h is the average headway in seconds.

Since s describes driver behavior, vehicle characteristics such as size and acceleration characteristics, traffic conditions, and environmental factors as well as driving habits affect the saturation flow. Thus the HCM [5.10] recommends the local study and derivation of ideal saturation flow levels. Studies have shown that saturation flows are higher in suburban areas [5.12], and lower in small urban areas [5.13] or under adverse weather conditions.

For intersection capacity analysis, an ideal saturation flow is selected first; s_0 is usually equal to 1800 pcphgpl (passenger cars per hour of green per lane). The ideal saturation flow represents driver behavior in large U.S. urban areas on facilities with specific geometric and operational characteristics. Then s_0 is adjusted to reflect actual conditions. Adjustments are not made for environmental conditions; daylight and dry pavement conditions are always assumed. The prevailing saturation flow for a specific lane group is estimated as follows:

$$s = s_0 N f_w f_{\mathrm{HV}} f_g f_p f_{bb} f_a f_{\mathrm{RT}} f_{\mathrm{LT}} \tag{5.4.3}$$

The following adjustments are incorporated:

Number of lanes (N) is the number of lanes serving the lane group.

Lane width (f_w), in feet. The wider the lanes, the more comfortable drivers feel (i.e., less interference with vehicles in adjacent lanes; also refer to Section 2.3.4), and the higher the saturation flow. This factor varies between 0.87 and 1.10 for lane widths varying between 8 and 15 ft, respectively; it is 1.00 for 12-ft-wide lanes.

Heavy vehicles (f_{HV}). Heavy vehicles have slow acceleration characteristics; they tend to slow down the discharging process; long headways are created and the saturation flow decreases. This factor varies between 1.00 and 0.87 for heavy vehicle proportions varying between 0 and 30%, respectively.

Grade (f_g). Uphill grade tends to decrease acceleration characteristics; thus headways elongate and saturation flow decreases The opposite is true for downhill grades. This factor varies between 0.97 and 1.03 for approach grades varying between +6 and −6%, respectively; it is 1.00 for level grade.

Parking (f_p). Parking adjacent to traffic streams tends to interfere with adjacent passing-by traffic, while parking maneuvers disrupt the normal discharge process. The fewer the lanes available, the greater the impact of parking. In addition, the number of parking maneuvers is related to saturation flow: the more parking maneuvers per hour, the lower the saturation flow. For a one-lane approach, this factor varies between 1.00 and 0.70 for parking maneuvers varying between 0 and 40 maneuvers per hour, respectively; the factor is smaller for approaches with two, three, or more lanes.

Bus blockage (f_{bb}). Often, public buses stop at intersection corners to serve passengers. This usually disrupts intersection operations. One lane may be temporarily blocked—during green—or following vehicles may have to slow down and maneuver around the stopped bus. Thus saturation flow decreases temporarily. For a one-lane approach, this factor varies between 1.00 and 0.83 for number of bus stops per hour varying between 0 and 40, respectively; it is smaller for multilane approaches.

Area type (f_a). The type of the area surrounding the intersection—CBD or non-CBD area—may have an impact on driving behavior and consequently on the saturation flow. Recent studies recommend the appropriate selection of ideal saturation flow and the abandonment of this factor (i.e., $s_0 = 1600$ for small urban areas, $s_0 = 2000$ for high-design intersections, and $s_0 = 1800$ pcphgpl for all other cases, including urban CBDs [5.9, 5.10]).

Turning movements (f_{RT} and f_{LT}). Adjustment factor for lane groups serving turning movements (exclusive turns or shared use). Turning movements often conflict with opposing traffic and/or with pedestrians. As a result, their respective saturation flows tend to be lower compared with through movements. The type of movement (right or left turn), the serving process (protected, permitted, or a combination of the two), opposing volumes, and number of pedestrians are necessary inputs for the estimation of these factors, which may range between 0.95 and 0.25. The analysis of permitted left-turn movements has many commonalities with unsignalized intersection operations (see Section 5.6).

The adjusted volumes and the derived saturation flows for each lane group are combined in the *capacity analysis*. The capacity for each lane group is estimated by

$$c_i = s_i \frac{g_i}{C} \tag{5.4.4}$$

where

c_i = capacity of lane group i, in vehicles per lane

s_i = prevailing saturation flow of lane group i

g_i = green time allotted to lane group i

C = cycle length

The degree of saturation is estimated as follows:

$$X_i = \frac{v_i}{c_i} \tag{5.4.5}$$

where

X_i = degree of saturation of lane group i

v_i = adjusted peak volume of lane group i

c_i = capacity of lane group i

In order to be able to derive a degree of saturation for the entire intersection, critical movements must be identified for each phase. If more than one lane group is served in one phase, the lane group with the highest flow ratio $(v/s)_i$ is the critical one. The process of critical movement selection is identical to the one presented in the cycle-length estimation process. The critical degree of saturation (X_c) for the entire intersection is estimated as follows:

$$X_c = \Sigma \left(\frac{v}{s}\right)_{\text{critical}} \frac{C}{C - L} \tag{5.4.6}$$

where L is the total lost time during a cycle, typically equal to the sum of all amber and all-red durations. The X_c factor is particularly useful at intersections with some oversaturated lane groups or approaches. For example, a specific lane group may have a degree of saturation X_i equal to, for example, 1.04; that is, demand exceeds capacity by 4%. If the X_c is less than 1.00, this means that the facility as a whole is not utilized to its capacity. Then, simple reallocation of green times within the same cycle length will improve operating conditions (i.e., they will no longer be oversaturated lane groups). Thus X_c provides a safeguard against leaping to drastic measures, such as new channelization, roadway widening, redirection of oncoming traffic, and so forth.

The last step in the intersection capacity analysis process is the *performance evaluation* of the facility. The performance evaluation is based on the average delay incurred by all vehicles utilizing the facility. There are several definitions of delay, two of the most common being travel delay and stopped delay. *Travel delay* for an individual vehicle is the difference between the time a vehicle passes a point downstream of the intersection where it has regained normal speed, and the time it would have passed that point had it been able to continue at its approach speed [5.8]. *Stopped delay* for an individual vehicle is the time duration of "substantially standing still" while waiting in queue at a signalized intersection approach. Substantially standing still is usually taken equal to 3 mi/h or less [5.8]. Empirical results show that division of the travel delay by 1.3 results in the stopped delay.

Two delay components are estimated for each lane group: the uniform delay (d_1) and the overflow delay (d_2). The former accounts for uniform arrivals, while the latter accounts for random arrivals. The two delay components are estimated as follows:

$$d_1 = 0.38C \frac{\left(1 - \frac{g}{C}\right)^2}{1 - \left(\frac{g}{C}\right)X} \tag{5.4.7}$$

$$d_2 = 173X^2 \left\{ X - 1 + \sqrt{(X - 1)^2 + 16\frac{X}{c}} \right\} \tag{5.4.8}$$

These equations result in *stopped delay*. The total delay for each lane group is estimated as follows:

$$TD_i = PF_i(d_{1i} + d_{2i}) \tag{5.4.9}$$

where

$$TD_i = \text{total delay for lane group } i$$

$$PF_i = \text{progression factor for lane group } i$$

The progression factor accounts for the process of vehicle arrivals in conjunction with the signal indications. When most arrivals take place while red is displayed for the lane group analyzed (poor progression), the delays are likely to be higher than average (PF > 1.0). Random arrivals result in average conditions (PF = 1.0). On the other hand, when most arrivals take place while green is displayed (good progression), the delays are likely to be lower than average (PF < 1.0).

The amount of estimated delay defines the level of service of a lane group, of an approach, and of the intersection as a whole. Approach delays result by weighting lane group delays with the respective lane group volumes. The intersection delay results by weighting approach delays with the respective approach volumes. According to the HCM, total delay per vehicle up to 5.0 s corresponds to level of service A; delay between 5.1 and 15.0 s corresponds to LOS B; delay between 15.1 and 25.0 s corresponds to LOS C; delay between 25.1 and 40.0 s corresponds to LOS D; delay between 40.1 and 60.0 s corresponds to LOS E; delay higher than 60.0 s corresponds to LOS F. Unequal performance among approaches served by different phases indicates that green times are not properly allocated.

Signalized intersection network analysis is a major concern of traffic engineering. Such analysis is usually assisted by network simulation models such as NETSIM and TRANSYT. Issues of signal networks, principles of analysis, and the basics of network simulation software packages are presented in Section 9.3.1. Section 9.2.6 presents a comprehensive example of signalized intersection capacity and performance analysis as part of a traffic impact study.

5.4.3 Planning Applications Procedure

The planning applications procedure [5.10] treats the various components of flow in terms of vehicles per hour (rather than passenger car equivalents), assuming an average vehicle mix. Consequently, explicit adjustments for heavy vehicles are not performed. Also, the effect of bus operations in the vicinity of the intersection is ignored. This procedure can be used to assess broadly the level of service that prevails at an existing intersection, to calculate the maximum service volume for a known level of service, to predict the impact of design changes on the level of service, and combinations of the three. Table 5.4.1 summarizes the required adjustment factors, and Fig. 5.4.4 outlines the steps involved in the procedure.

TABLE 5.4.1   LEFT- AND RIGHT-TURN EQUIVALENCE
FACTORS

Opposing through *plus* right flows (veh/h)	Equivalent "through" (veh/h)
Left	
0–199	1.1
200–599	2.0
600–799	3.0
800–999	4.0
1000+	5.0
Right	
Right-turn equivalent "through" is 1.0.	

Source: Transportation Research Board [5.10].

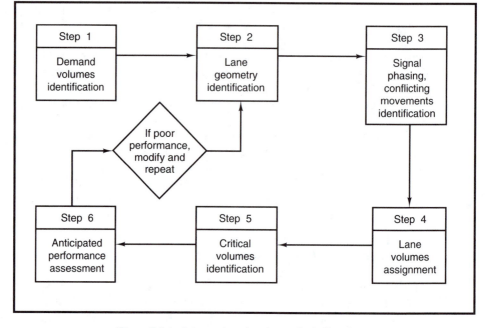

Figure 5.4.4 Intersection planning analysis flowchart.

Step 1: Identification of demand.   The left-turning, through, and right-turning volumes that use (or are expected to use) each approach are identified and expressed in vehicles per hour.

Step 2: Identification of lane geometry.   A diagram of the entire intersection is prepared, which shows all lanes and the types of movement(s) that are permitted on each lane (e.g., left-only or left-and-through).

Step 3: Identification of signal phasing.   The existing or contemplated phases that make up the signal cycle are identified.

Step 4: Assignment of lane volumes.   This step assigns the approach volumes to the available lanes. When examining an existing intersection, the observed lane utilization can be used. Otherwise, a procedure that estimates the lane choice of drivers is applied. When exclusive turn lanes are present, the turning volume is, naturally, assigned to them. If two turn lanes are provided for the same movement, one is assigned 55% and the other 45% of the turning volume. The volume not using as exclusive turn lane is divided between the lanes that are available to it considering the fact that vehicles going straight through the intersection show a preference to lanes that are not blocked by turning vehicles. The degree to which this phenomenon occurs depends on the number of lanes, the magnitude of the turning volumes, and the magnitude of the opposing volumes against which the turns are made. In the case of left turns, the opposing volume consists of the through *plus* right-turning vehicles that simultaneously proceed into the intersection area from the opposite approach. In the case of right-turning vehicles, the opposing volume most often consists of pedestrians on the cross street. The turning volumes are converted to "equivalent through vehicles per hour" (from Table 5.4.1), and the total approach volume (expressed in equivalent through vehicles per hour) is divided equally among the available lanes. The turning volumes are then converted back to vehicles per hour, and a check is made to ensure that all turning volumes have been assigned to lanes that permit the execution of turns.

Example 5.4

An intersection approach is expected to carry the following hourly volumes:

1000 veh/h going straight through the intersection

200 veh/h turning right

400 veh/h turning left

Three lanes are present: An exclusive left, a middle lane for through vehicles, and a curb lane that is shared by through and right-turning vehicles. Assuming that the vehicles executing right turns are free from pedestrian interference and that the left-turning vehicles face an opposing volume (through plus right) of 400 veh/h, assign the approach volume to three available lanes.

Solution   The entire left-turn volume is assigned to the exclusive left lane. Since there is no pedestrian interference, the remaining volume of 1200 veh/h is divided equally between the other two lanes, as shown in Fig. 5.4.5.

400 veh/h

600 veh/h

400 veh/h

Figure 5.4.5   Example of volume allo-

200 veh/h   cation per lane (3 lanes).

Example 5.5

Repeat the procedure of Example 5.4, assuming that the left lane is not present.

Solution   In this case, the center lane will be shared by the left-turning vehicles and a portion of the through volume. The likely distribution by lane is estimated as follows:

1. With an opposing volume of 400 veh/h, a through-vehicle equivalency factor for the left-turning vehicles is obtained by interpolation from Table 5.4.1. This factor is 2.0.
2. The left-turning volume of 400 veh/h is converted to through-vehicle equivalent of (400)(2.0) = 800.
3. The right-turn equivalency factor is 1.0.
4. The total approach volume, that is, (800 + 1000 + 200) = 2000 through vehicles per hour, is divided equally between the two lanes, each lane receiving 1000 veh/h.
5. Since the equivalent volume assigned to the center lane (1140) is greater than the left-turning volume (800 "through" vehicles per hour), the entire left-turning volume has, in effect, been assigned to the center lane.
6. The left-turning volume is converted back to vehicles per hour (i.e., 400 veh/h), and the lane assignment is completed as shown in Fig. 5.4.6.

400 veh/h left

1000 − 800 = 200 veh/h through

1000 − 200 = 800 veh/h through

Figure 5.4.6 Example of volume allocation per lane (2 lanes).

200 veh/h right

Step 5: Determination of critical volumes for each signal phase. For each green signal phase, there is a critical point within the intersection crossed by the highest volume for that phase (i.e., the *critical volume*). The critical point may be on a single path or at the intersection of two paths. Figure 5.4.7 shows a variety of possible critical points, a combination of which would appear during each phase. In Fig. 5.4.7(a), potential critical points on single paths are shown. In (b), points prior to diverging volumes are designated as possible critical points. Finally, (c) shows points where turning vehicles are in conflict with opposing movements. The volume that crosses such points of conflict is given by the sum of the two conflicting volumes. Although not drawn on the figure, the opposing volume includes through plus right-turning vehicles, if applicable. A fundamental

(a) Single lane volume   (b) Diverging lane volume

(c) Conflicting lane volumes

Figure 5.4.7 Examples of possible critical points.

assumption of the intersection analysis method described here is that the relative duration of signal phases is proportional to their critical volumes.

Example 5.6

The movements permitted from the east–west approaches to an intersection during a signal phase are shown in Fig. 5.4.8, along with their lane assignments. Find the critical volume for this phase.

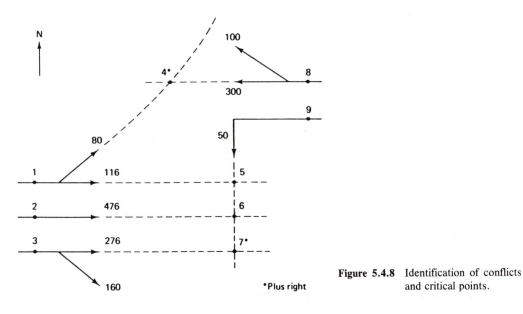

Figure 5.4.8   Identification of conflicts and critical points.

*Plus right

Solution   Nine potentially critical points are identified in the figure. The volumes associated with each point are calculated next:

Point		Volume (veh/h)
1	80 + 116	196
2		476
3	276 + 160	436
4	80 + (300 + 100)	480
5	50 + 116	166
6	50 + 476	526
7	50 + (276 + 160)	486
8	300 + 100	400
9		50

The critical volume for this phase is 526 veh/h at point 6. The critical volumes calculated for each phase are summed to arrive at a single measure of the intersection as a whole. In the case of the four-phase intersection of the preceding examples, the *sum of critical volumes* is 300 + 200 + 400 + 526, or 1426, veh/h.

Step 6: Assessment of level of service.   Table 5.4.2 is used to determine how well the intersection is likely to perform. Under capacity denotes that the delays are likely to be short (good LOS). Near capacity denotes that the delays may fluctuate substantially; they may reach large values at times (potentially poor LOS). Over capacity denotes that the intersection as planned is likely to provide a poor LOS with consistently high delays.

TABLE 5.4.2   INTERSECTION LOS: PLANNING LEVEL

Critical volume for intersection (veh/h)	Relationship to probable capacity
0–1200	Under capacity
1201–1400	Near capacity
≥1401	Over capacity

Source: Transportation Research Board [5.10].

Step 7: Modification of design.   The geometric configuration of the intersection, its signal phasing, or both may be modified. The effect of such modifications on the level of service can then be calculated by returning to Step 1.

5.5 TRAFFIC DATA COLLECTION METHODS

There is a long list of data that need to be collected to apply the *Highway Capacity Manual* procedure for the capacity estimation and performance evaluation of a signalized intersection. The required data may be grouped into static and dynamic (time dependent). Static data are measured once, while dynamic data are collected continuously during the data collection period. Geometric characteristics (i.e., lane widths and grades) as well as pretimed signal timings and the area type are static data. Time-dependent data are traffic volumes, traffic composition (i.e., percent of heavy vehicles in traffic), arrival type (i.e., percent of vehicles arriving in green), and signal timings of actuated controllers (i.e., cycle length and green time available to each movement). Other time-dependent data are the number of buses stopping at the intersection to serve passengers and the number of parking maneuvers per hour. In addition, actual saturation flows and delays can be measured directly in the field.

There are three common ways for collecting traffic data: (1) image recording with video or film cameras, (2) manual collection with a team of workers, and (3) automated collection with mechanical counters [5.14, 5.15]. The third approach is preferred only when daily volumes are desired. These volumes are appropriate for evaluating networks as well as for planning applications. The actual data collected are the number of vehicle axles that cross a specific approach or lane at any time (i.e., hourly, daily, monthly, or annual counts). Dynamic data collected by mechanical counters with tubes attached to the pavement cannot supply information on turning movements, arrivals on green, and traffic composition. Data collected with mechanical counters are least appropriate for capacity estimation and performance evaluation.

The videotaping or filming alternative requires image recording equipment as well as some experience for its appropriate location and use. To obtain a sufficiently wide field of view, an elevated point may be necessary. After the recording is complete, a substantial number of labor hours is required to translate pictures (frames) into numerical data. Specially manufactured film editors may be necessary because the intervals between frames must be precisely equal to a specified amount of time (e.g., 2 to 20 s).

A major problem with this approach is that the signal indications cannot be viewed at the same time as the queues of vehicles. This is a substantial disadvantage when the traffic signal controller is actuated or when arrivals during green are desired. Multiple cameras may resolve this problem, but then precisely synchronized film editors must be used for the derivation of numerical data from the tapes.

Image recognition technology promises to simplify these tasks by having a computer connected to the cameras and translate images (i.e., vehicles by type and signal displays) directly into numerical format. Such automated image processing devices have started entering the market. A device developed at the University of Minnesota (AUTOSCOPE, [5.16]) can automatically count volumes from video images and derive a multitude of traffic parameters.

The most common option for data collection is with a team of workers, each of whom takes measurements of a specific traffic element. For a specific approach with variable signal timings (actuated signal controller) the following measurement assignments are necessary for full coverage of all inputs required for signalized intersection analysis:

1. *Service volume* (i.e., vehicles crossing the stop-line) *for each movement of traffic* (i.e., through, right, and left turns) *along with the number of heavy vehicles in each movement*. It is preferred to record this information at the end of each cycle (end of green for the approach) because the peak 15 min can be identified accurately. In practice, it is common to take volume measurements every 15 min, following the suggestion in the HCM. Revisions of the recommendations for traffic counts for the analysis of intersections with actuated signal controllers have been proposed [5.17, 5.18].

2. *Total number of arrivals as well as the arrivals during green.* This results in the true demand for service for each approach, while it also furnishes accurate inputs for the type of arrival (i.e., if most vehicles arrive at the

beginning of green the arterial progression is good and the delays are reduced). Typically, these measurements are not done in small-scale, local
applications.

3. *Duration of green for each movement and cycle length.* These measurements
   are taken and recorded every cycle. If the intersection has a pretimed signal
   controller, cycle length and green times may be taken only once. Signal
   timings may also be provided by the city traffic engineer. For actuated controllers, average duration of phases is derived, which consequently compromises the accuracy of intersection capacity and performance.

The labor needed for the collection of traffic data for intersection capacity
analysis varies considerably with the design, operation, size, and load of the
intersection. In addition, the experience and reliability of the traffic counts team
is an important factor. Usually, experienced labor may accurately execute multiple assignments (i.e., volume data collection from more than one approach and
for all the movements of traffic).

For intersections with actuated signal controllers, the number of people
needed for full coverage (i.e., volume counts from all approaches and signal timing
data collection) varies between 3 and 10. Figure 5.5.1 shows a typical intersection
configuration with the traffic-count people positioned so as to minimize the personnel needs. The first volume-counting person (VC_1) is responsible for volume
counts on the eastbound and southbound approaches, while the second volume-
counting person (VC_2) takes care of the westbound and northbound volumes.
Consider VC_2: When any of the movements on approach A_1 have green, traffic
is counted at the stop-line of approach A_1 and approach B_2 is ignored since none
of the movements on approach B_2 have the right-of-way, except for right-turn-
on-red (RTOR), if permitted, and vice versa. Thus one person could take counts
from two approaches. The task of traffic counts may be difficult for two persons
to accomplish at intersections with multilane approaches and heavy traffic. In
such cases, one volume-counting person should be allocated for each approach.

Similarly, two to four persons are needed for the collection of signal timing
data, if they are variable. In Fig. 5.5.1 the intersection was assumed to operate
in two phases. In this case two persons are adequate for measuring signal timings.
One person (SM_1) times the duration of green for phase A (east–west traffic,
approaches A_1 and A_2) and the cycle length, while the other (SM_2) times the
duration of green for phase B (north–south traffic, approaches B_1 and B_2). For a
complex signal operation with protected left-turn phases and/or other features,
more persons are required, the maximum being five persons: one for each of the
four approaches and the fifth one for the cycle-length measurement [5.19].

Additional labor is required if field-measured saturation flows and stopped
delays are desired. Field delays can be estimated accurately by following a simple
procedure. Every 10, 15, or 20 s (the length of the sampling interval is defined a
priori) the number of stopped vehicles are recorded. Simultaneously, volume
counts are obtained. These recordings should be taken per lane or approach. Then

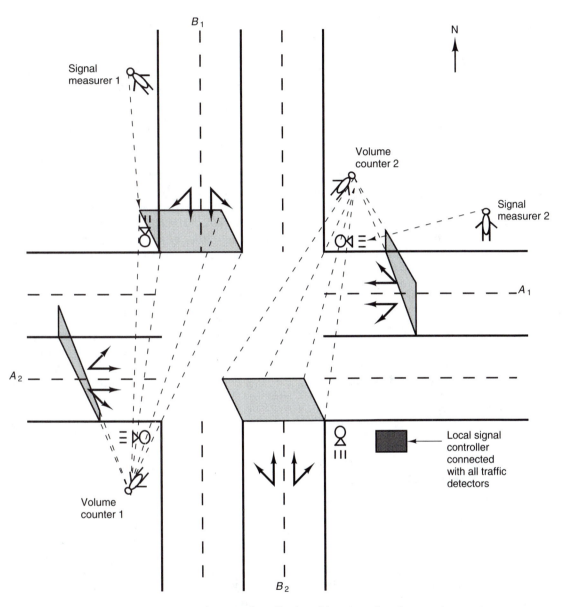

Figure 5.5.1   Personnel assignments for collection of time-dependent data at an intersection with a two-phase actuated signal controller.

field delay (stopped delay), in seconds per vehicle, is obtained by using the following formula:

$$\text{field delay} = \frac{V_s I}{v} \tag{5.5.1}$$

where

$$V_s = \text{sum of all stopped vehicles counted}$$

$$I = \text{length of time interval}$$

$$v = \text{volume count}$$

The field measurement of the saturation flow for a specific lane is simple as well. It requires the accurate measurement of the elapsed time between the 4th and the Nth vehicle as they discharge, with reference point the stop-line. All vehicles from the first to the Nth must be in queue to obtain a valid measurement. Usually the tenth vehicle in queue is utilized (i.e., time between the front bumper of the fourth and the front bumper of the tenth vehicle as they cross the stop-line). The field saturation flow can be estimated using the following formula:

$$S_{\text{field}} = \frac{3600}{t_{4 \text{ to } N}/(N - 4)} \tag{5.5.2}$$

Accuracy of a tenth of a second is essential. An elapsed time between the fourth and tenth vehicle equal to 10.8 s results in a saturation flow of 2000 pcphgpl. An error of ± 0.5 s results in saturation flows equal to 2100 and 1900 pcphgpl, respectively. Since the formula for estimating field saturation flow is sensitive to the elapsed time, accurate digital chronometers must be used and careful measurements must be taken.

5.6 CAPACITY ANALYSIS OF UNSIGNALIZED INTERSECTIONS

5.6.1 Introduction

The unsignalized intersection is the most common type of traffic intersection. At an unsignalized intersection the service discipline is typically controlled by signs (i.e., stop or yield signs). A primary objective of a traffic engineer studying an unsignalized intersection is to determine its capacity.

There are four types of unsignalized intersections, each one with different flow and traffic control characteristics. The first type consists of one major and one minor street with stop sign traffic control at the minor street. The second type consists of two streets of equal importance where the volume is neither too low (no traffic control required) nor too high (signalization is warranted); in this case, traffic is controlled by stop signs on all approaches (four-way stop). The third type consists of two streets (or one street and an offramp) where either the flow characteristics or the geometrics (i.e., channelization) warrant yield traffic control for the minor street. The fourth type consists of an intersection where the traffic volume is low. In these traffic facilities, the right-of-way is determined by a rule; usually, the rule is first-come, first-served; in case of ties, the vehicle on the right has the priority. The first two types are commonly subject to capacity analysis.

Estimation of the capacity along the minor street as well as of the left turns from the major to the minor street of an unsignalized intersection is the goal of unsignalized intersection analysis. The most common approach is stochastic (probabilistic) modeling. Implicit in the stochastic modeling are the issues of gap distribution and gap acceptance. The stochastic modeling approach is incorporated in the *Highway Capacity Manual* [5.10] analysis of unsignalized intersections.

Gap distribution represents the distribution of gaps on the major street flow. Long enough gaps give the opportunity of service to minor street traffic. Two alternative types of arrivals are usually assumed for the directional flows on the major street: random (Poisson) and platooned. Platooned arrivals are observed in the case where a signalized intersection exists upstream and/or downstream of the unsignalized intersection; after the stopped vehicles receive the green, they arrive at the unsignalized intersection in platoons.

The most common probability distribution representing the headways (gaps) on the major street is the exponential distribution (i.e., random arrivals correspond to exponential interarrival times). In the case of platooned arrivals, the lognormal distribution best approximates the distribution of headways [5.20].

Gap acceptance, on the other hand, describes the drivers' behavior, such as the probability of accepting a gap of certain size given the type of maneuver desired (i.e., cross the major street, or turn right or left on the major street). The driver's physical and mental condition, the perception of risk, and the characteristics of acceleration and handling of the vehicle that he or she drives play a certain role in the decision of gap acceptance or rejection [5.21].

5.6.2 Two-Way-Stop Controlled Intersections

The traffic flow process at an unsignalized intersection is complicated since there are many distinct vehicular movements to be accounted for, all of which operate stochastically. Most of these movements conflict with opposing vehicular volumes. These conflicts result in decreasing capacity, increasing delays, and increasing potential for traffic accidents.

Figure 5.6.1 illustrates conflicts at an unsignalized intersection with stop control on the minor street. T_c^{RT}, T_c^{TH}, and T_c^{LT} denote the critical gaps for the

Figure 5.6.1　Identification of conflicts at an unsignalized intersection (northbound movements on the minor street not shown).

right-turn, through, and left-turn movements from the minor street, respectively. For a specific movement, a gap equal to or longer than the critical gap may be accepted by a driver waiting on the minor street. Theory, intuition, and empirical results indicate that

$$T_c^{\text{RT}} < T_c^{\text{TH}} < T_c^{\text{LT}} \tag{5.6.1}$$

The left turns from the major street to the minor street have the top priority among all the permitted movements. Only after left-turning vehicles from the major street have been served can vehicles from the minor street be served.

Sometimes, servicing may occur simultaneously (i.e., left turn from major and right turn from minor executed at the same time). It is also proper to assume that long gaps may be utilized by more than one vehicle on the minor street (i.e., multiple utilization of gaps [5.22]).

The distribution of headways on the major street, together with the gap acceptance behavior, enable the derivation of the potential capacity of a stop-controlled minor street. This is the first step in the HCM procedure for analysis of unsignalized intersections (Fig. 5.6.2). The plots in Fig. 5.6.2 were derived by using the following formula for potential capacity estimation [5.23]:

$$C_p = \frac{e^{-(\alpha-\beta)}}{e^\beta - 1} V_c \quad \text{with } \alpha = \frac{V_c T_c}{3600}, \quad \beta = \frac{V_c T_s}{3600}, \quad T_s = \frac{1}{2} T_c + 0.5 \quad (5.6.2)$$

where

V_c = sum of major street traffic volumes which conflict with the movement analyzed

T_c = critical gap

T_s = follow-up gap; the gap in addition to T_c needed to serve the second, third, etc. vehicle in multivehicle gap utilization

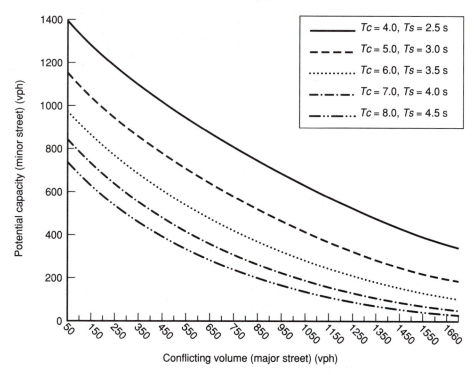

Figure 5.6.2   Potential capacity of minor street of an unsignalized intersection.

The plots in Fig. 5.6.2 are close to those illustrated in the HCM (Fig. 10-3, p. 10-7) but *not* identical, because the authors of the manual do not reveal the definition of T_s. Equation 5.6.2 incorporates K.G. Baass's definition of T_s [5.23].

The potential capacity needs adjustment according to the directional flows and the totals of opposing volumes for each movement on the minor street. The adjustments in the 1985 HCM process have been criticized with regard to their reasonableness and accuracy [5.23–5.25]. The British have abandoned this approach, while the Germans have revised their methodology (the HCM process is a modified version of an early German methodology).

This brings up a new stage of development in this area: unsignalized-intersection capacity analysis based on statistical models derived from empirical observations. According to this method, geometric characteristics of the intersec-

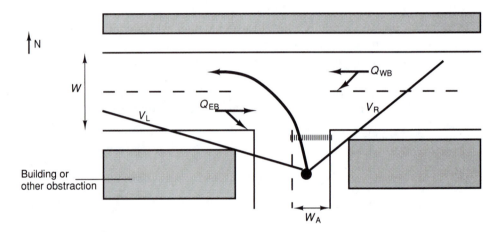

Capacity of the left-turn movement from the minor street:

$$C_{LT} = X_{LT}\,[\,\alpha - (1 - \beta W)\,(\gamma Q_{WB,TH} + \delta Q_{WB,LT} + \varepsilon Q_{EB,TH} + \zeta Q_{EB,RT})]$$

$$X_{LT} = [1 + \eta\,(W_A - \theta)][1 + \iota(V_L - 120)][1 + \kappa(V_R - 150)]$$

where
Greek letters represent empirically determined coefficients
W = width of the major street
W_A = width of the minor street approach at the stop-line
V_R, V_L = visibility distances, right and left, respectively
TH, RT, LT = through, right and left turn, respectively

Figure 5.6.3   Field data-based econometric approach for unsignalized intersection capacity estimation (model form developed at TRRL [5.25, 5.26]).

tion, visibility distances, and directional volumes on the major street are the inputs in the model for capacity estimation.

For example, the capacity of a left-turn movement at a T-intersection is estimated by the model in Fig. 5.6.3 [5.26]. Field data [5.25] indicate that speeds on the major street ranging between 15 and 50 mi/h do not have a significant effect on the minor street capacity. Daylight, night, and degree of illumination have an effect on minor street capacity: Capacity is highest under daylight conditions. These parameters are not incorporated in the statistical models because usually volumes on both major and minor street are light at night. Section 9.2.6 presents a comprehensive example of unsignalized-intersection capacity analysis as part of a traffic impact study.

5.6.3 All-Way Stop-Controlled Intersections

The capacity of all-way stop-controlled (AWSC) intersections is comparatively easy to assess. It should be clear to the reader that capacity is different from potential capacity. Several adjustments must be applied on potential capacity to yield capacity. The analysis of AWSC intersections is easier because all users must stop. Thus the service process becomes more mechanistic and less stochastic, which makes the derivation of representative models easier. Actually, the critical entity in AWSC intersection capacity is the average intersection departure headway. Secondary parameters are the number of cross lanes, turning percentages, and distribution of volume on each approach.

Figure 5.6.4 presents the basics of a proposed process [5.27] for calculating the capacity of each approach of an AWSC intersection. First an approach is selected for analysis. This becomes the subject approach. The approach opposite to the subject approach is called opposing approach, and the approaches on the sides of the subject approach are called conflicting approaches. The superscripts s, o, and c utilized below stand for subject, opposing, and conflicting approach, respectively.

The capacity is estimated as follows:

$$c = 1000V_\%^s + 700V_\%^o + 200L^s - 100L^o$$

$$- 300LT_\%^s + 200RT_\%^s - 300LT_\%^c + 300RT_\%^c \qquad (5.6.3)$$

where

$\qquad c$ = capacity of the subject approach, in vehicles per hour

$\qquad V_\%^s$ = proportion of the intersection volume on the subject approach

$\qquad V_\%^o$ = proportion of the intersection volume on the opposing approach

$\qquad L^s$ = number of lanes on the subject approach

$\qquad L^o$ = number of lanes on the opposing approach

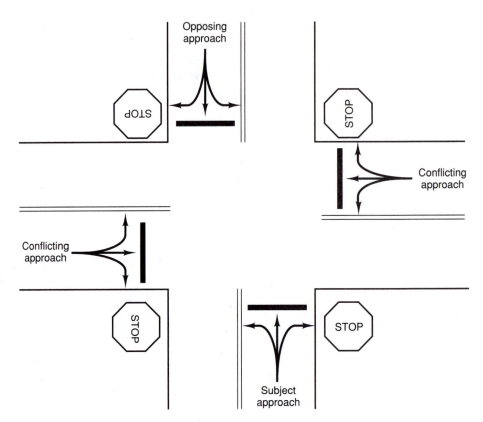

Figure 5.6.4   All-way stop-controlled intersection and example assignment of approaches for capacity and performance analysis.

$LT^o_\%$ = proportion of volume on the opposing approach turning left

$RT^o_\%$ = proportion of volume on the opposing approach turning right

$LT^c_\%$ = proportion of volume on the conflicting approaches turning left

$RT^c_\%$ = proportion of volume on the conflicting approaches turning right

The application of this formula is straightforward, as illustrated in Example 5.7 later in this section. The only required inputs are the number of lanes on each approach and accurate traffic volumes per movement for all approaches. Notably, the process is adaptable to T intersections or intersections with one or two one-way streets (simply, certain factors of Eq. 5.6.3 are not applicable).

The average delay on the subject approach is derived as follows:

$$D = e^{3.8(v/c)}$$ (5.6.4)

where

$$D = \text{delay on subject approach, in seconds per vehicle}$$

$$v = \text{volume on subject approach}$$

$$c = \text{capacity of subject approach (estimated by Eq. 5.6.3)}$$

After the first approach is done, another approach is selected and the roles of subject, opposing, and conflicting approaches are reassigned. The calculations continue until all approaches are analyzed.

It is suggested [5.27] that delay between 10 and 20 s corresponds to level of service C, which is acceptable in most cases. This is consistent with the British practice of utilizing $v/c = 0.85$ as the onset for long queues and delays [5.26]. For $v/c = 0.85$, Eq. 5.6.4 yields an average delay of 25 s per vehicle, which corresponds to LOS D (typically, not acceptable).

This empirically derived methodology for analysis of AWSC intersections should be applied only within a specified range of valid input conditions, as specified by its authors [5.27].

Example 5.7

An all-way stop-controlled intersection has one lane on each of its four approaches. The following traffic volumes were collected.

	Left turn	Through	Right turn	Total
Eastbound (EB)	75	300	50	425
Westbound (WB)	75	200	50	325
Northbound (NB)	50	250	50	350
Southbound (SB)	50	200	50	300

Estimate the capacity and delay of the NB approach.

Solution

$$V_\%^s = \frac{350}{425 + 325 + 350 + 300} = 0.25$$

$$V_\%^o = \frac{300}{425 + 325 + 350 + 300} = 0.214 \qquad L^s = 1 \qquad L^o = 1$$

$$LT_\%^o = \frac{50}{300} = 0.167 \qquad\qquad RT_\%^o = \frac{50}{300} = 0.167$$

$$LT_\%^c = \frac{75 + 75}{425 + 325} = 0.2 \qquad RT_\%^c = \frac{50 + 50}{425 + 325} = 0.133$$

Substitution in the capacity equation (5.6.3) results in $C = 463$ vehicles/hour. Then $D = e^{3.8}(350/463) = 17.7$ s/vehicle (LOS C).

5.6.4 Signalization Warrants

The type of intersection control is selected from the *Manual on Uniform Traffic Control Devices* (MUTCD) [5.28], which lists the criteria that need to be fulfilled before selecting a type of intersection control. MUTCD lists 11 alternative warrants for judging whether the signalization of an unsignalized intersection is appropriate. If one warrant is met, signal control should be considered. It is recommended that capacity analysis and safety investigation be conducted before a decision to signalize is made: The capacity, performance, and safety under signal control need to be assessed and compared to existing conditions.

The warrants for signalization are as follows:

1. *Vehicular volume*. A minimum total volume on the major street and a minimum volume on one of the minor street approaches is required.
2. *Interruption of continuous traffic*. Traffic on major street is heavy and continuous, which does not allow safe service to the vehicles on the minor street.
3. *Pedestrian volume*. Pedestrians crossing the major street exceed a stated minimum.
4. *School crossings*. The available gaps in traffic are not sufficient in number and length for the safe crossing of schoolchildren.
5. *Progressive movement*. Signalization should be considered if it will enhance the flow between neighboring signalized intersections which is interrupted by existing unsignalized intersection(s).
6. *Accident experience*. Signalization should be considered if all other measures for accident reduction are not applicable or if they were not effective enough.
7. *Systems*. Signalization may encourage concentration and organization of traffic flow along a signalized intersection network.
8. *Combination of warrants*. Signalization may be justified if 80% of the values stated in warrants 1 and 2 are satisfied.
9. *Four-hour volumes*. This is similar to warrant 1 but for any 4 h on a typical day.
10. *Peak-hour delay*. Signalization should be considered if undue delay is experienced along the minor street.
11. *Peak-hour volume*. This is similar to warrant 1 but for the peak hour on a typical day

MUTCD furnishes values or ranges of values for each of the aforementioned warrants so that existing conditions can be compared with minimum requirements.

It has been proposed [2.27] that compatibility should be established between the unsignalized intersection analysis of the HCM and the warrants of MUTCD. Presently, the potential capacity, capacity, and delay estimated with the HCM procedure are not linked to MUTCD warrants.

5.7 SUMMARY

In this chapter we addressed the topic of vehicular stream interruptions. The basic elements of transit stations were described, and a model of the capacity of on-line stations was developed. The analysis of urban signalized and unsignalized intersections was considered next. Various signal systems were presented and a method for coordinating a series of fixed-cycle, pretimed signalized intersections was discussed. Widely accepted methods for analysis of signalized and unsignalized intersections were presented, followed by a presentation of field measurement needs and techniques. The analysis of intersections is constantly being updated and revised. A new *Highway Capacity Manual* is planned by the year 2000. It is expected that the capacity analysis for signalized intersections will be modified to better accommodate intersections with actuated signal controllers, and the capacity of unsignalized intersections may be revised completely to conform to empirical evidence [5.27, 5.29]. It should be mentioned that a large number of computer programs are available for capacity analysis of signalized and unsignalized intersections: HCS, MONITOR, NCAP, SICA, SIGCAP, SOAP84, and many more. The reader may consult reference [5.30] and other university centers for lists of capacity analysis software.

5.8 EXERCISES

1. Using the data of Example 5.1, calculate and discuss the station capacity that would result from varying the number of vehicles per train from $N = 2$ to $N = 5$.
2. Computerize the solution procedure for Exercise 1.
3. Estimate the optimal cycle length and the green intervals for the intersection shown in Fig. E5.3. Assume that phase A serves the north–south traffic and phase B serves the east–west traffic. Lost time is equal to 3 s per phase and amber is equal to 4 s. The width of each lane is 10 ft and the prevailing saturation flows are as follows:

$$s(TH + RT) = 1700$$

$$s(LT) = 300 \text{ which reflects permitted operation.}$$

Figure E5.3

Figure E5.5

4. Estimate the signal timings for the intersection of Exercise 3 assuming a four-phase operation. Phase A serves north–south left turns only, phase B serves north–south traffic (no left turns permitted), phase C serves east–west left turns only, and phase D serves east–west traffic (no left turns permitted). Assume 3 s lost per phase and amber equal to 3 s. The saturation flow for protected left turns is 1700.

5. Evaluate two phasing schemes for the intersection and traffic loads illustrated in Fig. E5.5: (a) two-phase operation: north–south (phase A), east–west (phase B); and (b) a three-phase operation north–south (phase A), east–west left turns (phase B), and east–west right turns and through (phase C). Take lost times equal to 3 s per phase and amber equal to 4 s. The following saturation flows prevail: $s(TH,RT,LT) = 1200$, $s(TH,RT) = 1700$, $s(TH,LT) = 500$ (LT permitted), and $s(LT) = 1700$ (LT protected). Select the best of these two phasing schemes (must furnish quantitative proof other than cycle length which is not a description of efficiency).

6. At time $t = 485$ s after the reference time, a traffic signal is 22 s into its cycle. Assuming that the cycle length is 90 s, calculate the signal's offset.

7. Show graphically that the answers to parts (a) and (b) of Example 5.2 are correct.

8. For the system of intersections of Example 5.3, calculate the width of the through band that would result from changing the offsets at intersections A, B, and C to 10, 60, and 20 s, respectively.

9. Assuming that the street of Exercise 8 is a two-way street, calculate the width of the through band in the other direction.

10. Given a speed of 45 mi/h and the accompanying data, determine whether a balanced signal coordination exists.

Intersection	Green (s)	Amber (s)	Red (s)	Offset (s)	Distance from A (ft)
A	30	5	15	5	—
B	25	5	20	0	660
C		Unsignalized			1430
D	20	5	25	25	1980
E	30	5	15	5	3300

11. Construct a computer program that calculates the through band widths for a series of N intersections given (a) the signal cycles, (b) the signal offsets, (c) the distances between intersections, and (d) the design speed.

12. Given the intersection shown in Fig. E5.12 and the table of adjustment factors calculate the prevailing saturation flows for each lane, for two levels of ideal saturation flow: 1800 and 2000 vphgpl. If the cycle length is 60 s and the total lost time is equal to 7 s, what is the effect of the saturation flow estimates on overall level of intersection utilization (X_c)?

	f_w	f_{HV}	f_g	f_p	f_{bb}	f_a	f_{RT}	f_{LT}
Approach A	0.93	1.00	1.025	0.80	1.00	1.00	1.00	0.85
Approach B	1.00	0.93	1.00	0.70	0.96	1.00	0.85	1.00

Parking

300   250

N

A

700

12-ft lanes, 15% HV, level
grade, high parking
activity, 10 buses/hr stop,
non-CBD area

B

425

Bus stop

10-ft lanes, 0% HV, 5%
downhill, medium
parking activity, no bus
stops, non-CBD area

Figure E5.12

13. Conduct capacity analysis for the intersection approach illustrated in Fig. E5.13. Make a table with the following columns: v, s, v/s, g, C, g/C, c, v/c, d_1, d_2, PF, delay, LOS, whole approach delay, and whole approach LOS. It will be best if a spreadsheet is used for analysis.

14. For the intersection shown in Fig. E5.14, conduct analysis for each approach and for the intersection as a whole (delay and LOS). Deliver a table similar to the one in Exercise 13.

15. Derive better signal timings for the intersection of Exercise 14 and check to see whether the intersection performance improves. Maintain the same phasing scheme and assume total lost time of 10 s. Use of spreadsheet software is strongly recommended.

16. Consider the three factors that play an important role in average delay per vehicle: cycle length (C), green split (g/c), and degree of saturation (X or v/c). Conduct an analysis to identify which of these three factors has the most critical effect on delay. Assume that the progression factor is 1.0 and take $c = 1000$ for the overflow delay only. You need to conduct a sensitivity analysis. Select a range of values for each factor (e.g., 60 to 130 for C, 0.1 to 0.9 for g/c, and 0.2 to 1.2 for X). Then hold two factors constant at the midpoint of their range and vary the third factor. Take the delay estimates and discuss the results.

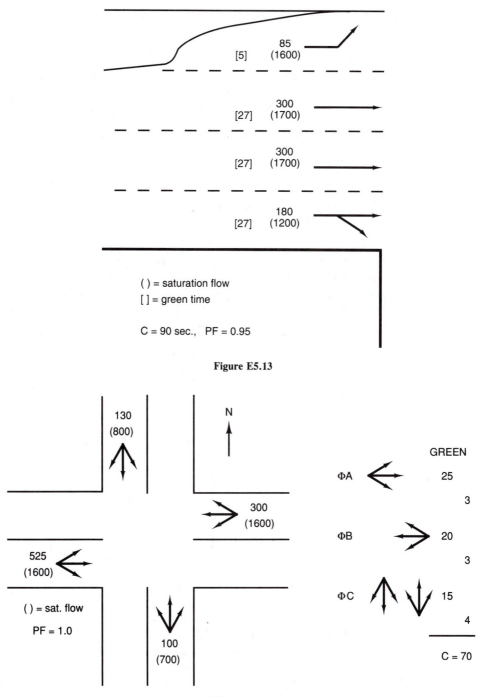

85
[5]   (1600)

300
[27]   (1700)

300
[27]   (1700)

180
[27]   (1200)

( ) = saturation flow

[ ] = green time

C = 90 sec.,   PF = 0.95

Figure E5.13

130
(800)

N

GREEN

ΦA   25

3

300
(1600)

ΦB   20

525
(1600)

3

ΦC   15

( ) = sat. flow

PF = 1.0

4

100
(700)

C = 70

Figure E5.14

17. The following data were collected in the field for the two through lanes of an approach. The stopped vehicle counts were

    10, 12, 18, 24, 16, 7, 0, 0, 3, 11, 16, 8, 0, 5, 13, 18, 28, 15, 9, 0

    every 20 s. If the corresponding vehicle volume is 178, what is the average delay per vehicle?

    Saturation flow measurements: A total of 15 measurements was obtained. They represent the elapsed time between the fourth and the Nth vehicle in queue. Estimate the mean saturation flow and the range of one standard deviation around the mean.

	1	2	3	4	5	6	7	8	9	10	11	12	13	14	15
Time	12.3	11.9	7.6	11.4	11.7	15.0	15.3	16.1	11.7	12.6	12.0	7.8	18.9	11.8	12.2
Nth	10	10	8	10	10	12	12	12	10	10	10	8	14	10	10

    Given these saturation flow measurements, can the hypothesis of $s = 1800$ be statistically rejected at the 95% confidence level? (*Hint*: Conduct a t test.)

18. Given the unsignalized T intersection illustrated in Fig. E5.18, calculate the potential capacity of each lane on the minor street using the HCM formula. If the volumes on the minor street are 140 and 190 for the left and right turns, respectively, would the

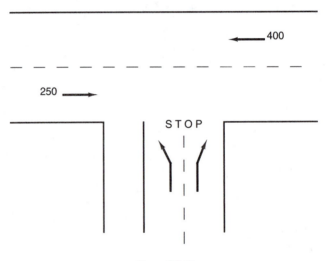

Figure E5.18

    minor street be expected to operate adequately, or are long delays likely to occur? The critical gap sizes are as follows: LT = 6.5 s, RT = 5.0 s.

19. Conduct potential capacity analysis for the intersection illustrated in Fig. E5.19 using the HCM formula and taking critical gaps equal to 5.0 s for right turns and 7.0 s for through and left turns. If the volumes per movement are as follows: (1) = 200, (2) =

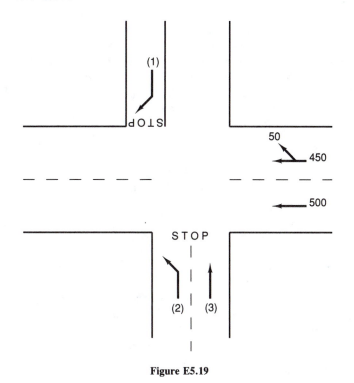

Figure E5.19

300, (3) = 250, what is the expected performance of each movement? If there is a capacity problem, what can be done about it?

20. Estimate the capacity and delay of the EB, WB, and SB approaches of Example 5.7.

21. Assume that the unsignalized intersection of Example 5.7 and Exercise 20 is signalized with a 60-s cycle evenly divided between two phases (east–west and north–south) and with amber duration of 3 s at the end of each phase. Using $s = 1700$ vphgpl for each approach, estimate the capacity and delay for each approach and compare them with those for AWSC operation. Which traffic control operation is better?

5.9 REFERENCES

5.1 HIGHWAY RESEARCH BOARD, *Highway Capacity Manual*, Special Report 87, National Research Council, Washington, D.C., 1965.

5.2 VUCHIC, VUKAN R., *Urban Public Transportation Systems and Technology*, Prentice Hall, Englewood Cliffs, N.J., 1981, p. 556.

5.3 PIGNATARO, LOUIS J, *Traffic Engineering Theory and Practice*, Prentice Hall, Englewood Cliffs, N.J., 1973.

5.4 INSTITUTE OF TRANSPORTATION ENGINEERS, *Transportation and Traffic Engineering Handbook*, Prentice Hall, Englewood Cliffs, N.J., 1976.

5.5 NATIONAL ELECTRICAL MANUFACTURERS ASSOCIATION, *Traffic Control Systems*, NEMA Standards Publication TS 1–1983, NEMA, Washington, D.C., 1983.

5.6 YAUGH, P. J., "Traffic Signal Control Equipment: State of the Art," National Highway Research Program, Synthesis of Highway Practice 166, Transportation Research Board, National Research Council, Washington, D.C., 1990.

5.7 MCSHANE, W. R., and R. P. ROESS, *Traffic Engineering*, Prentice Hall, Englewood Cliffs, N.J., 1990.

5.8 BERRY, D. S., *Notes on Traffic Engineering*, unpublished, Northwestern University, Evanston, Ill., 1978.

5.9 FEDERAL HIGHWAY ADMINISTRATION, *TRANSYT 7-F: User's Manual*, FHWA, Washington, D.C., 1987.

5.10 TRANSPORTATION RESEARCH BOARD, *Highway Capacity Manual*, Special Report 209, National Research Council, Washington, D.C., 1985.

5.11 ———, *Interim Materials on Highway Capacity*, Circular 212, National Research Council, Washington, D.C., 1980.

5.12 JOVANIS, P. P., P. D. PREVEDOUROS, and N. ROUPHIAL, *Design and Operation of Signalized Intersections in Illinois*, Final Report for the Illinois DOT, Northwestern University, Evanston, Ill., 1987.

5.13 JOVANIS, P. P., A. J. KHATTAK, and N. ROUPHIAL, *Design and Operation of Signalized Intersections in Small Urban Areas in Illinois*, Final Report for the Illinois DOT, Northwestern University, Evanston, Ill., 1988.

5.14 BOX, P. C., and J. C. OPPENLANDER, *Manual of Traffic Engineering Studies*, 4th ed., Institute of Transportation Engineers, Washington, D.C., 1976.

5.15 ORGANISATION FOR ECONOMIC CO-OPERATION AND DEVELOPMENT, *Traffic Measurement Methods for Urban and Suburban Areas*, OECD Publications, Paris, 1979.

5.16 MICHALOPOULOS, P. G., *Automated Extraction of Traffic Parameters through Video Image Processing*, Department of Civil Engineering, University of Minnesota, Minneapolis, 1989.

5.17 BERRY, D. S., "Volume Counting for Computing Delay at Signalized Intersections," *Institute of Transportation Engineers Journal*, 57, 5 (1987): 21–24.

5.18 TRANSPORTATION RESEARCH BOARD, *A Program of Research in Highway Capacity*, Transportation Research Circular 371, National Research Council, Washington, D.C., 1991.

5.19 PREVEDOUROS, P. D., "Actuated Signalization: Traffic Measurements and Capacity Analysis," *Proceedings of the 61st Annual Meeting of the Institute of Transportation Engineers*, Milwaukee, Wis., Sept. 1991.

5.20 ———, "A Model of Unsignalized Intersection Capacity Based on Erlang-3 Gap Distribution," in *Intersections Without Signals*, W. Brilon, ed., Springer-Verlag, Berlin, 1988, pp. 165–179.

5.21 DAGANZO, C., "Estimation of Gap Acceptance Parameters within and across the Population from a Direct Roadside Observation," *Transportation Research*, 15B (1981): 1–15.

5.22 TROUTBECK, R., "Average Delay at an Unsignalized Intersection with Two Major Streams Each Having a Dichotomized Headway Distribution," *Transportation Science*, 20, 4 (1986): 272–288.

5.23 BAASS, K. G., "The Potential Capacity of Unsignalized Intersections," *Institute of Transportation Engineers Journal* (1987): 43–46.

5.24 KHATTAK, A., and P. P. JOVANIS, "Capacity and Delay Estimation Approaches for Unsignalized Intersections: Conceptual and Empirical Issues," *Transportation Research Record* (1990).

5.25 TAYLOR, M. C., "UK Techniques for the Prediction of Capacities, Queues and Delays at Intersections without Traffic Signals," in *Intersections without Signals*, W. Brilon, ed., Springer-Verlag, Berlin, 1988, pp. 274–288.

5.26 KIMBER, R. M., "The Design of Unsignalized Intersections in the UK," in *Intersections without Signals*, W. Brilon, ed., Springer-Verlag, Berlin, 1988, pp. 20–34.

5.27 TRANSPORTATION RESEARCH BOARD, *Interim Materials on Unsignalized Intersection Capacity*, Transportation Research Circular 373, National Research Council, Washington, D.C., 1991.

5.28 FEDERAL HIGHWAY ADMINISTRATION, *Manual on Uniform Traffic Control Devices*, U.S. Department of Transportation, Washington, D.C., 1988.

5.29 TRANSPORTATION RESEARCH BOARD, *A Program of Research in Highway Capacity*, Transportation Research Circular 371, National Research Council, Washington, D.C., 1991.

5.30 MCTRANS, CENTER FOR MICROCOMPUTERS IN TRANSPORTATION, *1991 McTrans Catalog*, Transportation Research Center, University of Florida, Gainesville, Fla., 1991.

6

Urban Transportation

6.1 INTRODUCTION

The movement of people and goods within cities is a special area of transportation with several unique characteristics. A large number of modes compete or complement each other in providing transportation services in cities (Figure 6.1.1). Urban transportation is among the most important components ensuring the vitality of an urban area. A dense network of transportation services affects the efficiency of operations in an urban area. Furthermore, there is a direct connection between transportation and city growth: Transportation can promote or hinder development and expansion. The opposite is also true: Vibrant, growing urban areas invite expansion or implementation of new transportation facilities and services.

This chapter begins with an overview of the historical development of urban areas in the United States, followed by a presentation of the major transportation modes involved. Then a series of current urban transportation issues are presented. A special section focuses on emerging advanced technology techniques aimed at alleviating parts of urban transportation problems.

6.2 HISTORICAL BACKGROUND

The historical development of urban areas suggests that population settlements occurred beside harbors, lakes, canals, and rivers. These settlements evolved into cities. Later, cities were developed along and in crossroads of major railroad lines

(a)

(b)

(c)

Figure 6.1.1 Several urban transportation modes. (From *1990 Annual Report*, Transportation Research Board, National Research Council, Washington, D.C.)

and highway routes. All these interactions can best be put in perspective by observing the historical development of U.S. cities and their transportation networks. Figure 6.2.1 illustrates the *parallel* chronological evolution of cities and urban networks. In the beginning cities had a main street where most businesses and services were located. Residences were scattered along secondary "roads." Main streets were usually the "urban" parts of trails connecting neighboring settlements.

Expansion over time created a distinct city core where mostly businesses were located. The city core included a usually grid-shaped downtown road network on which horse-drawn carriages and trams were rolling. The city core was surrounded by residential neighborhoods. Public transportation (carriages and trams) were connecting the neighborhoods with the city core. Several industrial sites were adjacent to the city core at that time. Suburbs began their legal wars against encroachment of their sovereignty by the central city, thereby setting limits to the expansion of the central city. This is the prevalent way in which city limits were defined.

The next stage of evolution brought cities close to the shape recognized

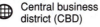

Main street
(stores) and
scattered
residences

City core and
residential
neighborhoods

CBD within the central city.
The city is surrounded by
primarily residential suburbs.

⊕ Central business
district (CBD)

• Neighborhood or ethnic
business centers

Explosive growth of suburbs
with satellite business districts.
Residences and employment
expand to exurbia.

○ Suburban (satellite)
business centers

◎ Previously independent
communities become part
of the metropolis, or large
cities form conurbations

(a)

Main
Street

Downtown network
and radial arterials

Radial network of urban
freeways and rail or transit
corridors to facilitate
suburb-to-CBD movement

▨▨ Rail / transit
▬▬ Freeways

Beltways and circumferential
connections of freeways to
facilitate suburb-to-suburb
movement. Bypasses direct
through traffic away from the
urban freeways

(b)

Figure 6.2.1 Historic evolution of (a) cities and (b) parallel evolution of urban transportation
networks.

today. The city core became an exclusive business center (central business district: CBD), often including high-rise office buildings. Pollution and efficiency concerns pushed industrial zones in the outskirts of the central city. Ethnic and neighborhood business centers were developed within the city limits.

The major trend at this stage was the exodus to the suburbs, which were viewed as quiet bedroom communities, providing a socially proper setting for raising a family. The transportation network followed as well as fostered this trend. Radial corridors of public transit and highways were developed to bring the suburban workers to their work places in the central city where most employers were located. Downtown areas began experiencing traffic congestion problems, pollution problems, and lack of adequate parking space. The oil crises of the 1970s gave a major boost for developing and expanding public transit systems.

The next stage represents present times in which cities still reshape and adjust to demographic, social, and economic trends. The worsened levels of pollution, density, services, and safety of central cities further encouraged people to move to the suburbs. An outer ring of suburbs growing at high rates started developing in the 1980s. At this stage, businesses and employers followed the residents in the exodus to the suburbs. As a result, satellite business districts were developed in the outer suburban ring (e.g., Tysons Corner in Washington, D.C., Naperville and Schaumburg in Chicago, Orange County in Los Angeles). Furthermore, the expansion of metropolitan limits swallowed small independent towns of the past and minimized the distance between neighboring metropolitan areas (e.g., Washington, D.C. and Baltimore, Chicago, and Milwaukee).

Most suburban development took place along major roadway and/or passenger rail thoroughfares. Beltways (circumferential expressways) were installed or are planned to be installed to divert through traffic away from congested urban freeways. On the other hand, public transportation started going through major adjustments while trying to operate under increasingly reduced subsidies. The ridership of central city buses and subways has been declining due to the increasing number of people working in the suburbs, while the ridership of commuter railroads and suburban bus operations has been increasing slowly. Traditional forms of public transportation may be losing the battle of ridership attraction and financial survival because their effectiveness is substantially reduced in low-density environs such as the suburbs.

6.3 SERVICES AND COSTS

A large number of city activities and services are heavily dependent on transportation: Emergency medical services, street and highway maintenance, police, mail collection and delivery, fire protection, utility connections and repairs, snowplowing, street cleaning, refuse collection and disposal, public transportation services, taxis, school bus service, commercial transport of people and goods, transportation of hazardous materials, and private transportation and mobility [6.1].

The costs of services requiring transportation vary with respect to densities (of people and activities), vertical buildup, and city size. There is a continuous debate regarding the size of the city at which the total cost of services per inhabitant is minimized. There does not seem to exist a unique answer to this issue, partly because of definition problems (i.e., decision makers tend to consider public costs only, while minimization of the total of both public and private costs would result in best public welfare) as well as complex relationships between costs of services and densities [6.2].

Pollution and congestion are additional costs related to transportation. The effects of pollution are twofold: negative effects on the health of humans, animals, and vegetation, and expenditures for pollution reduction and cleanup. Wasted productive time due to extended travel times is another cost component (i.e., value of time lost). This has occurred because of congestion, systems malfunction, and lengthened commutes (partly caused by the dispersion of activity locations). Costs and measures against pollution and traffic congestion are discussed in Section 6.6.

6.4 MODES

Urban transportation needs are served with a multitude of modes. The primary access mode of transportation in urban areas is walk. The share of this mode is negligible, however, for line-haul trips (i.e., home-to-work trips). Line-haul urban trips are served by the following modes or combinations of these modes.

1. *Private automobile,* which can be in the forms of drive alone, drive with passenger(s), or passenger in a private car. Carpooling is the organized commute to work by car with a minimum of two people aboard. The most common form of carpooling is intrahousehold, where two or more members of the household utilize the same car. Carpooling between co-workers is less popular despite its potential to reduce the net amount of traffic substantially.

2. *Van-pooling* is the voluntary or company-organized commute to work. Either a group of individuals agree to hire a commercial van-pool provider (thereby cutting down their commuting costs by forgoing the purchase and/or use of a car) or companies provide transportation to and from work. In several areas that experience severe congestion problems, pressure is applied on employers to reduce the number of trips generated by their employees through the institution of car and van pools.

3. *Taxis* are owner-operators or private companies that provide transportation to the general public. Major markets for taxis are tourists, visitors, and businesspeople. Also, people in a hurry and people who do not need a car at their destination tend to hire taxi services (i.e., airport dropoff).

4. *Buses* usually belong to a public mass transit system or to private operators and companies. Nonmass transit bus services include tour services, schoolchildren transportation, labor transportation, and company-organized van pools. Buses provide high accessibility because they can run through neighborhoods, but a lower level of service than that of fixed-guideway mass transit because they often have to use congested routes.

5. *Light rail* is the present name for trolleys or electric streetcars. Several U.S. cities have light rail systems in operation today (i.e., Portland, Pittsburgh, San Jose, San Francisco). This type of urban transportation is particularly common in older European cities. Light rail operations can be inefficient in congested urban sections since they operate on arterials along with vehicular traffic. In addition, their bulky and slow nature may worsen traffic conditions [6.3].

6. *Rail rapid-transit systems* are common in large U.S. cities. Atlanta, Boston, Chicago (Fig. 6.4.1), Los Angeles (a small system began operations in 1990), New York City, San Francisco, and Washington, D.C. have such systems. Operations include trains of four to 10 railcars with stations every $\frac{1}{4}$ to 5 mi, depending on densities. At present, all U.S. systems involve the classic technology of electric-powered cars with steel wheels running on steel rails. The major advantage of these systems in terms of operating efficiency is that they operate on an exclusive right-of-way that isolates them from other traffic, thereby giving them the ability to offer relatively fast (i.e., compared with private auto), on-time service. Major disadvantages of these systems are the high implementation cost, the high

Figure 6.4.1   Elevated rapid transit rail system (Chicago). *Source*: Photography by P. D. Prevedouros.

levels of subsidy required for their implementation and operation (i.e., typically, only a fraction of the operating costs is recovered from the fare boxes), and their inflexibility in following shifts in demand. In contrast, buses can easily be rerouted, so they can respond to changing demands more effectively.

7. *Commuter (or regional) rail systems* primarily connect distant suburbs with financially affluent population to suburban centers and the central business district of the central city. The average trip length of commuter rail passengers was 21.4 mi in 1988 [6.4]. Such systems are unique to a handful of cities (i.e., New York and Chicago). Commuter railroads use large passenger cars and often run on freight railroad lines. Commuter systems offer much shorter travel times compared with private automobiles and rapid-transit systems, due to the fewer stops and the high average speed between stations.

8. *Air and water services* are provided in a few metropolitan areas. Transportation of corporate executives and government officials with helicopters is quite common, while passenger ferry services are offered in some places (i.e., the Staten Island ferry in New York City).

Usual combinations of modes are *park-and-ride*, according to which individuals drive their autos to transit terminals, park, and use public transportation for the line-haul trip to work, and *kiss-and-ride*, according to which a car passenger is dropped off at a terminal. This mode is common among family members, particularly in families where the number of cars is fewer than the number of workers.

The use of various modes is heavily dependent on the pattern of origins and destinations, which is itself constantly changing. The changes have a strong effect on the number and types of trips needed as well as on the modes chosen.

6.5 URBAN TRANSPORTATION ISSUES

At present, three-fourths of the 250 million trips made by Americans each day are made in metropolitan areas, while over 80% of these trips are made by private motor vehicles [6.5]. Heavy trucks carry freight into and out of cities, and smaller trucks and vans are used for local delivery. Many cities have ports and airports which are primary entry or exit points for passengers and cargo originating from or destined to a broad area. All these functions generate substantial traffic loads for the urban networks.

Several transportation problems plague contemporary urban areas, the most prevalent being traffic congestion. Traffic congestion is created on fixed-capacity road networks when traffic grows beyond a point, after which the level of service deteriorates to unacceptable levels (Fig. 6.5.1). The capacity of the roadway system is to a large extent determined by the transportation system characteristics and policies, such as geometry, signalization characteristics, and traffic manage-

Figure 6.5.1 Generation of traffic congestion.

ment restrictions (i.e., high-occupancy vehicle lanes, bus lanes, reversible lanes). To a lesser extent, roadway system capacity is determined by the driving habits of the population, the size and average acceleration rate of vehicles, the weather conditions, and so forth.

The growth of traffic is affected by four major factors: (1) the natural growth of population, (2) locational patterns (i.e., spatial distribution of residence, work, shopping, and entertainment places), (3) transportation characteristics and policies, and (4) transport behavior of individuals and households manifested in their mode, departure time, and route choices.

The transport behavior of people is affected by the characteristics and norms of individuals and households, which along with the locational patterns of places and activities are affected by the evolution of the society, the economy, and the technology at a regional and national level. Furthermore, most of the factors affecting traffic growth are time dependent. As the society, the mix of households, and the culture evolves over time, the time and space characteristics of traffic change. (More will be said about transport behavior in Section 8.6.)

The effects of traffic congestion are multiple; they include (1) loss of productive time; (2) loss of fuel; (3) increases in pollutants (both because of the additional fuel burned and because more toxic gases are produced while engines are in idle or in stop-and-go traffic); (4) increases in the wear and tear of automobile engines; (5) high potential for (usually, low impact) traffic accidents; (6) slow and inefficient emergency response and delivery services; and last but not least, (7) people's moods are often affected, which has negative impacts on productivity at work and on personal relationships. The summation of all these effects yields a grand loss for the society and the economy of an urban area.

Other major urban transportation problems are the inefficient utilization of systems (i.e., peaks and valleys in travel demand), infrastructure financing (i.e., capacity expansion versus rehabilitation, highways versus transit; and source and share of financing: local, state, federal, and private), special transportation provisions for the elderly, disabled, and low-income people, environment (i.e. concerns of emissions and noise pollution as well as balancing the conflicting demands for environment quality and efficient and affordable transportation), safety, and incorporation of technological innovations for the partial solution of some of the problems above.

Solution strategies for alleviating urban transportation problems may be classified in three categories: pricing, policy and management, and technology-based. *Pricing* can be administered through roadway use tolls, parking charges, mass transit fares, fuel surtaxes, and area-wide road use pricing. The latter is discussed in Section 6.6.5. Objectives of pricing may be the following: (1) provision of disincentives for using private automobiles (through higher costs of utilization, e.g., parking pricing is a major disincentive against private automobile use.); (2) provision of disincentives for using private automobiles without passengers (i.e., reduce drive-alone mode share with free parking and/or other benefits for carpoolers); (3) provision of funds to operate and expand mass transit systems (cross-subsidization: use of fuel and other auto-specific taxes to finance public transit operations); and (4) development of fare structures aimed at spreading the morning and evening peaks on the public transit systems (i.e., offering lower off-peak fares).

Management and policy include measures such as:

1. Ramp metering that controls the flow entering freeway facilities so that they operate close to optimal flow levels (i.e., throughput maximization: q_{max} in Fig. 3.4.5).

2. City zoning,[†] which may enable authorities to (a) control the number of major traffic generators along congested corridors, (b) establishment of sensible allocations of land for future development given present constraints and expansion plans for the transportation network, and (c) enforcement of balanced employment and residential development, which has the potential to reduce long home-to-work trips [6.6].

3. Flex-time or staggered work hours, which may help spreading the morning and evening peaks of travel demand.

4. Restricted access, according to which private or all vehicles are prohibited from certain streets or urban sections (i.e., transitways and pedestrian malls).

---

†Zoning is discussed in detail in Chapter 7.

5. Regulation of parking, delivery zones, and times of certain operations, aimed at avoiding chaotic conditions (multiple parallel parking, bottlenecks, and other hazards).

6. Demand-responsive public transportation, which is a nonscheduled passenger service aimed at helping people with mobility problems or serving low-density locations where regular public transportation would be wasteful and less attractive to the public (i.e., fixed route stops may be too far from residences).

7. Incentive strategies aimed at reducing the number of automobiles on the roads and improving the efficiency of public services. High-occupancy vehicle (HOV) lanes, bus-only (often contra-flow) lanes to speed up bus operations, as well as incentives to use a car or van pool are primary options.

Advanced technology strategies include roadway applications (i.e., smart cars/smart highways, route guidance, collision avoidance, convoying, remote parking reservation, and area-wide road pricing), alternative fuels (i.e., electricity, methanol- or hydrogen-powered vehicles), and telecommunications (i.e., satellite office operations). Several of these technologies are presented in the next section.

6.6 EMERGING TRANSPORTATION TECHNOLOGIES

6.6.1 Introduction

Several urban transportation technologies are in the experimental or limited real-world application state today. These emerging technologies, herein referred to as advanced technologies, have a substantial potential in revolutionizing urban transportation as it is known today. The objectives of advanced urban transportation technologies are fivefold: systems efficiency improvements through information (informatics), safety, pricing, capacity enhancements, and pollution reduction.

6.6.2 Informatics

Highway surveillance with loop induction detectors or closed-circuit cameras, real-time variable message signs along highways and major thoroughfares, route guidance, vehicle navigation, and parking information and reservation are the basic technological components of informatics.

A substantial portion of delays are due to unpredictable events such as disabled vehicles, accidents, and bad weather conditions. Nearly 2 billion potentially productive hours are wasted annually due to traffic congestion. It is estimated that these delays cost over $16 billion in 1989 in lost productivity. By the turn of the century this estimate may reach $90 billion if nothing is done to reverse the causes of congestion [6.7].

Highway surveillance (smart highways) is a system that gathers information on traffic conditions and delays, and informs motorists quickly so that they can take alternative routes and avoid adding to congestion [6.7, 6.8]. The information to motorists can be disseminated with variable message sings, regular radio frequencies, overriding radio frequencies as well as directly on in-vehicle guidance systems, along with a suggested optimal path for going from a current position to the desired destination (smart cars).

Real-time route guidance [6.9] involves the keying-in of origin and destination points by the motorists on the in-vehicle guidance equipment (miniature display terminal as in Fig. 6.6.1, processor, and keypad). Essential components of route guidance are the automatic vehicle identification and communication of the in-vehicle guidance unit with a central computer that oversees the road network operations and advises individual motorists (in-vehicle equipment) or groups of motorists (variable message signs, etc.).

Navigation capabilities exist today, and they can be added to the route guidance equipment. Detailed city maps stored on optical disks can be accessed by the in-vehicle processor, which can suggest the shortest path from a given point to a desired destination, the location of which may be unknown to the vehicle operator. This service may be particularly useful in large urban areas, where most

Figure 6.6.1 Example of dashboard layout including route guidance devices. (From *TR News*, No. 152, Transportation Research Board, National Research Council, Washington, D.C., 1991.)

people are unfamiliar with several sections, and to people who are unfamiliar with the general area. Delivery operations and taxi companies may also benefit from the introduction of such systems. Navigation will suggest the shortest path between two points, distance-wise, while route guidance, given information from the central computer, will suggest the minimum path time-wise.

The integration of navigation, real-time route guidance, and continuous highway and signal network surveillance forms a management system called IVHS (intelligent vehicle-highway system). IVHS is rapidly becoming the center of attention for urban traffic management. Large pilot projects are being deployed in Europe, Japan, and the United States to assess the merits of such integrated, computer-aided information and control systems under real-world conditions [6.10]. Parking information and reservation involve similar equipment, which, in addition, will inform motorists about available parking places and charges at the destination point; it may also enable them to reserve a space if desired.

All the systems above involve a central processing unit which gathers information on roadway and parking utilization and then feeds back the users with proper information so that the whole system operates at its best, given the level of traffic demand [6.10, 6.11].

6.6.3 Safety

Roadway accidents costs reached $65 billion in 1989. This is the outcome of 45,450 deaths and hundreds of thousands of injuries. The estimated costs include medical expenses, property damage, lost time, and so forth [6.7]. Collision warning, collision avoidance, and night vision are the primary advanced technology components aimed at improving roadway safety. All systems engage a tele-sensing devise (radar) which gathers information for the conditions ahead (usually within 100 to 500 ft). Collision warnings are sounded or displayed if the driver fails to adjust the speed or position of the vehicle to maintain a safe distance or avoid an imminent collision.

Collision avoidance systems are more sophisticated. An in-vehicle computer controls engine and brake functions, which enable it to intervene and adjust speed, acceleration, or deceleration characteristics so that a collision will be avoided or its impact will be less severe.

Night vision or artificial vision are systems that are able to detect hazardous conditions ahead, which the driver ignores or has no ability to realize (e.g., pedestrians at night and in rain, approaching a curve too fast, hidden stop sign, yield sign, or red signal or approaching a sign too fast.)

6.6.4 Capacity

Collision avoidance with speed and headway keeping capabilities, along with lane keeping capabilities, are the essential technological components of convoying which would enable passenger cars to be driven on exclusive lanes at high speeds (i.e., 60 mi/h or higher) with a minimal distance between them. The result of this would be a substantial increase of the throughput of expressway facilities. This system involves the surrender of all driver functions to a computer in the automobile. This may be unacceptable for many road users, while the liability concerns from potentially disastrous accidents give this technology a lower priority than that of informatics-based technologies, which have the potential to improve the network-wide performance by better allocating demand (vehicles) on the roadway network [6.12].

Fixed guideway facilities for buses as in Fig. 6.6.2 is a technological innovation that increases the capacity and level of service of public bus transportation.

Figure 6.6.2   Fixed guideway bus system in Essen, Germany. (From Essener Verkehrs AG [6.13].)

This technology essentially provides an exclusive right-of-way for buses, primarily along congested corridors. Slightly modified buses can operate both on streets as well as on exclusive guideways. These systems require extensive infrastructure because the bus guideway is similar to the metro-rail guideway. This system, however, is inherently more flexible than rail systems because the same buses can operate off the guideway on regular streets. This, in turn, may create a disadvantage because schedules may not be maintained closely if bus routes include non-guideway portions (traffic congestion effects). Guided bus systems have been implemented in Essen, Germany and Adelaide, Australia [6.13].

6.6.5 Pricing

Many argue that the improvements of existing, and investments in new urban transportation systems should be absorbed by the users and not by the total tax-paying population. This would require an extensive vehicle identification and pricing system. Pricing could discourage driving into congested areas, while it will gather revenues for transportation systems improvements.

The first step would be automated tolls, where vehicles pass under a toll structure instead of stopping and remitting the toll. According to this technology, all vehicles will be equipped with a tamper-free transpondent that will be transmitting the license plate number to receivers located at the toll plazas. The charge will be done automatically, and the users will be receiving monthly bills of toll charges, much like the itemized telephone bills.

The system can be expanded to cover city zones. Each time a zone is crossed, a specific change is debited [6.14]. In addition, on- and off-street public parking could become automated in the same fashion; for example, instead of parking meters there will be receivers recording the duration of parking of each automobile, which, as mentioned earlier, electronically transmits its license number continuously or after request by a toll or parking receiver/transponder. Again, a central accounting computer will be receiving and processing the user charges.

A major problem with the vehicle identification technology is the ability to monitor citizens' activities (the Big Brother syndrome), which in several countries, including the United States, could be unacceptable constitutionally. Additional social equity concerns plague road pricing systems. Since the charges are going to be equal for every motorist, the impact of road use charges on lower-income users would be disproportionally high compared with the impact on financially affluent users (i.e., such a pricing system seemingly discourages use of the roads by low-income people).

6.6.6 Environment

Pollution can be improved with stricter emissions standards. Politically set standards, however, may be meaningless or counterproductive if technological advances cannot fulfill them at reasonable costs for the consumers and users [6.15]. For example, electric vehicles, which at present can carry up to three passengers, may be functional for urban activities, but additional conventional autos (i.e., equipped with internal combustion engines) will be required for large households as well as for excursion and long-distance business travel [6.16]. Also, complex trade-offs arise; for example, electric vehicles are practically emissions-free, but the plants that produce electricity are not. Thus the entire picture of pollution sources and consequences must be envisioned before decisions are made.

The emissions of internal combustion engines can be reduced with alternative fuels such as reformulated gasoline, methanol, compressed (or liquefied) natural gas, and hydrogen. Many tests are in progress for these fuels. The cleanest and most efficient of all is hydrogen, but production, distribution to stations, vehicle refueling, and fuel tank problems need much research and experimentation before actual implementation [6.15]. Of all alternative fuels, reformulated gasoline (i.e., M85 is 85% gasoline and 15% methanol) has reached several U.S. markets. Also, ceramic diesel engines for heavy vehicles, already in mass production by a Japanese manufacturer (HINO), are the most energy-efficient internal combustion engines today.

Extensive research in internal combustion and jet engine technology, exhaust systems, insulation methods and materials, tires, and noise barriers is aimed at reducing the transportation-generated noise. Curfews and noise standards provide additional incentives to researchers, manufacturers, and operators in reducing noise levels from transportation equipment.

6.6.7 Telecommunications

Telecommunication services [6.8] are being expanded continuously to improve the efficiency of information transactions, which may result in less dependence on transportation. Telecommunication per se is the transportation of information via electronic networks. Comprehensive transportation of information via electronic networks may result in fewer needs for travel.

Teleconferencing and teleshopping are two major applications that reduce the need for travel. Teleconferencing is the technology that allows people or parties to meet without being physically in the same room. Real-time picture and voice connections enable all parties to confer. The visual media are major users of teleconferencing today. Teleshopping is still in primitive stages in the United States. The old form of teleshopping is catalog shopping, followed by placement of order(s) by mail or telephone. The advanced form requires cable connections of television sets or personal computers. The individual teleshoppers can connect to a large network of banks, retailers, specialty shops, airlines, and so forth, and perform the desired transactions without having to visit the bank, the store, and so on.

Telecommuting [6.17] is another application according to which satellite offices are developed at which neighboring employees go to work and transmit their work to the central offices. This way, long commutes to the central location are replaced by telecommuting connections. Telecommuting also gives the ability to work at home for professions whose product of work is transmittable through electronic devices (i.e., writers, reporters, engineers, designers, data processing personnel, etc.).

An emerging technology in telecommunications is that of the integrated services digital networks (ISDN), which will permit the real-time transmission of all types of information (i.e., voice, text, and images). Such a service linked to upgraded telephone devices will improve human contact from a distance, thereby reducing some needs for travel.

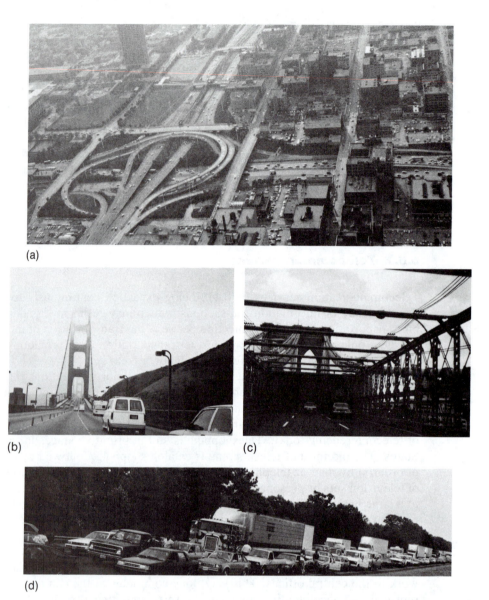

(a)

(b)   (c)

(d)

Figure 6.7.1 Urban roadway infrastructure is vital to the economic life of a city (a). Often, the supplied capacity falls far short of travel demand, while resources for maintenance and expansion are scarce (and opposition is often fierce). The problem is worse on arterials with bridges (b, c). Not only are bridges classic traffic bottlenecks during rush hours, but also their age and heavy utilization raise concerns about their safety. Congestion often reaches intolerable levels (d) and advanced technologies have been called upon to help drivers on alternative paths (e). Public transportation is a potential solution to congestion. However, the level of service offered as well as the safety and security must be nearly impeccable in order to attract large numbers of automobile users. Illustrations (f) and (g) depict rapid transit systems in New York City and Hamburg, Germany. For congested CBDs, the walk or taxi mode (h) may be most efficient over short distances. (Photographs by P. D. Prevedouros.)

(e)

(f)

(g)

(h)

Figure 6.7.1 *Continued*

6.7 SUMMARY

In this chapter we presented an overview of urban transportation. The presentation was largely focused on the historical development of urban areas and their respective transportation systems as well as on the modes serving their transportation needs. Current issues of urban transportation and procedures for the resolution of these issues were presented analytically. Figures 6.7.1 through 6.7.3 summarize most of the issues and elements of urban transportation systems.

Transportation is inseparably connected to cities. This is a two-way connection: A prosperous and expanding city generates needs for new transportation infrastructure and services. On the other hand, expansions of transportation infrastructure and improvements of services offered invariably invite urban growth

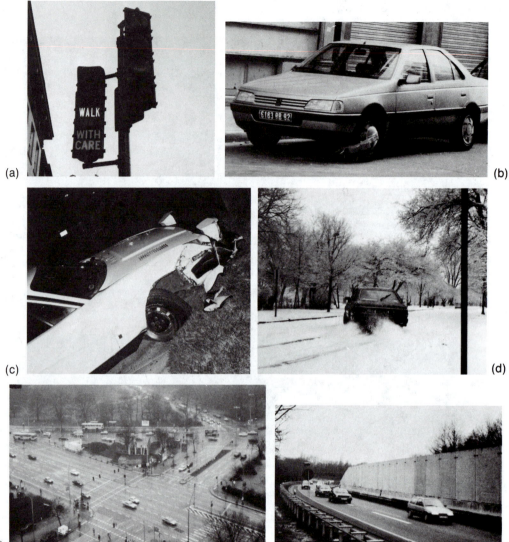

Figure 6.7.2 Signalized intersections are a necessity in urban areas. Great attention should be paid to the efficient movement of vehicles and the safe processing of pedestrians (a). Parking is a major issue in urban areas and increasingly severe penalties are imposed on violators (b). Traffic accidents in urban areas (c) are another major issue; congestion and, most importantly, intoxication, are the leading causes of these. In addition to loss of life or the loss of normal, productive life, and the losses due to material damages, a great impact of accidents is the critical deterioration of traffic flow, particularly on expressways and main arterial streets. Cities in snow-belt states face additional traffic problems and higher rates of accidents due to inclement weather (d, e). Two other problems in urban areas are pollutant emissions [smog is visible in Fig. 6.7.1(a)] and noise from traffic. Noise barriers are an (often esthetically unappealing) necessity for high-speed, heavy-traffic roadways adjacent to residential neighborhoods (f). (Photographs by P. D. Prevedouros.)

and stimulate local economies. This is the main reason behind the attention paid to urban transportation systems and the efforts for resolution of their problems. The solution of urban transportation problems is for the sake of the cities and the people and not for the sake of the systems per se.

Figure 6.7.3 The ever-increasing intercity movement via rural highways (a), rail (b) (which is becoming a most appealing option for fast intercity travel for distances less than 1000 miles), boat (c), or airplane (d) places heavy demands on urban transportation networks. Air travel has been and is expected to continue to grow. This places high demands on airfields (e) and airports (f) which are often managed by cities, as well as on air traffic control systems (g). Airfields need to expand but face great opposition due to noise and pollution impacts. Airport terminals need to expand to facilitate increasing numbers of passengers, but convenience is compromised by the long walking distances within. Air traffic control has to direct with utmost efficiency and safety an ever-increasing number of incoming and outgoing flights. (Photographs by P. D. Prevedouros.)

(f)   (g)

Figure 6.7.3   *Continued*

6.8 REFERENCES

6.1 LARSON, R. C., and A. R. ODONI, *Urban Operations Research*, Prentice Hall, Englewood Cliffs, N.J., 1981.

6.2 THOMSON, W. R., "A Preface to Suburban Economics," in the *Urbanization of the Suburbs*, Sage Publications, Beverly Hills, Calif., 1973, pp. 409–430.

6.3 EUROPEAN CONFERENCE OF MINISTERS OF TRANSPORT, *Changing Patterns of Urban Travel*, ECMT, Paris, 1985.

6.4 ENO FOUNDATION FOR TRANSPORTATION, *Transportation in America: A Statistical Analysis of Transportation in the United States*, 8th ed., EFT, Washington, D.C., 1990.

6.5 U.S. DEPARTMENT OF TRANSPORTATION, *Moving America: New Directions, New Opportunities,*, Vol. I: *Building the National Transportation Policy*, U.S. Government Printing Office, Washington, D.C., 1989.

6.6 CERVERO, R., *Suburban Gridlock*, Center for Urban Policy Research, Rutgers University, New Brunswick, N.J., 1986.

6.7 LARSON, T.D., "Transportation Innovation and Technology: Moving America into the 21st Century," *Institute of Transportation Engineers Journal* (1990): 17–20.

6.8 THE INSTITUTE OF ELECTRICAL AND ELECTRONICS ENGINEERS, "Europower: Looking Ahead to 1992, *IEEE Spectrum* (1990): 20–62.

6.9 ORGANISATION FOR ECONOMIC CO-OPERATION AND DEVELOPMENT, *Route Guidance: An In-Car Communications System*, Road Transport Research Series, OECD Publications, Paris, 1988.

6.10 ILLINOIS UNIVERSITIES TRANSPORTATION RESEARCH CONSORTIUM, *Scope, Feasibility and Cost of a Dynamic Route Guidance System Demonstration*, Final report to the Illinois DOT, Aug. 1990.

6.11 ORGANISATION FOR ECONOMIC CO-OPERATION AND DEVELOPMENT, *Dynamic Traffic Management in Urban and Suburban Systems*, Road Transport Research Series, OECD Publications, Paris, 1987.

6.12 UNDERWOOD, S. E., K. CHEN, and R. D. ERVIN, *The Future of Intelligent Vehicle-Highway Systems: A Delphi Forecast of Markets and Sociotechnological Determinants,* presented at the *69th Annual Meeting of the Transportation Research Board*, 1990.

6.13 ESSENER VERKEHRS, A. G., *Spurbus Essen: Information on the Research and Development Project Guided Bus Essen*, 1986.

6.14 COMMISSION OF THE EUROPEAN COMMUNITIES (DIRECTORATE F), *R+D in Advanced Road Transport Telematics in Europe*, CEC, 1990.

6.15 TRANSPORTATION RESEARCH BOARD, "Transportation and Air Quality," *TR News 148*, Special Issue, 1990.

6.16 WANG, Q., M. A. DELUCHI and D. SPERLING, *Emission Impacts of Electric Vehicles*, presented in the 69th annual meeting of the Transportation Research Board, 1990.

6.17 STATE OF HAWAII, DEPARTMENT OF TRANSPORTATION, *Hawaii Telework Center: Demonstrating Innovative Ways to Reduce Traffic Congestion*, Hawaii DOT, 1989.

7
Transportation Planning

7.1 INTRODUCTION

Many treatises and learned essays have been written about the subject of planning and the role of the professional planner in various societal functions. One hears of urban, economic, financial, corporate, industrial, water resource, environmental, and many other kinds of planning. In the field of transportation, professional designations such as highway planner, airport planner, and urban transportation planner, are common. It is thus clear that planning is considered to be an important function in modern society and that, whatever this function is, it has a specific focus—that is, it is concentrated in particular areas, subjects, or systems.

For the purposes of this book, planning may be defined as the activity or process that examines the potential of future actions to guide a situation or a system toward a desired direction, for example, toward the attainment of positive goals, the avoidance of problems, or both. Being the conceptual, premeditative process that precedes a decision to act in a certain way, planning is a fundamental characteristic of all human beings. However, as a focused professional discipline, planning is viewed in a wider, yet bounded, context.

The most important aspect of planning is the fact that it is oriented toward the *future*: A planning activity occurs during one time period but is concerned with actions to be taken at various times in the future. However, although planning may increase the likelihood that a recommended action will in fact take place, it does not guarantee that the planned action will inevitably be implemented exactly as conceived and on schedule. Another time element of importance to planning's forward-looking perspective is the lag between the time when the action is to be taken and the time when its effects are felt. This time lag depends on many factors, including the scope and magnitude of the contemplated action.

It is often said that everything is related to everything else. Therefore, any event or human action affects everything else, ultimately in ways that are beyond the limits of human comprehension. As a matter of practicality, planning is not a search for ultimate answers but only a means to specific ends that is based on the proposition that better conditions would result from premeditative as opposed to impulsive actions. How much premeditation is necessary (i.e., how much planning is good planning) in a particular situation is always an open question: Too little planning is almost like no planning, and too much planning is self-defeating, as it leads to inaction.

By necessity, any particular planning effort has a limited scope and is oriented toward bringing about specific desirable ends. Since desirability cannot be divorced from the value system of human beings, planning is necessarily directed toward the satisfaction of the goals and objectives of particular groups of people. However, within its social context, planning cannot afford to ignore the reactions of other groups; it must, in fact, anticipate these responses as well. In addition, when the group on behalf of which planning is undertaken is heterogeneous, the planning effort must deal with the presence of internal conflicts relating to specific objectives and aspirations. This is especially critical when the government participates in or regulates the planning effort.

The fundamental purpose of transportation is to provide efficient access to various activities that satisfy human needs. Therefore, the general goal of transportation planning is to accommodate this need for mobility. Within specific contexts, however, whose mobility, for what purpose, by what means, at what cost and to whom, and who should do the planning and how are questions that are not amenable to easy answers. Contemporary responses to these questions are largely rooted in history and have been influenced by a confluence of many factors, including *technological innovations, private interests*, and *governmental policies*.

The purpose of this chapter is to illustrate the dynamic nature of transportation planning by briefly tracing this evolutionary process for the case of land transportation. The main objective of the chapter is to bring about an appreciation of the complexity of the transportation-planning methodology, which cannot be said to have reached a historical finality, and to highlight, in broad strokes, its most fundamental elements. More detailed coverage of the colorful history of the U.S. transportation system and of evolving transportation planning issues may be found in the literature (e.g., [7.1–7.8]).

7.2 HISTORICAL DEVELOPMENT IN THE UNITED STATES

7.2.1 Colonial Era

The migration of European settlers to North America, which led to the establishment of cities, occurred by sea. Thereafter, water transportation using the coastline and natural inland channels was the major form of long-distance transportation. Chartered privately owned ferries offered for-hire service on the rivers. Movement over land utilizing human and animal power was cumbersome and was inhibited by topographic obstacles. Following English practice, the responsibility for planning, building, and maintaining roads rested with local jurisdictions. The use of these primitive roads by travelers was free of charge and their construction and maintenance was accomplished primarily by statute labor, an English practice that required all men over 16 years of age to work on the roads on appointed days.

7.2.2 Turnpikes and Canals

Following the War of Independence, the new nation was underdeveloped, and its immediate transportation needs were primarily related to simple *accessibility* between the cities lying primarily on the eastern seaboard and toward the unexplored lands to the west. The available technology to this end consisted of wagons and coaches for land transportation and boats and barges for movement on rivers and canals. Two major problems that had to be overcome were topography and finance. Because of debts incurred during the war, the states were not in a financial position to accommodate increasing demands to provide the needed facilities. Some states had been obliged a little earlier to adopt the practice, introduced in England a century earlier, of allowing private companies to plan and construct transportation linkages and to charge tolls for their use. This practice ushered in the turnpike and canal eras, during which hundreds of companies were chartered by the states to operate as regulated monopolies. Turnpikes were named for a pike, or pole, that was turned to allow access to the roadway after the payment of the toll. Minimum design standards such as roadway width and maximum gradients were usually included in the charter requirements. The states participated in varying degrees in the construction of these facilities by conferring the right to eminent domain for the taking of land and building materials, by subscribing to company stock, and in some cases by direct subsidies.

At the beginning, the role of the federal government was confined to the building of military roads. Otherwise, a strict interpretation of the U.S. Constitution commanded respect for the sovereignty of the states in matters of local concern including transportation. Indirectly, however, the federal government aided transportation development through land surveys of its territorial holdings, the sale of which was its major source of income. The first national transportation facility inventory was undertaken in 1807 by the secretary of the treasury, Albert Gallatin, who in his report a year later clearly recognized the importance of a good national transportation system to the growth and unity of the nation. Gradually, the federal government took carefully measured steps toward land grants to the states for roads and canals. It also moved toward the allocation of proceeds from land sales to the states to be used for transportation development, among other purposes. A notable exception to the hands-off federal policy was the construction, after bitter debate, of the first national road, the Cumberland Road, through Maryland, Virginia, and Pennsylvania. This road was later extended to Ohio, Indiana, and Illinois. Inadequate congressional appropriations for maintenance and a determination that the federal government was not empowered to charge user tolls led to the transfer of the road to the aforementioned states.

On the technological side, turnpike pavement construction of the heavily traveled routes initially employed the French method of building a heavy stone structural foundation. By 1820, the macadam method (named after the Scottish engineer John McAdam) was preferred. This method relied on the strength of the native soil, over which thin layers of small stones were packed for protection. In the area of water transportation, Fulton's successful, although not original, demonstration of steam power on the Hudson in 1807 enhanced the efficiency of this mode and eliminated the need to pull canal boats by horses, which walked along the shore. The network of individually planned turnpikes and water lines formed the basic long-distance transportation system of the nation until the arrival of the railroads.

7.2.3 Railroads

In their infancy during the early part of the nineteenth century, railroads were expected merely to provide a better roadbed for animal-drawn vehicles. The introduction of the railroad steam engine altered this notion and gave rise to railroad companies essentially as they are now known. Railroad planning and development followed the paradigm of turnpikes and canals but on a grander scale. The states extended charters to railroad companies on a line-by-line basis. When a standard gauge evolved, short lines were consolidated into fewer but larger entities. The superior performance and efficiency of the new technology caused the demise of most private turnpikes and canals.

The federal government contributed to the development of the railroads in the West via land surveys conducted by the U.S. Army Corps of Engineers between 1824 and 1838, by the imposition of tariffs on imported iron in 1832 to support the United States iron industry, and, beginning in 1850, by land grants to the railroads. In return, the recipients of land grants agreed to carry the United States mail and troops. The first transcontinental railroad was completed in 1869 with the driving of the golden spike at Promontory, Utah. The oligopolistic advantage enjoyed by the railroad companies began to be moderated by a series of government regulatory actions, which led to the passage of the 1877 Interstate Commerce Act. With regard to the railroads, this law provided for the regulation of rates and included several anticollusion clauses. The Interstate Commerce Commission (ICC) was established by this act to carry out its provisions.

As mentioned above, the railroads were favored by the government through the granting of eminent domain, that is, acquisition of privately owned land without the owner's consent. This, along with the fact that each railroad operates on its own right-of-way, generated excess capacity because of a multitude of parallel lines developed between destinations. Until 1975 the railroad industry was heavily regulated by the federal government. Due to their decline, abandonment of trackage was a necessary step for a large number of railroads. However, abandonment had the potential to cause major economic impacts to the regions served by the lines proposed to be abandoned; therefore, there was substantial resistance for the approval of such proposals. The 4R Act of 1976 made abandonment of trackage easier for railroads, while it was shown that hardship in the affected areas was hardly experienced because the motor carrier industry quickly filled the void. Furthermore, the 1980 Staggers Act gave the railroad industry the ability to compete under free-market conditions by making major changes in the regulation of rates.

7.2.4 Rural Highways

Under local control, statute labor laws, and other sources of local support, urban streets were kept in a reasonably adequate condition. Outside the cities, however, the same could be said only for short roadway spurs connecting farms and towns. The importance of good roads was appreciated but the means necessary to plan, finance, construct, and maintain them was lacking. Toward the end of the nineteenth century a good-roads movement swept the country. Newly formed associations of recreational bicyclists who had begun to brave the countryside played a pivotal role in this movement, which was consistent with the later-strengthened U.S. tradition of organized citizen participation in public planning and decision making.

The states assumed an active role in 1880 by extending aid to the counties and municipalities for the construction of public highways and by establishing highway or public roads commissions empowered with varying degrees of advisory, supervisory, and planning responsibilities. The Commonwealth Highway plan enacted by the Massachusetts legislature in 1894 was perhaps the first attempt at planning a connected statewide network of public roads.

Two experimental programs, both approved in 1893, marked the formal reentry of the federal government in the planning of rural highways. First, the U.S. Congress approved a mail-delivery experiment on specially designated rural routes beginning the 1896. Later program expansions provided a strong incentive to the states to improve certain roadways in order to qualify for mail-route designation. Second, a temporary Office of Road Inquiry (ORI) was established within the U.S. Department of Agriculture to undertake research in road-building methods and to disseminate its findings to the states. The ORI's 1899 successor, the Office of Public Road Inquiry (OPRI), was merged in 1905 with the Division of Tests of the Bureau of Chemistry that had played an instrumental role in road-building materials research to form the Office of Public Roads (OPR), the precursor of the Bureau of Public Roads (BPR). Much later, in 1966, the BPR was absorbed into the Federal Highway Administration within the then-formed U.S. Department of Transportation.

The early planning-related pioneering work of the ORI included the preparation of a national inventory of macadamized roads, the Good Roads National Map, and the compilation of statistics relating to road usage, including quantified data on trip lengths and user costs for the transportation of farm products. To help meet its charge to disseminate its findings relating to road-building technology, the ORI initiated the construction of short segments of demonstration roads. In the meantime, technological advances were rapidly bringing the motor vehicle (electric, steam, and gasoline-powered) to the forefront of U.S. transportation. In 1912, a congressional appropriation was approved, which authorized an experimental determination of the ability of good roads to effect savings to the U.S. Post Office's rural mail delivery. The first full-fledged federal highway aid was extended to the states via the Federal Road Act of 1916, which established a 50–50 construction-cost sharing between the federal government and the states, with the federal contribution to each state determined by a formula. During World War I the federal government seized the railroads and established the Federal Railway Administration to operate them. In addition, it designated a number of military highway routes for use by an increasing number of heavy trucks. This development had three major effects on highway planning after the war. First, it supported the growth of long-distance trucking; second, it renewed the need for improved road-building; and third, it emphasized the need for a physical continuity of the intrastate and interstate highway systems.

The Federal-Aid Highway Act of 1921 required each state to designate up to 7% of their existing highways as part of a national system that would be eligible for federal aid. The BPR established cooperative agreements with some states to aid in the planning and location of this system. In the process, innovative survey methods and studies were developed that had a profound effect on the shaping of transportation planning. These studies included:

> the ownership of motor vehicles; the seasonal, monthly and daily variations in traffic; the origin and destination of cargoes; the size and weight of trucks. . . . In later studies, they examined driver behavior—the average speeds of drivers traveling freely on the highway and their observance of traffic laws, such as those prohibiting passing on hills and curves. In Maine, the researchers discovered a historical relationship between vehicle ownership, population and traffic. By projecting historical trends ahead, they were able to make fair estimates of traffic 5 years in the future [7.1], p. 122.

Highway construction benefited during the Great Depression from federal work-relief programs. In 1934, the Hayden–Cartwright Act permitted the expenditure of up to 1.5% of federal highway funds to be used for "surveys, plans, and engineering investigations of projects for future construction." This led the states, through their highway departments, to undertake massive needs studies by projecting population, traffic volumes, and vehicle ownership trends into the future. The projections were used to identify highway capacity deficiencies, which in turn guided the overall highway planning effort.

The Federal-Aid Highway Act of 1944 set the nation's sights toward a national system of interstate highways and provided for urban extensions of this system. In 1945 the American Association of State Highway Officials (AASHO), a cooperative organization established in 1914 during the good-roads movement, adopted a set of geometric design policies, which became the precursors of the contemporary standards discussed in Chapter 2.

The worldwide political instabilities that followed World War II led to a requirement in the 1948 Federal-Aid Highway Act for a cooperative federal–state study to assess the nation's highway system from the perspective of national defense. This study revealed significant deficiencies in many aspects, including a lack of adequate and uniform geometric designs, and encouraged a stronger federal role in the planning of national highways. About the same time and because of insufficient highway revenues collected from user charges, the states embarked on the construction of high-standard toll highways that mostly followed or paralleled the national interstate system. Most such publicly owned turnpikes opened between 1948 and 1954, when this type of state financing appeared to be the direction of the future. This trend, however, was reversed after the extension of federal funding to the secondary system of highways and the passage of the Federal-Aid Highway Act of 1956. This act and its companion Highway Revenue Act redefined the roles of the federal government and the states in the area of highway planning and had a profound effect on the evolution of a formalized planning process. Among its major provisions were the following:

1. It mandated the construction of the *national system of interstate and defense highways*, the largest single public works undertaking of its kind, in accordance with high and uniform design standards.
2. It established a 90–10% federal–state funding basis for this interstate highway system and provided that the larger federal portion be paid from revenues collected in the form of user taxes and charges that were to be placed in a special *highway trust fund* for this purpose.
3. It required the conduct of supportive planning studies and extended the requirement for the conduct of related *public hearings* in relation to project location, first set forth in 1950, to all federal-aid projects.

7.2.5 Urban Transportation Planning

The extension of federal highway aid to urban areas that began with the 1944 Federal-Aid Act brought about a division of interests between state concerns for interstate highway system continuity on one hand and urban concerns related to local circulation and the growing urban-traffic problem on the other. This fusion of perspectives contributed to the refinement of formalized planning processes and methodologies.

During the preindustrial era, many European cities were laid out according to the conceptual designs of notable city planners. These physical plans reflected a primary concern with the aesthetic qualities of city form and with the dominant location of symbolic structures such as cathedrals and palaces. In this connection, several schools of thought evolved. Early American cities can be traced to these city-planning traditions. Williamsburg (Virginia), Savannah (Georgia), Philadelphia, and L'Enfant's plan of the nation's capital are notable examples of this trend.

During the late eighteenth and most of the nineteenth centuries, the growth patterns of U.S. cities were driven by a speculative fever, and city planning, as practiced earlier, disappeared from the scene. Most new cities and towns were built on land hastily subdivided into gridiron street patterns that followed the lines of government surveys. The same spirit permeated the growth of older cities as well; the original city plans were all but ignored, and random development of every available parcel of land ensued. Aided by the technological breakthroughs of the industrial revolution, cities entered a period of rapid expansion by absorbing a massive influx of people from rural areas and from abroad. Industrial and economic forces and the centralizing influence of railroad transportation necessitated the concentration of the population in cities. Among the major technological innovations were the steam engine, which facilitated the growth of the railroads, and the elevator and the frame-construction method, which made the skyscraper possible.

Urban planning reemerged as a professional discipline during the later part of the nineteenth century. This reemergence was aided by four developments that redefined the government's *power of eminent domain* (i.e., the power of taking private rights and property for public purposes) and the *police power* (i.e., the power to regulate the use of private property). Not necessarily in chronological order, the first development affecting modern city planning was related to an increasing involvement of city governments in the alleviation of slum conditions and the urban ills associated with them. New York enacted its first tenement law in 1867 to regulate building structures in an attempt to minimize fire hazards and to enhance the living conditions of the population. The origin of modern *building codes* can be traced here. The second trend was the practice of *districting*, or *zoning*, where the government assumes the power to regulate the use of land,— for example, for commercial, industrial, or residential purposes. Zoning was first applied in Germany in 1884 and spread through Europe before reaching the United States. The term *zone* originally referred to a concentric ring, or belt, with the central city at its center but was later taken to mean a land area of any shape and location. The first comprehensive zoning code in the United States was enacted by the city of New York in 1916. The third precursor of modern city planning is evident in the *parks movement* advocated by an emerging group of planners and landscape architects, who, praising the virtues of pastoral life, saw public parks as having a beneficial influence on the otherwise drab existence of urban populations. Land for the first major urban park in the United States, New York City's Central Park, was acquired in the 1850s. The fourth major antecedent of modern urban planning was an advocacy for the beautification of *public buildings* within dominating civic squares, the descendents of the cathedral and palace of the earlier planning philosophy. Taking its lessons from European city forms, this movement developed during the closing years of the nineteenth century. The city-beautiful planning movement of the early 1900s was a planning philosophy distilled from these trends, which emphasized the construction of monumental civic centers and urban park systems connected by wide boulevards. It helped legitimize the need for planning and brought into the planning process the civil engineering profession and its road-building and structural-engineering techniques. During this time, the cities began to establish planning commissions composed of influential civic leaders to guide the formulation and implementation of plans, relying on a cadre of consultants to carry out the work. Both practices are extant to this day.

The introduction of streetcar services (see Introduction) exerted a decentralizing influence on the urban form by facilitating an outward expansion that reached beyond the city limits in a spokelike pattern. This radial growth left an indelible impression on the way planners thought of cities for decades and directed their attention to the urban region rather than merely the city proper. Public transportation was provided by private companies franchised as public utilities and operated on city-owned streets. Proponents of city planning argued that the award of franchises should be made in an orderly fashion and in accordance with regional city plans.

Consistent with the age of mechanization, a new planning perspective gradually emerged that saw the city as a machine. Although more complex than other mechanical devices, the efficient functioning of its interrelated parts was considered to be amenable to scientific treatment. According to the developing *city practical* (also known as *city efficient* and *city scientific*) planning movement of the 1920s and 1930s, transportation was seen not only as the skeleton of a static city plan but as a force that affects the future shape of the city. As such, it was reasoned, transportation planning should become an integral part of urban planning.

The decentralizing influence of public transit was not confined to residential suburbanization but extended to industrial decentralization as well. Many new towns were built along the principles set forth in Graham R. Taylor's book *Satellite Cities* [7.9], which was influenced by Ebenezer Howard's earlier work on garden cities [7.10]. These principles are reflected in the design of modern suburban communities.

In step with the scientific approach to planning was an increasing reliance on measurement and prediction, for example, the conduct of physical, economic, and demographic inventories, the collection of transportation usage data, and the attempt to discern the relationships between these factors. This kind of planning activity was contemporaneously occurring in relation to intercity highways. Figure 7.2.1 is an early graphical display of transit route usage in the city of Newark, New Jersey [7.8]. The radial pattern of travel demand is clearly evident.

By accelerating residential and industrial decentralization not only along

Fundamental data on transit touching conditions past and present, showing routes, traffic density, time and fare zones, etc., will be required. Approximately 200,000 people enter and leave the "Four Corners" in the city of Newark upon the trolley cars each day from 7 A.M. to 7 P.M. The greatest proportion of this travel is north and west, as shown by the width of the bands in the diagram. These illustrate the proportion of travel upon each of the various routes.

Figure 7.2.1   Early transit patronage volume map: Newark, c. 1929. (From John Nolen, ed., *City Planning*. Copyright 1929 by D. Appleton & Co., renewed 1957 by John Nolen, Jr., Gerald Nolen, and Barbara Nolen Strong. A Hawthorn book. Reproduced by permission of E.P. Dutton, a division of New American Library.)

fixed radial routes but also in the spaces between them, the motor vehicle caused another revision of planning practice and also the evolution of a specialized profession, *traffic engineering*, the scope of which was primarily restricted to the orderly expansion of street capacity, parking facilities, and traffic-control strategies to accommodate the quality and safety of ever-increasing automobile flows. Among the major contributions of traffic engineering were advanced traffic and driver-behavior studies and the modeling of land use, population, and traffic demand relationships. A rudimentary model of land use and traffic was applied in San

Juan, Puerto Rico, to plan a freeway system serving a new airport. The invention of the high-speed digital computer made possible the analysis of large quantities of data and the development of more sophisticated planning methods.

By the 1940s, urban planning became an established function of city governments. The *master planning* era of the next two decades emphasized the production of comprehensive regional zoning maps and specifying the planned location of infrastructural systems, including transportation, water supply, and sewage facilities. Figure 7.2.2 shows a portion of the 1950 zoning map of the city of Honolulu, Hawaii [7.11].

The extension of federal aid to the urban portions of the national highway system in 1944 marked the definite entry of the states into the urban-planning scene. This development brought together three overlapping professional perspectives, the interaction of which was fundamental in the evolution of transportation planning: through their highway departments, the states that were predominantly concerned with the connectivity of the intrastate and interstate highway network; the city traffic engineering departments that were primarily concerned with accommodating the efficient and safe operation of the urban street network; and the city (or in some instances, regional) planning departments, which were concerned with regional land use planning, housing, and urban public transportation. Out of this interaction emerged a generally shared, quantitatively based land use–transportation planning methodology.

7.3 DEVELOPMENT OF A FORMAL PLANNING PROCESS

7.3.1 Housing Policies

Direct federal involvement in the area of housing is evident in the Home Loan Bank Act of 1932 and in the National Housing Act of 1934, which established the Federal Housing Administration (FHA). The Housing Act of 1949 set up the Housing and Home Finance Agency (HHFA) and appropriated funds for the elimination of urban blight through the clearance of slums and the redevelopment of the areas occupied by them. The Housing Act of 1954 shifted the emphasis of this program from leveling and rebuilding to urban renewal, which included the rehabilitation and preservation of existing structures in accordance with a general plan for each locality. Grants for transportation planning, including comprehensive traffic surveys and studies, were provided by the Housing Act of 1961 and administered by the HHFA, which in 1965 became part of the newly formed Department of Housing and Urban Development (HUD). The Demonstration Cities and Metropolitan Development Act of 1966 included additional assistance to urban transit and required the designation by each urbanized area of a regional organization to oversee the orderly development of the program.

Figure 7.2.2 Portion of a land-use map. (From City and County of Honolulu [7.11].)

7.3.2 The 3C Process

The federal-aid highway program was also gaining a planning perspective that was being adapted to the conditions found in urban areas. The Office of Planning was established within the BPR in 1961, and the Federal-Aid Highway Act of 1962 mandated that after 1965, state eligibility for federal highway aid in major cities would be conditioned on the existence of long-range plans that would

> be based on a *continuing, comprehensive* transportation planning process carried out *cooperatively* by states and local communities . . . [emphasis added]

It also declared that it is

> in the national interest to encourage and promote the development of transportation

PROPOSED LAND USES	
USE	ACRES
RESIDENTIAL	145
DUPLEX	—
HOTEL - APARTMENT	—
BUSINESS	—
LIGHT - INDUSTRIAL	—
HEAVY - INDUSTRIAL	—
AGRICULTURAL	685
MILITARY	—
PUBLIC USE	20
PARKS	5
CEMETERY	5

LEGEND

RESIDENTIAL
HEAVY INDUSTRIAL
PARKS
GOLF COURSE
CEMETERIES
CHURCHES
SCHOOLS
CIVIC CENTER
AGRICULTURAL
FLOOD PLAIN
MILITARY
PROPOSED ROADS
PROPOSED ROAD WIDENING

FUTURE LAND USE

EWA — HONOULIULI

systems, embracing various modes of transport, in a manner that will serve the states and local communities effectively and efficiently.

This act officially established the requirement for the *3C planning process*.

7.3.3 Social Concerns

Beginning with the movement for racial equality, which led to the passage of the Civil Rights Act of 1964 and other housing and equal opportunity laws, the decade of the 1960s was a decade of social concern. Social activists held the view, sometimes justified and sometimes exaggerated, that the slum clearance and urban highway programs were signs of a "bulldozer mentality" that was insensitive to social needs. These groups learned to organize and lobby at the local, state, and federal levels and to seek judicial relief of their grievances. The provision of public transportation was viewed as one means of addressing the needs of disadvantaged groups.

The Urban Mass Transportation Act of 1964 provided capital assistance for urban public transportation to be administered by HHFA. Federal responsibilities for urban mass transportation remained with HUD until 1968, when the Urban Mass Transportation Administration (UMTA) was established within the Department of Transportation (DOT).

The Federal-Aid Highway Act of 1968 amended the requirements of earlier highway acts relating to the economic effects of highway location to

> economic and social effects for such a location, its impact on the environment, and its consistency with the goals and objectives of . . . urban planning as has been promulgated by the community.

This law allowed the use of federal highway aid for the construction of fringe parking facilities and earmarked funding for traffic engineering measures known as the Traffic Operation Programs to Increase Capacity and Safety (TOPICS). To be eligible for matching funds, fringe parking and TOPICS projects had to be based on the 3C process.

The Urban Mass Transportation Assistance Act of 1970 provided a multiyear commitment for capital (but not operating assistance) for transit projects and encouraged the provision of mass transportation services to the elderly and handicapped, having recognized that

> elderly and handicapped persons have the same right as other persons to utilize mass transportation facilities and services.

7.3.4 National Environmental Legislation

The passage of the landmark National Environmental Policy Act (NEPA) of 1969 consolidated several trends relating to social, economic, environmental impact, and citizen participation in public decisions that were developing in various areas of federal concern including transportation. The act required that proposals for "Federal actions significantly affecting the quality of the human environment" be accompanied by

> a detailed statement by the responsible official on—
>
> (i) the environmental impact of the proposed action,
> (ii) any adverse environmental effects which cannot be avoided should the proposal be implemented,
> (iii) alternatives to the proposed action,

(iv) the relationship between local short-term uses of man's environment and the maintenance of long-term productivity, and

(v) any irreversible and irretrievable commitments of resources which would be involved in the proposed action should it be implemented.

Major transportation proposals required the preparation of such an *environmental impact statement* (EIS), the expressed purpose of which was a full and objective disclosure of positive and negative environmental effects in order to aid the decision-making process. Indirect transportation consequences (e.g., traffic congestion and needed capacity) were to be included among the impacts covered by the EIS for nontransportation actions. An important provision of NEPA was the requirement to analyze alternatives to a preferred action including a baseline (or do-nothing) alternative.

The Clear Air Act of 1970 established national ambient air-quality standards and required the states to develop plans to meet these standards. Motor-vehicle emissions were identified as major contributors to the problem. The Environmental Protection Agency (EPA), which played a central role in subsequent transportation laws, rules, and regulations, was created by this act, which was followed by a series of environmental laws relating to noise, management of coastal and other environmentally sensitive areas, protection of endangered species, water quality, and so on. The 1982 version of the guidelines issued by the Federal Highway Administration (FHWA) relating to the conduct of environmental assessments is included in Appendix A to illustrate the breadth of impacts and transportation alternatives that have been incorporated in the requirements of the 3C planning process.

The 1990 Clean Air Act Amendments tightened the pollution standards for motor vehicles and established a severity classification system for geographical areas not meeting ambient air quality standards. Nonattainment areas (as they are called) could be placed into the categories of marginal, moderate, serious, severe, and extreme. Depending on the area's category, increasingly severe requirements are set along with a timetable for compliance with the standards.

7.3.5 Toward Planning Coordination

The Intergovernmental Cooperation Act of 1968 recognized a need for a mechanism by which projects seeking federal aid could be reviewed by the various interested and affected agencies. A year later, the Bureau of the Budget issued Circular A-95, which set forth a requirement to designate specific state and metropolitan agencies as clearinghouses to facilitate the project-review process, which was thereafter referred to as the "A-95 review."

A series of highway- and mass-transportation-related laws enacted between 1970 and 1974 extended federal support to mass transit in urban and rural areas and increasingly placed federal aid for both highway and transit projects on essentially identical planning requirements. Both had to be produced by the 3C process; address the same social, economic, and environmental impacts; ensure community participation; and undergo similar agency and public reviews. This and functional overlaps between highways and transit systems using the highways motivated a closer degree of coordination between the FHWA and UMTA program requirements. In 1975, the two agencies issued joint regulations, which required each urban area to designate a single Metropolitan Planning Organization (MPO) with a widely based membership to coordinate the planning activities of the local communities and modal planning agencies within their respective regions. The MPOs were to be certified annually by both FHWA and UMTA to ensure the presence of a satisfactory 3C process. One of the duties of the MPOs was the preparation of an annually updated multimodal transportation plan for the entire metropolitan area consisting of

1. A long-range element addressing a time horizon of the order of 20 years
2. A transportation systems management element (TSME) containing the region's plan for low-cost operational improvements
3. A transportation improvement plan (TIP) specifying the region's 5-year priorities drawn from the other two elements and including an annual element (AE), which listed the programs and projects scheduled for the following year

Like its precursor (i.e., the 1969 TOPICS program), the TSM element addressed the need for short-term, low-cost operational improvements aiming for a better use of existing facilities, but in addition to traffic engineering measures, it included additional options such as carpooling, the use of taxis and other demand-responsive services, automobile restraints, changes in work schedules, and the like. The term *transportation demand management* (TDM) is often used to describe such options. TSM planning was first required by a 1976 UMTA policy statement as a possible alternative to major transit projects for which the UMTA purse was becoming insufficient. Eventually, the requirement for a separate TSM element in the annual plan was dropped, but by that time a regional TSM option became the de facto baseline alternative against which other proposals were being compared. The attempt to coordinate the FHWA and UMTA programs is also seen in the title of the Surface Transportation Assistance Act of 1978. This act shifted the emphasis of the highway program from construction of new facilities to the renovation of existing highways and authorized additional funding for transit development. Partly because of a financial inability to fund all heavy rail rapid-transit proposals, UMTA issued a policy toward rail transit in 1978, which promulgated its intent to fund such systems on an incremental basis rather than in toto and only when an alternatives analysis has shown them to be superior to all-TSM, light rail, busway, and other options.

Following a 1973 oil embargo by the Organization of Petroleum Producing Countries (OPEC), the Highway Trust Fund also experienced difficulties because of decreasing revenues from gasoline taxes and because of price inflation. Responding to this problem, the U.S. Congress enacted the National Transportation Assistance Act of 1982, which imposed an additional federal tax of 5 cents on each gallon of fuel, of which 4 cents was earmarked for highway purposes and 1 cent for transit assistance.

Toward the latter part of the 1970s, the nation showed signs of a change in mood away from federal intervention in the private sector. The federal government embarked on a trend to deregulate many sectors of the economy and to transfer the responsibility for many programs back to the states.

7.3.6 Intermodal Surface Transportation Efficiency Act of 1991

The Federal Intermodal Surface Transportation Efficiency Act (ISTEA), which was signed into law in December 1991, consisted of eight Titles as follows:

   I: Surface Transportation (mainly highways)
  II: Highway Safety
 III: Federal Transit Act Amendments of 1991
 IV: Motor Carrier Act of 1991
  V: Intermodal Transportation
 VI: Research
VII: Air Transportation
VIII: Extension of Highway-Related Taxes and Highway Trust Fund

This comprehensive transportation law gave States and urban areas unprecedented flexibility with respect to the transfer of funds between highways, transit, and other projects. The major provisions of the act included the following:

1. It mandated the designation, by 1955, of a National Highway System (NHS) consisting of approximately 155,000 miles of roadways. The NHS would include the entire Interstate Highway System, a large portion of urban and rural principal arterials, and other major roads which, collectively, are considered to be critical to interstate and international travel, national defense, and intermodal connectivity.

2. It provided increased funding for research and development in the areas of new technology including Intelligent Vehicle-Highway Systems (IVHS), high-speed ground transportation systems, magnetic levitation technologies, and electric vehicles.

3. It stipulated that each State must establish a statewide planning process and six management systems in the areas of highway pavement maintenance, bridge management, highway safety, traffic congestion, public transportation, and intermodal transportation facilities.

4. It required Metropolitan Planning Organizations (MPOs) to incorporate in their Transportation Improvement Programs (TIPs) and their long-range plans considerations of land use policies, intermodal connectivity, enhanced transit service, and management systems.

5. It permitted the use of federal transportation funds for projects aimed toward enhancing the environment such as wetland and wildlife habitat protection, air quality improvement measures, and highway beautification.

6. It strengthened the level of federal support for toll roads and allowed for private entities to own such facilities.

7. It renamed the Urban Mass Transportation Administration (UMTA) to the Federal Transit Administration (FTA) to reflect more accurately the broadened transit initiatives of the act, including an added emphasis on rural and intercity transit services.

8. It extended the Mass Transit and Highway Accounts of the Highway Trust Fund (HTF) by four years to Fiscal Year 1999, and established a National Recreational Trails Trust Fund. The federal share was set at 90% for interstate construction and maintenance projects, at 80% for most other highway-related projects and for transit capital improvements, and at 50% for transit operating assistance.

7.4 PLANNING STUDIES AND METHODS

7.4.1 Introduction

The preceding section traced the evolution of a formalized transportation planning process, by which transportation plans are produced, revised, and selected for implementation. It also identified the groups of participants in the process and the factors that were deemed relevant to the proper execution of the planning function.

The participating groups include bodies of elected officials, public agencies that have leading and supportive roles in the process, officially appointed citizen advisory commissions and committees, private- and public-transportation system operators, voluntary citizen and professional associations, and interested individuals. These groups and individuals bring into the process differing, often conflicting, and also changing goals and objectives. To complicate matters, not all these groups are particularly interested in a continuous and intensive participation in all aspects of the process; on the contrary, they often feel free to enter or exit the process at will. Moreover, the membership of these groups exhibits a considerable amount of fluidity. It is not unusual, for example, for a member of a voluntary organization to be elected or appointed to public office or for an agency representative to belong to a professional organization and to also reside in the path of a proposed facility.

Institutionalized procedures, such as the requirements for planning documents, interagency reviews, and public hearings and other means of citizen participation have evolved within the larger sociopolitical system specifically to ensure that the factors considered to be relevant to a particular situation are
adequately addressed and in order to facilitate the formation of local consensus
in an orderly manner. Transportation engineers participate in various aspects of
this complex process. One aspect of engineering involvement that merits further
treatment here is the conduct of supportive planning studies that attempt to model
and estimate *some* of the many travel, economic, social and environmental factors
that have been deemed to be important to transportation planning.

7.4.2 Antecedents to Planning Studies

The first step toward the development of the contemporary transportation-planning methodology may be traced to the conduct of land surveys that supported
the layouts of cities and towns and the locations of turnpike, canals, and—later—
railroads. The second step was the need to conduct facility inventories, such as
the first national inventory of 1807. The third step commenced when the Office
of Road Inquiry, toward the end of the nineteenth century, extended data-col-
lection efforts to include information relating to facility use, that is, traffic levels,
trip lengths, and user costs. The expanded usage studies that followed the pre-
scription of the Federal-Aid Highway Act of 1921 to plan a connected national
network and the transition to studies emphasizing highway planning to meet future
needs made possible by the Hayden–Cartwright Act of 1934 established the fundamental elements of transportation planning.

7.4.3 Planning for Future Needs

A major breakthrough of the needs studies of the 1930s and 1940s was the recognition that planning highway network extensions should not be based merely
on the static criterion of connectivity but also on continuous efforts to anticipate
future demands for travel. Initially, this was accomplished by projecting current
traffic measurements into the future by using traffic-growth factors based on discerned relationships between population and economic growth on one hand and
traffic levels on the other. For example, based on annual rates of growth in the
gross national product (GNP), traffic-growth factors in the range of 3 to 4% were
considered to be reasonable. The projected traffic levels could then be checked
against the capacity of existing highways to anticipate future capacity deficiencies
and, within financial constraints, to plan and schedule capacity improvements
accordingly. Figure 7.4.1 illustrates a 1948 statewide traffic-flow map that bears
a similarity to the urban-transit usage map of Fig. 7.2.1: The widths of the bands
shown along the various highway links are proportional to the measured link flows.
The inserted heavy flow bands in and around urbanized areas portend the need
to pay special attention to these areas.

Figure 7.4.1 A 1948 statewide traffic flow map. (From Stevens et al. [7.12].)

7.4.4 Large-Scale Urban Travel Surveys

Figure 7.4.2 shows a similar traffic flow map of pre–World War II Milwaukee and perhaps the intent of transportation planners to apply the rural travel needs methodology to urban areas. Significant differences in the patterns of urban travel, however, necessitated the development of more refined techniques. An important difference was (and still is) the fact that in urban areas, street capacities between various parts of the city involved multiple rather than single routes. If needed, capacity enhancements should consider this combined supply of roadways. Figure 7.4.3 illustrates a *desire line diagram*, which shows the region divided into smaller sectors, or *traffic (analysis) zones*, and the flows between these zones irrespective of individual roadway links. To obtain this type of information, new travel-survey and data-reduction methods were developed during the 1940s, including the *origin-and-destination (O-D) surveys* consisting of home interviews, truck interviews, taxi interviews, and parking surveys. The data on travel habits obtained from interviewing a sample consisting of 4 to 5% of the total households in the region and about 20% of the truck and taxi companies were expanded to the overall population by computer-based statistical techniques, and the actual traffic counts crossing selected *screen lines* were used to check the accuracy of the statistical expansion of the sample data [7.13]. The first large-scale travel survey of this type was conducted in Detroit.

Figures 7.4.4 through 7.4.7 illustrate the application of the needs study methodology as applied to the city of Baltimore to project 1957 (*base year*) measurements to 1980 (*target*, or *horizon, year*) freeway needs. The desire line diagram of Fig. 7.4.4 superposes the base and target year interzonal flows exclusive of the downtown area, Fig. 7.4.5 identifies the anticipated screen-line capacity deficiencies, Fig. 7.4.6 summarizes the results of a special analysis across a particular screen line, and Fig. 7.4.7 specifies the location of additional freeways selected to rectify the capacity problems disclosed by the planning study.

7.4.5 Travel Demand Forecasts

Initially, the projection of the interzonal *trip distribution* toward the target year was accomplished by applying simple growth factors to the base-year travel desire volumes in a manner that was similar to rural highway practice. Gradually, however, it became evident that the need for added capacity and parking facilities in urban areas was not uniform throughout the region but was dependent on the specific types (e.g., residential, commercial, or industrial) and intensities (residential density, workers per acre, shopping floor space, and the like) and the *land uses* found in each zone. Moreover, the expected regional growth of the population and the economic system was unevenly distributed among the zones owing to differences in the availability and suitability of developable land for various purposes, urban-planning policies (such as zoning), and accessibility. The first computer-based quantitative *land use* and *socioeconomic projection models* were de-

Figure 7.4.2   Early urban traffic flow map. (From Gamble and Ilgner [7.13].)

Figure 7.4.3   Desire-line diagram. (From MacLachlan [7.14].)

veloped by transportation planners in this connection and were later adopted eagerly by other urban planners. Mathematical *trip generation models* relating the trip-producing capability of residential areas and the trip-attracting potential of various types of nonresidential land use classes were postulated, calibrated, and validated.

Since the emphasis of these studies was placed on the urban highway system, transit trips had to be subtracted from the projected total interzonal traffic volumes to arrive at an estimate of future highway demands. *Modal split models*, such as the one illustrated by Fig. 7.4.8, were developed to help divide the total flows

Figure 7.4.4 Observed and projected desire-line diagram. (From Voorhees and Booth [7.15].)

between the two modes, highway and transit [7.16]. The planning for mass-transit services was generally left to the operators and was considered to be of secondary importance, since transit patronage was experiencing a steady decline.

Of relevance to urban highway design was a prior knowledge of the degree to which arterial street traffic would be attracted to new freeways. Having this

Figure 7.4.5   Screen-line deficiencies. (From Voorhees and Booth [7.15].)

knowledge before designing a new facility was important in determining the capacity (e.g., the number of lanes) that it should provide. Models of traffic diversion from arterials to freeways similar in shape to the model choice curve of Fig. 7.4.8 resulted. These route-choice models were later extended to cover large networks and became known as *traffic assignment models*. Thus trip-generation, trip-dis-

NATURE OF DEFICIENCIES
ACROSS JONES FALLS

— — JONES FALLS SCREEN LINE

A STUDY AREAS

2,000 4,000 6,000 8,000 10,000

PEAK HOUR VEHICULAR TRIPS

PEAK HOUR VEHICULAR TRIPS BETWEEN AREAS

AREAS	A	B	C	D	TOTAL
1	1200	685	1455	262	3,602
2	1083	—	421	205	1,709
3	5000	3840	4749	288	13,877
4	2516	295	—	—	2,871
TOTAL	9859	4820	6625	755	22,059

Figure 7.4.6   Screen-line special analysis. (From Voorhees and Booth [7.15].)

tribution, modal choice, and traffic-assignment models evolved, each intended to describe and forecast a different component of travel behavior.

The Chicago Area Transportation Study (CATS) was the first to combine land-use and socioeconomic projection models with these travel demand models to analyze regional long-range transportation alternatives. This urban transportation planning methodology was then applied to other U.S. metropolitan areas and was also taken to major cities throughout the world by U.S. consulting firms. In the process, the methodology was further refined and applied to various planning contexts.

Figure 7.4.9 is a simplified flowchart of steps involved in applying the original methodology after the conduct of planning inventories and surveys (e.g., land-

Figure 7.4.7   Identified freeway needs. (From Voorhees and Booth [7.15].)

use data, economic investigations, and travel surveys) and the postulation and calibration of models forecasting land use and travel demand to fit local conditions.

Step 1:   Forecasts for the target year of the regional population and economic growth for the subject metropolitan area.

Figure 7.4.8   Early modal split curve. (From Voorhees and Morris [7.16].)

Step 2: Allocation of land uses and socioeconomic projections to individual analysis zones according to land availability, local zoning, and related public policies.

Step 3: Specification of alternative transportation plans partly based on the results of Steps 1 and 2.

Step 4: Calculation of the capital and maintenance costs of each alternative plan.

Step 5: Application of calibrated demand-forecasting models to predict

Figure 7.4.9 Simplified version of the original urban transportation planning process.

the target year equilibrium flows expected to use each alternative, given the land-use and socioeconomic projections of Step 2 and the characteristics of the transportation alternative (Step 3).

Step 6:   Conversion of equilibrium flows to *direct user benefits*, such as savings in travel time and travel cost attributable to the proposed plan.

Step 7:   Comparative evaluation and selection of the "best" of the alternatives analyzed based on estimated costs (Step 3) and benefits (Step 6).

This methodology was (and continues to be) refined and expanded to cover additional social, economic, and environmental benefits and costs; to admit a wider range of multimodal transportation alternatives; to be more sensitive to the relationship between land-use and transportation planning; and to admit multi-agency and public participation.

7.5 OTHER PLANNING ISSUES

7.5.1 Introduction

A significant problem of the long-term transportation master-planning procedure as typically applied during the 1960s and early 1970s was the problem of joint transportation and land-use planning, the treatment of uncertainty about future policy changes, and the problem of coordinating long-range and ongoing planning. This section addresses these issues in very general terms.

7.5.2 Transportation and Land Use

That there exists an intimate relationship between transportation and land de-velopment has been understood for centuries [7.17, 7.18]. An understanding of this interaction is also evident in the principles of the city practical approach. In that case, the city form preferred by certain planners was closely related to the transportation technology of the day: radially expanding urban development along heavily traveled fixed-route streetcar and heavy rail lines. The subsequent pro-liferation of the ubiquitous automobile all but eliminated the search for ideal city forms and facilitated a wider range of urban structure possibilities. Gradually, the prescriptive nature of early master planning gave way to an adaptive approach that aimed instead at providing guidance for an orderly development of the region. To this day, zoning maps accompanied by zoning ordinances and other land-use policies remain the major tools of this approach. The zoning map specifies the type (e.g., residential, manufacturing, mixed, open space) and intensity (e.g., high-rise, low-density) of the land uses permitted at designated locations within the region. However, if developed to the limits permitted by the zoning map, the population and land-based activities in the region would far exceed the growth that is typically anticipated within normal planning horizons. The land-use policy expresses the community's principles and procedures that are intended to guide land development in desirable directions. Among these rules are provisions for the issuance of *zoning variances* (special permission to private or public-sector developers to deviate from the specifications of the current zoning map). In ad-dition to zoning-map revisions, major changes in land-development policies take place in response to changing economic, social, and political conditions.

Since the basis of long-term regional-transportation prediction models is the future land-use pattern and since the zoning map provides room for a variety of future patterns, there exists a need to forecast the most likely pattern subject to zoning constraints and current land-use policy. This is precisely the purpose of the land-use prediction phase shown in Fig. 7.4.9. However, the accumulated effect of zoning variances, the sequence in which major projects are implemented, and possible revisions of the underlying land-use policies introduce a significant degree of uncertainty to a single land-use forecast. Moreover, if implemented, major recommended modifications in the regional transportation system that are partly based on these forecasts would have an effect on the future land use by making certain areas within the region more accessible than others. This gives rise to the problem of model consistency on the grand scale: The predicted transportation demand may not be consistent with the assumptions of the land-use projection. Conceptually, the modeling of this dynamic effect may be rectified by introducing a feedback link between the output of the travel-forecasting procedure and the land-use prediction phase to facilitate an iterative equilibrium solution. If such an approach were to be taken, the transportation forecasting models used would most probably need to be simplified, at least for the larger urban areas. Specifically, the number of traffic-analysis zones would have to be kept at a minimum, whereas the transportation network would be specified at an aggregate (e.g., corridor) level rather than at the individual-facility link level. Planning analysis at a relatively high level of aggregation is known as *sketch*, or *strategic*, planning.

An alternative to the closed-form equilibrium-solution method just described is an approach that examines several alternative land-use scenarios in connection with the alternative transportation options. In this manner, the analysis of combined transportation and land-use alternatives may provide some guidance for joint planning. Although not attempting to predict a single future pattern, this approach can address a larger set of alternatives, including land-use and transportation combinations that appear to be consistent with each other. For example, a fixed-guideway rapid-transit system may be examined in relation to a potential land-use policy that guides land development along the transit corridor and especially in the vicinity of transit stations [7.19]. Sketch planning models would seem more appropriate for this type of analysis as well.

A relatively recent development in connection with land-use and transportation planning is a practice first begun in California: assessing land developers special *traffic impact fees* as a precondition for approving land development. Traditionally, this practice has been used in connection with providing other public services, such as sewers, where those residents that would gain from the new service are asked to pay part of the associated costs. In connection with traffic impact fees, the courts have held that a municipality can impose them only if it can show that the proceeds from the assessment will be used to ameliorate traffic impacts that are attributable to the proposed land development. This relationship is legally known as *rational nexus* between the development and the traffic impact fees.

7.5.3 Project, System, and Operational Planning

Long-term regional strategic planning may disclose a need to enhance the capacity of a certain travel corridor either in general terms or specifically in terms of highways or transit. In either case, it would normally not be able to supply sufficiently detailed information for *project-level* planning. Depending on the way in which the problem is expressed and its specificity regarding the admissible range of alternative options, a series of increasingly detailed planning studies leading to the stage of final design would normally be undertaken. The following quotation from a request for consultation services issued by the Honolulu Department of Transportation Services (DTS) in July 1985 illustrates this point.

> CONCEPTUAL ENGINEERING FOR HONOLULU RAPID TRANSIT. To reactivate specific planning and engineering elements of the Honolulu Area Rapid Transit Study. Develop architectural, engineering, and operating system design criteria. Develop elements of definitive engineering, architectural and operating system plans, and geotechnical investigations as necessary. Develop elements of supplemental EIS as necessary to handle major alignment and/or station shifts from current approved HART EIS. Develop materials for the conduct of public information and citizen involvement programs to keep people apprised on program development and to obtain inputs to aid system design. Perform new ridership estimates based on land use changes based on the approved Development Plans and the OMPO Long-Range Program ([7.20], p. D-10).

OMPO is the metropolitan planning organization that has been designated as the 3C process-coordinating agency for the island of Oahu, where the city of Honolulu is located. Close study of this terse statement can help the reader appreciate the issues discussed in this and earlier chapters of the book.

In addition to multimodal regional sketch planning and planning for new capital-intensive projects, there exists a variety of ongoing planning studies at various geographical scales and time horizons for the modal components of the regional system. To illustrate this point, consider the following requests for consulting services issued by the Honolulu DTS at the same time as the one quoted earlier.

> COMPREHENSIVE ISLAND-WIDE TRANSIT SYSTEM STUDY. Develop short-, intermediate-, and long-range bus transit plans including improvements for bus fleet, maintenance facilities, and transit operations. Other tasks include on-board bus survey, evaluation of existing system, transit financing feasibility of use of small shuttle bus concept and contract supplemental bus service.

With regard to traffic operations:

> OAHU VEHICLE COUNTS AND TRAVEL DATA. Collect and process current traffic data in order to permit evaluation of both the effectiveness of short-term improvements and the accuracy of travel forecasts on both State and County facilities.

The three planning studies just described would be undertaken more or less at the same time by different consultants under the coordination of the DTS, which is one of the many agencies participating in the 3C planning process. Moreover, other such land-use and transportation-related issues that were being addressed at the time in Honolulu included a major freeway project that was in litigation in the federal court system, a major deep-draft harbor, the expansion of the Honolulu International Airport, the selection of a site for a general aviation airport, and several proposals for major industrial centers and residential developments, some of which involved applications for zoning variances. The sequence in which some of these projects would be implemented might require revisions of the regional long-range plan to incorporate committed, programmed, and implemented projects. The last sequence of the quotation relating to planning for the Honolulu rapid-transit system illustrates that uncommitted projects may subsequently have to be restudied.

7.5.4 Planning at the Statewide and National Levels

The examples given in the preceding subsection were drawn from the urban context. Planning for single-mode and multimodal transportation systems in larger areas (i.e., statewide and national) are also undertaken by various planning entities. As an illustration, consider the following quotation from the National Airport System study conducted by the Federal Aviation Administration (FAA) [7.21].

> The 1978 National Airport System Plan (NASP) provides, in accordance with Section 12 of the Airport and Airway Development Act of 1970, as amended, a compilation of development needs for the Nation's civil airports in the decade ahead. The NASP, although published periodically, represents a continuous planning process and is constantly being updated. It is a traditional "needs" study and, as such, does not consider alternative levels of service related to different investments commitments. The generation of such assessments will require the development of performance measures and an appropriate data base . . . .
>
> Aviation as well as other forms of transportation must compete for limited resources at the state and local levels and must be reconciled with other, sometimes conflicting, priorities such as environmental and energy considerations ([7.21], p. iii).

The need for strategic, project-level, and operational planning is expressed in this context as well.

7.6 SUMMARY

In this chapter we defined planning as the forward-looking, organized, and premeditative process that precedes the undertaking of actions intended to guide a particular situation or system in desirable directions but not as a search for the ultimate. The fundamental objective of transportation is to provide the efficient and safe levels of mobility needed to support a wide spectrum of other human needs for a heterogeneous variety of societal groups. Since these needs, goals, and objectives are continuously changing, transportation planning is also an ever-evolving process.

The evolution of contemporary transportation planning in the United States was traced along the historical path of land transportation, paying particular attention to the confluence of three important factors: technological progress, private interests, and changing governmental policy.

The merging and interaction of three disparate planning perspectives (the facility orientation of intercity highway planning, the traffic-operations-oriented traffic engineering approach, and the social consciousness of urban planning) produced the basic elements of the contemporary urban transportation planning process, incorporating technical analyses, widely based citizen participation, and a concern for a large variety of social, economic, and environmental impacts in addition to connectivity and accessibility.

7.7 EXERCISES

1. Obtain an EIS for a major transportation project and write a short report summarizing its major contents.

2. Prepare a synopsis of the transportation impacts covered in an EIS for a nontransportation project such as a residential development, an industrial plant, or a commercial center.

3. Present your own arguments for or against governmental actions to improve the mobility of the elderly and handicapped.

4. What is the major difference between the *needs* studies described in this chapter and the urban transportation-planning methodology illustrated by Fig. 7.4.9?

5. How can the methodology of Fig. 7.4.9 be applied to aid in the planning of a statewide system of airports?

6. Prepare a list of the major ways by which the federal government has been involved in planning land transportation.

7. Review the material included in Appendix A and, in your own words, discuss the potential impacts of building a freeway in a large city.

8. In your own words, describe the major consequences of implementing a high-capacity rapid-transit system in a major urban area.

9. Review an article from the technical literature that addresses the topic of TSM.

10. Discuss the major advantages and disadvantages of privately owned highways.

11. Discuss the major advantages and disadvantages of privately owned urban bus systems.

12. Compile a dossier containing clippings from your local newspaper of transportation-related stories over a 2-week period. Arrange this material in an organized way of your choosing.

13. If a major transportation-related decision is pending in your city or state, identify the major groups involved and briefly describe the thrust of their arguments. Distinguish between qualititatively and quantitatively supported claims.

14. What kinds of transportation impacts do you think that construction of a multistory residential building in a densely populated area would possibly have?

15. Prepare a short report describing the zoning ordinances of your city or town.

16. List the various types of planning-related surveys discussed in this chapter.

17. Make a list of alternative strategies that have the potential of alleviating urban-traffic congestion.

18. Briefly compare the various urban-planning schools of thought described in this chapter. What was the basic view that each held with regard to the role of transportation in the urban milieu?

19. What is the purpose of the Highway Trust Fund?

20. Give several specific examples of the way in which technological development has affected the structure of cities.

21. What do you think was the rationale behind placing provisions for federal aid to urban mass-transit systems in housing laws?

22. What were the objectives of the TOPICS program?

23. How can you adapt the methodology of needs study to the planning of a system of parks and playgrounds within a city?

24. Describe how the methodology discussed in Section 7.4.5 can be adapted to help plan a regional water supply system.

25. What are some major components of travel demand?

26. You have been assigned the task of developing materials for the conduct of public-information and citizen-involvement programs as specified in the request for consulting services quoted in Section 7.5.3. Research the topic and write a report not to exceed 10 typewritten pages.

7.8 REFERENCES

7.1 FEDERAL HIGHWAY ADMINISTRATION, *America's Highways 1776-1976: A History of the Federal-Aid Program*, U.S. Department of Transportation, U.S. Government Printing Office, Stock No. 050-001-00123-3, Washington, D.C., 1976.

7.2 NATIONAL TRANSPORTATION POLICY STUDY COMMISSION, *National Transportation Policies through the Year 2000*, Final Report, U.S. Government Printing Office, Washington, D.C., June 1979.

7.3 TRANSPORTATION RESEARCH BOARD, *Urban Transportation Alternatives: Evolution of Federal Policy*, Special Report 177, National Research Council, Washington, D.C., 1977.

7.4 HOFFMAN, H. W., *Sagas of Old Western Travel and Transport*, Howell-North Books, San Diego, Calif., 1980.

7.5 GRAY, G. E., and L. A. HOEL, eds., *Public Transportation: Planning, Operations and Management*, Prentice Hall, Englewood Cliffs, N.J., 1979.

7.6 Martin, J., *Mule to MARTA*, vols. I and II, Atlanta Historical Society, Atlanta, Ga., 1977.

7.7 Goodman, W. I., and E. C. Freund. *Principles and Practice of Urban Planning*, International City Manager's Association, Washington, D.C., 1968.

7.8 Nolen, J., ed., *City Planning*, D. Appleton and Company, New York, 1929.

7.9 Taylor, G. R., *Satellite Cities: A Study of Industrial Suburbs*, D. Appleton and Company, New York, 1915.

7.10 Howard, E., *Garden Cities of To-morrow*, first published in 1898 as *Tomorrow: A Peaceful Path to Real Reform*, Faber and Faber Limited, London, 1902.

7.11 City and County of Honolulu, *General Plan for Urban and Urbanizing Areas*, Planning Department, Honolulu, Aug. 1960.

7.12 Stevens, J. C., A. W. Maner, and T. E. Shelburne, "Pavement Performance Correlated with Soil Areas." *Proceedings of the 29th Annual Meeting*, Highway Research Board, National Research Council, Washington, D.C., 1949, pp. 445–466.

7.13 Gamble, R. W., and H. F. Ilgner, "Purpose, Analysis and Application, Origin and Destination Survey, Milwaukee Metropolitan Area," *Proceedings of the 26th Annual Meeting*, Highway Research Board, National Research Council, Washington, D.C., 1946, pp. 404–421.

7.14 MacLachlan, K. A., "The Coordinate Method of O and D Analysis," *Proceedings of the 29th Annual Meeting*, Highway Research Board, National Research Council, Washington, D.C., 1949, pp. 349–367.

7.15 Voorhees, A. M. and J. W., Booth, *Application of O-D Data in the Baltimore Region*, Highway Research Board Bulletin 224, National Research Council, Washington, D.C., 1959, pp. 115–123.

7.16 Voorhees, A. M., and R. Morris, *Estimating and Forecasting Travel for Baltimore by Use of a Mathematical Model*, Highway Research Board Bulletin 224, National Research Council, Washington, D.C., 1959, pp. 105–114.

7.17 Hall, P., ed., *Von Thunen's Isolated State*, Pergamon Press, Oxford, 1966.

7.18 Losch, A., "The Nature of Economic Regions," *Southern Economic Journal*, 5 (1938):71–78.

7.19 U.S. Subcommittee on the City, *New Urban Rail Transit: How Can Its Development and Growth-Shaping Potential Be Realized*, Committee on Banking, Finance and Urban Affairs. U.S. House of Representatives, 96th Congress, First Session, U.S. Government Printing Office, Washington, D.C., 1980.

7.20 *Honolulu Star-Bulletin*, July 30, 1985.

7.21 Federal Aviation Administration, *National Airport System Plan 1978–1987*, U.S. Department of Transportation, U.S. Government Printing Office, Washington, D.C., 1977.

Sequential Demand-Forecasting Models

8.1 INTRODUCTION

In Chapter 7 we explained that the purpose of the travel forecasting phase of the urban transportation-planning process is to perform a conditional prediction of travel demand in order to estimate the likely transportation consequences of several transportation alternatives (including the do-nothing alternative) that are being considered for implementation. This prediction is also conditional on a predicted target-year land-use pattern. The major components of travel behavior were identified as:

1. The decision to travel for a given purpose (trip generation)
2. The choice of destination (trip distribution)
3. The choice of travel mode (modal choice)
4. The choice of route or path (network assignment)

Figure 8.1.1 illustrates that travel-demand models can be chained together in a sequence. In this *sequential-demand-modeling* arrangement, the outputs of each step become inputs to the following step, which also takes relevant inputs from the specification of the alternative plan under study and from the land-use and socioeconomic projection phase. Figure 8.1.2 is a more elaborate description of the urban transportation-planning process [8.1]. This figure shows the continuing aspect of the planning process and the need for data collection and model calibration as well. The most frequently used models for each of the four steps

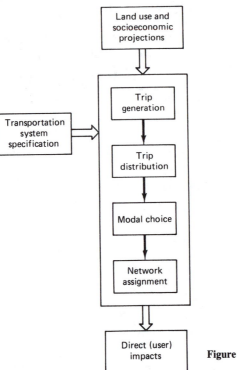

Figure 8.1.1 Sequential forecasting process.

of the sequential process are covered in this chapter. For each model, the relevant dependent and independent variables are identified, and the method of calibration is described. Additionally, the advantages and disadvantages of each model are discussed. Model selection, of course, should be guided by the rules discussed in Appendix C in relation to modeling in general.

8.2 TRIP GENERATION

8.2.1 Introduction

The objective of a trip-generation model is to forecast the number of person-trips that will begin from or end in each travel analysis zone within the region for a typical day of the target year. Prior to its application, a trip-generation model must be calibrated using observations taken during the base year by means of a variety of travel surveys (see Chapter 7). The total number of person-trips generated constitutes the dependent variable of the model. The independent or explanatory variables include land use and socioeconomic factors that have been shown to bear a relationship with trip making. When applying a calibrated trip-

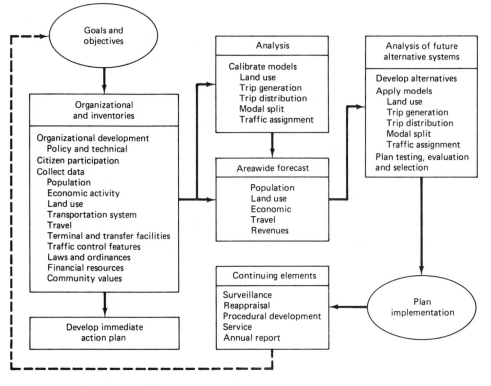

Figure 8.1.2   Continuing urban transportation planning process. (From Federal Highway
Administration [8.1].)

generation model for predictive purposes, the numerical values of the independent
variables must be supplied by the analyst. These values are obtained from the
areawide land use and socioeconomic projection phase, which precedes the trip-
generation step. As Fig. 8.2.1 illustrates, the output of a trip-generation model

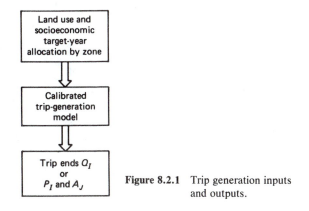

Figure 8.2.1   Trip generation inputs
and outputs.

consists of the amount of trip making or the *trip ends* Q_I of each zone *I* within the region.

8.2.2 Trip Purpose

In contemporary transportation planning, the zonal trip making Q_I is estimated separately for each of a number of trip purposes, typically including work trips, school trips, shopping trips, and social or recreational trips. In certain special-context studies, other categories are considered appropriate as well. For example, a study that examined the travel behavior of users of a special service for elderly and handicapped persons in Honolulu, Hawaii, considered travel for medical and rehabilitational purposes to be relevant categories to that analysis [8.2].

The reason separate trip-generation models are usually developed for each trip purpose is that the travel behavior of trip-makers depends on the trip purpose. For example, work trips are undertaken with daily regularity, mostly during the morning and afternoon period of peak traffic, and overwhelmingly from the same origins to the same destinations. This is also true in the case of school trips. Social and recreational trips, on the other hand, are clearly of a different character. Figure 8.2.2 illustrates that the time-of-day distribution of trips also varies among purposes [8.3].

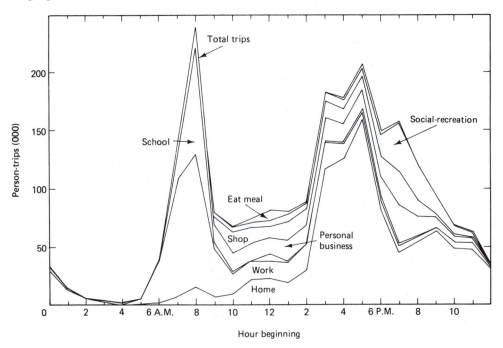

Figure 8.2.2 Hourly distribution of internal person-trips by trip purpose. (From Keefer [8.3].)

8.2.3 Zonal- versus Household-Based Models

A transportation-planning study cannot possibly trace the travel patterns of every individual residing within a region. As a result, the geographical patterns of trip making are summarized by dividing the region into smaller travel-analysis zones and by associating the estimated trips with these zones. Early models of trip generation considered the zone to be the smallest entity of interest as far as trip making was concerned. Consequently, these models are calibrated on a *zonal basis*, meaning that the overall zonal characteristics were used as independent or explanatory variables. These zonal attributes included variables such as the zonal population, the average zonal income, the average vehicle ownership, and the like. Using zonal averages, however, tends to mask internal (or intrazonal) variability and affects the accuracy of the estimated trip levels. For example, two zones may have the same average income (in the middle-income range, for example) but one may be composed of a homogenous group of households with respect to income, whereas the second may be composed of two heterogeneous groups, one at high and the other at low income. If income is not linearly related to trip generation, a *zone-based* (or *aggregate*) model will not be sensitive to the intrazonal income differences. *Household-based* (or *disaggregate*) models of trip generation are also available.

The rationale of household-based models is that households with similar characteristics tend to have similar travel propensities irrespective of their geographical location within the region. The calibration of household-based models employs a sample of households rather than a sample of zones. These models are known as disaggregate models because they decompose (or disaggregate) each zone into smaller units. However, this disaggregation is not geographical, as households of the various types may be interspersed throughout a zone. Consequently, this decomposition is not necessarily equivalent to delineating smaller zones. In order to arrive at the required estimates of zonal trip generation (thus retaining the spatial characteristics of travel within the region), it is necessary to recombine the contribution of each group of similar households found within the zone into a zonal total. For this reason, the land-use projections that provide the inputs to a trip-generation model must specifically forecast the number of households by type. Disaggregate models are further discussed in Section 8.6.

8.2.4 Productions and Attractions

The trips that are predicted by a trip-generation model for each zone are often referred to as the trip ends associated with that zone. Trip ends may be classified either as origins and destinations, or as productions and attractions. As used in trip-generation studies, the terms *origin* and *production* on one hand and *destination* and *attraction* on the other are not identical. To understand this difference, consider the two zones I and J of Fig. 8.2.3. Typically, each of these zones will

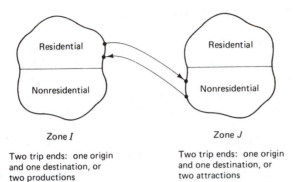

Zone *I*

Two trip ends: one origin
and one destination, or
two productions

Zone *J*

Two trip ends: one origin
and one destination, or
two attractions

Figure 8.2.3   Trip-end definitions.

contain residences as well as nonresidential land uses, such as places of business, schools, and commercial establishments. The figure captures this fact by showing a portion of each zone as residential and a portion as nonresidential, even though the two types of activity within each zone may be intermingled. Now consider a single worker whose residence is located in zone *I* and whose place of employment is in zone *J*. On a typical workday, this trip-maker will travel from zone *I* to zone *J* in the morning and back from zone *J* to zone *I* in the evening. In the morning, zone *I* is the trip-maker's *origin* and zone *J* is the trip-maker's *destination*. In the evening, zone *J* becomes the origin and zone *I* the destination. Thus origins and destinations are defined in terms of the direction of a given interzonal trip. In this example, each of the two zones experienced two trip ends during the day: one origin and one destination.

The terms *production* and *attraction*, on the other hand, are *not* defined in terms of the directions of trips but in terms of the land use associated with each trip end. A *trip production* is defined as a trip end connected with a residential land use in a zone, and a *trip attraction* is defined as a trip end connected to a nonresidential land use in a zone. On the basis of these definitions, zone *I* of Fig. 8.2.3 has *produced* two trips, while zone *J* has *attracted* two trips. This distinction is made because the zonal trip productions can be more easily estimated from the socioeconomic characteristics of the zone's population and the related travel needs of the population for various purposes, whereas the zonal trip attractions depend on the availability and intensity of nonresidential opportunities found within the zone. For example, if a significant portion of the population of a zone consisted of working-age adults, that zone would produce a high number of work trips. On the other hand, if a zone were predominantly nonresidential (a downtown employment zone, for instance), it would be likely to attract many work trips produced by zones that are dispersed throughout the region.

Thus, a typical trip-generation study involves the application of residential trip-production and nonresidential trip-attraction models. The former contain a set of explanatory variables that describe the demographic makeup of the zone's population. The latter rely on a set of explanatory variables that capture the type and intensity of nonresidential activities within the zone. In the general case, each zone I will have a number of productions P_I and a number of attractions A_I.

While the vast majority of the trips occurring within urban areas have a production and an attraction trip end, there are trips for which the definition is not directly applicable, for example, trips that take place between two nonresidential activities, such as a trip from the place of employment to a shopping area. Trips can also be classified as *home-based* or as *non-home-based*. The former category consists of trips that either begin or end at a residence, whereas the latter neither begin nor end at a residence. This leaves a small percentage of trips usually occurring during the noncritical off-peak periods of the day that have both their origins and their destinations in a residence (e.g., a trip to a friend's house). Depending on the prevalence of non-home-based and (to employ an unconventional term) home-to-home trips within the particular region under study and the degree of detail required, special-context studies may be appropriate. The three most common mathematical formulations of trip generation are regression models, trip-rate analysis models, and cross-classification models.

8.2.5 Regression Models

Appendix C presents the underlying theory of least squares regression and shows regression models as linear or nonlinear on one hand and as simple or multiple on the other. All these types of regression models can be employed in connection with trip-generation studies. The selection of the most appropriate form in a particular case is usually based on experience and preliminary investigations into the matter. A frequently used regression model is the linear multiple-regression model, which has the form

$$Y = a_0 + a_1 X_1 + \cdots + a_r X_r \tag{8.2.1}$$

where Y is the dependent variable, the X's are the relevant independent or explanatory variables, and the a's are the parameters of the model that must be estimated prior to applying the model. In a trip-production multiple regression model, the dependent variable can estimate either the total trips produced by a zone P_I if it is an aggregate model or the household trip-production rate if it is a household-based model. The independent variables included in a zone-based model are characteristics of the zone as a whole, whereas the independent variables employed by a disaggregate model are household characteristics. The calibration of the former is based on a set of observations for a number of zones, each observation corresponding to a zone; the calibration of a disaggregate model employs a number of base-year observations, each corresponding to an individual household in a sample of households drawn randomly from the region. In the case of multiple regression models of trip attractiveness, the independent variables consist of nonresidential attributes.

In all cases, each term of the equation can be interpreted as the contribution of the corresponding independent variable to the magnitude of the dependent variable. That is, a unit change in an independent variable is seen to result in a change in the dependent variable, which equals the magnitude of the coefficient of the independent variable. The constant term a_0 captures effects that are not explicitly included in the model.

When calibrating a multiple regression model, the analyst is faced with the questions of how many and which independent variables to include in the equation. The following rules of thumb provide some guidance in this respect. Regarding the number of independent variables to be included in a model, practical experience has shown that the law of diminishing returns holds true with respect to accuracy resulting from increasing the number of independent variables. Figure 8.2.4 illustrates the point by plotting the accuracy obtained by increasingly complex models versus the number of variables employed [8.4]. The figure shows that a point is reached beyond which the extra cost and complexity associated with adding another variable (which includes the need to forecast this variable toward the target year) may not be warranted by the increasingly smaller improvements in accuracy obtained.

The following four guidelines are helpful in deciding which explanatory variables to include in a linear regression model. The selected explanatory variables

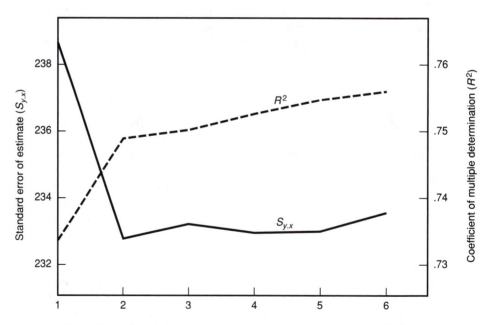

Figure 8.2.4   Graphical representation of the stepwise change in standard error of estimate and coefficient of multiple determination. (From Federal Highway Administration [8.4].)

1. Must be linearly related to the dependent variable
2. Must be highly correlated with the dependent variable
3. Must not be highly correlated between themselves
4. Must lend themselves to relatively easy projection

The first rule states that the relationship between a selected explanatory variable and the dependent variable must be linear, as required by the mathematical specification of the model. If this is not true, an appropriate transformation of the explanatory variable may be performed as explained in Appendix C. The second rule states that the explanatory variable must be highly associated with the dependent variable; otherwise, it would have no explanatory power. The third rule states that variables that are highly correlated among themselves must not be included in the same equation. If two potential explanatory variables are highly correlated, they essentially measure the same effect or, in other words, they are not independent. If both were to be included in the same equation, double counting would result. Moreover, the resulting equation would not be easy to interpret, as the sensitivity of the dependent variable to a single explanatory variable could not be captured by that variable's coefficient alone. The fourth rule states that the selected explanatory variables must be such that they can be forecast toward the target year with relative ease. The reason that trip-generation models are used in the first place is because it is extremely difficult to project the dependent variable directly. Consequently, the model is calibrated in terms of a set of factors (or independent variables) that explain the dependent variable. Unless these factors are relatively easy to project into the future, the entire effort will prove to be of little value.

By applying these rules, the number of potentially useful alternative specifications of a trip-generation model can be considerably reduced. What remains is to select the best model for this reduced set on the basis of statistical tests for goodness of fit and, not to be underestimated, the application of professional judgment to ensure the reasonableness of results [8.1, 8.4].

Example 8.1

The following correlation matrix contains the simple correlation coefficients between pairs of variables computed by Eq. C.3.4 using base-year data. Discuss the question of which explanatory variables X should be included in a linear multiple regression model.

	Y	X_1	X_2	X_3	X_4
Y	1.00	0.32	0.92	0.95	0.62
X_1		1.00	0.25	0.19	0.03
X_2			1.00	0.99	0.29
X_3				1.00	0.33
X_4					1.00

Solution Variable X_1 is not highly correlated with the dependent variable Y. Hence it may be eliminated from further consideration. Although highly correlated with Y, variables X_2 and X_3 are also highly correlated with each other. Therefore, they should not appear together in the same equation. Variable X_4 is not highly correlated with either X_1 or X_2. Hence it can appear in the same equation with either of the two. Based on this discussion, the following alternative linear multiple regression models may be considered:

1. $Y = a_0 + a_2X_2$
2. $Y = b_0 + b_3X_3$
3. $Y = c_0 + c_4X_4$
4. $Y = d_0 + d_2X_2 + d_4X_4$
5. $Y = e_0 + e_3X_3 + e_4X_4$

Discussion The simple correlation matrix is symmetric, and only the upper or lower half need be specified. The diagonal elements are equal to unity because the correlation between any variable with itself is perfect. The five potential models specified in the solution meet the rules of selection given earlier. Further analysis is required to discover the best among them (consult Appendix C).

8.2.6 Trip-Rate Analysis

Trip-rate analysis refers to several models that are based on the determination of the average trip production or trip attraction rates associated with the important trip generators within the region. Table 8.2.1, for example, displays the trip-generation rates associated with various land-use categories in downtown Pittsburgh,

TABLE 8.2.1 GOLDEN TRIANGLE FLOOR-SPACE TRIP GENERATION RATES GROUPED BY GENERALIZED LAND-USE CATEGORIES

Land-use category[a]	Thousands of square feet	Person trips	Trips per thousand square feet
Residential	2,744	6,574	2.4
Commercial			
Retail	6,732	54,833	8.1
Services	13,506	70,014	5.2
Wholesale	2,599	3,162	1.2
Manufacturing	1,392	1,335	1.0
Transportation	1,394	5,630	4.0
Public buildings	2,977	11,746	3.9
Total[b]	31,344	153,294	
Average[b]			4.9

[a] Net floor space as regrouped to match trip-end land-use categories will not match totals in Table 7.

[b] Includes trips to public open spaces.

Source: Keefer [8.3].

that were obtained by one of the very first major urban-transportation studies
[8.3]. Table 8.2.2, taken from the same source, presents the land-area trip rates
in terms of person-trips per acre for several land-use types and locations with
respect to the central business district (ring 0). The land-use types include both
residential and nonresidential categories, and the location is specified by a series
of concentric rings.

The hypothetical trip-attraction rates of Table 8.2.3 are expressed in terms
of the number of trips attracted per employee for the case of retail and nonretail

TABLE 8.2.2 PERSON-TRIPS PER ACRE BY GENERALIZED LAND USE AND RING

		Commercial			Manu-factur-ing	Trans-porta-tion	Public build-ings	Public open space	Average	
Ring	Residen-tial	Retail	Services	Whole-sale					Used land	All land
1	51	340	178	54	141	29	238	2	51	40
2	43	169	103	36	73	10	106	1	30	20
3	37	225	202	46	33	14	150	4	32	22
4	30	268	154	29	29	10	98	2	26	17
5	22	185	146	24	22	5	36	2	17	8
6	18	194	135	19	21	7	19	1	14	5
7	15	152	131	16	14	6	4	1	11	3
Average[a]	24	226	198	31	26	9	46	2	20	9

[a] Includes ring 0.
Source: Keefer [8.3].

TABLE 8.2.3 EXAMPLE OF PROCEDURE FOR TRIP-ATTRACTION ESTIMATES PERSON-TRIP ATTRACTIONS[a]

	Trips per employee							
				Retail				
Trip purpose	Trips per household	Nonretail	CBD	Shop center	Other	University	High school	Other
Home-based work		1.70	1.70	1.70	1.70			
Home-based shop			2.00	9.00	4.00			
Home-based school						0.90	1.60	1.20
Home-based other	0.70	0.60	1.10	4.00	2.30			
Non-home-based[b]	0.30	0.40	1.00	4.60	2.30			

[a] Illustration data only—not to be used directly.
[b] Non-home-based productions and attractions have same rate and are used to allocate to zones and areawide control total developed in the trip-production model.
Source: Federal Highway Administration [8.1].

land uses and in terms of school trips attracted per student enrolled in each of three types of educational institutions [8.1, 8.5].

Trip rates for a large number of commercial developments and land uses are supplied in the *Trip Generation* manual of the Institute of Transportation Engineers. They are presented in detail in Chapter 9.

8.2.7 Cross-Classification Models

Cross-classification (or category analysis) models may be thought of as extensions of the simple trip-rate models discussed previously. Although they can be calibrated as area- or zone-based models, in trip-generation studies they are almost exclusively used as disaggregate models. In the residential-generation context, household types are classified according to a set of categories that are highly correlated with trip making. Three to four explanatory variables, each broken into about three discrete levels, are usually sufficient.

The trip rates associated with each type of household are estimated by statistical methods, and these rates are assumed to remain stable over time. Table 8.2.4 presents a cross-classification table that shows the calibrated nonwork home-based trip-production rates for various types of households defined by (1) four levels of household size (i.e., number of persons per household), (2) three levels of car ownership (i.e., vehicles available per household), and (3) three levels of residential density (i.e., dwelling units per acre).

The documentation of the study that produced this table [8.6] specifies points of demarcation between the levels of density denoted as high (urban), medium (suburban), and low (rural). Each cell of the table contains the calibrated daily trip-production rate per household expressed in terms of person-trips per household per day. Given projections relating to the target-year household composition of a zone, the application of this calibrated model for predictive purposes is straightforward, as the following example example illustrates.

TABLE 8.2.4 EXAMPLE: TOTAL HOME-BASED, NONWORK TRIP RATES

Cross class	Vehicles available per household area type	Persons per household			
		1	2, 3	4	5+
1. Urban—high density	0	0.57	2.07	4.57	6.95
	1	1.45	3.02	5.52	7.90
	2+	1.82	3.39	5.89	8.27
2. Suburban—medium density	0	0.97	2.54	5.04	7.42
	1	1.92	3.49	5.99	8.37
	2+	2.29	3.86	6.36	8.74
3. Rural—low density	0	0.54	1.94	4.44	6.82
	1	1.32	2.89	5.39	7.77
	2+	1.69	3.26	5.76	8.14

Source: Oahu Metropolitan Planning Organization [8.6].

Example 8.2: Cross Classification

An urban zone contains 200 acres of residential land, 50 acres devoted to commercial uses, and 10 acres of park land. The following table presents the zone's expected household composition at some future (target) year.

Vehicles per household	Persons per household			
	1	2, 3	4	5
0	100	200	150	20
1	300	500	210	50
2+	150	100	60	0

Using the calibrated cross-classification table of Table 8.2.4, estimate the total non-work home-based trips that the zone will produce during a typical target-year day. The rates are given as trips per household per day.

Solution   The total productions are estimated by summing the contribution of each household type:

$$P_I = \sum_h N_h R_h$$

where N_h and R_h are the number of households of type h and their corresponding production rate. For example, the 300 single-person one-car households contribute $(300)(1.45) = 435$ nonwork home-based trips per day. Summing over all household types gives

$$P_I = 5760 \text{ trips per day}$$

Discussion   Only the residential-land-use sector of the zone entered into the solution because trip productions are associated with the residential characteristics of the zone. The commercial and recreational characteristics of the zone would be relevant to the estimation of the attractiveness of the zone for these purposes. In that case, properly calibrated attractiveness models would be required.

8.2.8 The FHWA-Simplified Trip-Production Procedure

Figure 8.2.5 presents a hypothetical example of a residential trip-generation procedure developed by the FHWA [8.1]. This procedure combines several of the concepts discussed in this section. Curve A represents the distribution of households by income and auto ownership. In the example shown, the auto ownership of a group of households with an annual income of $12,000 is distributed as follows: 2% own no autos, 32% own one auto, 52% own two autos, and 14% own three or more autos. Incidentally, depending on the way in which curve A is calibrated, it may represent a zonal (aggregate) distribution, in which case the income variable would be a zonal average, or it may represent a household-based (disaggregate)

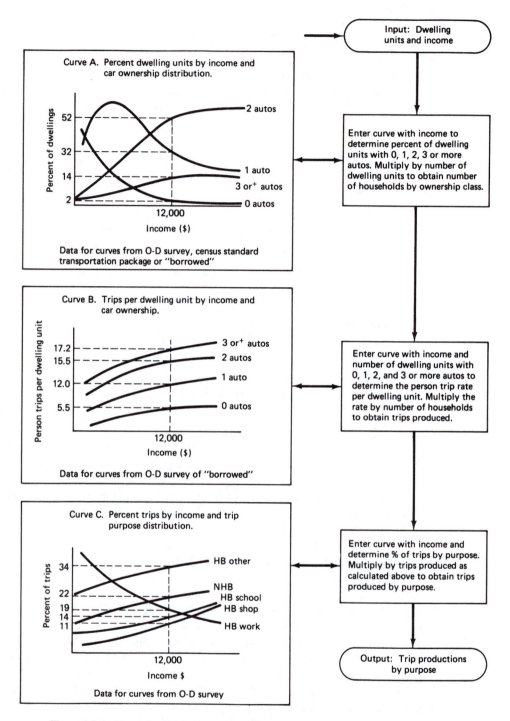

Figure 8.2.5 Example of urban trip-production procedure. (From Federal Highway Administration [8.1].)

distribution, in which case the group of households illustrated may correspond to a subset of all the households in a zone. In the latter case, the percentages obtained can be interpreted as probabilities; for example, the probability that any $12,000 per year household will own two cars is 0.52. (Note that the $12,000 in Figure 8.2.5 roughly correspond to $45,000 in 1992.)

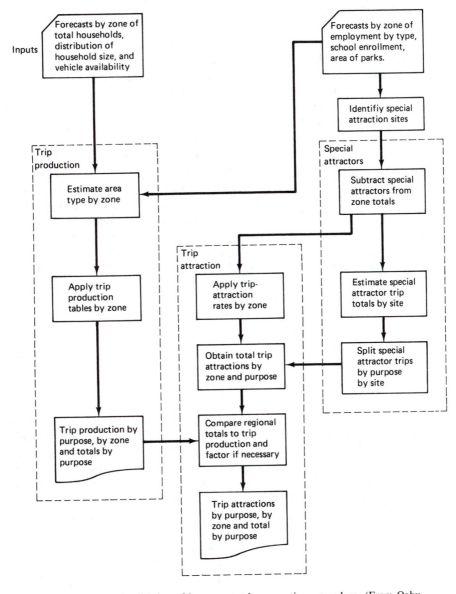

Figure 8.2.6   Application of long-range trip-generation procedure. (From Oahu Metropolitan Planning Organization [8.6].)

The regression lines of curve B provide the person-trip rates for household types defined by income and auto ownership, and curve C divides these trips among several trip purposes. Adherence to the instructions that accompany the figure leads to the target-year estimate of trip productions by purpose.

8.2.9 Summary

The purpose of trip generation is to estimate the target-year trip-ends by travel purpose for each zone within the region. Commonly, these trips are expressed as residential trip productions and nonresidential trip attractions. The most common mathematical forms of trip generation models are multiple regression equations, trip-rate models, cross-classification models, and their combinations.

Figure 8.2.6 illustrates the trip-generation procedure used to obtain long-range forecasts in a particular urban area. This figure shows that two sets of inputs, residential and nonresidential characteristics, were first obtained from zonal socioeconomic and land use projections. The specific variables used are listed among the inputs. Residential projections were used by the trip-production models, which took the form of household-based cross-classification tables to estimate the target-year zonal trip productions by purpose. The nonresidential land-use projections were used primarily in relation to the trip-attraction model, which was of the form of multiple regression. Several special attractors, including airports, major shopping centers, and universities, have been given special treatment because of their unique trip-attraction characteristics. The final outputs were the zonal productions and attractions by trip purpose.

8.3 TRIP DISTRIBUTION

8.3.1 Introduction

The next step in the sequential forecasting model system is concerned with the estimation of the target-year trip volumes Q_{IJ} that interchange between all pairs of zones I and J, where I is the trip-producing zone and J is the trip-attracting zone of the pair. The rationale of trip distribution is as follows: all trip-attracting zones J in the region are in competition with each other to attract trips produced by each zone I. Everything else being equal, more trips will be attracted by zones that have higher levels of "attractiveness." However, other intervening factors affect the choice of J as well. Consider, for example, the case of two identical shopping centers (i.e., of equal attractiveness) competing for the shopping trips produced by a given zone I. If the distances between zone I and each of the two centers are different, shoppers residing in zone I will show a preference for the closer of the two identical centers. Thus the intervening difficulty of travel between the producing zone I and each of the competing zones J has a definite effect on the choice of attraction zone. In the shopping center example, distance is cited as a measure of this difficulty of travel, but other measures of this effect may be used, such as travel time or some generalized cost that includes travel time, out-of-pocket cost, and the like. The notation W_{IJ} is used for this generalized cost which is also known as travel *impedance*, or *disutility*. When applying a specific model for predictive purposes, care must be exercised to use the same measure of impedance that was employed to calibrate the model.

Figure 8.3.1 conceptually illustrates that a trip-distribution model estimates the interzonal person-trip volumes Q_{IJ} based on the productions of each zone I, the attractiveness of zone J, and the interzonal impedance W_{IJ}. The production and attraction inputs are obtained from the preceding trip-generation phase, and estimates of the target-year interzonal impedances are obtained from the specification of the alternative transportation plan under investigation.

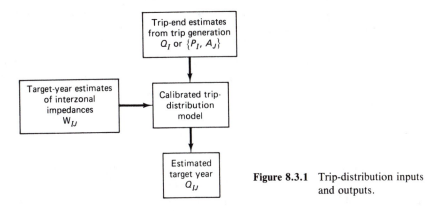

Figure 8.3.1   Trip-distribution inputs and outputs.

The most common mathematical formulations of trip distribution include various growth factor models, the gravity model, and a number of *opportunities* models. The following sections discuss the gravity model and one growth factor model (the Fratar model).

8.3.2 The Gravity Model

The gravity model gets its name from the fact that it is conceptually based on Newton's law of gravitation, which states that the force of attraction between two bodies is directly proportional to the product of the masses of the two bodies and inversely proportional to the square of the distance between them, or

$$F = k\frac{M_1 M_2}{r^2} \tag{8.3.1}$$

Variations of this formula have been applied to many situations involving human interaction. For example, the volume of long-distance telephone calls between cities may be modeled in this manner, with the population sizes of the cities replacing the masses of particles and the distance between cities or the cost of telephone calls taking the place of r. The exponent of the impedance term in the denominator, however, need not be exactly equal to 2 but may be replaced by a model parameter c.

The application of this concept to trip distribution takes the form

$$Q_{IJ} = k\frac{P_I A_J}{W_{IJ}^c} \tag{8.3.2}$$

Equation 8.3.2 states that the interchange volume between a trip-producing zone I and a trip-attracting zone J is directly proportional to the magnitude of the trip productions of zone I and the trip-attractiveness of zone J and is inversely proportional to a function of the impedance W_{IJ} between the two zones.

Using the usual mathematical modeling terminology, the interzonal volume is the dependent variable; the productions, attractions, and impedances are the independent variables; and the constants k and c are the parameters of the model that must be estimated through calibration using base-year data.

The parameter k can be eliminated from Eq. 8.3.2 by applying the *trip-production balance* constraint, which states that the sum over all trip-attracting zones J of the interchange volumes that share I as the trip-producing zone must equal the total productions of zone I, or

$$P_I = \sum_x Q_{Ix} \tag{8.3.3}$$

Equation 8.3.3 ensures that the model will distribute to the competing zones J exactly as many trips as are produced by zone I.

Substituting Eq. 8.3.2 into Eq. 8.3.3 and taking the terms not involving the index x outside the summation, we obtain

$$P_I = kP_I \sum_x \frac{A_x}{W_{Ix}^c} \tag{8.3.4}$$

Solving for k yields

$$k = \left[\sum_x \frac{A_x}{W_{Ix}^c}\right]^{-1} \tag{8.3.5}$$

which is the expression for k that ensures that the trip balance Eq. 8.3.3 is satisfied.

Substituting Eq. 8.3.5 into Eq. 8.3.2 leads to the classical form of the gravity model:

$$Q_{IJ} = P_I \left[\frac{A_J/W_{IJ}^c}{\sum_x (A_x/W_{Ix}^c)}\right] \tag{8.3.6}$$

The bracketed term is the proportion of the trips produced by zone I that will be attracted by zone J in competition with all trip-attracting zones x. Note that the numerical value of this fraction would not be affected if all attraction terms were multiplied by a constant. This implies that the attraction terms can measure the relative attractiveness of zones. For example, one employment zone may be said to be twice as attractive as another, for instance, based on the number of employment opportunities available. In this context, the estimated target-year trip attractions of a zone J (denoted by A_J^* to distinguish them from the relative attractiveness term used earlier) may be computed by applying the following *trip-attraction balance* equation to the results of the model:

$$A_J^* = \sum_x Q_{xJ} \tag{8.3.7}$$

The gravity formula is often written alternatively as

$$Q_{IJ} = P_I\left(\frac{A_J F_{IJ}}{\sum_x A_x F_{Ix}}\right) \tag{8.3.8}$$

where

$$F_{IJ} = \frac{1}{W_{IJ}^c} \tag{8.3.9}$$

is known as the *travel-time* (or *friction*) *factor*. Note that the calibration constant c is now implicit in the friction factor.

Finally, a set of interzonal *socioeconomic adjustment factors* K_{IJ} are introduced during calibration to incorporate effects that are not captured by the limited number of independent variables included in the model. The resulting gravity formula becomes

$$Q_{IJ} = P_I\frac{A_J F_{IJ} K_{IJ}}{\sum_J A_J F_{IJ} K_{IJ}} = P_I p_{IJ} \tag{8.3.10}$$

where p_{IJ} is the probability that a trip generated by zone I will be attracted by zone J. A table that contains the interzonal impedances W_{IJ} is known as a *skim table*.

Example 8.3

Perform a localized application of the basic gravity model for trips between a proposed site (attractor) and three surrounding zones. The site receives 1,524 incoming trips during the morning rush hour. Assume that all incoming trips are from the surrounding zones. Average travel times from each zone to the site as well as the population of each zone are given in Fig. 8.3.2. Estimate the number of trips from each zone to the site.

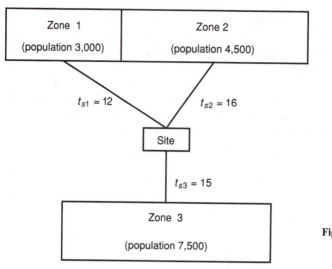

Figure 8.3.2 Zone population and travel times between zones and site.

Solution

$$G_{s1} = k \frac{(1524)(3,000)}{12} = 381,000k$$

$$G_{s2} = k \frac{(1524)(4500)}{16} = 428,625k$$

$$G_{s3} = k \frac{(1524)(7500)}{15} = 762,000k$$

The sum of all "gravities" should be equal to the number of trips destined to the site. Thus

$$G_{s1} + G_{s2} + G_{s3} = 1524$$

which yields $k = 0.0009697$. After substitution of k, we have

$$G_{s1} = 369, \qquad G_{s2} = 416, \qquad G_{s3} = 739$$

These flows are shown in Fig. 8.3.3.

Example 8.4: Application of the Gravity Model

The target-year productions and relative attractiveness of the four-zone city have been estimated to be as follows:

Zone	Productions	Attractiveness
1	1500	0
2	0	3
3	2600	2
4	0	5

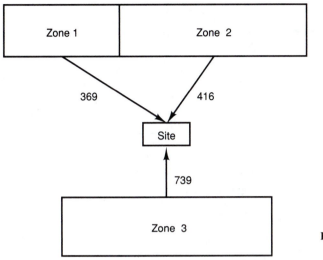

Figure 8.3.3   Resultant trips from zones to site.

The calibration of the gravity model for this city estimated the parameter c to be 2.0 and all socioeconomic adjustment factors to be equal to unity. Apply the gravity model to estimate all target interchanges Q_{IJ} and to estimate the total target-year attractions of each zone given that the target-year interzonal impedances W_{IJ} will be as shown in the following skim table.

I \ J	1	2	3	4
1	5	10	15	20
2	10	5	10	15
3	15	10	5	10
4	20	15	10	5

Solution   The gravity model calculations of the interchange volumes are shown in tabular form for the two trip-producing zones ($I = 1$ and $I = 3$). For $I = 1$, $P_1 = 1500$:

J	A_J	F_{1J}	K_{1J}	$A_J F_{1J} K_{1J}$	p_{1J}	Q_{1J}
1	0	0.0400	1.0	0	0	0
2	3	0.0100	1.0	0.0300	0.584	875
3	2	0.0044	1.0	0.0089	0.173	260
4	5	0.0025	1.0	0.0125	0.243	365
				0.0514	1.000	$1500 = P_1$

For $I = 3$, $P_3 = 2600$:

J	A_J	F_{3J}	K_{3J}	$A_J F_{3J} K_{3J}$	p_{3J}	Q_{3J}
1	0	0.0044	1.0	0.0	0	0
2	3	0.0100	1.0	0.03	0.188	488
3	2	0.0400	1.0	0.08	0.500	1300
4	5	0.0100	1.0	0.05	0.312	812
				0.16	1.000	$2600 = P_3$

To find the total target-year trip attractions of the nonresidental zones ($J = 2$, $J = 3$, and $J = 4$), apply the trip-attraction balance (Eq. 8.3.7) to get

$$A_2^* = 875 + 488 = 1363$$

$$A_3^* = 260 + 1300 = 1560$$

$$A_4^* = 365 + 812 = 1177$$

The solution is summarized by the following *trip table:*

I \ J	1	2	3	4	Sum
1	0	875	260	365	1500
2	0	0	0	0	0
3	0	488	1300	812	2600
4	0	0	0	0	0
Sum	0	1363	1560	1177	4100

Discussion The trip-generation data indicate that there are three types of zones in this city: Zone 1 is purely residential since it is shown to have productions only, zones 2 and 4 are purely nonresidential because they produce no trips, and zone 3 is a mixed land-use zone because it has both productions and attractions. The impedance matrix represents an estimate of interzonal impedances for the target year. The diagonal elements of this matrix represent intrazonal impedances, that is, the impedances associated with trips that begin *and* end within each zone. It is possible, of course, that trips produced by the mixed-land-use zone 3 to be attracted by the nonresidential sector of the same zone. The sum of each row of the trip table produces the total productions of the corresponding zone I, whereas the sum of each column represents the total attractions of each zone J. Again note that the purely residential zone has no attractions and the purely nonresidential zones have no productions. The mixed zone has both.

Example 8.5: The Generation-Distribution Chain

You are a planning consultant to a trading firm that is considering the construction of a major shopping center in the city of Trinity. At present, the city consists of three residential zones and the central business district (CBD), where all shopping activity is concentrated. Your clients can acquire land for the proposed center at the location shown and are interested in your prediction of the patronage that the center will attract if built to compete with the CBD. The following data have been made available to you:

1. *Daily shopping trip production* (*trips per person*):

X_1 \ X_2	0	1	2
≤2	0.2	0.3	0.4
3	0.1	0.2	0.3
≥4	0.1	0.2	0.3
	$X_3 = $ I		

X_1 \ X_2	0	1	2
≤2	0.3	0.4	0.5
3	0.2	0.2	0.4
≥4	0.2	0.2	0.5
	$X_3 = $ II		

where

$$X_1 = \text{household size, in persons/household}$$

$$X_2 = \text{auto ownership, cars/household}$$

$$X_3 = \text{household income level (I or II)}$$

2. *Relative shopping attractiveness:* The relative shopping attractiveness of commercial zones has been found to be given by the following multiple regression equation:

$$A = 5X_a + 3X_b$$

where

$$X_a = \text{area of shopping floor space provided, in acres}$$

$$X_b = \text{available parking area, in acres}$$

3. *Land-use and socioeconomic projections:*

RESIDENTIAL ZONES

Zone	X_1	X_2	X_3	Number of households Base year	Number of households Target year
1	2	0	I	300	500
	2	1	I	300	400
	3	1	I	200	300
	2	2	II	0	50
2	2	1	I	400	500
	2	1	II	300	200
	3	2	I	200	300
	3	0	I	100	400
3	1	1	II	200	200
	2	2	II	300	400
	3	2	II	400	300
	4	2	II	200	400

COMMERCIAL ZONES

Zone	Base year		Target year	
	X_a	X_b	X_a	X_b
4 (CBD)	3.0	2.0	3.0	2.5
5	0.0	0.0	2.0	3.0

4. *Gravity model parameters:*

(a) $\ln F = -\ln W$ where W is the interzonal impedance, in minutes (see Fig. 8.3.4).

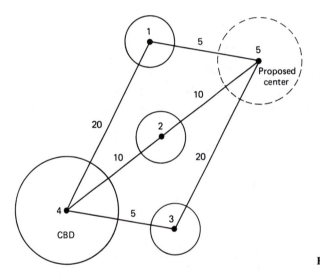

Figure 8.3.4 Interzonal impedances.

(b) K_{IJ}

I \ J	4 (CBD)	5 (center)
1	1.0	0.9
2	0.9	1.2
3	1.0	1.0

You are asked to calculate all target-year interchange volumes and the target-year patronage of the two commercial zones.

Solution First, apply the calibrated trip-generation models and the available land-use and socioeconomic projections to find the target-year productions and relative attractiveness of the five zones. The shopping-trip-production model is a disaggre-gated cross-classification model. Considering the units of the calibrated production rate, the contribution of each household type to the total zonal productions is

(number of households)(household size)(trips per person)

Hence, for each of the trip-producing zones:

Zone 1	Zone 2	Zone 3
$500 \times 2 \times 0.2 = 200$	$500 \times 2 \times 0.3 = 300$	$200 \times 1 \times 0.4 = 80$
$400 \times 2 \times 0.3 = 240$	$200 \times 2 \times 0.4 = 160$	$400 \times 2 \times 0.5 = 400$
$300 \times 3 \times 0.2 = 180$	$300 \times 3 \times 0.3 = 270$	$300 \times 3 \times 0.4 = 360$
$50 \times 2 \times 0.5 = \underline{50}$	$400 \times 3 \times 0.1 = \underline{120}$	$400 \times 4 \times 0.5 = \underline{800}$
$P_1 = 670$	$P_2 = 850$	$P_3 = 1640$

The target-year attractiveness of the two competing commercial zones is calculated via the calibrated trip-attractiveness equation and the relevant land-use projections, as follows:

$$A_4 = 5 \times 3 + 3 \times 2.5 = 22.5$$

$$A_5 = 5 \times 2 + 3 \times 3.0 = 19.0$$

The target-year interchange volumes are computed using the gravity model with the given $c = 1$ and the given K_{IJ} factors. Proceeding as in Example 8.4, the following trip table results:

I \ J	4 (CBD)	5 (center)	P_I
1	166	504	670
2	400	450	850
3	1354	286	1640
A_J	1920	1240	

Thus 1240 of the estimated 3160 daily shopping trips (or 39% of the total) will be attracted by the proposed shopping center if built.

Discussion   This example illustrates the application of the demand-forecasting models discussed so far and shows how the steps of the sequential forecasting procedure are chained together. The prerequisite selection and calibration of the given models had already been carried out using base-year data. Also, the target-year land-use and socioeconomic projections are given.

The production model is of the cross-classification type, and the production rates are given as trips per person. This is reflected in the calculations where this rate multiplies the total number of persons belonging to each socioeconomic category. The attraction model is a zonal (aggregate) multiple regression equation using shopping floor space and parking availability as the determinants of attractiveness. The dependent variable is relative attractiveness and not trip attractions.

The gravity model of trip distribution incorporates the effect of interzonal impedance, which is clearly seen in the results. Since the productions and attractions are defined irrespective of direction, the actual patronage of the two centers will be half the attractions just calculated. Note, however, that the same result would be obtained by using half the productions of each zone in the gravity model.

8.3.3 Calibration of the Gravity Model

The calibration of the gravity model in the form of Eq. 8.3.6 involves the determination of the numerical value of the parameter c that fixes the model to the one that reproduces the base-year observations. Equation 8.3.8 is simply another way of expressing Eq. 8.4.6 by substituting Eq. 8.3.9 in the latter. Hence, knowledge of the proper value of c fixes the relationship between the travel-time factor and the interzonal impedance.

Unlike the calibration of a simple linear regression model where the parameters can be solved for by a relatively easy minimization of the sum of squared deviations (see Appendix C), the calibration of the gravity formula is accomplished through an iterative procedure: An initial value of c is assumed and Eq. 8.3.6 is applied using the known base-year productions, attractions, and impedances to compute the interzonal volumes Q_{IJ}. These results are then compared with those observed during the base year. If the computed volumes are sufficiently close to the observed volumes, the current value of c is retained as the calibrated value. Otherwise, an adjustment to c is made and the procedure is continued until an acceptable degree of convergence is reached. Most commonly, the friction-factor function F rather than the parameter c is used in the calibration procedure. In that case, Eq. 8.3.8 is employed in the place of Eq. 8.3.6.

The results of calibration are then expressed in terms of the appropriate equation relating the friction factor and the interzonal impedance. Example 8.6 illustrates this procedure and clarifies the role of the socioeconomic adjustment factors K_{IJ} as well [8.5].

The comparison between the computed and the observed values of Q_{IJ} is accomplished by using the *trip-length frequency distribution*. This distribution consists of a plot of the percentages of the regionwide trips versus their interzonal impedance and has the general shape illustrated by Fig. 8.3.5; The frequency of trips eventually decreases with increasing impedance, as should be expected [8.7].

The base-year trip-length frequency distribution may be compared with that resulting from applying the model during each iteration of the calibration procedure until the latter sufficiently conforms to the former. The following example illustrates the major thrust of the gravity-model calibration procedure (Fig. 8.3.6).

Example 8.6: Calibration of the Gravity Model

Consider the five-zone city shown by Fig. 8.3.7(a). Two of the zones are purely residential, and the remaining three are purely nonresidential. The base-year interzonal impedances are specified in terms of travel time in minutes and are shown in parentheses on the arcs joining pairs of zones. The observed base-year productions,

Figure 8.3.5   Frequency distribution in a work-trip survey by travel distance. (From Bock [8.7].)

attractiveness, and trip-interchange volumes are inserted in the figure. It is required to find the value of c and the values of K_{IJ} that cause Eq. 8.3.8 to reproduce the observed base-year data.

By taking the natural logarithm of both sides, Eq. 8.3.9 may be rewritten as

$$\ln F = -c \ln W \qquad (8.3.11)$$

In other words, the negative of the parameter c is the slope of a straight line relating the logarithmic transformations of the friction factor and the interzonal impedance.

Figure 8.3.8 plots the base-year trip-length frequency distribution using the base-year observations. Impedance is shown in 5-min increments, and the ordinate represents the percent of total trips that travel at the corresponding impedance level.

The calibration procedure begins by assuming an initial estimate for c, say 2.0. This assumption is reflected in the plot of Eq. 8.3.11 shown by Figure 8.3.9, which plots the initially assumed relationship between F and W.

Application of the gravity formula using the assumed value of c leads to the interzonal volume estimates shown in Fig. 8.3.10 along with the *calculated* trip-length frequency distribution superposed on the *observed* trip-length frequency distribution

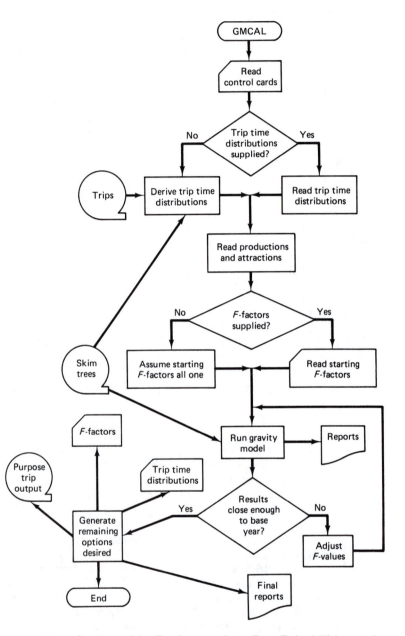

Figure 8.3.6 Gravity model calibration procedure. (From Federal Highway Administration [8.5].)

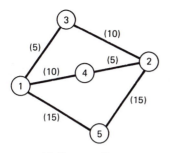

(a) Five-zone city

Zone I	P_I	A_I
1	500	0
2	1000	0
3	0	2
4	0	3
5	0	5

(b) Base-year generation

I \ J	3	4	5
1	300	150	50
2	180	600	220

(c) Base-year distribution

Figure 8.3.7   Base-year data for Example 8.5.

Frequency computation:

W	ΣQ_{IJ}	$f = (2)/\text{sum}$
5	300 + 600 = 900	0.60
10	150 + 180 = 330	0.22
15	50 + 220 = 270	0.18
	Sum = 1500	1.00

(a) Frequency calculation

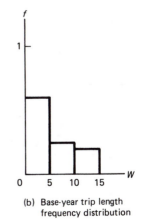

(b) Base-year trip length frequency distribution

Figure 8.3.8   Trip length–frequency distribution.

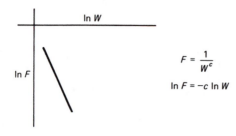

$$F = \frac{1}{W^c}$$

$$\ln F = -c \ln W$$

Figure 8.3.9 $\ln F$ versus $\ln W$ for $c = 2$.

to illustrate the discrepancy between the two. The assumption that $c = 2.0$ is seen to overestimate the percentage of trips at low impedances and to underestimate the percentage at the high-impedance end. To rectify this situation, the F-factors are adjusted to cause a shift of the calculated distribution toward the observed distribution. A commonly used formula for this adjustment is

$$F^* = F \frac{\text{observed}}{\text{calculated}} \qquad (8.3.12)$$

I \ J	3	4	5
1	303	114	83
2	123	741	136

W	ΣQ_{IJ}	f
5	1044	0.70
10	237	0.16
15	219	0.14

(a) First iteration ($c = 2$)

I \ J	3	4	5
1	251	145	104
2	176	654	170

W	ΣQ_{IJ}	f
5	905	0.60
10	321	0.21
15	274	0.19

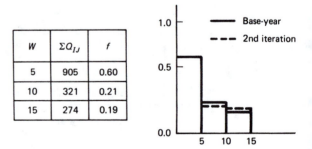

(b) Second iteration (F_{IJ} from Eq. 8.3.12)

Figure 8.3.10 Results of first two iterations.

where

$$F* = \text{adjusted friction factor at a given impedance}$$

$$\text{observed} = \text{corresponding base-year percentage of trips}$$

$$\text{calculated} = \text{current estimate of the percentage of trips at that impedance level}$$

For example, the assumed friction factor corresponding to an impedance level of 5 min is equal to 5^{-2}, or 0.04. After the first iteration, the adjusted factor becomes

$$F_5^* = 0.04\left(\frac{0.6}{0.7}\right) = 0.034$$

The adjusted friction factors obtained in this manner are plotted against the interzonal impedances on Fig. 8.3.11. If a single value of c were desired, simple linear regression could be used to fit the best-fitting straight line through this scatter diagram. However, at this point it becomes clear that the friction factor function need not be linear; it could be allowed to take the form that best describes the scatter diagram. The following general function relating F and W has been suggested by the FHWA [8.5].

$$F = aW^b e^{-cW} \tag{8.3.13}$$

where e is the base of natural logarithms and a, b, and c are calibration constants. Figure 8.3.12 shows the range of shapes that this smoothing function can yield depending on the magnitude of parameter b. The adjusted friction-factor function is used in the next iteration and the calibration procedure continues until the computed

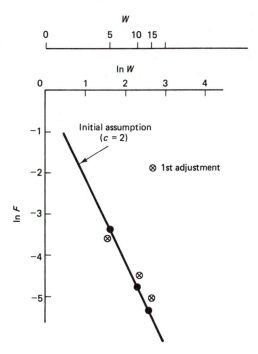

Figure 8.3.11   Friction factor adjustment.

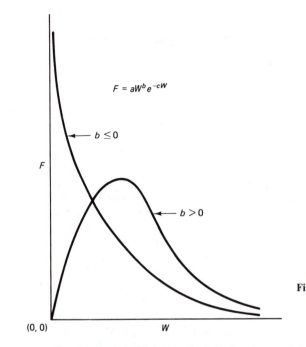

$$F = aW^b e^{-cW}$$

$b \leq 0$

F

$b > 0$

(0, 0) W

Figure 8.3.12 Shapes assumed by the F factor. (From Federal Highway Administration [8.5].)

distribution is sufficiently close to the observed distribution. The friction-factor function used last provides the desired calibration parameters.

Figure 8.3.10 also includes the results of the second iteration of the simple example being described. For simplicity, the new friction factors were applied directly, as computed by Eq. 8.3.12. The new trip-length frequency distribution is now closer to the observed base-year distribution.

Even though the regional trip-length frequency distribution is now close to the observed distribution, certain pronounced discrepancies remain at the interchange level. To adjust for these, the calibration procedure fine tunes the model by introducing a set of *zone-to-zone* socioeconomic adjustment factors

$$K_{IJ} = R_{IJ} \frac{1 - X_1}{1 - X_I R_{IJ}} \tag{8.3.14}$$

where

R_{IJ} = ratio of observed to calculated Q_{IJ}

X_I = ratio of the base-year Q_{IJ} to P_I, the total productions of zone I

The following values of K_{IJ} would result if Eq. 8.3.14 were applied at the end of the second iteration of the example problem.

I \ J	3	4	5
1	1.7	1.0	0.5
2	1.0	0.8	1.4

8.3.4 The Fratar Model

Several naive trend or simple growth-factor models have also been developed for use in special situations. Among these, the Fratar model [8.8] is often used to estimate *external* trips, that is, trips that are either produced and/or are attracted outside the boundaries of the region under study from outlying areas whose character is not explicitly analyzed.

The Fratar model begins with the base-year trip-interchange data as illustrated by Fig. 8.3.13(a). Usually, this model does not distinguish between productions and attractions and considers the interzonal trips irrespective of their direction. Consequently, the values shown represent the total interchange volumes between two zones, and $Q_{IJ} = Q_{JI}$. Since no distinction is made between productions and attractions, the trip generation of each zone is denoted by Q_I; the following trip balance equation provides the necessary relationship between the trip generation of a zone I and the trip interchanges that involve zone I:

$$Q_I = \sum_x Q_{Ix} \tag{8.3.15}$$

The estimate of the target-year trip generation $Q_I(t)$, which precedes the trip-distribution phase, is computed by multiplying the base-year trip generation, $Q_I(b)$, by a simple *growth factor*, G_I. This growth factor is based on the anticipated land-use changes that are expected to occur within the zone between the base year and the target year. Thus:

$$Q_I(t) = G_I[Q_I(b)] \tag{8.3.16}$$

Subsequently, the Fratar model estimates the target-year trip distribution $Q_{IJ}(t)$ that satisfies the trip balance (Eq. 8.3.15) for that year. Mathematically, the model consists of successive approximations and a test of convergence in an iterative procedure. During each iteration, the target-year trip-interchange volumes are

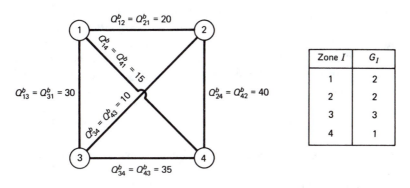

Zone I	G_I
1	2
2	2
3	3
4	1

(a) Base-year trip-interchange data   (b) Estimated growth factors

Figure 8.3.13   Fratar model inputs.

computed based on the anticipated growth of the two zones at either end of each interchange. The implied *estimated* target-year trip generation of each zone is then computed according to Eq. 8.3.15 and compared to the *expected* target-year trip generation (Eq. 8.3.16). A set of *adjustment factors, R_I,* are then computed by

$$R_I = \frac{Q_I(t)}{Q_I(\text{current})} \tag{8.3.17}$$

If the adjustment factors are all sufficiently close to unity, the trip-balance constraint is satisfied and the procedure is terminated. Otherwise, the adjustment factors are used along with the current estimate of trip distribution Q_{IJ} (current) to improve the approximation. A comparison of Eqs. 8.3.16 and 8.3.17 shows that the adjustment factors that are used in all but the first iteration and the original growth factors that are applied during the first iteration play the same mathematical role. Their interpretation, however, is not the same: The growth factors constitute a prediction of the actual growth of each zone between the base year and the target year, but the subsequent adjustment factors are merely mathematical adjustments that facilitate the convergence of the solution to the predicted zonal-trip generation.

The basic equation employed by the Fratar model to calculate the portion of the target-year generation of zone I that will interchange with zone J is

$$Q_{IJ}(\text{new}) = \frac{[Q_{IJ}(\text{current})]R_J}{\sum_{x} [Q_{Ix}(\text{current})]R_x} Q_I(t) \tag{8.3.18}$$

This equation is similar to that of the gravity model. The expected trip generation of zone I is distributed among all zones so that a specific zone J receives its share according to a zone-specific term divided by the sum of these terms for all "competing" zones x. When Eq. 8.3.18 is applied to all zones, two estimated values result for each pair of zones: The first represents the portion of the generation of zone I allotted to the interchange due to the influence of zone J (or Q_{IJ}), and the second is the portion of the generation of zone J allotted to the interchange due to the influence of zone I (or Q_{JI}). As the following example shows, these two values are not necessarily equal. Since the Fratar model employs only one interzonal volume estimate $Q_{IJ} = Q_{JI}$, the two values are simply averaged; that is,

$$Q_{IJ}(\text{current}) = Q_{JI}(\text{current}) = \frac{Q_{IJ}(\text{new}) + Q_{JI}(\text{new})}{2} \tag{8.3.19}$$

and these values are used to calculate the new adjustment factors as explained previously.

An asymmetric form of the Fratar model begins with a base-year trip table in the production-attraction format. In this case the sum of each row represents the base year productions, whereas the sum of each column represents the base-year attractions of the corresponding zone. Each zone is given two growth factors: one associated with the expected growth in residential activity (and, therefore, productions), whereas the second captures the zone's nonresidential growth (i.e., attractions).

Example 8.7: Application of the Fratar Model

Consider the base-year trip distribution of the simple four-zone system of Fig. 8.3.13. Assuming that the growth factors for the four zones are as shown, find the target-year trip distribution.

Solution The accompanying trip table summarizes the base-year data. Note that $Q_{IJ} = Q_{JI}$, as required by the Fratar model.

I \ J	1	2	3	4	$Q_I(b)$	$\times$	G_I	$=$	$Q_I(t)$
1	0	20	30	15	65		2		130
2	20	0	10	40	70		2		140
3	30	10	0	35	75		3		225
4	15	40	35	0	90		1		90
$Q_J(b)$	65	70	75	90					

Step 1: Use the trip balance Eq. 8.3.15 to compute the base-year trip generation for each of the four zones and multiply this total by the corresponding growth factor to calculate the target-year trip generation of each zone.

The marginal sums of each row or column of the trip table represent the base-year trip generation for the respective zones. The computation of the target-year generation using the row sums is also shown.

Step 2: For the first iteration, equate the adjustment factors to the growth factors and the current interchange flows to the base-year interchange volumes.

Step 3: Apply Eq. 8.3.18 to all pairs of zones I, J to get

I \ J	1	2	3	4
1	0	36	81	13
2	51	0	38	51
3	117	39	0	69
4	13	33	44	0

Step 4: Apply Eq. 8.3.19 to arrive at single volume estimates for each interchange:

I \ J	1	2	3	4	Q_I(current)
1	0	43.5	99.0	13.0	155.5
2	43.5	0	38.5	42.0	124.0
3	99.0	38.5	0	56.5	194.0
4	13.0	42.0	56.5	0	111.5
Q_J(current)	155.5	124.0	194.0	111.5	

Step 5: Apply Eq. 8.3.15 to calculate the target-year trip generation of each zone that is implied in the results of Step 4. The results of this step are shown in the marginal column and row of the preceding table.

Step 6: Apply Eq. 8.3.17 to compute the adjustment factors:

$$R_1 = \frac{130}{155.5} = 0.84 \qquad R_2 = 1.13 \qquad R_3 = 1.16 \qquad R_4 = 0.81$$

These adjustment factors show that the current solution overestimates the target-year generation of zones 1 and 4 (i.e., the adjustment factors are less than unity) and underestimates it for zones 2 and 3. If a better approximation is desired, the procedure returns to Step 3, using the given adjustment factors and the contents of the trip table of Step 4 as the current interchange volumes.

8.3.5 Limitations of the Fratar Model

The Fratar model suffers from three major drawbacks. First, it breaks down mathematically when a new zone (e.g., a new housing development) is built after the base year, since all base-year interchange volumes involving such a zone would be equal to zero; second, convergence to the target-year generation totals is not always possible; and third, the model is not sensitive to the impedance W_{IJ}, which has been shown to affect significantly the interzonal distribution of trips. For these reasons, the application of the Fratar model is restricted to situations where the more sophisticated models (such as the gravity model) cannot be used.

8.3.6 Summary

The aim of trip distribution is to estimate the target-year interchange volumes between all pairs of zones. The trip productions of each zone I obtained from the earlier trip generation phase are distributed among the trip-attracting zones J. The trip volume that a zone J would attract depends on its relative attractiveness (i.e., the availability of nonresidential activities vis-à-vis all competing zones of attraction) and the relative impedance between the producing zone I and the subject zone J. Estimates of the interzonal impedances are obtained from the specification of the transportation alternative plan under consideration.

The most common formulation of trip distribution is the gravity model, which is conceptually based on Newton's law of gravitation. This section presented the mathematical development of the model, described how it can be calibrated, and illustrated its application. The gravity model can be calibrated separately for each of several trip purposes if the outputs of the antecedent trip generation phase permit it. Also, it may be calibrated for total daily volumes (i.e., person-trips per day) or for smaller time periods of the day (e.g., person-trips per peak period).

A simple growth-factor model, the Fratar model, was described. Although insensitive to interzonal impedance, this model can be useful in special situations where the detailed data required by more sophisticated models are not available.

8.4 MODAL CHOICE

8.4.1 Introduction

In a typical travel situation, trip-makers can select between several travel modes. These may include driving, riding with someone else, taking the bus, walking, riding a motorcycle and so forth. A *modal choice,* or *modal split,* model is concerned with the trip-maker's behavior regarding the selection of travel mode. The reasons underlying this choice vary between individuals, trip type, and the relative level of service and cost associated with the available modes. If the reader were to contemplate the reasons behind his or her choice of travel mode to and from school or work, the reader would have a tangible example of what these factors mean. Additionally, it is likely that the reader has established a pattern of modal choice that remains relatively constant as long as these conditions remain the same. When significant changes in these conditions occur, trip-makers respond to varying degrees by shifting from one mode to another. For example, a significant increase in the parking fees charged at a destination may induce some people to shift from driving a car to riding a bus.

The characteristics of the trip also have an effect on the choice of mode. It seems more likely, for example, that a person would choose to travel to work or school by a mass-transit system but prefer the private automobile, if available, for social trips. As discussed in relation to trip generation and trip distribution, it is not unusual for a regional transportation study to decompose trip making into trip-purpose categories and to model each component separately. This practice could then be extended to the modal choice phase as well.

In addition to the attributes of the available modes and the trip type, the socioeconomic status of the trip-maker affects the choice of travel mode. Thus trip-makers may also be classified or disaggregated into finer categories, such as income or age, and separate estimates may be obtained for each of these socioeconomic subgroups. In many transportation planning studies, a particular subgroup (referred to as the *transit-captive* subgroup) has been singled out for special treatment. As this group's name implies, it consists of people who for various reasons do not have ready access to private transportation and, hence, whose mobility is almost exclusively dependent on the public-transit system. Included in this group are many of the elderly, the poor, the very young, and even the second primary individual of one-car households. Because this group is of considerable size, public transportation policy at the federal, state, and local levels has specifically addressed the needs of the members of this group.

Since transit captives do not have access to private transportation, they may be identified on a zonal basis as a percentage of the trip generation. The remaining trip-makers who do have a choice between competing private and public modes are treated by the modal split model, which estimates the percentage of trip-makers who choose to use the public-transportation system (i.e., the *choice riders*). The total ridership of the public transportation system can be obtained by summing the estimated captive and choice riders.

Depending on their positions in the demand-forecasting sequence, modal choice models are classified either as *predistribution* (*trip-end*) models or as *post-distribution* (*trip-interchange*) models (Fig. 8.4.1). As their name implies, the former are applied before the trip distribution step—or, to put it in another way, they operate on the trip ends (i.e., P_I) resulting from the trip-generation step. This practice carries the behavioral implication that trip-makers choose their modes of travel prior to deciding where to go; that is, the choice of attraction-zone J has no effect on their choices of modes. As Table 8.4.1 illustrates, in these models, the variables that capture the service attributes of the competing modes cannot be specified at the zonal-interchange level; they can only be gross estimates of the regionwide service offered by these modes. This assumption is appropriate for urban areas where public-transportation service is minimal. On the other hand, if the public-transportation system is or is expected to be extensive, it becomes

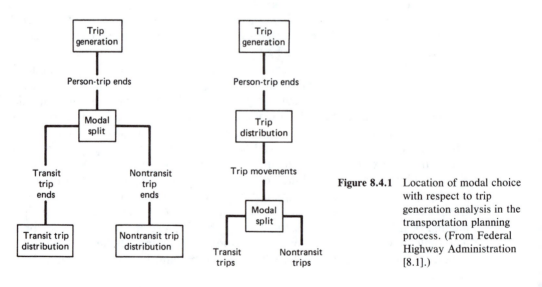

Figure 8.4.1 Location of modal choice with respect to trip generation analysis in the transportation planning process. (From Federal Highway Administration [8.1].)

TABLE 8.4.1   VARIABLES USED IN MODAL SPLIT MODELS

Variables	Trip-end models					Trip-interchange models			
	Chicago	Pittsburgh	Erie	Puget Sound	Southeastern Wisconsin	Washington D.C.	Twin Cities	San Juan	Buffalo
Trip characteristics									
Number of trip purposes used	2	3	1	4	7	2	3	2	2
Length of trip									x
Time of day						x			x
Orientation to CBD	x	x							
Trip-maker characteristics									
Auto ownership	x	x		x	x			x	x
Residential density		x		x			x		
Income				x		x	x		
Workers per household									x
Distance to CBD		x							
Employment density							x		
Transportation-system characteristics									
Travel time						x	x	x	x
Travel cost						x		x	
Parking cost						x	x		x
Excess travel time[a]						x			
Accessibility[b]			x	x	x				

[a] Time spent outside the vehicle during a trip: walk, wait, and transfer times for transit trips and parking-delay time for auto trips.

[b] A measure of the level of travel service provided by the transit or highway system to trip ends in the study area.

Source: Fertal et al. [8.9].

necessary to capture the relative service attributes of the competing modes at the interchange level, since the relative levels of service offered by the competing modes are likely to vary between interchanges. Thus trip-interchange models are applied after trip distribution. In some studies, trip-end and trip-interchange models are used in combination.

To summarize, the mode-choice behavior of trip-makers can be explained by three categories of factors: the characteristics of the available modes; the socioeconomic status of the trip maker; and the characteristics of the trip. These are the categories of independent variables that would be included in mathematical models of modal choice, the dependent variable being the market share or the percent of travelers that are expected to use each of the available modes.

One of the simplest modal split models employs simple *diversion curves*, such as the one illustrated by Fig. 7.4.8. A more elaborate empirical stratified *diversion-type model* and the probability-based *multinomial logit* formulation of modal choice are discussed in this section. Another form of the logit model, known as the nested logit formulation, is beyond the scope of this book. (See [8.34] for detailed coverage on this topic.)

8.4.2 The Stratified Diversion-Curve Model

Figure 8.4.2 illustrates a typical stratified diversion-curve model of the modal choice, which superposes the calibration results obtained in Washington, D.C., Philadelphia, and Toronto for work trips and two competing modes (i.e., auto and transit). Similar curves were also calibrated for other trip purposes. The independent variables employed by this model include three characteristics of the competing modes—the ratio of transit to auto travel time (TTR), the ratio of transit to auto costs (CR), and the ratio of transit to auto service (L), which is defined as the time spent outside the vehicle—and one characteristic of the trip makers, income category (EC). Each cell of the table corresponds to an income range and a cost-ratio level and contains a family of regression curves relating the travel-time ratio to the percentage of trips choosing transit for each of the four levels of relative service.

The modal characteristics employed by this particular model are given separately for each interchange between a pair of zones. For this reason, this model has come to be known as *the* trip-interchange model even though trip-interchange models of other mathematical forms are possible.

The application of this model is straightforward: The interchange volume obtained from the trip distribution phase is multiplied by the appropriate percentage obtained from Fig. 8.4.2 to arrive at the market shares of the two competing modes of travel.

Example 8.8

The peak-hour target-year work-trip interchange volume between two zones has been estimated to be 2000 person-trips as follows: 200 of these trips are made by captive riders, 600 are made by trip-makers from households of income category EC_3, and the remaining 1200 from economic category EC_5. Apply the Washington, D.C., stratified model of Fig. 8.4.2 to find the market share of the transit system assuming that this model has been calibrated as a disaggregate model based on household-income categories. The following data apply to the interchange under consideration:

$$TTR = 2.0$$

$$CR = 0.8$$

$$L = 4.0$$

Solution   For a disaggregate model, the contribution of each economic subgroup to the transit patronage must be computed separately and then summed to arrive at an estimate of the total transit share:

$$\text{Captives: } 200 \times 1.0 = 200 \text{ person-trips}$$

$$EC_3 \text{ group: } 600 \times 0.25 = 150$$

$$EC_5 \text{ group: } 1200 \times 0.2 = 240$$

Figure 8.4.2 Work-trip modal split relationships for Washington, Philadelphia, and Toronto. (From Deen et al. [8.10].)

Figure 8.4.2 *Continued*

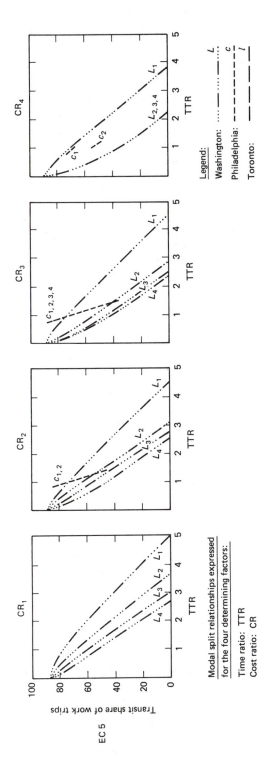

Modal split relationships expressed
for the four determining factors:

Time ratio: TTR
Cost ratio: CR
Service ratio: L
Economic status: EC

Figure 8.4.2 *Continued*

351

The transit patronage for this interchange is 590 person-trips per peak hour (or about 30% of the total interchange volume).

Discussion   This problem assumed that the modal split curves had been calibrated on a disaggregate basis, and the same assumption was retained in the solution. To be able to do this, the trip-generation data were disaggregated into the three market segments. If the modal split curves were calibrated on a zonal basis, two consequences would be observed. First, the curves resulting from a zone-based calibration would not be identical to those resulting from a household-based calibration. Second, assuming that economic status were still the relevant variable, it would represent a zonal-level characteristic (say, the average zonal-income level) and only a single target-year value of this variable would be projected forward. Based on this zonal variable, a single percentage of trips using transit would be obtained and applied to the entire interchange volume rather than the separately calculated contributions to the total by each economic subgroup. It should be noted that, in actuality, the diversion curves of the model had been calibrated on a zonal basis. Hence, their application as disaggregate curves is questionable.

8.4.3 Probabilistic Models

Although simple in concept, the model described previously is awkward to calibrate and use, especially if more than two competing travel modes are to be included. In its full form, which involved a number of trip purposes, the Washington, D.C., model consisted of 160 different curves. More computationally efficient probability-based models of modal choice have been developed including discriminant analysis models, probit analysis models, and the most popular logit analysis models [8.11, 8.12, 8.34]. These models of human choice have been applied to many situations to explain how people select between competing alternatives. Each alternative is described by a utility (or disutility) function, and the probability associated with an individual's choosing of each of the competing alternatives is expressed mathematically in terms of these utilities. Extended to groups of individuals via the theory of probability, these models estimate the proportion of the group that is likely to choose each of the competing alternatives. The development of each model involves two steps: the selection of its mathematical form and the calibration of appropriate utility functions that render the selected model capable of reproducing the available base-year data.

8.4.4 Utility and Disutility Functions

A *utility* function measures the degree of satisfaction that people derive from their choices. A *disutility* function represents the generalized cost (akin to the concept of impedance) that is associated with each choice. The magnitude of either depends on the characteristics (or *attributes*) of each choice and on the characteristics (or socioeconomic status) of the individual making that choice. In the case of modal choice, the characteristics of the trip (e.g., trip purpose) also bear a relationship to the utility associated with choosing a particular mode of travel. To specify a utility function, it is necessary to select the relevant variables from this list and to select the particular functional form relating the selected variables. In addition, the analyst or planner is faced with the now-familiar question relating to the level of disaggregation of the modeling effort. Simply stated, this decision relates to whether a calibration will be at the regional, zonal, household or individual level, and also whether the calibration will include different models for other categories, such as trip purpose or time of day. This decision, of course, affects the types of variables that must be included. For example, when separate models are calibrated for each socioeconomic class of trip-makers and for each trip purpose, the utility function contains only variables that are related to the attributes of the competing modes.

The utility (or disutility) function is typically expressed as the linear weighted sum of the independent variables or their transformation, that is,

$$U = a_0 + a_1X_1 + a_2X_2 + \cdots + a_rX_r \qquad (8.4.1)$$

where U is the utility derived from a choice defined by the magnitudes of the attributes X that are present in that choice and that are weighted by the model parameters a.

Early attempts to describe the utility associated with travel modes calibrated a *separate* utility function for each mode, as illustrated by the following hypothetical three-mode case:

$$U_1 = 6.2 + 2.4X_1 + 3.5X_2 \qquad (8.4.2a)$$

$$U_2 = 3.4 + 3.1X_1 + 2.9X_3 \qquad (8.4.2b)$$

$$U_3 = 4.3 + 2.9X_1 + 3.2X_3 \qquad (8.4.2c)$$

The three modes in this hypothetical example may be the private auto, a local bus system, an express bus system, respectively, and the independent variables (or attributes) may represent the cost, level of service, and convenience associated with a mode. This type of formulation is known as a *mode-specific* (and, in the general case, *choice-specific*) model, because the same attributes are assigned different weights for different modes. It is not even necessary to include the same variables in the utility equations of different modes. This, of course, is the same as saying that some attributes are either absent or are given zero weights in certain modes. Although there may be some validity in this hypothesis, it causes a problem when a new mode is introduced. In that case, it would be next to impossible to estimate the utility associated with the new mode because the necessary base-year data required for the calibration of its utility function would be unavailable. This new-product problem has haunted consumer-behavior analysts as well. A way to resolve it was proposed by Lancaster [8.13] as a new approach to consumer theory, where he postulated the idea of a *choice-abstract* (or *attribute-specific*) approach. This theory is based on the hypothesis that when making choices, people perceive goods and services indirectly in terms of their attributes, each of which is weighted identically across choices. Thus trip-makers perceive two distinct modes offering the same cost, level of service, and convenience as being identical. Continuing with the three-mode example, a *mode-abstract* model of modal choice would use a single equation to measure utility; for example,

$$U = 3.1 + 2.8X_1 + 1.2X_2 + 0.9X_3 \qquad (8.4.3)$$

Differences in the utilities U associated with each of the competing modes arise because of differences in the magnitudes of the attributes X of these modes. For example, one mode may be faster but costlier than another, and this fact is reflected in their calculated utilities. The attribute-specific approach has a strong conceptual foundation. However, in practical applications, it is not possible to enumerate all the relevant attributes involved in the choice of mode. The first constant term in Eq. 8.4.3 is meant to capture the effect of variables that are not explicitly included in the model. Since it is unlikely that a given set of competing modes will be identical in these excluded attributes, it is reasonable to attempt to capture these unexpressed differences by calibrating for alternative-specific constants by weighting the explicitly identified attributes equally across modes. The calibrated utility function in the case of the three-mode example may then become

$$U_K = a_K + 2.5X_1 + 1.5X_2 + 0.8X_3 \qquad (8.4.4)$$

where U_K is the utility of mode K and a_K is the calibrated mode-specific constant for the same mode. The new-product problem resurfaces but in a milder form, since the selection of a mode-specific constant for a new mode is much more amenable to professional judgement vis-à-vis the mode-specific models, where none of the coefficients are known.

     A utility-based modal-choice model estimates the market share of each mode based on the utility associated with it. In a *deterministic* model, it would seem reasonable that all travelers (if they know what is good for them) will select the mode with the highest utility. However, the models being discussed are not deterministic but *probabilistic* (see Appendix D). In other words, the calculated modal utilities are related to the likelihood that a given mode will be selected or, when dealing with groups of travelers, the proportion or fraction that will select each mode of travel. The relationship between this fraction and the utilities of competing modes has been cast in various forms, the most popular of which is the logit model, which can be applied to the case of two [8.14] or multiple [8.15] competing modes.

8.4.5 The Multinomial Logit Model

The multinomial logit model calculates the proportion of travelers that will select a specific mode K according to the following relationship:

$$p(K) = \frac{e^{U_K}}{\sum_x e^{U_x}} \qquad (8.4.5)$$

The general form of this equation resembles the fractional term employed by the gravity model of trip distribution: A term relating to the subject mode K appears as the numerator and the summation of the similar terms corresponding to all competing modes is placed in the denominator. This specification ensures that all trips that have been estimated to occur on a specific interchange are assigned to the available modes; that is, the following trip-balance equation is satisfied:

$$Q_{IJ} = \sum_x Q_{IJx} \qquad (8.4.6)$$

Equation 8.4.6 would still be satisfied by writing the proportion attracted by each mode as

$$p(K) = \frac{U_K}{\sum_x U_x} \qquad (8.4.7)$$

For reasons that lie beyond the scope of this book, the logistic transformation of the utilities (Eq. 8.4.5) is preferred.

Example 8.9: Application of the Logit Model

A calibration study resulted in the following utility equation:

$$U_K = a_K - 0.025X_1 - 0.032X_2 - 0.015X_3 - 0.002X_4$$

where

$$X_1 = \text{access plus egress time, in minutes}$$

$$X_2 = \text{waiting time, in minutes}$$

$$X_3 = \text{line-haul time, in minutes}$$

$$X_4 = \text{out-of-pocket cost, in cents}$$

The trip-distribution forecast for a particular interchange was a target-year volume of $Q_{IJ} = 5000$ person-trips per day. During the target year, trip-makers on this particular interchange will have a choice between the private automobile (A) and a local bus system (B). The target-year service attributes of the two competing modes have been estimated to be:

Attribute:	X_1	X_2	X_3	X_4
Automobile:	5	0	20	100
Local bus:	10	15	40	50

Assuming that the calibrated mode-specific constants are -0.12 for the automobile mode and -0.56 for the bus mode, apply the logit model to estimate the target-year market share of the two modes and the resulting fare-box revenue of the bus system.

Solution   The utility equation yields

$$U(A) = -0.745 \qquad \text{and} \qquad U(B) = -1.990$$

According to the logit equation (Eq. 8.4.5),

$$p(A) = 0.78 \quad \text{and} \quad p(B) = 0.22$$

Therefore, the market share of each mode is

$$Q_{IJ}(A) = (0.78)(5000) = 3900 \text{ trips/day}$$

$$Q_{IJ}(B) = (0.22)(5000) = 1100 \text{ trips/day}$$

The fare-box revenue estimate is

$$(1100 \text{ trips/day})(\$0.50/\text{trip}) = \$550 \text{ per day}$$

Discussion   The terms of the utility function used in this example are negative. As negative quantities they represent cost (that is, disutility) components. The more negative this quantity, the less attractive the mode. Because of the exponential trans-formation of the utilities, the market shares are not directly proportional to the mag-nitudes of utility. Division of the numerator and denominator of Eq. 8.4.5 by $e^{U(A)}$ results in the following form:

$$p(B) = \frac{e^{U*}}{1 + e^{U*}} \quad \text{and} \quad p(A) = \frac{1}{1 + e^{U*}} \tag{8.4.8}$$

where $U*$ is the difference in the utilities of the two modes. This form resembles that advanced by Stopher [8.14]. In the bimodal case, the logistic transformation results a sigmoidal curve, as illustrated by Fig. 8.4.3.

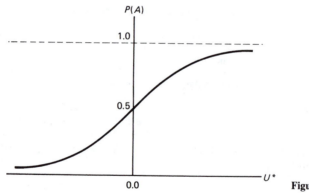

Figure 8.4.3   Binomial logit model.

Example 8.10: Introduction of a New Mode

It is desired to examine the effect of introducing a rapid-transit (RT) system in the city of Example 8.9. A related study has projected that the service attributes of the proposed system for the interchange under consideration will be:

$$X_1(RT) = 10 \qquad X_2(RT) = 5 \qquad X_3(RT) = 30 \qquad X_4(RT) = 75$$

Based on professional experience, the mode-specific constant for the new mode is somewhere between the other two but closer to the bus system, say -0.41. Find the market shares of the three modes that will result from implementing the rapid-transit proposal and the effect on the revenues of the public transportation authority, which operates both the local bus and the rapid-transit systems.

Solution   Assuming that the attributes of the existing modes will not be affected by the introduction of the new mode, the utilities of the three alternatives will be

$$U(A) = -0.745 \qquad U(B) = -1.990 \qquad U(RT) = -1.420$$

Proceeding as before, we obtain

$$
\begin{array}{llll}
p(A) & = 0.56 & Q_{IJ}(A) & = 2800 \\
p(B) & = 0.16 \qquad \text{and} \qquad & Q_{IJ}(B) & = 800 \\
p(RT) & = 0.28 & Q_{IJ}(RT) & = 1400
\end{array}
$$

The revenue will be $800 \times 0.5 + 1400 \times 0.75 = \$1450$ per day.

Discussion   One of the attractive characteristics of the logit model is the fact that it could be so easily extended to this situation. In this example, the proposed system is seen to attract 28 percent of the interchange volume, or 1400 person-trips, reducing the auto usage by 1100 trips and the local bus patronage by 300 daily trips. In this connection, it is appropriate to mention that the specification of competing modes does not have to be restricted to the generic categories illustrated by this example. Depending on special concerns, finer categories of modes or submodes may be considered for calibration. For example, a study in Honolulu, Hawaii [8.6], which addressed the question of car-pooling, has calibrated mode-specific constants for the following modes:

1. Driving alone
2. Auto with 2 occupants
3. Auto with 3+ occupants
4. Regular bus
5. Express bus

The fare-box revenue on this interchange increased from \$550 to \$1450 per day. This, however, is not necessarily a sufficient reason to implement the proposed system. This decision must also consider the costs of constructing and operating the system as well as other impacts.

Example 8.11: Sensitivity to Other Policies

A city council is contemplating a proposal to charge a rapid-transit fare of \$1.50 rather than \$0.75. Determine the effect of this policy on the utilization of the three modes and on the public transportation authority's revenues.

Solution   The proposed policy will cause a change in the utility of the rapid-transit system to -1.57 and will affect the patronage of all modes. Proceed as before.

Mode	Proportion	Market share
Auto	0.58	2900
Local bus	0.17	850
Rapid transit	0.25	1250

The revenue will be $850 \times 0.5 + 1250 \times 1.50 = \$2300$ per day.

Discussion   This example shows how the response of trip-makers to various public policies and combinations of policies can be examined. The fare increase induced some patrons to shift back to the auto and bus modes. Although the public-transit share decreased, the revenues increased. In order words, the extra fare revenue collected outweighed the losses that resulted from patronage losses. This is not always the case, however (see the discussion of price elasticity in Section 8.7.5).

8.4.6 Summary

The purpose of a modal choice model is to predict the trip-makers' choice of travel mode. The factors that explain this behavior include:

1. The characteristics of the trip-maker
2. The characteristics of the trip
3. The attributes of the available modes of travel

Trip-end or predistribution models are applied after trip generation and hence can incorporate the attributes of the available modes only on a regionwide level. These models may be applicable to urban areas offering only limited public transportation service. Trip-interchange or postdistribution models are applied after trip distribution and thus operate on estimates of interchange volume. In either case, modal split models may be aggregate or disaggregate, depending on the level at which they are calibrated and applied.

The purely empirical diversion-curve method and the probability-based multinomial logit formulation were presented in this section and the concepts of utility and disutility employed by the latter were explained. The difference between choice-specific and attribute-specific models of consumer behavior was drawn and illustrated.

8.5 NETWORK OR TRIP ASSIGNMENT

8.5.1 Introduction

The last phase of the sequential transportation-forecasting process is concerned with the trip-makers' choice of path between pairs of zones by travel mode and with the resulting vehicular flows on the multimodal transportation network. This step may be viewed as the equilibration model between the demand for travel (Q_{IJK}) estimated earlier in the process and the supply of transportation in terms of the physical facilities and, in the case of the various possible mass-transit modes, the frequency of service provided. Incidentally, this conceptual framework of economic theory is applicable to earlier steps of the process as well and has been so treated by many authors. Examples 8.9 through 8.11 illustrate how people respond to changes in the availability and price of transportation services. If the price of one mode increases relative to another, its market share will decrease.

Returning to the topic of network assignment, the question of interest is: Given Q_{IJK}, that is, the estimate of interzonal demand by mode, determine the trip-makers' likely choice of paths between all zones I and J along the network of each mode K and predict the resulting flows q on the individual links that make up the network of that mode (Fig. 8.5.1). The estimates of link utilization can be used to assess the likely level of service and to anticipate potential capacity problems.

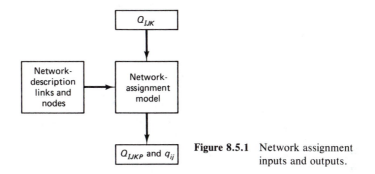

Figure 8.5.1   Network assignment inputs and outputs.

The number of available paths between any pair of zones depends on the mode of travel. In the case of private-transportation modes, a driver has a relatively large set of possible paths and path variations and also a good deal of freedom in selecting between them. On the other hand, typical mass-transit modes offer a limited number of path (or route) choices.

Three preliminary questions must be dealt with prior to the performance of network assignment. The first is related to the difference between interzonal person-trips and interzonal vehicle-trips, the second is related to the difference between daily trips (that is, the estimate of the 24-h demand) versus the diurnal distribution of this demand, and the third is concerned with the direction of travel of the trips to be assigned on the transportation network.

8.5.2 Person-Trips and Vehicle-Trips

The forecasts of the person-trip and vehicle-trip flows that are expected to use the transportation system are both relevant to the assessment of its performance.

The estimate of person-trips that desire to use a highway, for example, provides an indication of the passenger throughput that will be accommodated. On the other hand, the level of service (see Chapter 4) that the trip-makers experience when traveling on a highway is related to the *vehicular* flow (e.g., vehicles per hour) that desires to use the highway. For this reason, the estimated interzonal person-trips must be translated into vehicular-trips prior to performing the high-way-trip assignment (also known as *traffic assignment*). *Car occupancies* (i.e., persons per car) vary between cities and also between trip types.

The estimate of person-trips that desire to use a highway, for example, provides an indication of the passenger throughput that will be accommodated. On the other hand, the level of service (see Chapter 4) that the trip-makers experience when traveling on a highway is related to the *vehicular* flow (e.g., vehicles per hour) that desires to use the highway. For this reason, the estimated interzonal person-trips must be translated into vehicular-trips prior to performing the high-way-trip assignment (also known as *traffic assignment*). *Car occupancies* (i.e., persons per car) vary between cities and also between trip types.

Mass-transit (or *transit assignment*) must address another issue as well. In this case, the specification of an alternative system consists not only of the fixed facilities that constitute the modal network but also the scheduling of transit services. This means that the analysis of a particular transit alternative must address the question of whether a proposed fleet size and operating schedule and the related vehicular frequencies (i.e., flows) provide sufficient capacity to meet the anticipated interzonal person-trip demand.

8.5.3 Diurnal Patterns of Demand

In Chapters 4 and 5, the highway flows and intersection-approach volumes that are used to calculate the prevailing level of service are expressed in vehicles per hour. On the other hand, the estimates of interzonal flows that are obtained by the trip generation-distribution modal choice sequence are often based on a 24-h period. As Fig. 8.2.2 illustrates, the demand for transportation exhibits a highly peaked pattern with a sharp peak period in the morning and a generally longer but less pronounced peak period in the evening. It is appropriate, therefore, to investigate the performance of the transportation system under peak-demand conditions, when capacity limitations become most critical. The time variation of demand is most relevant to mass-transit planning because the scheduling of service is typically tailored to the variation of demand over the 24-h period.

The diurnal distribution of demand may be estimated through the use of factors taken from observations during the base year, or it may be explicitly modeled in the preceding steps of the demand-forecasting process. Typically, the morning peak period demand is in the range of 10 to 20% of the total daily demand.

8.5.4 Trip Direction

In the discussion of trip generation, a distinction was drawn between productions and attractions on one hand and origins and destinations on the other. It was also explained why most trip-generation models estimate productions rather than origins. However, it is desirable that the assignment of trips (especially by time of day) retain the direction of these trips. The predominant direction of travel during the morning peak period is toward major activity centers (i.e., CBDs or schools), and the reverse is true during the evening rush hour. The experience and knowledge accumulated through studies of the travel patterns within the region aid in the accomplishment of this task.

8.5.5 Historical Context

The origin of traffic assignment can be traced to the 1950s and early 1960s, when the majority of urban freeways were constructed in United States cities. Typically, highway engineers wanted to know how many drivers would be diverted from arterial streets to a proposed freeway in order to make decisions related to the geometric design and capacity of proposed urban freeways. The *diversion-curve model* was developed to answer this question. This model employs empirically derived curves to compute the percentage of trips that would use the freeway route between two points on some measure of relative impedance between the freeway route and the fastest arterial route between the two points. Figure 8.5.2 shows that the California diversion curves use travel time and travel distance differences between the two alternative paths to estimate the percentage of trips that use the freeway. Figure 8.5.3 illustrates a diversion curve developed by the BPR [8.17], where the ratio of travel times via the two routes serves as the impedance measure.

A shortcoming of the diversion-curve method is the fact that drivers between two points have path options that contain both freeway segments and arterial street segments rather than two distinct all-freeway and all-arterial paths. Moreover, these combinations become computationally complex as the number of zonal pairs and the size of the transportation network increase. Developments in digital computer technology have made it possible to expand the traffic assignment procedure to large networks. A network assignment procedure requires

1. A way of coding the modal network for computer processing
2. An understanding of the factors affecting the trip-makers' path preferences
3. A computer algorithm capable of producing the trip-makers' preferred paths

8.5.6 Highway Network Description

Figure 8.5.4 shows a street map of a hypothetical urban highway network consisting of facilities of the various classes discussed in Chapter 2, ranging from local streets to high-type facilities such as freeways and expressways. The figure also shows the boundaries of travel-analysis zones [8.17, 8.18].

Figure 8.5.5 contains only those elements of the highway network that would normally be included in the coded traffic assignment network. A comparison of the two figures shows that local and minor streets are not included in the coded network and the remaining fixed facilities (i.e., major arterials, expressways, and freeways) are specified by a set of *nodes* (i.e., intersections and interchanges) and *links*. Each node is specified by a numerical code and each link is described

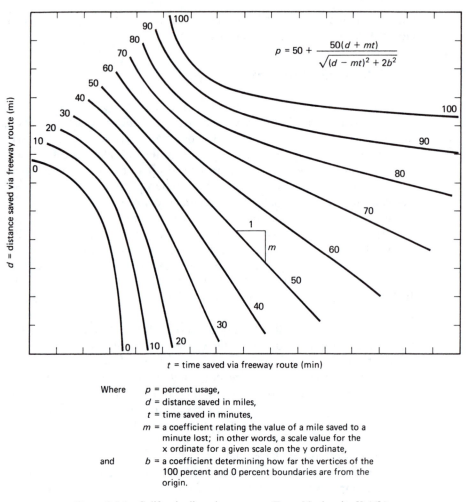

$$p = 50 + \frac{50(d + mt)}{\sqrt{(d - mt)^2 + 2b^2}}$$

t = time saved via freeway route (min)

Where   *p* = percent usage,
        d = distance saved in miles,
        t = time saved in minutes,
        m = a coefficient relating the value of a mile saved to a
            minute lost; in other words, a scale value for the
            x ordinate for a given scale on the y ordinate,
and   *b* = a coefficient determining how far the vertices of the
            100 percent and 0 percent boundaries are from the
            origin.

Figure 8.5.2   California diversion curves. (From Moskowitz [8.16].)

by its end nodes. Important characteristics of each link (such as its capacity, free-flow speed or travel time) are also specified. It is often advantageous to select the coding scheme judiciously to reflect other link attributes as well. For example, nodes that lie exclusively on arterial streets may be denoted by one range of numerical codes (say, between 100 and 1000), whereas nodes that lie on higher-type facilities may be coded with numbers in another range (say, greater than 1000). Thus a link connecting nodes 525 and 666 is clearly a segment of an arterial street, while link 1212-1213 is a segment of freeway. Moreover, links 729-1432 and 1198-888 represent an on-ramp (i.e., connecting an arterial to a freeway) and an off-ramp (i.e., connecting a freeway to an arterial).

Figure 8.5.3   Bureau of Public Roads diversion curve. (From Bureau of Public
Roads [8.17].)

Travel-analysis zones are coded as a set of imaginary nodes referred to as
zonal centroids. To distinguish them from the actual network nodes, they are
usually designated by numerical codes at the lower range of positive integers (see
the heavy nodes of Fig. 8.5.5). Their geographical location is often taken to coincide with the activity or population centroid of the zones they represent, hence
their name. Finally, a set of imaginary links known as *centroidal connectors*
(shown by dashes in Fig. 8.5.5) are introduced to connect the zonal centroids to
the assignment network. Although not real links, they are typically given link
attributes corresponding to the average conditions that trip-makers experience on
the noncoded local- and minor-street system.

The simple network of Fig. 8.5.6 consists of five zonal centroids (i.e., nodes
1 to 5), six centroidal connectors, nine street intersections (i.e., nodes 6 to 14),
and 13 arterial street links. The numerical values in parentheses correspond to
the link impedances in the direction shown. This network is described by the *link*

Figure 8.5.4 Street classification and base map. (From Bureau of Public Roads [8.17].)

Figure 8.5.5 Sample traffic assignment network map. (From Bureau of Public Roads [8.17].)

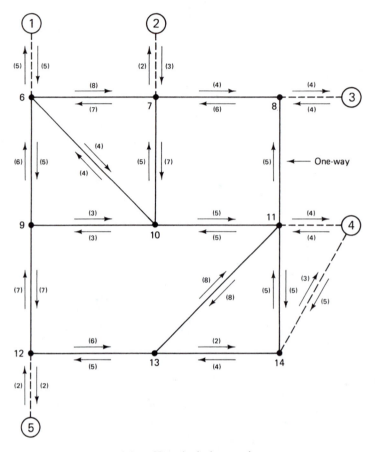

Figure 8.5.6　Hypothetical network.

array (Table 8.5.1), each cell of which represents a possible direct link between the row and column nodes. A numerical entry in a cell means that there is in fact such a link, the cell value being, say, the link's impedance. The dimensions of the link array may be increased to include other link attributes as well, such as free-flow speed, length, and capacity.

8.5.7 Link Flows and Interzonal Flows

A careful distinction must be made between the terms *interzonal flows* (Q_{IJ}) and *link flows* (q_{ij}). The former refer to the demand for travel between a pair of zones. The latter is the flow that occurs on a specific link (i,j) of the transportation network and is the sum of all interzonal flows that happen to include that particular link on their preferred paths. For the sake of clarity, uppercase letters are employed in this book to denote *zones* (I and J) and *interzonal* flow (Q), and low-

TABLE 8.5.1   LINK ARRAY

$i \backslash j$	1	2	3	4	5	6	7	8	9	10	11	12	13	14
1						5								
2							3							
3								4						
4											4			5
5												3		
6	5							8		5	4			
7		2				7		4		7				
8			4			6								
9						6				3		7		
10					4	5			3		5			
11				4				5		5			8	5
12					2				7				6	
13											8	5		2
14				3							5		4	

ercase letters are used to denote traffic assignment network *nodes* (i and j) and link flows (q).

8.5.8 Route-Choice Behavior

The key to assigning users on the network is the underlying behavioral assumption of route choice. In 1952, Wandrop established two mutually independent principles of route choice. According to the first principle, users choose the route that minimizes their own travel time. According to the second principle, users distribute themselves on the network in such a way that the average travel time for all users is equal (on each route leading from origin to destination).

The first rule defines the *user equilibrium*, whereupon each user goes on the shortest path. The second rule defines the *system equilibrium*, whereupon the total cost of using the system is minimized. The terms "shortest" and "cost" typically refer to travel time, but elaborate equilibrium formulations account for *generalized costs*, which include travel time, fuel consumption or fare price, average speed, number of stops, and so forth.

A later development in equilibrium principles recognizes the fact that users have only limited information about the network and their transportation options (mode and route) for going from origin to destination. Thus it is more logical to base the equilibrium on the perceptions of users. This way, each user assigns himself/herself on a path that he or she thinks is the shortest. This is called *stochastic equilibrium*.

The effect of these three types of equilibria is most notable on networks. According to the user equilibrium, all used paths between origin and destination require the same travel time (or cost), while all unused paths have times that are greater than the shortest time. It is likely that several paths between origin and destination will not have any flow.

According to system equilibrium, all possible paths are evaluated and users are assigned in a way to minimize the network-wide travel time or cost. This equilibrium rule is useful during the planning stage of large traffic studies: Signal timing, channelization, lane allocations, and other traffic elements can be used to encourage or discourage particular routes so that the network-wide travel time, pollution, or congestion level is kept at a minimum.

Finally, according to the stochastic equilibrium, all reasonable paths (i.e., paths that logically go from origin to destination) between an origin and a destination will have flow; if two paths have equal impedance, they will have equal flows; while a path k with impedance higher than that of path m will have a flow less than that on path m.

8.5.9 Minimum Path Algorithms

Assume that it is required to find the minimum (impedance) path between zones 3 and 5 on the network of Fig. 8.5.6. This task may be accomplished by identifying all possible paths between the two zones, computing their impedances, and choosing the path with the lowest impedance. But even in the case of this extremely simple network, the path-enumeration procedure is time-consuming and inefficient. More efficient minimum-path algorithms have been developed as variations on a theme advanced by Moore [8.19]. Some determine the minimum path between a pair of zones, while others compute the *minimum tree,* which contains all the interzonal minimum paths that emanate from a zone of origin [8.20].

The basic minimum-tree algorithm begins at the node of origin and proceeds outward, successively eliminating links that clearly do not belong on any minimum path emanating from the origin. Figure 8.5.7 illustrates this concept. Suppose that the minimum tree emanating from node 1 and terminating in all other nodes of the network is being sought. The minimum path to node 5 passes through node 4. But there are two possible paths to node 4: one via node 2 and the other via node 3. The first takes 5 and the second 8 units of impedance. Therefore, the first is the minimum path to node 4 and to any subsequent node whose path passes through node 4. The last link of the longer path (in this case link 3–4) is eliminated from the minimum tree shown by Fig. 8.5.7(b).

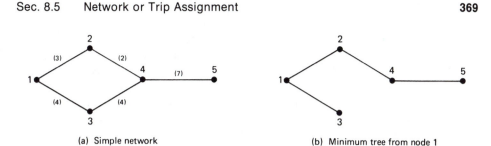

(a) Simple network   (b) Minimum tree from node 1

Figure 8.5.7   Link elimination.

The minimum tree may be described numerically by a *tree table,* as shown by Table 8.5.2. The first column of the tree table contains all network nodes j including the origin. The second column contains the total impedance of the minimum path from the origin to each node j. The last column specifies the node i that immediately precedes node j on the minimum path from the origin to node j. In other words, the pair of nodes (i, j) defines the last link on the minimum path from the origin to node j. Thus the fourth row of the table says that the minimum path from node 1 to node 4 takes 5 units of impedance and that node 4 is immediately preceded by node 2.

TABLE 8.5.2   SIMPLE TREE TABLE

Node (j)	Total impedance to node j	Node preceding j
1	0	—
2	3	1
3	4	1
4	5	2
5	12	4

The tree table describes a specific path, say to node 5, as follows: Node 5 is preceded by node 4 (last column of row 5), node 4 is preceded by node 2 (last column of row 4), and node 2 is preceded by node 1 (last column of row 2), which is the origin (last column of row 1). Reversing this order, the path from node 1 to node 5 consists of the following sequence of links: 1–2, 2–4, and 4–5.

Most transportation planning packages (see Section 9.2) incorporate assignment algorithms. The more sophisticated of them incorporate *vine building* algorithms. A vine building algorithm, when seeking minimum paths, takes into account both delays at intersections (nodes) and turn prohibitions.

8.5.10 A Minimum-Tree-Seeking Procedure

The following procedure produces the tree table that contains every minimum path emanating from the node of origin:

Step 1:   Initialize the path impedances of the tree table at zero for the node of origin and a very large number for all other nodes. This large number ensures that the first encountered actual path to a node will be chosen.

Step 2:   Enter into a list the links (i,j) that emanate directly from any node i just added to the tree.

Step 3:   For each node j included in the list, add the impedance of link (i, j) to the tree table's current total impedance to node i. This quantity represents the total impedance to node j via node i. If this value is smaller than the current tree table entry for node j, replace the current total impedance to j with the new total impedance and enter node i as the node that immediately precedes j. This operation replaces the longer path to node j with the shorter one just discovered. If the new total impedance is greater than the current tree table entry, proceed to the next link in the list.

Step 4:   Return to Step 2, unless the list is empty, in which case the tree table contains the solution.

Example 8.12: Minimum-Tree Algorithm

Find the minimum tree emanating from node 1 for the network described by the link array of Table 8.5.1

Solution   The graphical solution to this problem is summarized by Fig. 8.5.8. The related calculations are shown by Tables 8.5.3 and 8.5.4. Table 8.5.3 shows the changes performed on the tree table as the tree is built outward from the origin (node 1). The second and third columns of the table have been expanded to show these

TABLE 8.5.3   TREE-TABLE CHANGES AT THE END OF EACH STAGE

Node	Total impedance to node j						Node preceding j					
(j)	I	II	III	IV	V	VI	I	II	III	IV	V	VI
1	0						—					
2	∞			15						7		N
3	∞				21						8	O
4	∞				18						11	
5	∞				19						12	
6	∞	5					1					C
7	∞		13						6			H
8	∞			17						7		A
9	∞		10						6			N
10	∞		9						6			G
11	∞			14						10		E
12	∞			17						9		
13	∞				22						11	
14	∞				19						11	

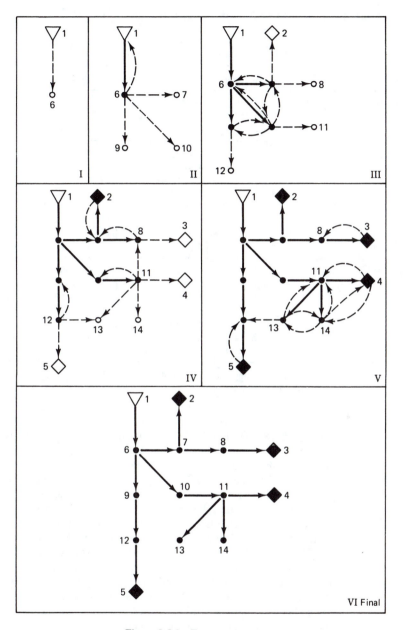

Figure 8.5.8 Tree stages.

changes as they occur during the procedure. The initial condition (stage I) contains only the node of origin. All links emanating from node 1 are next entered in the list (Table 8.5.4) and are also shown by dashed lines on the graph of the partial tree (Fig. 8.5.8). These links and their link impedances are found in row 1 of the link

TABLE 8.5.4 LIST CHANGES AND RELATED CALCULATIONS

Stage N	Links i	j	Compute new path impedance	Compare to tree table stage N − 1	Decision
II	1	6	0 + 5 = 5	5 < ∞	Accept
III	6	7	5 + 8 = 13	13 < ∞	Accept
		9	5 + 5 = 10	10 < ∞	Accept
		10	5 + 4 = 9	9 < ∞	Accept
IV	7	2	13 + 2 = 15	15 < ∞	Accept
		8	13 + 4 = 17	17 < ∞	Accept
		10	13 + 7 = 20 Reject	---	Reject
	9	10	10 + 3 = 13	13 > 9	Reject
		12	10 + 7 = 17	17 < ∞	Accept
	10	7	9 + 5 = 14	14 > 13	Reject
		9	9 + 3 = 12	12 > 10	Reject
		11	9 + 5 = 14	14 < ∞	Accept
V	8	3	17 + 4 = 21	21 < ∞	Accept
	11	4	14 + 4 = 18	18 < ∞	Accept
		8	14 + 5 = 19	19 > 17	Reject
		13	14 + 8 = 22	22 < ∞	Accept
		14	14 + 5 = 19	19 < ∞	Accept
	12	5	17 + 2 = 19	19 < ∞	Accept
		13	17 + 6 = 23 Reject	---	Reject
VI	All links emanating from nodes 3, 4, 5, 13, and 14 are rejected; the list is now empty and the procedure ends.				

array (Table 8.5.1). In this case, there is only one entry, link 1-6 with a link impedance of 5 units. The calculations of stage II are shown in Table 8.5.4. The impedance of the new path is computed by adding the impedance of link (1,6) to the current tree table entry for mode $i = 1$ (i.e., $0 + 5 = 5$). This value is compared to the current tree table entry for node $j = 6$ (i.e., infinity). Since the new path to node 6 is shorter than the current value, the new path is accepted. Stage II of the tree table and the tree diagram reflect this modification. All links emanating from the newly added node (node 6) are placed in the list to be considered at the next stage. They are also shown by dashed lines on the partial tree diagram. At the end of stage III, nodes 7, 9, and 10 are added to the tree, and the links emanating from these nodes (that is, the links found in rows 7, 9, and 10 of the link array) are placed in the list. Note that the stage IV entries to the list contain two alternative paths to node 10: One via node 7 and one via node 9. Of these two, the second is shorter, so the first may be rejected immediately. The path to node 10 via node 9 is also rejected in favor of the current path to 10, which the tree table shows to be via node 6. The procedure continues until stage VI, when all the list entries are rejected, that is, the list is empty. The final tree table emanating from node 1 and the corresponding diagram are shown on Table 8.5.5.

TABLE 8.5.5 FINAL TREE TABLE

Node (j)	Total impedance to node j	Node preceding j
1	0	—
2	15	7
3	20	8
4	18	11
5	19	12
6	5	1
7	13	6
8	17	7
9	10	6
10	9	6
11	14	10
12	17	9
13	22	11
14	19	11

Discussion This example found the minimum tree emanating from node 1 and terminating in all other nodes of the network. It does not contain any other paths. Thus, the sequence of links shown on the tree of Fig. 8.5.8 joining node 3 and node 14 does not represent the minimum path between these nodes. In order to find the minimum tree emanating from node 3, the procedure must be repeated, starting with the appropriate initialization of the tree table.

8.5.11 Free/All-or-Nothing Traffic Assignment

The free/all-or-nothing assignment technique allocates the entire volume interchanging between pairs of zones to the minimum path calculated on the basis of free-flow link impedances. After all interchange volumes are assigned, the flow on a particular link is computed by summing all interzonal flows that happens to include that link on their minimum paths.

Example 8.13

Assign the following interzonal vehicular trips emanating from zone 1 to the network of Example 8.12.

$$J: \quad 2 \quad 3 \quad 4 \quad 5$$
$$Q_{1J}: \quad 800 \quad 500 \quad 600 \quad 200$$

Solution The minimum tree emanating from zone 1 is reproduced in Fig. 8.5.9. The interzonal flows using each link of the tree are summed to compute the total contribution of the given flows to these links. Thus link 7–2 takes only the total interchange between zones 1 and 2, and link 7–8 takes the flow from zone 1 to zone 3. Link 6–7 takes the sum of the flows from zone 1 to zone 2 and from zone 1 to zone 3, since it belongs to both minimum paths. These links may also be assigned addi-

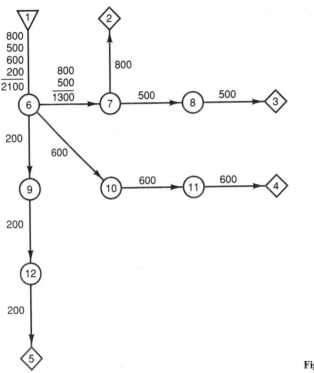

Figure 8.5.9   Minimum tree.

tional flows if they happen to be part of minimum paths that originate from zones other than zone 1.

8.5.12 Free/Multipath Traffic Assignment

In essence, a free/all-or-nothing assignment assumes that all trip-makers traveling between a specific pair of zones actually select the same path. In reality, interchange volumes are divided among a number of paths, and algorithms capable of determining several paths between each pair of zones in order of increasing impedance are available. Therefore it is possible to apportion the interchange volume between these paths according to some realistic rule. The diversion-curve method described earlier is a case where the interzonal flows are allocated to two competing paths. Other allocation rules are also possible. For example, Irwin and von Cube [8.21] suggested the following inverse-proportion function to compute the fraction to be assigned to each of a number of interzonal routes:

$$p(r) = \frac{W_{IJr}^{-1}}{\sum_x W_{IJx}^{-1}} \tag{8.5.1}$$

where W_{IJr} is the impedance of route r from I to J. As the following example illustrates, the use of the multinomial logit model (see Section 8.4.5) with disutilities based on path impedances is another possibility.

Example 8.14

A multipath algorithm found the interzonal impedances of the four shorter paths between a pair of zones to be 1.0, 1.5, 2.0, and 3.0 units of disutility. Estimate the percentage of trips to be assigned to each of the four routes according to the multinomial logit model.

Solution   Applying Eq. 8.4.5 with the negative of the path disutilities in place of the utility terms, we obtain

$$p(1) = 0.47$$

$$p(2) = 0.29$$

$$p(3) = 0.17$$

$$p(4) = 0.07$$

Discussion   This example merely illustrates how the multinomial logit model may be applied to the unrestrained multipath assignment problem. Whether this model is adequate for a particular planning study must also be the subject of inquiry. The computational complexity of these models must not escape the student's attention, but computerized algorithms that deal effectively with the repetitive nature of the calculations are available. Of greater complexity are *capacity-restrained* algorithms that incorporate the effect of traffic flow on link impedance.

8.5.13 Capacity-Restrained Traffic Assignment

In Chapter 3 we showed that as the flow increases toward capacity, the average stream speed decreases from the free-flow speed (u_f) to the speed at maximum flow (u_m). Beyond this point, the internal friction between vehicles in the stream becomes severe, the traffic conditions worsen (i.e., levels of service E and F), and severe shock waves and slow-moving platoons develop.

The implication of this phenomenon on the results of free-traffic assignment presents the following paradox: The interzonal flows are assigned to the minimum paths computed on the basis of free-flow link impedances (usually travel times). But if the link flows were at the levels dictated by the assignment, the link speeds would be lower and the link travel times (i.e., impedances) would be higher than those corresponding to free-flow conditions. As a result, the minimum paths computed *prior* to trip assignment may not be the minimum paths *after* the trips are assigned. Several iterative assignment techniques address the convergence between the link impedances assumed prior to assignment and the link impedances that are implied by the resulting link volumes. These techniques are known as *capacity-restrained* methods or techniques that employ *capacity restraints*.

The relationship between link flow and link impedance is described the *link-capacity function*. Several such functions are found in the technical literature (e.g., [8.22]). Figure 8.5.10 presents the form developed by the BPR, which is

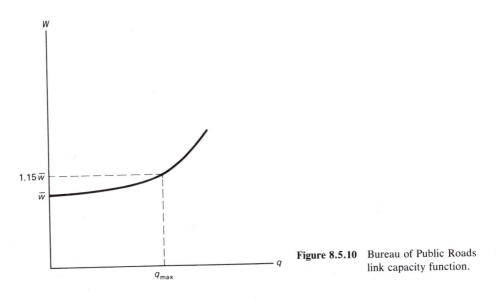

Figure 8.5.10 Bureau of Public Roads link capacity function.

expressed mathematically as

$$w = \overline{w}\left[1 + 0.15\left(\frac{q}{q_{max}}\right)^4\right] \qquad (8.5.2)$$

where

$$w = \text{impedance of a given link at flow } q$$

$$\overline{w} = \text{free-flow impedance of the link}$$

$$q = \text{link flow}$$

$$q_{max} = \text{link's capacity}$$

This function states that at capacity, the link impedance is 15% higher than the free-flow impedance. If the demand were to exceed the capacity of the link, the resulting shock waves and their dissipation times (see Chapter 3) would cause a rapid deterioration in the link flow conditions.

Capacity-restrained algorithms incorporate link capacity functions in their search for convergence to an equilibrium state. They may be either all-or-nothing or multipath. An example of the former is the algorithm developed by CATS [8.23], where the following assignment procedure is applied: An interchange is chosen at random, the minimum path is determined using the free-flow impedances, and the entire interchange volume (i.e., all-or-nothing) is assigned to this minimum path. The impedances of the links that make up this path are updated according to the assigned flows, and another interchange is randomly chosen for similar treatment. The procedure ends when all interchanges are considered. Although not realistically reproducing particular interchange flows, the incremental updating of link impedances is expected to result in realistic estimates of the equilibrium link flows.

The 1973 edition of the FHWA's traffic-assignment manual [8.18] describes a multipath extension of the CATS method developed by the Control Data Corporation. This method begins with an uncongested network, finds all the minimum paths, and assigns a portion (say, 20%) of each interchange volume to these paths. It then updates the link impedances according to the resulting partial link flows, recomputes the minimum paths, and assigns the next increment of the interchange volumes. The procedure continues until 100% of the interzonal flows are assigned.

The method originally developed by the BPR [8.17] first performs an all-or-nothing assignment based on free-flow link impedances. It then updates all loaded links and repeats the all-or-nothing assignment using the new impedances. After several iterations, paths between pairs of zones are assigned a portion of the interzonal flow in proportion to the number of times that each appeared to be the minimum path. Figure 8.5.11 illustrates the results of this procedure on a small hypothetical network after four iterations.

The Urban Transportation Planning System (UTPS), a battery of computer programs developed by the FHWA, includes a method that is based on the linear-programming optimization technique [8.25]. Figure 8.5.12 illustrates this method, which begins with a free/all-or-nothing assignment (iteration 0). The simple two-zone diagram shows that 100% of the interzonal flow is assigned to the minimum path. The BPR function (Eq. 8.5.1) is then applied to update the impedances of the loaded links. Iteration 1 repeats the all-or-nothing assignment based on the updated link impedances. At this stage, the linear-programming algorithm is applied to calculate the value of the variable λ, which is used to divide the interzonal volume between the first two paths. The link impedances are updated accordingly, and the procedure continues until λ is close to zero, a sign that an equilibrium stage has been reached.

Other capacity-restrained assignments have been reported in the literature (e.g., [8.26, 8.27]), including a two-pass Markov model, which allocates traffic to links based on reasonable transition probabilities [8.28].

8.5.14 Transit Assignment

The assignment of interzonal trips to a transit network presents certain complications that are not encountered in traffic assignment. In addition to the transit network of links and nodes, transit operations involve the identification of transit routes and schedules. The temporal pattern and directional orientation of demand coupled with resource limitations (e.g., available fleet size, operating costs) always dictate a service coverage that is not ubiquitous. Overlapping routes, the

Tree computed using speeds obtained in the travel-time study

Tree computed after first iteration of capacity restraint

Tree computed after second iteration of capacity restraint

Tree computed after third iteration of capacity restraint

1   Zone number

104   Node number

Figure 8.5.11   Illustration of the Bureau of Public Roads multipath assignment procedure. (From Humphrey [8.24].)

need to transfer between routes, differences between exclusive right-of-way lines and mixed traffic operations [8.29, 8.30], and variabilities of service in time and space add to the challenges associated with transit assignment. But the methods of transit-network analysis (e.g., [8.31]) are beyond the scope of this book.

8.5.15 Summary

Network or trip assignment simulates the way in which trip-makers select their paths between zones. Traffic assignment estimates the expected flows that the

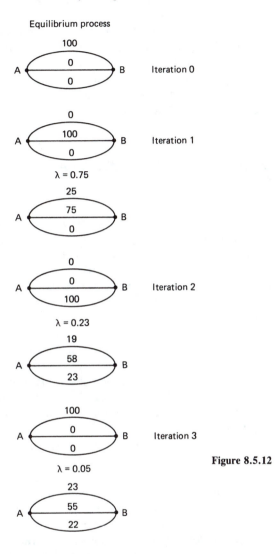

Equilibrium process

Iteration 0

Iteration 1

Iteration 2

Iteration 3

Figure 8.5.12   Urban Transportation Planning System capacity-restrained assignment procedure. (From Levinsohn et al. [8.25].)

links of the highway network are likely to experience to help anticipate potential capacity problems and to plan accordingly. It requires a behavioral hypothesis of route choice, a method of describing the highway network for computer processing, a way of selecting the appropriate interzonal paths, and a way of realistically allocating (i.e., assigning) the interzonal volumes on these paths. Several traffic-assignment models were described in this section, including a simple two-path diversion-curve model. In addition, traffic-assignment models that are more appropriate for the analysis of large networks were described. These models were classified in two ways. First, they were identified either as capacity-restrained or as free-assignment models, depending on whether they explicitly account for the effect of congestion or not. Second, they were categorized as either all-or-nothing or multipath models, depending on whether they allocate the interzonal demand on a single or on multiple paths.

In addition to path (or route) allocation, transit assignment must contend with complexities that are not present in traffic assignment. The study of this topic falls outside the scope of this book.

8.6 *TRANSPORT BEHAVIOR OF INDIVIDUALS AND HOUSEHOLDS*

In this section we focus on behavioral aspects of transportation demand. The prevailing trend in demand analyses is toward focusing on the household and its individual members in an effort to achieve a better understanding of transport demand. This focus reveals that a large number of factors (i.e., from most tangible factors, such as gender, age, and income, to most elusive ones, such as personality and lifestyle) affect transport behavior and consequently, the utilization of transportation systems and modes.

It is well known that transportation is by and large a derived demand. Individual and household needs generate the demand for transportation. The transport behavior of individuals and households results from their transport-related decisions, which may be classified into long- and short-term decisions. The long-term decisions are referred to as *mobility choices* and include decision relations to residential location, employment location, automobile ownership, and mode to work. The short-term decisions are referred to as *travel choices* and include frequency of travel for various purposes, mode, destination, route, and time of day of trips.

In disaggregate transport behavior analyses, one important element is the unit of analysis (i.e., the entity upon which the analysis is focused): It could be the individual or the household. Individuals can be viewed independently, with their own unique aspirations, goals, and idiosyncratic personalities. However, the behavior of individuals belonging to households is constrained and will necessarily conform to certain role assignments usually defined to meet household as well as individual goals with reasonable efficiency. Therefore, it is important to recognize the effects of household characteristics while trying to account for the personal attributes of each person in the household.

Several conceptual models describing the process generating the transport behavior of people have been developed. The process generating the transport behavior of people founded upon work by Hartgen and Tanner [8.32], Field et al. [8.32], Salomon [8.33], Ben-Akiva and Lerman [8.34], and Prevedouros [8.35] is presented in Fig. 8.6.1.

The environment within which households and individuals exist may be represented by a set of activities, defined by location, time, and money requirements

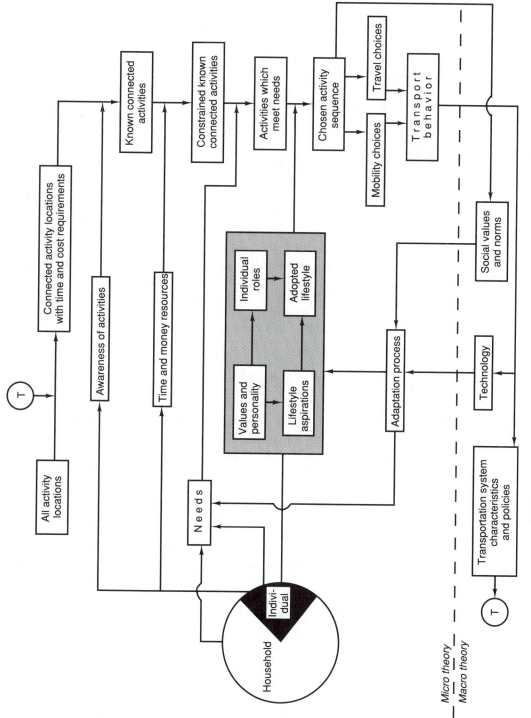

Figure 8.6.1 Conceptual model of factors affecting transport behavior.

381

as well as constraints (e.g., food store closes at 9 P.M., favorite restaurant is closed on Thursdays, the movie show costs $3 before 5:00 P.M. and $6 after 5:00 P.M., etc.) The activity locations are connected with a transportation system that has distinct characteristics (e.g., network structure, modes, performance, costs to the traveler) and policies (e.g., parking regulations, transit hours of operation, time-dependent transportation services pricing, etc.)

The personal and joint needs of individuals create the set of household needs. Some needs must be fulfilled (i.e., work, school, maintenance) at certain time periods, while some others are optional (i.e., recreational activities). When the set of needs that can or must be fulfilled and the resulting set of activities that will meet those needs have been identified, the personal characteristics and responsibilities of each person determine the chosen activity sequence for each household member (which will result in the fulfillment of needs). This is a dynamic process with much variation around an "average" activity pattern as well as longer-term changes of the average pattern.

Focus on the personal characteristics and responsibilities of each individual reveals that each person has a set of values and a distinct personality. These elements interact with the surrounding world generating their lifestyle. Lifestyle, according to Salomon [8.33], is a person's orientation in life through three major decisions: The decision to form a household, the decision to participate in the labor force, and decisions about spending free time (leisure). Many more detailed components can be attributed to lifestyle, which are complements or parts of this broad definition (i.e., preference for residence location, degree of career orientation, preference for specific types of automobiles, entertainment preferences, etc.)

Two major underlying components of a person's lifestyle are his or her personality and occupational status, both of which are responsible to a large degree for the orientation of each person in life. Lifestyle is important because it underlies the decision-making process of individuals. Certainly, the chosen lifestyle of each person is not a straight, narrow line connecting points in the person's life. It is better to be viewed as a broad path through life. In other words, individuals make decisions and perform activities that broadly fulfill their lifestyle aspirations.

Another important element for each individual household member is that of the role and role commitments (i.e., provision of shelter, food gathering, schooling, working, etc.) The role is tied to a function or a set of functions; by performing a set of activities that fulfills those functions, a person assumes a role. Functions are defined by the needs of individuals and household members. Thus the role constitutes a link between needs and patterns of fulfilling needs. The needs cluster in four broad groups: household/familial, work/career, interpersonal/social, and leisure/recreation [8.32]. The responsibility for the fulfillment of roles within each group is divided among members in the household. The basis for this division is a result of a mix of factors, such as social norms, past experience, time and opportunity constraints, sociocultural and personality factors, and negotiation.

There are short and long-term role commitments. Over time, roles change for household members as the household evolves through the life-cycle stages† [8.36].

All these result in the activity sequence chosen by the individual household member. This sequence allows fulfillment of the needs of the household and achievement of the person's lifestyle aspirations. The chosen activity sequence then serves as the input for the mobility and travel choices of the household members, which, in turn, define the transport behavior (see Fig. 8.6.1).

The sum of the chosen activity sequence and the transport behavior across all individuals in the population feeds back the set of values and norms of the society as well as the technology and the transportation system and policies to the household (macro theory, Fig. 8.6.1). This dynamic interaction modifies the environment in which individuals live. An adaptation process then takes place and the household needs and standards and aspirations for each person are adjusted.

The critical elements of this framework are the individual and household needs as well as the lifestyles of the individual household members. There are some basic elements of needs and lifestyles that can be found in most individuals at most places (i.e., work, shelter, household formation, transportation). A large number of factors (i.e., culture, environment, available technology, etc.) shape and differentiate needs and lifestyles across individuals, households, or places. The process in Fig. 8.6.1 suggests that people's transport behavior is affected by such factors as:

- Household structure
- Availability and cost of activities
- Personality and lifestyle
- Technology available to users
- Location patterns
- Personal or household income
- Social values and norms
- Transportation system characteristics and policies

Detailed knowledge of the factors affecting transport behavior enables the estimation of realistic models for transport demand forecasting, including models of automobile ownership, trip generation, mode choice, residence location choice, and diversion choice (i.e., response of drivers to real-time information on traffic conditions). The latter is critical in the rapidly approaching IVHS era (intelligent vehicle-highway systems, discussed in Chapter 6).

---

† The basic life-cycle stages of a household are the following, in chronological order: single person, couple without children, couple or single parent with dependent children, couple or single parent with independent children (children at driving age or older living at the parental household), couple of seniors, senior single person.

In addition to the factors mentioned above, perception of quality of service and attitudes toward transportation modes can be included in quantitative representations of transport behavior (models) to enrich the coverage of factors affecting transport behavior and to obtain a better understanding of the impact of each factor on transport behavior [8.37, 8.38].

Knowledge of transportation systems and services varies among people, as does the degree of accuracy with which characteristics of transportation systems and services are known to people. Two major characteristics affecting the choice of mode are travel time and travel cost. One's perception may be that the travel time from A to B by bus is 25 min and 10 to 12 min by private car. Although the actual travel time by bus is 15 to 18 min, this objective fact is not the input utilized by the person considered when deciding his or her mode of transportation from A to B. Misperceptions also apply to travel cost. Typically, people tend to count only the out-of-pocket cost of using an automobile (i.e., gasoline, parking, and tolls) and forget the substantial costs of vehicle depreciation, insurance, and maintenance. The aforementioned misperception of characteristics may bias the judgment of the merits of private auto and public transportation, which would result in a higher-than-normal proportion of people selecting private auto as their means of transportation.†

It may take an extensive and expensive marketing campaign by a transit authority to partially correct public misperceptions. It is critical, however, that public transit agencies and private travel industries utilize models and planning tools which reflect their customers' perceptions and not objective system characteristics.

The feelings or attitudes toward a transportation mode also affect travel choices in important ways. People tend to have a less favorable attitude toward public transportation (i.e., in terms of scheduling, privacy, convenience, and safety) than toward the private auto [8.37], especially in the United States.

In the remainder of this section we discuss two basic models: an automobile ownership and a trip-generation model. *Automobile ownership* is considered as one of the key determinants of transport behavior and is included in virtually every model of trip generation and mode choice [8.39]. A basic classification of automobile ownership models results from the unit of analysis. A model is disaggregate when the unit of analysis is the individual or the individual household. When characteristics of individuals or households are aggregated in any way (i.e., in tracts, zones, etc.) for model estimation, the resulting model is aggregate. The data also characterize the geographic area of application of a model. There are models built to fit specific urban environs, states, and nations.

---

† Similar misperceptions are evident in intercity transportation as well. In this context, modes are often selected based on their terminal-to-terminal performance, thereby ignoring substantial access and waiting times. This way, a bias toward fast traveling modes is created in the mind of individuals about to choose a mode for travel to another city. For example, the bus or rail modes may be disadvantaged against air travel for trips up to 200 mi if only terminal-to-terminal performance is accounted for.

Regression models are used to estimate levels of automobile ownership (e.g., the number of automobiles owned by a household). Poisson regression and logit models are used to estimate a household's probability of having 0, 1, 2, . . . automobiles. Recent studies [8.35, 8.40] show that the number of household drivers, the number of dependent children (i.e., before the age of driving), and location (i.e., high- and low-density locations) play an important role in automobile ownership and usage (refer to the example later in this section).

The classification of *trip generation* models (i.e., aggregate, disaggregate, local, regional, etc.) is similar to that for automobile ownership models. A usual method for model estimation is regression. Trip generation models are often segmented either by gender or by level of automobile ownership. Common factors used in trip generation models are number of automobiles available (i.e., owned plus rented or company-provided), household structure (i.e., size, life-cycle stage, and number of workers), residential location, and income.

Recent advancements in travel behavior focus on activity analysis. This is an exciting area of research which, however, has not produced any major breakthroughs so far, particularly in regard to direct applicability to planning [8.41]. Activity analysis involves the integration of concepts from psychological theory, sociological theory, economic theory, and geography, and it aims at developing a clear understanding of the people who make the trips (i.e., motivational structure and psychological profile), the interdependencies among people both within and outside the household, the people's opportunity set, transport services, and options.

Examples of disaggregate automobile ownership and trip-generation models are presented in Table 8.6.1. The automobile ownership model includes the following variables, in the order listed in Table 8.6.1:

1. Number of household members who are eligible to drive (i.e., at age 16 or older)

2. Number of household full-time workers

3. Number of household workers who are employed in the suburbs

4. A binary variable that identifies households with dependent children (i.e., variable is equal to 1 if there exist children younger than 16 years of age)

5. A binary variable that identifies households with senior members (i.e., no children present and at least one member at the age of 65 or older)

6. Income in 1989 U.S. dollars

7. A binary variable that accounts for public transit use (i.e., it is equal to 1 if one household worker used mass transit to commute to work)

8. A binary variable that is equal to 1 if the household resides at a low-density location (it is equal to 0 otherwise, same as the other binary variables in the model)

TABLE 8.6.1 EXAMPLES OF AUTOMOBILE OWNERSHIP AND TRIP-GENERATION MODELS

Automobile ownership model [8.35]		Trip-generation model [8.42]	
Dependent variable: number of household automobiles		Dependent variable: household trips to work	
Independent variables	Parameter	Independent variables	Parameter
Number of drivers	0.58	Number of workers	3.933
Number of full-time workers	0.11	Number of adult females	0.416
Number working in the suburbs	0.11	Number of adult males	0.918
Household with dependent children	0.11	Household size	0.282
Household with senior members	−0.13	Number of nondrivers	−0.457
Income (thousand 1989 U.S. dollars)	0.04	(High-education) (workers)	0.23[a]
Use of mass transit to work	−0.28	(Low-education) (workers)	−0.35[a]
Low-density residence location	0.14	$\sqrt{\text{Income (in DFI)}}/100$ (workers)	0.22[a]
Constant	0.23	(High-density) (workers)	−0.11[a]
		(Low-density) (workers)	−0.43[a]
		Constant	−0.36[a]
R^2	0.54	R^2	0.56
Number of cases	1372	Number of cases	1739
Source of data: Survey in Chicago, Illinois		*Source of data:* Survey in the Netherlands	

[a] Parameter not statistically significant; otherwise, significant at $\alpha = 0.05$.

Example 8.15

Given a suburban (low-density) zone with 250 households with the following average characteristics: 2.2 drivers, 1.4 full-time workers, 70% employed in the suburbs, 33% of all households have dependent children, 8% of all households are senior households, income is $43,000, and 6.5% use mass transit to work, apply the model in Table 8.6.1 to estimate the average automobile ownership per household.

Solution Using the model in Table 8.6.1 and substituting the given inputs, the average automobile ownership per household is estimated as

$$
\begin{aligned}
&+ \ 0.58(2.2) \\
&+ \ 0.11(1.1) \\
&+ \ 0.11(1)(0.70) \\
&+ \ 0.11(1)(0.33) \\
&- \ 0.13(1)(0.08) \\
&+ \ 0.04(43,000 \div 10,000) \\
&- \ 0.28(1)(0.065) \\
&+ \ 0.14(1) \\
&+ \ 0.23 = 2.06 \quad \text{automobiles per household}
\end{aligned}
$$

Discussion   This estimate translates into a total of 515 automobiles in the zone examined. If this population was at a high-density location and 15% were using mass transit to work, the average household automobile ownership would be equal to 1.92 automobiles, which would translate into 475 automobiles in the zone examined, a 7.8% reduction in the number of automobiles owned.

The latter part reflects another utility of such models: ability to assess the effect of each factor upon the element of transport behavior examined. In addition, sensitivity analysis (i.e., how much a Δx change of factor x affects the dependent variable) may assist in policies aimed at encouraging or discouraging specific transportation decisions of people. Also, the effects on transport behavior of dynamic changes in the society, such as aging, increases in the workforce population, and economic downturns that affect people's incomes, can be assessed.

The trip-generation model includes the following variables, in the order listed in Table 8.6.1:

1. Number of workers in the household
2. Number of adult females in the household
3. Number of adult males in the household
4. Number of persons in the household
5. Number of household persons at age 12 or older who do not drive
6,7. Level of education, which is defined by two binary variables: high education is equal to 1 if a household member has a college degree (it is 0 otherwise), and low education is equal to 1 if the household member with the highest education has an elementary school degree (it is 0 otherwise)
8. Income is used after the square root of the annual gross income in DFl is taken and then divided by 100
9,10. Density, which is represented by two binary variables: high density is equal to 1 if the household resides in a large metropolitan area served by transit systems (it is 0 otherwise), and low density is equal to 1 if the household resides in a community without transit service (it is 0 otherwise)

Example 8.16

Consider a zone with 250 households with the following average characteristics: household size is 3.2, number of workers per household is 1.1, 1.4 adult females and 1.3 adult males per household, 0.9 nondrivers per household, 35% of households have a member with a college degree, 12% of households belong to the low-education category, income is 23,000 DFl, and the entire zone is in a high-density area. These data are similar to the types of data that can be taken from census reports by tract or zip code. Apply the model in Table 8.6.1 to estimate the expected number of trips in the zone.

Solution By applying the trip-generation model in Table 8.6.1, the expected work trips generated in the zone are

250 [(3.993)(1.1)
    + 0.416(1.4)
    + 0.918(1.3)
    + 0.282(3.2)
    − 0.457(0.9)
    + 0.230(1)(0.35)(2.1)
    − 0.350(1)(0.12)(2.1)
    + 0.220($\sqrt{23{,}000}$ ÷ 100)
    − 0.110(1)(2.1)
    − 0.430(0)(2.1)
    − 0.360] = 250(6.5) =   1622 worktrips produced from the households
                          residing in the examined zone

The trip-generation model presented above results in the total number of trips produced by a group of households. An older practice consists of the separate estimation of household trips using two models: a model estimating home-based trips and a model estimating non-home-based trips. Then the separate estimates are combined to yield the total number of trips for a zone or area. The implicit assumption in the combination of home-based and non-home-based trips is that these two types of trips are mutually independent. This convenient assumption is hardly realistic [8.41].

The weakness of the combination of dependent trip rates is absent in *trip chaining* models. These models comprise a theoretically sound trip generation modeling basis which is gaining acceptance. Trip-chaining modeling employs a procedure that links trips originating from home according to purpose and other characteristics. Separate models for work, school, social activities, household maintenance, and so forth, are developed. These models are connected to a trip chaining model that identifies applicable chains [8.42, 8.43]. This combination of models provides a more realistic representation of the household trip-making behavior and it maintains the ability to produce home and non-home-based trip rates for application in older model structures.

The models presented in Table 8.6.1 are not meant to be applied to single households. These models produce meaningful estimates when applied to zones with fairly homogeneous populations. For example, it is likely that if applied to a single household, the models may estimate 6.88 trips or 1.65 automobiles, which of course have little physical meaning. On the other hand, these numbers may well represent household averages for a number of households in an area.

Caution should be exercised in the use of behavioral models, particularly when they have been derived from small sample sizes and/or from a specific population group (i.e., survey in affluent suburbs), which may not be representative of the whole population in an area. Great attention should be exercised in the application of such models in areas other than the area where the data used for the estimation of the model were collected. The issue of model transferability is important and simple conversion of units (i.e., present worth of past incomes, pounds to dollars, kilometers to miles, etc.) is hardly sufficient for application of a model in another area [8.44]. This is due largely to the substantial cultural, spatial, economic, and transportation differences between locations, even within the same nation. Similar concerns undermine the validity of empirically derived models over time; caution should be exercised when applying a 1970s behavioral model in the 1990s.

8.7 OTHER DEMAND-FORECASTING MODELS

8.7.1 Introduction

Efforts to improve the modeling of transportation demand have followed two main paths. The first represents a move away from purely empirical models and toward models that are grounded on an improved theoretical understanding of travel behavior. The ultimate test of the appropriateness of these theoretical constructs, however, is not their theoretical eloquence but their ability realistically to describe and predict the real world. The second major thrust of modeling has been toward the discovery of simple models that can facilitate decision making by providing useful information quickly and inexpensively. Of course, the availability of parsimonious models that are also soundly based on a realistic theory of travel behavior is ideal, but theoretical difficulties and practical constraints often prevent the attainment of this ideal.

In earlier sections we surveyed alternative formulations for each of the four components of travel behavior, for example, trip generation, trip distribution, modal choice, and trip assignment. In addition, two alternative calibration approaches (aggregate or disaggregate) and two alternative choice theories (choice-specific and choice-abstract) were discussed. Additional modeling options available to the transportation planner are presented next.

8.7.2 Demand-Model Consistency

Model consistency is an important consideration relating to modeling the demand for transportation. Consider, for example, the difference between free and capacity-restrained traffic-assignment models. As explained earlier, a free assignment allocates the interzonal flows based on the free-flow interzonal impedances associated with alternative routes between zones. Because the impedances implied by the assigned flows could be significantly different from their assumed values, various capacity-restrained algorithms have been developed to ensure internal consistency between the two sets of interzonal impedances.

The question of consistency between the four steps of the sequential process was also addressed. For instance, it was argued that a conformance must be sought between the interzonal impedances used by the trip-distribution phase and those that result from trip assignment; as a matter of fact, several studies have introduced a feedback link between the two models for this purpose. Figure 8.7.1 illustrates an early attempt made by the Toronto Transportation Study [8.45] to introduce feedbacks between trip distribution and traffic assignment. Note that the modal choice step does not appear. Iterating among all four steps in search of overall model consistency is more difficult and resource-intensive than it may seem.

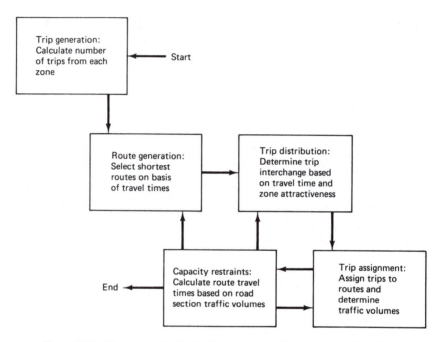

Figure 8.7.1   Toronto study feedback mechanism. (From Irwin et al. [8.27].)

8.7.3 Simultaneous or Direct Demand Formulations

A related travel-demand theory states that an individual makes travel choices simultaneously rather than in a sequence of discrete steps and that a demand model should be calibrated to reflect this behavior. An often-cited example of *simultaneous* models is the Quandt and Baumol [8.46] formulation of intercity travel demand, which, using the notation of this book, takes the general form

$$Q_{IJK} = a_0(P_I)^{a_1}(P_J)^{a_2}(C_{IJ*})^{a_3}\left(\frac{C_{IJK}}{C_{IJ*}}\right)^{a_4}(H_{IJ*})^{a_5}\left(\frac{H_{IJK}}{H_{IJ*}}\right)^{a_6}\left(\frac{D_{IJK}}{D_{IJ*}}\right)^{a_7}(Y_{IJ})^{a_8}$$

$$(8.7.1)$$

where

$$Q_{IJK} = \text{travel flow between cities } I \text{ and } J \text{ via mode } K$$

$$P_I, P_J = \text{populations of } I \text{ and } J$$

$$C_{IJ*} = \text{least cost of travel between } I \text{ and } J$$

$$C_{IJK} = \text{cost via mode } K$$

$$H_{IJ} = \text{shortest travel time between } I \text{ and } J$$

$$H_{IJK} = \text{travel time via mode } K$$

$$D_{IJ}* = \text{departure frequency of the most frequent mode}$$

$$D_{IJK} = \text{departure frequency of mode } K$$

$$Y_{IJ} = \text{weighted average incomes of } I \text{ and } J$$

$$a_0, \ldots, a_8 = \text{calibration parameters}$$

This model is a simultaneous trip-generation/trip-distribution modal choice equation employing land-use variables (populations), socioeconomic characteristics (income levels), and interzonal impedances by mode (costs, travel times, and frequency of service) to estimate the interzonal demands by mode (Q_{IJK}). In keeping with the purpose of the demand-estimating methodology, these interzonal flows would presumably be assigned to the networks of the modes K serving the region to find the equilibrium link flows. The earlier-raised question of consistency between the assumed levels of some of the explanatory variables (travel times, for example) and the levels implied in the results of the assignment phase resurfaces.

In urban situations, the calibration and application of such large models is, to say the least, cumbersome. However, they may be useful for rather coarse estimates at the regional level if the number of zones and the degree of detail in specifying the transportation network are kept to a minimum.

8.7.4 Combined Modeling Strategies

Between the two extremes of sequential model arrangements and large simultaneous models there exist a plethora of options that are partly sequential and partly simultaneous. The following excerpt from a modeling undertaking in Canberra, Australia [8.47], that was intended to be sensitive to the short-term effects of various TSM-type options illustrates this point:

If all travel choice decisions for all purpose groups were to be modelled, the scope of modelling required would be extensive and consequently very expensive. It is however possible to reduce the scale and range of models by making some *a priori* assumptions as to the travel choice processes exercised by individual travellers or potential travellers. For example it seems reasonable to assume, certainly for the short term, that workplace and schooling location and the frequency of work and school trips are relatively stable and do not vary significantly under the range of practical conditions which are likely to occur. In these particular cases travel mode choice would therefore appear to be the most important travel decision. Using these and similar reasonings for other purpose categories, a listing of the necessary models was prepared. Specifically these models were:

(a) work, mode choice,
(b) school, mode choice,
(c) shopping, mode choice,
(d) shopping, frequency,
(e) shopping, destination,
(f) shopping, mode choice/destination,
(g) social/recreation, mode choice,
(h) social/recreation, destination, and
(i) social/recreation, mode choice/destination.

Other purpose groups were reasoned to be either less significant in terms of scale than the above purpose groups or they were to be less responsive to the specific policy measures, which can be manipulated by Canberra transport planners ([8.47], p. 62).

Models (d) and (e) are trip-generation and trip-distribution models, respectively, calibrated for shopping trips that could be chained in the sequence d-e-c. Model (f) is a simultaneous modal choice and trip-distribution model that may be applied after estimating trip generation [i.e., model (d)]. Similarly, (g) and (h) are modal choice and trip-distribution models, respectively, and (i) is a simultaneous model of these two choices.

Careful contemplation of the quoted terse statement will reveal the wide variety of modeling choices available to the contemporary transportation planner, the need to tailor specific models and model arrangements to particular levels of planning and policy issues, and the importance of professional judgment in this most important phase of transportation planning.

One common form of simultaneous models of trip distribution and modal choice is the following *share model:*

$$Q_{IJK} = P_I \frac{A_J e^{U_{IJK}}}{\sum_{X,Y} A_X e^{U_{IXY}}} \tag{8.7.2}$$

Note that the inputs to this model are the exogenously estimated zonal trip productions P_I, zonal trip attractiveness A_J, and interzonal modal utilities U_{IJK}. The output of this simultaneous logit model consists of interzonal flows by mode. Any change in the values U_{IJK} is permitted to affect both the trip distribution and the modal shares of the interzonal demand at the same time.

8.7.5 Models of Demand Elasticity

Many planning situations are concerned with immediate or short-term actions or with relatively small changes to the system that do not warrant an elaborate and detailed analytical treatment. Several simplified methods have been developed for this purpose. For example, consider the situation of a planner who has been hired by a private developer to estimate the traffic impacts of a proposed high-rise residential building as part of an EIS that is a prerequisite to securing the necessary building permits. In this case, a rough estimate of the trip generation based on published trip rates for different types of land uses (e.g., [8.48]) would probably suffice. Simple models are also appropriate to planning studies for rural areas, small- and medium-size urban areas, and certain elements of planning for larger cities [8.49–8.51].

A transportation-demand model that can be used to provide broad predictions of the response of trip-makers to changes in the transportation system is founded in the economic concept of price elasticity of demand.

Definition of price elasticity of demand.   In economic theory, the law of demand states that, everything else being constant, the quantity Q of goods or services that consumers demand decreases as their price P increases, and, conversely, when the price is reduced, the quantity demanded rises. Figure 8.7.2 illustrates this law. The parallel to transportation viewed as a service that is subject to market forces is inescapable. For example, a patronage drop should be expected

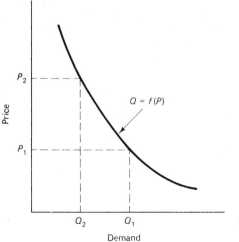

Figure 8.7.2   A hypothetical demand curve.

to occur following an increase in transit fares. Similarly, lowering the downtown parking fees should encourage an increase in automobile use.

The price elasticity of demand, E, is defined as

$$E = \frac{dQ/Q}{dP/P} = \frac{dQ}{dP} \frac{P}{Q} \tag{8.7.3}$$

In words, it is the ratio of the *relative* change in the quantity demanded to the *relative* change in price.

Example 8.17: Linear-Demand Functions

Given a demand function of the form

$$Q = a - bP \tag{8.7.4}$$

express the price elasticity of demand as a function of price.

Solution   Applying Eq. 8.7.3, we obtain

$$E = \frac{-Pb}{Q}$$

Substituting Eq. 8.7.4 in this, gives

$$E = \frac{-Pb}{a - bP}$$

Discussion   The negative sign of elasticity reflects the fact that a percentage increase in P will cause a percentage decrease in Q. The solution illustrates that, depending on the demand function, the price elasticity of demand is not constant for all points on the curve. In addition, the value of the price elasticity of demand reflects the implication of a price change on the total revenue (PQ) of the supplier. For example, when $E < -1$, the percent decrease in Q (i.e., the numerator of Eq. 8.7.3) is larger than the percent increase in P (i.e., the denominator of Eq. 8.7.3). In that case, the demand is said to be *elastic* and the total revenue after the price increase decreases because the loss of sales volume outweighs the extra revenue obtained per unit sold. When $E > -1$, the demand is said to be *inelastic* and the total revenue after raising P increases. When $E = -1$, the demand is *unitarily elastic* and the revenue derived from selling less units at a higher price is equal to the total revenue prior to raising the price, for example, more units at a lower price. Thus an upward or downward price change may result in an increase, a decrease, or a constancy of revenue. The value of the price elasticity of demand reflects this fact.

Example 8.18: Product Forms

The demand for a particular transit service has been assessed to be a function of fare F and travel time T as follows:

$$Q = aF^bT^c \tag{8.7.5}$$

Calculate the elasticity of demand with respect to (a) fare and (b) travel time.

Solution   The two elasticities can be computed via Eq. 8.7.3 except that partial derivatives should be taken.

The fare elasticity of demand is

$$E_f = \left(\frac{F}{Q}\right) abF^{b-1}T^c$$

Substituting Eq. 8.7.5 in this relationship yields

$$E_f = b$$

Similarly, the travel time elasticity of demand is

$$E_t = c$$

Discussion   This example illustrates that if the demand function is of the product form 8.7.5, the exponents of the price components represent the elasticity of demand with respect to each component. This is the basic reason why Quandt and Baumol have selected this particular functional form for their simultaneous demand equation (8.7.1). A disadvantage of this form is that it assumes that the elasticities are constant. This may be reasonable for price-level changes near the base-data conditions.

Direct and cross elasticities.   So far, the discussion of elasticity was confined to the effect of changes in the price of a product on the demand for the *same* product. This type of elasticity is called a *direct* elasticity. On the other hand, a price change in one product often affects the demand for *another* product. Price elasticities reflecting this effect are called *cross* elasticities. Cross effects may be positive or negative depending on whether the two products are complementary or substitutes for each other. An increase in the cost of automobile travel would be expected to cause a decrease in automobile use (direct effect) and an increase in transit patronage (cross effect). Another possible cross effect is a decrease in the demand for automobile tires.

Measurement of elasticities.   The discussion of Example 8.18 implies that one way of obtaining elasticity estimates is to apply Eq. 8.7.3 to calibrated demand models such as those described earlier and Eqs. 8.7.1 and 8.7.2. Note that if certain important cost or level-of-service variables are not included in a particular model, their associated effect on demand cannot be derived. It would be distributed among the variables included in the model. Also, if a calibrated model is not readily available, this method of elasticity estimation may be very expensive and time consuming.

Another method of obtaining estimates of elasticities is by observing the effects of actual price changes in the system under study [8.52, 8.53]. When undertaking this task, special care must be exercised to account properly for demand changes due to factors other than price, such as secular trends attributable to population and demographic changes. When the observed situation involves changes in more than one cost component, it is important to separate the overall demand response to its corresponding individual components. An excellent treatment of these issues may be found in the work reported by Parody and Brand [8.52] relating to a study of the transit system of the city of Jacksonville, Florida.

In that study, various elasticities for several user subgroups were derived and used to predict the transit-demand effects of alternative fare structures. Incidentally, the practice of calibrating demand models specifically for individual market subgroups (known as *market segmentation*) is a matter of increasing concern to planners, especially as it relates to tailoring transportation services to the needs of these groups and, also, as it relates to the investigation of how transportation benefits and costs are distributed among them.

Given an actual price change, say from P_1 to P_2 as shown in Fig. 8.7.2, and an observed demand change from Q_1 to Q_2, the implicit price elasticity of demand (Eq. 8.7.3) may be approximated in several ways:

1. The *shrinkage ratio,* defined as

$$E_{shr} = \frac{(Q_2 - Q_1)/Q_1}{(P_2 - P_1)/P_1} \tag{8.7.6}$$

2. The midpoint (or linear) *arc elasticity,* computed as

$$E_{arc} = \frac{(Q_2 - Q_1)/(Q_1 + Q_2)}{(P_2 - P_1)/(P_1 + P_2)} \tag{8.7.7}$$

3. The *log-arc elasticity,* calculated as

$$E_{log-arc} = \frac{\log Q_2 - \log Q_1}{\log P_2 - \log P_1} \tag{8.7.8}$$

These three measures of elasticity yield approximately equal values for relatively small price changes. For larger differences, the shrinkage ratio begins to deviate significantly from the other two.

Example 8.19: Application of Elasticities

Given that the log-arc elasticity of demand is -0.28, calculate the effect of an increase in transit fares from 50 to 80¢ given that the patronage prior to the price increase is 20,000 riders per day.

Solution   Equation 8.7.8 yields

$$-0.28 = \frac{\log Q_2 - \log 20,000}{\log 80 - \log 50}$$

Solving for Q_2 gives

$$Q_2 = 17,534 \text{ riders per day}$$

Discussion   Since the given direct elasticity was of the log-arc form, Eq. 8.7.8 was applied. To illustrate the differences between the three measures of elasticity, the shrinkage ratio and the arc elasticity implied in the results above may be computed.

Equation 9.3.4 with $Q_2 = 17,534$ yields $E_{shr} = -0.21$, and Eq. 8.7.7 gives $E_{arc} = -0.29$. As stated previously, the shrinkage ratio tends to deviate from the other two measures.

Example 8.20: Multiple Price Changes

The shares of the automobile and a transit mode along a corridor are 4500 and 1000 persons per peak period, respectively. The prevailing out-of-pocket costs and travel times associated with the two modes are as follows:

	Time (min)	Cost
Auto	35	$2.00
Transit	50	1.00

The shrinkage ratios with respect to transit prices have been estimated to be

	Time (min)	Cost
Auto	0.05	$ 0.04
Transit	-0.52	-0.30

In other words, the direct elasticity of transit demand with respect to transit travel time is -0.52, the cross elasticity of auto demand with respect to transit cost is 0.04, and so forth. The shrinkage ratios with respect to auto prices are

	Time (min)	Cost
Auto	-0.58	$-0.20
Transit	0.12	0.03

The city department of transportation services is contemplating the opening of an exclusive bus lane that would save an average of 10 min per trip. At the same time, the city council is holding public hearings on a proposal to raise downtown parking rates and thus cause an increase in automobile travel costs to $2.60. Estimate the likely effects on peak-hour travel demand of both actions combined.

Solution   The direct effect of reducing the transit travel time on transit patronage may be predicted by Eq. 8.7.6, which may be rewritten as

$$Q_2 - Q_1 = \frac{E_{shr}Q_1 (T_2 - T_1)}{T_1}$$

$$= \frac{(-0.52)(1000)(40 - 50)}{50}$$

$$= 104$$

Thus the transit patronage would increase by 104 peak-hour trips, or by 10.4% in relation to the initial demand of 1000, as a result of a 20% decrease in travel time. Because of the way in which shrinkage ratios are defined, the same answer could have been obtained by proportioning the given shrinkage ratio. Specifically, this ratio states that a 1% increase (decrease) in travel time would result in a 0.52% decrease (increase) in transit patronage. Since the contemplated decrease in travel time is 20%, the percentage of increase in patronage would be $20 \times 0.52 = 10.4\%$ of the original demand, or $1000 \times 0.104 = 104$ trips.

The remaining likely direct and cross effects are summarized next:

	Demand changes	
Action	Automobile	Transit system
20% Transit-time reduction	-45	$+104$
30% Auto-cost increase	-270	$+9$
Combined effects	-315	$+113$

Discussion   In combination, the two actions would result in a decrease of 315 auto person-trips per peak and an increase in transit patronage of 113. The available information precludes any definite answers to the question of what would happen to the net loss of 202 peak-hour person-trips, for example, whether they would shift to another time period, whether they would be given up, or whether they would shift to another mode not included in the analysis. The question of internal consistency discussed in Section 8.7.2 merits consideration: The predicted decrease in auto trips may, in fact, cause a reduction in auto travel times, whereas the added transit patronage may induce the scheduling of additional departures, thus decreasing the average waiting times and, consequently, travel times. These changes may have further direct and cross effects on the peak hour demand before a new equilibrium is reached.

8.8 SUMMARY

In this chapter we presented the fundamental elements of the sequential demand-forecasting process, the purpose of which is to predict how a proposed regional transportation system will be used at some future time. The process is driven by scenaria describing the distribution of future land uses and socioeconomic characteristics between small analysis zones in the region and a description of a regional multimodal transportation system. Consequently, it constitutes a conditional prediction of future demand given these inputs. The process is called *sequential* because it applies a chain of models in sequence to predict the number of trips that each zone will either produce or attract (trip generation), the interchange volumes between pairs of zones (trip distribution), the shares of interzonal volumes that will use each of the available travel modes (modal choice), and the allocation of interzonal trips to the interzonal paths provided by the transportation network (network assignment). The resulting interzonal volumes by mode can be translated to link flows in order to aid in the assessment of the ability of the transportation system to accommodate the demands that will be placed on it.

Given a land-use pattern, several proposed transportation system alternatives (including the do-nothing alternative) are typically examined. The outputs of the demand-forecasting models for each alternative are included among the consequences or impacts (see Chapter 10) that enter the process of system evaluation and selection (see Chapter 11). The demand-forecasting process can also aid in predicting the transportation consequences of land use changes (see Chapter 9) and to provide guidance to related public policies.

The transport behavior of individuals and households was examined as well. Analyses based on disaggregate units such as individuals and/or households offer insights on the effects of personal and household characteristics on travel behavior and trip patterns. Factors ranging from household structure and income to lifestyles and personality were addressed along with applications of household variables in automobile ownership and trip-generation modeling.

Principles of simultaneous model structures, demand elasticity models (which are particularly useful in assessing the effects of price or service changes on transport demand), and strategies that combine a wide spectrum of transport demand forecasting methodologies were presented as well.

Finally, the fact that large-scale transportation-demand forecasting is a monumental enterprise must not escape the attention of the student. The task is facilitated by the availability of computer-software packages that can be used for the calibration and application of the models described in this chapter as well as those covered in the following chapter.

8.9 EXERCISES

1. An origin–destination survey in 10 travel-analysis zones provided the following data relating to zonal residential densities (households/acre) and average daily trip productions per household. Calibrate and plot a model of the form $10^Y = AX^{-B}$.

    Density X: 42   5   25   10   4   15   20   12   14   22
    Trip rate Y: 1.5   4.0   2.1   2.6   4.8   2.0   2.5   3.3   1.9   2.0

2. A transportation engineer was hired by the city planning department to calibrate a multiple regression model for trip productions. The department has collected base-year data for the following variables:

$$P_I = \text{trip productions}$$

$$X_1 = \text{zone population}$$

$$X_2 = \text{median income}$$

$$X_3 = \text{median age}$$

$$X_4 = \text{car registrations}$$

$$X_5 = \text{number of dwelling units}$$

A preliminary analysis of the data resulted in the following simple correlation matrix.

	P_I	X_1	X_2	X_3	X_4	X_5
P_I	1.00	0.95	0.83	0.41	0.82	0.85
X_1		1.00	-0.21	0.22	-0.29	0.91
X_2			1.00	0.82	0.89	-0.43
X_3				1.00	-0.19	-0.15
X_4					1.00	-0.22

Specify at least five possible equations that may be tried and give the specific reasons for their selection.

3. A zone in the CBD is projected to contain 1,525,000 ft^2 of residential space; 3,675,000 ft^2 of service establishments; and a total retail activity floor area of 2,100,000 ft^2. Government and other public buildings occupy a total area of 615,000 ft^2. Using the data obtained in Pittsburgh, calculate the trip generation of this zone.

4. An international hotel chain is planning the construction of a model/office development in a resort town. The preliminary design includes 2100 rooms, a sit-down restaurant having a total floor space of 2500 ft^2, and 5000 ft^2 of office space, which the company is planning to lease to various local firms. Apply the trip rates published by the Institute of Transportation Engineers to estimate the total trip attractions during the afternoon traffic peak hour. (Instructor must furnish tables or formulas.)

5. A high-rise apartment building containing 350 units is planned for a residential area of a city. Because the area is zoned for low-density residential land uses, the developer has applied for a zoning variance. At the legally required public hearing, several residents of the area have opposed the zoning change, claiming that the proposal will add to the traffic-congestion problem during the peak hours, but they were unable to substantiate their claim. Calculate the likely peak-hour trip generation of the proposed project. (Instructor must furnish tables or formulas.)

6. Use the cross-classification table (Table 8.2.4) to calculate the total nonwork-home-based productions of each of the zones that are expected to contain the following mixtures of households (HH):

Zone 1: Suburban

Persons/HH \ Veh/HH	0	1	2+
1	50	150	100
2, 3	10	500	300
4	100	400	100

Zone 2: Rural

Persons/HH \ Veh/HH	0	1	2+
1	300	50	100
2, 3	100	200	100
4	400	300	150

7. A residential zone is expected to have 1500 dwelling units. For a $12,000 average income, calculate (a) the person trips per dwelling unit for units that own 0, 1, 2, and 3+ autos and (b) the total trip generation by trip purpose. Use the income–auto-ownership distribution given in Fig. 8.2.5 and assume that curve C applies to all subgroups within the zone.

8. Given

1.

Zone	Productions	Attractiveness
1	1000	2
2	0	5
3	2000	1

2. W_{IJ}:

I \ J	1	2	3
1	5	20	10
2	20	5	10
3	10	10	5

K_{IJ}:

I \ J	1	2	3
1	1.1	1.5	0.8
2	0.6	1.2	0.5
3	1.0	1.4	1.3

3. $\ln F = -1.5 \ln W$

Apply the gravity model to calculate all interchange volumes.

9. Complete the following table given that $P_1 = 1000$ trips per day, $C = 2.0$, and all $K_{IJ} = 1.0$.

Zone	A_J	W_{IJ}	F_{IJ}	Q_{IJ}
1	0	—		
2	400	20		
3	300	5		
4	100	5		
5	200	10		

10. Assuming that the relationship between F and W is of the form $F = AW^{-c}$, apply the method of least squares to the following data to estimate the parameters A and c.

$$F: \quad 0.03 \quad 0.04 \quad 0.02 \quad 0.03$$
$$W: \quad 7 \quad\quad 5 \quad\quad 12 \quad\quad 8$$

11. The final iteration in a calibration of the gravity model yielded the following friction-factor and impedance values:

$$F: \quad 1.0 \quad 4.0 \quad 0.5 \quad 0.3$$
$$W: \quad 12 \quad\; 4 \quad\; 15 \quad\; 20$$

(a) Calibrate a relationship of the form $F = aW^{-b}$.
(b) Apply your results to the following case: Two residential zones (1 and 2) are expected to produce 6500 and 3800 person-trips per day, respectively. Two nonresidential zones (3 and 4) are competing for these trips. The planning commission has received a proposal to improve parts of the transportation system, which, if implemented, would affect certain interzonal impedances as shown.

Do-nothing:

I \ J	3	4
1	10	14
2	8	14

Proposed plan:

I \ J	3	4
1	10	10
2	8	8

Given the following additional information, calculate the effect of the proposal on the total trips attracted by the nonresidential zones.

$$A_3 = 10 \qquad A_4 = 15 \qquad \text{all } K_{IJ} = 1.0$$

12. A base-year trip-generation study obtained the data shown relating to the daily person-trip productions per dwelling unit (Y) and residential density (X dwelling units per acre).

$$
\begin{array}{lcccc}
Y: & 3.5 & 6.5 & 4.0 & 2.2 \\
X: & 30.0 & 10.0 & 50.0 & 70.0
\end{array}
$$

(a) Calibrate and plot and relationship $Y = (a + bX)^{-1}$.
(b) Apply your answers to part (a) to the following situation: A residential zone I has an area of 500 acres and contains 7500 dwelling units. Two zones (J and L) are competing for the trips produced by I. Given the following information, calculate the trip interchange volumes Q_{IJ} and Q_{IL} if $W_{IJ} = 12$, $W_{IL} = 8$, $\ln F = -1.5 \ln W$, $A_J = 0.5A_L$, and all $K_{IJ} = 1.0$.

13. A gravity-model calibration study obtained the following final values for the travel-time factors and the interzonal impedances:

$$
\begin{array}{lcccc}
F: & 0.19 & 0.10 & 0.07 & 0.05 \\
W: & 4 & 7 & 9 & 12
\end{array}
$$

Using F as the dependent variable, calculate the parameter c of Eq. 8.3.9.

14. Given the following data:

I	P	A
1	2000	4
2	0	10
3	0	12

W_{IJ}:

I \ J	1	2	3
1	5	10	15
2	10	4	10
3	15	10	15

Estimate all interchange volumes assuming that $c = 1.9$ and that all socioeconomic adjustment factors are equal to unity.

15. After calibrating Eq. 8.3.13, the following interzonal information became available. The observed and calculated interzonal flow interchanging between I and J were 2500 and 2100, respectively. The data corresponding to the interchange between zones I and L were 1960 and 2060. Given that the total production of zone I was 12,000 trips, calculate the socioeconomic adjustment factors for the two interchanges.

16. Computerize the application of the gravity model of trip distribution.

17. Perform a second Fratar model iteration using the results of Example 8.7.

18. Computerize the Fratar model, making sure to place an upper limit on the number of iterations in order to avoid infinite looping.

19. Given the utility equation

$$U_K = a_K - 0.003X_1 - 0.04X_2$$

where X_1 is the travel cost in cents and X_2 is the travel time in minutes.
(a) Calculate the market shares of the following travel modes:

Mode K	a_K	X_1	X_2
Automobile	−0.20	120	30
Express bus	−0.40	60	45
Regular bus	−0.60	30	55

(b) Estimate the effect that a 50% increase in the cost of all three modes will have on modal split.

20. Given the utility expression

$$U_K = A_K - 0.05T_a - 0.04T_w - 0.02T_r - 0.01C$$

where T_a is the access time, T_w is the waiting time, T_r is the riding time, and C is the out-of-pocket cost.
(a) Apply the logit model to calculate the shares of the automobile mode ($A_K = -0.005$) and a mass-transit mode ($A_K = -0.05$) if

Mode	T_a	T_w	T_r	C
Auto	5	0	30	100
Transit	10	10	45	50

(b) Estimate the patronage shift that would result from doubling the bus out-of-pocket cost.

21. Computerize the application of the multinomial logit model allowing for N choices and M attributes per choice, where N and M are input variables.

22. The application of a route-building algorithm resulting in the following final tree table:

Node to	Total time	Node from
1	0	—
2	8	3
3	3	1
4	7	3
5	17	6
6	10	2
7	8	4
8	19	5
9	13	6
10	14	9
11	17	10
12	18	9
13	18	10
14	25	12
15	23	13
16	22	13

Sketch the minimum tree, and specify the link travel times.

23. Complete the tree table that describes the minimum tree shown in Fig. E8.23.

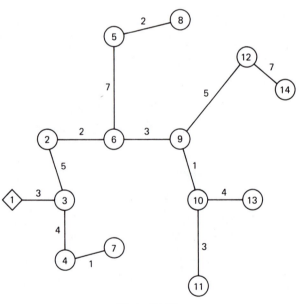

Figure E8.23

24. Without drawing the entire network described by the accompanying link table, find and sketch the minimum tree emanating from node 1.

i	j	w_{ij}
1	4	2
2	5	4
2	6	3
3	8	5
4	1	2
4	5	6
4	8	10
5	2	4
5	4	6
5	6	4
6	2	3
6	5	4
6	7	9
7	6	9
7	8	7
8	3	5
8	4	10
8	7	7

25. Given the link table of Exercise 8.24 (a) find graphically the minimum tree emanating from node 1; (b) using your answer to part (a), calculate Q_{1-2} and Q_{1-3} if $P_1 = 2500$ trips per day, $A_2 = 1.5$, $A_3 = 3.5$, all other P_I and $A_J = 0$, and all $K_{IJ} = 1.0$; and (c) perform an all-or-nothing assignment to allocate the interzonal volumes calculated in part (b) to the links of the network.

26. Write a computer program for the minimum-tree-seeking procedure described in this chapter.

27. Allocate the following peak-hour interchange volumes produced by zone 10 to the network described.

J:	11	12	13	14	15	16	17
Q_{IJ}:	200	150	190	270	320	110	540

LINK TABLE

i	j	w_{ij}	i	j	w_{ij}
10	14	6	14	13	15
10	15	5	14	15	7
10	16	12	15	10	5
11	14	5	15	11	3
11	15	3	15	14	7
11	17	8	15	16	8
12	14	21	16	10	12
12	16	4	16	12	4
12	17	3	16	13	7
13	14	15	16	15	8
13	16	7	16	17	2
13	17	6	17	11	8
14	10	6	17	12	3
14	11	5	17	13	6
14	12	21	17	16	2

If the capacity of link 10–16 is 1000 veh/hr calculate this link's travel time as implied by your answer.

28. A roadway connection is planned between cities A and B, which at present have no direct connection. The cities are approximately 800 miles apart. There is no passenger rail connection between A and B, but there are four commercial flights a day from each city to the other. City A has a population of 250,000, and B has 350,000. The median household income is $22,000 and $23,500 in A and B, respectively.

   The model below provides estimates on the expected daily volume (DV) of passenger traffic between two cities. Assuming that (1) the average vehicle occupancy will be 1.5 passengers per vehicle, (2) each lane can serve up to 1,700 vehicles per hour, and (3) 40% of the expected daily volume will occur in 1 h (peak, or design hour), estimate and decide how many lanes are required (even number):

$$DV = 2000 + 30 \quad \text{[population in largest of the two cities (in thousands)]}$$
$$+ 25 \quad \text{[population in smallest of the two cities (in thousands)]}$$
$$+ 240 \quad \text{[median household income in largest of the two cities (in thousands)]}$$
$$+ 200 \quad \text{[median household income in smallest of the two cities (in thousands)]}$$
$$- 1.5 \quad \text{[Distance between the two cities (miles)]}$$
$$- 0.005 \quad \text{(distance between the two cities squared)}$$
$$- 500 \quad \text{[passenger rail connection (1 if exists, 0 otherwise)]}$$
$$- 150 \quad \text{(number of daily commercial flights between the two cities)}$$

The standard error of estimate (SEE) for the dependent variable is $\pm 1,000$.

29. Focus on the model in Exercise 28 and answer the following questions: (a) What type of model is this? (b) Would you be confident in using this model for a real application? Why? (c) Why do population and income have positive contributions to daily passenger traffic, and why do distance and commercial airline flights have a negative contribution? (It may be necessary to consult Appendix C to answer this part.)

30. Identify the characteristics of the following three transportation-demand models and indicate their role in the demand-forecasting process.

$$Q_{IJ} = aP_IA_JW_{IJ}^b$$
$$Q_{IJ} = aY_I^bX_I^cW_{IJ}^d$$
$$Q_{IJK} = aX_I^bY_I^cZ_J^dW_{IJK}^e$$

where

$$P_I = \text{productions of zone } I$$
$$A_J = \text{attractions of zone } J$$
$$W_{IJ} = \text{travel impedance from } I \text{ to } J$$
$$Y_I = \text{average income in zone } I$$
$$X_I = \text{population of zone } I$$
$$Z_J = \text{total employment in zone } J$$
$$W_{IJK} = \text{impedance from } I \text{ to } J \text{ via mode } K$$

31. Specify and discuss the forecasting model structures that are possible given the models calibrated for Canberra, Australia (see Section 8.7.4).

32. Calculate and interpret the income elasticity of demand in model 2 of Exercise 30 assuming that $a, b, c, d,$ and e are constants.

33. An increase of transit fares from 40 to 60¢ has resulted in a decrease in transit patronage from 500,000 to 450,000 trips per day. Calculate the shrinkage ratio, the linear-arc elasticity, and the log-arc elasticity.

34. An increase in gasoline prices from $1.00 to $1.30 per gallon resulted in a decrease of automobile use from 1,000,000 to 960,000 trips. Estimate the likely impact of an increase in gasoline prices from $1.30 to $1.50. Solve this problem using the three alternative measures of elasticity.

35. A special service for the elderly and handicapped currently serves 2500 persons per day. Given that the current fare is 50¢ and that the linear-arc fare elasticity of demand is -0.45, calculate (a) the loss of patronage that would result from doubling the fare, (b) the effect on fare-box revenues, (c) the implied shrinkage ratio, and (d) the implied log-arc elasticity.

36. A 20% increase in automobile costs has been observed to cause a 5% increase in transit patronage relative to the patronage prior to the increase and a 10% decrease in auto usage. Calculate the implied direct and cross elasticities of demand as measured by $E_{sh}, E_{arc},$ and $E_{log\text{-}arc}$.

37. A zonal interchange is served by a local bus route and an express bus route. The current travel times and fares associated with the two types of service are

	Travel time (min)	Fare
Local	50	$0.50
Express	30	1.00

Given the following linear-arc elasticities of demand and that the current transit patronage of 4000 trips per peak period is split 40–60 between the express and local bus services, calculate the effect of raising the express bus fare to $1.50.

	Local		Express	
	Time	Fare	Time	Fare
Local	-0.02	-0.03	$+0.01$	$+0.02$
Express	$+0.09$	$+0.62$	-0.08	-0.15

38. For the system of Exercise 37, estimate the effect of expanding the number of express buses and thus reducing the express bus travel time to 25 min.

39. Examine the effect that a 10-min reduction in the travel time offered by the local bus service would have on the total peak-hour transit usage between the two zones described in Exercise 37.

40. Assuming that the elasticities given in Exercise 38 are shrinkage ratios, estimate the combined effect of raising express bus fares to $1.30 *and* lowering the local bus fare to $0.40.

41. Repeat Exercise 37 assuming that the given elasticities are log-arc elasticities.
42. Repeat Exercise 37 assuming that the given elasticities are shrinkage ratios.

8.10 REFERENCES

8.1 FEDERAL HIGHWAY ADMINISTRATION, *Trip Generation Analysis,* U.S. Department of Transportation, U.S. Government Printing Office, Stock No. 050-001-00101-2, Washington, D.C., 1975.

8.2 PAPACOSTAS, C. S., "Honolulu's Handi-Van: Use and Implications," *Traffic Quarterly,* 34, 3 (July 1980): 429–440.

8.3 KEEFER, L. E., Director, *Pittsburgh Area Transportation Study,* vol. I, Study Findings, Nov. 1961.

8.4 FEDERAL HIGHWAY ADMINISTRATION, *Guidelines for Trip Generation Analysis,* U.S. Department of Transportation, U.S. Government Printing Office, Washington, D.C., June 1967.

8.5 ———, *Computer Programs for Urban Transportation Planning: PLANPAC/BACKPAC General Information,* U.S. Department of Transportation, U.S. Government Printing Office, Stock No. 050-001-00125-0, Washington, D.C., Apr. 1977.

8.6 OAHU METROPOLITAN PLANNING ORGANIZATION, *Oahu Model Update Study: User's Manual and Training Information,* Honolulu, Dec. 1982.

8.7 BOCK, F. C., *Factors Influencing Modal Trip Assignment,* National Cooperative Highway Research Report 57, Highway Research Board, National Research Council, Washington, D.C., 1968.

8.8 FRATAR, T. J., "Forecasting the Distribution of Interzonal Vehicular Trips by Successive Approximations," *Proceedings of the 33rd Annual Meeting,* Highway Research Board, National Research Council, Washington, D.C., 1954.

8.9 FERTAL, M. J., et al., *Modal Split: Documentation of Nine Methods for Estimating Transit Usage,* Bureau of Public Roads, U.S. Department of Commence, U.S. Government Printing Office, Washington, D.C., Dec. 1966.

8.10 DEEN, T. B., W. L. MERTZ, and N. A. IRWIN, *Application of a Modal Split Model to Travel Estimates for the Washington Area,* Highway Research Record 38, Highway Research Board, National Research Council, Washington, D.C., 1963, pp. 97–123.

8.11 KANAFANI, A., *Transportation Demand Analysis,* McGraw-Hill, New York, 1983.

8.12 HUTCHINSON, B. G., *Principles of Urban Transport Systems Planning,* McGraw-Hill, New York, 1974.

8.13 LANCASTER, K. J., "A New Approach to Consumer Theory," *Journal of Political Economy,* 64 (1966): 132–157.

8.14 STOPHER, P. R., *A Probability Model of Travel Mode Choice for the Work Journey,* Highway Research Record 283, Highway Research Board, National Research Council, Washington, D.C., 1969, pp. 57–65.

8.15 RASSAM, P. R., R. H. ELLIS, and J. C. BENNET, *The n-Dimensional Logit Model:*

Development and Applications, Highway Research Record 369, Highway Research Board, National Research Council, Washington, D.C., 1971, pp. 135–147.

8.16 Moskowitz, K., *California Model of Assigning Diverted Traffic to Proposed Freeways,* Highway Research Record 130, Highway Research Board, National Research Council, Washington, D.C., 1956, pp. 1–26.

8.17 Bureau of Public Roads, *Traffic Assignment Manual,* U.S. Department of Commerce, U.S. Government Printing Office, Washington, D.C., June 1964.

8.18 Federal Highway Administration, *Traffic Assignment,* U.S. Department of Transportation, U.S. Government Printing Office, Stock No. 5001-00060, Washington, D.C., Aug. 1973.

8.19 Moore, E. F., "The Shortest Path Through a Maze," *Proceedings of the International Symposium on the Theory of Switching,* Harvard University, Cambridge, Mass., 1957.

8.20 Martin, B. V., *Minimum Path Algorithms for Transportation Planning,* Research Report R63-52, Department of Civil Engineering, Massachusetts Institute of Technology, Cambridge, Mass., 1963.

8.21 Irwin, N. A., and H. G. von Cube, *Capacity Restraint in Multi-travel Mode Assignment Programs,* Highway Research Board, Bulletin 347, National Research Council, Washington, D.C., 1962, pp. 258–289.

8.22 Huber, M. J., H. B. Boutwell, and D. K. Witheford, *Comparative Analysis of Traffic Assignment Techniques with Actual Highway Use,* National Cooperative Highway Research Report 58, Highway Research Board, National Research Council, Washington, D.C., 1968.

8.23 Schneider, M., *A Direct Approach to Traffic Assignment,* Highway Research Record 6, Highway Research Board, National Research Council, Washington, D.C., 1963, pp. 71–75.

8.24 Humphrey, T. F., *A Report on the Accuracy of Traffic Assignment When Using Capacity Restraint,* Highway Research Record 191, Highway Research Board, National Research Council, Washington, D.C., 1967, pp. 53–75.

8.25 Levinsohn, D., et al. *UTPS Highway Network Development Guide,* Federal Highway Administration, U.S. Department of Transportation, Washington, D.C., Jan. 1983.

8.26 Smock, R., *An Iterative Assignment Approach to Capacity Restraint on Arterial Networks,* Highway Research Board Bulletin 347, National Research Council, Washington, D.C., 1962, pp. 60–66.

8.27 Irwin, N. A., N. Dodd, and H. G. von Cube, *Capacity Restraint in Assignment Programs,* Highway Research Board Bulletin 297, National Research Council, Washington, D.C., 1961, pp. 109–127.

8.28 Dial, R. A., "A Probabilistic Traffic Assignment Model Which Obviates Path Enumeration," *Transportation Research,* 5, 2 (1971): 83–222.

8.29 Papacostas, C. S., *Development and Application of the Bimodal Travel Behavior Model,* Masters thesis, Department of Civil Engineering, Carnegie-Mellon University, Pittsburgh, Pa., 1971.

8.30 ——, *Pollution and Energy Implications of Bus-Automobile Alternatives,* Ph.D. dissertation, Department of Civil Engineering, Carnegie-Mellon University, Pittsburgh, Pa., 1974.

8.31 DIAL, R. B., G. S. RUTHERFORD, and L. QUILLIAN, *Transit Network Analysis: INET,* Report UMTA-UPM-20-79-3, Urban Mass Transportation Administration, U.S. Department of Transportation, Washington, D.C., July 1979.

8.32 HAVENS, J. J., "New Approaches to Understanding Travel Behavior: Role, Life-Style and Adaptation," in *New Horizons in Travel Behavior Research,* Lexington Books, Lexington, Mass., 1981.

8.33 SALOMON, I.,"Life-Styles: a Broader Perspective on Travel Behaviour," in *Recent Advances in Travel Demand Analysis,* Gower, Aldershot, Hampshire, England, 1983.

8.34 BEN-AKIVA, M., and S. LERMAN, *Discrete Choice Analysis: Theory and Application to Travel Demand,* MIT Press, Cambridge, Mass., 1985.

8.35 PREVEDOUROS, P. D., *Demographic, Social, Economic and Personality Factors Affecting Suburban Transport Behavior,* Ph.D. dissertation, Department of Civil Engineering, Northwestern University, Evanston, Ill., 1990.

8.36 TOWNSEND, T. A., *The Effects of Household Characteristics on the Multi-day Time Allocations and Travel Activity Patterns of Households and Their Members,* Ph.D. dissertation, Department of Civil Engineering, Northwestern University, Evanston, Ill., 1987.

8.37 KOPPELMAN, F. S., and E. I. PAS, *Travel-Choice Behavior: Models of Perceptions, Feelings, Preference and Choice,* Transportation Research Record 765, Transportation Research Board, National Research Council, Washington, D.C., (1980):26–33.

8.38 KOPPELMAN, F. S., and P. K. LYON, "Attitudinal Analysis of Work/School Travel," *Transportation Science,* 15, 3 (1981).

8.39 KITAMURA, R., "A Panel Analysis of Household Car Ownership and Mobility," *Proceedings of Japan Society of Civil Engineers,* No 383/IV-7 (1987): 13–27.

8.40 GOLOB, T. F., "The Dynamics of Household Travel Time Expenditures and Car Ownership Decisions," presented at the *International Conference on Dynamic Travel Behavior Analysis,* Kyoto University, Kyoto, Japan, July 18–19, 1989.

8.41 JONES, P. M., F. S. KOPPELMAN, and J. P. ORFEUIL, "Activity Analysis: State-of-the-Art and Future Directions," in *Developments in Dynamic and Activity-Based Approaches to Travel Analysis,* Avenbury, London, 1990.

8.42 GOULIAS, K. G., and R. KITAMURA, *Recursive Model System for Trip Generation and Trip Chaining,* Transportation Research Record, 1236, Transportation Research Board, National Research Council, Washington, D.C., 1989; pp. 59–66.

8.43 GOULIAS, K. G., R. M. PENDYALA, and R. KITAMURA, *Practical Method for the Estimation of Trip Generation and Trip Chaining,* Transportation Research Record, 1285, Transportation Research Board, National Research Council, Washington, D.C., 1990; pp. 47–56.

8.44 KOPPELMAN, F. S., and G. ROSE, "Geographic Transfer of Travel Choice Models: Evaluation and Procedures," *Proceedings of the International Symposium on New Directions in Urban Modelling,* University of Waterloo, Canada, July 1983.

8.45 HAMBURG, J. R., G. T. LATHROP, and E. J. KAISER, *Forecasting Inputs to Transportation Planning,* National Cooperative Highway Research Program Report 266, Transportation Research Board, National Research Council, Washington, D.C., December 1983.

8.46 QUANDT, R. E., and W. J. BAUMOL, "The Demand for Abstract Modes—Theory and Measurement," *Journal of Regional Science,* 6, 2 (1966): 13–26.

8.47 WIGAN, M. R., ed., *New Techniques for Transport Systems Analysis,* Special Report 10, Australian Road Research Board and Bureau of Transport Economics, Vermont, Victoria, 1977.

8.48 INSTITUTE OF TRANSPORTATION ENGINEERS, *Transportation and Traffic Engineering Handbook,* Prentice Hall, Englewood Cliffs, N.J., 1976.

8.49 SOSSLAU, A. B., et al., *Travel Estimation Procedures for Quick Response to Urban Policy Issues,* National Cooperative Highway Research Program Report 186, Transportation Research Board, National Research Council, Washington, D.C., 1978.

8.50 TRANSPORTATION RESEARCH BOARD, *Transportation Planning for Small and Medium-Sized Communities,* Special Report 187, National Research Council, Washington, D.C., 1980.

8.51 ————, *State Transportation Issues and Actions,* Special Report 189, National Research Council, Washington, D.C., 1980.

8.52 PARODY, T. E., and D. BRAND, *Forecasting Demand and Revenue for Transit Prepaid Pass and Fare Alternatives,* Transportation Research Record 719, Transportation Research Board, National Research Council, 1979, pp. 35–41.

8.53 FEDERAL HIGHWAY ADMINISTRATION, *Traveler Response to Transportation System Changes,* 2nd ed., U.S. Department of Transportation, Washington, D.C., July 1981.

9 Traffic Impact and Parking Studies

9.1 INTRODUCTION

In this chapter we provide an overview of two common types of traffic engineering studies: traffic impact studies and parking studies. The former assess the impact of proposed new developments or expansions of existing developments on traffic networks (i.e., impact of anticipated traffic on existing road networks surrounding the site). The latter focus on the analysis of needs and on the principles of design of parking facilities. A number of comprehensive and widely used traffic and planning analysis personal computer software packages are presented as well.

9.2 TRAFFIC IMPACT STUDIES

9.2.1 Introduction

Few people realize the connection between transportation analysis and proposed developments. Why should transportation analysis be necessary in the design of a shopping mall, a large apartment building, a new employment center, and so forth? All of the above may require some internal circulation design and parking lots or parking structures. However, the role of transportation analysts goes far beyond the aforementioned traffic engineering applications.

New or expanded developments generate new or additional traffic: new shoppers, new residents, and new employees in the examples mentioned above. In general, developments attract people, because certain needs of people can be fulfilled in a new development. For example, the new development may include a supermarket which is larger or closer to the one previously used (the underlying need is household maintenance), or the new development may host offices, restaurants, and movie theaters (the underlying needs are work and entertainment) that would attract people. Users of these facilities would travel to the new development by various travel modes (i.e., driving, sharing a ride, using public transportation, bike, walk, or a combination of the above).

To quantify the transportation implications of new developments, the new or additional trips have to be estimated; their origins and destinations must be determined and the modes and routes selected have to be established. Furthermore, traffic is dynamic. Directional flows vary by the time of day and with time. New transportation facilities and services are implemented or terminated over time. Thus the characteristics of the generated trips and their impact on traffic must be forecast and assessed. This requires specialized traffic engineering knowledge.

9.2.2 Basic Characteristics

Traffic impact studies (TIS) are necessitated by the increasing levels of congestion in growing areas, particularly those that are located within the boundaries of large urban areas. In an attempt to control unplanned growth and unmanageable loads of traffic, traffic impact studies became a requirement to examine whether the road network surrounding a proposed development will be able to handle the additional traffic while still offering acceptable levels of service (e.g., performance at level C or better). TIS are required by municipalities or counties which, individually, determine the acceptable levels of intersection performance. For example, in some locations LOS D is acceptable for peak periods.

Traffic impact studies provide answers to the following questions:

1. What are the existing traffic conditions on the network surrounding the proposed development?
2. How much additional traffic will be generated by the proposed development?
3. How will additional traffic affect existing conditions?
4. What roadway improvements or changes in the site plan would be necessary to minimize the traffic impact of the proposed development?

Traffic impact studies are not required for all developments. A traffic impact study may be necessary if at least 100 new inbound (i.e., entering the site) or outbound (i.e., exiting from the site) trips are generated along the peak direction of traffic. This corresponds to developments of substantial size: 160 single-family houses, or 220 multifamily units, or 10,000 ft^2 of retail space, or 60,000 ft^2 of office space. Smaller developments that (1) may generate traffic safety hazards or (2) are located in traffic congested areas may necessitate a traffic impact study. The municipalities may request a TIS for reasons other than the ones mentioned before. The roles of developers, traffic consultants, and government agencies vary between localities.

Several assumptions are put forth in traffic impact studies, particularly for large developments, because proposed developments may be fully operational in the near future, whereas their impact will be felt over a longer period.

The following are some of the issues needing resolution:

- Determination of the appropriate size of the study area surrounding the proposed development
- Peak periods to be analyzed (i.e., morning, noon, evening, weekends, etc.)
- Time frame of analysis, which includes the base year when the proposed facility opens and the target or horizon year for assessment of impacts
- Anticipated background growth (e.g., overall growth of the surrounding area)
- Identification of committed transportation improvements or changes until the horizon year
- Study methodology (i.e., analysis of intersections using the HCM [9.1] or Circular 212 [9.2] method, utilization of nationwide or area-specific rates)
- Requirements for additional analyses (e.g., accidents, sight distance, gap availability, weaving, queuing, etc.)

The size of the development largely dictates the number of intersections to be analyzed (i.e., two to four for a 300,000 ft^2 strip mall), which, in turn, suggests the equipment to be utilized. Small developments can be analyzed by hand, or computers are used for simple bookkeeping tasks and calculations. Large developments are typically analyzed with the aid of personal computers. Traffic network flow models are utilized for the proper assignment of flows on the network and the faster repetition of calculations for future scenarios. Also, for large developments, traffic impact studies are required during various phases of design and issuance of requisite permits, because the final site plan is likely to be different from the original plan (e.g., redesign to respond to new economic or demand trends, public reaction, etc.) Computer processing of the traffic impact study vastly improves responsiveness and efficiency.

The basic inputs and outputs of traffic impact studies are as follows: *inputs*: traffic volumes by movement and direction, link volumes, network characteristics (street system: link lengths, capacities, signal timings), land-use patterns, trip-generation rates, and distribution by direction (i.e., percent of traffic entering and leaving the site); *outputs*: link and intersection volumes, capacity and performance analysis of intersections (usually with the HCM method; see Chapter 5), and recommendations for improvements within the site and of the surrounding network.

9.2.3 Overview of Steps

The methodology of a traffic impact study includes the following steps [9.3]:

1. Meetings with the municipality to discuss the scope and extent of the study, and the assumptions and horizon years to be used for analysis. At this stage, the municipality may agree to provide data on traffic volumes, signal timings, accidents, and planned transportation improvements.
2. Field surveys, which usually include the following observations: detailed reconnaissance of project site, roadway network in the area, traffic control devices, signal phasings and timings at signalized intersections, roadway geometrics, parking regulations, transit routes and stops, adjacent land uses, and driveway locations.
3. Traffic counts and surveys. The standard traffic counts (detailed in Chapter 5) are conducted during the agreed time periods, days, and seasons. Surveys of pass-by motorists, neighboring residents, and employees may be collected for guidance in modal split, trip distribution, and traffic assignment.
4. Analysis, which consists of the following tasks listed in the order in which they are often conducted:
    a. Trip generation: estimation of trip rates and application of modal split based on experience (historical data in the area) or from local surveys.
    b. Trip distribution.
    c. Estimation of nonsite traffic. The impact of such traffic should not be attributed to the site studied; else unreasonable demands for roadway improvements or downsizing of the development may be placed on the developer of the project under study.
    d. Assignment of site and nonsite trips on the roadway network based on a network equilibrium rule or an empirical technique.
    e. Capacity and performance analysis of signalized and unsignalized intersections.
    f. Evaluation of results and recommendations for improvements.
5. Revisions of the site plan and incorporation of selected improvements.
6. Production of reports for the client and the municipality.

9.2.4 Major Components of Traffic Impact Studies

In this section we focus on components of a traffic impact study which require specific analyses. These components are trip generation, modal split, trip distribution, traffic assignment, and intersection analyses. Methodologies of these fundamental steps of transportation analysis are detailed in Chapters 5 and 8. In this section we present some basic examples of the application of these transportation analysis techniques to conduct traffic impact studies.

Trip generation.   Trip-generation estimation is conducted separately for site and nonsite traffic. Nonsite traffic includes all through traffic that has neither origin nor destination at the site as well as the traffic generated by developments within the study area, but outside the specific site under analysis. In the absence of locally derived rates, ITE's *Trip Generation* manual [9.4] is utilized for assessing site and nonsite traffic. An example of the form of the data in this manual is given in Fig. 9.2.1.

The *Trip Generation* manual employs simple additive or multiplicative models of the form

$$T = a + bX \qquad \text{(additive)} \tag{9.2.1}$$
$$\ln T = a + b \ln X \qquad \text{(multiplicative; original form } T = a'X^b)$$

where

$$T = \text{total number of generated trips}$$
$$X = \text{total GFA or GLA or another characteristic of the site}$$
$$a, b = \text{given model parameters}$$
$$\text{GFA} = \text{gross floor area}$$
$$\text{GLA} = \text{gross leasable area}$$

Example 9.1

Estimate the peak-hour number of trips generated by an office park with 190,000 ft^2 GFA for 1 h during the morning and evening peak periods.

Solution   The appropriate formulas from the *Trip Generation* manual are (see Fig. 9.2.1):

$$\text{AM peak:} \quad \ln T = 0.818 \ln X + 1.679 \tag{9.2.2a}$$

$$\text{PM peak:} \quad \ln T = 0.825 \ln X + 1.418 \tag{9.2.2b}$$

Simple substitution of $X = 190$, since inputs should be in thousands, results in 392 vehicle trips in the morning peak hour (Eq. 9.2.2a), and 315 in the evening peak hour (Eq. 9.2.2b).

The present traffic in the area (assessed with traffic counts) needs to be projected to the horizon year. This is done by augmenting traffic using a specified annual growth rate (one of the assumptions mentioned earlier) or by using historical growth rates for the general area. More sophisticated forecasting tools incorporating demographic and socioeconomic parameters may be employed for large-scale developments (see Chapter 8). The simpler the forecasting method (i.e., constant annual growth rate) and the farther the horizon year, the more

Office Park
(750)

Average Vehicle Trip Ends vs:	**1000 Sq. Feet Gross Floor Area**
On a:	**Weekday,**
	Peak Hour of Adjacent Street Traffic,
	One Hour Between 7 and 9 a.m.

Number of Studies: 27
Average 1000 Sq. Feet GFA: 331
Directional Distribution: 89% entering, 11% exiting

Trip Generation per 1000 Sq. Feet Gross Floor Area

Average Rate	Range of Rates	Standard Deviation
1.84	0.98 - 5.89	1.50

Data Plot and Equation

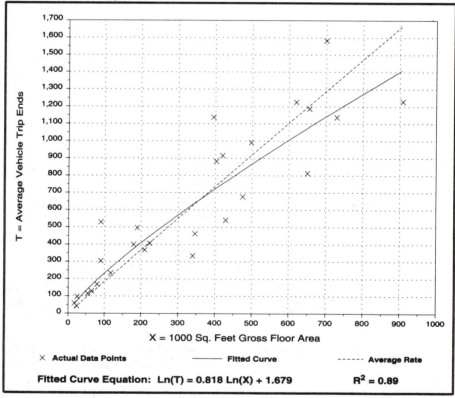

Fitted Curve Equation: Ln(T) = 0.818 Ln(X) + 1.679 $R^2 = 0.89$

Figure 9.2.1 Example of trip rates (office park development). (Reprinted with permission from *Trip Generation*, 5th ed., ©1991 Institute of Transportation Engineers, Washington, D.C.)

Office Park
(750)

Average Vehicle Trip Ends vs: 1000 Sq. Feet Gross Floor Area
On a: Weekday,
P.M. Peak Hour

Number of Studies: 25
Average 1000 Sq. Feet GFA: 285
Directional Distribution: 15% entering, 85% exiting

Trip Generation per 1000 Sq. Feet Gross Floor Area

Average Rate	Range of Rates	Standard Deviation
1.51	0.73 - 4.50	1.34

Data Plot and Equation

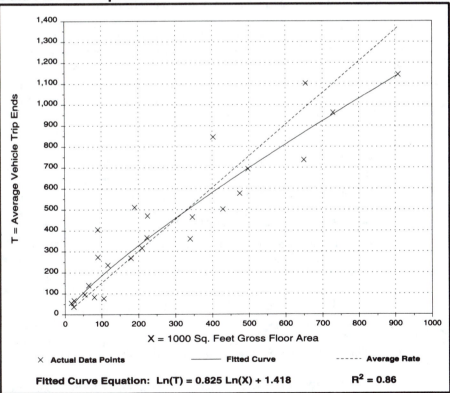

Fitted Curve Equation: Ln(T) = 0.825 Ln(X) + 1.418 $R^2 = 0.86$

Figure 9.2.1   *Continued*

uncertain the forecasts are. In such cases it may be wise to employ alternative growth scenarios, such as constant growth, accelerated growth, tapering growth, and so forth. Examples are given below.

		Growth (%)	
Years from present	Constant	Accelerated	Tapering
1– 5	3	2	8
5–10	3	3	5
10–15	3	4	2

A simple method in common use is a compounded growth equation (see Appendix B). For example, 1000 vehicle trips in 1995 will correspond to 1344 trips in 2005, assuming a constant 3% growth rate. As the reader may calculate, the same number of trips in 1995 will correspond to 1394 trips in 2005, assuming a 5% growth rate for the first 4 years, 3% growth rate for the next 4 years, and 1% growth rate for the last 2 years (high growth that tapers off).

Modal split.   The estimated trips need to be adjusted to reflect public transit use and ride sharing. Usually, the prevailing modal split in similar developments in the general area is adopted, if no locally calibrated modal split is available. Modal split is essential because it varies substantially from place to place. The *Trip Generation* data are from suburban locations with nearly 100% auto modes share.

Example 9.2

For 1000 generated trips estimate the number of vehicle trips for the following scenarios: (1) 100% automobile use with average occupancy equal to 1.2 persons per car, and (2) 65% automobile use with average occupancy equal to 1.2, 25% ride sharing with average occupancy equal to 2.5, and 10% public transit (in this case, this corresponds to 29 buses per hour).

Solution   Scenario 1 results in 833 vehicle trips ($1000/1.2 = 833$). Scenario 2 results in 671 vehicle trips, which reflects a 19% reduction of the trips estimated in scenario 1 [$1000(0.65)/1.2 + 1000(0.25)/2.5 + 29 = 671$].

Note that the rates resulting from the *Trip Generation* manual implicitly account for average occupancy rates for the drive-alone mode (i.e., average occupancy equal to 1.2 persons per car); thus the occupancy adjustment illustrated above should be avoided when rates from that source are used.

Trip distribution.   Trip generation results in the total number of trips generated by the site analyzed. Some of these trips are entering the site while others are leaving the site. Knowledge of the destination of exiting trips and the origin of entering trips is necessary so that the routes followed and the impact on in-tersections can be assessed in the steps of traffic assignment and intersection performance analysis. Trip distribution enables identification of the general di-rection of origin or destination of the trips (i.e., 12% of traffic is coming from zone *x*) and trip assignment enables the assignment of trips along specific routes.

The split of trips in entering and exiting can be taken by surveying neigh-boring similar sites or from the *Trip Generation* manual, as shown in the example below.

Example 9.3

Based on Example 9.1, estimate the number of trips entering and exiting the site for the morning and evening peak hours.

Solution   For the particular kind of site development, the *Trip Generation* manual specifies the following average values (see Fig. 9.2.1):

A.M. peak hour: 89% entering and 11% exiting

P.M. peak hour: 15% entering and 85% exiting

Given the 392 and 315 trips estimated for the A.M. and P.M. peak hours, respectively, the directional distribution is as follows:

A.M. peak hour: 349 entering and 43 exiting

P.M. peak hour: 47 entering and 268 exiting

The directions from which the traffic will access the site, or depart from the site, depend on:

- The type of proposed development
- Competing developments in the surrounding area
- The size of the proposed development
- The land uses in the area and its population
- The flow conditions and the characteristics of the surrounding street system

So far the location of the site as well as the study area have been established. The study area is defined by the intersections to be analyzed. To apply trip dis-tribution, an influence area (a perimeter surrounding the study area) needs to be established. This area should include at least 80% of the trips ending at or departing from the site. One way to define the influence area is by setting a reasonable upper bound travel time between the site and the limits of the influence area. Some examples of travel times are: shopping mall, 15 to 30 min; office park, 30 to 45 min [9.4]. Then the influence area is divided in zones (i.e., census tracts, physical or legal boundaries, etc.) A basic method for distributing of trips from many origins to one (the site in this case) or several destinations is the gravity model, which is presented in detail in Chapter 8 (also see Example 8.3).

Note that the smaller the zones and the more accurate the distances or travel times utilized, the more accurate the trip distribution results. Large zones are inhibited with large aggregation errors, and inaccurate travel characteristics result in a biased trip distribution (the distribution favors shorter distances or travel times). Distances and travel times are discussed further in the next section.

Traffic assignment.   The traffic assignment step determines the amount of traffic that will use certain routes of the roadway network between the site and the surrounding zones (within the influence area). Links of the network will be loaded differentially, depending on the origins and destinations, as well as on the traffic conditions on each link. As a result, some links or network segments may receive the bulk of the site-generated traffic, while others may receive no additional traffic.

As discussed in Chapter 8, the fundamental methodology for traffic assignment is based on some principle of network equilibrium. There are three mutually exclusive principles: *user* equilibrium (assign users on the shortest path from their origin to their destination), *system* equilibrium (assign flows to minimize the total travel time spent by all users in the network), and *stochastic* equilibrium (assign users on paths that *they think* are the shortest). The latter incorporates the notion of perception of travel times, while it implicitly assumes that all reasonable paths between origin and destination will have some flow; realistically, this is a better equilibrium principle [9.5].

A measure of travel cost is necessary to perform traffic assignment: usually, travel time or distance. The use of travel time instead of distance is preferred because it represents actual flow conditions on the network. Distance remains constant over time, whereas travel time fluctuates by the *time of day* (e.g., it is shortest during off peak hours and it is much longer during peak hours; thus travel time accounts for the level of congestion) or by the *type of the facility* (e.g., under uncongested conditions, 5 mi on an expressway can be traversed in shorter time than on an urban arterial, which typically has a lower speed limit as well as traffic signals and other interruptions). Thus travel time accounts for facility-specific characteristics as well.

The traffic assignment phase can be hand-solved only for very small networks (i.e., up to eight nodes and/or 12 links). Usually, computer programs are employed for conducting the traffic assignment (see Section 9.3). The process is often iterative in an attempt to estimate realistic traffic loads.

Intersection analysis.   After the trip assignment is complete, all additional (site and nonsite) volumes are known for the base as well as for the horizon year. The calculation of volumes by movement (i.e., through, right and left) is the next step; it is illustrated in the detailed example in Section 9.2.6. At this point all site-generated volumes at each intersection are available by movement. Simple superposition of these volumes to the preexisting ones results in the final volumes to be used for intersection analysis. Thus the final traffic volumes for intersection analysis are the summation of (1) existing traffic, (2) growth of existing traffic at the horizon year, (3) site-generated traffic, and (4) anticipated nonsite traffic (i.e., from neighboring proposed development sites).

The intersection capacity and performance analysis is conducted as illustrated in Chapter 5. The total number of intersection analyses required are given in Fig. 9.2.2. For example, if five intersections were to be analyzed for morning and evening peak periods, a total of $5 \times 2 \times 5 = 50$ intersection analyses would be required. This is because present time, base, and horizon year analyses are required and traffic conditions with and without the site are analyzed, so that present, base-year and future-year conditions as well as the impact of the subject project can be evaluated.

In the horizon year analyses, planned roadway improvements such as widened approaches, installation of signal control, and so forth, should be included.

Figure 9.2.2 Intersection analysis reporting of results. (Only a selected number of time periods is usually considered; for example, A.M. and P.M. peak hours only.)

Other detailed factors, such as elimination of curb parking and scheduling of new transit service, may be included if sufficient information is available.

The analysis of intersections has the potential to reveal service deficiencies, such as approaches or whole intersections performing at unacceptable levels of service. These deficiencies have to be dealt with before seeking approval from the municipality. Potential deficiencies and remedies are discussed in Section 9.2.5.

Queue lengths as well as weaving areas at interchanges may need investigation to assure that safe and efficient traffic operations are maintained. Traffic simulation packages are usually employed for this type of analyses. Small or large signalized-intersection networks can be analyzed efficiently and accurately with standard traffic simulation packages such as TRANSYT and NETSIM. A description of these two packages is presented in Section 9.3.1.

9.2.5 Site and Network Improvement Alternatives

The traffic impact study may reveal a number of traffic-related deficiencies that need to be improved. In some cases the deficiencies are so substantial that large elements of the design or the size of the whole project may need to be changed. In this section improvements that may be within the site or in the surrounding roadway network are presented.

There are a number of improvements that can reduce and/or improve the flow of traffic within the site. They are grouped in three categories: (1) access locations, (2) internal circulation, and (3) demand management programs. Most of these improvements pertain to large-scale developments. In some cases, however, the access and internal circulation design of small or medium-sized sites need to be improved before approval from the municipality can be granted.

Access improvements facilitate the flow entering or leaving the site. Potential improvements may be the widening of entrance and exit points, which may include the placement of bays (exclusive lanes) for turning movements. Queues should not impede the internal circulation as well as the out-of-site traffic. Exit and entrance lanes should supply enough capacity and storage so that the performance and safety of operations is not compromised.

Internal circulation improvements facilitate the flow within the site. Proper pavement markings as well as signs must be placed to assure the safety of operations. Major concerns arise from the expected presence of heavy vehicles in the internal traffic of the site (i.e., public transportation buses, employee transportation buses, and pick-up, delivery or waste removal trucks). Thus turning radii should be designed to accommodate the movement of large vehicles, the parking layout should allow sufficient space for the maneuvering of heavy vehicles, and vertical clearances should account for the potential presence of oversized vehicles, while small bridges and other landscaping elements should be able to withstand the stress from heavy vehicles. Finally, the loading and unloading ramps should be carefully designed: They should be practical, spacious, and concealed from public view, if possible, to enhance aesthetics.

Demand management programs could also be considered. They aim at the reduction of the number of vehicles using the road network to go to the site, and using the internal network and the parking space of the site. Cooperation with the local public transit authority for rerouting buses through the site and programs matching commuters as well as incentives for ride sharing (i.e., bonuses, free parking, privilege to park closer to entrance) have a potential to reduce the number of vehicles on site. In the case of large employment facilities, the institution of flexible work hours has the potential to reduce local congestion for accessing and circulation in the facility during peak hours (i.e., peak demand spreading).

On the surrounding roadway system, improvements may take place on intersections, arterial streets, and freeway interchanges. The operation of intersections may be improved easily by altering the signal phasing and timings as well as the progression settings (offsets). Other improvements include the addition of lanes and/or different channelization schemes (i.e., allocation of lanes for turning movements). Often, the addition of lanes is infeasible due to lack of available adjacent land and right-of-way. Also, due to the site-generated traffic, signal control may be warranted for previously unsignalized intersections. Semiactuated controllers at the access points of large sites may facilitate the safe and efficient processing of traffic flows.

Several improvements may take place along arterials. Additional lanes increase capacity, walkways and curbs facilitate the safe processing of pedestrians, and lighting, particularly near access points and busy intersections, improves night driving conditions and safety, whereas new or altered regulations can affect the operational and safety characteristics (i.e., revision of speed limits and parking regulations).

If the site is close to an expressway facility, new access ramps may be installed, or the design of existing ramps, channelization, and weaving areas may need revisions. There are two major concerns at interchanges: the processing of flow moving at considerable speeds (particularly in the merging and weaving areas on the freeway) and the elimination of spilling over queues, which have the potential to clog ramps or parts of arterials. Ramp metering at freeway entrances can control the number of vehicles entering the facility so that uncongested flow conditions may be maintained.

The effectiveness of the selected improvements should be assessed and the least costly or most cost-effective options should be identified. This is an additional reason for having the whole traffic impact analysis done on a computer.

In general, states, counties, and municipalities are increasingly hesitant in expending on infrastructure improvements to facilitate the traffic generated by one or several developments in an area. Roadway infrastructure improvements are costly and the small tax base of suburban communities can hardly provide the funds for such projects. Thus in many places *impact fees* have been instituted and schemes for shared funding of network improvements from the public and the private sector have been established. Certainly, both the developer and the municipality try to minimize their share in the contribution for roadway improvements. Comprehensive and accurate information from the transportation analysts will guarantee that each party pays only its fair share of the expenditures.

9.2.6 Comprehensive Example

This example illustrates analyses for a small-scale site development traffic impact study. At the corner of East-West Road and Oahu Avenue in Ocean County a site will be developed in the next few years after the county issues a permit. The TIS study will be used in the application for site development. This site is planned to be developed as an office park. The developer suggested that the gross floor area (GFA) of the office park is going to be equal to 157,300 ft^2. The development is expected to be fully operational in 1999. No other sites have been proposed for development in the neighborhood of the site to be analyzed. Access to the project is provided at the north side of its boundaries; it is planned to be an unsignalized intersection with STOP control at the exit from the project, unless the TIS study indicates otherwise.

There are two communities close to the project: Northtown, with 18,000 residents, and Easttown, with 25,000 residents. These population estimates are average estimates for year 1995 (present year). The county statistics indicate that Northtown grows at an annual rate of 3.2%, while Easttown grows by a rate of 1.5%. The county is expected to grow at an average rate of 2.0% for the next 10 years. The county's planners advised that 100% of the site traffic will be coming from or going to the two neighboring communities.

Both communities are roughly equally far away from the site, approximately 10 mi. The county insists that detailed volume-travel time surveys be conducted to estimate the functions that would enable accurate assignment of traffic.

The traffic analysts have agreed with county planners that the evening rush should be considered at this early stage of the proposal, while only the intersection of East-West Road with Oahu Avenue should be analyzed (for both 1995 and 1999 conditions). Figure 9.2.3 contains most of the information required for this preliminary TIS. Ocean County requires that (1) all lanes or lane groups should operate under LOS C or better, and (2) the traffic (demand) for each movement of the unsignalized intersection should be at most 50% of the potential capacity of the corresponding movement.

The analysis proceeds as follows:

Step 1: Evaluation of the performance of the signalized intersection at present time that the project is not in place.

Step 2: Site and nonsite traffic.
Step 2.1: Estimation of the project-generated traffic.

Figure 9.2.3 Description of site and surrounding area.

Step 2.2:   Traffic distribution.

Step 2.3:   Traffic assignment on the roadway network.

Step 2.4:   Imposition on the augmented volumes on the signalized and the unsignalized intersection.

Step 3:   Evaluation of the performance of the signalized intersection assuming that the project is in place and fully functioning.

Step 4:   Assessment of the capacity and performance of the unsignalized intersection.

Step 5:   Provision of recommendations to the developer so that the requirements set forth by Ocean County will be met.

The performance of the intersection under present conditions is analyzed and evaluated in Table 9.2.1 using the HCM procedure presented in Chapter 5. The analysis reveals that under the present timings, all left-turning movements operate at level of service (LOS) D, which is unacceptable. The intersection timings should be revised.

This intersection is also evaluated under future (1999) conditions without the site. Table 9.2.2 presents the base future scenario assuming an average growth of 2.0% a year, which translates into a growth factor of 1.0824 (2.0% growth for 4 years: $(1 + 0.02)^4 = 1.0824$). All average delays per lane group increase marginally, while all left turns operate at an unacceptable level of service.

Trips generated by the proposed site are estimated as follows. A model supplied by the *Trip Generation* manual [9.4] is used; it is identical to the one in Eq. 9.2.2b. This model is for the evening peak period (1 h during the evening peak period), and the proportions for entry and exit are 15% and 85%, respectively. Thus

$$\ln T = 0.825 \ln X + 1.418 \quad \text{for } X = 157.3 \to T = 268 \text{ trips}$$

and

$$\text{ENTER} = 40 \text{ trips}, \quad \text{EXIT} = 228 \text{ trips}$$

The future populations of the surrounding communities need to be estimated before the site-generated traffic is distributed. The specified growth rates are used, while "future" is 4 years ahead (i.e., 1995 is present and 1999 is future).

$$\begin{aligned}
\text{Northtown:} & \quad 18,000(1 + 0.032)^4 = 20,417 \\
\text{Easttown:} & \quad 25,000(1 + 0.015)^4 = \underline{26,534} \\
& \quad \quad \quad \quad \quad \quad \quad \quad 46,951 \text{ total}
\end{aligned}$$

The description of the site development states that there are no other sites to be developed in the neighborhood of the site under analysis at present. Thus there is no nonsite, other than the background traffic to be considered. If there

TABLE 9.2.1 PRESENT CASE: 1995 WITHOUT SITE

Approach 1	Move-ment 2	Volume 3	PHF 4	Peak volume 5	Lane group 6	Lane group volume 7	Satura-tion flow 8	Flow ratio 9	Critical move-ment 10	Green time 11	Cycle length 12	Capacity 13	Degree of satura-tion 14	Delay 15	LOS 16
EB	LT	75	0.85	88	LT	88	1650	0.053	!	9	90	165	0.53	31.8	D
	TH	415	0.85	488	TH	294	1800	0.163	!	24	90	480	0.61	23.6	C
	RT	45	0.85	53	TH+RT	247	1700	0.145		24	90	453	0.54	22.6	C
WB	LT	35	0.85	41	LT	41	1650	0.025		9	90	165	0.25	28.6	D
	TH	100	0.85	118	TH	118	1800	0.066		24	90	480	0.25	19.7	C
	RT	180	0.85	212	RT	212	1650	0.128		24	90	440	0.48	21.8	C
NB	LT	30	0.85	35	LT	35	1650	0.021		12	90	220	0.16	26.3	D
	TH	595	0.85	700	TH	441	1800	0.245	!	33	90	660	0.67	20.0	C
	RT	110	0.85	129	TH+RT	388	1700	0.228		33	90	623	0.62	19.2	C
SB	LT	110	0.85	129	LT	129	1650	0.078	!	12	90	220	0.59	30.8	D
	TH	235	0.85	276	TH	171	1800	0.095		33	90	660	0.26	15.2	C
	RT	40	0.85	47	TH+RT	152	1700	0.089		33	90	623	0.24	15.1	C

TABLE 9.2.2 BASE FUTURE SCENARIO: 1999 WITHOUT SITE (2% ANNUAL VOLUME GROWTH)

Approach 1	Movement 2	Volume 3	PHF 4	Peak volume 5	Lane group 6	Lane group volume 7	Saturation flow 8	Flow ratio 9	Critical movement 10	Green time 11	Cycle length 12	Capacity 13	Degree of saturation 14	Delay 15	LOS 16
EB	LT	81	0.85	96	LT	96	1650	0.058	!	9	90	165	0.58	33.1	D
	TH	449	0.85	528	TH	318	1800	0.177	!	24	90	480	0.66	24.7	C
	RT	49	0.85	57	TH+RT	267	1700	0.157		24	90	453	0.59	23.3	C
WB	LT	38	0.85	45	LT	45	1650	0.028		9	90	165	0.28	28.7	D
	TH	108	0.85	127	TH	127	1800	0.070		24	90	480	0.26	19.9	C
	RT	195	0.85	229	RT	229	1650	0.139		24	90	440	0.52	22.3	C
NB	LT	32	0.85	38	LT	38	1650	0.023	!	12	90	220	0.17	26.3	D
	TH	644	0.85	758	TH	477	1800	0.265		33	90	660	0.72	21.4	C
	RT	119	0.85	140	TH+RT	421	1700	0.248		33	90	623	0.68	20.3	C
SB	LT	119	0.85	140	LT	140	1650	0.085	!	12	90	220	0.63	32.1	D
	TH	254	0.85	299	TH	185	1800	0.103		33	90	660	0.28	15.4	C
	RT	43	0.85	51	TH+RT	165	1700	0.097		33	90	623	0.26	15.2	C

was such traffic, the analysis of nonsite traffic would be identical to the analysis of the site-generated traffic. Then, both site and nonsite traffic would have to be combined to result in the proper intersection loadings (volumes in the future year), before the intersection analyses can proceed.

The site-generated traffic is distributed using a simplified version of the gravity model. The distances between the communities and the site are excluded because they are nearly identical.

Entering Trips		*Exiting Trips*	
Northtown to site	$40 \dfrac{20{,}415}{46{,}951} = 17$	Site to Northtown	$228 \dfrac{20{,}415}{46{,}951} = 99$
Easttown to site	$40 \dfrac{26{,}534}{46{,}951} = 23$	Site to Easttown	$228 \dfrac{26{,}534}{46{,}951} = 129$

The assignment of traffic on specific routes is the next step. There is only one practical way for traffic to go between the site and Easttown: along East-West Road. It is not conceivable that such traffic will utilize the route via North-town (e.g., a 21-mi trip instead of a 10-mi trip). Thus the traffic from the site to Easttown and from Easttown to site can readily be assigned on East-West Road.

The traffic between the site and Northtown has two options. It may follow the 9-mi route (East-West Road and Pacific Boulevard) or the 10-mi route (Oahu Avenue and Kona Street). For the assignment to satisfy county requirements, volume–travel time surveys were conducted. The following models were esti-mated:

$$\text{East-West/Pacific:}\quad TT = 2 + 2.5\,(V/2000)^2 \tag{9.2.3a}$$

$$\text{Oahu/Kona:}\quad TT = 2 + (V/2140)^2 \tag{9.2.3b}$$

where

$$TT = \text{travel time per mile}$$

$$V = \text{traffic volume present}$$

First, the future time volumes (without the site) along the routes identified above need to be estimated. Figure 9.2.4(a) presents these calculations. Then the 99 trips from the site to Northtown and the 17 trips from Northtown to the site need to be assigned on the network.

Call x the proportion of the 99 trips to be assigned on the East-West/Pacific route. To reach equilibrium, the following relationship must be true:

East-West/Pacific Route   **Oahu/Kona Route**

$$9\left[2 + 2.5\left(\frac{687 + 129 + x}{2000}\right)^2\right] = 10\left[2 + \left(\frac{920 + (99 - x)}{2140}\right)^2\right] \tag{9.2.4}$$

$(75 + 375 + 220 + 180) \times (1 + 0.02)^4 = 920$

$(250 + 165 + 110 + 110) \times (1 + 0.02)^4 = 687$

$(40 + 90 + 145 + 110) \times (1 + 0.02)^4 = 417$

$(180 + 0 + 100 + 35) \times (1 + 0.02)^4 = 341$

(a)

40

69

129 + 30

(b)

Oahu Avenue and
East-West Road
intersection

Eastbound
approach
REDESIGN

Site

(c)

East-West Road   184   40   228

290   289

Site Grounds

Site access

Permitted movements

(d)

N

Figure 9.2.4 Volume calculations and traffic assignment. (a) Existing volumes for traffic assignment; (b) Intersection loadings from site-generated traffic; (c) Lane configuration and intersection layout after redesign; (d) Traffic volumes per movement of the unsignalized (STOP-controlled) intersection at the access point of the site.

Note: 129 are the trips from the site to Easttown which have already been assigned to East-West Road. Travel times equate at $x = 30$. The equilibrium travel time is 22 min, which corresponds to an average speed of 24.5 mi/h along the East-West/Pacific route and to 27.3 mi/h on the Oahu/Kona route. The analyst should always check results for reasonableness: average speeds below 15 mi/h or above 45 mi/h may be unreasonably slow or fast, respectively.

The 17 trips from Northtown to site are all assigned on the East-West/Pacific route because after all the site-generated traffic is added, the resulting travel time is shorter than that on the Kona/Oahu route:

East-West/Pacific: total volume $= 341 + 23 + 17 \rightarrow TT = 19$ min

Kona/Oahu: total volume $= 417 + 0$ $\qquad \rightarrow TT = 22$ min

Note: 23 represents the trips from Easttown to the site, which have already been assigned to East-West Road.

All traffic assignment calculations were based on the assumption that travelers will choose the route providing the minimum travel time between origin and destination, until equilibrium is reached (user equilibrium).

Figure 9.2.4(b) presents the final assignment of traffic and the corresponding loading on the intersection under analysis. The site traffic needs to be allocated on specific lanes. The allocation is as follows.

1. *Westbound traffic.* The 40 added vehicle-trips (through movement) are all assigned to the center lane because the rightmost lane already carries a higher volume:

$$180(1 + 0.02)^4 > 100(1 + 0.02)^4 + 40$$

2. *Eastbound traffic.* The 159 vehicle-trips (through movement) need to be distributed on the center and rightmost lanes. If x is the portion to be assigned on the center lane, then:

$$\underset{\text{Before}}{\frac{45 + 165}{250}} = \underset{\text{After}}{\frac{45 + 165 + (159 - x)}{250 + x}} \rightarrow x = 86$$

Thus 86 vehicle-trips are added to the center lane and 73 vehicle trips are added to the rightmost lane.

At this point the performance of the intersection adjacent to the site at the time in the future when the site becomes fully operational can be assessed. Table 9.2.3 details the analysis of the intersection. The site-generated volumes have been added to the future background traffic; bold type in columns 3 and 7 highlights the cells containing additions of background and site-generated traffic. The results indicate that six out of 12 lane groups will be providing unacceptable LOS.

Since the distribution of traffic has been changed (i.e., the eastbound ap-

TABLE 9.2.3 FUTURE SCENARIO: 1999 WITH SITE

Approach 1	Movement 2	Volume 3	PHF 4	Peak volume 5	Lane group 6	Lane group volume 7	Saturation flow 8	Flow ratio 9	Critical movement 10	Green time 11	Cycle length 12	Capacity 13	Degree of saturation 14	Delay 15	LOS 16
EB	LT	150	0.85	177	LT	177	1650	0.108	!	9	90	165	1.08	112.4	F
	TH	608	0.85	716	TH	419	1800	0.233	!	24	90	480	0.87	35.3	D
	RT	49	0.85	57	TH+RT	354	1700	0.208		24	90	453	0.78	29.1	D
WB	LT	38	0.85	45	LT	45	1650	0.028		9	90	165	0.28	28.7	D
	TH	148	0.85	174	TH	174	1800	0.097		24	90	480	0.36	20.6	C
	RT	195	0.85	229	RT	229	1650	0.139		24	90	440	0.52	22.3	C
NB	LT	32	0.85	38	LT	38	1650	0.023	!	12	90	220	0.17	26.3	D
	TH	644	0.85	758	TH	477	1800	0.265		33	90	660	0.72	21.4	C
	RT	119	0.85	140	TH+RT	421	1700	0.248		33	90	623	0.68	20.3	C
SB	LT	119	0.85	140	LT	140	1650	0.085	!	12	90	220	0.63	32.1	D
	TH	254	0.85	299	TH	185	1800	0.103		33	90	660	0.28	15.4	C
	RT	43	0.85	51	TH+RT	165	1700	0.097		33	90	623	0.26	15.2	C

Overall intersection performance delay = 30.0 s/vehicle; LOS = D

434

proach has been loaded with a large amount of additional traffic) and the whole traffic load has been increased (i.e., due to the expected area-wide growth of 2.0%), new signal timings should be estimated. They may be able to alleviate the problem of poor intersection performance. Note that the entire intersection is expected to operate at LOS D.

Webster's formula for the estimation of optimal cycle length is utilized (see Chapter 5). The total time lost is 12 s ($L = 4$ phases $\times$ 3 s per phase), while the sum of the flow ratios for each critical movement per phase is $Y = 0.696$. These inputs result in $C_o = 74.4$ s. A 75-s cycle length is selected. The green allocation is presented in column 11 of Table 9.2.4. Now only two of the 12 intersection lane groups are likely to operate under unacceptable LOS, while the total LOS of the intersection is acceptable.

Intersection rechannelization combined with revised signal timings should provide sufficient improvement. A proposed intersection redesign is presented in Fig. 9.2.4(c). All channelization improvements are concentrated in the eastbound approach. A left-turn lane has been added for a total of two left-turn lanes. A right-turn lane has been added as well. This channelization results in two lanes for exclusive use by the through movement.

These improvements are reflected in Table 9.2.5. New signal timings were devised since several flow ratios changed. The optimal signal timings were slightly altered to achieve better performance for the left-turning movements. These modifications are explained in column 17 of Table 9.2.5.†

After these improvements, all approaches as well as the intersection as a whole are expected to operate under acceptable conditions. Observe that in the base future scenario (without the site) the average delay for the intersection as a whole is 30 s per vehicle (Table 9.2.3), while in the last scenario, with the site in place along with some intersection redesign and retiming, the average delay is expected to be about 17 s per vehicle.

The intersection redesign (lane additions) was accomplished with minimal expansion of the right-of-way. The extra left-turn lane was added within the existing configuration, largely because the westbound through traffic utilizes one lane only), and space was taken from the site to add the extra right-turn lane.

The next step is the evaluation of the performance of the unsignalized intersection, which provides access to the site. Figure 9.2.4(d) presents the intersection configuration and the traffic volumes present when the site becomes fully operational. Two movements need to be analyzed: the left turn from the major street into the site, and the right turn exiting from the site. The potential capacity of each permitted movement is estimated separately using the following equation

---

† These modifications are necessary for combating the resulting long uniform delay (i.e., the shorter the green time allocated within the cycle and the longer the cycle length, the longer the vehicles served by the particular phase are likely to wait on idle). This modification is expected to have a reduction in queue formation as well; shorter queues will be developed, thus shorter storage bays need to be provided.

TABLE 9.2.4 FUTURE SCENARIO: 1999 WITH SITE-IMPROVED SIGNAL TIMINGS

Approach 1	Movement 2	Volume 3	PHF 4	Peak volume 5	Lane group 6	Lane group volume 7	Saturation flow 8	Flow ratio 9	Critical movement 10	Green time 11	Cycle length 12	Capacity 13	Degree of saturation 14	Delay 15	LOS 16
EB	LT	150	0.85	177	LT	177	1650	0.108	!	10	75	220	0.81	37.1	D
	TH	608	0.85	716	TH	419	1800	0.233	!	21	75	504	0.83	27.1	D
	RT	49	0.85	57	TH+RT	354	1700	0.208		21	75	476	0.74	23.0	C
WB	LT	38	0.85	45	LT	45	1650	0.028		10	75	220	0.21	22.1	C
	TH	148	0.85	174	TH	174	1800	0.097		21	75	504	0.34	16.5	C
	RT	195	0.85	229	RT	229	1650	0.139		21	75	462	0.50	17.9	C
NB	LT	32	0.85	38	LT	38	1650	0.023		8	75	176	0.22	23.4	C
	TH	644	0.85	758	TH	477	1800	0.265	!	24	75	576	0.83	24.8	C
	RT	119	0.85	140	TH+RT	421	1700	0.248		24	75	544	0.77	22.3	C
SB	LT	119	0.85	140	LT	140	1650	0.085	!	8	75	176	0.79	39.2	D
	TH	254	0.85	299	TH	185	1800	0.103		24	75	576	0.32	14.8	B
	RT	43	0.85	51	TH+RT	165	1700	0.097		24	75	544	0.30	14.7	B

Overall intersection performance delay = 23.6 s/vehicle; LOS = C

TABLE 9.2.5 FUTURE SCENARIO: 1999 WITH SITE-IMPROVED SIGNAL TIMINGS AND INTERSECTION CHANNELIZATION

Approach 1	Movement 2	Volume 3	PHF 4	Peak volume 5	Lane group 6	Lane group volume 7	Saturation flow 8	Flow ratio 9	Critical movement 10	Green time 11	Cycle length 12	Capacity 13	Degree of saturation 14	Delay 15	LOS 16	Timings alterations (see col. 11) 17
EB	LT	150	0.85	177	LT	177	**3300**	0.054	!	5	60	275	0.65	23.8	C	4+1
	TH	608	0.85	716	TH	716	**3600**	0.199	!	15	60	900	0.80	19.5	C	16−1
	RT	49	0.85	57	**RT**	57	**1650**	0.035		15	60	413	0.14	13.3	**B**	16−1
WB	LT	38	0.85	45	LT	45	1650	0.028		5	60	138	0.33	20.2	C	4+1
	TH	148	0.85	174	TH	174	1800	0.097		15	60	450	0.39	14.5	B	16−1
	RT	195	0.85	229	RT	229	1650	0.139		15	60	413	0.56	16.2	C	16−1
NB	LT	32	0.85	38	LT	38	1650	0.023	!	7	60	193	0.20	18.3	C	
	TH	644	0.85	758	TH	477	1800	0.265		21	60	630	0.76	16.8	C	
	RT	119	0.85	140	TH+RT	421	1700	0.248		21	60	595	0.71	15.5	C	
SB	LT	119	0.85	140	LT	140	1650	0.085	!	7	60	193	0.73	28.0	C	
	TH	254	0.85	299	TH	185	1800	0.103		21	60	630	0.29	10.8	B	
	RT	43	0.85	51	TH+RT	165	1700	0.097		21	60	595	0.28	10.7	B	

Overall intersection performance delay = 17.3 s/vehicle; LOS = C (see Chapter 5 for explanation of factors):

$$C_p = \frac{e^{-(\alpha - \beta)}}{e^\beta - 1} V_c \qquad (9.2.5)$$

The analysis of the unsignalized intersection proceeds as follows:

1. *Left turn from major street.* From HCM: critical gap $=$ 5.0 s; follow-up gap $= \frac{1}{2}(5.0) + 0.5 = 3.0$ s; conflicting volume $(V_c) = 579$ vehicles per hour.

$$\alpha = \frac{579(5.0)}{3600} = 0.8082 \quad \text{and} \quad \beta = \frac{579(3.0)}{3600} = 0.4825$$

Substitution in (9.2.5) results in $C_p = 674$ vehicles. The demand (40 vehicles) is well below the 50% of the potential capacity (337 vehicles). Thus for this movement the county's criterion is fulfilled.

2. *Right turn from minor street.* From HCM: critical gap $=$ 5.5 s; follow-up gap $= \frac{1}{2}(5.5) + 0.5 = 3.25$ s; conflicting volume $=$ 289 vehicles per hour.

$$\alpha = \frac{289(5.5)}{3600} = 0.4415 \quad \text{and} \quad \beta = \frac{289(3.25)}{3600} = 0.2609$$

Substitution in (9.2.5) results in $C_p = 809$ vehicles. The demand (228 vehicles) is well below the 50% of the potential capacity (405 vehicles). Thus for this movement the county's criterion is fulfilled.

The study of this intersection may not be complete at this point. Some potential problems that may require further study are the following:

1. The left-turn movement from the major street into the site may be overloaded in the morning peak period. This is likely to cause a substantial disruption to the westbound through traffic, while the queue may back up all the way to the intersection of East-West Road with Oahu Avenue. A left-turn bay may be required.
2. A number of vehicles exiting from the site (right turn) may need to take a left turn at the intersection of East-West Road with Oahu Avenue. It is not certain that under rush-hour conditions such weaving can be safely accomplished. This problem may be ameliorated by moving the access point to the west end of the site. If this does not solve the problem, semiactuated signal control with detectors at the access site and the lane for left turn into the site may be required.

This traffic impact study indicates that if certain modifications are implemented, the surrounding road network will be able to handle the additional volumes generated by the site in 1999. Two lanes must be added to the eastbound approach of the intersection adjacent to the site. The timings of the signalized intersection must be altered as well. After these modifications take place, the site may be developed according to the original plan. However, detailed analysis of morning conditions (i.e., a left-turn bay for accessing the site may be required) as well as of a potential weaving problem between the site access and the adjacent signalized intersection is required to assure the safety of operations when the site becomes operational.

The TIS example above is substantially simplified compared with a real-world TIS. However, all fundamental elements of a TIS have been preserved. A similar real-world TIS would likely include the following:

- Requirement to analyze more intersections.
- Morning peak traffic should be evaluated.
- Other proposed developments in the immediate area are likely to exist.
- The traffic should be distributed to a larger number of smaller zones.
- More routes could be available between the site and each zone.
- Identified problems (such as the weaving problem of the illustrated example) should be analyzed and specific treatment should be recommended.

9.3 COMPUTER SOFTWARE FOR TRAFFIC AND PLANNING STUDIES

9.3.1 Traffic Simulation Models: TRANSYT and NETSIM

Two common traffic simulation software packages are TRANSYT and NETSIM. The fundamental difference between the two packages is the unit of simulation. TRANSYT simulates platoons (groups) of vehicles (*macroscopic simulation*), whereas NETSIM simulates individual vehicles (*microscopic simulation*). Both approaches have their merits. Microscopic simulation is more detailed and it can provide real-time visual display of the traffic process. Simulation at a microscopic level demands large, often excessive computer processing time. On the other hand, macroscopic simulation is more efficient in terms of processing time; while the lesser requirements for memory and processing allow for the detailed representation of functions governing the flow of traffic (i.e., platoon dispersion, gap acceptance, etc.)

TRANSYT.   The acronym for this package stands for TRAffic Network StudY Tool [9.6]. The original version of TRANSYT was developed by Dennis Robertson at the Transport Road Research Laboratories (U.K.) in 1967.

As mentioned in the introduction, TRANSYT processes platoons of vehicles. Figure 9.3.1 illustrates this process. The smooth curves represent the actual

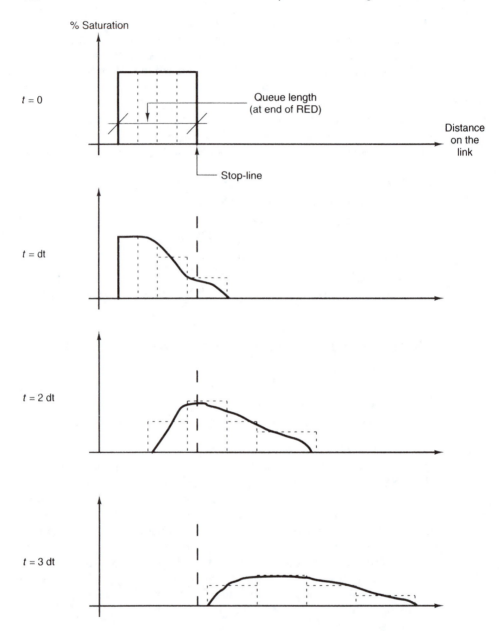

Figure 9.3.1   Example of platoon dispersion as modeled in TRANSYT.

process of vehicle dispersion as they move downstream from the intersection after they were released at the beginning of green. The dashed blocks represent the way TRANSYT handles this process. In the actual simulation process the blocks are substantially smaller, while the analyst can control the size of the simulation steps, which essentially control the size of the platoons.

In Fig. 9.3.1 the queue gradually dissipates, the speed of vehicles increases, and thus the average headway between successive vehicles elongates (i.e., car-following distance increases as speed increases), thereby causing a substantial decrease in the saturation flow.

Optimization is achieved through the minimization of an objective function called the Performance Index (PI):

$$PI = \sum_{i=1}^{n} d_i + kS_i \qquad (9.3.1)$$

where

d_i = total delay at node (intersection) i
S_i = total number of stops at node i
n = number of intersections in the network
k = user-defined parameter determining the importance of stops relative to delays (i.e., greater emphasis on stops corresponds to a greater emphasis on arterial progression)

Since the PI is the sum of "negative" factors (i.e., high delays and large number of stops denote poor signal operations), TRANSYT tries to minimize it.

TRANSYT uses volumes, saturation flows, average link lengths and speeds, signal phasings, minimum intervals (i.e., minimum duration of green to satisfy pedestrian crossing requirements), and cycle lengths as inputs. Then, in an optimization run, it calibrates the durations of greens and the progression offsets to minimize delays and improve progression. At the end of each run it produces output that includes average delays per approach and intersection, intersection and network-wide PIs, and fuel consumption and emissions estimates.

Furthermore, TRANSYT can assist in the identification of the optimal network-wide cycle length. Alternative runs are submitted with various cycle lengths (e.g., runs for cycle lengths ranging from 50 to 120 s at 5- or 10-s intervals). The cycle length that results in the lowest PI is the best for the given network. This is the cycle length to be used in consecutive optimization runs for determination of optimal signal settings for each intersection in the network.

TRANSYT can perform plain simulation (not optimization), which will result in a summary of the performance of the existing network without any alterations. This output typically serves as the base case upon which the evaluation of the improvements of the consequent optimization runs is based.

The output includes a number of measures of effectiveness (MOEs), such as various measures of delays, average speeds, queue lengths, fuel consumption as well as time-space and progression diagrams, and optimal signal timing settings for ready use by signalization technicians.

NETSIM.   The name of this package stands for "NETwork SIMulation." The model was originally called UTCS-1 because its development was supported by the Office of Research of the U.S. Federal Highway Administration (FHWA) as part of the Urban Traffic Control System (UTCS) program. Two earlier models (DYNET and TRANS) were incorporated in the development of the UTCS-1 model [9.7].

NETSIM is a microscopic, interval-scanning simulation model capable to represent complex urban networks, traffic control systems, and vehicle performance characteristics. The model is microscopic because it treats each vehicle as an independent entity; it is an interval-scanning model because it computes the state of the system at regular time intervals, specifically every second. The model traces the trajectory of each vehicle as it progresses through the network. The motion of each vehicle is governed by car-following rules, lane-changing and overtaking behavior, turning movements, and response to the traffic control system. Several of the characteristics of each vehicle are assigned probabilistically using the Monte Carlo method described in Appendix D.

Being a microscopic simulation model, NETSIM requires a considerable number of inputs, including the following:

1. *Topology of the roadway network.* The network is described by nodes and one-way links. The nodes represent intersections and points where the roadway geometric characteristics change, such at lane drop locations. The links represent one-directional roadway segments between nodes.

2. *Characteristics of each roadway link.* These include the link's length; the link's free-flow speed; and the number and channelization of lanes, including full lanes, turning lanes, and turning bays. In addition, the mean values of startup delays, lost time, and discharge headways at the downstream end of each link are specified. Pedestrian interference at the upstream end of the link is also input. Related links that receive traffic from the subject link are described as illustrated by Fig. 9.3.2.

3. *Traffic control system.* The input stream includes the characteristics of the traffic control system. NETSIM is capable of simulating the operation of STOP and YIELD sign control, pretimed signals, and actuated signal detector/controller combinations for semiactuated and fully actuated operations as described in Section 5.3.2.

4. *Traffic demand.* The traffic volumes entering and exiting the network and the distribution of turning volumes at each intersection are specified.

5. *Traffic composition.* The composition of the simulated vehicles is given in terms of four fleet components (i.e., automobiles, trucks, car pools, and buses). Several types of vehicles may be specified for each fleet component. Each type is described in terms of its operational characteristics, including maximum acceleration, maximum speed, speed–acceleration relationship,

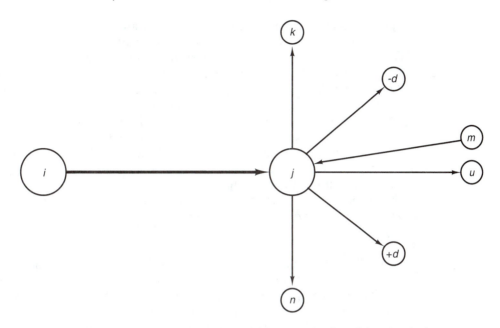

Figure 9.3.2   Possible configurations of links emanating from link (i, j). i, beginning of link; j, end of link; k, left turns; m, through traffic; n, right turns; $\pm d$, diagonal movements; u, movement opposing left turns.

headway characteristics, fuel consumption rates, and pollutant emission rates.

6. *Bus operations.* Optionally, the user may specify the operating characteristics of a bus transit system in terms of bus routes, stations, and frequencies of service.

NETSIM provides a wealth of output information on a link-specific basis and aggregated over the entire network. Output MOEs include travel times, total and stopped delays, timing data, queue lengths, signal-phase failures, vehicle occupancies, fuel consumption, pollution emissions, and so on.

Recent microcomputer versions of NETSIM are accompanied by editing programs to facilitate the preparation of the input stream, enhanced graphics to display inputs and outputs, and animation software.

9.3.2 Planning Models: EMME/2, QRS II, and TRANPLAN

Planning software automates the four-step process of trip generation, trip distribution, modal split, and traffic assignment. A large number of inputs is required, such as a full description of the network, the existing traffic and transit volumes, and origin–destination tables by zones. Most software planning packages allow the user to insert and calibrate models for each of the four steps.

The major advantage of all planning packages is that after inputting the data, complex analyses can be undertaken and a large number of alternatives can be evaluated in a short time. The packages presented next greatly facilitate analyses for new transportation facilities (i.e., new, extended or widened roadway facilities, new public transportation service, expansion of airport or port facilities, etc.) They are also useful in analyzing large developments such as a residential sub-division, a new shopping mall, an office park, and so forth. At a grand scale, these packages permit the analysis of entire metropolitan areas and the evaluation of proposed new installations or alterations.

The major features of three popular transportation packages are presented next. These packages are continuously updated by their developers in response to user needs.

EMME/2.   The major advantage of this software package is the incorporation of *multimodal equilibrium*: In all applications both auto- and transit-related characteristics can be incorporated simultaneously, which closely approximates real-world conditions (i.e., auto and transit modes are competing in an urban environment). This property not only offers the ability to assess the impact of transit services on road networks, but also aids in the identification of more efficient routes for transit services.

The inputs required are a network representation that can be input by coordinates, or it can be digitized directly from maps. On each node and link the pertinent modes, transit lines, turns, and volumes are input. Different types of transit vehicles can be incorporated and a total of 30 modes can be handled. Zone characteristics such as demand, socioeconomic variables, and travel impedances are inputs. Network or zone data such as traffic surveys, accident statistics, pavement characteristics, and other custom information can be incorporated with user-defined attributes. In addition, existing traffic characteristics of roadway or transit links such as volumes, travel times, and speeds can be input for comparisons (i.e., observed versus estimated). The user can specify unlimited expressions (models) representing demand, volume–delay relationships, turn penalties, and mode-choice behavior, which reflects the objective of the developers of EMME/2, to design a package with a glass-box rather than a black-box philosophy [9.8].

EMME/2 provides a framework for implementing a wide variety of travel demand forecasting: From simple road or transit assignments or the classical four-step model (trip generation, distribution, mode choice, assignment) to the implementation of multimodal equilibration procedures that *integrate demand functions* into the assignment procedures (i.e., multimodal traffic assignment under constant or variable demand conditions). Both aggregate and disaggregate input models can be used, in either a *sequential* or *simultaneous* manner. Other detailed inputs include the explicit modeling of dedicated lanes (i.e., HOV lanes and transitways), the incorporation of walk connections between transit lines, and the modeling of people's different perceptions of the various travel-time components.

Validation and checking procedures are supplied for the continuous identification and control of counterintuitive inputs (i.e., unconnected links, dead-end links with entering traffic, etc.) The program will make automatic corrections if requested, given a set of user-specified criteria.

The main output of EMME/2 is the overall network equilibrium assignment and the presentation of comprehensive results (most in a graphical, interactive way). This output can be used in traffic simulation models for the establishment of signal settings and evaluation of network performance. Updated network characteristics can be fed back to EMME/2 for the derivation of optimum network assignment. Other optional outputs are economic evaluation and traffic impact analysis. Detailed outputs include performance estimates of HOV lanes and truck traffic, location analysis of existing and future transit and roadway facilities, and computation of least-cost paths according to any desired cost function.

The list of modeling options and consequent outputs is practically limitless because the open architecture of EMME/2 allows for the building of numerous specialized analysis procedures. Given the current ability of the program to use geographic information system (GIS) data bases (see Section 9.3.3), the major future improvement would be the incorporation of a traffic simulation and optimization algorithm so that traffic and transit operating deficiencies can be identified and optimal settings can be derived within the same software package.

QRS II.   The Quick Response System was developed in the 1970s as a set of manual travel demand analysis techniques intended to provide a means for the quick analysis of policy issues, particularly at a small-area level. Detailed descriptions of these techniques for trip generation, trip distribution, modal choice, auto occupancy, time-of-day travel demand distribution, traffic assignment, and capacity analysis were documented in a 1978 National Cooperative Highway Research Program Report [9.9]. A stand-alone gravity model for trip distribution and a simultaneous trip distribution/modal choice model similar to the share model (i.e., Eq. 8.7.2) were included. In 1981, the U.S. Federal Highway Administration (FHWA) released a microcomputer version of the system as Quick Response System I (QRS I). This implementation was capable of handling larger problems than those that could be analyzed via the earlier manual methods, but it proved to be awkward to use. A more flexible system, known as QRS II, was subsequently developed and upgraded at the Center for Urban Transportation Studies of the University of Wisconsin at Milwaukee (e.g., [9.10]).

QRS II features a powerful interactive graphics General Network Editor (GNE) which can be used to quickly draw and modify highway and transit networks on the computer screen and to display and plot networks and the results of travel demand analyses. All data needed by the system are entered via the GNE. The system is capable of performing both the routine calculations required by the manual techniques described above and more complex and detailed analyses using the forecasting model combinations described in this book. Algorithms for trip generation, trip distribution, modal choice, highway and transit path finding, traffic assignment, and transit assignment are part of QRS II. Default equations and parameters are provided for the three trip purposes. These may be overridden or adapted to local conditions by experienced users.

The trip-generation step estimates the trip productions and trip attractions of each zone as person-trips per day. The embedded default trip production model first calculates the total zonal productions based on average household trip rates. Either household income or household automobile ownership may be selected as the independent variable. The total zonal productions are then split into three purposes (home-based work, home-based nonwork, and non-home based) according to embedded parameters. Trip attractions are estimated via a multiple linear regression equation.

The trip distribution model is accomplished by a gravity type of model with options as to the choice of travel-time factor. One option is the *power* function expressed by Eq. 8.3.9; the other is an *exponential* form:

$$F = e^{-aW} \tag{9.3.2}$$

The basic modal choice employed by QRS II splits interzonal demands (by purpose) between highways and transit based on the difference in the disutilities of the two modes and on the degree of "captivity" associated with the trip-producing zone. The form of the mathematical model is similar to the binomial logit equation. Additional modes can be included by multiple applications of the model.

Directional, time-of-day distributions and vehicle occupancy factors are applied prior to assignment as described in Section 8.5. QRS II is capable of performing all-or-nothing, iterative capacity restrained, and through a feature that averages the results of successive iterations, a true equilibrium traffic assignment. Transit assignment is based on a variation of the probabilistic multipath algorithm developed by Dial (see [8.31]). QRS II requires the specification of a separate network for each of the modes involved in a multimodal system. Consequently, special attention is called for to ensure consistency between modal networks that share network elements.

Finally, the package provides several programs for exporting QRS-formatted files to spreadsheet and ASCII formats. Because of this feature, it is possible to perform some calculations (e.g., trip generation) using other programs (such as spreadsheets), which can be interfaced with other components of the package.

TRANPLAN. The TRANPLAN software is a toolbox of more than 40 "functions" that are grouped in the following categories: trip generation, distribution/modal choice models, networks, paths, loading, matrix utilities, reporting, and plotting. A graphics package, the Network Information System (NIS), is available for the development, display, and maintenance of highway and transit networks and related data. The NIS is available in a standard edition and an extended edition. The latter is a rudimentary Geographic Information System (see Section 9.3.3) that provides the capability for defining, displaying, and updating up to 15 types of polygon boundaries that may be used to represent traffic analysis zones, census tracks, and so on. TRANPLAN, however, is a *batch* rather than an interactive system. This means that a control file containing the instructions associated with a particular run of the model must be prepared off-line. The control file specifies the combination of functions to be run and for each function the needed inputs, options, and desired outputs. The user may develop certain parts of an application (e.g., trip generation) by other programs and interface the results with TRANPLAN functions. This is necessary when the user wishes to apply a model that is not directly supported by TRANPLAN.

The TRANPLAN trip-generation model for the estimation of trip productions and trip attractions is of the multiple regression form. For trip distribution, TRANPLAN supports the gravity model and the Fratar model. The modal choice model is of the diversion-curve type that "splits" interzonal trips between two modes (i.e., automobile versus public transit) based on either the difference of the ratio of the corresponding interzonal impedances. The network functions allow for the definition and updating of highway and transit networks. Subarea networks can be extracted. The highway minimum paths are produced based on a vine algorithm which accounts for turn prohibitors and turn penalties; the transit path algorithm was originally developed by Alan M. Voorhees for the U.S. Department of Housing and Urban Development [9.11]. Supported traffic assignment (or highway loading) models include the free/all-or-nothing method, the capacity restrained algorithm, incremental loading, and a user equilibrium algorithm developed initially in connection with the Urban Transportation Planning Package (UTPS). The transit assignment model loads interzonal passenger trips on the minimum paths generated by the transit path functions. Transit trips may be split among competing transit lines in one of three ways: in proportion to the frequencies of the competing lines, equally among them, or only on selected lines.

9.3.3 Geographic Information Systems

It is clear that regional transportation planning is a data-intensive activity: It requires a vast amount of information about the type, intensity, and geographical distribution of land uses and population characteristics within a region. In addition, it requires the specification of the existing and proposed multimodal transportation networks. The collection, management, and use of such data are expensive, labor-intensive, and time-consuming tasks that require the participation of many organizations and individuals. Computerized methods in general, and Geographic Information System (GIS) technology in particular, are well suited to the management and sharing of transportation-related data.

A GIS has been defined as "an information technology composed of hardware, software, and data used to gather, store, edit, display, and analyze geographic information [9.12]''. GIS is suitable to transportation systems because transportation systems have a strong geographical (spatial) aspect.

In general, a GIS retains data in several "layers." For example, a GIS layer may be allotted to land-use information, another to soil conditions, a third to environmentally sensitive areas, a fourth to the transportation network, and so forth. All of these layers use the same geographic coordinate system and make possible the simultaneous consideration of data from multiple layers. For example, sensitive environmental areas from one layer, soil conditions from a second layer, and the layer containing the existing highway network may be superimposed to help in the identification of possible network extensions that meet environmental

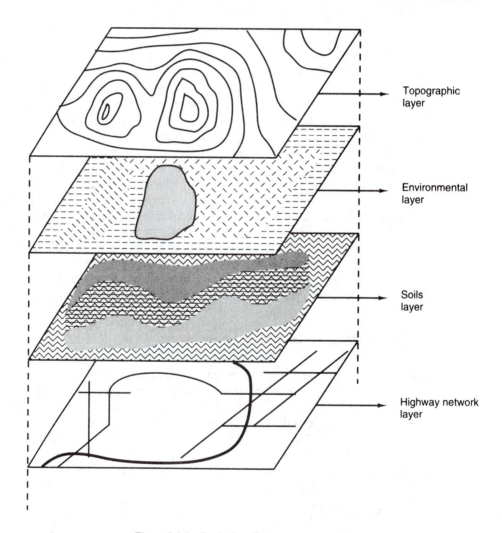

Topographic layer

Environmental layer

Soils layer

Highway network layer

Figure 9.3.3 Typical multilayer structure of GIS.

and geotechnical requirements (see Fig. 9.3.3). Geographic Information Systems use computer graphics and mapping that greatly enhance the visualization of complex spatial data.

GIS technology combines the principles of topology and database management. Topology refers to the representation of features in terms of their location, shape, and spatial relationship. The features (or entities) may be described as points, lines, and polygons. In a particular application, points may be used to represent the locations of traffic accidents, in another they may represent zonal centroids, and so on. Lines are used to describe elements such as roadway segments, utility lines, and the like. Polygons represent areal features such as traffic analysis zones, political jurisdictions, land subdivisions, and rainfall intensity zones. The principles of topology are applied to define both the location of entities and their spatial relationships (e.g., line A lies within polygon P, or polygons C and D are adjacent to each other). The topological specification of transportation networks involves some special requirements, the discussion of which is beyond the scope of this book [9.13, 9.14].

The nonspatial (or *thematic*) attributes of the features included in a GIS are usually described in a relational database. Examples of thematic attributes include the population of a traffic analysis zone; the length, capacity, and free-flow speed of a highway link; or the severity and property damage associated with a traffic accident. Thus a GIS system may be thought of as an "intelligent" map (or drawing) because, in addition to its ability to represent objects graphically, it "knows" how the objects are related and it also associates thematic information with these objects. For this reason GIS technology is finding increasing use in many subject areas, including transportation engineering, planning, and decision making. The latter are usually referred to as GIS-T.

9.4 PARKING STUDIES

9.4.1 Introduction

Parking is an important urban transportation element. As such, it has various long- and short-term impacts on individuals, societies, and transportation systems. First, parking affects mode choice. Individuals having an automobile available will probably choose to access their destination by automobile if parking is available and conveniently located at the destination, and if the cost of parking is reasonable. In other words, inexpensive (or free) and plentiful parking is an incentive for using private automobiles; whereas scarce, inconvenient, and/or expensive parking is a substantial disincentive for using private automobiles [9.15].

Parking also affects the vitality of communities, commercial and business centers, transit systems, and airports as well as the efficiency of traffic circulation in downtown areas. For example, in certain European cities it is estimated that 40% of the total travel time to work is consumed in searching for parking [9.16].

Parking has certain direct economic impacts as well. At a micro scale, parking costs may result in tax benefits for both employers and employees. At a macro scale, parking generates revenues for both public (i.e., municipality revenue from metered parking and citations) and private institutions (i.e., for profit development of land).

As a result, most individuals and institutions are concerned with parking: automobile users, local governments (i.e., service to residents and visitors, economic vitality of businesses plus revenue for the community), private businesses (i.e., customer attraction, convenience to employees plus for-profit parking development), hospitals, schools and colleges, public services, and so forth.

9.4.2 Types of Parking

There are two broad categories of parking: public and private. *Public* parking may be curb-side (on streets and alleys) or off-street. Curb-side parking may be free or not, and it may be regulated or unregulated (i.e., no parking during rush hours, no parking overnight, etc.) In downtown areas curb-side parking is usually metered and regulated.

Off-street parking is usually in lots, decks (within multipurpose buildings), or in exclusive parking structures. Private firms or public agencies may be operating these facilities, which are open to the public. Some facilities may operate under certain rules (e.g., parking on a long-term/contract basis).

Private parking includes home or apartment building garages, stalls and driveways, or affilitate-specific parking (i.e., permit-required employee parking).

The arrangement of stalls and pricing schemes are two important characteristics of parking. Stalls may be parallel or angled (varying from 20 to 90°). Pricing schemes usually try to maximize revenue as well as to fulfill certain objectives. Some pricing schemes are designed to encourage short stay (high turnover): $1 for up to ½ h, $3 if ½ h is exceeded and $2 for every hour thereafter, or parking meters with short-duration dials (this hinders convenience because coins must be inserted frequently, while the likelihood of getting a citation increases). Other pricing schemes are designed to encourage long stay (low turnover): $3 for 1 h or less, $0.50 for each hour thereafter.

9.4.3 Types of Parking Studies

Parking studies include financial feasibility, functional design, structural design, and demand studies. This chapter focuses on demand and functional design studies. There are three major types of parking demand studies: comprehensive, limited, and site-specific [9.17]. *Comprehensive studies* cover an entire area, such as central business district.

A major objective is to estimate demand for parking. The status quo reveals utilization forced by existing conditions and does not represent actual demand. Usually, surveys are employed to assess the demand for parking: both need for parking and preferred locations for parking. Careful sampling design and analysis is necessary to compensate for the natural bias toward oversampling short-term parkers [9.17].†

In comprehensive studies, the future parking demand is estimated with the use of forecasting models, which include population growth, demographic, social and economic trends, as well as trends of the local economy and use of transportation modes. Analytic and comprehensive inventories of on- and off-street parking are gathered along with detailed information on utilization patterns. From these, current deficiencies of the parking supply are identified (i.e., lack of supply, negative interference with traffic circulation). Then, proposed scenarios for alleviating current deficiencies and for fulfilling anticipated demands are developed and evaluated for judgment by officials and/or private interests. The development and evaluation of scenarios or *alternatives analysis* is conducted with a number of criteria, such as (1) encouragement or discouragement of private automobile use, (2) identification of primary recipients of service and ways to screen out nonprimary parkers, (3) derivation of a pricing schedule, (4) issues regarding access distance (i.e., convenience and safety for walking), (5) satisfaction of municipal and private perspectives, (6) zoning requirements, and (7) budget and future costs/income flows.

Limited studies are similar to comprehensive studies but with reduced geographic coverage and fewer requirements. Typically, in limited studies only one type of parking may be investigated (i.e., curb-side parking only), while the estimation of future demand may not be required.

Site-specific studies are geographically narrow but analytically extensive. Focus sites may include existing, planned or expanding hospitals, campuses, shopping malls, residential, office, and industrial developments. Detailed inventories of existing supply and utilization are taken and future demands are forecast. In addition, attention is paid in regard to the various types of users of the parking supply: people who do business or work at the site (i.e., primary recipients of parking service) and people who park at the site to go elsewhere. Information on the users' access mode, the mix of users in regard to their parking occupancy (i.e., in hospitals, visitors stay up to a few hours, doctors and nurses may stay in excess of 16 h, and other staff stays 8 to 9 h) are often measured. Change of shifts and the overlapping parking utilization patterns of land uses such as industrial parks are of critical importance, due to concerns in parking availability and turnover, internal circulation, and potential congestion at access points.

---

† Assume a 100-stall lot, where 50 stalls are filled with long-term parkers with zero turnover rate during the sampling period and the other 50 stalls are filled with short-term parkers with a turnover rate of five. Assume, for the sake of the argument, that all parkers were sampled. If so, 300 surveys were collected, 50 from long-term parkers and 250 from short-term parkers; the bias toward sampling short-term parkers is quite obvious.

Assessment of site parking demand.   Parking demand for proposed sites is commonly estimated from ITE's *Parking Generation* manual [9.18], which is conceptually and presentationally identical to the *Trip Generation* manual [9.4]. Figure 9.4.1 presents two graphs, one for general-purpose office buildings and one for movie theaters.

Parking demand dictates the size of the parking facility. A substantial parcel of land is always required for the establishment of a parking lot or structure. To achieve better utilization of a parking lot, it is preferred to develop land uses with complementary parking use requirements. An office building and a movie theater complex sharing the same parking lot is a good example. Typically, the office

GENERAL OFFICE BUILDING (711–716)
Peak Parking Spaces Occupied vs: **1,000 GROSS SQUARE FEET BUILDING AREA**
On a: **WEEKDAY**

PARKING GENERATION RATES

Average Rate	Range of Rates	Standard Deviation	Number of Studies	Average 1,000 GSF Building Area
2.79	0.75–32.93	2.25	207	168

DATA PLOT AND EQUATION

X = 1000 GROSS SQUARE FEET BUILDING AREA
□ ACTUAL DATA POINTS   —— FITTED CURVE

Fitted Curve Equation: $Ln(P) = 0.93 Ln(X) + 1.253$
$R^2 = 0.870$

Figure 9.4.1   Examples of parking demand rates for general-purpose office buildings and movie theaters. (Reprinted with permission from *Parking Generation*, 2nd ed., ©1987 Institute of Transportation Engineers, Washington, D.C.)

building causes peak parking use between 8 A.M. and 5 P.M. during weekdays, while the movie theater complex causes peak parking use between 6 P.M. and midnight during weekends. The following example illustrates this point.

Example 9.4

A joint development of a general-purpose office building with 200,000 ft² gross building area and a movie theater complex with 1500 seats is planned. The facilities will be served by a common parking lot. Estimate the number of stalls required and assess whether the efficiency improves with shared use of a parking lot as opposed to separate parking lots for each of the developments.

MOVIE THEATER (443)

Peak Parking Spaces Occupied vs: **SEATS**
On a: **SATURDAY**

PARKING GENERATION RATES

Average Rate	Range of Rates	Standard Deviation	Number of Studies	Average Number of Seats
0.26	0.11–0.42	0.11	9	1562

DATA PLOT AND EQUATION

Fitted Curve Equation: $P = 0.50(X) - 322.0$
$R^2 = 0.837$

Figure 9.4.1 *Continued*

Solution   The parking generation equations are as follows:

Office building (weekday): $\ln P = 0.93 \ln X + 1.253$ (Fig. 9.4.1)
Movie theaters (weekday): $P = 0.32X - 174.0$ ([9.18], p. 60)
Movie theaters (weekend): $P = 0.50X - 322.0$ (Fig. 9.4.1)

Based on the inputs supplied, the required parking is:

Office building (weekday):   483 stalls
Movie theaters (weekday):   306 stalls
Movie theaters (weekend):   428 stalls

It would be erroneous and excessive to suggest that for the shared use of the parking lot $483 + 306 = 789$ stalls are required in a typical weekday. Better efficiencies may be realized if the parking demand is assessed separately for (1) regular work hours, (2) weekday evenings, and (3) weekends, and then select the highest estimate as the required parking size.

During weekdays, assume that up to 30% of the maximum weekday movie patronage occurs before 5 P.M., since many people work, go to school, or run errands during daylight [9.19]. Thus the parking demand during work hours is

$$483 + 0.3(306) = 575 \text{ stalls}$$

which is 27% less than the original estimate of 789 stalls.

For weekday evenings assume that up to 30% of the office building tenants will be working overtime (i.e., after 5 P.M.) during hours that the movie theater experiences high rates of patronage [9.19]. Thus, after 5 P.M., $483(0.3) + 306 = 451$ stalls are required, which is less than the 575 stalls required during regular work hours.

During weekends assume that no more than 10% of the office building tenants will come to work (particularly on a Saturday evening) [9.19], and as a result, the maximum weekend parking demand is

$$428 + 0.1(483) = 476 \text{ stalls}$$

which is less than the amount required during regular work hours. Thus a 575-stall parking lot will serve both developments sufficiently.

The following calculations explain why the overall utilization of the parking lot improves when complementary land uses are sharing the use of the same lot.

Scenario 1: use of separate lots for the office building and the movie theaters. The average utilizations for certain periods of a weekday (i.e., work-day and evening) as well as for a weekend day are estimated below. Then they are divided by the total availability of the lot in a week, which is the product of total capacity by the 7 days in a week. It is assumed that from around midnight to 7 A.M. the lot is empty.

$$\left[\frac{8(450)}{24}(5) + \frac{4(0.3)(450)}{24}(5) + \frac{8(0.1)(450)}{24}(2) \right] \bigg/ [483(7)] = \frac{892.5}{3381} = 26.4\%$$

average work day	average work day overtime	average weekend overtime

OFFICE BUILDING LOT

$$\left[\frac{8(0.3)(300)}{24}(5) + \frac{6(300)}{24}(5) + \frac{6(0.3)(400)}{24}(2) + \frac{6(400)}{24}(2)\right] \bigg/ [428(7)] = \frac{785}{2996} = 26.2\%$$

average weekday daylight patronage	average weekday evening patronage	average weekend daylight patronage	average weekend evening patronage

MOVIE THEATER LOT

These figures include rounded estimates of average parking demand by day period. The weighted efficiency of these two facilities is

$$\frac{483(26.4) + 428(26.2)}{483 + 428} = 26.3\%$$

Scenario 2: joint use of a 575-stall parking lot. In this case the overall efficiency of the single parking lot is

$$\frac{892.5 + 785}{7(575)} = 41.7\%$$

which represents a substantial improvement of the lot utilization over time. This way, (1) a substantial parcel of land was preserved: land for 575 instead of 911 (i.e., 483 + 428 stalls, for separate lots), which represents a 37% reduction in land consumption, while the unused land may be landscaped or put in other revenue/utility-generating uses); and (2) the efficiency of land utilization increased from 26% to 42%.

Figure 9.4.2 presents an approximate plot of shared parking lot utilization during a weekday for the example illustrated above. Separate plots for the two developments are presented together with the occupancy count of the lot per hourly interval. The lot fills quickly in the morning, then occupancy drops around the lunch hour, and then it returns to the morning levels. Around 4 P.M., patronage for the movie theater starts increasing and the lot reaches its maximum utilization, followed by a substantial decrease in occupancy due to the departure of most workers of the office building. Around 10 P.M., a spike in occupancy is observed. It is caused by the theater patrons coming for the late show, while several patrons of the evening show have not yet departed. After 1 A.M. all patrons and theater personnel have departed.

9.4.4 Parking Measurements and Analysis

There are four major indices describing the parking utilization of the area or site of focus: occupancy, accumulation, turnover, and average duration of occupancy. In all these measurements, 85 to 95% instead of 100% of the available parking capacity is used in the calculations. This is because levels of utilization higher than 95% are hard to attain due to efficiency losses in turnover and circulation [9.17]. In other words, when the utilization of the capacity exceeds 95%, it becomes very difficult to find an empty parking stall. The supply or capacity results directly from the inventory measurements.

The four indicators are defined as follows:

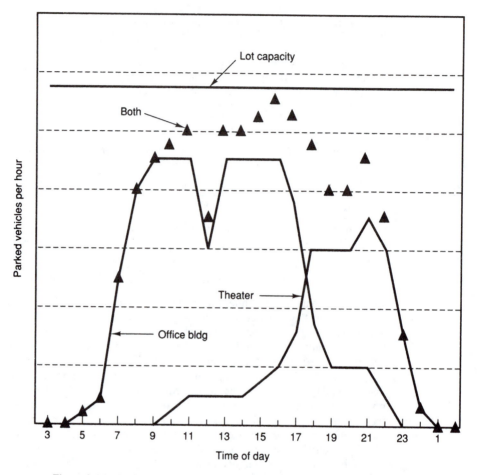

Figure 9.4.2 Parking occupancy profiles of a parking lot shared by an office building and a movie theater complex (approximate profiles during a weekday).

$$occupancy \ (\%) = 100 \ \frac{number \ of \ spaces \ occupied}{total \ spaces \ available}$$

$accumulation$ = number of vehicles parked at a given time

$turnover$ = number of vehicles utilizing the same stall over a given period of time
(4 or more during an 8-h period indicates a high turnover rate)

$$average \ duration = \frac{total \ vehicle \ hours}{total \ number \ of \ vehicles \ which \ parked} = \frac{\sum_{i=1}^{N} t_i}{N}$$

where t_i is the duration of parking occupancy of vehicle i.

There are various methods of collecting the data required for the estimation of these four indices. Three of the most common methods are *ins and outs*, *fixed period*, and *license plate* surveys.

According to *ins and outs*, all vehicles parked in the focus area are counted at the beginning of the survey period. Then vehicles entering and exiting the area are counted (i.e., lot accesses and/or streets carrying traffic into or out of the area of focus are monitored continuously). Another occupancy count is conducted at the end of the survey period to check whether measurements balance. This method can yield the overall accumulation and occupancy only; turnover rates and average duration cannot be estimated.

According to *fixed-period* sampling, all vehicles parked in the focus area are counted at the beginning of the survey period. Then the same area is covered in increments of $\frac{1}{2}$ to 4 h; that is, occupancy counts are conducted every $\frac{1}{2}$ to 4 h. This method may miss short-term parkers and it may be difficult to conduct in areas with private garages.

License plate surveys result in the most accurate and realistic data because essentially every parking stall is monitored at fixed intervals (the shorter the intervals, the higher the accuracy; i.e., avoid missing short-term parkers). This method is very labor intensive, while it entails certain liability problems (i.e., close monitoring of private property by copying vehicle license numbers). This can be partly alleviated by copying only the first or last three digits of the license plate.

The basic principles of a license plate survey are discussed next. Every surveyor is assigned to specific parking stalls (i.e., the floor of a parking structure or a stretch of roadway with curb parking). For each parking stall there is a corresponding box on the survey form. Both standardized and project-specific forms are used. Typically, every 30 min the surveyor walks along his or her inspection area marking on the form the license number of each vehicle parked on the corresponding box on the form. For the next 30 min, the same is repeated on another row of the form. Usually, symbols are defined for denoting empty stalls as well as stalls occupied by the same vehicles as in the previous 30 min. At the end of the survey period, the data are manually consolidated for each stall and input to computer (i.e., spreadsheet software) for analysis.

9.4.5 Design, Operation, and Other Considerations

Extensive information on parking lot and structure designs is presented in various manuals and textbooks [9.20–9.23]. Figure 9.4.3 illustrates a basic lot or deck design. Several principles of design are discussed below.

Parallel on-street parking is preferred to angled parking, for reasons of safety. When parked at an angle, backing into traffic may be dangerous due to poor visibility. In addition, the width of one traffic lane may not be sufficient for maneuvering out of the parking stall.

Figure 9.4.3 Parking lot layout (approximate scale). 1, Access gates; 2, vehicle presence detector to open gate; 3, vehicle departure detector to close gate; 4, transition from roadway to pavement; 5, internal circulation directions; 6, dedicated handicapped parking stalls; 7, space provisions for bicycles and motorbikes; 8, lighting; 9, curb; 10, street.

458

Angling stalls at 60° result in most efficient utilization of space in lots and decks, although other angles may provide a larger number of stalls for specific lot footprints. Unutilized corners should be landscaped or designated for motor-bike or bicycle parking.

Due to the continuous downsizing of automobiles (particularly of those de-signed for urban commuting) a large number of "tighter" stalls with the desig-nation "compact" should be supplied. This increases the overall parking capacity as well as the land-use efficiency.

Special attention should be paid to parking for handicapped persons. Local ordinances may require a specific number or percentage of stalls designated for use by handicapped drivers. These stalls should be located closest to the facility access points and be clearly noted for the exclusive use by handicapped drivers.

Security in parking lots is important, for both drivers and passengers and for vehicles. At a minimum, proper illumination should be supplied, while fencing, retractable gates, and security personnel are additional options of security, de-pending on the form and the size of the lot, the crime risk at the area, and the hours of operation. Often in hospitals and campuses, escort services are offered instead of or in addition to parking security.

There are many options in collecting parking fees: manual or electronic (digital) parking meters, collection boxes, coin/token collectors, authorization cards, time-stamped cards, collector (manual or automatic) at the exit, and permits (visually displayed or electronic: signal transmitted to sensor).

Automated parking with computer-controlled robotic dollies, which auto-matically park and retrieve automobiles, eliminates ramps at multistoried parking structures as well as valet parking operators. For the same capacity, smaller structures are required—which are easier to design to look like an ordinary office building—while noise, fumes, internal congestion, accidents, and security prob-lems are almost completely eliminated. Backup computers and electricity gen-erators are essential for reliable operation. Systems with ability to process up to 240 automobiles in 1 h are currently in operation in the United States and else-where [9.24].

9.5 SUMMARY

In this chapter we have focused on practical applications of traffic and transpor-tation engineering and on some of the established computer tools utilized in traffic impact and planning studies. Traffic impact studies are essentially small-scale (localized) planning studies where the impacts of a proposed development on the existing roadway network are assessed and evaluated. The results of traffic impact studies permit a site to be developed as proposed, or after certain modifications to the site per se and/or the surrounding roadway network and traffic controls.

Large-scale traffic analyses, including urban signalized-intersection networks, are conducted with powerful simulation packages such as NETSIM or TRANSYT. Planning studies and traffic impact studies of large-scale projects are conducted with powerful planning packages such as EMME/2, QRS II, and TRANPLAN. Geographic Information Systems increasingly become a valuable source of computerized transportation planning data and are often interfaced with planning packages.

Parking studies analyze parking, which is an indispensable component of urban transportation. Parking studies are either site-specific or area-specific. In a typical parking study, the demand for parking is assessed, the present conditions are evaluated, and strategies for alleviating parking problems are suggested. Principles of parking design were also discussed.

9.6 EXERCISES

1. Consider a proposed office park with 3250 people employed in it. Estimate the morning and evening flows of vehicle trips for a weekday and sketch the flows at the single access point of the site, which is at a midblock location. The site is located along an east–west road, and 30% of the site-generated traffic comes from (or is destined to) east. Identify high flow movements and potential operation deficiencies. The following trip generation models apply: $T = 1/(1.97/X - 0.000053)$ with 92% enter and 8% exit (A.M.), and $\ln T = 0.75 \ln X + 0.87$ with 15% enter and 85% exit (P.M.)

2. Based on Exercise 1, estimate three modal split assignment scenarios. Scenario 1: 100% auto. Scenario 2: 70% auto, 20% carpooling with average occupancy 2.2 persons per car and 10% bus transit (one bus every 10 min enters site from each direction). Scenario 3: 40% auto, 25% carpooling with average occupancy 2.2 persons per car, 10% bus transit (one bus every 10 min enters site from each direction), and 25% rail transit, which stops near the site (walk access). Estimate the vehicle trips for each scenario as well as the reduction from scenario 1. Is the reduction significant? Sketch A.M. volumes at the access point for all scenarios.

3. The site in Fig. E9.3 is expected to generate 2480 trips of which 90% will be from zones 1 through 9. Estimate the flows from each zone to the site. Assume that the rate of attraction is inversely proportional to the square of the distance between the site and each zone centroid.

4. Consider Exercise 3 and assume that the rate of attraction is inversely proportional to the square root of the distance between the site and each zone centroid. Do flows change, and how much? What is the underlying difference in people's behavior, which in one case suggests that the square of the distance should be used (Exercise 3), while in the other case the square root of the distance should be used?

5. Figure E9.5 presents the proposed layout of a site and the expected flows of traffic. Identify problematic spots at the access point of the site and in the internal circulation. Then, design an improved layout which corrects most of the problems. Note: numbers on the drawing represent traffic volumes, unless noted otherwise.

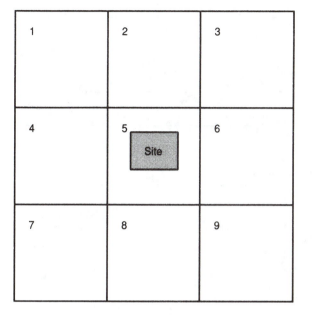

Zone	Population	Average distance
1	1300	10
2	3000	7
3	7000	9
4	800	6
5	3000	3
6	5500	6
7	500	10
8	1800	6
9	4400	10

Figure E9.3

6. A proposed movie theater is expected to generate 250 new trips during the evening rush hour (80% enter and 20% exit). The consultant and the municipality have agreed to distribute the trips empirically. To accomplish this, vehicle counts were taken at a nearby supermarket and an intersection during the evening rush hour. Figure E9.6 shows these counts. Estimate the site-generated number of vehicle trips by direction and movement at the site access point and at intersection I.

7. Consider the following data generated by a TRANSYT simulation run:

	Averages per cycle ($C = 75$ s)	
Node	Delay per vehicle	Number of stopped vehicles
1	18	20
2	25	34
3	5	8
4	12	30
5	22	41
6	36	17

Calculate the performance index for $k = 1$ and $k = 5$. What is the percent increase? Use the following model to estimate the hourly fuel consumption in the network of nodes 1 through 6.

$$FC = 4TTT + 0.5TD + 0.003TSV$$

NOTES: 1) buildings not to scale, 2) AM peak flows; reverse flows at PM peak.

Figure E9.5

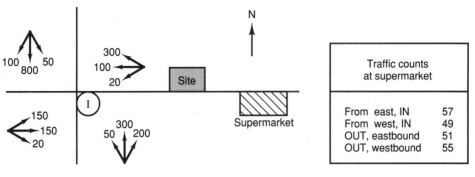

Figure E9.6

	Traffic counts at supermarket
From east, IN	57
From west, IN	49
OUT, eastbound	51
OUT, westbound	55

where FC is the network-wide fuel consumption in gallons per hour, TTT is the total travel time in 1 h (use 12.8 vehicle-hours per hour), TD the total delay in vehicle-hours per hour, and TSV the total number of stopped vehicles per hour.

8. A developer plans to install a large movie theater complex with approximately 4000 seats. The developer's site is next to a large office building that has a parking structure attached to it. The developer's site has no room for parking and he considers whether to accept the offer of the office building management to provide him with up to 1000 stalls of parking on weekdays and up to 2000 stalls of parking during weekends for a cost of $3 per stall (validated parking to be absorbed by the developer) or to lease part of an adjacent parcel of vacant land at $2.75 per square foot per annum. Approximately one-half of theater sitting capacity is expected to be utilized in weekdays (100% in weekends) and 250 ft^2 is needed for each parking stall (includes parking space, access, and space for maneuvering). Round parking demand estimates upward to the closest hundred increment. Which option should he choose?

9. Design an open parking lot with space for 120 passenger cars. Use a square lot layout and place the access point in the middle of one of its sides. Angle stalls by 60° and use 9 × 19 ft stall size and 20-ft-wide aisles for access and maneuvering.

10. The following table presents a sample of parking observations of 15 curb stalls. Estimate the occupancy, accumulation, turnover, and average duration for this sample of parking stalls.

	1	2	3	4	5	6	7	8	9	10	11	12	13	14	15
9:00	Y	Y	N	Y	N	N	N	Y	Y	N	N	Y	Y	Y	N
9:30	Y*	N	Y	Y	Y	Y	Y	N	Y	Y	Y	N	Y*	Y	Y
10:00	Y	Y	Y*	Y	Y*	Y	N	Y	Y*	Y	Y	Y	Y	N	Y
10:30	N	Y*	N	Y*	Y	Y*	Y	Y	Y*	N	Y	Y	Y*	Y	Y*
11:00	N	Y*	Y	Y	Y	Y	Y	Y	Y*	Y	Y*	Y*	N	Y*	Y*
11:30	Y	Y	Y	N	N	Y*	Y*	Y*	N	Y*	N	Y	Y	Y	N
12:00	Y	N	N	N	Y	N	N	N	N	Y	N	N	N	Y	Y

Y, stall occupied; N, stall empty; *, occupancy by different vehicle than in preceding time period.

11. [Class Project] On the map shown in Fig. E9.11, a site will be developed as an office
park which will house 1700 workers. Conduct a traffic impact study and a parking

Figure E9.11

study for this site. The time points to be considered are (1) the present time, (2) the
time when the development becomes fully operational (3 years from present time; 3%
annual growth of background traffic), and (3) a target year set at 7 years from the time
when the development becomes operational (1.5% annual growth of background
traffic).

It is likely that signalized control should be placed at the site access point. This T
intersection along with intersections I_1 and I_2 must be analyzed for 1 hr in the A.M.
and P.M. weekday peak period. New signal timings should be estimated and up to two
additional lanes per approach may be placed (in $t = t + 10$) if approach LOS worse
than C results. Estimates of through traffic at the access point should result from the
volumes of intersection I_2. All three intersections must operate under comparable cycle
lengths so that arterial progression is maintained.

The expected modal splits are as follows:

Opening time ($t + 3$): 80% drive alone, 20% carpool (occupancy 2.4)
Target time ($t + 10$): 60% drive alone, 30% carpool (occupancy 2.0),
                         10% use rail transit

These modal splits should be used in both the traffic impact and the parking study.
Figure E9.11 includes the expected distribution of traffic. Existing conditions of intersections I_1 and I_2 are shown in Fig. E9.12. Regarding the parking lot design, design
an open, rectangular lot with one of its sides limited to 200 ft. Use the design specifications in Exercise 9. The parking demand may be estimated from the following
function: $P = [(1.2/X) + 0.0005]^{-1}$, where X is the number of employees.

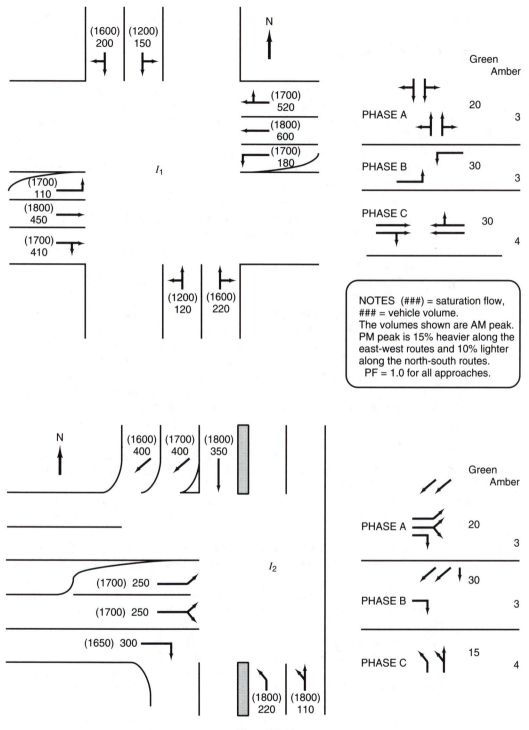

Figure E9.12

9.7 REFERENCES

9.1 TRANSPORTATION RESEARCH BOARD, *Highway Capacity Manual*, Special Report 209, National Research Council, Washington, D.C., 1985.

9.2 ———, *Interim Materials on Highway Capacity*, Circular 212, National Research Council, Washington, D.C., 1980.

9.3 INSTITUTE OF TRANSPORTATION ENGINEERS, *Traffic Access and Impact Studies for Site Development: a Recommended Practice*, Final Report by the Transportation Planners Council, ITE, Washington, D.C., Sept. 1989.

9.4 ———, *Trip Generation*, 5th ed., ITE, Washington, D.C., 1991.

9.5 DIAL, R. B., "A Probabilisitic Multipath Traffic Assignment Model Which Obviates Path Enumeration," *Transportation Research*, 5 (1971): 83–104.

9.6 FEDERAL HIGHWAY ADMINISTRATION, *TRANSYT 7-F: Users Manual*, U.S. Department of Transportation, Washington, D.C., July 1987.

9.7 ———, *TRAF-NETSIM User's Manual*, U.S. Department of Transportation, Washington, D.C., 1989.

9.8 INRO CONSULTANTS, *EMME/2: User's Manual*, INRO, Montreal, 1989.

9.9 SOSSLAU, A. B., et al., *Quick-Response Urban Travel Estimation Techniques and Transferable Parameters*, *User's Guide*, National Cooperative Highway Research Program Report 187, National Research Council, Washington, D.C., 1978.

9.10 HOROWITZ, A. J., *Quick Response System II Reference Manual*, Version 2.2., prepared for the Federal Highway Administration, U.S. Department of Transportation, Center for Urban Transportation Studies, University of Wisconsin, Milwaukee, 1988.

9.11 THE URBAN ANALYSIS GROUP, *TRANPLAN User's Manual*, UAG, Danville, Calif., 1990.

9.12 ABKOWITZ, M., S. WALSH, E. HAUSER, and L. MINOR, "Adaptation of Geographic Information Systems to Highway Management," *Journal of Transportation Engineering*, 116, 3 (May/June 1990).

9.13 TRANSPORTATION RESEARCH BOARD, *Geographic Information Systems 1990*, Transportation Research Record 1261, National Research Council, Washington, D.C., 1990.

9.14 ———, *Implementation of Geographic Information Systems (GIS) in State DOTs*, Research Results Digest 180, National Research Council, Washington, D.C., Aug. 1991.

9.15 SURBER, M., D. SHOUP, and M. WACHS, *Effects of Ending Employer-Paid Parking for Solo Drivers*, Transportation Research Record 957; National Research Council, Washington, D.C., 1984, pp. 67–70.

9.16 ORGANIZATION FOR ECONOMIC CO-OPERATION AND DEVELOPMENT, *Evaluation of Urban Parking Systems*, OECD Publications, Paris, Dec. 1980.

9.17 KROHN, R. A., *Parking Studies: General Procedures and Case Studies*, Graduate Report UCB-ITS-GR-85-2, Institute of Transportation Studies, University of California at Berkeley, Apr. 1985.

9.18 INSTITUTE OF TRANSPORTATION ENGINEERS, *Parking Generation*, 2nd ed., ITE, Washington, D.C., 1987.

9.19 URBAN LAND INSTITUTE, *Shared Parking*, a study conducted by Barton–Aschman Associates, Washington, D.C., 1983.

9.20 HIGHWAY RESEARCH BOARD, *Parking Principles*, Highway Research Special Report 125, National Academy of Sciences, Washington, D.C., 1971.

9.21 PARKING CONSULTANTS COUNCIL, *The Dimensions of Parking*, Urban Land Institute and National Parking Association, Washington, D.C., 1979.

9.22 INSTITUTE OF TRANSPORTATION ENGINEERS, "Employment Center Parking Facilities," a summary report by the ITE Technical Council Committee 6F-24, *Institute of Transportation Engineers Journal* (1988):29–35.

9.23 FEDERAL SIGN CORPORATION, *How to Plan Parking Areas*, FSC, Hinsdale, Ill., 1979.

9.24 Editorial, "Robots Could Take Anxiety Out of Parking," *Civil Engineering* (June 1989):21–22.

10 Air Quality, Noise, and Energy Impacts

10.1 INTRODUCTION

The main objective of the travel-demand-forecasting models examined in Chapters 8 and 9 is to estimate the impacts of transportation systems that are directly related to travel. These impacts include the amount of trip making, the geographical distribution and orientation of trips, the utilization of the available and proposed modes of travel, and the consequences of these travel choices on the loading of the transportation network in terms of link flows, and in terms of the impedances (e.g., travel times) experienced by the users of the system.

Up to the 1960s, transportation decisions in the public sector were generally based on the assessment of the capital and operating costs of transportation facilities vis-à-vis the expected direct improvements in the levels of service and travel times experienced by the user. The explicit consideration of indirect and nonuser impacts was generally confined to practical cost-related items such as the appropriate or just compensation of individuals and businesses for right-of-way acquisition and relocation.

As described in Chapter 7, the civil rights and the environmental movements of the 1960s contributed to the evolution of an altered perspective. Civil rights concerns affected the understanding of the role of transportation by addressing issues relating to the rights to mobility and accessibility to employment and other opportunities on the part of various societal subgroups. The environmental movement resulted in an increasing awareness about many indirect socioeconomic and environmental effects of transportation decisions (see Appendix A).

In this chapter we address three of the many transportation-related impacts that have become an integral part of contemporary transportation planning and decision-making. These are air quality, noise generation, and energy consumption. For each of these impacts, a brief historical note is presented, several mitigation strategies are described, and practical models for estimating the impact are illustrated.

10.2 AIR POLLUTION

10.2.1 Introduction

The release of air pollutants in the atmosphere is a concomitant result of human activities. In some instances, naturally produced air pollutants outweigh man-made pollution, but the latter tends to be concentrated in urbanized areas where people live and work. The problem of air pollution is not new. In early fourteenth-century London, the smoke and odor consequences of coal burning became such a public nuisance that several commissions were appointed to combat them. In his book on the subject of air pollution, Perkins [10.1] quotes the following declaration by King Edward I:

> Be it known to all within the sound of my voice, whosoever shall be found guilty of burning coal shall suffer the loss of his head.

More recently, connections between air pollution and respiratory disease have been demonstrated and detrimental environmental effects on the global scale have been discerned. Several localized pollution episodes have resulted in documented deaths and have highlighted the severity of the problem. A December 1948 episode in Donora, Pennsylvania, and a December 1956 episode in London are most notable.

The first major law enacted by the U.S. Congress in relation to air pollution was the 1955 Air Pollution Act, which provided federal support for research into the subject. The Clean Air Act of 1963 recognized the contribution of "urbanization, industrial development, and increasing use of motor vehicles" to the problem and encouraged automobile manufacturers to address it. Two years later, the 1965 Motor Vehicle Air Pollution Control Act provided for the establishment of vehicle-emission standards and opened the way to a series of amendments that led to the Air Quality Act of 1970, which provided for national ambient air-quality standards, for a reduction of vehicle emissions of several pollutants by 90% of their 1970 levels, and for state implementation plans to conform to these provisions. The 1970 Federal-Aid Highway Act explicitly required that highway planning must be consistent with implementation plans to attain and maintain established regional ambient air quality standards. Table 10.2.1 presents the national

TABLE 10.2.1 1971 NATIONAL AMBIENT AIR-QUALITY STANDARDS

Pollutant	Type of standard	Averaging time	Frequency parameter	Concentration	
				mg/m^3	ppm
Carbon monoxide	Primary[a] and	1 h	Annual maximum[c]	40,000	35
	secondary[b]	8 h	Annual maximum	10,000	9
Hydrocarbons (nomethane)	Primary and secondary	3 h (6–9 A.M.)	Annual maximum	160[d]	0.24[d]
Nitrogen dioxide	Primary and secondary	1 year	Arithmetic mean	100	0.05
Photo-chemical oxidants	Primary and secondary	1 year	Annual maximum	160	0.08
Particulate matter	Primary	24 h	Annual maximum	260	—
		24 h	Annual geometric mean	75	—
	Secondary	24 h	Annual maximum	150	—
		24 h	Annual geometric mean	60[e]	
Sulfur dioxide	Primary	24 h	Annual maximum	365	0.14
		1 h	Arithmetic mean	80	0.03
	Secondary	3 h	Annual maximum	1,300	0.5
		24 h	Annual maximum	260[f]	0.1[f]
		1 h	Arithmetic mean	60	0.02

[a] Primary standards are those required to protect   .ic health.

[b] Secondary standards are those required to , ..ect public welfare.

[c] Not to be exceeded more than once per year.

[d] As a guide in devising implementation plans for achieving oxidant standards.

[e] As a guide to be used in assessing implementation plans for achieving the annual maximum 24-h standard.

[f] As a guide to be used in assessing implementation plans for achieving the annual arithmetic mean standard.

Source: Environmental Protection Agency [10.2].

ambient standards for several air pollutants as issued by the EPA in 1971. This requirement resulted in an accelerated level of activity regarding the monitoring and modeling the air-quality impacts of transportation systems and in the integration of air-quality considerations into the transportation-planning process. The subsequent legislative history of the issue has been, to say the least, tumultuous. Nevertheless, the problem has come to the forefront and has claimed a special place in the planning, design, and implementation of transportation projects. The 1990 Amendments to the Clean Air Act imposed more stringent requirements on geographical areas that did not comply with tightened pollution standards.

10.2.2 Problem Dimensions

The combustion of transportation fuels releases several contaminants into the atmosphere, including carbon monoxide, hydrocarbons, oxides of nitrogen, and lead and other particulate matter. Hydrocarbons, of which more than 200 have been detected in exhaust emissions, are the result of the incomplete combustion of fuel. Particulates are minute solid or liquid particles that are suspended in the atmosphere; they include aerosols, smoke, and dust particles. Photochemical smog is the result of complex chemical reactions of oxides of nitrogen and hydrocarbons in the presence of sunlight.

Once emitted into the atmosphere, air pollutants undergo mixing or diffusion, the degree of which depends on topographic, climatic, and meteorological conditions. These include wind speed and direction, and atmospheric stability.

The assessment of the air-pollution effects of transportation may be undertaken at three levels: microscale analysis in the immediate vicinity of a transportation facility such as a highway, mesoscale analysis in areas that are somewhat removed from the facility, which includes the contribution of other mobile and stationary sources of pollution, and macroscale analysis, extending from the regional to the global levels. Available air-pollution estimation models range from simple models that provide rough estimates of emission levels to very complex numerical models that trace the diffusion of pollutants in space and time and also simulate the chemical processes that follow.

10.2.3 Emission Levels

Vehicular emissions of air pollutants are usually measured in grams per vehicle-mile of travel and are related to several factors, including vehicle type and age, ambient temperature, and altitude. The operating cycle, which consists of starts and stops, speed changes, and idling time, is also an important factor. A disproportionate fraction of carbon monoxide and hydrocarbons are emitted during cold starts of the engine. The EPA periodically issues reports relating to emission factors for various types of vehicles [10.3].

The general relationships between speed and emissions are illustrated by Fig. 10.2.1. Carbon monoxide emissions generally decrease with speed, partly due to the air-to-fuel ratio supplied to the engine at different speeds. Up to about 30 to 40 mi/h, a similar relationship occurs in the case of hydrocarbons, but a mild increase in emissions is seen thereafter. The emission of nitrogen oxides exhibits a different pattern—that is, it generally increases with speed.

Figure 10.2.1   General relationship between speed and emissions.

A number of emission models utilizing these factors have been developed and many traffic-simulation models (e.g., [10.4]) have been supplemented by emission-estimating subroutines. The EPA has developed [10.5] a computer program that estimates the emissions that result from various combinations of traffic flows, vehicle mixes, and other factors. A simplified model for carbon monoxide based on the EPA program has been proposed by Raus [10.6]. This model uses several nomographs that are based on a typical 1980 vehicle mix for various altitudes and ambient temperatures and is included here for illustrative purposes. The family of curves corresponding to altitudes up to 4000 ft above sea level is shown in Fig. 10.2.2.

Example 10.1

According to a traffic forecast, a proposed 4-mi highway is expected to carry 3500 veh/h during the 2-h peak period of the day at an average travel time of 16 min. Apply the Raus model to estimate the total peak-hour emissions of carbon monoxide on the highway for the typical autumn day (60°F).

Solution   The total number of vehicle-miles traveled during the typical peak period is

$$(3500 \text{ veh/h})(2 \text{ h/peak})(4 \text{ mi}) = 28,000 \text{ veh-mi/peak period}$$

The estimated average speed is 15 mi/h and, according to Fig. 10.2.2, the emission rate corresponding to this speed is 78g/veh-mi. As a result, the total emissions of carbon monoxide are estimated to be 2,184,000 g, or 4811 lb, per peak period.

10.2.4 Air-Pollution Dispersion

While the emission level is an important measure of the air-pollution impact of various sources, it is the concentration of pollutants in the atmosphere that defines the levels and times of exposure. Following the emission of pollutants, dispersion and chemical oxidation take place in the atmosphere. The dispersion of a pollutant is affected by the strength of the source and by topographic and meteorological conditions. The topography of the terrain in the vicinity of the source of pollution affects, among other items, the wind profile near the ground and the generation of turbulence in the form of eddies. Special conditions related to highway facilities also affect the dispersal of highway-generated pollution. For example, the EPA HIWAY model [10.7] analyzes at-grade and depressed highways differently to estimate the concentrations of nonreactive pollutants from highway traffic at various downwind locations. Also, air pollutants released on roadways passing through densely developed urban areas tend to be trapped in the street canyons that are formed by rows of buildings at both ends of the roadway.

One of the most important meteorological conditions that affect the mixing of pollutants is the temperature lapse rate, which is defined as the rate of change of temperature with altitude. This rate is usually referenced to the *adiabatic lapse rate* of −5.4°F per 1000 ft, which corresponds to an atmosphere that is charac-

Figure 10.2.2   Carbon monoxide emission factors—1980 vehicle mix. (From Raus [10.6].)

terized by neutral stability, that is, a situation where air particles tend to maintain their positions. When the temperature drops at a faster rate than the adiabatic (i.e., at a *superadiabatic lapse rate*), the atmosphere is unstable, and vigorous mixing takes place. On the other side of the adiabatic lapse rate, *subadiabatic lapse rates* tend to inhibit mixing. Due to various meteorological combinations, sometimes certain layers in the atmosphere experience an increase of temperature with altitude. This is known as a *temperature inversion* and is critical especially when it occurs in a layer close to the ground because pollutants are trapped within this layer. The *mixing height* is the height of the atmospheric layer within which mixing occurs. This height varies from locality to locality and also exhibits daily and seasonal variation. The degree of mixing is a function of the atmospheric stability of this layer. Typically, the atmosphere near the earth's surface becomes unstable in the morning, allowing for energetic mixing within the mixing layer, which attains its maximum height in the afternoon [10.7].

One of the simplest mathematical models of air pollution diffusion is the box model, which is described in the next subsection. More sophisticated models employing numerical integration of complex Gaussian equations [10.8] and the modeling of chemical processes [10.9] usually require the use of computer algorithms.

10.2.5 The Box Model

The *box model* may be used to approximate the concentration of air pollution within an atmospheric volume defined by a rectangular area and extending to the altitude of the mixing height H, as shown by Fig. 10.2.3. Pollutants emitted into the box at a constant rate E in pollutant weight per unit time are assumed to be

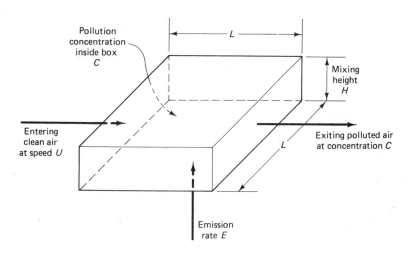

Figure 10.2.3 Box model.

mixed instantaneously with the air volume of the box. Clean air is assumed to enter the box at a speed U, and air containing the same concentration as the interior of the box is assumed to exit from the opposite side. The concentration $C(t)$ at any time t inside the box is expressed in pollutant weight per unit volume. Based on these assumptions, the following balance equation applies:

$$E - FC = V\left(\frac{dC}{dt}\right) \tag{10.2.1}$$

where

$$F = ULH = \text{airflow (volume per unit time)}$$

$$V = L^2H = \text{box volume}$$

Equation 10.2.1 expresses the rate of change of pollution inside the box as the difference between the amount of pollution entering the box (E) and the amount of pollution exiting the box (FC).

Example 10.2

Solve Eq. 10.2.1 for concentration as a function of time assuming that the air within the box is initially clean (i.e., $C_0 = 0$) and that U, E, and H are constant.

Solution Rewrite Eq. 10.2.1 as

$$\frac{dC}{dt} + \frac{F}{V}C = \frac{E}{V} \tag{10.2.2}$$

Equation 10.2.2 is a first-order linear differential equation of the form

$$\frac{dy}{dx} + p(x)y = g(x) \tag{10.2.3}$$

which can be solved by multiplying both sides by the integrating factor

$$f(x) = e^{\int p(x)\,dx} \tag{10.2.4}$$

thus rendering the left-hand side into the exact differential of the product $yf(x)$. In this case the integrating factor is

$$f(t) = e^{(F/V)t} \tag{10.2.5}$$

Hence

$$\frac{d}{dt}(Ce^{(F/V)t}) = \frac{E}{V}e^{(F/V)t}$$

Integrating with respect to t gives us

$$Ce^{(F/V)t} = \frac{VE}{FV}e^{(F/V)t} + K$$

or

$$C = \frac{E}{F} + Ke^{-(F/V)t} \tag{10.2.6}$$

where K is the constant of integration, which can be evaluated at the initial condition $C(0) = 0$ to be

$$K = -\frac{E}{F}$$

As a result, the solution to Eq. 10.2.1 becomes

$$C = \frac{E}{F}[1 - e^{-(F/V)t}] \tag{10.2.7}$$

which is plotted in Fig. 10.2.4. Thus, under the simplifying assumptions of this model, the pollution concentration of the interior of the box tends toward a steady-state level of E/F.

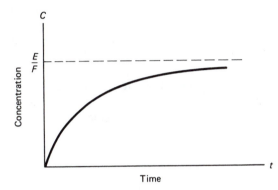

Figure 10.2.4 Pollutant concentration as a function of time.

10.3 NOISE GENERATION

10.3.1 Introduction

Sound is acoustical energy released into the atmosphere by vibrating or moving bodies. Therefore sound is amenable to objective scientific measurement and investigation. On the other hand, noise is undesirable or unwanted sound and as such it is cloaked with a certain degree of subjectivity. Extended exposure to excessive sound has been shown to produce physical and psychological damage. Because of its annoyance and disturbance implications, noise adds to mental stress and hence affects the general well-being of those that are exposed to it. Undoubtedly, noise has always been a major source of friction between individuals.

Transportation operations are major contributors to noise in the modern urban environment. Noise is generated by the engine and exhaust systems of vehicles, by aerodynamic friction, and by the interaction between the vehicle and its support system (e.g., tire–pavement and wheel–rail interactions). Because noise diminishes with distance from the source, the most serious transportation-related noise problems are confined to transportation corridors (e.g., highway and railway corridors and aircraft flight paths) and at major transportation hubs (e.g., airports and transit terminals).

Seiff [10.10] reports that in 1970 the Bureau of Motor Carrier Safety issued rules relating to noise levels in the interior of commercial vehicles based in the belief that the safety of these operations would be compromised by the resulting driver fatigue and hearing problems. About the same time, various states and local communities began to establish community noise regulations, including motor-vehicle noise standards. The passage of the Noise Control Act of 1972 at the federal level, marked the recognition of the problem as a major detriment to urban living of nationwide proportions. Pursuant to the provisions of this act, the FHWA issued the 1973 Policy and Procedure Memorandum [10.11], which promulgated noise standards for various types of land use and stated that the FHWA:

> ... encourages the application of the noise standards at the earliest appropriate stage in the project development process.

Table 10.3.1 presents the noise standards issued by the FHWA in 1973 for several categories of land use. Thus concern about the noise impacts of transportation vehicles and facilities officially entered the calculus of transportation design, planning, and implementation.

10.3.2 Noise Measurement

The quantity of energy or the intensity of a single sound is usually measured on a relative logarithmic scale that employs a unit called a *bel* or in terms of its subdivision, the *decibel*. A bel represents a 10-fold increase in energy and is measured in relation to a reference intensity I_0, which is usually taken at the threshold of human hearing. The intensity I of a sound corresponding to L bels is

$$I = 10^L I_0 \qquad (10.3.1)$$

Solving for L yields

$$L = \log_{10}\left(\frac{I}{I_0}\right) \qquad \text{B} \qquad (10.3.2)$$

At the threshold of hearing, $I = I_0$ and the noise level L is equal to zero. When L is about 14, the sound becomes painful to the human ear.

For finer scaling, the bel is divided into 10 dB, and Eq. 10.3.2 becomes

$$L = 10 \log_{10}\left(\frac{I}{I_0}\right) \qquad \text{dB} \qquad (10.3.3)$$

An alternative formulation of Eq. 10.3.2 is based on the fact that the sound energy

TABLE 10.3.1 FHWA NOISE STANDARDS

(a) Design noise level/land-use relationships

Land-use category	Design noise level, L_{10}	Description of land-use category
A	60 dBA (exterior)	Tracts of land in which serenity and quiet are of extraordinary significance and serve an important public need, and where the preservation of those qualities is essential if the area is to continue to serve its intended purpose. Such areas could include amphitheaters, particular parks or portions of parks, or open spaces which are dedicated or recognized by appropriate local officials for activities requiring special qualities of serenity and quiet.
B	70 dBA (exterior)	Residences, motels, hotels, public meeting rooms, schools, churches, libraries, hospitals, picnic areas, recreation areas, playgrounds, active sports areas, and parks.
C	75 dBA (exterior)	Developed lands, properties or activities not included in categories A and B.
D	—	For requirements on undeveloped lands see paragraphs 5a(5) and (6), this PPM.
E[a]	55 dBA (interior)	Residences, motels, hotels, public meeting rooms, schools, churches, libraries, hospitals, and auditoriums.

[a] See part (b).

(b) Noise-reduction factors

Building type	Window condition	Noise reduction due to exterior of the structure (dB)	Corresponding highest exterior noise level that would achieve an interior design noise level of 55 dBA (dBA)
All	Open	10	65
Light frame	Ordinary sash		
	Closed	20	75
	With storm windows	25	80
Masonry	Single glazed	25	80
	Double glazed	35	90

Source: Federal Highway Administration [10.11].

is proportional to the square of the frequency f of the sound, that is,

$$I = af^2 \qquad (10.3.4)$$

where a is a proportionality factor. Substitution of this equation in Eq. 10.3.2 yields

$$L = 20 \log_{10}\left(\frac{f}{f_0}\right) \qquad \text{dB} \qquad (10.3.5)$$

where f is the frequency of the sound being measured and f_0 is the reference frequency at the threshold of hearing.

Equations 10.3.1 through 10.3.5 apply to sounds that consist of a single frequency. However, typical environmental noises consist of combinations of frequencies of which only those in the approximate range from 500 to 10,000 Hz are detectable by humans. A single noise-level scale in decibels that combines the effect of multifrequency noises in a manner that simulates the sensitivity and response of humans discriminates or weighs against frequencies that lie outside

Sound levels and human response		
Common sounds	Noise level (dB)	Effect
Carrier deck jet operation Air raid siren	140	Painfully loud
	130	
Jet takeoff (200 ft)		
Thunderclap Discotheque	120	Maximum vocal effort
Auto horn (3 ft)		
Pile drivers	110	
Garbage truck	100	
Heavy truck (50 ft) City traffic	90	Very annoying Hearing damage (8 hrs)
Alarm clock (2 ft) Hair dryer	80	Annoying
Noisy restaurant Freeway traffic Man's voice (3 ft)	70	Telephone use difficult
Air conditioning unit (20 ft)	60	Intrusive
Light auto traffic (100 ft)	50	Quiet
Living room Bedroom Quiet office	40	
Library Soft whisper (15 ft)	30	Very quiet
Broadcasting studio	20	
	10	Just audible
	0	Hearing begins

Figure 10.3.1 Sound levels and human response. (From Environmental Protection Agency [10.12].)

this range. The most common weighting scheme is referred to as the *A-weighted scale* and gives measurements that are measured in A-weighted decibels, or dBA. Figure 10.3.1 presents the A-weighted decibel levels of several common environmental sounds that lie between the threshold of hearing (i.e., dBA = 0) and the level of physiological pain [10.12].

10.3.3 Noise Propagation and Mitigation Strategies

Once generated at a source, unshielded noise spreads out spherically as it travels through the air away from the source. Consequently, the intensity of the sound diminishes with distance from the source. In addition to these losses in intensity due to spreading, absorption losses also take place as the sound energy is transferred between air particles. When the sound waves encounter natural and manufactured solid objects, they undergo bending or diffraction and reflection, the degree of which depends on the characteristics of the object. Trees and other vegetation, for example, tend to reflect the sound waves in a diffused pattern and are considered to be good interceptors of noise.

The major thrust of noise-control strategies is to minimize the noise levels to which the population is exposed. Figure 10.3.2 summarizes the overall problem of community noise and amelioration strategies as described by Borthwick [10.13]. Part (a) enumerates the various sources of community noise that have been identified in 1974 by the noise-control section of the Florida Department of Pollution Control. Part (b) specifies three categories of transportation noise-control strategies: source controls, noise-path controls, and receiver-side controls. Part (c) lists a variety of potential source controls, including vehicle-control devices, vehicle-maintenance practices, traffic controls, and highway-design controls. Part (d) shows that noise-path controls include the erection of appropriately designed noise barriers that reflect and diffuse noise and the provision of buffer zones between the transportation facility and the population to provide a distance over which noise can be attenuated. Finally, part (e) lists a series of noise-control strategies at the receptor site, including public-awareness programs and building-design practices. Figure 10.3.3 illustrates the effects of elevating or depressing the highway.

10.3.4 Noise Measures

Figure 10.3.4 shows that the noise levels generated by transportation facilities show a good amount of variability with respect to time. It is, therefore, necessary to establish meaningful statistical noise measures that describe the magnitude of the problem while capturing this variability. Commonly used statistical measures include the following:

  1. L_p denotes the noise level at a receptor site that is exceeded p percent of the time. Commonly used levels of this measure include the noise level that

(a) Noise identification system.

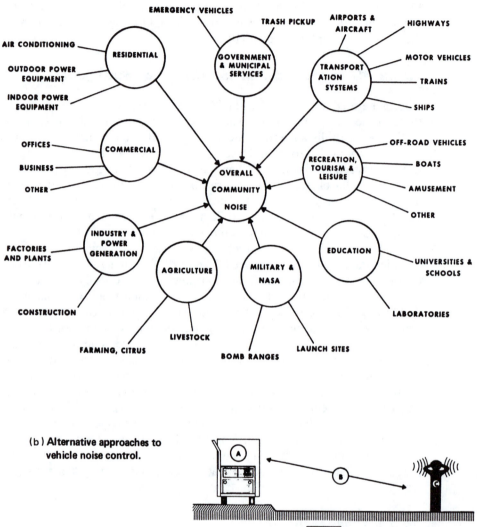

(b) Alternative approaches to vehicle noise control.

Figure 10.3.2   Florida noise control program elements. (From Borthwick [10.13].)

(c) **Noise source control strategies.**

(d) **Noise path control strategies.**

(e) **Noise receiver control strategies.**

Figure 10.3.2 *Continued*

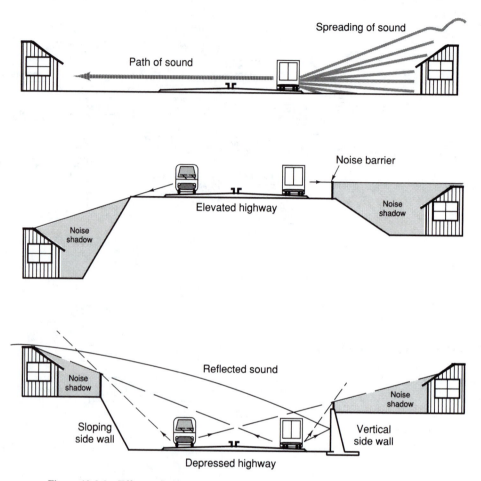

Figure 10.3.3 Effects of elevating and depressing highways, and noise barriers on noise exposure of adjacent land uses.

is exceeded 10, 50, and 90% of the time. L_{10} is a peak noise level used by most highway departments in the United States and endorsed by the FHWA. Noise level L_{90} is a background level that is exceeded most of the time.

2. The equivalent noise level denoted by L_{eq} is defined as

$$L_{eq} = 10 \log_{10}\left(\frac{1}{T} \int_0^T \frac{f^2}{f_0^2}\, dt\right) \qquad (10.3.6)$$

where T is the period of time over which the measurement is made. The equivalent noise level may be approximated by a series of N discrete measurements as follows:

Figure 10.3.4   Noise-level variability. (From U.S. Department of Transportation [10.14].)

$$L_{eq} = 10 \log_{10}\left(\frac{1}{N} \sum_i 10^{(L_i/10)}\right) \qquad (10.3.7)$$

where L_i is the average noise level during interval i.

Other noise-impact measures for the assessment of transportation noise have been proposed. Some of these combine the above measures in various ways that attempt to capture the annoyance caused by the noise. Hall and Allen [10.15] summarize several of these alternative measures.

10.3.5 Mathematical Models of Transportation Noise

Wesler [10.16] traces the first mathematical formulation of traffic noise to the following empirical equation presented in the 1952 Wright Air Development Center *Handbook of Acoustic Noise Control* [10.17]:

$$L_{50} = 68 + 8.5 \log V - 20 \log D \qquad \text{dB} \qquad (10.3.8)$$

where

$$V \stackrel{.}{=} \text{traffic volume, in veh/h}$$

$$D = \text{distance from a traffic line to the observer, in feet}$$

Since then, many researchers have attempted to calibrate highway-related noise models for various traffic conditions. The state of the art has recently been greatly enhanced, and various manual and computer-based models are available for the analysis of noise impacts and for the design of noise-amelioration devices such as noise barriers. The FHWA, for example, has published several models, which have been subsequently enhanced and refined [10.18]. These models include several manual and computerized solution procedures. Figure 10.3.5 is a nomograph that can be used to estimate the unshielded noise level (i.e., in the absence of noise barriers) at some distance from a highway. Inputs to this model are the volumes and speeds of automobiles, medium trucks, and heavy trucks using the highway, and the output consists of an estimate of L_{10} at a given distance away. The noise level caused by each component is calculated by the procedure

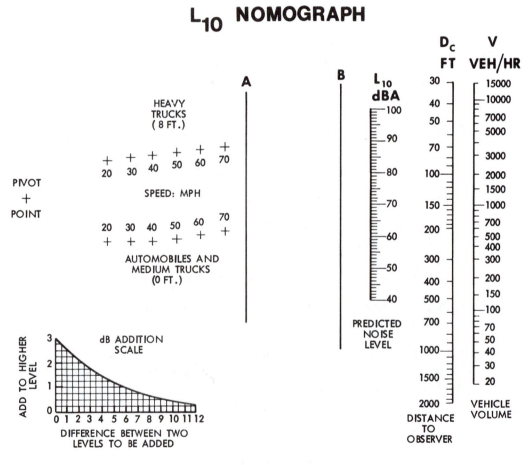

Figure 10.3.5 L_{10} nomograph. (From Kugler et al. [10.18].)

described next and added logarithmically to arrive at the total highway noise level. The medium-truck volume is converted to automobile equivalents by a factor of 10. If the speeds of medium trucks and automobiles are equal, the two can be combined into one group. Heavy trucks are always analyzed separately. Automobiles and medium trucks differ from heavy trucks in that the major part of the noise emitted by the former is at the pavement level, due to the interaction between the tires and the pavement. Heavy-truck noise, on the other hand, is emitted from exhaust systems, which are located about 8 ft above the pavement level. This difference is denoted on the noise nomograph but is more important to the design and analysis of barriers than to the simplified estimation of unshielded noise addressed here. To estimate the noise level produced by highway traffic, the first three steps of the following procedure are applied to each vehicular volume component and the results are combined, as explained in Step 4.

Step 1.   A straight line joining the pivot point at the extreme left-hand side of the nomograph to the point corresponding to the mean speed is extended until it intersects line A. Note that two sets of speed-related points are included: one for automobiles and medium trucks and the other for heavy trucks.

Step 2.   A second straight line is drawn from the above point of intersection of the traffic volume V on the scale located at the extreme right-hand side of the chart. The point of intersection of the second line and line B is noted.

Step 3.   A third line is drawn from the point of intersection of line B to the distance D_c for which the noise level is calculated. The intersection of the third line and the L_{10} scale next to line B represents the required L_{10} estimate. The distance to the observer D_c may be either taken approximately from the middle of the highway or, if desired, from the middle of individual lanes. In the latter case, the volume and speed inputs must be known by lane.

Step 4.   The calculated L_{10} levels for the various highway flow components are combined. Because of the logarithmic nature of the dBA scale, the L_{10} levels cannot be added arithmetically. Instead, if two sounds are to be added, an incremental amount, depending on the difference in the two noise levels, is added to the higher of the two. The insert located at the lower left-hand side of the chart gives the magnitude of the incremental amount. Thus two sounds of equal intensity (i.e., zero difference) combine into a level that is only 3 dBA higher. The proof of this fact is given in Example 10.3.

Example 10.3

Prove that two sounds of equal intensity produce a decibel level that is only 3 dBA higher.

Solution   The energy contained in the two sounds combined is equal to two times the sound energy I of either of the two alone. By Eq. 10.3.3, the combined level L is

$$L = 10 \log_{10}\left(\frac{2I}{I_0}\right)$$

$$= 10 \log_{10}\left(\frac{I}{I_0}\right) + 10 \log_{10}2$$

$$= 10 \log_{10}\left(\frac{I}{I_0}\right) + 3$$

Discussion   The first term on the right side is the decibel level corresponding to the sound intensity I to which 3 dB is added when the two sounds are combined. In conjunction with the sound-addition insert to Fig. 10.3.5, when more than two noise sources are to be added, their magnitudes are first listed in decreasing order. The increment contributed by lowest level to the next lowest is read from the graph and added to the latter. The result is then combined with the next list entry, and the procedure continues until all components have been included.

Example 10.4

A straight at-grade highway accommodates 3600 passenger cars and 40 medium trucks per hour. The average speed of the two vehicle types is the same and equals 40 mi/h. Plot the relationship between the noise level, L_{10}, and distance from the highway.

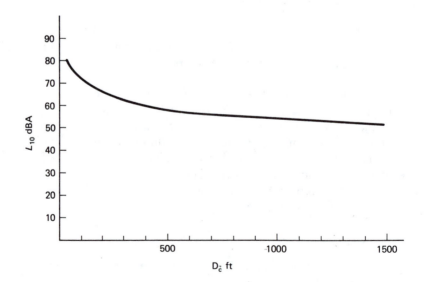

Figure 10.3.6   Noise level and distance from highway.

Solution   The procedure relating to Fig. 10.3.4 is applied, using a combined volume of

$$3600 + 40 \times 10 = 4000 \text{ automobile equivalents per hour}$$

and the results obtained in relation to various distances D_c are plotted in Fig. 10.3.6. The figure illustrates the attenuation of noise over distance from about 78 dBA at a distance of 30 ft to about 51 dBA at a distance of 1500 ft.

10.4 ENERGY CONSUMPTION

10.4.1 Introduction

The enormous strides in industrial and economic growth that occurred in the United States during the twentieth century have been closely related to an ample supply of inexpensive energy, particularly energy derived from fossil fuels. Around 1970, the population of the United States constituted about 6% of the world's population but used approximately 30% of the global petroleum consumption. A little more than half of the petroleum used in this country is expended for transportation-related purposes, and of this amount the private automobile accounts for close to two-thirds, or about one-third of the total petroleum consumed in the United States. The potential impact that energy shortages can have was experienced during World War II, when strict rationing and allocation of energy and other resources had to be imposed. After the war, energy consumption resumed its upward spiral and the problem came to the forefront in 1973 when the Organization of Petroleum Exporting Countries (OPEC) imposed an oil embargo and subsequently raised the price of crude oil. The economic effects of this action reverberated around the globe.

10.4.2 National Response to the Energy Embargo

The immediate response of the nation to the 1973–1974 energy embargo was to first deal with the emergency situation at hand. Among the earliest actions of the U.S. Congress was the passage of the 1973 Emergency Petroleum Allocation Act, which empowered the executive branch to establish an allocation plan for various sectors of the economy and geographical regions. Related actions included extensions of the Daylight Savings Time, the establishment of a national highway speed limit of 55 mi/h, which became effective in 1974, and the creation of a Federal Energy Office to deal with the problem. The 1975 Energy Policy and Conservation Act provided for the development of a national energy contingency plan, which was issued by the Federal Energy Administration in 1976. The same act mandated a schedule for improving the fuel economy of new automobiles sold in the United States. At that time energy-related responsibilities were scattered among several agencies and programs. Pursuant to Executive Order 12009, the U.S. Congress established in 1977 the Department of Energy (DOE). This new federal department combined the Energy Research and Development Administration (ERDA) and the Atomic Energy Commission (AEC) and was charged with the lead role in coordinating the national response to the problem of energy and to seek short-, medium-, and long-term solutions under a multifaceted program, which came to be known as "Project Independence" [10.19].

A second fuel shortfall occurred in 1979 and caused significant disruptions despite the implementation in the meantime of various gasoline rationing schemes. In the same year, the U.S. Congress passed the 1979 Emergency Energy Conservation Act, which directed the executive branch to establish energy conservation targets for the federal government and the states and required the states to submit their plans, including a transportation element, within 45 days of the issuance of the targets. In 1980, the newly elected administration ushered in a different perspective toward the problem by shifting the emphasis from central management to a reliance on a free-market approach. Proposals directed toward the abolishment of the DOE were sent forth and, in 1981, Executive Order 12287 was issued, which eliminated the then-existing allocation and price controls on crude oil and petroleum products. Both approaches to the problem of energy have their strong proponents, and the nation's response to the problem continued to be the subject of national debate.

10.4.3 Transportation-User Reactions

The 1973–1974 oil embargo found the nation's transportation system ill prepared, and long queues at gasoline stations became commonplace. According to subsequent reviews of the major events that occurred during the period of low fuel supplies, the general reaction of highway users was to curtail automobile usage by about 20%, mainly by reducing recreational and nonessential trips [10.20]. Localized differences not withstanding, modal shifts to transit on a national scale were minimal during the emergency. This has been attributed to a lack of adequate transit capacity and to uncertainties about the the expected duration of the emergency situation. However, a trend toward the use of more efficient motor vehicles and other transportation equipment became evident. In this connection, the 1975 Energy Policy and Conservation Act prescribed a time schedule for fuel economy improvements and required the sales-weighted average fuel economy of each domestic manufacturer to adhere to this schedule.

Other transportation-intensive sectors of the economy responded similarly to the fact that an increasing share of their operating costs were attributed to fuel costs. For example, Johnson and Saricks [10.21] report that most intercity freight carriers began to convert to more fuel-efficient equipment and devices through replacement and retrofit programs and to modify their maintenance and scheduling practices. Similarly, Horn [10.22] reports that the airline industry also moved toward the purchase of fuel-efficient aircraft, implemented new operational and maintenance practices, and reduced cruise speeds. In 1974, the airlines dropped a few thousand daily flights in order to increase passenger-load factors and thus minimize their consumption of fuel. Highway- and transit-operating agencies also took measures to improve their own consumption rates. Among the actions taken by highway agencies was a conversion to fuel-efficient highway-lighting systems.

10.4.4. Energy-Related Transportation Actions

The predominant view of the energy problem among transportation-planning agencies at the local, state, and federal levels was driven by the possibility of petroleum-supply interruptions, and the secret to the solution of the energy problem was understood to lie in emergency preparedness and in conservation. This view is reflected in the requirement of the 1979 Emergency Energy Conservation Act of Transportation Energy Contingency Plans [10.23, 10.24] and in proposed rules issued by the DOT in 1980, which required that energy conservation be considered in transportation-planning programs receiving federal support. Possible energy-conservation strategies may be classified into those that are aimed to cause:

1. Technological innovations
2. Improvements in traffic flow
3. Reductions in the total vehicle miles of travel (VMT).

Technological innovations include improvements in the fuel efficiency of in-use technology. By converting to more fuel-efficient vehicles, highway users were able to sustain their trip-making levels while expending less, although more-expensive, fuel. An interesting side effect of this development has been its impact on the revenues of agencies responsible for the construction, operation, and maintenance of highway facilities, because the source of funding for these activities had been primarily in the form of user charges, mainly gasoline taxes levied on a per gallon basis. Another development in relation to technological innovation was an accelerated level of often federally sponsored research and development in the areas of new engines and toward the utilization of alternate transportation fuels. Examples of new engine types include various external combustion engines such as the Stirling and the Rankine engines, continuous-combustion turbine devices, and various configurations of electric and hybrid electric vehicles. Fuels that have been proposed as replacements for conventionally derived petroleum products in existing and new engine designs include gasoline and distillates (diesel fuel), which can be derived from coal and shale, alcohol fuels such as methanol and fuel blends, hydrogen, and electricity, which can be derived from various sources.

Highway level of service and the search for traffic-flow improvements have always been matters of direct concern to transportation engineers. In addition, the effect of highway design and maintenance (e.g., grades, curvature, and pavement condition) on fuel-consumption rates had traditionally been included in the calculation of motor-vehicle operating costs [10.25]. It was, therefore, natural that the inclusion of fuel-consumption considerations in the evaluation of highway designs and congestion-reducing schemes would be given new emphasis in view of the evolution of the global energy situation. A sampling of related investigations includes the use of freeway shoulders as low-cost traffic lanes to improve traffic flow, allowing right turns on red to reduce idling times, providing left turn lanes at signalized and unsignalized intersections, improving arterial access, and implementing signal systems. The energy effects of other strategies such as the spreading of the peak-period demand for highway travel through the implementation of staggered work schedules and other transportation system management (TSM) actions have also been addressed.

Strategies aimed at reducing the vehicle-miles traveled represent a departure from the other two categories of actions in that they require significant changes in the public's travel habits. Ways to reduce the VMT range from policies that encourage high vehicle occupancies to urban-planning processes that emphasize the joint development of transportation and land-use to minimize the need for travel without adversely affecting the accessibility of the population to activities.

10.4.5 Vehicle-Propulsion Energy

The propulsion energy expended by individual vehicles is typically reported either in terms of *energy economy rates* (i.e., distance traveled per unit energy) or in terms of its reciprocal, that is, the *energy consumption rate*. The energy measure is usually specified either in terms of the amount of a particular fuel or, when applicable, in terms of electrical energy. Thus the energy economy of passenger cars is specified as gallons of gasoline per vehicle mile and for electrically propelled transit vehicles, as kilowatt-hours per vehicle mile. In order to be able to compare the energy efficiency of vehicles using different types of fuel, several analysts resort to the conversion of energy requirements to a common unit such as the British thermal unit (Btu) or the joule. Comparisons based on such conversions, of course, are not sensitive to the particular source of the energy used (i.e., crude oil, coal, or nuclear energy), which have certain important policy implications.

A considerable body of research exists relative to the propulsion efficiency of highway vehicles and the factors that influence it. Among these factors are vehicular characteristics (e.g., vehicle type, weight, age, and engine displacement), highway geometrics and condition (e.g., grades, curvature, and pavement maintenance), and traffic-flow conditions (i.e., free-flow to jammed). Figure 10.4.1 illustrates the general shape of the relationship between sustained uniform speed and fuel consumption for highway vehicles. This figure shows that the minimum fuel-consumption for highway vehicles. This figure shows that the minimum fuel-consumption rate corresponds to a uniform speed of about 35 mi/h, depending on vehicle type and the other factors just mentioned. Fuel-consumption curves similar to Fig. 10.4.1 are available in the technical literature for different types of

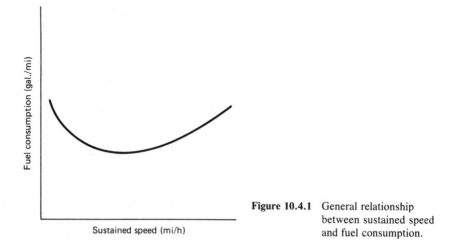

Figure 10.4.1 General relationship between sustained speed and fuel consumption.

vehicles, including passenger cars, light and heavy trucks, buses, and composite vehicles reflecting various vehicle combinations [10.26].

Regarding the propulsion efficiency of nonhighway transit vehicles and systems, it suffices to state that a great variability is found, depending on the type of system, its propulsion technology, and geometric characteristics, including station spacing and gradients.

To calculate the propulsion-energy requirements for a transportation network, estimates of the vehicle mixes and traffic-flow conditions are required, which, in a planning context, may be provided by transportation demand-forecasting model systems such as those described in Chapters 8 and 9 [10.27]. Observed before and after traffic-flow conditions may also be used to assess the energy effects of various short-term policies. Vehicular volumes can then be translated to fuel consumption by the use of appropriately calibrated fuel relationships.

In the case of travel on urban arterials, the traffic-flow characteristics involve interruptions by the control system and flow variations due to factors that are internal to traffic streams. The General Motors Research Laboratory [10.28] has calibrated a model relating consumption to travel time for various types of vehicles and vehicle mixes in urban arterial driving conditions. The following linear relationship was found to apply for average arterial system speeds of up to 35 mi/h.

$$f = k_1 + k_2 t \tag{10.4.1}$$

where

f = fuel-consumption rate (e.g., gallons per mile)

t = travel time (e.g., hours per mile)

k_1 = calibration constant, in gal/veh-mi

k_2 = calibration constant, in gal/h

Equation 10.4.1 may be rewritten in terms of average speed as

$$f = k_1 + \frac{k_2}{u} u < 35 \text{ mi/h} \tag{10.4.2}$$

which has a shape similar to Fig. 10.4.1 but is actually calibrated for the average speed over an urban-trip cycle rather than for sustained uniform speeds.

To calculate the fuel consumption F for a single vehicular trip in urban traffic, Eq. 10.4.1 is multiplied by the length of the trip D to yield

$$F = k_1 D + k_2 T \tag{10.4.3}$$

where T is the travel time for the entire trip.

Figure 10.4.2 represents General Motors' (GM) calibrated relationship for a typical passenger car mix consisting of 1973 to 1976 car models [10.6] with calibration constants $k_1 = 0.0362$ gal/veh-mi and $k_2 = 0.746$ gal/h. A similar relationship relating to diesel engine tractor-trailers with gross vehicle weights (GVW) of 33,000 lb and over is illustrated by Fig. 10.4.3. Finally, Fig. 10.4.4 shows the fuel-consumption rates of city buses in reference to the number of stops per mile rather than to the average trip speed. The number of stops per mile u ed to enter the graph includes scheduled stops, stops that are caused by the traffic-flow conditions, and interruptions due to the control system.

Example 10.5

During the typical 1976 weekday peak period, 4000 passenger cars traveled from a suburb to the CBD along a 6-mi arterial route at an average speed of 18 mi/h. One of the lanes on the route was subsequently reserved for car pools. This action resulted in a mild reduction in the peak period vehicle trips. A postimplementation count showed that the special lane was used by 1000 vehicles (which included previous and new carpoolers) at an improved speed of 24 mi/h. However, 2800 vehicles used the regular lanes, and this caused a speed reduction to 12 mi/h for this component. Calculate the fuel consumed during the peak period (a) prior to and (b) subsequent to the opening of the carpool lane.

Solution   (a) Prior to the project, the fuel consumption of the average vehicle over the 6 mi route was, according to Eq. 10.4.3 and the GM calibration constants,

$$F = (0.0362)(6) + \frac{0.746}{3} = 0.466 \text{ gal/veh}$$

A total of 4000 vehicles traversed the route during the peak period. Hence the total fuel consumption was

$$(4000)(0.466) = 1864 \text{ gal per peak period}$$

(b) Following the opening of the carpool lane, the flow was segregated into regular lane traffic, and carpool lane traffic. Applying Eq. 10.4.3 twice and summing the results, the total consumption became

$$(2800)(0.590) + (1000)(0.0404) = 2066 \text{ gal/peak}$$

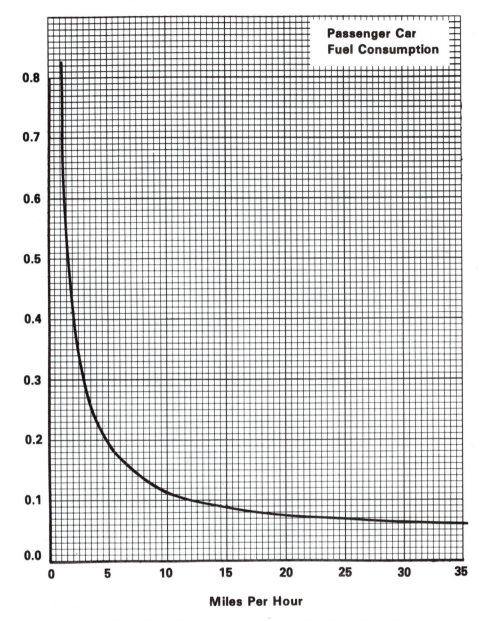

Figure 10.4.2   Passenger-car fuel consumption. (From Raus [10.6].)

Discussion   The peak-period propulsive fuel consumption on an arterial route was calculated for two operational strategies. In this particular case, the fuel consumption following the opening of a carpool lane increased even though the vehicle-miles traveled during the peak actually decreased from 24,000 (i.e., 4000 veh × 6 mi) to

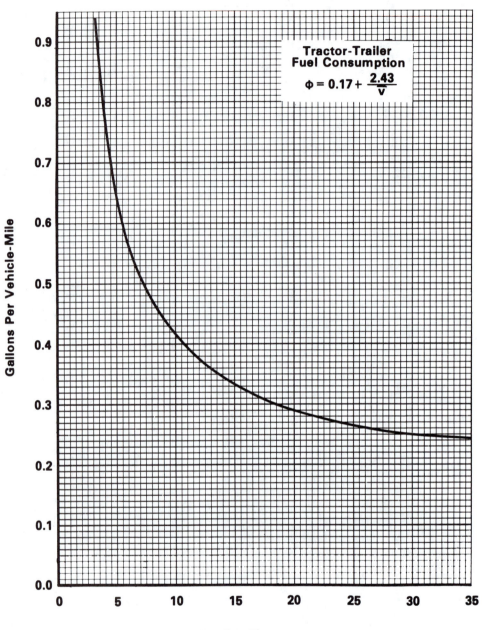

Figure 10.4.3 Tractor–trailer fuel consumption. (From Raus [10.6].)

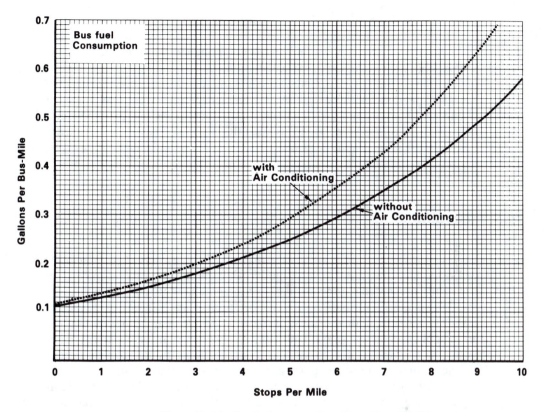

Figure 10.4.4   Bus fuel consumption. (From Raus [10.6].)

22,800. This was due to the resulting traffic-flow conditions given in the problem and should not be considered as the inevitable result of all carpool-lane situations. The route fuel consumption for each case may be reported in terms of the aggregate economy rate (AER) by dividing the total vehicle-miles by the total fuel consumption. Thus the AER for the pre- and the post-carpool-lane situations was, respectively, 12.9 and 11.0 veh-mil/gal. The conclusion reached by comparing these two rates is identical to that drawn on the basis of the fuel consumption alone. However, neither of these two vehicle-mile-based measures provides definite information about the number of passenger-miles accommodated by the two alternatives, which may be an important policy question.

10.4.6 Indirect Energy Consumption

The foregoing discussion has concentrated on the propulsive, or direct, energy consumption of transportation systems. A complete accounting of the energy requirements of transportation systems, on the other hand, also includes indirect energy expenditures, consisting of construction, maintenance, and operational energy expenditures. Several analysts have attempted to estimate the total (i.e., direct *and* indirect) energy needs of various modes and systems. It suffices to state that these estimates depend on the components of indirect energy that each analyst chose for inclusion in the calculation. Any attempt to trace the full energy implications of transportation systems is ultimately difficult, as it may include the energy expended for the extraction, refinement, conversion, and transportation of energy resources and fuels and even items such as the energy imbedded in the manufacturer of the vehicles. Consequently, a detailed review of total transportation energy studies and their energy policy and economic implications is beyond the scope of this book.

10.5 SUMMARY

This chapter discussed the air quality, noise, and energy impacts of transportation, described and illustrated several models that can be used to estimate these impacts, and presented strategies that have the potential of addressing these issues.

The major contribution of transportation to air pollution is in the form of carbon monoxide, hydrocarbons, nitrogen oxides, lead and other particulate matter, and photochemical smog. The degree of this contribution depends on emission levels, which are related to vehicle technology, traffic-flow levels, and traffic characteristics, and on the subsequent processes of mixing, diffusion, and chemical oxidation. A method developed by Raus of the FHWA for calculating the emission rates on highway facilities and a simple mathematical pollutant diffusion model (the box model) were described.

Noise was defined as undesirable or unwanted sound and was related to physical and mental health problems. It is typically measured in terms of A-weighted decibel levels on a logarithmic scale that simulates human responses. The intensity of noise decreases with distance from the source because of spreading and absorption energy losses and is also intercepted and reflected by solid objects. These attributes of noise suggest mitigation strategies that include the placement of noise barriers and buffer zones between the source and the receiver in addition to vehicle related and other actions. The simplest of several noise-estimation models was included. This model applies to long, straight segments of highways in the absence of noise barriers.

A significant portion of the national consumption of energy, particularly petroleum-based, is expended for transportation purposes. A recognition of the ultimate depletion of crude oil and international developments involving oil producing countries have brought this issue into sharp focus. The problem elicited differing reactions from several perspectives, including the users of transportation fuels, the highway- and transit-operating agencies, the transportation-planning organizations, and the regional and national energy policy analysts. A method for estimating the propulsive energy requirements of transportation systems was included.

Suggested actions that have important implications with respect to all three impacts covered in this chapter were classified into those that aim at the technological performance of vehicles, those that are concerned with geometric design and traffic flow operations, those that encourage significant changes in travel behavior, particularly modal choice, and those that propose alternative urban structural forms.

10.6 EXERCISES

1. The one-directional speed–concentration relationship for a 10-mi-long segment of a two-lane rural highway is

$$u = 45.0 - 0.3k$$

   Apply the Raus model to estimate the total emissions of carbon monoxide assuming that the highway operates at capacity for an entire hour. The ambient temperature at the low-altitude highway is 40°F.

2. A proposed increase of parking fees in a downtown area is expected to cause a reduction in the one-directional peak-hour flow of a radial six-lane highway from 5100 veh/h to 4200 veh/h. Given that the flow–concentration relationship for each highway lane is

$$q = 42.0k - 0.25k^2 \text{ mi/h per lane}$$

   estimate the effect that the parking policy would have on the emission of carbon monoxide during the peak hour. Assume that the flow is distributed equally among the three lanes of traffic, the ambient temperature is 0°F, and the highway was originally operating at level of service F.

3. The pollutant emission rate E has been estimated to change with respect to time as

$$E = Ae^{-Bt}$$

   where A and B are constants. Assuming a constant air flow F and a box volume V, apply the box model to express the pollutant concentration as a function of time. The initial concentration in the box at time $t = 0$ is K.

4. Repeat Exercise 3 assuming that the emission rate is given by

$$E = A(1 - e^{-Bt})$$

5. The air-pollution emission rate E in a parking lot may be approximated by step function shown in Fig. E10.5. Assuming a constant airflow F and zero initial pollutant concentration, plot the C as a function of time.

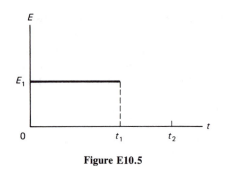

Figure E10.5

6. At a given location, the measured noise level during 15 consecutive time intervals was

   80, 75, 76, 75, 71, 72, 72, 73, 74, 76, 75, 72, 74, 73, 72

   dB. Use this limited set of data to (a) approximate the cumulative distribution of noise level, (b) estimate the L_{10}, L_{50}, and L_{90} levels, and (c) calculate the L_{eq} noise level.

7. Bicyclists A and B rode along the bikeways shown at 15 and 20 mi/h, respectively. Bicyclist A encountered 180 vehicles during his 1.2-mi ride against traffic, and bicyclist B was overtaken by 30 more vehicles than she overtook during her 1.2-mi ride with traffic (see Fig. E10.7). Assuming that the traffic stream consisted of passenger cars only, calculate the L_{10} noise level to which each of the bicyclists was exposed.

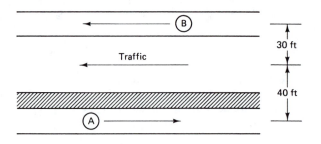

Figure E10.7

8. The traffic flows on each of the two lanes of a highway are shown in Fig. E10.8. Calculate the L_{10} noise level at point P.

9. Apply Eq. 10.3.2 to calculate the combined effect of the following four decibel levels:

   71, 77, 72, and 73.

10. Combine the four noise levels given in Exercise 9 by means of the insert to Fig. 10.3.5.

11. The combined noise level from two sources is 68.5 dBA. The noisier of the two sources produces a noise level of 68.0 dBA. Estimate mathematically the level produced by the other source.

Figure E10.8

12. The flow on a highway consists of 100 heavy trucks per hour traveling at 50 mi/h, 30 medium trucks per hour traveling at 40 mi/h, and 600 passenger cars per hour traveling at 50 mi/h. Assuming a highway width of 50 ft, specify the width of a buffer zone that ensures that the noise level in an adjacent park will not exceed the 1973 FHWA standard.

13. How close to the highway of Exercise 12 can a single-glazed masonry school building be located and still meet the FHWA noise standard?

14. The flow–concentration relationship for a roadway is

$$q = 60.0k - 4.0k^{1.5} \text{ veh/h}$$

Using the GM model, derive and plot the fuel consumption rate f as a function of traffic stream concentration (veh/mi). Assume that the traffic stream consists of passenger cars only.

15. Find the fuel consumption rate corresponding to q_{max} for the roadway of Exercise 14.

16. A bus line operates in mixed traffic and carries 4000 passengers per peak hour at an average speed of 10 mi/h. Typically, each bus makes two scheduled stops per mile and is interrupted by the traffic control system and by other vehicles six times per mile. Given an average occupancy of 50 persons per bus and a 5-mi trip, calculate the number of buses needed to serve the passenger demand and the total amount of fuel consumed during a typical peak hour.

17. Calculate the effect on the fleet size and the fuel consumption of the bus system of Exercise 16 assuming that an exclusive bus lane were to be implemented. The resulting conditions include a reduction of nonscheduled stops from six to two, and an average speed of 15 mi/h.

10.7 REFERENCES

10.1 PERKINS, H. C., *Air Pollution*, McGraw-Hill, New York, 1974.

10.2 ENVIRONMENTAL PROTECTION AGENCY, *Federal Register*, 36, 84 (Friday, Apr. 30, 1971).

10.3 ——, *Compilation of Air Pollution Emission Factors*, Publication AP-42, Office of Air Quality Planning and Standards, Research Triangle Park, N.C., various annual revisions.

10.4 LEE, C. E., and LEE, F.-P., *Simulation of Traffic Performance, Vehicle Emissions, and Fuel Consumption at Intersections: The TEXAS-II Model*, Transportation Research Record 971, Transportation Research Board, National Research Council, Washington, D.C., 1984, pp. 133–140.

10.5 ENVIRONMENTAL PROTECTION AGENCY, *User's Guide to MOBILE I: Mobile Source Emissions Model*, Office of Air, Noise, and Radiation, EPA, Washington, D.C., 1978.

10.6 RAUS, J., *A Method for Estimating Fuel Consumption and Vehicle Emissions on Urban Arterials and Networks*, Report FHWA-TS-81-210, Office of Research and Development, Federal Highway Administration, Washington, D.C., 1981.

10.7 ZIMMERMAN, J. R., and R. S. THOMPSON, *User's Guide for HIWAY, A Highway Air Pollution Model*, Office of Research and Development, U.S. Environmental Protection Agency, Research Triangle Park, N.C., 1975.

10.8 TURNER, B.D., *Workbook on Atmospheric Dispersion Estimates*, U.S. Environmental Protection Agency, Research Triangle Park, N.C., 1970.

10.9 DEMERJIAN, K. L., *Oxidant Modeling Status*, Transportation Research Record 670, Transportation Research Board, National Research Council, Washington, D.C., 1978, pp. 1–6.

10.10 SEIFF, H. E., "Enforcement of Control of Interstate Motor Carrier Noise: A Federal Perspective," *Motor Vehicle Noise Control*, Special Report 152, Transportation Research Board, National Research Council, Washington, D.C., 1975, pp. 66–72.

10.11 FEDERAL HIGHWAY ADMINISTRATION, *Noise Standards and Procedures*, Policy and Procedure Memorandum, Transmittal 279, 90-2, FHWA, Washington, D.C., Feb. 8, 1973.

10.12 ENVIRONMENTAL PROTECTION AGENCY, *Noise and Its Measurement*, Office of Public Affairs, EPA, Washington, D.C., Feb. 1977.

10.13. BORTHWICK, J. O., "A Status Report on the Florida Motor Vehicle Noise Control Plan," *Motor Vehicle Noise Control*, Special Report 152, Transportation Research Board, National Research Council, Washington, D.C., 1975, pp. 85–93.

10.14. U.S. DEPARTMENT OF TRANSPORTATION, *Organization and Content of Environmental Assessment Materials*, Notebook 5, U.S. Government Printing Office, Stock No. 050-000-00109-1, Washington, D.C., 1975.

10.15. HALL, F. L. and B. L. ALLEN, *Toward a Community Impact Measure for Assessment of Transportation Noise*, Transportation Research Record 580, Transportation Research Board, National Research Council, Washington, D.C., 1976, pp. 22–35.

10.16. WESLER, J. E., *Introduction and History of Highway Noise Prediction Methods*, Transportation Research Circular 174, Transportation Research Board, National Research Council, Washington, D.C., 1975, pp. 9–13.

10.17 Wright Air Development Center, *Handbook of Acoustic Noise Control*, WADC Technical Report 52-204, 1952.

10.18 KUGLER, B. A., D. E. COMMINS, and W. J. GALLOWAY, *Highway Noise: A Design Guide for Prediction and Control*, National Cooperative Highway Research Program Report 174, Transportation Research Board, National Research Council, Washington, D.C., 1976.

10.19 U.S. FEDERAL ENERGY ADMINISTRATION, *Project Independence Report*, U.S. Government Printing Office, Stock No. 4118-000019, Washington, D.C., Nov. 1974.

10.20 CHESLOW, M. D., "Potential Use of Carpooling during Periods of Energy Shortages," *Considerations in Transportation Energy Contingency Planning*, Special Report 191, Transportation Research Board, National Research Council, Washington, D.C., 1980, pp. 38–43.

10.21 JOHNSON, L. R., and C. L. SARICKS, *An Evaluation of Options for Freight Carriers during a Fuel Crisis*, Transportation Research Record 935, National Research Council, Washington, D.C., 1983, pp. 5–11.

10.22 HORN, K. W., "Energy and the Airline Industry," *Considerations in Transportation Energy Contingency Planning*, Special Report 191, Transportation Research Board, National Research Council, Washington, D.C., 1980, pp. 69–70.

10.23 TRANSPORTATION RESEARCH BOARD, *Considerations in Transportation Energy Contingency Planning*, Special Report 191, National Research Council, Washington, D.C., 1980.

10.24 ———, *Proceedings of the Conference on Energy Contingency Planning in Urban Areas*, Special Report 203, National Research Council, Washington, D.C., 1983.

10.25 CURRY, D. A., and D. G. ANDERSON, *Procedures for Estimating Highway User Costs, Air Pollution, and Noise Effects*, National Cooperative Highway Research Program Report 133, Transportation Research Board, National Research Council, Washington, D.C., 1972.

10.26 CLAFFEY, P. J., *Running Costs of Motor Vehicles as Affected by Road Design and Traffic*, National Cooperative Highway Research Program Report 111, Transportation Research Board, National Research Council, Washington, D.C., 1971.

10.27 PAPACOSTAS, C. S., *Pollution and Energy Implications of Urban Bus-Automobile Alternatives*, Ph.D. dissertation, Carnegie-Mellon University, Pittsburg, Pa., 1974.

10.28 CHANG, M. F., et al., *The Influence of Vehicle Characteristics, Driver Behavior, and Ambient Temperature on Gasoline Consumption in Urban Areas*, General Motors Corporation, Warren, Mich., 1976.

11   Evaluation and Choice

11.1 *INTRODUCTION*

Even when presented a single proposal, decision makers have a choice between it and doing nothing. Therefore, every decision involves at least two options. *Evaluation* facilitates decision-making by appraising the merits (*positive impacts*) and demerits (*negative impacts*) of alternative options in terms of either a single or multiple decision criteria. Determining which impacts are relevant to a particular decision and specifying the appropriate decision criteria are related to the value system within which the choice is to be made. In the case of transportation decisions in the public sector, the operating value system is not that of any single individual or subgroup but that of the community as a whole. In the Introduction to this book and in Chapter 7 we recognized the existence of conflicting value systems within society. Consequently, transportation decision making also entails the resolution of conflicts.

Two types of evaluation studies are commonly undertaken: preimplementation studies, which facilitate the choice of the best course of action from among several alternative proposals, and postimplementation studies, which assess the performance of already implemented actions. Postimplementation studies are important for two reasons. First, they help to discover whether or not the implemented alternative performs well, and second, they help to determine whether or not it continues to perform properly over time. This is especially important in the case of transportation systems, which are subject to changing conditions and also to evolving goals and objectives. Continuous monitoring and periodic performance evaluation can help identify emerging problems and also provide guidance to the design of possible improvements.

To be selected for implementation, an alternative must be both feasible *and* superior to all other alternatives. The prerequisites to the admission of an alternative to the list of acceptable options include the conditions of technological feasibility, economic efficiency, and cost-effectiveness, and availability of the needed resources. In this chapter we present the fundamental elements of efficiency and effectiveness evaluation techniques, along with a brief description of their conceptual foundations and their major strengths and weaknesses.

11.2 FEASIBILITY AND IMPACT ENUMERATION

11.2.1 Measures of Feasibility

Technological feasibility refers to the ability of a system to function according to the laws of nature and not to its desirability: A perpetual-motion machine may be highly desirable but technologically impossible. Engineers and other technologists are qualified to deal with questions relating to technology. Research and development are on-going activities that occasionally lead to technological breakthroughs. The vast majority of practical applications, however, involve the use of existing technology. Even then, innovative and creative ways of combining off-the-shelf technology are common. Consequently, the question of technological feasibility is an aspect of evaluation that cannot be ignored.

Efficiency is defined as the ratio of the quantity produced (*output*) to the resources required for its production (*input*). *Physical* or *machine efficiency* is the ratio of the energy delivered by a machine or a process to the energy supplied to it. Although expressed in the same unit of measurement, the input and the output energy differ in form, for example, energy in the form of electricity vis-à-vis energy in the form of work done by the system. Machine efficiency is always less than unity because of the unavoidable energy losses that are incurred in the process. This waste can be justified only when the usefulness, or utility, of the output exceeds that of the input. When both the numerator and the denominator are converted to the same measure of economic value, their ratio is referred to as the *economic efficiency* of the machine, which must be greater than unity if the machine is to be economically feasible. The idea of economic efficiency has been extended to the evaluation of systems to contrast the economic value of the advantages (or benefits) that are derived from the system to its disadvantages (or costs).

Effectiveness is defined as the degree to which an action accomplishes its stated objectives. It differs from efficiency in that it need not have to explicitly express all impacts in the same scale of measurement. For example, the effectiveness of a regional transportation system for elderly and handicapped persons may be expressed as the proportion of eligible users that live within the service area of the system or as the total number of persons served, whereas its operating costs may be expressed in terms of dollars. *Cost-effectiveness* evaluation is the attempt to determine the efficacy of alternatives by comparing their cost to their effectiveness. Of course, if an objective method for collapsing all impacts to the same dimension were available, efficiency and effectiveness would lead to identical results, but no such method exists. Consequently, both evaluative methods are used, sometimes separately and sometimes in combination [11.1, 11.2].

An alternative may be technologically feasible, economically efficient, and cost-effective and yet not be a prudent choice for implementation because of the unavailability of the financial and other resources that are needed for its implementation. Problems of affordability or resource availability are not uncommon. Consider, for example, the case of financial resources. Usually, there exists a lag between the time when financial resources are expended and the time when the returns of the investment are realized. Lack of access to financial resources during this critical time lag would render the investment infeasible. Another common problem of financial affordability that is especially true in the case of public projects is related to the fact that the benefits derived by a public investment do not usually return in the form of money to the agency that expends the financial costs for the project. Unless the agency is in a position to afford these expenditures, it would not be able to produce the benefits for whomever they would otherwise accrue.

11.2.2 Impact Trade-Offs

Determining the feasibility of each alternative is only half of the evaluation process. The other half involves the comparison of all proposals (including the do-nothing alternative) in order to select the best one among them. Based on the assignment of relative weights to the impacts of each alternative, this step involves *impact trade-offs*. Consider, for example, a choice between two transportation alternatives requiring equal and available financial expenditures. Further, assume that one of the two would provide a higher level of mobility than the other but would also discharge higher quantities of atmospheric pollutants. This statement implies that three impacts have been identified as relevant to the choice, that appropriate measures of performance have been established to express them, and that the likely levels of these impacts have been predicted for each alternative, perhaps using the methods of Chapter 8 through 10. When comparing the two alternatives, a trade-off between mobility on one hand and environmental quality on the other becomes apparent. In the final analysis, the evaluation method used to aid this decision must incorporate the assignment of relative weights to the impacts.

11.2.3 Generalized Impact Matrices

The foregoing example of evaluation raises a problem that is inherent in situations where the decision makers are faced with multiple decision criteria. On the side of costs, the direct cost of operating the system and a *negative externality* (i.e., the unintended undesirable impact of air pollution) were identified. Direct benefits (e.g., mobility) and potential *positive externalities* are typically included in the evaluative calculus. All recognizable impacts, whether intended or concomitant, can be classed into positive impacts (i.e., advantages or benefits) and negative impacts (i.e., disadvantages or costs) and the results of the impact estimation process that precedes the evaluation phase (see Chapters 8, 9, and 10) may be summarized in an *impact matrix*, as illustrated by Fig. 11.2.1.

Impact category	$ costs		Mobility		Environmental quality			Social
Measures of performance	Capital	O & M	Travel time	Travel cost	Air	Noise	· · ·	· · ·
Do nothing								
Alternative A								
Alternative B								
⋮								

Figure 11.2.1 Generalized impact matrix.

This array lists the estimated impacts associated with each alternative expressed in terms of the applicable measures of performance, which differ with regard to their units of measurement. Moreover, some are expressed in terms of quantitative measures (i.e., carbon monoxide concentration), and others are qualitative.

Table 11.2.1 lists the impacts that were considered in the EIS for a proposed Honolulu Area Rapid Transit (HART) System [11.3]. The first column summarizes the goals and objectives set forth in the regional general plan for the island of Oahu, where the city of Honolulu is located. The second column presents the specific goals identified by an earlier Oahu transportation study. Following are the objectives established by two previous Preliminary Engineering Evaluation Program studies of transit alternatives (PEEP I and II). The fourth column lists the criteria that were selected to measure the performance of alternative systems. Also noted is the potential applicability of these criteria to three characteristics of alternative proposals, that is, route location, transit system type, and system length. The rapid transit alternatives are augmented by feeder bus services.

Table 11.2.2 summarizes the analytical results obtained by applying the se-

TABLE 11.2.1 EXAMPLE OF GOALS, OBJECTIVES, AND CRITERIA

Transportation goals Oahu general plan	Transportation goals Oahu transportation study	Transit development objectives PEEP I and II	Transit development criteria for alternatives analysis	Applicable criteria for specific alternative analysis		
				Route location	System type	System length
1. Provide transportation facilities to enable travel from any point in the region to any other point within reasonable travel time by one or more modes	1. [a]Provide transportation facilities for ease of movement throughout Oahu; and provide a variety of modes of travel which will best serve the different requirements of the community	1. *Improve accessibility by service and interconnecting existing and future urbanized areas of Oahu*	a. Availability & coverage	—	✓	✓
			b. Average trip time	✓	✓	✓
			c. Service reliability	—	✓	✓
			d. Rider convenience	✓	✓	✓
			e. Rider comfort	✓	✓	
2. A transportation system which will provide the greatest efficiency and service to the community with the least overall expenditure of resources	2. Provide a balanced transportation system which will result in optimum service with the least public expenditure	2. [a]*Provide a balanced transportation system of transit and highways*	a. System patronage	✓	✓	✓
			b. System capacity	✓	✓	✓
		3. [a]*Minimize expenditure of resources and disruption to community*	a. Consumption of land	—	✓	✓
			b. Displacement of residents	✓	✓	✓
			c. Displacement of businesses	✓	✓	✓
			d. Reduction of comm. amenities	✓	✓	✓
			e. Disruption to future dvlpmt.	✓	✓	✓
			f. Disruption to local circulation	✓	✓	✓
			g. Disruption—constr. activity	—	✓	✓
			h. Savings in energy	—		✓
			i. Technical risk	—		✓

(continued)

509

TABLE 11.2.1 (Continued)

Transportation goals Oahu general plan	Transportation goals Oahu transportation study	Transit development objectives PEEP I and II	Transit development criteria for alternatives analysis	Route location	System type	System length
3. A transportation system to be designed as an integral part of and complementary to land use policies	3. Integration of the transportation system with land use	4. *Support land use and development policies*	a. Support regional development	✓	✓	✓
			b. Support comm. development	✓	✓	✓
4. Preserve and maintain significant historic sites, scenery and natural assets of Oahu	4. Preserve Oahu's beauty and amenities	5. *Preserve environment*	a. Reduction air pollution	✓	✓	✓
			b. Noise level	✓	✓	✓
			c. Visual intrusion	✓	✓	✓
			d. Vistas	✓	✓	✓
			e. Historic sites	✓	✓	✓
5. Safety	5. Safety	6. *Safety*	a. Reduce accident exposure	—	✓	✓
			b. Security	—	✓	✓
6. bProvide a transportation system which will provide the greatest efficiency and service to the community with the least overall cost	6. bProvide a balanced transportation system which will result in optimum service at the least cost to the public	7. *Provide the most economical system which best meets all other objectives*	a. Total annual cost	✓	✓	✓
			b. Cost per trip	—	✓	✓
			c. Benefit-cost ratio	—	✓	—
aStated as one of the general goals; bStated separately from 2 to differentiate between expenditure of resources and least cost	aCombines Goals 1 & 3 of OTS; bStated separately from 2 to differentiate between expenditure of resources and least cost	aGoal 2 stated as two separate objectives				

Source: Urban Mass Transportation Administration [11.3].

TABLE 11.2.2 EXAMPLE SUMMARY OF ANALYTICAL RESULTS

System	Travel characteristics						Operating characteristics				Cost[a]	
	Total Daily Transit Trips	Mode Split (Total) %	Daily Trips on Gwy.	% Pk. Hr. Work Trips By Transit	Avg. Trip Length (Mi.)	Avg. Trip Time (Min.)	Vehicles required (with spares) Gwy.	Feeder	Vehicle Miles Operated Daily Gwy.	Feeder	Total Capital Cost ($1,000)	Annual Operating Cost ($1,000)
7-mi busway	456,250	13.8	288,200	42.4	7.31	36.3	179	752	30,308	121,408	414,411	49,510
LRT												
28 mi	474,520	14.4	358,750	44.6	7.22	32.4	410	443	79,515	71,645	712,289	47,660
23 mi	474,520	14.4	353,700	44.6	7.21	32.3	325	477	75,530	75,910	646,537	46,320
14 mi	473,300	14.3	306,900	44.2	7.26	33.7	198	580	45,840	94,260	529,321	44,310
7 mi	459,300	13.9	277,300	42.8	7.19	35.2	109	774	23,580	124,605	406,808	50,170
Fixed guideway												
23 mi	490,000	14.8	332,600	46.0	7.50	31.6	421	493	111,495	78,390	647,900	46,940
14 mi	473,300	14.3	306,900	44.2	7.26	33.7	264	580	64,225	94,260	517,318	43,890
7 mi	459,300	13.9	277,300	42.8	7.19	35.2	161	774	34,335	124,605	398,676	50,070

[a] All costs shown are in 1975 dollars.

Source: Urban Mass Transportation Administration [11.3].

TABLE 11.2.3 EXAMPLE OF COMPARISON MATRIX FOR ALTERNATIVE SYSTEMS

	Busway	Short 7-mi length		Medium 14-mi length		Long 23- and 28-mi lengths		
		LRT	Fixed guideway	LRT	Fixed guide.	23-mi LRT	28-mi LRT	23-mi F.G.
Objective 1								
a. Availability & coverage	Same	Same	Same	Same	Same	Same	Same	Same
b. Avg. trip time (min.)	36.3	35.2	35.2	33.7	33.7	32.3	32.4	31.6
c. Service reliability	(2)[a]	(1)	(1)	Same	Same	(2)	(2)	(1)
d. Rider convenience	(1)	(2)	(2)	Same	Same	(2)	(1)	(2)
e. Rider comfort	(2)	(1)	(1)	Same	Same	Same	Same	Same
Objective 2								
a. System patronage (million)	137.8	138.7	138.7	142.9	142.9	143.3	143.3	148.0
b. System capacity	*[b]	Same	Same	Same	Same	Same	Same	Same
Objective 3								
a. Consumption of land (acres)	42	21	20	23	22	36	36	32
b. Displacement of residents (units)	233	152	148	166	162	179	179	167
c. Displacement of businesses (units)	257	168	164	187	183	194	194	184
d. Reduction of community amenities	Same	Same	Same	Same	Same	Same	Same	Same
e. Disruption to future dvlpmt.	Same	Same	Same	Same	Same	Same	Same	Same
f. Disruption to local circulation	Same	Same	Same	Same	Same	(2)	(3)	(1)
g. Disruption from constr. activities	Same	Same	Same	Same	Same	(1)	(2)	(1)

	10.0	8.5	8.9	8.5	9.4	5.0	4.8	8.5
h. Savings in energy (million gal/yr.)	10.0	8.5	8.9	8.5	9.4	5.0	4.8	8.5
i. Technical risk	(3)	(1)	(2)	(1)	(2)	(1)	(1)	(2)
Objective 4								
a. Support regional dvlpmt.	Same	Same	Same	Same	Same	Same	Same	Same
b. Support comm. dvlpmt.	Same	Same	Same	Same	Same	Same	Same	Same
Objective 5								
a. Reduction Air pollution (tons/yr.)	2,970	3,240	3,260	4,110	4,150	4,120	4,140	4,930
b. Noise level (dBA)	86–88	77–81	77	77–81	77	77–81	77–81	77
c. Visual intrusion	(3)	(2)	(1)	(2)	(1)	(2)	(2)	(1)
d. Vistas	(2)	(3)	(1)	(2)	(1)	(1)	(1)	(2)
e. Historic sites	Same	Same	Same	Same	Same	Same	Same	Same
Objective 6								
a. Reduce accident exposure	Same	Same	Same	Same	Same	Same	Same	Same
b. Security	Same	Same	Same	Same	Same	Same	Same	Same

Objective 7[c]

	Interest Rates	4%	10%
a. Total annual cost ($ million)	10.0	77.43	96.90
	8.5	76.98	96.17
	8.9	76.41	95.21
	8.5	77.38	102.60
	9.4	76.26	101.01
	5.0	85.73	116.66
	4.8	90.73	124.84
	8.5	86.51	117.48
b. Cost per trip	10.0	56.2¢	70.3¢
	8.5	55.5¢	69.3¢
	8.9	55.1¢	68.6¢
	8.5	54.1¢	71.8¢
	9.4	53.4¢	70.7¢
	5.0	59.8¢	81.4¢
	4.8	63.3¢	87.1¢
	8.5	58.5¢	78.4¢
c. Benefit-cost ratio	10.0	2.24	1.50
	8.5	2.28	1.55
	8.9	2.31	1.58
	8.5	2.40	1.47
	9.4	2.47	1.51
	5.0	2.06	1.24
	4.8	1.87	1.13
	8.5	2.19	1.32

[a] Numbers in parentheses show ranking of alternatives based on how well they met the objective.

[b] Practical capacity for busways is unknown and assumed to be less than for guided systems.

[c] All costs shown are in 1975 dollars.

Source: Urban Mass Transportation Administration [11.3].

quential transportation demand-forecasting process described in Chapter 8. This table includes only direct impacts.

Table 11.2.3 is the generalized impact matrix developed in connection with the HART EIS. It includes the direct and indirect impacts of each alternative either in quantitative terms or qualitatively.

11.3 ENGINEERING ECONOMIC ANALYSIS

11.3.1 Introduction

Traditional engineering economic analysis is based on the principle that the quantified impacts of alternatives should and can be converted to their monetary equivalents and treated just as if they were money. With this conversion, the calculation of economic efficiency and the comparison of alternatives on the basis of their costs and benefits can be conducted. The basic unit of measurement employed (i.e., money) has certain attributes that must be retained in the calculation of benefits and costs. A fundamental characteristic of money is its time value. Simply stated, this says that "a dollar today is not the same as a dollar tomorrow." To illustrate this point, consider the situation where an amount of $100 is deposited in a bank at an interest rate of 10%. One year from the day of deposit, $110 may be withdrawn from the bank. In this case, $100 today is equivalent to $110 dollars a year from today. The *interest* or *discount* rate affects this equivalency.

11.3.2 Project Evaluation

Based on the axiom that the consequences that are relevant to the impending decision can be equated with money, each alternative may be considered to consist of two cash flows: a cash flow of benefits and a cash flow of costs, both shown as money equivalents at the times when they are expected to occur (Fig. 11.3.1).

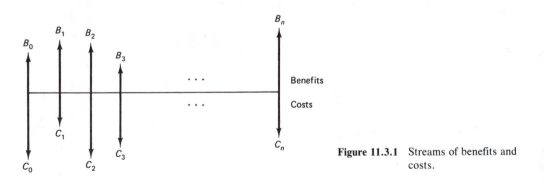

Figure 11.3.1 Streams of benefits and costs.

A proposed alternative is considered to be economically feasible when the benefits to be derived from it exceed its costs. This comparison between benefits and costs is legitimate only when the two cash flows are placed on the same time basis. Given an appropriate interest rate, the *present worth of benefits* (PWB) and the *present worth of costs* (PWC), or their equal series cash-flow equivalents, may be calculated. Appendix B develops the appropriate formulas that can be used for this task, which the reader may wish to review before continuing with the rest of this chapter.

The *net present worth* (NPW) of an alternative is defined as the present worth of its benefits minus the present worth of its costs. Hence a positive NPW implies economic feasibility. Another way of contrasting benefits and costs is the use of the *benefit-cost* (B/C) *ratio*, in which case the economic feasibility criterion requires a B/C ratio that is greater than unity. A third method of assessing the economic feasibility of an alternative is one that calculates the *internal rate of return* (IRR), which is defined as the interest rate that just equates benefits and costs, that is, the rate at which the NPW equals zero and the B/C ratio equals unity. This rate is then compared with a predetermined *minimum attractive rate of return* (MARR) reflecting managerial policy and profit expectations to assess whether the project is attractive or not.

11.3.3 Independent and Mutually Exclusive Alternatives

Before discussing the mechanics of economic evaluation of alternatives, it is appropriate to explain several principles that are explicitly or implicitly encompassed by the final choice. First, the set of alternatives being considered should include the do-nothing, or baseline, alternative. Second, pairs of alternatives can be either *independent* or *mutually exclusive*. Two alternatives are *independent* when the selection of one does not necessarily prohibit the selection of the other. For example, a state department of transportation may be contemplating the provision of subsidies to the bus systems of two different cities. Assuming that the necessary resources are available to the department, a decision to subsidize one city does not necessarily eliminate a favorable outcome for the other. By contrast, a pair of alternatives are said to be *mutually exclusive* if the choice of one renders the other impossible. A metropolitan transit authority engaged in the comparative evaluation of two technologically incompatible transit systems on a single alignment is faced with mutually exclusive alternatives. Third, the do-nothing alternative and each of the do-something alternatives are mutually exclusive. Fourth, the list of options under consideration includes all possible combinations of independent alternatives. For example, when two independent projects are being considered, the list of available options contains four entries: the do-nothing alternative, each of the two projects alone, and the two in combination. When viewed in this manner, the four options are actually mutually exclusive, as it is not possible to implement one project alone and both projects together at the same time. The problem of economic evaluation and project selection becomes one of discovering the alternative combination of feasible projects that maximizes the benefits to be derived from the expenditure of available resources.

Example 11.1

A regional planning organization is considering the following proposals: two mutually exclusive alignments for a highway in county A (projects A1 and A2), two mutually exclusive alignments for a highway in county B (projects B1 and B2), and a special transportation system for handicapped persons in city C. What is the number of available options?

Solution Considering that with regard to the first and second highways, three possibilities exist (that is, not building, selecting alternative 1, and selecting alternative 2) and that two choices are possible with regard to alternative C, the total number of proper combinations is $3 \times 3 \times 2 = 18$, as illustrated by Fig. 11.3.2. If any one

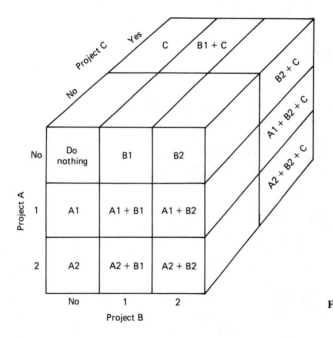

Figure 11.3.2 Alternative combinations of options.

of the projects is infeasible, the total number of options is reduced accordingly. If, for example, alternative A1 were judged to be infeasible, the total number of options would become $3 \times 2 \times 2 = 12$. Similarly, if project C were found to be infeasible, the remaining options would number $3 \times 3 \times 1 = 9$.

11.3.4 Evaluation of Mutually Exclusive Alternatives

Consider two mutually exclusive do-something alternatives with the following discounted benefits and costs expressed in millions of dollars.

Alternative	PWB	PWC	NPW	B/C
A	1.8	1.2	0.6	1.50
B	2.9	2.2	0.7	1.32

According to the NPW criterion, alternative B is superior to alternative A, but, according to the B/C criterion, alternative A is better than alternative B. This inconsistency between the two methods can be rectified by augmenting the B/C evaluation with an *incremental analysis*. To understand the rationale of incremental analysis, consider the simplified situation where the total $2.2 million is in hand and no other investment option is possible; that is, the available amount of money could either be expended in one of the two projects or placed in a safe deposit box, where it would earn no interest. Under these assumptions, the *overall* investment strategies associated with each of the two alternatives are (1) to invest $1.2 of the $2.2 million in the less costly alternative A, which will return $1.8 million in benefits, and place the remaining $1.0 million in the safe deposit box, which will return no additional benefits, and (2) to invest the entire $2.2 million in the more costly alternative, which will derive total benefits of $2.9 million. The present worth of the benefits resulting from the first strategy would equal $1.8 million plus $1.0 million, or $2.8 million, as compared to the $2.9 million associated with the more costly alternative. Hence, investing in the second option is the more prudent choice. Another way of stating the above is that the *incremental benefits* ($2.9 − $1.8 = $1.1 million) derived from the costlier alternative outweigh the *incremental costs* ($2.2 − $1.2 = $1.0 million) it entails, or that the *incremental B/C* ratio between the two options is greater than unity. Thus when both alternatives are feasible in themselves, the incremental B/C ratio and the NPW criteria lead to identical conclusions. The incremental ratio analysis of feasible options is conducted as follows: The feasible alternatives are listed according to increasing cost, with the least costly alternative at the top of the list. If the incremental ratio between the first two entries is greater than unity, the more costly alternative is selected; otherwise the less costly alternative is retained. The chosen alternative is then compared with the next list entry and the procedure continues until all alternatives have been considered and all but the best alternative have been eliminated.

Example 11.2

The benefits and costs associated with the following five mutually exclusive alternatives have been discounted to their present worth and the alternatives have been listed according to increasing cost. Apply the B/C ratio method to select the best option.

Alternative	PWC	PWB	B/C
A	100	150	1.50
B	150	190	1.27
C	200	270	1.35
D	300	290	0.97
E	320	350	1.09

Solution   After forming the B/C ratio, alternative D is found to be infeasible and therefore is dropped from further consideration. The incremental B/C between A and B is $(190 - 150)/(150 - 100) = 0.8$, and the costlier alternative B is dropped. The incremental ratio between A and the next feasible alternative in the list (i.e., C) is equal to $(270 - 150)/(200 - 100) = 1.2$ and C is favored over A. Finally, the comparison between C and E yields an incremental ratio of 0.67. Since this is less than unity, the less costly alternative C is retained as the best option.

Discussion   Alternative C has been selected even though alternative A has a larger individual B/C ratio. It can easily be shown that the NPW criterion leads to the selection of the same alternative. The incremental ratio analysis must be preceded by an individual ratio analysis to eliminate all infeasible alternatives. If the incremental ratio analysis were to be applied directly to a list that happened to contain only infeasible alternatives, it would result in the selection of the least infeasible without any indication that the selected option is, in fact, infeasible. Serious problems related to this point arise in situations where, for practical reasons, the benefits and costs of do-something alternatives are calculated relative to the do-nothing alternative. For example, travel time or fuel savings are often considered to be benefits associated with proposed highways as compared to the do-nothing alternative. In that case, the B/C analysis is an incremental analysis from the start. To illustrate this point consider the following simple example: The benefits and costs associated with an existing highway (do-nothing) and a proposed highway are:

Alternative	PWB	PWC
Existing	1.2	1.8
Proposed	1.9	2.4

Clearly, neither of the two is feasible. However, if the benefits and costs of the proposed highway were to be reported only in relation to the do-nothing alternative, the proposed project would have an appearance of feasibility and an incremental B/C ratio of 1.17. Moreover, the NPW of the relative benefits and costs would also be misleading. To avoid problems of this nature, ways of measuring benefits and costs in absolute rather than relative terms have been proposed. One such method is based on the *theory of consumer surplus* [11.4], but although conceptually attractive, these attempts are not without practical difficulties.

11.3.5 Identification and Valuation of Benefits and Costs

The conduct of economic evaluation procedures for the selection of the best alternative requires the conversion or valuation of quantified impacts to monetary terms. Impact valuation presents varying degrees of difficulty. Some impacts, such as construction and maintenance costs, are already expressed in monetary terms. The rest must be translated into monetary equivalents. As an illustration, Fig. 11.3.3 presents a family of curves suggested by a 1977 AASHTO Manual

Figure 11.3.3   Value of time saved by trip purpose. (From AASHTO [11.5].)

[11.5] for the conversion of travel time savings to dollars. These curves are based on extensive economic explorations into the matter and—unlike earlier versions, which assumed a linear relationship between time saved and dollar value irrespective of trip purpose—the 1977 version provides for a nonlinear relationship and for a sensitivity to trip purpose. A linear relationship at, say, $1.50 or $2.80 per hour saved would be highly inappropriate if millions of daily trips, each saving a few minutes, were to be simply added together. According to Fig. 11.3.3, such small time savings are insignificant individually. Other impacts of transportation projects (e.g., effect on rural lifestyles or aesthetics) are much more difficult to quantify, let alone express in dollar equivalents. However, in order to be included in a B/C economic evaluation, they must be quantified and valuated.

11.3.6 Limitations of Economic Evaluation

The foregoing commentary brings to light the fact that economic efficiency analysis is not as objective as it may seem at first glance. Its strongest advantage is that it provides a useful quantitative but partial picture of the subject matter. Its major limitations may be classed into problems of impact enumeration, valuation, and distribution. The selection of an appropriate interest rate and the treatment of price inflation and deflation are also problematic.

The question of *impact enumeration* refers to the fact that not all impacts considered to be important can be included in the analysis. Even though no evaluation technique can possibly include all ramifications of major transportation projects, economic efficiency analysis further restricts the admissible set.

The problem of *impact distribution* refers to the fact that the benefits and costs are distributed unevenly between individuals and groups. For example, some persons may have to relocate their residences or businesses to permit the construction of a highway that could result in travel time and fuel savings for another group, the users of the new highway. Similarly, it may be argued that subsidizing a public-transportation system entails the taking of tax dollars from everyone in order to enhance the mobility of the few that ride the system. In this connection, the first piece of federal legislation to require a B/C analysis for public projects explicitly stated that public projects are justified:

> . . . if the benefits *to whomsoever they may accrue* are in excess of the estimated costs ([11.6], emphasis added).

Of course, counterarguments are possible in both examples just cited, but this is not the proper place to address them. It is clear, however, that *those who perceive that they will be adversely affected by a proposed project are not obliged to acquiesce on the grounds that the calculated overall B/C ratio is greater than unity.*

11.4 EFFECTIVENESS ANALYSIS

11.4.1 Introduction

The preceding discussion has pointed out that, even when they can be quantified in terms of specific measures of performance, the various impacts associated with proposed alternatives are often difficult to express in monetary terms. *Effectiveness*, which has been defined as the degree to which the performance of an alternative attains its stated objectives, seeks to rectify this problem by explicitly accounting for such impacts and for providing a framework within which these impacts can be clearly defined and traded off via the choice of alternative. The effectiveness approach to evaluation and decision-making is founded on the axiom that more-informed and, hence, better decisions would result if the decision makers were presented with the maximum amount of available information about the subject. Within this framework, the basic role of the analyst becomes more concerned with facilitating the decision-making process by devising well-organized ways to summarize and transmit to the decision makers the data required for the decision and less with applying a specific technique that presumes to determine unambiguously the "best" alternative. At the same time, the role of the decision makers becomes more demanding as they are given the added responsibility of ultimately assigning relative values to the merits and demerits of the alternatives being considered. The vast technical literature on specific techniques that may be used to measure effectiveness (ranging from purely subjective to highly quantitative) as well as the decision-making processes and the institutional structures for which these techniques are best suited spans several disciplines. Only the basic elements of effectiveness analysis are discussed here.

11.4.2 Cost-Effectiveness

The application of economic efficiency methods to public projects had its origins in the civilian sector and the provision flood protection. Cost-effectiveness, on the other hand, was first applied in connection with the evaluation of military systems. In its strictest sense, it was an extension of the principles of economic efficiency, as it was concerned with maximizing the returns (in terms of effectiveness) of public expenditures described in terms of the monetary costs associated with the life cycles of proposed systems. The following simple example illustrates the essence of the method.

Suppose that the administration team of a university (i.e., the decision-making body) is faced with the task of selecting a new computer system for the college of engineering. Because the system is to be used primarily for undergraduate instruction, it has been agreed that it should maximize the number of users it can accommodate simultaneously and that this number must be at least equal to that supported by the existing system. On the other hand, the administration has established a maximum cost constraint as well. Several computer manufacturers responded to a request for bids with the six mutually exclusive proposals shown in Fig. 11.4.1. In accordance with the agreed-upon rules, alternative A would be dropped because it fails to meet the minimum effectiveness level and alternative F would be eliminated as its costs exceed the maximum available resources. Furthermore, alternatives B and C and the do-nothing alternative would also be eliminated, as they cost at least as much but offer no better level of effectiveness than alternative D. The final choice would rest between alternatives D and E and would involve a trade-off between dollars and the number of potential users. This choice is an incremental consideration, but unlike the incremental analysis applied to the B/C ratio, the relative worth of the two impacts being traded off would be implicit in the final choice. The choice of alternative E would imply that the extra benefits are *at least* equivalent to the extra costs required. Conversely, the selection of alternative D would carry the implication that the worth of the incremental effectiveness associated with alternative E is less than the worth of the incremental dollar costs it would entail.

The problem of selecting the best computer system would be further com-

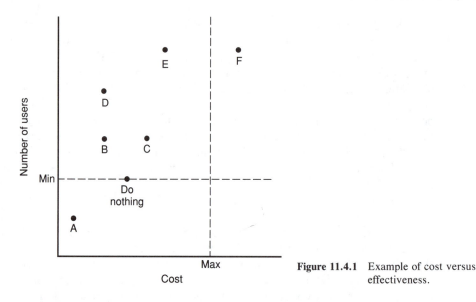

Figure 11.4.1 Example of cost versus effectiveness.

plicated if the system's effectiveness were multidimensional—for example, if the availability of engineering software (however measured) were also considered to be important. Thus, as the dimensions of effectiveness increases, so does the complexity of determining the relative worth of the alternatives (i.e., evaluating them). Consequently, an individual decision maker soon becomes overwhelmed with vast amounts of often-conflicting information. The matter becomes worse as the number of individuals constituting the decision-making group increases. Hence, a need arises to organize the available information and to establish procedures that aid the attainment of consensus.

Several ways by which the relative assessment of alternatives may be accomplished are as follows:

1. The decision makers select the best based on their unexpressed subjective judgments.
2. Aided by the analyst, decision makers *rank* alternative options in an ordinal sense (that is, A is better than B) and make selection by one of several *rank-ordering* procedures.
3. Aided by the analyst and other sources, the decision makers assign a score (usually based on the relative weights of impacts) to each alternative and select the one with the highest score.

11.4.3 Rank-Ordering Techniques

One rank-ordering technique with obvious application to the topic is one that Sage [11.7] treats with mathematical formalism and which has been applied in several variations by others. In simplified form, the method works as follows.

The decision maker, faced with n alternatives, is asked to compare them in pairs according to a contextual relationship, such as "alternative i is superior to alternative j." After the decision maker has completed the consideration of all pairs, the following rules are examined to ensure consistency. First, an alternative cannot be superior to itself. Second, if i is superior to j, then j cannot be superior to i. Third, if i is superior to j and j is superior to k, then i is superior to k. If the decision maker violates any of these rules, an inconsistency is detected that should be resolved.

Example 11.3

Considering four options, a decision maker has completed the following array by placing a 1 in cell (i, j) if the answer to the question "option i is superior to option j" was affirmative and a 0 otherwise. Check for any inconsistencies in the decision maker's logic, and, if none are found, identify the rank order of the four options.

i \ j	A	B	C	D
A	0	0	1	1
B	1	0	0	1
C	1	1	0	1
D	0	0	0	0

Solution The diagonal elements are all 0, as expected. However, A has been designated to be superior to C at the same time that C was considered to be superior to A. Moreover, a circularity exists between A, B, and C: B was considered to be superior to A, C superior to A, and C superior to B. Therefore, a defect in the assessment is revealed. The same conclusion may be reached by drawing the directed graph shown in Fig. 11.4.2., where each arrow is directed from the inferior to the superior option.

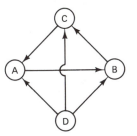

Figure 11.4.2 Graphic identification of rank-ordering deficiencies.

Example 11.4

Assume that the inconsistency of Example 11.3 was pointed out to the decision maker and that, after considerable thought, the decision maker revised the original assessment by rating option A inferior to option C. Revise the solution of Example 11.3.

Solution   The revised directed graph is shown in Fig. 11.4.3. Furthermore, by eliminating redundant arrows (e.g., from D to C), a clear rank order emerges.

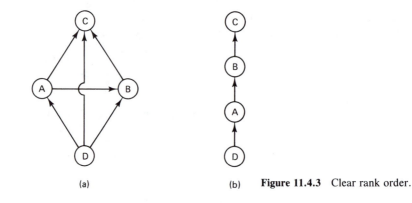

(a)   (b)   **Figure 11.4.3**   Clear rank order.

Discussion   This method produces a consistent ranking of the options based on the subjective judgment of the decision makers that can provide guidance to the discovery of inconsistencies that need to be clarified and resolved. When the decision-making body consists of many individuals, an overall compromise must be made. One way of accomplishing this is the method by which the "number 1 college football team" is selected in the United States: a panel of experts (i.e., football coaches and sports reporters) are asked to rank the top teams and the team that receives the most first-place votes is ranked as being the best. Alternatively, each first-place, second-place, and so on, vote is weighted and combined to derive an overall score.

Table 11.4.1 illustrates the application of the ranking techniques to eight alternatives considered in the 1979 Honolulu study, which is described in subsection 11.2.3. Note that the number of firsts, seconds, and thirds have been tabulated as well. Table 11.4.2 is a similar summary of rankings for the baseline alternative, an alternative consisting of a combination of TSM strategies and a 14-mi-long fixed-guideway rapid-transit alternative. Table 11.4.3 presents some details relating to the basis on which several of the rankings of Table 11.4.2 were derived.

11.4.4 Scoring Techniques

The objective of *scoring techniques* is the assignment of meaningful grades to the alternatives in a manner that reflects the degree to which they differ from each other. Numerous scoring techniques and procedures are reported in the technical literature. The following discussion is an amalgamation of these methods, emphasizing their rationale rather than an in-depth examination of any one in particular.

TABLE 11.4.1 SUMMARY OF RANKINGS FOR EIGHT ALTERNATIVES

	Bus.	7 mi LRT	FG	14 mi LRT	FG	23 mi LRT	28 mi LRT	23 mi FG
Objective 1								
a. Availability & coverage	–	–	–	–	–	–	–	–
b. Avg. trip time (min.)	2	1	1	–	–	2	3	1
c. Service reliability	2	1	1	–	–	2	2	1
d. Rider convenience (transfers per trip)	1	2	2	–	–	2	1	2
e. Rider comfort	2	1	1	–	–	–	–	–
Objective 2								
a. System patronage	2	1	1	–	–	2	2	1
b. System capacity	2	1	1	–	–	–	–	–
Objective 3								
a. Consumption of land (acres)	3	2	1	2	1	2	2	1
b. Displacement of residents (units)	3	2	1	2	1	2	2	1
c. Displacement of businesses (units)	3	2	1	2	1	2	2	1
d. Reduction of community amenities	–	–	–	–	–	–	–	–
e. Disruption to future development	–	–	–	–	–	–	–	–
f. Disruption to local circulation	–	–	–	–	–	2	3	1
g. Disruption from constr. activities	–	–	–	–	–	1	2	1
h. Savings in energy (million gal/year)	1	3	2	2	1	2	3	1
i. Technical risk	3	1	2	1	2	1	1	2
Objective 4								
a. Support regional development	–	–	–	–	–	–	–	–
b. Support comm. development	–	–	–	–	–	–	–	–
Objective 5								
a. Reduction air pollution (tons/year)	3	2	1	2	1	3	2	1
b. Noise level (dBA)	3	2	1	2	1	2	2	1
c. Visual intrusion	3	2	1	2	1	2	2	1
d. Vistas	2	3	1	2	1	1	1	2
e. Historic sites	–	–	–	–	–	–	–	–

(*continued*)

TABLE 11.4.1 (*Continued*)

	Bus.	7 mi LRT	FG	14 mi LRT	FG	23 mi LRT	28 mi LRT	23 mi FG
Objective 6								
a. Reduce accident exposure	—	—	—	—	—	2	2	1
b. Security	—	—	—	—	—	—	—	—
Objective 7								
a. Total annual cost	3	2	1	2	1	1	3	2
b. Cost per trip	3	2	1	2	1	2	3	1
c. B/C ratio	3	2	1	2	1	2	3	1
No. of firsts	2	6	15	1	11	4	3	15
No. of seconds	6	10	3	11	1	14	10	4
No. of thirds	10	2	0	0	0	1	6	0

Source: Urban Mass Transportation Administration [11.3].

TABLE 11.4.2 SUMMARY OF RANKINGS: BASELINE, TSM,
AND FIXED GUIDEWAY

	Approach A		
Evaluation factors	Baseline	TSM	14-mi fixed gwy.
Objective 1			
a. Availability & coverage	2	1	1
b. Avg. trip time	3	2	1
c. Service reliability	3	2	1
d. Rider convenience	2	2	1
e. Rider comfort	2	2	1
Objective 2			
a. System patronage	3	2	1
b. System capacity	3	2	1

(*continued*)

TABLE 11.4.2 (*Continued*)

Evaluation factors	Approach A		
	Baseline	TSM	14-mi fixed gwy.
Objective 3			
a. Consumption of land	1	2	3
b. Displacement of residents	1	1	2
c. Displacement of businesses	1	2	3
d. Reduction of community amenities	1	1	2
e. Disruption of future development	1	1	2
f. Disruption of local circulation	3	2	1
g. Disruption from constr. activities	1	1	2
h. Savings in energy	3	2	1
i. Technical risk	1	1	2
Objective 4			
a. Support regional development	2	2	1
b. Support comm. development	2	2	1
Objective 5			
a. Reduction Air pollution	3	2	1
b. Noise level	2	2	1
c. Visual intrusion	1	1	2
d. Vistas	1	1	2
e. Historic sites	1	1	2
Objective 6			
a. Reduce accident exposure	3	2	1
b. Security	2	2	1
Objective 7			
a. Total annual cost	1	2	3
b. Total annual cost per trip	1	2	3
c. Benefit-cost ratio	—	2	1
No. of firsts	12	9	16
No. of seconds	7	19	8
No. of thirds	8	0	4

Source: Urban Mass Transportation Administration [11.3].

TABLE 11.4.3 COMPARATIVE EVALUATION MATRIX: BASELINE, TSM, AND FIXED GUIDEWAY

Evaluation factors	Approach A		
	Baseline	TSM	14-mi fixed gwy.
Objective 1			
a. Availability & coverage[a]	(2)	(1)	(1)
b. Avg. trip time (min.)	40.7	40.1	33.7
c. Service reliability[a]	(3)	(2)	(1)
d. Rider convenience[a]	(2)	(2)	(1)
e. Rider comfort*	(2)	(2)	(1)
Objective 2			
a. System patronage-1985 (million/year)	64.7	83.6	102.4
b. System capacity[a]	(3)	(2)	(1)
Objective 3			
a. Consumption of land (acres)	—	3	22
b. Displacement of residents (units)	—	—	162
c. Displacement of businesses (units)[a]	—	2	183
d. Reduction of community amenities[a]	(1)	(1)	(2)
e. Disruption of future development[a]	(1)	(1)	(2)
f. Disruption of local circulation[a]	(3)	(2)	(1)
g. Disruption from constr. activities[a]	(1)	(1)	(2)
h. Savings in energy (million gal/year)	—	0.9	4.5
i. Technical risk[a]	(1)	(1)	(2)
Objective 4			
a. Support regional development[a]	(2)	(2)	(1)
b. Support comm. development[a]	(2)	(2)	(1)
Objective 5			
a. Reduction Air pollution (tons/year)	—	220	2260
b. Noise level (dBA)	86–88	86–88	77
c. Visual intrusion[a]	(1)	(1)	(2)
d. Vistas[a]	(1)	(1)	(2)
e. Historic sites[a]	(1)	(1)	(2)

(*continued*)

TABLE 11.4.3   (*Continued*)

	Approach A		
Evaluation factors	Baseline	TSM	14-mi fixed gwy.
Objective 6			
a. Reduce accident exposure[a]	(3)	(2)	(1)
b. Security[a]	(2)	(2)	(1)
Objective 7			
a. Total annual cost[b]-1985 ($ million)	32.9	45.0	66.2
b. Total annual cost per trip ($)	0.508	0.538	0.647
c. B/C ratio[c]	—	1.12	1.13

[a] For comparative measures, alternatives are ranked in the order of how well they met the objective.

[b] All costs based on constant 1975 dollars and interest rate of 7%.

[c] Based on constant 1975 dollars.

Source: Urban Mass Transportation Administration [11.3].

Figure 11.4.4 is an expanded version of the generalized impact matrix of Fig. 11.4.1 as it relates to one of the alternatives being evaluated. The impacts that are considered to be relevant to the evaluation are listed in the first row of Fig. 11.4.4. Related *impacts* are combined into a smaller number of evaluation *criteria*, which are themselves combined to yield the alternative's *overall score*. Conceptually, the combination of a set of impacts into a criterion is identical to the derivation of the overall score from a set of quantified criteria. Furthermore,

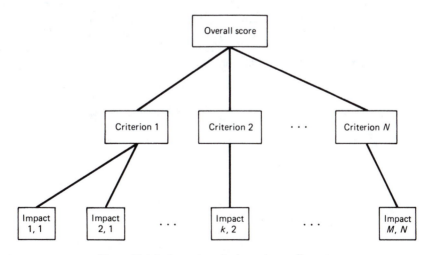

Figure 11.4.4   Impacts, criteria, and overall score.

the evaluation of very complex systems may require more than the three levels of aggregation illustrated. At the other extreme, the simplest case involves a scoring scheme that is based on a single criterion, which is identical to a single impact. A slightly more complex case entails a single criterion that is composed of several impacts. The composite grade of any criterion involves the following steps:

1. The impacts that constitute the criterion are identified and quantified, usually on different scales of measurement.
2. The quantified impacts are placed on the same scale of measurement.
3. The scaled impacts are assigned relative weights and combined.

For instance, the NPW which incorporates the net effect of many impacts, may serve as one of several evaluation criteria. As explained in Section 11.3, the NPW of an alternative is derived by first predicting the likely impacts of the alternative (Step 1), translating the disparately quantified impacts to dollar equivalents (Step 2), and weighting them equally as if they were, in fact, dollars (Step 3). The general scoring methods discussed here allow for (1) the use of a common scale other than a monetary scale, and (2) the assignment of unequal weights to the impacts. This is the essential difference between measures of economic efficiency on one hand and measures of effectiveness on the other.

Example 11.5

An elected official wishes to evaluate three transportation proposals on the basis of three criteria: economic worth, aesthetic quality, and electorate reaction. The economic worth of the alternatives is measured by their NPW, which has been calculated by a consulting firm according to accepted practice. The aesthetic attributes of the alternatives have been assessed by a survey conducted by a marketing-research company and is measured by the percent of respondents that are pleased with each alternative. The probable electorate reaction has been reported by the official's staff, who maintain contacts with the voters in the official's district. The following table summarizes the available information.

Alternative	NPW (millions of dollars)	Aesthetics (%)	Electorate
A	6	70	Neutral
B	13	40	Favorable
C	14	90	Unfavorable

Three possible scoring ways are presented.

1. *Combined rankings.* The alternatives may first be ranked according to each criterion from worst (lowest ranking) to best (highest ranking), and a composite score may be derived by summing the rankings of each alternative. Thus

$$S_i = \sum_j R_{ij} \qquad (11.4.1)$$

where S_i is the score of alternative i and R_{ij} is the rank of alternative i with respect to criterion j.

For the current example, the scores of the three alternatives become:

Alternative	NPW	Aesthetics	Electorate	Score
A	1	2	2	5
B	2	1	3	6
C	3	3	1	7

This method applies equal weights to the criteria. Moreover, it is oblivious to the degree to which the alternatives differ from each other with respect to each criterion.

2. *Weighted rankings.* The criteria may be assigned relative weights, which will affect the contribution of each criterion to the overall scores:

$$S_i = \sum_j w_j R_{ij} \qquad (11.4.2)$$

where w_j is the relative weight of criterion j. Assuming that the official considers satisfying the electorate to be four times as important as aesthetics and twice as important as economic worth, that is,

$$w(\text{NPW}) = 2 \qquad w(\text{aesthetics}) = 1 \qquad w(\text{elect.}) = 4$$

the scores of three alternatives become:

Alternative	Score
A	$2 \times 1 + 1 \times 2 + 4 \times 2 = 12$
B	$2 \times 2 + 1 \times 1 + 4 \times 3 = 18$
C	$2 \times 3 + 1 \times 3 + 4 \times 1 = 13$

The weights assigned to each criterion are reflected in the overall score of the alternatives. However, the problem of scaling the magnitudes associated with the alternatives with respect to each criterion still remains unsolved. Thus the differences in NPW between alternatives A versus B on one hand and B versus C on the other are not captured by this method.

3. *Scaled criteria.* The three criteria used in this example are measured on different scales: The NPW is a quantitative measure that is unbounded at either end. The scale that has been selected to measure aesthetic quality ranges from 0 to 100. Finally, electoral reaction has been reported on an ordinal scale. If the three criteria are to be combined into a single score, they must be placed on a common scale. For the sake of illustration, consider a common ordinal scale ranging from 0 to 100. The criterion relating to aesthetics is already measured on this scale. The NPW of each alternative may be mapped onto the

common scale by assigning a grade, say 90, to alternative C and proportioning accordingly the grades of the other two. With respect to the third criterion, a neutral reaction may be used as an anchor midway on the scale.

Alternative	NPW	Aesthetics	Electorate	Score I	Score II
A	40	70	50	160	350
B	85	40	80	205	580
C	90	90	40	200	450

Two scores are shown in this table. Score I was derived using a function similar to Eq. 11.4.1 with the criteria levels associated with each alternative replacing the raw rankings. Score II is based on a weighting scheme, as in Eq. 11.4.2.

Discussion This example illustrates the mechanics of only four out of a very large number of possible scoring techniques. Theoretically inclined individuals may even be tempted to apply one or more of the scoring techniques described here to combine the various scores derived above into a super score, but such a process has no bound. The potential for an infinite number of scoring variations, each leading to a different decision, may give to the process the appearance of capriciousness or arbitrariness. But no evaluation technique can be an end in itself. Thus, the usefulness of any technique lies in its ability to help organize the decision-making process in an explicit and systemic way and not in its ability automatically to yield an unequivocable result. This presupposes a predisposition on the part of the decision maker to participate actively in all stages of the process, including the identification of impacts and criteria, their scaling and weighing, and, ultimately, the final decision. As to the choice of technique, it is largely situational, and it depends on the quantity and quality of the available information.

11.4.5 Group Consensus

Perhaps the major source of difficulty associated with effectiveness analysis is the dependence on the subjective judgment of the decision maker. This dependence is often moderated by the reliance on decision-making bodies that consist of many individuals. But precisely because of the differences that exist between individuals, group decision-making requires the attainment of group consensus. Traditional means for reaching consensus include group discussion, debate, argumentation, and brainstorming. The advantages of these methods include the exposure of the group to differing points of view. A major drawback is that certain individuals tend to dominate the process because of rank, strength of conviction, or persuasive ability. Several methods that attempt to eliminate this difficulty have been devised. Theoretically, the group's consensus may be revealed by statistically summarizing the responses of the members of a panel to the questions required by the ranking and scoring techniques discussed above. The *delphi method*, originally proposed by the Rand Corporation [11.8], encompasses several procedures that attempt to facilitate collective decisions via a series of questionnaires administered to all members of a panel and accompanied by summaries of the panel's earlier responses. The final decision is enhanced by anonymity, by equal treatments of all points of view, and by the fact that the participants are free to revise their positions.

11.5 SUMMARY

In this chapter we introduced the concepts of project evaluation and described the elements of some commonly used methods that can aid the evaluation of alternative courses of action and can facilitate the selection of an alternative for implementation. The complex nature of transportation-related decisions was conveyed only by implication because a detailed examination of the political, legislative, and judicial reverberations of transportation decisions is beyond the scope of this introductory book.

Evaluation methods were classified into economic efficiency methods and effectiveness methods. The former require that the quantified impacts that are relevant to evaluation be translated into money equivalents and be treated as such. The traditional economic efficiency evaluation measures of net present worth and B/C analysis were then described and illustrated. Finally, the case was made for expanding the evaluation framework to incorporate impacts that are either impossible or difficult to quantify in terms of dollars. Within this expanded framework various measures of effectiveness as well as measures of economic efficiency can serve as evaluative criteria for the ranking and scoring of alternatives.

11.6 EXERCISES

1. Drawing on the store of knowledge you have amassed so far, discuss the contents of Table 11.2.1.
2. Discuss several possible ways by which each of the travel, operating characteristics, and costs listed in Table 11.2.2 could have been estimated. Be as specific as you can.
3. Referring to Table 11.2.2, explain why the projected total daily transit patronage is different for each transportation alternative studied. Which part of the sequential travel-demand forecasting methodology do you think produced these results? Explain specifically the most likely model variables that capture this effect.
4. In reference to Table 11.2.2, why do you think the estimated daily trips on the 7-mi fixed-guideway alternative are the same as those corresponding to the 7-mi LRT?
5. Perform an incremental B/C analysis of the alternatives listed in Table 11.2.3, assuming an interest rate of 4%. Why is the interest rate important in the B/C ratio method of evaluation?
6. Repeat Exercise 5 assuming an interest rate of 10%.

7. With reference to objective 7 of Table 11.4.2, why wasn't the B/C ratio of the baseline alternative reported? What implication can this fact have on the feasibility of the other two alternatives?

8. Perform an incremental analysis of the three alternatives listed in Table 11.4.3 and discuss your results.

9. Determine the preferred alternative of a decision maker who has completed the following array on the basis of the contextual relationship alternative i is better than alternative j.

i \ j	A	B	C	D
A	0	0	0	0
B	1	0	0	1
C	1	1	0	1
D	0	0	0	0

10. Using the data given in Table 11.4.2, (a) calculate the simple combined rankings score of each of the three alternatives with respect to each of the seven objectives; (b) rank the alternatives for each objective according to the scores derived in part a; (c) apply the simple combined rankings technique to the results of part b; (d) use the following weights to calculate the weighted-ranking scores derived in part (b).

$$i: \quad 1 \quad 2 \quad 3 \quad 4 \quad 5 \quad 6 \quad 7$$
$$w: \quad 2 \quad 4 \quad 1 \quad 4 \quad 5 \quad 2 \quad 7$$

Explain any assumptions you felt were necessary to complete this exercise and explain why a universally applicable effectiveness analysis method is not possible.

11. Three alternative plans (A, B, and C) have been ranked with respect to four criteria (I to IV) as follows:

	I	II	III	IV
A	2	1	3	2
B	1	2	2	1
C	3	3	1	3

where 1 means best. Apply the single combined-rankings technique to derive an overall score for each alternative.

12. Given the following weights for the four criteria of Exercise 11, compute the weighted-rankings scores for the three alternatives.

$$i: \quad I \quad II \quad III \quad IV$$
$$w: \quad 2 \quad 4 \quad 1 \quad 2$$

13. Discuss the steps you would follow in order to apply the B/C ratio method to evaluate alternative highway-safety proposals consisting of all possible combinations of 12 ac-

cident-reducing actions such as signalization, curve widening, street lighting, and so on.

14. From the government documents section of your school's library, obtain a planning study for a major transportation action and report on the evaluation method employed.

15. Discuss the possible differences in the perspectives of an environmentalist, a construction firm president, and a federal judge regarding a proposal to build a multilane highway through a conservation district. Use Appendix A as a guide to your answer.

11.7 REFERENCES

11.1 THOMAS, E. N., and J. L. SCHOFER, *Strategies for the Evaluation of Alternative Transportation Plans*, National Cooperative Highway Research Program Report 96, Highway Research Board, National Research Council, Washington, D.C., 1970.

11.2 MANHEIM, M. L., et al., *Transportation Decision-Making: A Guide to Social and Environmental Considerations*, National Cooperative Highway Research Program Report 156, Transportation Research Board, National Research Council, Washington, D.C., 1975.

11.3 URBAN MASS TRANSPORTATION ADMINISTRATION, *Draft Environmental Impact Statement: Honolulu Area Rapid Transit Project*, UMTA Project Report HI-03-0005, U.S. Department of Transportation, Washington, D.C., July 1979.

11.4 WOHL, M., *Transportation Investment Planning: An Introduction for Engineers and Planners*, Lexington Books, Lexington, Mass., 1972.

11.5 American Association of State Highway and Transportation Officials, *A Manual on User Benefit Analysis of Highway and Bus-Transit Improvements 1977*, AASHTO, Washington, D.C., 1978.

11.6 *United States Code*, U.S. Government Printing Office, Washington, D.C., 1940, p. 2964.

11.7 SAGE, A. P., *Methodology for Large-Scale Systems*, McGraw-Hill, New York, 1977.

11.8 DALKEY, N., and O. HELMER, "An Experimental Application of the Delphi Method to the Use of Experts," *Management Science*, 9, 3 (Apr. 1963): 458–467.

A

1982 Guidelines for the Preparation of Environmental Documents†

Federal Highway Administration
U.S. Department of Transportation

INTRODUCTION

The purpose of this material is to provide guidance to FHWA field offices and project applicants on National Environmental Policy Act (NEPA) actions and to provide the public with a further explanation of FHWA internal operating procedures in the development of the reports and documentation required by NEPA. This material also provides the guidance required by 23 U.S.C. 109(h) to assure the full consideration of possible adverse economic, social, and environmental effects of proposed FHWA projects. While the material was developed primarily to provide guidance in the development of environmental impact statements (EISs), it is also applicable, to the extent appropriate, for environmental assessments and other environmental studies deemed necessary prior to the advancement of a project with a categorical exclusion determination or a finding of no significant impact. This material is not regulatory, but has been developed to provide uniform and consistent guidance for the development of environmental documents. Each project will need to be carefully evaluated and the appropriate environmental document developed based on each individual situation.

The FHWA fully subscribes to the Council on Environmental Quality (CEQ) philosophy that the goal of the NEPA process is better decisions and not more documentation. As noted in the CEQ regulations, EISs should normally be less than 150 pages for most projects and not more than 300 pages for the most complex projects.

† FHWA Technical Advisory T 6640.8, February 24, 1982.

The FHWA considers the early coordination process to be a valuable tool to assist in identifying and focusing on the significant environmental issues. On April 30, 1981, the CEQ issued a memorandum entitled "Scoping Guidance," which discusses various techniques that will ensure participation in the scoping process. The CEQ also issued, on March 6, 1981, a memorandum entitled "Questions and Answers about the NEPA Regulations." Both of the documents are nonregulatory; however, they do provide CEQ views on various issues and are available from the FHWA Office of Environmental Policy (HEV-10).

A.1 ENVIRONMENTAL ASSESSMENT (EA)

Title 23, Code of Federal Regulations, Part 771, Environmental Impact and Related Procedures, describes those circumstances where the preparation of an EA is appropriate. The CEQ regulations require that an EA is to include the information listed in 40 CFR Part 1508.9. The following format, which assures this coverage, is suggested:

   a. *Cover sheet.* There is no *required* format for the EA. However, it is recommended the EIS cover sheet format, as shown on page 540, be followed *where appropriate*. Since the EA is not formally circulated, there is no need to include the "comments due" paragraph on page 541.

   b. *Description of the proposed action.* Describe the locations, length, termini, proposed improvements, etc.

   c. *Need.* Identify and describe the problem which the proposed action is designed to correct. Any of the items discussed under the "Need" section in Section 3 (EIS—Format and Content) may be appropriate.

   d. *Alternatives considered.* Discuss all reasonable alternatives to the proposed action which were considered. The EA may either discuss (1) the preferred alternative and the alternatives considered or (2) if the applicant has not identified a preferred alternative, the alternatives under consideration.

e. *Impacts.* Discuss the social, economic and environmental impacts of the alternatives considered and describe why these impacts are considered not significant.

f. *Comments and coordination.* Describe coordination efforts and comments received from government agencies and the public. If the EA includes a Section 4(f) evaluation, the EA and the Section 4(f) evaluation may be circulated to the appropriate agencies for Section 4(f) coordination, or the Section 4(f) evaluation may be supplemented by any additional information necessary to properly explain the project and circulated as a separate document.

g. *Appendices (if any).* Include only analytical information that substantiates an analysis which is important to the document. Other information should be incorporated by reference only.

A.2 FINDING OF NO SIGNIFICANT IMPACT (FONSI)

771.121 of 23 CFR 771, entitled Environmental Impact and Related Procedures, describes the approval process for a FONSI. Section 1508.13 of the CEQ regulations describes the content of a FONSI. The EA should be modified to reflect all applicable significant environmental comments received as a result of the public hearings or other significant environmental comments received as a result of the public and clearinghouse notification process. The EA, revised as appropriate, including appropriate responses to any comments received, is then submitted to the FHWA Division Administrator along with the applicant's recommendation. The basis for the applicant's recommendation should be documented in the EA. After review of the EA and any other appropriate information, the FHWA Division Administrator may determine that the proposed action has no significant impacts. This is documented by attaching to the EA a separate statement (example follows) which clearly sets forth the FHWA analysis of the EA along with any other supporting documentation that has resulted in a FONSI. As appropriate, the FHWA Division Administrator may choose to expand on the discussion in the sample FONSI to identify the basis for the decision. The EA/FONSI should document compliance with the requirements of all applicable environmental laws, Executive Orders, and other related requirements. If full compliance is not possible by the time the FONSI is prepared, it should reflect consultation with the appropriate agencies and provide reasonable assurance that the requirements will be met.

FEDERAL HIGHWAY ADMINISTRATION
FINDING OF NO SIGNIFICANT IMPACT
FOR
(Title of Proposed Action)
The FHWA has determined that this project will not have any significant impact on the human environment. This finding of no significant impact is

based on the attached environmental assessment (reference other environmental documents as appropriate) which has been independently evaluated by the FHWA and determined to adequately and accurately discuss the environmental issues and impacts of the proposed project. It provides sufficient evidence and analysis for determining that an environmental impact statement is not required. The FHWA takes full responsibility for the accuracy, scope, and content of the attached environmental assessment.

_____   _____   _____

Date   Responsible Official   Title

A.3 EIS—FORMAT AND CONTENT

Each EIS should have a cover sheet containing:

(EIS number)

(Route, Termini, City or County, and State)
Draft (Final)
Environmental Impact Statement
Submitted Pursuant to 42 U.S.C. 4332(2)(c) (and
where applicable, 49 U.S.C. 1653(f) by the
U.S. Department of Transportation
Federal Highway Administration
and
State highway agency (HA)
and
(As applicable, local highway agency (HA))

Cooperating Agencies
List Here

_____   _____

Date of Approval   For FHWA   Title

The following persons may be contacted for additional information concerning this document:

(Name, address,   (Name address, and telephone
and telephone   number of HA contact)
number of FHWA
division office
contact)

A one-paragraph abstract of the statement.

Comments on this draft EIS are due by (*date*) and should be sent to (*name and address*).

The top left-hand corner of the cover sheet of all draft and final EISs contains a number parallel to that in the following example:

FHWA-AZ-EIS-81-01-D(F)(S)

FHWA—name of Federal agency

AZ—name of State (cannot exceed four characters)

EIS—environmental impact statement

81—year draft statement was prepared

01—sequential number of draft statement for each calendar year

D—designates the statement as the draft statement

F—designates the statement as the final statement

S—designates supplemental statement

The EISs should be printed on $8\frac{1}{2} \times 11$-inch paper with all graphics folded for insertion to that size. The wider sheets should open to the right with the title or identification on the right. The use of a standard size will facilitate administrative recordkeeping.

Summary

The summary should include:

a. A brief description of the proposed FHWA action indicating route, termini, type of improvement, number of lanes, length, county, city, state, etc., as appropriate.

b. A description of any significant actions proposed by other government agencies in the same geographic area as the proposed FHWA action.

c. A summary of major alternatives considered. (The final EIS should identify the preferred alternative).

d. A summary of *significant* environmental impacts, both beneficial and adverse.

e. Any areas of controversy (including issues raised by both agencies and the public).

f. Any significant unresolved issues.

g. A list of other federal actions required because of this proposed action (i.e., permit approvals etc.).

Table of Contents

a. Cover sheet
b. Summary
c. Table of contents
d. Purpose of and need for action
e. Alternatives including proposed action
f. Affected environment
g. Environmental consequences
h. List of preparers
i. List of agencies, organizations, and persons to whom copies of the statement are sent
j. Comments and coordination
k. Index
l. Appendices (if any)

Purpose of and Need for Action

Identify and describe the transportation problem(s) which the proposed action is designed to address. This section should clearly demonstrate that a "need" exists and must define the "need" in terms understandable to the general public. This discussion will form the basis for the "no action" discussion in the "Alternatives" section. The following is a list of items which may assist in the explanation of the need for the proposed action. It is by no means all-inclusive or applicable in every situation and is intended only as a guide.

a. *System linkage.* Is the proposed project a "connecting link"? How does it fit in the system? Is it an "essential gap" in the Interstate System?
b. *Capacity.* Is the capacity of the present facility inadequate for the present traffic? Projected traffic? What capacity is needed? What is the level of service?
c. *Transportation demand.* Includes relationship to any statewide plan or adopted urban transportation plan.
d. *Federal, State, or local governmental authority (legislation) directing the action.*
e. *Social demands or economic development.* New employment, schools, land use plans, recreation, etc. What projected economic development/land use changes indicate the need to improve or add to the highway capacity?
f. *Modal Interrelationships.* How will the proposed facility interfere with and serve to complement airports, rail and port facilities, mass transit services, etc.

g. Is the proposed project necessary to correct an existing or potential safety hazard? Is the existing accident rate excessively high? Why? How will the proposed facility improve it?

Alternatives Including Proposed Action

The "Alternatives" section of the draft EIS should begin with a concise discussion of how the "reasonable alternatives" were selected for detailed study. It should also describe those "other alternatives" that were eliminated early in project development and the basis for their elimination. The alternatives to be considered in this section will normally include the following:

a. The "no-action" alternative, which would include those usual short-term minor reconstruction types of activities (safety improvements, etc.) that are a part of an ongoing plan for continuing operation of the existing roadway system in the project area.

b. A Transportation System Management (TSM) alternative which would include those types of activities designed to maximize the utilization and energy efficiency of the present system. Possible subject areas to include in this alternative are options such as fringe parking, ridesharing, high-occupancy vehicle (HOV) lanes on existing roadways, and traffic signal timing optimization. This limited construction alternative should be given appropriate consideration when major urbanized area construction activities are proposed. On major new urbanized area highway projects, the option of including and/or designating HOV lanes should be a consideration. Consideration of this alternative may be accomplished by reference to the regional transportation plan, when that plan considers this option. In the case of regional transportation plans which do not reflect consideration of this option, it may be necessary to evaluate the feasibility of this alternative. The effects that reducing the scale of a link in the regional transportation plan will have on the remainder of the system will need to be discussed during the evaluation of this alternative. While this discussion relates primarily to major projects in urbanized areas, the concept of achieving maximum utilization of existing facilities is equally important in rural areas. Before major projects on new location are proposed, it is important to demonstrate that reconstruction and rehabilitation of the existing system will not adequately correct the identified deficiencies. Appendix A of 23 CFR 450 provides additional discussion on the goals and scope of the TSM concept.

c. All other proposed "construction" alternatives discussions should include, where relevant, those reasonable and feasible alternatives (i.e., transit options) which may not be within the existing funding authority of FHWA. Some urban projects may be multimodal, thus requiring close coordination with the Urban Mass Transportation Administration (UMTA). In these situations, UMTA should be consulted early in the project development process. Depending on the extent of UMTA involvement and the possible use of UMTA funds for portions of the proposal, the need to request UMTA to be either a "lead agency" or a "cooperating agency" should be considered at the earliest stages of project development. Where applicable, cost-effectiveness studies that have been performed should be summarized in the EIS.

The discussion of alternatives in this section can be best accomplished by a brief written description of each alternative, supplemented with maps and other appropriate visual aids such as photographs, drawings, or sketches which would assist the reader in better understanding the various alternatives, impacts, and mitigation measures. In some situations, design level details may be appropriate to evaluate impacts. However, final design details are not normally available at this stage in project development. The material should provide a clear understanding of each alternative's termini, location, costs, and major design features (number of lanes, right-of-way requirements, median width, etc.) which will contribute to a reader's better understanding of each alternative's effects on its surroundings or the community.

Generally, each alternative should be developed to a comparable level of detail in the draft EIS. Normally, the draft EIS should state that all alternatives are under consideration and that a decision will be made only after the public hearing transcript and comments on the draft EIS have been evaluated. However, in those situations where the HA has identified a "preferred" alternative based on its early coordination and environmental studies, the HA may so indicate in the draft EIS. However, the EIS should include a comment to the effect that the final selection will not be made until the results of the EIS circulation and the public involvement process have been fully evaluated. The final EIS must identify the preferred alternative and discuss the basis for the selection.

Affected Environment

This section should provide a *concise* description of the existing social, economic, and environmental setting for the area affected by all of the alternative proposals. The description should be a single general description for the area rather than a separate one for each alternative. All environmentally sensitive locations or features should be identified. However, it may be desirable to exclude from environmental documents certain specific location data on archeological sites to prevent vandalism.

To reduce paperwork and eliminate the presentation of extraneous background material, the discussion should focus on significant issues and values. Prudent use of photographs, illustrations, and other graphics within the text can be effective in giving the reviewer an understanding of the area. The statement should describe other related Federal activities in the area, their interrelationships, and any significant cumulative environmental impacts.

Data and analyses in the statement should be in proportion to the significance of the impacts which will be discussed later in the document. Less important material should be summarized or referenced. This section should also describe the scope and status of the planning process for the area. The inclusion of a map of any adopted land use and transportation plan for the area would be helpful in relating the proposed project to the areawide planning process.

Environmental Consequences

This section will discuss the probable social, economic, and environmental effects of the alternatives and the measures to mitigate adverse impacts.

There are several ways of preparing this section. Normally, it is preferable to discuss the impacts and mitigation measures separately for each of the alternatives. However, in some cases (such as where there are few alternatives), it may be advantageous to present this section with the impacts as the headings. Where possible, a subsection should be included which would discuss the general impacts and mitigation measures that are the same regardless of the alternative selected. This would reduce or eliminate repetition under each of the alternative discussions.

When the final EIS is prepared, the impacts and mitigation measures associated with the selected alternative may need to be discussed in more detail than in the draft EIS. In discussing the impacts, both beneficial and adverse, the following should be included in both the draft and final EIS.

a. A summary of studies undertaken and major assumptions made, with enough data or cross referencing to determine the validity of the methodology.
b. Sufficient information to establish the reasonableness of the conclusions concerning impacts.
c. A discussion of mitigation measures. Prior to completion of the final EIS, these measures normally should be investigated in appropriate detail so that a commitment can be included in the final EIS.

Charts, tables, maps, and other graphics illustrating comparisons between the alternatives (i.e., costs, residential displacements, noise impacts, etc.) are useful as a presentation technique.

In addition to normal FHWA program monitoring of design and construction activities, special instances may arise when a formal program for monitoring impacts or mitigation measures will be appropriate. In these instances, the final EIS should describe the monitoring program.

Listed below are examples of the potentially significant impacts of highway projects. These factors should be discussed *to the extent applicable* for each alternative. This list is by no means all-inclusive and on specific projects there may be other significant impacts that require study.

Social and Economic Impacts

The statement should discuss:

a. Changes in the neighborhoods or community cohesion for various groups as a result of the proposed action. These changes may be beneficial or adverse, and may include splitting neighborhoods, isolating a portion of an ethnic group, new development, changed property values, or separation of residences from community facilities, etc.

b. Changes in travel patterns and accessibility (e.g., vehicular, commuter, bicycle, or pedestrian). If any cross streets are terminated, the EIS should reflect the views of the involved city or county on such street closings.

c. Impacts on school districts, recreation areas, churches, businesses, police and fire protection, etc.

d. The impacts of alternatives on highway and traffic safety as well as on overall public safety.

e. Regional economic impacts, such as the effects of the project on development, tax revenues and public expenditures, employment opportunities, accessibility and retail sales. Any significant impacts on the economic viability of affected municipalities should also be discussed together with a summary of any efforts taken and agreements reached for using the transportation investment to support both public and private development plans. To the extent possible, this discussion should rely upon reviews by affected state, county, and city officials and upon studies performed under 23 U.S.C. 134.

f. For projects that might lead to or support large commercial development, the EIS should provide information on any significant effects the pending action would have on established business districts, and any opportunities for mitigation by the public and/or private sectors.

g. The general social groups specially benefitted or harmed by the proposed action should be identified. Particular effects of a proposal on the elderly, handicapped, nondrivers, transit-dependent, or minorities should be described to the extent these can be reasonably predicted. For example, where minority impacts may be a significant concern, EISs should contain, when applicable, the following information, broken down by race, color, and national origin: the population in the study area, the number of displaced residents, the type and number of displaced businesses, and the type and number of displaced employees. Secondary sources of information such as census data reports can be utilized for obtaining this type of background information. Changes in minority employment opportunities, the relationship of the proposed action to other Federal actions which may serve or affect the minority population, and proposed mitigation measures to reduce or avoid impacts on minority populations should also be discussed.

Relocation Impacts

The relocation information necessary for the draft EIS may be included in the draft statement, either in the form of a complete conceptual stage relocation plan, or summarized in sufficient detail to adequately explain the relocation situation along with a resolution of anticipated or known problems. When the relocation information is summarized, the conceptual stage relocation plan should be referenced in the draft EIS.

A discussion of the information listed below is to be included in the draft EIS *to the extent appropriate* for the project.

a. An estimate of households to be displaced, including the family characteristics (e.g., minorities, handicapped, income levels, the elderly, large families, length of occupancy, and owner/tenant status). Where the project is not complex from a relocation viewpoint and the impact on the community is slight, this information may be obtained by visual inspection and from available secondary sources. On complex relocation projects where the relocation will have a major impact on the community, a survey of affected occupants may be needed. This survey may be accomplished by a sampling process.

b. A discussion of available housing in the area and the ability to provide suitable relocation housing for each type of family to be displaced within the financial capabilities of the relocatees.

c. A description of any special advisory services that will be necessary for unique relocation problems.

d. A discussion of the actions proposed to remedy insufficient relocation housing, including a commitment to housing of last resort, if necessary.

e. An estimate of the number, type, and size of businesses to be displaced. The approximate number of employees for each business should be included along with the general impact on the business dislocation(s) on the economy of the community.

f. A discussion of the results of early consultation with the local government(s) and any early consultation with businesses potentially subject to displacement, including any discussions of potential sources of funding, financing, planning for incentive packaging (e.g., tax abatement, flexible zoning, and building requirements), and advisory assistance which has been or will be furnished along with other appropriate information.

g. Impact on the neighborhood and housing community services where relocation is likely to take place. If there will be extensive residential and/or business displacement, the affected community may want to investigate other sources of funding from local and state entities as well as HUD, the Economic Development Administration, and other federal agencies, to assist in revitalization of the community.

h. The results of discussions with local officials, social agencies, and such groups as the elderly, handicapped, nondriver, transit-dependent, and minorities regarding the relocation impacts.

i. A statement that the housing resources are available to all relocatees without discrimination.

The effects on each group should be described to the extent reasonably predictable. The analysis should discuss how the relocation caused by the proposed project will facilitate or inhibit access to jobs, educational facilities, religious institutions, health and welfare services, recreational facilities, social and cultural facilities, pedestrian facilities, shopping facilities, and public transit services.

Air Quality Impacts

The EIS should contain a brief discussion of air quality effects or a summary of the carbon monoxide (CO) analysis if such an analysis is performed. The following provides additional guidance:

a. A microscale CO analysis to determine air quality impacts is probably unnecessary where such impacts are judged to be minimal or insignificant. The judgment on the degree of CO impacts may be based on: (1) previous analyses for similar projects, (2) previous general analyses for various classes of projects, or (3) simplified graphical or "table look-up" analyses.

b. If the impacts of CO are judged to be minimal or insignificant, a brief statement to this effect is sufficient. The basis for the statement should be given in the EIS.

c. If the project CO contribution plus the background level are known to be well below the 1- and 8-hour National Ambient Air Quality Standard or other applicable standard, then the air quality CO impact is judged to be insignificant.

d. For those projects where a CO microscale analysis is performed, then the total CO concentration (project contribution, plus estimated background) at identified reasonable receptor sites for all alternatives should be reported and compared with applicable State and national standards.

e. If a CO analysis is performed, a brief summary of the methodologies and assumptions used should be given in the EIS.

f. In addition to the CO impact assessment, one of the two following statements should be included in the EIS:

    (1) This project is in an area where the State implementation plan does not contain any transportation control measures. Therefore, the conformity procedures of 23 CFR 770 do not apply to this project.

    (2) This project is in an air quality nonattainment (or attainment) area which has transportation control measures in the State implementation plan (SIP) which was (conditionally) approved by the Environmental Protection Agency on (date). The FHWA has determined that both the transportation plan and the transportation improvement program conform to the SIP. The Federal Highway Administration has determined that this project is included in the transportation improvement program for the (indicate 3C planning area). Therefore, pursuant to 23 CFR 770, this project conforms to the SIP.

Noise Impacts

The EIS should contain a summary of the noise analysis including the following:

a. A brief description of noise sensitive areas, including information on the numbers and types of activities which may be affected. If the project has significant noise impacts, noise contours of the proposed action and alternatives may be appropriate to assist in understanding those impacts.

b. The extent of the impact (in decibels). This should include a comparison of the predicted noise levels with both the FHWA design noise levels and the existing noise levels.

c. Noise-abatement measures which have been considered and those measures that would likely be incorporated into the proposed project.

d. Noise problems for which no prudent solution is reasonably available and the reasons why.

Energy

Draft and final EISs should discuss in *general terms* the energy requirements and conservation potential of various alternatives under consideration. This general discussion might recognize that the energy requirements of various construction alternatives are similar and are generally greater than the energy requirements of the no-build alternative. Additionally, the discussion could point out that the post-construction, operational energy requirements of the facility should be less with the build alternative as opposed to the no-build alternative. In such a situation, one might then conclude that the savings in operational energy requirements would more than offset construction energy requirements and thus, in the long term, result in a net saving in energy usage. For most projects, a detailed energy analysis including computations of Btu requirements, etc., is not needed, but the discussion should be reasonable and supportable.

For major projects with potentially significant energy impacts (an example would be the Westway project in New York City), both the draft and final EIS should discuss any *significant* direct and/or indirect energy impacts of the proposed action. Direct energy impacts refer to the energy consumed by vehicles using the facility. Indirect impacts include construction energy and such items as the effects of any changes in automobile usage. The action's relationship and consistency with any State and/or regional energy plan should also be indicated.

The final EIS should identify any energy conservation measures that will be implemented as a part of the recommended alternative. Measures to conserve energy include the use of high-occupancy vehicle incentives, measures to improve traffic flow, and also pedestrian and bicycle facilities.

Wild and Scenic Rivers

If the proposed action could have an adverse effect on a river on the National Wild and Scenic Rivers System or a river listed in the Nationwide Inventory of rivers with potential for inclusion in the National Wild and Scenic Rivers System, there should be early coordination with the National Park Service (NPS) or the Department of Agriculture (USDA). The EIS should identify any potential significant adverse effects on the natural, cultural, and recreational values of the inventory river. Adverse effects include alteration of the free-flowing nature of the river, alteration of the setting, or deterioration of water quality. If it is determined that the proposed action could foreclose options to designate the river under the act, the EIS should reflect consultation with the NPS or USDA on avoiding or mitigating the impacts. The final EIS should indicate measures which will be included in the action to avoid or mitigate impacts. The October 3, 1980, memorandum from the Office of Environmental Policy provides additional information on this subject area.

Floodplain Impacts

The draft EIS should contain a summary of the "Location Hydraulic Studies" required by FHPM 6-7-3-2, Location and Hydraulic Design of Encroachments on Floodplains. Exhibits defining the floodplains or regulatory floodway, as appropriate, should be provided whenever possible. When there is no practicable alternative to an action which includes a significant encroachment, the final EIS should contain the finding required by FHPM 6-7-3-2, paragraph 8, in a separate subsection titled "Only Practicable Alternative Finding." When there is a regulatory floodway affected by the proposed action, the final EIS should contain a discussion of the consistency of the project with the regulatory floodway.

Coastal Zone Impacts

Where the proposed action is within, or may affect land or water uses within, the area covered by a State Coastal Zone Management Program (CZMP) approved by the Department of Commerce, the environmental document should briefly describe the CZMP plan, identify the potential impacts, and include evidence of coordination with the State Coastal Zone Management agency or appropriate local agency. For FHWA assisted activities, the EIS should include the State Coastal Zone Management agency's determination as to whether the project is consistent with the State CZMP plan. For direct Federal actions, the EIS should include the lead agency's consistency determination. If it is determined that the proposed action is inconsistent with the state's approved CZMP, FHWA will not approve the action except upon a finding by the Secretary of Commerce that the proposed action is consistent with the purposes or objectives of the Coastal Zone Management Act or is necessary in the interest of national security. The final environmental document for the proposed action will document all findings.

Wetlands Impacts

a. All draft EISs for projects involving new construction in wetlands should include sufficient information to: (1) identify the type of wetlands involved, (2) describe the impacts to the wetlands, (3) evaluate alternatives which would avoid these wetlands, and (4) identify practicable measures to minimize harm to the wetlands. Exhibits showing the wetlands in relation to the alternatives, including the alternatives to avoid construction in the wetlands, should be provided.

b. Executive Order 11990, Protection of Wetlands, requires federal agencies ". . . to avoid to the extent possible the long and short term adverse impacts associated with the destruction or modification of wetlands and to avoid direct or indirect support of new construction in wetlands wherever there is a practicable alternative. . . ." In evaluating the impact of the proposed project on wetlands, the following two questions should be addressed: (1) what is the importance of the impacted wetlands? and (2) what is the significance of this impact on the wetlands? Merely listing the number of acres taken by the various alternatives of a highway proposal does not provide sufficient information upon which to determine the degree of impact on the wetland's ecosystem. The wetlands analysis should be sufficiently detailed to allow a meaningful discussion of these two questions.

c. In evaluating the importance of the impacted wetlands, the analysis should consider such factors as: (1) the primary functions of the wetlands (e.g., flood control, wildlife habitat, erosion control, etc.), (2) the relative importance of these functions to the total wetlands resource of the area, and (3) other factors such as uniqueness that may contribute to the wetlands importance.

d. In determining the significance of the highway impact, the analysis should focus on how the project affects the stability and quality of the wetlands.

This analysis should consider the short- and long-term effects on the wetlands and the significance of any loss such as: (1) flood control capacity, (2) erosion control potential, (3) water pollution abatement capacity, and (4) wildlife habitat value. Knowing the importance of the wetlands involved and the significance of the impact, the SHA and FHWA will be in a better position to determine what mitigation efforts are necessary to minimize harm to these wetlands.

e. For purposes of analyzing alternatives and the wetlands finding, "located in wetlands" means that the proposed right-of-way or easement limits of the highway are located wholly or partially in wetlands or that the highway is located in the vicinity of the wetlands and there is evidence that the new construction will directly cause long-term damage or destruction of the wetlands.

f. Mitigation measures which should be considered include enhancement of existing wetlands, creation of new wetlands, and erosion control. It should be noted that any mitigation measure should be related to the actual adverse impact caused by the project and that acquisition of privately owned wetlands for purposes of protection should only be considered as a last resort.

g. When there is no practicable alternative to an action which involves new construction located in wetlands, the final EIS should contain the finding required by Executive Order 11990 and by DOT Order 5660.1A, entitled Preservation of the Nation's Wetlands, August 24, 1978, in a separate section or exhibit titled "Wetlands Finding." Approval of the final EIS containing this finding will document compliance with the requirements of Executive Order 11990. The finding should contain in summary form and with reference to the detailed discussions contained elsewhere in the final EIS:

   (1) a reference to executive Order 11990;

   (2) a discussion of the basis for the determination that there are no practicable alternatives to the proposed action;

   (3) a discussion of the basis for the determination that the proposed action includes all practicable measures to minimize harm to wetlands; and

   (4) a concluding statement as follows: "Based upon the above considerations, it is determined that there is no practicable alternative to the proposed new construction in wetlands and that the proposed action includes all practicable measures to minimize harm to wetlands which may result from such use."

h. A formal wetlands finding is required for all projects processed with EIS's or FONSI's that involve new construction in wetlands. In the case of a project processed as a categorical exclusion, the division office's administrative record should document evaluations of alternatives and measures to minimize harm for these actions.

Land Use Impacts

This discussion should begin with a description of current development trends and the state and/or local government plans and policies with regard to land use and growth in the area. These plans and policies will be reflected in the area's comprehensive development plan, including land use, transportation, public facilities, housing, community services, and other areas.

The land use impact analysis should assess the consistency of the alternatives with the comprehensive development plans adopted for the area. The secondary social, economic, and environmental impacts of *significant* induced development should be presented.

The EIS should note any proposed alternatives which will stimulate low density, energy intensive development in outlying areas and will have a significant adverse effect on existing communities. Throughout this discussion, the distinction between planned and unplanned growth should be clearly identified.

Joint Development

When applicable, the EIS should discuss how the implementation of joint development projects will preserve or enhance the community's social, economic, environmental, and visual values. This discussion should be included as part of the land use impact presentation.

Historic and Archeological Preservation

The draft EIS should contain a discussion demonstrating that a survey meeting the requirements of 36 CFR Part 800.4 has been performed for each alternative under consideration. The discussion should begin by describing the resources and summarizing the impacts that each alternative will have on these resources that might meet the criteria for inclusion on the National Register of Historic Places. There should be a record of coordination with the State Historic Preservation officer concerning the significance of the identified resources, the likelihood of eligibility for the National Register, and an evaluation of the effect of the project on the resources.

The draft EIS can serve as a preliminary case report for Section 106 requirements if the document indicates this and it contains the necessary information (36 CFR 800.13). The transmittal memorandum to the Advisory Council on Historic Preservation should specifically request consultation.

The final EIS should demonstrate that all the requirements of 36 CFR Part 800 have been met. If the selected alternative has an effect on a resource that is on or eligible for inclusion on the National Register, the final EIS should contain (a) a determination of no adverse effect concurred in by the Executive Director of the Advisory Council on Historic Preservation or (b) an executed memorandum of agreement or (c) in the case of a unique situation where FHWA is unable to conclude the memorandum of agreement (MOA), a copy of comments transmitted from the Advisory Council to the Secretary of Transportation. When necessary, the discussion should indicate that archeological recovery will be performed. The proposed use of land from a site on or eligible for inclusion on the National Register will normally require a determination pursuant to Section 4(f) of the DOT Act. The treatment of archeological sites is discussed in 23 CFR 771.135(f). Additional details regarding the type of information needed at the draft EIS and final EIS stages are contained in the May 14, 1980, memorandum from the Office of Environmental Policy to all regional offices.

Water Quality Impacts

This discussion should include summaries of analyses and consultations with the state and/or local agency responsible for water quality. Coordination with the Environmental Protection Agency (EPA) under the Federal Clean Water Act may provide assistance in this area. The EIS should discuss any locations where roadway runoff may have a significant affect on downstream water uses, including existing wells. A 1981 FHWA research report entitled "Constituents of Highway Runoff" contains procedures for estimating pollutant loading from highway runoff.

Section 1424(e) of the Safe Drinking Water Act requires that proposed actions which may impact those areas that have been designated as principal or sole-source aquifers be coordinated with EPA. The EPA will furnish information on whether any of the alternatives affect the aquifer. If none of the alternatives affect the aquifer, the requirements of the Safe Drinking Water Act are satisfied. If an alternative is selected which affects the aquifer, a design must be developed to assure, to the satisfaction of EPA, that it will not contaminate the aquifer.

If a rest area is involved, a Section 402 permit is required for point source discharge. Any potential Section 402 permits should be identified in the EIS. Also, for both the Section 402 and Section 404 permits, a water quality certification from the State agency responsible for water quality is necessary.

The MOA with the Corps of Engineers allows for application for permit as soon as the preferred alternative is identified (i.e., final EIS stage). Use of the procedures in the MOA is encouraged to minimize possible delays in the processing of Section 404 permits later in project development. The final EIS should indicate the general location of the fill or dredged activity, approximate quantities of fill or dredged material, general construction grades, and proposed mitigation measures, and should include evidence of coordination with the Corps.

Threatened or Endangered Species

The HA shall request from the Departments of the Interior (DOI) and/or Commerce (DOC) information on whether any species listed or proposed as endangered or threatened may be present in the area of the proposed construction project. If those departments advise that there are no such species in the area, the requirements of the Endangered Species Act have been met. If those departments advise that such a species may be present, the FHWA/HA shall undertake a biological assessment to identify any threatened or endangered species which are likely to be affected by the proposed action. This biological assessment should include:

a. An on-site inspection of the area affected by the proposed project.
b. Interviews with recognized experts on the species at issue.
c. A literature review to determine the species distribution, habitat needs, and other biological requirements.
d. An analysis of possible impacts to the species.
e. An analysis of measures to minimize impacts. This biological assessment should be forwarded to DOI/DOC for a biological opinion. The Fish and Wildlife Service (F&WS) is responsible for the protection of terrestrial and fresh-water species and the National Marine Fisheries Service (NMFS) is responsible for the protection of marine species.

Upon completing their review of the biological assessment, the F&WS/NMFS may request additional information and/or a meeting to discuss the project or issue a biological opinion stating that the project: (a) is not likely to jeopardize, or (b) will promote the conservation of or (c) is likely to jeopardize the threatened or endangered species. In selecting a preferred alternative, jeopardy to an endangered or threatened species must be avoided. If either a finding of (a) or (b) is given, the requirements of the Endangered Species act are met. If a detrimental finding is presented, the proposed action may be modified so that the species is no longer jeopardized. In unique circumstances, an exemption may be requested. If an exemption is denied, the action must be halted or modified. The final EIS should document the results of the coordination of the biological assessment with the appropriate agencies.

Prime and Unique Agricultural Lands

Information on prime and unique agricultural lands should be solicited through early consultation with the Department of Agriculture (USDA), and the EIS should identify the direct and indirect impacts of the proposed action on these lands, including:

a. An estimate of the number of acres that might be directly affected by right-of-way acquisition.
b. Areas where agricultural operation might be disrupted.

    c. Potential indirect effects such as those related to project-induced changes in land use.

The EIS should contain a map showing the location of prime and unique agricultural lands in relation to the project alternatives, summarize the results of consultations with the USDA, and include copies of correspondence with USDA regarding the project. Specific actions to avoid or, if that is not possible, to reduce direct and indirect effects on these lands should be identified.

Construction Impacts

The EIS should discuss significant impacts (particularly air, noise, water, detours, safety, visual, etc.) associated with construction of each of the alternatives. Also, where applicable, the impacts of disposal and borrow areas should be discussed along with any proposed measures to minimize these impacts.

Considerations Relating to Pedestrians and Bicyclists

Section 682 of the National Energy Policy Act of 1978 recognizes that bicycles are an efficient means of transportation, represent a viable commuting alternative to many people, and deserve consideration in a comprehensive national energy plan. The FHWA recognizes that bicyclists are legitimate highway users and that FHWA has a responsibility to provide for their transportation needs. Section 109(n) of 23 U.S.C. provides that "the Secretary shall not approve any project under this title that will result in the severance or destruction of an existing major route for nonmotorized transportation traffic and light motorcycles, unless such project provides a reasonable alternate route or such a route exists." The FHWA policy regarding Bicycle Program Activities is further defined in an August 20, 1981, memorandum from Administrator Barnhart to all regional administrators. Where appropriate, the EIS should consider pedestrian and bicycle use as an integral feature of the project and include a discussion of the relationship of the proposed project to local plans for bicycles and pedestrian facilities and evidence that the project is consistent with 23 U.S.C. 109(n).

Stream Modification and Wildlife Impacts

Title 16 U.S.C. 662(a) requires consultation with the Fish and Wildlife Service and the appropriate State agency regarding any federal action which involves impoundment (surface area of 10 acres or more), diversion, channel deepening, or other modification of a stream or body of water. Exhibits should be used to identify stream modifications. The use of the stream or body of water for recreation or other purposes should be identified. It should also discuss any significant impacts on fish and wildlife resources, including direct impact to fish and wildlife, loss or modification of habitat, and degradation of water quality.

Visual Impacts

This discussion should include an assessment of the visual impacts of the proposed action, including the "view from the road" and the "view of the road." Where relevant, the EIS should document the consideration given to design quality, art, and architecture in the project planning. These values may be particularly important for facilities located in sensitive urban settings. Where relevant, the draft EIS should be circulated to officially designated state and local arts councils and, as appropriate, other organizations with an interest in design, art, and architecture.

List of Preparers

This section will include lists of:

a. State (and local agency) personnel, including consultants, who were primarily responsible for preparing the EIS or performing environmental studies, and their qualifications, including educational background or experience
b. The FHWA personnel primarily responsible for preparation or review of the EIS, and their qualifications
c. The areas of EIS responsibility for each preparer

List of Agencies, Organizations, and Persons to Whom Copies of the Statement are Sent

List all entities from which comments are being requested (draft EIS) and identify those that submitted comments (final EIS).

Comments and Coordination

a. The draft EIS should summarize the early coordination process, including scoping, meetings with community groups and individuals, and the key issues and pertinent information received from the public and government agencies through these efforts.
b. The final EIS should include a copy of all substantive comments received (or summaries thereof, where the response has been exceptionally voluminous), along with a response to each substantive comment. When the EIS is revised as a result of the comments received, a copy of the comments should contain marginal references indicating where revisions were made,

or the discussion of the comments should contain such references. The FHWA comment(s) on the draft EIS should not be included in the final EIS. However, the document should include adequate information for the FHWA reviewer to ascertain the disposition of the comment(s). Formal comments by the Department of Transportation should be included in the final EIS along with an appropriate response to each comment.

c. The final EIS should document compliance with requirements of all applicable environmental laws, Executive Orders, and other related requirements. To the extent possible, all environmental issues should be resolved prior to the submission of the final EIS. Where this is not possible, the final EIS should clearly identify any remaining unresolved issues, the change taken to resolve the issues, and the positions of the respective parties.

d. The final EIS should contain a summary and disposition of substantive comments on social, economic, and environmental issues made at any public hearing or other public involvement activity or which were otherwise considered.

Index

The index should include major subjects and areas of significant impacts so that a reviewer need not read the entire EIS to obtain information on a specific subject or impact.

23 CFR 771 requires compliance to the extent possible with other applicable environmental laws, Executive Orders, and other related requirements. This includes the certifications and reports required by 23 U.S.C. 128 relating to public hearings, considerations of social, economic, and environmental (SEE) effects and consistency of the project with urban planning goals promulgated by the community. The certifications normally are made at the time the final EIS or FONSI is submitted to the FHWA Division Administrator. The report of SEE effects required by 23 U.S.C. 128 will normally be satisfied by the final EIS, FONSI, or identification of the project as a categorical exclusion.

Appendices

Material prepared as appendices to the EIS should:

a. consist of material prepared in connection with the EIS (is distinct from material which is not so prepared and which is incorporated by reference);

b. consist of material which substantiates an analysis which is fundamental to the EIS;

c. by analytic and relevant to the decision to be made; and

d. be circulated with the EIS or be readily available on request. Other reports and studies referred to in the EIS should be readily available for review or for copying at a convenient location

Alternate Process for Final EISs

Paragraph 1503.4 of the CEQ regulation (40 CFR 1500, et seq.) provides the opportunity for expediting final EIS preparation in those instances when, after receipt of comments resulting from circulation of the draft EIS, it is apparent that the changes in the proposal or in the EIS in response to the comments received are minor and that:

a. all reasonable alternatives were studied and discussed in the draft EIS, and
b. the analyses in the draft EIS adequately identified and quantified the environmental impacts of all reasonable alternatives.

When these two points can be established, the final EIS can consist of the draft EIS and an attachment containing the following:

a. Errata sheets making corrections to the draft EIS, if applicable.
b. A section identifying the preferred alternative and a discussion of the reasons it was selected. The following should also be included in this section, if applicable:
   (1) Final Section 4(f) evaluations containing the information described in Section 6 of these guidelines
   (2) Wetlands finding(s)
   (3) Floodplain finding(s)
   (4) A list of commitments for mitigation measures for the preferred alternative
c. Copies (or summaries) of comments received from circulation of the draft EIS and public hearing and responses thereto.

A.4 DISTRIBUTION OF EISs AND SECTION 4(f) EVALUATIONS

Environmental Impact Statements

a. Copies of all draft EISs should be circulated for comments to all public officials, private interest groups, and members of the public having or expressing an interest in the proposed action or the draft EIS, and to all government agencies expected to have jurisdiction, responsibility, interest, or expertise in the proposed action. Internal FHWA distribution of draft and final EISs is subject to change and is noted in memorandums to the Regional Administrators as requirements change. The FHWA transmittal letter to the Washington Headquarters should include a recommendation regarding the need for the prior concurrence of the Washington Headquarters in accordance with 23 CFR 771(e).

b. Copies of all approved final EISs should be distributed to all cooperating agencies, to all federal, state, and local agencies and private organizations, and members of the public who commented substantively on the draft EIS. A copy of all approved delegated EISs should be forwarded to the FHWA Washington Headquarters (HEV-10) for recordkeeping purposes.

Copies of all draft and final EISs in the categories listed in 23 CFR 771(e) should be provided to the Regional Representative of the Secretary of Transportation at the same time as they are forwarded to the FHWA Washington Headquarters.

c. Copies of all EISs should normally be distributed as follows, unless the agency has indicated to the FHWA offices the need for a different number of copies:

(1) The EPA Headquarters: five copies of the draft EIS and five copies of the final EIS (this is the "filing requirement" in Section 1506.9 of the CEQ regulation; the correct address is listed therein).

(2) The appropriate EPA regional office responsible for EPA's review pursuant to Section 309 of the Clean Air Act: five copies of the draft EIS and five copies of the final EIS.

(3) The DOI Headquarters:

(a) All States in FHWA Regions 1, 3, 4, and 5, plus Hawaii, Guam, American Samoa, Arkansas, Iowa, Louisiana, Missouri, and Puerto Rico: 12 copies of the draft EIS and 7 copies of the final EIS.

(b) Kansas, Nebraska, North Dakota, Oklahoma, South Dakota, and Texas: 13 copies of the draft EIS and 8 copies of the final EIS.

(c) New Mexico and all states in FHWA Regions 8, 9, and 10, except Hawaii, North Dakota, and South Dakota: 14 copies of the draft EIS and 9 copies of the final EIS.

Section 4(f) Evaluation

If the Section 4(f) evaluation is included in an EIS, DOI Headquarters should receive the same number of copies listed above for EISs for consultation in accordance with the requirements of 23 U.S.C. 138. If the Section 4(f) evaluation is processed as a separate document or as part of an EA, the DOI should receive seven copies of the draft Section 4(f) evaluation for coordination and seven copies of the final Section 4(f) statement for information.

In addition, draft Section 4(f) evaluations, whether in a draft EIS, an EA, or a separate document, are required to be coordinated where appropriate with HUD and USDA.

A.5 RECORD OF DECISION—FORMAT AND CONTENT

The record of decision (ROD) must set forth the reasons for the project decision, based on the material contained in the environmental documents. While cross referencing and incorporation by reference of other documents is appropriate, the ROD should explain the basis for the project decision as completely as possible.

   a. *Decision.* Identify the selected alternative. Reference to the final EIS may be used to reduce detail and repetition.

   b. *Alternatives considered.* This information can be most clearly organized by briefly describing each alternative (with reference to the final EIS, as above), then explaining and discussing the balancing of values underlying the decision. This discussion must identify the alternative or alternatives which were considered preferable from a strictly environmental point of view. If the selected alternative is other than the environmentally preferable alternative, the ROD should clearly state the reasons for that decision. In addition, if use of Section 4(f) land is involved, the required Section 4(f) approval should be summarized.

   For each individual decision (final EIS), the values (economic, environmental, safety, traffic service, community planning, etc.) which are significant factors in the decision-making process may be different and may be given different levels of relative importance. Accordingly, it is essential that this discussion clearly identifies each significant value and the reasons some values were considered more important than others. While any decision represents a balancing of the values, the ROD should reflect the manner in which these values were considered in arriving at the decision.

   It is also essential that legislation requirements in 23 U.S.C. be given appropriate weight in this decision-making process. The mission of FHWA is to implement the federal-aid highway program to provide safe and efficient transportation. While this mission must be accomplished within the context of all other federal requirements, the beneficial impacts of transportation improvements must be given proper consideration and documentation in this ROD.

   c. *Measures to minimize harm.* Describe all measures to minimize environmental harm which have been adopted for the proposed action. State whether all practicable measures to minimize environmental harm have been incorporated into the decision and, if not, why.

   d. *Monitoring or enforcement program.* Describe any monitoring or enforcement program which has been adopted for specific mitigation measures, as outlined in the final EIS.

A.6. SECTION 4(f) EVALUATIONS—FORMAT AND CONTENT

Draft Evaluation—Format

   a. Describe proposed action (if separate document)
   b. Describe Section 4(f) resource
   c. Impacts on resource (by alternative)
   d. Avoidance alternatives and their impacts
   e. Measures to minimize harm
   f. Coordination with appropriate agencies
   g. Concluding statement (final document only)

In the case of a complex Section 4(f) involvement, it is desirable to include the analysis in a separate section of the draft EIS, EA, or for projects processed as categorical exclusions, in a separate document. A Section 4(f) evaluation should be prepared for each location within the project where the use of Section 4(f) land is being considered.

Draft Evaluation—Content

The following information should be included in the Section 4(f) evaluation, as appropriate:

   a. A brief description of the project and the need for the project (when the Section 4(f) evaluation is circulated separately).
   b. A detailed map or drawing of sufficient scale to identify essential elements of the highway/Section 4(f) land involvement.
   c. Size (acres or square feet) and location (maps or other exhibits such as photographs, sketches, etc.) of involvement.
   d. Type of property (recreation, historic, etc.)
   e. Available activities at the property (fishing, swimming, golfing, etc.).
   f. Description and location of all existing and planned facilities (ball diamonds, tennis courts, etc.).

g. Usage (approximate number of users/visitors, etc.).

h. Relationship to other similarly used lands in the vicinity.

i. Access (pedestrian and vehicular).

j. Ownership (city, county, state, etc.).

k. Applicable clauses affecting the title, such as covenants, restrictions, or conditions, including forfeiture.

l. Unusual characteristics of the Section 4(f) land (flooding problems, terrain conditions, or other features that either reduce or enhance the value of portions of the area).

m. The location (using maps or other exhibits such as photographs or sketches) and the amount of land (acres or square feet) to be used by the proposed project including permanent and temporary easements.

n. The probable increase or decrease in environmental impacts (noise, air pollution, visual, etc.) of the alternative locations and designs considered on the Section 4(f) land users.

o. A description of all reasonable and practicable measures which are available to minimize the impacts of the proposed action on the Section 4(f) property. Discussions of alternatives in the draft EIS or EA may be referenced rather than repeated.

p. Sufficient information to evaluate all alternatives which would avoid the Section 4(f) property. Discussions of alternatives in the draft EIS or EA may be referenced rather than repeated. However, this section should include discussions of design alternatives (to avoid Section 4(f) use) in the immediate area of the Section 4(f) property.

q. The determination that there are no feasible and prudent alternatives is not normally addressed at the draft EIS, EA, or preliminary document stage until the results of the formal coordination have been completed.

r. The results of preliminary coordination with the public official having jurisdiction over the Section 4(f) property and with regional (or local) offices of DOI and, as appropriate, the regional (or local) office of USDA and HUD.

Section 4(f) Discussion in Final Document

When the selected alternative involves the use of Section 4(f) land, a Section 4(f) evaluation may be included as a separate section in the final EIS or FONSI or for projects processed as categorical exclusions, in a separate final Section 4(f) evaluation. The final evaluation should contain:

a. All information required above for a draft evaluation.

b. A discussion of the basis for the determination that there are no feasible and prudent alternatives to the use of the Section 4(f) land. The supporting information must demonstrate that there are unique problems or unusual factors involved in the use of alternatives and that the cost, environmental impact, or community disruption resulting from such alternatives reaches extraordinary magnitudes.

c. A discussion of the basis for the determination that the proposed action includes all possible planning to minimize harm to the Section 4(f) property.

d. A summary of the appropriate formal coordination with the Headquarters Offices of DOI, and as appropriate, the Headquarters Offices of USDA and HUD.

e. Copies of all formal coordination comments received and an analysis and response to any questions raised.

f. Concluding statement as follows: "Based upon the above considerations, it is determined that there is no feasible and prudent alternative to the use of land from the (Section 4(f) property) and that the proposed action includes all possible planning to minimize harm to the (Section 4(f) property) resulting from such use."

A Section 4(f) approval is the written administrative record which documents the approval required by 23 U.S.C. 138. The Section 4(f) approval will be incorporated into either the final EIS or the ROD. When the Section 4(f) approval is contained in the ROD, the information noted in items (a) through (e) above may be incorporated by reference to the EIS. For a project processed as a categorical exclusion, any required Section 4(f) approval will normally be prepared as a *separate* document.

A.7 PREDECISION REFERRALS TO CEQ

a. Any FHWA office receiving a notice of intent of referral from another agency should provide a copy of that intent of referral to the FHWA Washington Headquarters, Office of Environmental Policy (HEV-10), and the involved Regional Office, Division Office, and HA. This notice of intent of referral would generally be received as part of an agency's comments on the draft EIS. The exception would be when an agency indicates that the draft EIS did not contain adequate information to permit an assessment of the proposal's environmental acceptability. Every reasonable effort should be made to reach agreement with the agency prior to filing of the final EIS. If agreement cannot be reached, the final EIS should document the attempts to resolve the issues and summarize the remaining differences. Prior concurrence of the Washington Headquarters is necessary in the case of government opposition on environmental grounds.

b. The response to the notice of referral will be prepared by the Washington Headquarters with input from the regional, division, and state offices. The

FHWA Washington Headquarters will obtain the concurrence of the Department of Transportation prior to the response to CEQ.

c. Upon reviewing the draft EIS from another federal agency, if the FHWA Regional or Division Office believes a referral will be necessary, it should so advise HEV-1. The Office of Environmental Policy (HEV-1) will review the proposed referral and, if appropriate, will advise the Departmental Office of Environment and Safety (P-20), which will coordinate DOT comments on the draft EIS, including the notice of intended referral. Every reasonable effort should be made to resolve the issues after providing notice of intent to refer and prior to the lead agency's filing of the final EIS with EPA. In the event that the issues have not been resolved, the appropriate field office should prepare a referral to CEQ to be submitted through HEV to P-20 for a determination as to whether a referral to CEQ is appropriate.

A.8 OTHER AGENCY STATEMENTS

a. The FHWA review of statements prepared by other agencies will consider the environmental impact of the proposal on areas within FHWA's functional area of responsibility or special expertise.

b. Agencies requesting comments on highway impacts usually forward the draft EIS to the FHWA Washington Headquarters for comment. The FHWA Washington Headquarters will normally distribute these EISs to the appropriate regional office and will indicate where the comments should be sent. The regional office may elect to forward the draft statement to the division office for response.

c. When a field office has received a draft EIS directly from another agency, it may comment directly to that agency if the proposal does not fall within the types indicated in item (d) of this section. If more than one DOT Administration is commenting at the regional level, the comments should be coordinated by the DOT Regional Representative to the Secretary or designee. Copies of the FHWA comments should be distributed as follows:

(1) Requesting agency—original and one copy

(2) P-20—one copy

(3) DOT Secretarial Representative—one copy

(4) HEV-10—one copy

d. The following types of action contained in the draft EIS require FHWA Washington Headquarters review and such EISs should be forwarded to the Associate Administrator for Right-of-Way and Environment (HRE-01), along with regional comments, for processing:

(1) Actions with national implications

(2) Legislation or regulations having national impacts or national program proposals

A.9 PROPOSALS FOR LEGISLATION OR REGULATIONS

Proposals for regulations and legislation will be evaluated by the initiating Washington Headquarters office for compliance with the appropriate NEPA requirements. The proposal may require the development of an EA and FONSI, or an EIS which will be the responsibility of the initiating office in consultation with HEV-10. When a draft EIS for proposed legislation is appropriate, it will be submitted to OST for transmittal to the Office of Management and Budget for circulation in the normal legislative clearance process. Any comments received on the EIS will be transmitted to Congress. Except as provided in 40 CFR Part 1506(b)(2) there need not be a final EIS.

B   Elements of Engineering
                          Economy

B.1 MONEY AND ITS TIME VALUE

Money's *raison d'être* is its acceptability as a medium of exchange. It can be used in exchange for goods and services much more efficiently than the direct trading of goods and services (i.e., barter). Because money can be used for the purchase of many items, it can serve as a standard of value for them, at least in a relative sense. Because it can retain the ability to be exchanged for other commodities at various times, money is also a store of value.

In one view, the term *value* of a commodity is synonymous with the number of monetary units (or the *price*) that it commands. Others use the term value to refer to the degree to which a particular good or service satisfies the needs of individuals and employ the term *utility* to clarify this difference. The fact is that such a difference between price and utility exists and that the term value is often used for both. The context in which it is used usually clarifies the connotation intended.

Often, the *value of money* is defined as the reciprocal of the prices of the goods and services for which it can be exchanged. Thus if for various reasons the number of monetary units (e.g., dollars or yen) required to obtain a given item were to increase, the situation could be described either as an increase in the price of that item or, conversely, a decrease in the value of the monetary unit. A major difficulty associated with this definition for the value of money lies in the fact that the prices of the myriad of goods and services that are daily exchanged in markets do not all behave in the same way. The prices of some may be on the decrease, whereas the prices of others are either stable or increasing. These price changes are caused by many conditions, including changes in the quantities demanded, technological breakthroughs that result in more efficient or less costly production methods, and changes in the availability of resources (or factors of production) through depletion, new discoveries, or even catastrophic events such as wars. To complicate matters, the supply of money in the form of currency and credit also affects prices. Even though the prices of individual goods and services vary differentially, the general behavior of prices may, nevertheless, be described by several indicators. The most well known of these indicators is the *consumer price index* (CPI), which is compiled by the U.S. Bureau of Labor Statistics to capture the price changes of a combination of goods that the typical family considers essential. When the general price level is on an upswing, the economy is said to experience price *inflation*. When prices are falling the economy is in a *deflationary period*. The value of money as defined in this way decreases with price inflation and increases with price deflation.

People and firms exchange goods and services in order to maximize the satisfaction (i.e., utility) they derive from them. For example, firms give up money (and, indirectly, other goods and services) to purchase the services of employees and needed factors of production for the purpose of deriving profits from the sale of the goods and services they produce. Exchange is possible because the utility that individuals and other economic entities attach to the items being exchanged is not identical. Both parties to the exchange give up something they consider less desirable for something they consider more desirable. Since, as a store of value, money stands for the opportunities it represents to consumers and producers, it is imbued with the characteristics shared by all commodities, including the ability to satisfy human wants—that is, utility. As a major factor of production, it carries the ability to earn profits, and this earning power of money is reflected in the *time value of money*. Simply stated, a dollar in hand at present is not the same as a dollar in hand at some future date, because in the future, the present dollar would be incremented by the return it would earn in the meantime. Economic entities are willing to borrow and lend money at a premium because of the various profit-making opportunities they are able to pursue. Typically, the lender is satisfied with the "rental" to be received from a borrower for the use of the lender's money, whereas the borrower is looking for an opportunity to put the borrowed money to some use that would gain for the borrower a satisfactory profit above the cost of "renting" the money.

B.2 INTEREST AND DISCOUNT

The premium paid or received for the use of money is known as *interest*. The rate at which interest accumulates (i.e., the *interest rate*) is quoted as the percentage gained over a specified time period, known as the *interest period*. Thus the interest rate relates a sum of money presently in hand to its equivalent sum at some future date. The rate that relates a sum of money at some future date to its equivalent at present is known as the *discount rate*.

The value of money is affected by price instabilities. Consequently, the interest rate that lenders seek and borrowers are willing to pay is affected by (1) their expectations relating to potential movements of the price level (i.e., the *purchasing power* of money) and (2) their desired return or profit (i.e., the *earning power* of money). Assuming constant dollars (i.e., ignoring inflation) facilitates the understanding of the basic concepts covered by this section. Incidentally, the term *current dollar* refers to the reciprocal of the general price level at any given time, and, therefore, includes the effect of inflation. Current or real rates account for inflation. The real interest rate results after subtracting inflation from the prime rate (i.e., $7\% - 2\% = 5\%$).

Example B.1

A business firm borrows $10,000 and agrees to pay back $10,200 at the end of one month. Calculate the interest rate involved in the transaction.

Solution   The total interest paid at the end of the month is $200. The interest period is 1 month and the interest rate is

$$\frac{\$200}{\$10,000} = 0.02 \text{ or } 2\% \text{ per month}$$

Discussion   The interest rate translates a present sum to a future sum. The terms *present* and *future* are defined in relation to each other and not to specific calendar times. In other words, the previous calculation would be the same as long as the two times are separated by one month. The discount involved in this transaction is also $200. It relates the future sum ($10,200) to its present equivalent ($10,000). By definition, the discount rate is 2% per month, that is, the difference between the future and present sums divided by the *present sum* (see Example B.2).

Example B.2

An investor purchases a zero coupon bond for $867.98. The bond has a face value of $1000 and matures in 1 year. This means that the bond can be cashed after 1 year for $1000. Calculate the discount rate involved in the transaction.

Solution   The future sum ($1000) was discounted by $132.02. The discount rate was $132.02/867.98 = 0.1521$, or 15.21% per year.

Discussion   The same transaction may be viewed as follows: The investor's principal of $867.98 earned an interest of $132.02 in 1 year at an interest rate of 15.21% per year.

B.3 SIMPLE AND COMPOUND INTEREST

In the preceding two examples, the time over which the interest was earned (i.e., 1 month and 1 year, respectively) coincided with the interest period for which the interest and the discount rates were either calculated or quoted. This need not always be the case. The interval of time between the present and the future can be longer than a single interest period, in which case the present sum continues to earn interest at the quoted rate. *Simple interest* refers to the case where the percentage of the *original* sum of money is added at the end of each interest period. In the case of *compound interest*, both the original sum (principal) and the interest earned are allowed to earn interest during subsequent periods. The difference between the two is illustrated next.

Example B.3

A person who has a sum of $10,000 to invest is faced with the options of (a) earning simple interest at an annual rate of 9% per year or (b) earning compound interest at an annual rate of 8% per year. In both cases, the principal and interest are to be withdrawn at the end of a 5-year period. Compare the two investment options.

Solution   The consequences of each of the two options are tabulated as follows.

Year	Principal and interest at the start of the year	Interest added at the end of the year	Principal and interest at the end of the year
	Option (a): Simple interest at 9% per year		
1	$10,000.00	$ 900.00	$10,900.00
2	10,900.00	900.00	11,800.00
3	11,800.00	900.00	12,700.00
4	12,700.00	900.00	13,600.00
5	13,600.00	900.00	14,500.00
	Option (b): Compound interest at 8% per year		
1	$10,000.00	$ 800.00	$10,800.00
2	10,800.00	864.00	11,664.00
3	11,664.00	933.12	12,597.12
4	12,597.12	1007.77	13,604.89
5	13,604.89	1088.39	14,693.28

Discussion   From the borrower's perspective, the annual 9% simple interest rate is superior to the 8% annually compounded rate up to the end of the third year. Beyond that, the latter becomes the better option. From the lender's point of view, the reverse is true. Thus, both the magnitude of the interest rate and the number of interest periods affect the relative consequences of the two types of interest. The future worth F of a present sum P can be calculated by

$$F = P(1 + in) \qquad\qquad (B.3.1)$$

for the case of simple interest and by

$$F = P(1 + i)^n \qquad\qquad (B.3.2)$$

for the case of compound interest, where

$$i = \text{interest rate (percent per period divided by 100)}$$

$$n = \text{number of interest periods separating } P \text{ and } F$$

The term multiplying the single sum P in Eq. B.3.2 is one of several useful factors and is known as the *single-sum* (or single-payment) *compound-amount factor* for an interest rate i per period and n periods separating P and F (CAF',i,n). Solving Eq. B.3.2 for P yields

$$P = F \frac{1}{(1 + i)^n} \qquad (B.3.3)$$

and the factor that discounts a future sum F to a present sum P is known as the *single-sum present-worth factor* (PWF',i,n).

Example B.4

A sum of \$100,000 is invested at an annually compounded interest rate of 8% per year. Calculate its equivalent at the end of 20 years.

Solution   For $P = \$100,000$, $i = 0.08$, and $n = 20$, Eq. B.3.2. yields

$$F = \$100,000(1 + 0.08)^{20}$$

$$F = \$100,000(4.66096) = \$466,096$$

The single-sum compound-amount factor is 4.66096.

B.4 NOMINAL AND EFFECTIVE INTEREST RATES

Frequently, interest rates are specified on the basis of a period (usually a year) when compounding occurs more frequently than the specified period. By convention, the magnitude of the quoted *nominal interest rate* is equal to the product of the interest rate per interest period times the number of interest periods in the specified period. For example a nominal annual rate of 12% compounded semiannually means that the interest rate is 6% per 6-month interest period. Similarly, a nominal interest rate of 12% compounded monthly implies an interest rate of 1% per month. The following example shows that the *effective interest rate* is larger than the nominal interest rate because the interest earned at the end of each interest period is subsequently allowed to earn interest as well.

Example B.5

Compute the equivalent of \$1,000,000 at the end of 5 years if the annual interest rate is (a) 8% per year compounded quarterly and (b) 8% per year compounded semiannually. For each case, calculate the effective *annual* interest rate.

Solution   For part (a), the effective quarterly rate is 2% per quarter. A 5-year period contains 20 quarters. Therefore, substituting $i = 0.02$ and $n = 20$ in Eq. B.3.2 results in

$$F = \$1,000,000(1 + 0.02)^{20} = \$1,485,947$$

To find the effective annual rate, consider compound-amount factor for 1 year expressed in terms of the annual effective rate i and the annual nominal rate r compounded m times a year. The two must yield the same relationship between P and F 1 year apart. Therefore,

$$(1 + i) = \left(1 + \frac{r}{m}\right)^m$$

Consequently, the effective annual rate i is

$$i = \left(1 + \frac{r}{m}\right)^m - 1 \tag{B.4.1}$$

Therefore the effective annual rate for part (a) of this example is

$$i = (1 + 0.02)^4 - 1 = 0.082432 \quad \text{or} \quad 8.2432\% \text{ per year}$$

To illustrate its use, Eq. B.4.1 is applied to the solution of part (b) of this example. With $m = 2$ interest periods per year, the effective annual rate is

$$i = (1 + 0.04)^2 - 1 = 0.0816 \quad \text{or} \quad 8.16\% \text{ per year}$$

Using this effective annual rate, at the end of 5 years, the initial $P = \$1,000,000$ becomes

$$F = \$1,000,000(1 + 0.0816)^5 = \$1,480,244$$

The same result would have been obtained by using an effective semiannual interest rate of 4% per 6-month period and 10 interest periods (i.e., 5 years times two 6-month periods in a year).

B.5 DISCRETE AND CONTINUOUS COMPOUNDING

In the foregoing examples, compounding was considered to occur with finite interest periods such as a year, 6-months, a quarter of a year, a month and so forth. This is called *discrete compounding*, since the interest is paid at the end of each dicrete interest period. *Continuous compounding* represents the limiting case when the interest period approaches zero. Given a nominal interest rate r under continuous compounding, the effective interest rate would be the limit of i in Eq. B.4.1 as the number of interest periods m approaches infinity. In that case, the *effective interest rate for continuous compounding* is equal to $(e^r - 1)$, where e is the base of natural logarithms.

According to Eq. B.3.2, when interest is compounded continuously at a nominal interest rate r per specified period, the relationship between single sums separated by n periods is:

$$F = Pe^{rn} \tag{B.5.1}$$

$$P = Fe^{-rn} \tag{B.5.2}$$

The multiplier of P in Eq. B.5.1 is known as the *single-sum compound amount* factor (CAF′,r,n) and the multiplier of F in Eq. B.5.2. is called the *single-sum present-worth factor* (PWF′,r,n), both with continuous compounding. The subscript r refers to the *nominal* interest rate per period.

Example B.6

Solve Example B.5 for the case of continuous compounding.

Solution　The nominal annual rate is still 8%. Hence, for a 5-year period between P and F,

$$F = Pe^{(0.08)(5)} = \$1,491,825$$

The effective annual interest rate is approximately equal to 8.33% per year.

Discussion　For the same nominal interest rate, the magnitude of F increases as the number of compounding interest periods m increases. The maximum occurs when m approaches infinity, that is, when the interest is compounded continuously.

B.6 CASH FLOWS

Up to this point, the discussion of money equivalencies was restricted to the case of two single sums (or payments) separated by a time interval. The general case of a *cash flow* such as the one illustrated by Fig. B.6.1 is frequently encountered, and the equivalent single sum E_k of the cash flow at a time k may be desired. This task can be accomplished by summing the equivalent sums at time k of each single payment in the cash flow using the appropriate single-sum present-worth or compound-amount factors as follows:

$$E_k = \sum_{j=0}^{k} S_j \, (\text{CAF}'*, k - j) + \sum_{j=k+1}^{n} S_j \, (\text{PWF}'*, j - k) \qquad \text{(B.6.1)}$$

The first subscript of the factors, which is designated by the asterisk, is either the effective interest rate per period, i, for discrete compounding or the nominal interest rate, r, per period for continuous compounding. Note that the single payment S_k has been included as the last term of the first summation but the fact that, when $j = k$, $(k - j) = 0$ leaves that single payment intact. The terms S_j can be positive, zero, or negative. When they are specified by difference

Figure B.6.1　Cash flow.

between receipts and payments at each time j, the cash flow is referred to as the *net cash flow*.

Example B.7

Given the following cash flow, calculate its equivalent single sum at (a) the end of the sixth period, (b) the end of the fourth period, and (c) time zero. Assume discrete compounding at 10% per period.

Solution   This problem entails the application of Eq. B.6.1. The solution to part (a) is tabulated next. It involves only the first summation shown in the equation because $k = n$.

j:	0	1	2	3	4	5	6
S_j:	100.00	200.00	50.00	0.00	150.00	50.00	200.00
$(k - j)$:	6	5	4	3	2	1	0
$S_j(CAF')$:	177.16	322.10	73.21	0.00	181.50	55.00	200.00

$$\text{Sum} = 1{,}008.97$$

The solution to part (b) may be obtained by applying Eq. B.6.1 with $k = 4$. However, since the single sum obtained in part (a) is equivalent to the original cash flow, all that is needed is to find its equivalent at the end of the fourth period, or two periods earlier than the sixth. The single-sum present-worth factor for discrete compounding with an interest rate $i = 0.10$ and $n = 2$ yields:

$$E_4 = (1008.96)(0.82645) = 833.86$$

Similarly, the equivalent single payment at time zero can be computed by Eq. B.6.1 with $k = 0$. Alternatively, it can be calculated by discounting E_6 to its equivalent six periods earlier, or by discounting E_4 to its equivalent four periods earlier. Either one of the last two methods is simpler than the direct application of the long equation. Hence

$$E_0 = (1008.96)(0.56447) = 569.54$$

or

$$E_0 = (833.86)(0.68301) = 569.54$$

Discussion   This example illustrates the fact that individual components of a cash flow can be treated separately and the final result obtained by superposition. Care must be exercised to move the individual components to the desired point in time using (1) the appropriate time separation by noting that the terms *present* and *future* refer to a *relative* time difference, and (2) the correct present worth and compound-amount factors. Equation B.6.1 automatically takes care of these requirements. It also accounts properly for the situation where no payment exists at the end of one or more periods (e.g., the third period in this problem), since the corresponding term in the summation reduces to zero. The same equation may be used for discrete cash flows under continuous compounding. In that event, the present worth and compound-amount factors corresponding to continuous compounding must be used.

B.7 EQUAL SERIES OF PAYMENTS

A special cash flow profile is a series of n equal payments as shown by Fig. B.7.1(a). The first and last payments occur *at the end* of the first and last periods, respectively. The single-sum equivalent of the entire series either at time zero (i.e., the beginning of the first period; see Fig. B.7.1(b)) or at the end of the last period may be desired [Fig. B.7.1(c)]. Conversely, a single sum at the beginning of the first period or at the end of the last period may be converted to their equivalent series of equal payments [Fig. B.7.1(a)]. Rather that having to apply Eq. B.6.1 each time such a conversion is needed, four *equal-payment factors* have been developed. These are summarized in Table B.7.1 along with the two single-sum factors discussed earlier. Note that the acronyms for the single-sum factors have primes attached to distinguish them from the equal-payment factors of the same name.

As a mathematical illustration, the formulas for the equal-payment com-

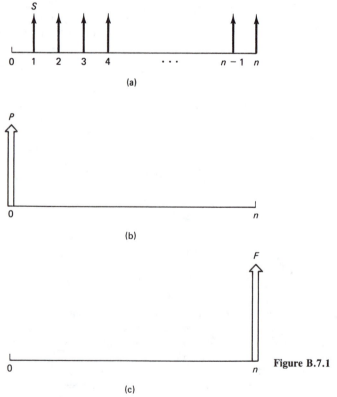

(a)

(b)

(c)

Figure B.7.1 Equal series, present, and future single-payment equivalents.

TABLE B.7.1 DISCRETE COMPOUNDING FACTORS[a]

Factor	Notation	Formula	Given	Find
1. Single-sum factors				
a. Compound-amount factor	(CAF',i,n)	$(1 + i)^n$	P	F
b. Present-worth factor	(PWF',i,n)	$\dfrac{1}{(1 + i)^n}$	F	P
2. Equal-series factors				
a. Compound-amount factor	(CAF,i,n)	$\dfrac{(1 + i)^n - 1}{i}$	S	F
b. Sinking fund factor	(SFF,i,n)	$\dfrac{i}{(1 + i)^n - 1}$	F	S
c. Present-worth factor	(PWF,i,n)	$\dfrac{(1 + i)^n - 1}{i(1 + i)^n}$	S	P
d. Capital recovery factor	(CRF,i,n)	$\dfrac{i(1 + i)^n}{(1 + i)^n - 1}$	P	S

[a] P, "present" single sum; F, "future" single sum; S, single sum in a series; n, number of periods.

pound amount and sinking factors under discrete compounding are derived as follows:

Applying Eq. B.6.1 to the series of equal payments of Fig. B.7.1(a) with $h = 0$, $k = n$, $S_0 = 0$, and all other $S_j = S$,

$$F = S[(1 + i)^{n-1} + \cdots + (1 + i)^2 + (1 + i) + 1]$$

Multiplying this equation by $(1 + i)$ and subtracting it from the result,

$$F(1 + i) - F = S[(1 + i)^n - 1]$$

Solving for F yields

$$F = S\left[\frac{(1 + i)^n - 1}{i}\right] \tag{B.7.1}$$

The bracketed term is the *equal-series compound-amount factor for discrete compounding* (CAF,i,n). Solving Eq. B.7.1 for S, the corresponding *sinking-fund factor* (SFF,i,n) that converts a single sum F to an equal-payment series is seen to be the reciprocal of the (CAF,i,n). The rest of the equal-payment factors for discrete compounding as well as those corresponding to continuous compounding (see Table B.7.1) can be derived in a similar manner. Also, useful relationships between the six factors for each compounding method may be reasoned out. For example, to find S given P, the latter is multiplied by the CRF. If P were to be multiplied by CAF' to find F and if this result were to be multiplied by SFF, the same equivalent equal-payment series would result. Therefore,

$$CRF = (CAF')(SFF) \tag{B.7.2}$$

In fact, all six factors can be expressed in terms of one single-sum and one of the equal-payment factors. Moreover, the continuous-compounding factors can be derived by substituting the effective rate per period $i = e^r - 1$ into the discrete compounding factors.

Example B.8

An automobile salesperson has offered the following terms to a customer who is interested in purchasing a $10,000 car: No down payment and 48 equal monthly payments, the first to be paid at the end of the first month after the purchase. Calculate the monthly payments and the equivalent single sum at the end of the 48-month period if the interest rate were 12% per year compounded monthly.

Solution   The effective interest rate per month is 1%, $i = 0.01$, and $n = 48$. Hence, the monthly payment S is:

$$S = P(\text{CRF},i,48) = \$(10,000)(0.026338) = \$263.34 \text{ per month}$$

To find the equivalent single sum after 48 months, this equal-payment series can be converted using the CAF:

$$F = S(\text{CAF},i,48) = (263.38)(61.22258) = \$16,122.26$$

or the original single sum can be converted using the single-sum compound-amount factor:

$$F = P(\text{CAF}',i,48) = (10,000)(1.612226) = \$16,122.26$$

Moreover, the same result can be obtained by first determining the effective annual interest rate via Eq. B.4.1 to be equal to 0.126825 and then applying the discretely compounded single-sum compound amount factor with this rate and 2 periods (i.e., 48 months = 2 years).

Discussion   In addition to the use of equal-payment factors, this example reviews several important principles. First, the interest period was matched with the payment period by converting the given monthly compounded annual nominal rate of 12% to a monthly effective rate of 1%. Second, three possible alternative methods of obtaining the single future sum were illustrated. The first two imply the following relationship between factors:

$$(\text{CRF})(\text{CAF}) = (\text{CAF}')$$

The third method by which F was obtained shows that the effective annual interest rate is larger than the quoted nominal annual rate (i.e., 12.6825% versus 12.00%).

B.8 SUPERPOSITION OF CASH FLOWS

A cash flow may be described as the superposition of its individual single payment components. The same principle of superposition applies to the case of complex cash flows that can be decomposed into several simpler cash flows. In each case, several alternative ways of decomposing and superposing the cash flow's parts are possible. It is advisable to contemplate these alternatives in order to discern the simplest way of solving the problem prior to undertaking any calculations. This principle is illustrated by the following example.

Example B.9

Find the *present worth* (i.e., the equivalent single sum at time zero) of the cash flow shown in Fig. B.8.1. The effective interest rate is 8% per period.

Solution   The series shown may be decomposed into simpler series in several ways. Three possibilities are:

1. A series of nine $6 million payments plus a series of five $4 million payments, both series beginning at the end of the first period.
2. A series of five $10 million payments beginning at the end of the first period plus a series of four $6 million payments beginning at the end of the fifth period.
3. A series of nine $10 million payments beginning at the end of the first period minus a series of four $4 million payments beginning at the end of the fifth period.

In this particular case, the first method of decomposition seems to be the simpler of the three. However, for the purpose of illustration, several solutions are attempted.

Using the first method of decomposition, the present worth of the original series is equal to

$$P = 6(\text{PWF},i,9) + 4(\text{PWF},i,5)$$

$$= 6(6.24689) + 4(3.99271) = \$53.45 \text{ million}$$

Using the second method of decomposition, the following two solutions are equivalent:

(a) $P = 10(\text{PWF},i,5) + 6(\text{PWF},i,4)(\text{PWF}',i,5)$

$$= 10(3.99271) + 6(3.31213)(0.68058) = \$53.45 \text{ million}$$

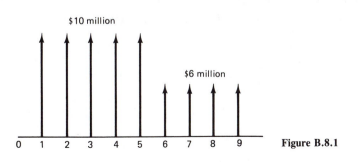

Figure B.8.1

or

(b) $P = 10(\text{PWF},i,5) + 6(\text{CAF},i,4)(\text{PWF}',i,9)$

$= 10(3.99271) + 6(4.50611)(0.50025) = \$53.45 \text{ million}$

Using the third method of decomposition, the following two solutions are also equivalent:

(a) $P = 10(\text{PWF},i,9) - 4(\text{PWF},i,4)(\text{PWF}',i,5)$

$= 10(6.24689) - 4(3.31213)(0.68058) = \$53.45 \text{ million}$

or

(b) $P = 10(\text{PWF},i,9) - 4(\text{CAF},i,4)(\text{PWF}',i,9)$

$= 10(6.24689) - 4(4.50611)(0.50025) = \$53.45 \text{ million}$

B.9 EXERCISES

1. A school transportation company has purchased a new bus on the following terms: $20,000 down and a monthly payment of $2704 for 5 years at a nominal annual interest rate of 9%. What was the cash price?
2. Find the equivalent of the cash price of the bus described in Exercise 1 at the end of the 5-year period.
3. Using an annual interest rate $i = 8\%$, find the present worth of the cash flows given in Fig. EB.3.
4. Find the worth of the cash flows of Exercise 3 at the end of the tenth year.
5. Referring to the cash flow shown in Fig. EB.5, which of the following equations are true?

$$P = 20 + [4(\text{CAF},i,5) + 4(\text{PWF},i,10)](\text{PWF},i,5)$$

$$P = 20 + 8(\text{PWF},i,15) - 4(\text{PWF},i,5)$$

$$P = 20 + [4(\text{CAF},i,15) + 4(\text{CAF},i,10)](\text{SFF},i,15)$$

$$P = 8(\text{CAF}',i,15) + 4(\text{PWF},i,15)(\text{CAF}',i,15) + 4(\text{CAF},i,10)$$

$$P = 20 + 4(\text{PWF},i,15) + 4(\text{CAF},i,10)(\text{PWF}',i,15)$$

$$P = [20(\text{CAF}',i,15) + 4(\text{CAF},i,15) + 4(\text{CAF},i,10)](\text{PWF}',i,15)$$

Figure EB.3

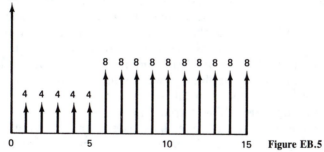

Figure EB.5

C
Model Calibration and Testing

C.1 EXPERIMENTAL DATA AND MODEL PARAMETERS

In many engineering and scientific applications, relationships between variables are established by conducting experimental studies either in the laboratory or in the field. The data collected in this manner may be plotted and the relationship between them discerned. Figure C.1.1 represents a plot (known as a *scatter diagram*) of such observations, each described in terms of a pair of values X and Y that resulted from an experiment. The two variables may represent the stress and strain of steel samples, the speed and concentration of a traffic stream, or city population and volume of long-distance telephone calls. Because of experimental and other errors of measurement, the points shown on the scatter diagram will not fall precisely on a smooth curve. For this reason, the task of the analyst becomes threefold: To hypothesize the mathematical form of the relationship between the two variables (*model postulation*), to estimate the parameters of the model based on the experimental data (*model calibration*), and to determine how well the calibrated relationship explains the observed data (*goodness of fit*).

One method of deriving the relationship between the two variables X and Y plotted in Fig. C.1.1 is freehand approximation. However, the resulting relationship between the variables as well as the assessment of the goodness of fit will be highly subjective. For this reason, a well-defined and rigorous technique of curve fitting is usually preferred. The *method of least squares* is a technique that yields the best-fitting line of a postulated form to a set of data. For example, the following are two possible mathematical forms that may be postulated in the

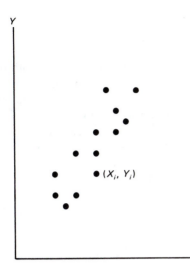
Figure C.1.1   Scatter diagram.

case of a relationship involving two variables Y and X:

$$Y = a + bX \qquad\qquad (C.1.1a)$$

$$Y = c + dX + eX^2 \qquad\qquad (C.1.1b)$$

where X is the independent, or explanatory, variable, Y is the dependent, or explained, variable, and the constant coefficients are the model parameters. Since a set of paired values of (X_i, Y_i) are the known results of an experiment, *calibrating the model means determining the unknown values of the parameters that fix the postulated equation to the one that best fits the data.* The method of least squares determines the numerical values of the coefficients that minimize the sum of square deviations between the observed values of the dependent variable Y_i and the estimated values $\hat{Y}_i$ that would be obtained by applying the calibrated relationship.

C.2 SIMPLE LINEAR REGRESSION

Consider the scatter diagram of Fig. C.2.1. If it can be assumed that the relationship between X and Y is linear, then the method of least squares linear regression can be used to find the one straight line that best fits the data shown. An infinite number of straight lines can be drawn through the scatter diagram, each having its unique pair of parameters, that is, the Y-intercept a and the slope b. Hence, the problem reduces to finding those values of a and b that define the best-fitting straight line. This line will then be used to describe the relationship between X and Y as

$$Y = a + bX \qquad\qquad (C.2.1)$$

Considering the ith observation shown on Fig. C.2.1, a difference exists between the observed value of Y_i corresponding to X_i and the estimated value of Y that would be obtained by substituting X_i in Eq. C.2.1. The estimated value of Y is denoted by $\hat{Y}_i$ to distinguish it from the observed value Y_i. The difference between the two is known as the *error*, *deviation*, or *residual*. The straight line that minimizes some measure of the sum of all such deviations would appear to be the best-fitting straight line. In order to weigh equally the positive and negative deviations (in other words, in order to ensure that the straight line passes *through* the scatter diagram), the deviations are squared and their sum is minimized, that is to say, the specific values of a and b are selected in such a way as to minimize the sum of square deviations.

In mathematical terms, find the values of a and b that minimize the sum:

$$S = \sum_{i=1}^{N} (Y_i - \hat{Y}_i)^2 \qquad\qquad (C.2.2)$$

To minimize S with respect to a and b, Eq. C.2.2 must be expressed in terms of these two parameters. This is accomplished by substituting Eq. C.2.1 in Eq. C.2.2:

$$S = \sum_{i=1}^{N} (Y_i - a - bX_i)^2 \qquad\qquad (C.2.3)$$

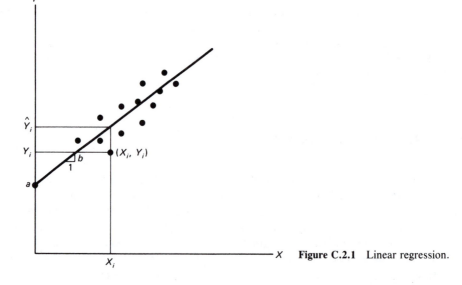

Figure C.2.1   Linear regression.

Setting the partial derivatives of S with respect to a and b equal to zero,

$$\frac{\partial S}{\partial a} = \sum_{i=1}^{N} [2(Y_i - a - bX_i)(-1)] = 0 \tag{C.2.4a}$$

$$\frac{\partial S}{\partial b} = \sum_{i=1}^{N} [2(Y_i - a - bX_i)(-X_i)] = 0 \tag{C.2.4b}$$

Dividing by 2 and rearranging terms gives

$$Na + \left(\sum_{i=1}^{N} X_i\right)b = \sum_{i=1}^{N} Y_i \tag{C.2.5a}$$

$$\left(\sum_{i=1}^{N} X_i\right)a + \left(\sum_{i=1}^{N} X_i^2\right)b = \left(\sum_{i=1}^{N} X_i Y_i\right) \tag{C.2.5b}$$

These two equations, known as the *characteristic equations*, are linear with two unknowns a and b, since the coefficients of the two unknowns and the constant terms on the right-hand side can be computed using the known data of the original experiment.

Application of *Cramer's rule* leads to

$$b = \frac{\begin{vmatrix} N & \Sigma Y_i \\ \Sigma X_i & \Sigma X_i Y_i \end{vmatrix}}{\begin{vmatrix} N & \Sigma X_i \\ \Sigma X_i & \Sigma X_i^2 \end{vmatrix}} = \frac{N(\Sigma X_i Y_i) - (\Sigma X_i)(\Sigma Y_i)}{N(\Sigma X_i^2) - (\Sigma X_i)^2} \tag{C.2.6}$$

Substituting the mean values of the observations $\overline{X}$ and $\overline{Y}$ defined as

$$\overline{X} = \frac{\sum_{i=1}^{N} X_i}{N} \quad \text{and} \quad \overline{Y} = \frac{\sum_{i=1}^{N} Y_i}{N} \tag{C.2.7}$$

where N is the total number of experimental data, Eq. C.2.6 can be rewritten as

$$b = \frac{\Sigma(X_i - \overline{X})(Y_i - \overline{Y})}{\Sigma(X_i - \overline{X})^2} \tag{C.2.8}$$

Dividing Eq. C.2.5a by the number of observations N and substituting Eqs. C.2.7,

$$\overline{Y} = a + b\overline{X} \tag{C.2.9}$$

In other words, the point $(\overline{X}, \overline{Y})$ satisfies the equation of the best-fitting line. This means that *the best-fitting straight line always passes through the mean of the observations*.

By substituting the value of b obtained from either Eq. C.2.6 or Eq. C.2.8 into Eq. C.2.9, the Y-intercept a becomes:

$$a = \overline{Y} - b\overline{X} \qquad (C.2.10)$$

Thus, given a set of N observations (X_i, Y_i), the parameters of the best-fitting straight line are given by Eqs. C.2.8 and C.2.10.

Example C.1

Given the following measurements of traffic speed u and concentration k, apply the method of least squares to find the best-fitting straight line $u = a + bk$.

$$u: \quad 50 \quad 45 \quad 40 \quad 30 \quad 25$$

$$k: \quad 10 \quad 20 \quad 36 \quad 39 \quad 70$$

Solution Speed is the dependent variable, concentration is the independent variable, and a and b are the desired parameters of the postulated linear model. These parameters are calibrated by using Eqs. C.2.8 and C.2.10 arranged in tabular form below:

u	k	$u - \overline{u}$	$k - \overline{k}$	$(u - \overline{u})(k - \overline{k})$	$(k - \overline{k})^2$
50	10	12	−25	−300	625
45	20	7	−15	−105	225
40	36	2	1	2	1
30	39	−8	4	−32	16
25	70	−13	35	−455	1225
190	175	0	0	−890	2092

where
$\overline{u} = 190/5 = 38$
$\overline{k} = 175/5 = 35$

Hence

$$b = \frac{-890}{2092} = -0.43$$

$$a = \overline{u} - b\overline{k} = 38 + (0.43)(35) = 53.05$$

and

$$u = 53.05 - 0.43k$$

The scatter diagram and the best-fitting straight line are shown in Fig. C.2.2.

Discussion The coefficient b turned out to be negative, as one would expect from the discussion of the general speed-concentration relationship. Also, it should be noted that the technique did not determine the mathematical form of the relationship: A linear form was postulated and the best straight line according to the regression criterion was the result.

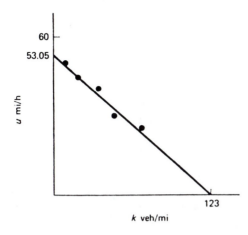

Figure C.2.2   Scatter diagrams and best-fitting line (small spread of data).

Example C.2

Repeat the procedure of Example C.1 using the following set of observations:

$$u: \quad 70 \quad 20 \quad 15 \quad 50 \quad 35$$

$$k: \quad 10 \quad 23 \quad 39 \quad 38 \quad 65$$

Solution   Proceeding as before,

u	k	$u - \bar{u}$	$k - \bar{k}$	$(u - \bar{u})(k - \bar{k})$	$(k - \bar{k})^2$
70	10	32	−25	−800	625
20	23	−18	−12	216	144
15	39	−23	4	−92	16
50	38	12	3	36	16
35	65	−3	30	−90	1225
190	175	0	0	−730	1694

where
$\bar{u} = 190/5 = 38$
$\bar{k} = 175/5 = 35$

Hence

$$b = \frac{-730}{1694} = -0.43$$

$$a = \bar{u} - b\bar{k} = 38 + (0.43)(35) = 53.05$$

and

$$u = 53.05 - 0.43k$$

The best-fitting straight line through the given data is shown in the accompanying Fig. C.2.3.

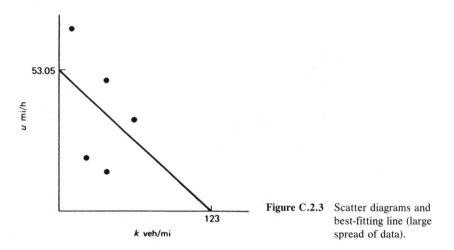

Figure C.2.3   Scatter diagrams and best-fitting line (large spread of data).

Discussion As far as the calculation of the model's parameters is concerned, this problem is identical to the preceding problem. In both cases, the best straight lines passing through the respective scatter diagrams were found. Note, however, that both problems led to identical regression equations. But a comparison of the two diagrams reveals that the first represents a tighter fit to the data than the second. Although the two sets of data led to the same relationship, the analyst would have more confidence in using the equation in the case represented by the first than the second set of experimental observations. A quantitative way of quantifying the "goodness of fit" is needed. The next section addresses this question.

C.3 CORRELATION

The sum

$$\text{TSS} = \sum (Y_i - \overline{Y})^2 \tag{C.3.1}$$

called the *total sum of square deviations from the mean*, or the *total variation*, is a measure of the degree to which the Y-observations are spread around their average value. It can be shown (see the exercises) that

$$\sum (Y_i - \overline{Y})^2 = \sum (Y_i - \hat{Y}_i)^2 + \sum (\hat{Y}_i - \overline{Y})^2 \tag{C.3.2}$$

The first term on the right side of Eq. C.3.2 is the *error sum of squares* (ESS) that the regression technique minimizes. It is also known as the *unexplained variation*. The second term represents the sum of squares of the difference between the estimated values of $\hat{Y}$ that lie on the regression line and the average value of $\overline{Y}$, which, as proven in the previous section, also lies on the regression line. Thus these differences are explained by the presence of the line. The sum of the squares of these quantities is known as the *explained variation*. The goodness of fit of a regression line increases with the proportion of the total variation that is explained by the line. The *coefficient of determination*

$$r^2 = \frac{\text{TSS} - \text{ESS}}{\text{TSS}} = \frac{\Sigma(\hat{Y}_i - \overline{Y})^2}{\Sigma(Y_i - \overline{Y})^2} \qquad (\text{C.3.3})$$

quantifies this fact. It ranges from zero when none of the total variation is explained by the regression line to unity when all the variation is explained by the line. It is denoted as a squared quantity to capture the fact that it is always nonnegative. The square root of the coefficient of determination is called the *coefficient of correlation*. Its value can range from -1 to $+1$. In the case of linear regression, the sign of r is the same as the sign of the slope b of the regression line. Figure C.3.1 illustrates that if r is near $+1$, there exists a high positive correlation; if it is near -1, there exists a high negative correlation; and if it is around zero, there exists no correlation between X and Y. The following formula gives the proper magnitude *and* sign of r:

$$r = \frac{N(\Sigma X_i Y_i) - (\Sigma X_i)(\Sigma Y_i)}{\{[N(\Sigma X_i^2) - (\Sigma X_i)^2][N(\Sigma Y_i^2) - (\Sigma Y_i)^2]\}^{1/2}} \qquad (\text{C.3.4})$$

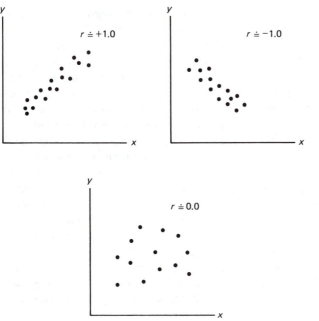

Figure C.3.1   Correlation.

Example C.3

Compute the coefficient of correlation between X and Y using the data of Examples C.1 and C.2.

Solution   Using Eq. C.3.4, we obtain

$$r = -0.95 \qquad \text{for the data of Example C.1}$$

and

$$r = -0.39 \qquad \text{for the data of Example C.2}$$

Discussion   As expected, both correlations are negative and the first case represents a better fit than the second.

C.4 MULTIPLE LINEAR REGRESSION

Simple linear regression involves only *two* variables. But often, it is appropriate to postulate relationships that include two or more independent variables, each of which partially explains the value of the dependent variable Y. A relationship between the dependent and the independent variables of the form

$$Y = a_0 + a_1 X_1 + a_2 X_2 + \cdots + a_p X_p \qquad (C.4.1)$$

calibrated by the method of least squares is known as a *multiple linear regression* model.

Although a detailed treatment of the method of multiple regression is beyond the scope of this book, it is of some value to point out certain characteristics of the model. First, it should be understood that every experimental observation used in the calibration process must consist of $(p + 1)$ observations (Y_i, X_{1i}, $X_{2i}, \ldots, X_{pi}$). Calibration of the relationship means, as before, the estimation of the numerical values of the parameters of the model (i.e., the constant a_0 and the coefficients $a_1, \ldots, a_p$ in order to minimize the sum of squared deviations).

Second, the independent variables to be included in the relationship must be chosen so that they are not highly correlated among themselves. The simple correlation coefficient between pairs of potential independent variables may be computed via Eq. C.3.4. When this criterion is satisfied, each of the terms on the right side of Eq. C.4.1 would be independent of the rest, capturing the effect of that specific variable X on the value of the dependent variable Y. If, on the other hand, two X's included in the equation were highly correlated, then it would be very difficult to examine the effect of each on the dependent variable, since varying one of the two X's necessarily involves a change in the other.

Third, each of the selected independent variables must be highly correlated with the dependent variable Y; otherwise, it would have no explanatory power.

Several calibration procedures are available for multiple-regression relationships. One technique adds the independent variables one at a time and assesses the degree to which the addition of the last variable improves the relationship. On this basis, a final relationship emerges, which includes the set of independent variables that provide the best fit. A *coefficient of multiple correlation* and various statistical tests can aid in assessing the goodness of fit.

C.5 DIRECT NONLINEAR REGRESSION

Linear regression (whether simple or multiple) assumes that the relationship between dependent and independent variables is, in fact, linear. Thus, when linear regression is applied to the observations illustrated by the scatter diagram of Fig. C.5.1, the result will be the best-fitting straight line (see the dashed line), even though the underlying relationship is clearly not linear.

To calibrate nonlinear relationships, one of two methods is frequently used. The first method involves specifying a nonlinear model and proceeding through the minimization of the sum of squared deviations, as in the case of simple linear regression, except that the postulated nonlinear form is substituted in Eq. C.2.2 prior to the minimization step. This is illustrated next for the best-fitting parabola to a set of experimental data.

Example C.4: Least Squares Parabola

Fit an equation of the form $Y = a + bX + cX^2$ to the following data:

$$Y: \quad 30 \quad 40 \quad 65 \quad 85$$

$$X: \quad 2 \quad 3 \quad 4 \quad 5$$

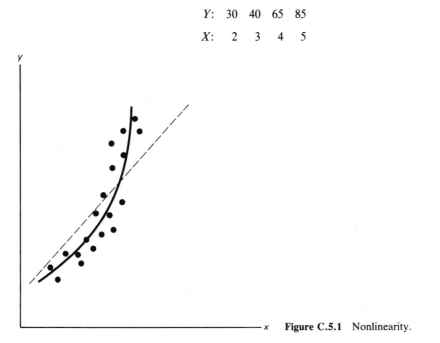

Figure C.5.1   Nonlinearity.

Solution The unknown parameters a, b, and c are computed by minimizing the sum of squared deviations, or

$$\min S = \sum (Y_i - \hat{Y}_i)^2$$

$$= \sum (Y_i - a - bX_i - cX_i^2)^2$$

The following characteristic equations result from setting the partial derivatives of S with respect to a, b, and c equal to zero and separating variables:

$$\sum Y_i = aN + b\left(\sum X_i\right) + c\left(\sum X_i^2\right)$$

$$\sum\left(X_i Y_i\right) = a\left(\sum X_i\right) + b\left(\sum X_i^2\right) + c\left(\sum X_i^3\right)$$

$$\sum\left(X_i^2 Y_i\right) = a\left(\sum X_i^2\right) + b\left(\sum X_i^3\right) + c\left(\sum X_i^4\right)$$

Substituting the given data in the characteristic equations,

$$220 = 4a + 14b + 54c$$

$$865 = 14a + 54b + 224c$$

$$3645 = 54a + 224b + 978c$$

which, when solved simultaneously, yield the following values:

$$a = 16, \quad b = 1.5, \quad \text{and} \quad c = 2.5$$

Thus the best-fitting parabola of the postulated type becomes

$$Y = 16 + 1.5X + 2.5X^2$$

Discussion Again, it must be emphasized that the technique did not select the functional form but merely determined the best line of the form supplied by the analyst. Care must be taken to express the sum of squared deviations to be minimized in terms of the postulated form. The reader is encouraged to find the least squares equations of the forms $Y = aX + bX^2$, $Y = a + bX^2$, and $Y = bX^2$ using the same data and to compare the results of the three regression lines. The first and last of these equations "force" the line to pass through the origin.

C.6 LINEAR REGRESSION WITH TRANSFORMED VARIABLES

The second method of calibrating nonlinear relationships applies when a nonlinear relationship can be transformed to a linear relationship, as Fig. C.6.1 illustrates. In this case, *linear regression is applied to the transformed relationship* to de-

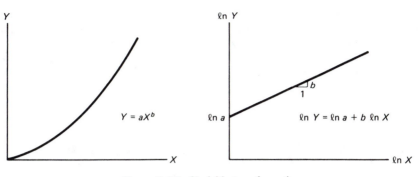

Figure C.6.1   Variable transformation.

termine the values of *its* parameters, which are then transformed back to the parameters of the original model.

Example C.5

The following speed and concentration measurements were taken on a highway:

$$u: \quad 50 \quad 35 \quad 35 \quad 25 \quad 20$$

$$k: \quad 10 \quad 40 \quad 50 \quad 80 \quad 100$$

It is desired to calibrate a speed–concentration equation of the form proposed by Underwood, that is, $u = u_f \exp(-k/k_m)$. Determine the parameters of this model using simple linear regression.

Solution   The postulated relationship is not linear. However, taking the natural logarithm of both sides,

$$\ln u = \ln u_f - \frac{k}{k_m}$$

The following substitutions render this equation in the proper linear regression form:

$$Y = \ln u \quad X = k \quad a = \ln u_f \quad b = \frac{-1}{k_m}$$

Performing simple linear regression of X on Y as before leads to

$$a = 4.01 \quad b = -0.01 \quad Y = 4.01 - 0.01X$$

To find the values of the parameters of the original model, make the inverse transformation:

$$u_f = e^a = 55 \text{ mi/h} \quad \text{and} \quad k_m = \frac{-1}{b} = 100 \text{ veh/mi}$$

and

$$u = 55 \, e^{-k_i 100}$$

Discussion   The free-flow speed of 55 mi/h and the concentration at capacity of 100 veh/mi represent the best-fitting Underwood relationship to the given data. This equation may be applied as in Section 3.4 to find the implied $q - k$ and $u - k$ curves and to estimate the capacity of the roadway, which (the reader could verify) happens to be 2023 veh/h.

C.7 HYPOTHESIS TESTING AND MODEL EVALUATION

A number of hypotheses are formulated and tested statistically to evaluate the goodness of fit of a linear model estimated with empirical data. The basic steps of hypothesis testing are the following.

Step 1:   Formulation of a null hypothesis (H_0); e.g., parameter value is equal to the estimated value.

Step 2:   Formulation of an alternative hypothesis (H_1); e.g., parameter value is equal to zero or a value different from the estimated one.

Step 3:   Identification of a test statistic distribution based on H_0; usually, Student's t, F, or χ^2 distribution is used, depending on the test.

Step 4:   Performance of comparison and rejection of H_0 if test statistic has very low probability of occurrence when H_0 is true.

These basic steps are applied to three common tests: single parameter test, test of a linear model as a whole, and test of equality of segmented linear models. These three tests are detailed below.

C.7.1 Single-Parameter Test

As the name of the test indicates, one parameter at a time is tested. It is compared with an alternative value (most commonly with zero). The test is formulated as follows:

$$H_0: \beta_1 = \beta_1^*$$

$$H_1: \beta_1 \neq \beta_1^*$$

$$\text{Statistic} = |\,\hat{\beta}_1 - \beta_1^*\,|/S_{\beta_1}$$

$$\text{Criterion: reject } H_0 \text{ if } |\,\hat{\beta}_1 - \beta_1^*\,|/S_{\beta_1}/\sqrt{N} > t_{N-J-1,\alpha/2}$$

where

$$\hat{\beta}_1 = \text{average estimated value (mean)}$$

$$S_{\beta_1} = \text{standard deviation of } \beta_1$$

$$N = \text{sample size}$$

$$J = \text{number of degrees of freedom}$$

(i.e., number of independent variables in the model)

$$1 - \alpha = \text{level of statistical confidence desired}$$

(e.g., for $\alpha = 0.05$ the level of statistical confidence is 95%)

The most common test of this type is setting $H_0: \beta_1 = 0$ and $H_1: \beta_1 \neq 0$.

Example C.6

The following data were gathered for saturation flow (see Chapter 5 for definition):

1820 1700 1780 1620 1810 1850 1690 1750 1750 1900 1860 1830

Compare these measurements with the recommended value of 1800 for a 95% level of statistical confidence and decide which is the preferred value for the saturation flow.

Solution   First the mean and standard deviation of the sample must be estimated. Treat saturation flow as parameter β.

$$\beta(\text{mean}) = 1780$$

$$S_\beta = 81.2$$

$$N = 12$$

Then the hypotheses are formulated.

$$H_0: \beta_1 = 1800$$

$$H_1: \beta_1 \neq 1800$$

$$\text{Statistic} = |\,1780 - 1800\,|/(81.2/\sqrt{12}) = 0.85 < 2.19 = t_{12-1,\ 0.025}$$

The criterion value of the t statistic (2.19) was taken from statistical tables attached to any standard book on probability and statistics ([C.1] and many others). Since this is a single-parameter estimate, the J factor is not applicable.

Discussion   The test does not support the rejection of the null hypothesis that the saturation flow should be equal to the recommended value of 1800.

C.7.2 Test of a Linear Model

This procedure tests the overall validity of a linear model by comparing all its parameter estimates to zero. If the test is not passed, this means that there is substantial probability that all parameters may be equal to zero, and thus the model is by and large worthless. The hypothesis testing for this is as follows:

$$H_0: \overline{\beta} = \overline{0}$$

$$H_1: \overline{\beta} \neq \overline{0}$$

$$\text{Statistic} = \frac{\text{RSS}/J}{[\text{ESS}/(N - J - 1)]}$$

$$\text{Criterion: reject } H_0 \text{ if } \frac{\text{RSS}/J}{[\text{ESS}/(N - J - 1)]} > F_{J,N-J-1,(1-\alpha)}$$

where

$$\overline{\beta}, \overline{0} = \text{vector matrices}$$

$$\text{RSS} = \text{TSS} - \text{ESS as defined by Eqs. C.3.1 and C.3.2}$$

$$N = \text{sample size}$$

$$J = \text{number of estimated parameters}$$

$$F \text{ statistic} = \text{criterion number taken from statistical tables [C.1]}$$

Example C.7

A multiple linear regression model was estimated on a computer with the aid of a statistical package. The output includes the following: ESS = 45.0, TSS = 95.8, N = 1220, J = 8. Check whether the equality of all dependent variable parameter estimates to zero can be rejected with 95% statistical confidence.

Solution From tables [C.1] the F statistic results as $F_{8,1211,95\%} = 1.94$. The statistic and comparison is as follows:

$$\frac{(95.8 - 45.0)/8}{45.0/(1220 - 8 - 1)} = 171 > 1.94$$

Discussion The F test is generally not a powerful test; it helps reject models with very weak associations between the dependent and the independent variables. For $N - J - 1 > 10$, the F-statistic value is less than 3.0, and usually the estimated statistic can easily exceed the F-statistic value, unless if ESS approaches TSS. For instance, in the example above, if ESS is 95.0, the statistic becomes $1.27 < 1.94$.

C.7.3 Test of Equality of Segmented Linear Models

Data for the analysis of a specific factor (dependent variable) are gathered from a population. Often, specific characteristics of the population suggest or necessitate the estimation of the same linear model for various subgroups of the population. Examples of this are (1) flow characteristics of two-, four-, or six-lane highways may be basically similar, but segmentation according to the size of the facility may provide better estimates for a specific flow characteristic; (2) trip characteristics of people may be assessed more accurately if segmentation by gender is applied; (3) automobile ownership may vary significantly between urban and rural communities; and so forth.

In the case of segmented estimation, the corresponding parameters of each model should be checked for equality. If the hypothesis of equality between the corresponding parameters of the models for each segment cannot be rejected, the segmentation is largely worthless.

Assume a straightforward linear model with three independent variables which was estimated as follows.

Pooled model (p):

$$\text{All data:}\quad Y = \beta_0 + \beta_1 X_1 + \beta_2 X_2 + \beta_3 X_3$$

Segmented models (g):

$$\text{Segment 1:}\quad Y = \beta_{01} + \beta_{11} X_{11} + \beta_{21} X_{21} + \beta_{31} X_{31}$$

$$\text{Segment 2:}\quad Y = \beta_{02} + \beta_{12} X_{12} + \beta_{22} X_{22} + \beta_{32} X_{32}$$

The hypothesis testing is formulated as follows.

$$H_0: \beta_{11} = \beta_{12},\ \beta_{21} = \beta_{22},\ \beta_{31} = \beta_{32}$$

$$H_1: \beta_{11} \neq \beta_{12},\ \beta_{21} \neq \beta_{22},\ \beta_{31} \neq \beta_{32}$$

$$\text{Statistic} = \frac{[\text{ESS}(p) - (\text{ESS}_1 + \text{ESS}_2)]/(J + 1)}{(\text{ESS}_1 + \text{ESS}_2)/[(N_1 - J_1 - 1) + (N_2 - J_2 - 1)]}$$

Criterion: reject H_0 if

$$\frac{[\text{ESS}(p) - (\text{ESS}_1 + \text{ESS}_2)]/(J + 1)}{(\text{ESS}_1 + \text{ESS}_2)/[(N_1 - J_1 - 1) + (N_2 - J_2 - 1)]}$$

$$> F_{J + 1,[(N_1 - J_1 - 1) + (N_2 - J_2 - 1)],(1 - \alpha)}$$

In this illustration, J is equal to 3 (β_1, β_2, β_3). ESS (p) is the ESS of the pooled model (an identical model estimated with all the data, without segmentation.)

Example C.8

The following summary statistics were obtained after the pooled and segmented estimation of a linear model. Test the equality of parameter estimates between the segmented models for $\alpha = 0.05$.

	Pooled	Segment 1	Segment 2
ESS	180	60	73
TSS	400	190	210
J	5	5	5
N	645	305	340

Solution   The F statistic is estimated from tables [C.1]: $F_{6,633,95\%} = 2.10$. The test statistic is calculated as follows:

$$\frac{[180 - (60 + 73)]/6}{(60 + 73)/633} = 37.3 > 2.10$$

Thus the equality of parameter estimates between the segmented models can be rejected.

C.7.4 Comprehensive Judgment of Linear Model

Five major checks should be conducted for judging the quality and acceptability of an empirically estimated linear model:

1. Overall model fit (coefficient of determination, r^2 or R^2)
2. Significance of parameter estimates (t test of all β_i)
3. Equality of all parameters to zero (overall model worthiness, F test)
4. Standard error of estimate of the dependent variable
5. Sign and size of parameter estimates (intuitiveness of parameters)

A model estimated from household survey data is utilized to illustrate the application of the whole set of tests.

$$Y = 0.26 + 0.71X_1 + 0.17X_2 + 0.052X_3 - 0.28X_4$$
$$\;\;(0.63)\;\;\;\;(0.07)\;\;\;(0.02)\;\;\;\;\;(0.03)\;\;\;\;\;\;\;(0.013)\;\;\;\;\;\;\;(0.05)$$

Results

$$R^2 = 0.49 \qquad F = 326 \qquad N = 1400$$

Dependent variable:

Y = number of household automobiles (automobile ownership level: 0, 1, 2, . . .)

Independent variables:

X_1 = number of drivers in the household

X_2 = residential density variable:
1 if household resides in a low density (suburban) location,
0 if in a high density (urban) location

X_3 = income per person calculated as the ratio of the total household income to the number of people in the household (in thousand 1989 U.S. dollars)

X_4 = number of household workers who commute to work by public transportation

The numbers in parentheses represent the standard error of estimate.

The overall model fit is deemed good since $R^2 = 0.49$, which means that 49% of the variance of the dependent variable can be explained by the model. R^2 scores ranging between 0.30 and 0.60 generally denote a good model fit. R^2 scores less than 0.20 represent poor model fit, and such models should be used with particular caution for real-world applications. R^2 scores greater than 0.70 when derived from large samples (i.e., a few hundred observations or more) may be suspicious. Collinearity effects and other problems may be resulting in exaggerated goodness of fit.

The t test for each parameter shows that all of them are statistically significant at the 99% level ($\alpha = 0.01$). The t statistic (tables [C.1]) for more than 120 observations and $\alpha = 0.01$ is 2.6. The t value for each parameter is estimated by dividing the parameter estimate by the corresponding standard error of estimate. For example, for X_4, $t = 0.28/0.05 = 5.6$, which is greater than 2.6. Thus the hypothesis that this parameter may be equal to zero can be rejected with 99% certainty. Same applies to all the other independent variables of the model.

The F score for the model is very high (i.e., $326 > 2.37$), which permits the rejection of the hypothesis that all parameter estimates are equal to zero, with 99% certainty.

The standard error of estimate for the dependent variable is 0.63. The standard error is equivalent to the standard deviation, and it means that 68% of the observations fall within one standard deviation and 95% fall within two standard deviations from the mean. The smaller the standard deviation, the more confident one can be for the estimates of the dependent variable. For the data set utilized for the estimation of this model, the mean automobile ownership level (dependent variable) is 2.02, thus the magnitude of the standard deviation is acceptable. In the case where the standard deviation is larger than the mean, the model is clearly unacceptable.

Finally, an intuitive test should be undergone with respect to the sign and size of parameters. The parameter estimates of the model examined are intuitive:

X_1 = (positive) larger number of drivers corresponds to higher automobile ownership level because of the higher mobility needs and the ability to drive a car

X_2 = (positive) low density tends to increase automobile ownership level (indeed, public transportation is not extensive in low density locations and walking distances tend to be long, thus the use of automobile may be necessary to fulfill mobility needs)

X_3 = (positive) higher income per person corresponds to more funds being available for automobile acquisition

X_4 = (negative) high number of household drivers commuting by public transportation translates into less need for automobiles for trips to work; thus automobile ownership tends to decrease.

Regarding the size of variables, prior experience is necessary for judgment. Based on historical evidence, the contribution of income should be small compared with the contribution of other variables such as number of drivers. This is because automobile ownership tends to be driven largely by the need for mobility. Income plays a secondary role: Low-income households tend to purchase inexpensive automobiles, and high-income households tend to purchase more luxurious automobiles. The model examined fulfills this anticipation. Consider a household with three drivers and $15,000 income per person. The respective contributions to automobile ownership (refer to the model) are as follows:

$$\text{Drivers:} \quad 3(0.71) = 2.13$$

$$\text{Income per Person:} \quad 15(0.052) = 0.78$$

Overall, the model passes all tests and it should be considered reliable for real-world use (in the context where the model was derived and estimated).

C.8 EXERCISES

C1. Show that Eqs. C.2.6 and C.2.8 are equivalent.

C2. Use the data of Example C.4 to fit a curve of the form $Y = aX^2$ by direct nonlinear regression.

C3. Repeat Exercise C2 assuming that $Y = aX^b$ by linear regression with transformed variables.

C4. Plot and compare the results of Example C.4 and Exercises C2 and C3.

C5. The following data were obtained from an experiment:

$$X: \quad 1 \quad 3 \quad 4 \quad 6 \quad 8 \quad 9 \quad 11 \quad 14$$

$$Y: \quad 9 \quad 8 \quad 7 \quad 5 \quad 4 \quad 4 \quad 2 \quad 1$$

Fit a line of the form $Y = a + bX$, and calculate and interpret the coefficient of correlation.

C.9 REFERENCE

C.1 BENJAMIN, J. R., and C. A. CORNELL, *Probability, Statistics and Decision for Civil Engineers*, McGraw-Hill, New York, 1970.

D

Probability, Queuing, and Simulation Models

D.1 INTRODUCTION

When the outcome of a situation or process can be known in advance with absolute certainty, the situation or process is said to be *deterministic*. It may be argued that, in a cause-and-effect universe, the outcome of every situation can be anticipated, assuming that all the factors affecting the situation are clearly understood. Knowing everything about something, however, requires knowing everything about everything else, and this is not a pragmatic claim. Engineering decisions are almost always based on limited information. Hence, all situations entail some degree of uncertainty. When the degree of uncertainty is very low, the situation may be treated as if it were deterministic. Otherwise, some way of incorporating uncertainty is needed. The *theory of probability* is the branch of mathematics that addresses this question. It had its origins in an attempt by Pascal to predict the likely outcome of interrupted gambling games to aid a group of friends in settling their bets and has since been applied to innumerable situations including the study of traffic systems. Queuing (waiting-line) models and computer-simulation models are two examples of *probabilistic models* that may be used to analyze traffic phenomena.

The practical methods of analysis discussed in Chapter 5 are based on knowledge that has been obtained from observing the operation of many facilities, and they approximate the effects of the various factors that influence capacity by the use of empirically derived charts and tables. The percentage of the total approach volume that wishes to execute turning maneuvers, for example, is clearly a major factor affecting the' operation of an intersection. However, it is reasonable to expect that not only the percentage, but also the pattern with which the left-turning vehicles arrive at the intersection would affect its operation. For example, turning vehicles arriving one after another during a short interval of time within the hour would result in different conditions than if they were spread out uniformly throughout the hour. Thus, having the knowledge that 20%, for example, of the approach volume consists of left-turning vehicles and that 10% of the approaching vehicles plan to turn right does not specify unequivocally either the sequence in which turning vehicles appear or the movement desire of any one vehicle in the approaching stream; it simply quantifies the likelihood, or probability, with which each vehicle is expected to execute each maneuver. When a more detailed investigation of a system characterized by a high degree of variability is desired, methods that are explicitly based on the theory of probability are often employed.

D.2 ELEMENTS OF PROBABILITY THEORY

D.2.1 Introduction

The theory of probability is concerned with situations (conventionally referred to as *experiments*) that have many possible *outcomes*. For example, a vehicle approaching an intersection (experiment) may choose one of three possible movements (outcomes): It may go straight through, it may turn right, or it may turn left. Similarly, casting a single die has six possible outcomes: the numbers 1 through 6. Thus for each experiment there exists a set of possible outcomes collectively known as the *sample*, *outcome*, or *event space*, usually denoted by the uppercase Greek capital letter omega (Ω). An *event* is a subset of the sample space. It is *simple* if it consists of a single outcome and *compound* if it contains a combination of single outcomes. For example, when casting a die, "rolling a 2" is a simple event A, whereas "rolling an even number" is a compound event B such that:

$$A = \{2\} \quad \text{and} \quad B = \{2,4,6\}$$

The following definitions from set theory are also relevant to the discussion of probability. The *complement* of an event A is denoted by $\overline{A}$ and is defined as the subset of Ω that contains all elements not belonging to A. Thus the complements of the events A and B are:

$$\overline{A} = \{1,3,4,5,6\} \quad \text{and} \quad \overline{B} = \{1,3,5\}$$

The *empty* (or *null*) *set*, denoted by $\varnothing$, is a set that contains no elements. The *union* of two events A and B, denoted by $A \cup B$, is the set that contains the elements belonging to A or B or both. For example,

$$A \cup B = \{2,4,6\} \quad \text{and} \quad A \cup \overline{B} = \{1,2,3,5\}$$

The *intersection* of two events A and B, denoted by $A \cap B$, is the set that contains only the elements that the two events share in common. Thus

$$A \cap B = \{2\} \quad \text{and} \quad \overline{A} \cap B = \{4,6\}$$

When two events have no elements in common, they are *mutually exclusive*. Clearly, an event and its complement are mutually exclusive. As just defined, pairs of simple events (i.e., single outcomes) are also mutually exclusive.

D.2.2 Definition of Probability

Probability is a measure of the likelihood with which events are expected to occur. Suppose we toss a coin 10 times and record the outcome of each trial as follows:

$$H H T T T H H T H H$$

The observed frequencies of heads (H) and tails (T) were 6 and 4 times, respectively. The *relative frequencies* of the two outcomes can be obtained by dividing the observed frequencies by the total number of trials. In this example,

$$f(H) = 0.6 \quad \text{and} \quad f(T) = 0.4$$

Intuitively, one would expect the two outcomes of tossing a fair coin to occur with equal frequencies. This could be the case when the number of trials is very large. Note that after only one trial, this long-term expectation cannot possibly be satisfied as the relative frequencies would be 1 for one outcome (H in this case) and 0 for the other. The *limiting value* of the relative frequency of an event as the number of trials approaches infinity is defined as the *probability* of occurrence of that event on any one trial. The probability of each outcome may be derived intuitively, or it may be estimated by repeating the experiment a large number of times and computing the relative frequencies of the outcomes. It must be borne in mind that when estimating the probabilities of events by experimentation, the chance always exists that the computed frequencies may deviate significantly from the theoretical probabilities.

It follows from this definition that the probability, $P[A]$, of an event A cannot be negative and cannot exceed 1. Also, the sum of the probabilities of all simple events contained in the sample space of an experiment always equals 1.

Other useful axioms of probability include the following. The probability of the event defined as the union of two events A and B is

$$P[A \cup B] = P[A] + P[B] - P[A \cap B] \tag{D.2.1}$$

The probability of the event defined by the intersection of A and B is subtracted from the sum of the probabilities of the two events to avoid double counting. Since two mutually exclusive events share no elements in common, the probability of the event defined by their union is equal to the sum of the probabilities of the two events. Also,

$$P[\Omega] = 1 \tag{D.2.2}$$

and

$$P[\varnothing] = 0 \qquad \text{(D.2.3)}$$

Equation D.2.2 states that the probability of the event defined as the union of all (mutually exclusive) simple events associated with an experiment is equal to 1. Thus, on any trial, *one* of the possible outcomes is certain to occur. Equation D.2.3 is an alternative way of stating the same concept: It is impossible to obtain none of the single outcomes of an experiment on a given trial. Since the intersection of the two mutually exclusive events E and $\bar{E}$ is equal to the null set, it follows from Eqs. D.2.1 through D.2.3 that

$$P[E \cup \bar{E}] = P[\Omega] = P[E] + P[\bar{E}] - P[\varnothing] = 1$$

and

$$P[\bar{E}] = 1 - P[E] \qquad \text{(D.2.4)}$$

Example D.1

Consider the experiment of casting a single die. Identify all simple events (outcomes) of the experiment, and calculate the probability of each.

Solution   The outcome space for this experiment contains six possible outcomes:

$$\{1,2,3,4,5,6\}$$

Assuming that the die is not loaded, the six simple events are equiprobable, each having a probability of occurrence on any trial of $\frac{1}{6}$. Note that all probabilities are nonnegative, and their sum equals unity. Moreover, the probability associated with any outcome not included in the sample space of the experiment (e.g., 9) is 0; that is, such an event is *impossible* given this experiment.

Example D.2

For the experiment of Example D.1, define two events A and B as

$$A: \text{the outcome is odd} \qquad \text{and} \qquad B: \text{the outcome is less than 5}$$

Find (a) the probability of each of the two compound events, (b) the probability of their union, and (c) the probability of their intersection.

Solution   The two events are defined as

$$A = \{1,3,5\} \qquad \text{and} \qquad B = \{1,2,3,4\}$$

Events A and B contain three and four equiprobable (mutually exclusive) simple events, respectively, each having a probability of $\frac{1}{6}$. Therefore,

$$P[A] = \frac{1}{6} + \frac{1}{6} + \frac{1}{6} = \frac{3}{6} = \frac{1}{2}$$

and

$$P[B] = \frac{1}{6} + \frac{1}{6} + \frac{1}{6} + \frac{1}{6} = \frac{4}{6} = \frac{2}{3}$$

The union of the two events, {1,2,3,4,5}, contains five equiprobable events. Hence $P[A \cup B] = \frac{5}{6}$. Their intersection contains only the elements 1 and 3. So, $P[A \cap B] = \frac{2}{6} = \frac{1}{3}$.

Discussion According to Eq. D.2.1, the probability of the event defined as the union of A and B is less than the sum of their individual probabilities by an amount that equals the probability of their intersection. Thus

$$P[A \cup B] = P[A] + P[B] - P[A \cap B]$$

$$= \frac{3}{6} + \frac{4}{6} - \frac{2}{6} = \frac{5}{6}$$

which is the same result obtained by enumerating the simple events that belong to the union of A and B.

D.2.3 Conditional Probability and Independence

The estimation of the probability of event A is often affected by prior knowledge that event B has occurred because the outcome is restricted to the subset of the sample space B. The *conditional probability* of A given B is

$$P[A \mid B] = \frac{P[A \cap B]}{P[B]} \qquad (D.2.5)$$

If events A and B are mutually exclusive, their intersection is the null set, which has a probability of 0. Hence, in the case of mutually exclusive events, the probability that A has occurred given that B has taken place is 0. In other words, the occurrence of B excludes the occurrence of A.

When the occurrence of B does not alter the probability associated with A, the two events are known as *independent events*. For independent events:

$$P[A \mid B] = P[A] \qquad (D.2.6a)$$

Substituting Eq. D.2.6a into Eq. D.2.5 and solving for the probability of the intersection of A and B,

$$P[A \cap B] = P[A]P[B] \qquad (D.2.6b)$$

Thus, for *independent events*, the probability of joint occurrence is equal to the product of the probabilities of the individual events.

Example D.3

For the two events defined in Example D.2, calculate the conditional probability $P[A \mid B]$.

Solution Substitution of the probabilities obtained in the earlier example into Eq. D.2.5 yields

$$P[A \mid B] = \frac{\frac{1}{3}}{\frac{2}{3}} = \frac{1}{2}$$

Discussion   The calculated conditional probability for event A is equal to the unconditional probability of the same event. Therefore, the knowledge that event B has occurred does not affect the probability of event A. Hence the two events are independent.

Example D.4

If the probability that a vehicle approaching an intersection will turn left is $P[L] = 0.25$ and the probability that it will turn right is $P[R] = 0.15$, calculate the probability that the vehicle will turn right given that it does not turn left.

Solution   Event B (i.e., "the vehicle does not turn left") is the complement of event L. According to Eq. D.2.4, $P[B] = 1 - P[L] = 0.75$. Compound event B contains the simple events of "turning right" (R) and "going through" (T), which are mutually exclusive. Hence, the probability of the intersection of events B and R is simply equal to the probability of R, or 0.15. The probability that the vehicle will turn right given that it does not turn left is

$$P[R \mid B] = \frac{P[R \cap B]}{P[B]} = \frac{(0.15)}{(0.75)} = 0.20$$

Discussion   Since $P[R \mid B]$ does not equal $P[R]$, events R and B are not independent. The results just obtained could have been reached by intuitive reasoning. The likelihood that the vehicle will turn right increases when it is known that it will not turn left. The solution, however, applies the formal relationships to illustrate the concept of conditional probability.

D.2.4 Discrete Distributions

A *random variable* is a variable that takes on the values of the outcomes of an experiment. When the number of possible outcomes is finitely or infinitely countable, the random variable is said to be *discrete*. Otherwise, the random variable is *continuous*. Examples of continuous random variables include the time between failures of a machine and the distance from a reference point on a highway where the next accident will occur. In this textbook, random variables are denoted by uppercase letters (e.g., X, Y, or Z) and the particular values that they assume are denoted by lowercase letters (e.g., x, y, z). Thus $X = x$ means the random variables X takes on a particular value x.

A function $p(x) = P[X = x]$, which associates each value of a discrete random variable to its probability, is known as the *probability (mass) function* (pmf), or the *discrete probability distribution*. The histogram of Fig. D.2.1(a) illustrates graphically the probability function associated with casting a die, and Fig. D.2.1(b) illustrates the probability function of the vehicle described in Example D.4. In the case of the former, the values assumed by the random variable are identical to the numerical values of the outcomes of the experiment and can be given that interpretation. In the case of the latter, the numerical values assigned to the random variable are arbitrary and are selected merely for convenience.

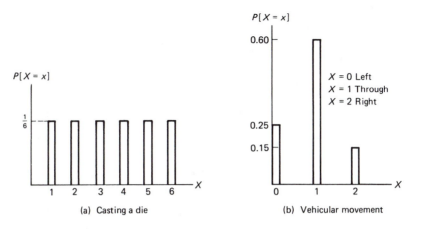

Figure D.2.1   Discrete probability functions.

Since the values of $p(x)$ represent the probabilities of simple events, they must satisfy the following conditions:

$$0 \leqslant p(x) \leqslant 1 \qquad \text{for all } x \qquad \text{(D.2.7a)}$$

$$\sum p(x) = 1 \qquad \text{(D.2.7b)}$$

The probability of the union of several (mutually exclusive) outcomes is equal to the sum of the probabilities of the individual outcomes. The condition of Eq. D.2.7b simply states that the sum of the probabilities of all single outcomes in the sample space of the experiment is equal to unity. This is merely a restatement of Eq. D.2.2.

Another useful function of a discrete random variable is its *cumulative distribution function* (cdf), which is defined as

$$F(x) = P[X \leqslant x] \qquad \text{(D.2.8)}$$

In words, the cdf is a function that assumes the values of the probability that a random variable X is less than or equal to a particular value x. Because $p(x)$ is nonnegative, a plot of the cdf against increasing values of x must necessarily be a nondecreasing step function, as illustrated by Fig. D.2.2. Moreover, the lower and upper limits of this function are 0 and 1, respectively. The upper limit corresponds to the condition described by Eq. D.2.7b.

Two characteristics of a probability function are its *mean* (or *expected value*) and its *variance*. The mean is a measure of the central tendency or the average value of the distribution and the variance is a measure of dispersion or the degree to which the distribution is spread out around the mean.

The mean is usually denoted by the Greek lowercase letter mu (μ) or by $E[X]$, the latter read "expected value." The mean is calculated by

$$E[X] = \sum_{x} x p(x) \qquad \text{(D.2.9)}$$

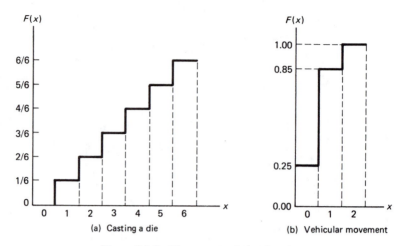

Figure D.2.2   Discrete cumulative functions.

The variance of a discrete distribution, denoted by σ^2 or by $V[X]$, is defined as the second moment about the mean, or

$$V[X] = \sum_x (X - E[X])^2 \, p(x) \tag{D.2.10}$$

The square root of the variance is known as the *standard deviation* of the distribution, that is,

$$\sigma = S[X] = V[X]^{1/2} \tag{D.2.11}$$

Example D.5

Calculate the mean, variance, and standard deviation of the discrete distributions of Fig. D.2.1.

Solution   (a) By Eq. D.2.9, the mean of the distribution shown on Fig. D.2.1(a) is

$$E[X] = (1)\left(\frac{1}{6}\right) + (2)\left(\frac{1}{6}\right) + \cdots + (6)\left(\frac{1}{6}\right) = \frac{21}{6} = 3.5$$

The variance is given by Eq. D.2.10:

$$V[X] = (1 - 3.5)^2\left(\frac{1}{6}\right) + (2 - 3.5)^2\left(\frac{1}{6}\right) + \cdots + (6 - 3.5)^2\left(\frac{1}{6}\right) = 2.92$$

The standard deviation is the square root of the variance, or

$$S[X] = 1.71$$

(b) Similarly, for the distribution of Fig. D.2.1(b),

$$E[X] = (0)(0.20) + (1)(0.60) + (2)(0.15) = 0.9$$

$$V[X] = (0 - 0.9)^2(0.20) + (1 - 0.9)^2(0.60)$$

$$+ (2 - 0.9)^2(0.15) = 0.35$$

$$S[X] = 0.6$$

Discussion   The mean of the distribution does not necessarily coincide with one of the outcomes of the experiment. It simply represents the average of a series of trials as the number of trials approaches infinity. In part (a) of this problem, the average represents a value that is meaningful in terms of the magnitudes of the outputs of the experiment. By contrast, the mean value of part (b) depends on the numerical codes selected for the three outcomes. The variance and standard deviation measure the dispersion of each distribution about its mean value.

D.2.5 Some Common Discrete Distributions

Any discrete function that satisfies the conditions of Eqs. D.2.7 can conceivably be the distribution for some experiment. This subsection presents a number of discrete distributions that are frequently encountered in practice, the characteristics of which are well known. The work of the analyst can be simplified when the problem at hand fits the specifications of one of these common distributions. Formal mathematical derivations for these functions may be found in the technical literature (e.g., [D.1]).

The *uniform distribution* describes experiments that have a finite number of N equiprobable outcomes. The casting of a fair die and the tossing of a fair coin are but two examples of this distribution. In general,

$$p(x) = P[X = x] = \frac{1}{N} \quad \text{for all } x \text{ in } \Omega \qquad (D.2.12)$$

The mean and variance of this distribution can be calculated by Eqs. D.2.9 and D.2.10. In the special case when X takes on the values $x = 1, 2, \ldots, N$, the following apply:

$$E[X] = \frac{N + 1}{2} \quad \text{and} \quad V[X] = \frac{N^2 - 1}{12} \qquad (D.2.13)$$

The *Bernoulli distribution* applies to experiments that have only two outcomes, often referred to as a "success" S and a "failure" F. Tossing a coin, fair or unfair, is a Bernoulli trial. If, on any trial, the probability of success is p and the probability of failure is q, by Eq. D.2.7,

$$P[F] = q = 1 - P[S] = 1 - p \qquad (D.2.14)$$

In the special case when a success is coded as 1 and a failure as 0, the mean and variance of the Bernoulli distribution become

$$E[X] = 1p + 0q = p \tag{D.2.15a}$$

and

$$V[X] = pq = 1(1 - p) \tag{D.2.15b}$$

The *binomial distribution* expresses the probability of x successes in a sequence of n independent Bernoulli trials. The random variable takes on the values $x = 0,1,2, \ldots , n$. The binomial probability function is

$$p(x) = P[X = x] = \frac{n!}{x! \, (n - x)!} \, p^x q^{n-x} \tag{D.2.16}$$

The mean and variance of the binomial distribution are

$$E[X] = np \tag{D.2.17a}$$

and

$$V[X] = npq \tag{D.2.17b}$$

The Bernoulli distribution is a particular case of the binomial when $n = 1$.

The *geometric distribution* is also based on a sequence of independent Bernoulli trials. It represents the probability that the first success will occur on the xth trial. This means that A: the first $(x - 1)$ independent trials result in a failure and B: the last trial is a success. Considering that events A and B are, by definition, independent, Eq. D.2.6b yields the following probability that the first success will occur on the xth trial:

$$p(x) = q^{x-1}p \qquad x = 1,2, \ldots \tag{D.2.18}$$

This is an example of a discrete random variable X that takes on an *infinitely countable* number of values. The mean and variance of the geometric distribution are

$$E[X] = p^{-1} \tag{D.2.19a}$$

and

$$V[X] = qp^{-2} \tag{D.2.19b}$$

The *negative binomial* (or *Pascal*) *distribution* measures the probability that the kth success will occur on the xth trial of a Bernoulli process. For this to be true, two events must occur, A: there must be $(k - 1)$ successes in the first $(x - 1)$ trials *and* B: the last trial must be a success. The probability of event A is given by the binomial (Eq. D.2.16) and the probability of event B is p. Since the two events are independent, the probability that the kth success will occur on the xth trial becomes

$$p(x) = \frac{(x-1)!}{(k-1)!\,(x-k)!}\, p^k q^{x-k} \qquad \text{for } x = k, k+1, \ldots \quad \text{(D.2.20)}$$

The mean and variance of the negative binomial are

$$E[X] = kp^{-1} \tag{D.2.21a}$$

and

$$V[X] = kqp^{-2} \tag{D.2.21b}$$

The geometric distribution is a special case of the Pascal distribution when $k = 1$.

Finally, a discrete distribution that has found wide application in traffic situations is the *Poisson distribution*. It describes the probability of x occurrences of an event (successes) within a given interval of time (or space) t and applies to experiments that satisfy the following conditions.

1. There exists a small interval dt within which the probability of one occurrence is $\lambda\,dt$, whereas the probability of additional occurrences is negligible.
2. The occurrences (or nonoccurrences) of the event in nonoverlapping intervals are mutually *independent*.

The total interval t may be thought to consist of a sequence of small intervals dt, each representing an independent Bernoulli trial with $p = \lambda\,dt$. In other words, the probability of x successes within the total interval t is given by the binomial. In the limit, that is, when the number of small intervals is very large and the probability of success p is small, the Poisson distribution is obtained:

$$p(x) = \frac{(\lambda t)^x}{x!}\, e^{-\lambda t} \qquad \text{for } x = 0,1, \ldots \tag{D.2.22}$$

The mean and variance of the Poisson distribution are

$$E[X] = V[X] = \lambda t \tag{D.2.23}$$

Example D.6

The probability that a vehicle will turn left at an intersection is known to be 0.15. Assuming independence, calculate the probabilities of the following events:

(a) The tenth vehicle is not turning left.
(b) Exactly three out of 10 vehicles will turn left.
(c) At least three out of 10 vehicles will turn left.
(d) No more than three out of 10 vehicles will turn left.
(e) The first left-turning vehicle will be the fourth vehicle.
(f) The eighth vehicle will be the third to turn left.

Solution The movement of each vehicle is a Bernoulli trial with $p = 0.15$ and $q = 0.85$.

(a) The probability that the tenth vehicle, and any other vehicle, will not turn left is $q = 0.85$ (Bernoulli distribution).

(b) According to the binomial distribution, the probability that three out of 10 vehicles will turn left is

$$p(3) = 0.130$$

(c) The complement of event A: at least three out of 10 is event B: zero or one or two out of 10 and

$$P[A] = P[X > 2] = 1 - P[B] \quad \text{for } n = 10$$

But B is the union of three mutually exclusive simple events, the probability of which is given by the binomial. Hence

$$P[A] = 1 - \{p(0) + p(1) + p(2)\}$$
$$= 1 - (0.197 + 0.347 + 0.276) = 0.180$$

(d) The binomial still applies. The probability of the compound event A: no more than three in 10 is

$$P(A) = P[X < 4] = p(0) + p(1) + p(2) + p(3)$$
$$= 0.197 + 0.347 + 0.276 + 0.130 = 0.950$$

(e) This question may be answered either by using the geometric distribution or the negative binomial (Pascal) distribution with $k = 1$. Thus

$$p(4) = (0.85)^3(0.15) = 0.092$$

(f) The Pascal distribution provides the answer to the question of the probability that the kth (i.e., third) left turner is the eighth vehicle, x, is the sequence

$$p(8) = 0.031 \quad \text{for } k = 3$$

Discussion The event of which the probability is being sought must be clearly understood. For example, the difference between "exactly three," "at least three," and "no more than three" was illustrated in parts (a), (b), and (c). Also, the appropriate distribution must be selected. It should be remembered that the notation $p(x)$ has a different meaning depending on the particular distribution used. Thus in the case of the binomial, $p(4)$ represents "the probability of four occurrences in n trials," and in the case of the geometric, it represents "the probability that the first occurrence is on the fourth trial."

Example D.7

It is known that 8% of the drivers in a resort town drive under the influence of alcohol. Assuming independence, calculate the probability of the following events:

(a) No driver in five stopped is under the influence.
(b) Exactly 10 out of 100 stopped are drunk.
(c) Fifty out of 500 are under the influence.

Solution   Considering the discovery of a drunken driver to be a "success," each act of stopping a driver is a Bernoulli trial with $p = 0.08$.

(a) The probability of finding no driver to be under the influence of alcohol in five independent Bernoulli trials is the product $q^5 = 0.659$ (see Eq. D.2.6b). The same result can be obtained by applying the binomial distribution with zero successes in five trials.

(b) In this case, the binomial yields a probability of discovering exactly 10 drunken drivers:

$$p(10) = 0.102 \quad \text{when } n = 100$$

Since p is small and n is large, the Poisson with a mean $np = 8$ (Eq. D.2.17a) may be applied to approximate the binomial distribution, that is,

$$p(10) = P[X = 10] = 0.099 \quad \text{when } n = 100$$

(c) Repeating the procedure of part (b), the binomial distribution yields $p(50) = 0.0167$, and the Poisson approximation (with mean 40) results in $p(50) = 0.0177$.

Discussion   The Poisson approximation to a binomial improves as the number of trials increases. In this particular case, the same conclusion is reached by comparing the mean and variance of the binomial distribution. For part (b) the mean is 8 and the variance is $npq = 7.36$. For part (c), the mean and variance are 40 and 36.8, respectively.

Example D.8

Cars arrive at a parking garage at a rate of 90 veh/h according to the Poisson distribution. Compute the cumulative distribution for the random variable X that represents "the number of arrivals per minute."

Solution   The mean arrival rate is 1.5 veh/min. Hence Eq. D.2.22 becomes

$$p(x) = P[X = x] = \frac{(1.5)^x}{x!} e^{-1.5} \quad x = 0,1,2, \ldots$$

The cumulative distribution $F(x) = P[X \leq x]$ is obtained by summing the probabilities of the simple events $0,1, \ldots, x$. The results are:

x	$p(x) = P[X = x]$	$F(x) = P[X \leq x]$
0	0.223	0.223
1	0.335	0.558
2	0.251	0.809
3	0.126	0.935
4	0.047	0.982
5	0.014	0.996
—	—	—
—	—	—
—	—	—

Discussion   Properly, the cumulative distribution approaches 1 as x approaches infinity. According to the Poisson distribution, the random variable X is defined up to this limit. In practical situations, however, X is usually bounded at some lower value. In the situation examined here, for example, the number of cars arriving at the garage within a minute cannot be very large. Thus, at best, the Poisson distribution can serve only as an approximation to this situation. Noting, however, that the calculated probability of more than five arrivals per minute is only 0.004, it is not unreasonable to expect that this approximation would be satisfactory.

D.2.6 Continuous Random Variables

The random variables discussed in the preceding section were allowed to assume a countable number of values. On the other hand, many situations are characterized by an uncountable number of possible outcomes that can be described only by continuous random variables. For example, consider the measurement of the headways between persons as they enter a hall. Conceivably, the headway between any two persons can vary from zero (when they enter simultaneously) to infinity (following the last person *ever* to enter the hall). Assuming that the headways can be measured with absolute precision, the probability of obtaining *exactly* any particular value is zero. In the continuous case, probability is associated with *ranges of the outcome* rather than with single values. The following definitions clarify this statement.

The range over which a continuous random variable is defined (e.g., zero to infinity in the example relating to headways) can be divided into infinitesimal intervals, dx. If the probability that the outcome of an experiment will fall within dx is equal to the area $f(x)\,dx$, then the function $f(x)$ is defined as the *probability density function* (pdf) or the *continuous probability distribution* for that experiment.

Since the probability of the occurrence of any event is nonnegative, a pdf is also nonnegative. Moreover, according to Eq. D.2.2, the sum of the probabilities of the (mutually exclusive) events defined by each dx over the range of the random variable X must necessarily equal unity. In mathematical terms,

$$f(x) \geq 0 \qquad \text{for all } x \qquad\qquad (D.2.24a)$$

and

$$\int_{-\infty}^{+\infty} f(x)\,dx = 1 \qquad\qquad (D.2.24b)$$

These conditions correspond to the requirements that must be satisfied by discrete probability distributions expressed by Eqs. D.2.7. The area under the pdf between points a and b is equal to the probability that the outcome will fall in the interval $\{a,b\}$, or

$$\int_{a}^{b} f(x)\,dx = P[a \leq X \leq b] \qquad\qquad (D.2.25)$$

When $a = b$, the area under the curve is zero. Hence the probability associated with any single value of the random variable is zero.

The mean, the variance, and the standard deviation of a pdf are defined as

$$E[X] = \int_{-\infty}^{+\infty} xf(x)\, dx \tag{D.2.26}$$

$$V[X] = \int_{-\infty}^{+\infty} (x - E[X])^2 f(x)\, dx \tag{D.2.27}$$

and

$$S[X] = \{V[X]\}^{1/2} \tag{D.2.28}$$

Equation D.2.26 describes the first moment of the area under the curve about the y-axis. Considering that this area equals unity, the expected value is the x-coordinate of its centroid. Equation D.2.27 describes the second moment of the area about the centroidal y-axis.

The *cumulative distribution function* (cdf) of a continuous random variable is defined as

$$P[X \leq x] = \int_{-\infty}^{x} f(x)\, dx \tag{D.2.29}$$

The cdf is a nondecreasing function with a lower limit of 0 and an upper limit of 1. In this respect, it is identical to the cumulative distribution function of a discrete random variable.

D.2.7 Some Common Continuous Distributions

The best-known probability density function is the *normal distribution*, or the "bell-shaped" curve. Because of its mathematical intractability, however, it is not discussed here, even though it is fundamental to the theory of probability.

The *uniform distribution* is defined as

$$f(x) = \begin{cases} \dfrac{1}{b - a} & \text{for } a \leq x \leq b \\[2ex] 0 & \text{otherwise} \end{cases} \tag{D.2.30}$$

In words, it consists of a horizontal line over the range $\{a,b\}$ in such a way that the area under the curve is equal to 1. The mean and variance of the uniform pdf are

$$E[X] = \frac{a + b}{2} \quad \text{and} \quad V[X] = \frac{(b - a)^2}{12} \tag{D.2.31}$$

The *(negative) exponential distribution* bears a special relationship to the discrete Poisson distribution. When the occurrence of an event follows the Poisson distribution, the interval between occurrences is distributed according to the negative exponential. For example, if vehicles arrive at an intersection according to the Poisson distribution, the interarrival times (i.e., the headways between successive vehicles) are exponentially distributed. The negative exponential pdf is

$$f(x) = ae^{-ax} \tag{D.2.32}$$

where e is the base of natural logarithms. The mean and variance of the negative exponential are

$$E[X] = \frac{1}{a} \quad \text{and} \quad V[X] = \frac{1}{a^2} \tag{D.2.33}$$

The mean of this distribution is equal to its standard deviation. Moreover, it is the reciprocal of the mean of the Poisson distribution.

Numerous distributions have been used to describe vehicular headways and other traffic phenomena (e.g., [D.2]). Those just discussed will be sufficient for the purposes of this book.

Example D.9

Given the arrival pattern of Example D.8, calculate (a) the mean headway, (b) the probability that a headway is less than or equal to 45 s, and (c) the probability of headways longer than 2 min.

Solution   (a) The average, or mean, headway is the reciprocal of the average number of arrivals per unit time. The latter was calculated in Example D.8 to be 1.5 veh/min. Therefore,

$$E[X] = \frac{1}{a} = \frac{1}{1.5} \text{ min (per vehicle)}$$

     (b) This probability is given by the integral of the pdf from 0 to 0.75 min, or the value of the cdf at $x = 0.75$ min. Hence

$$P[X \leqslant 0.75] = F(0.75) = 1 - e^{-(1.5)(0.75)} = 0.675$$

(c) $P[X > 2] = 1 - P[X \leqslant 2] = e^{-3} = 0.050$

Example D.10

Given that the instantaneous location of vehicles along a highway is Poisson distributed and that the average concentration is 100 veh/mi, calculate (a) the probability that 30 vehicles will be found on any quarter of a mile, and (b) the probability that the spacing between any two vehicles is less than or equal to 0.02 mi.

Solution   (a) The average number of vehicles per quarter mile is 25 and the probability that exactly 30 vehicles occupy a quarter mile, according to the Poisson, is

$$p(30) = P[X = 30] = 0.045$$

(b) If the location of the vehicles is Poisson distributed, their spacing is exponentially distributed. With an average spacing of 0.01 mi (i.e., $a = 100$),

$$F(0.02) = P[X \leq 0.02] = 1 - e^{-(100)(0.02)} = 0.865$$

Discussion   The relationship between the negative exponential and the Poisson distributions is clearly illustrated by the last two examples. Both are "memoryless." This property implies that the occurrences of events described by the Poisson are mutually independent. Similarly, the intervals between events described by the negative exponential are mutually independent. Specifically, when the negative exponential is used to describe the time interval between successive occurrences, the memoryless property means that occurrences in the future are not influenced by what has happened in the past. In the case of vehicular headways, the negative exponential is most appropriate in the case of low concentration conditions, when the interactions between vehicles are at a minimum and vehicular events occur at random. When used to describe the headways between vehicular arrivals at an intersection, it seems reasonable that the intersection should be isolated, or removed, from other intersections, which—because of the signal control regularity—may impart a definite pattern to the arrivals at the intersection under study.

D.3 QUEUING MODELS

D.3.1 Introduction

Queuing, or waiting-line, phenomena are everyday occurrences. Examples include vehicles waiting to be served at a gasoline station, passengers or vehicles lined up at a transit terminal, airplanes awaiting clearance for take-off or landing, patients scheduled for use of a hospital's operating room, component parts stockpiled at an assembly plant, computer jobs awaiting execution or printing, vehicles at an intersection, and so forth. Continuous processes may also be described as queuing systems: for example, drinking water in a reservoir "waiting" to be used by households. No matter how complex, queuing systems are characterized by an *arrival pattern*, a *service facility*, and a *queue discipline*. When all three components are constant, the system can be analyzed by deterministic methods. Probabilistic systems, however, are more common.

The arrival pattern describes the way in which the items (or "customers") to be served enter the system. For instance, some examples of the preceding section considered the case of vehicles arriving according to the Poisson distribution, which meant that their interarrival times were exponential distributed.

The service facility is characterized by the *number and arrangement of servers* and by a *service pattern*. A service facility can be a *single-server* or a *multiserver* facility. Service counters may be arranged in parallel, in series, or in any combination of the two. The service pattern usually measures either the rate at which customers are processed (i.e., vehicles per minute) or the time required to serve individual customers. These characteristics may also be described by appropriate probability functions.

The queue discipline refers to the rules by which the next customer to be served is chosen. Some of the most common rules include the following. A *first-in, first-out* (FIFO) scheme serves customers in the order they arrive: The customer at the front of the waiting line is always selected. Another rule is the *last-in, first-out* (LIFO) rule. For example, program instructions in a computer's stack memory are executed in the reverse order of placement into the stack. The service rule may allow either a *single queue* or *multiple queues*. The customers may be treated equally or they may be treated according to some *priority*. Examples of priority rules include carpool lanes for use by vehicles carrying a specified minimum number of passengers, express lanes at a supermarket, business-transactions-only counters at a bank, scheduling patients for an operation according to the severity of their maladies, and computer processing of administrative jobs before the jobs submitted by faculty and students. The priority rule may be either *preemptive* or *nonpreemptive*, depending on whether or not a higher-priority customer is permitted to interrupt the processing of a lower-priority customer. For example, emergency vehicles on the roadways have a preemptive priority over other vehicles.

A signalized intersection may be modeled as a multichannel system with complex queue disciplines controlled by the traffic signal. The description of transit stations in Chapter 5 reveals the possibility of analyzing their operations by employing queuing models. Also, platoons of vehicles on the road may be viewed as moving queues. The pervious discussion illustrates that queuing systems can range from the very simple to the very complex. Relatively simple systems may be examined by formulating the appropriate mathematical equations and solving them *analytically*. More complex systems become mathematically intractable and are usually solved by *numerical* methods.

The solution to a queuing problem entails the assessment of a system's performance, which, in turn, is described by a set of *measures of performance* (mop's). These may include the number of customers served per unit time, the average delay per customer, the average and maximum length of the waiting lines, the percent of time each service counter is idle, the cost of operating the system, and so forth.

D.3.2 Single-Server FIFO Systems

One of the simplest queuing problems that is amenable to analytical solution is the single-server FIFO system with Poisson arrivals and exponentially distributed customer service times. When in the system, customers are assumed to be patient, that is, they do not leave prematurely. The system is assumed to have an unlimited holding capacity: There is no upper limit on the number of customers that can be in the waiting line. The *state of the system* is described by the random variable

X representing the number of customers in the system at any given time, including those that are being served. Any reference book on queuing theory (e.g., [D.3]) may be consulted for a mathematical proof that the steady-state conditions of the above system when the mean arrival rate (λ arrivals per unit time) is less than the mean service rate (μ items served per unit time), X is distributed according to the following function:

$$f(x) = P[X = x] = r^x (1 - r), \qquad x = 0, 1, 2, \ldots \qquad \text{(D.3.1)}$$

where

$$r = \frac{\lambda}{\mu}$$

The expected value, that is, the average number of customers in the system at any time, is

$$E[X] = \frac{r}{1 - r} \qquad \text{(D.3.2)}$$

Other useful measures of performance include the following. The average number of customers in the waiting line (*queue length, L_q*) is

$$E[L_q] = \frac{r^2}{1 - r} \qquad \text{(D.3.3)}$$

The expected time each customer spends in the system and in the queue are calculated, respectively, by dividing the last two equations by λ. Thus

$$E[T] = \frac{1}{\mu - \lambda} \qquad \text{(D.3.4)}$$

and

$$E[T_q] = \frac{\lambda}{\mu(\mu - \lambda)} \qquad \text{(D.3.5)}$$

Example D.11

Bank customers arrive at a single drive-in window at an average rate of 15 veh/hr. On the average, the customers need 3 min each to transact their business. Given that the arrival pattern is described by the Poisson distribution and that the departure time is exponentially distributed, calculate the following:

(a) The percent of time that the bank teller will be idle.
(b) The probability that five customers will be in the system.
(c) The average number of customers in the system.
(d) The average queue length.
(e) The average time each customer spends in the system.

Solution   The average arrival rate is 15 customers per hour, the average service rate is $60/3 = 20$ customers per hour and $r = 0.75$. Since the service rate of this FIFO system is larger than the arrival rate, the equations just developed apply.

(a) The teller is idle when there are no customers in the system. Hence

$$p(0) = P[X = 0] = (0.75)^0(1 - 0.75) = 0.25$$

or 25% of the time.

(b) The probability that five vehicles will be in the system is given by Eq. D.3.1:

$$p(5) = (0.75)^5(1 - 0.75) = 0.059$$

or 5.9% of the time.

(c) The average number of customers in the system is

$$E[X] = \frac{15}{20 - 15} = 3 \text{ customers}$$

(d) By Eq. D.3.3, the average queue length is

$$E[L_q] = 2.25 \text{ customers}$$

(e) The average time in the system is

$$E[T] = (20 - 15)^{-1} = 0.2 \text{ h, or 12 min}$$

Discussion   The average number of customers in the queue is not equal to the average number of customers in the system less one because when the system is empty (25% of the time in this example), one customer cannot be meaningfully subtracted from zero customers in the system. As explained in Section D.2, the average of a discrete distribution need not coincide with an outcome. Thus an average queue length of 2.25 customers is meaningful as a long-term average.

D.3.3 Multiserver FIFO Systems

A more complex queuing system is a FIFO system with N identical service counters in parallel. The average service rate *per counter* is μ and the remaining variables are defined as before. In this case, the distribution of X is as follows.

For $x = 0$:

$$p(0) = \left[\left(\sum_{x=0}^{N-1} \frac{r^x}{x!} \right) + \frac{r^N}{(N - 1)! \, (N - r)} \right]^{-1} \qquad \text{(D.3.6a)}$$

For $1 \leq x \leq N$:

$$p(x) = \frac{r^x}{x!} p(0) \qquad \text{(D.3.6b)}$$

For $x > N$:

$$p(x) = \frac{r^x}{N! \, N^{x-N}} \, p(0) \tag{D.3.6c}$$

The average number of customers in the system is

$$E[X] = r + \left[\frac{r^{N+1}}{(N-1)! \, (N-r)^2} \right] p(0) \tag{D.3.7}$$

The average queue length is

$$E[L_q] = \left[\frac{r^{N+1}}{(N-1)! \, (N-r)^2} \right] p(0) \tag{D.3.8}$$

The expected time in the system is

$$E[T] = \frac{E[X]}{\lambda} \tag{D.3.9}$$

Finally, the expected time in the queue is

$$E[T_q] = \frac{E[L_q]}{\lambda} \tag{D.3.10}$$

Example D.12

Solve Example D.11 again, assuming that an identical service counter is added in parallel to the existing one.

Solution The new arrangement is also a FIFO system but one that provides two service counters (i.e., $N = 2$). This means that customers line up in single file and up to two customers can be served simultaneously. The ratio of the arrival to the service rate of a single counter is $r = 0.75$, as before.

(a) The percent of time that *both* tellers are idle is given by Eq. D.3.6a:

$$p(0) = \left[\left(\frac{0.75^0}{0!} + \frac{0.75^1}{1!} \right) + \frac{0.75^2}{1! \, (2 - 0.75)} \right]^{-1}$$

$$= 0.455 \text{ or } 45.5\% \text{ of the time}$$

The percent of the time that only one of the two tellers is idle is given by the probability that only one customer is in the system. By Eq. D.3.6b:

$$p(1) = \frac{0.75}{2!} \, (0.455) = 0.171 \quad \text{or} \quad 17.1\% \text{ of the time}$$

Thus $45.5 + 17.1 = 62.6\%$ of the time either one or both of the tellers are idle.

(b) The probability that five customers are in the system is given by Eq. D.3.6c:

$$p(5) = \frac{0.75^5}{2! \, 2^{(5-2)}} \, (0.455) = 0.007 \quad \text{or} \quad 0.7\% \text{ of the time}$$

(c) Equation D.3.7 gives the average number of customers in the system:

$$E[X] = 0.75 + \left[\frac{0.75^3}{1! \, (2 - 0.75)^2}\right](0.455) = 0.873 \text{ customers}$$

(d) According to Eq. D.3.7 and D.3.8, the relationship between the average queue length and the average number of customers in the system is

$$E[L_q] = E[X] - r$$

Hence

$$E[L_q] = 0.873 - 0.75 = 0.123 \text{ customer}$$

(e) By Eq. D.3.9, the average time each customer spends in the system is

$$E[T] = \frac{0.873}{15} = 0.058 \text{ h} \quad \text{or} \quad 3.49 \text{ min}$$

Discussion   The new arrangement greatly reduces the queue length from 2.25 to 0.123 customers and the average waiting time from 12 to 3.49 min, but at the expense of having either one or both of the tellers idle 62.6% of the time as compared to 25% of the time for the single-server situation of Example D.11. Thus there exists a trade-off between the customers' convenience and the cost of running the system. The equations governing the two simple queuing systems just examined clearly show that the mathematical complexity of queuing models increases rapidly. In fact, satisfactory analytical models are unavailable for many problems, especially for those that involve priority scheduling. The next section discusses the elements of digital computer simulation, a numerical technique that can be applied to the investigation and design of complex systems, including queuing systems.

D.4 COMPUTER SIMULATION

D.4.1 Introduction

The study of complex systems that cannot be sufficiently simplified to be amenable to analytical solution requires alternative methods, the use of simulation models being one possibility. A successful simulation model is an abstraction of a real system that retains the system's essential aspects. The model can be used either to enhance the understanding of how the system works or to investigate the potential effects of proposed modifications to the system. Being an abstraction of a real system, a model cannot be identical to it in all respects. Consequently, a model is employed when direct experimentation with a real system is impossible, too costly, or unsafe. To be useful, any model of a system must realistically represent the system. Although more involved, the steps of model calibration and validation (see Appendix C) are very important, but a detailed discussion of these topics is beyond the scope of this book.

Simulation models can be either deterministic or probabilistic. In addition, simulation models can be either *physical* or *mathematical*. Vehicle crash tests using anthropomorphic dummies are examples of physical models. A model of the Mississippi River system used by the U.S. Corps of Engineers at Vicksburg, Mississippi, is another example. This section is concerned with mathematical models.

D.4.2 Monte Carlo Simulation

Monte Carlo simulation employs an artificial probabilistic experiment (model), the repeated application of which leads to an approximation of the outcome of a system or process. The basic idea of this method is illustrated next.

Consider the now-familiar process of a sequence of independent Bernoulli trials, specifically the tossing of a fair coin. The authors repeated a Bernoulli sequence of 10 tosses four times and obtained the following results:

1.	*T*	*T*	*T*	*H*	*T*	*H*	*H*	*H*	*H*	*T*
2.	*T*	*H*	*H*	*T*	*H*	*H*	*H*	*H*	*H*	*H*
3.	*T*	*H*	*T*	*T*	*T*	*T*	*H*	*H*	*H*	*H*
4.	*T*	*H*	*H*	*T*	*T*	*T*	*T*	*H*	*T*	*T*

Without any knowledge of the underlying process, these four *realizations* of the process may seem to be totally random. Yet it is known in this case that each single outcome listed was the result of a Bernoulli trial with $p = q = 0.5$. In fact, the frequencies of heads and tails in all 40 trials taken together are nearly equal, as would be expected in the long run.

Section D.2 discussed various distributions that may be used to calculate the probability of compound events, such as the probability of getting x successes in n trials and the probability of obtaining the first success on the xth trial. By contrast, a Monte Carlo model of the previous experiment is intended to produce sequences of outcomes (i.e., realizations) that are consistent with the underlying process, in this case a series of independent Bernoulli trials. If desired, the long-run probabilities of various events can be approximated by analyzing the results of the model for a large number of repetitions. To understand how the technique works, consider the cumulative probability distribution of the coin toss experiment shown in Fig. D.4.1. The horizontal axis shows the two possible outcomes of each trial, labeled $X = H$ and $X = T$ for head and tail, respectively. The vertical axis represents the cumulative probability $P[X \leq x]$. The difference in the values of the cumulative function for two adjacent outcomes is the probability of the second outcome. Consequently, the range from 0 to 1 on the vertical axis has been divided according to the probabilities of the outcomes of the experiment under discussion. For a sequence of independent and uniformly distributed numbers in the range between 0 and 1, the long-run frequencies with which these *random numbers* would fall within each segment of the vertical axis would be proportional to the probability of the corresponding outcome.

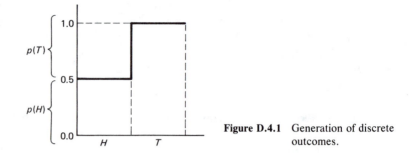

Figure D.4.1   Generation of discrete outcomes.

Example D.13

It is known that 15% of the vehicles approaching an intersection will turn left, 60% will go straight through, and the rest will turn right. Construct the corresponding cumulative distribution and translate the following 10 *random numbers* to outcomes of this process: 0.5954, 0.4501, 0.2590, 0.7081, 0.1405, 0.9740, 0.8676, 0.2729, 0.4474, 0.0166.

Solution   On the cumulative distribution for each trial (i.e., approaching vehicle) shown, the ranges on the vertical axis corresponding to left, right, and through movements are {0.00, 0.15}, {0.15, 0.40}, and {0.40, 1.00}, respectively (see Fig. D.4.2). The first random number (0.5954) falls in the range corresponding to a through movement. Thus the first *simulated* vehicle is going straight ahead. Continuing with the remaining random numbers, the following results are obtained.

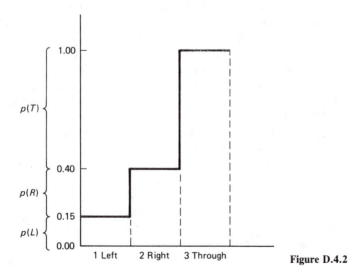

Figure D.4.2

Vehicle number	Movement
1	Through
2	Through
3	Right
4	Through
5	Left
6	Through
7	Through
8	Right
9	Through
10	Left

Discussion   The coding scheme selected to represent the three possible outcomes was arbitrary in this case because there exists no natural ordering of the acts of turning left, turning right, and going straight through. Had a different coding scheme been chosen, the generated sequence of approaching vehicles would not have been identical to the one shown in this example. However, both would be consistent with the underlying distribution.

D.4.3 Simulation of Outcomes of a Continuous Random Variable

A similar method can be used to generate a sequence of outcomes for a continuous random variable. Figure D.4.3 illustrates how a random number in the range of 0.0 to 1.0 can be transformed to a particular outcome x. The transformation entails equating the cumulative distribution to a random number R_N and solving the resulting equation for x. For example, consider the cumulative negative exponential distribution

$$F(x) = 1 - e^{-ax}$$

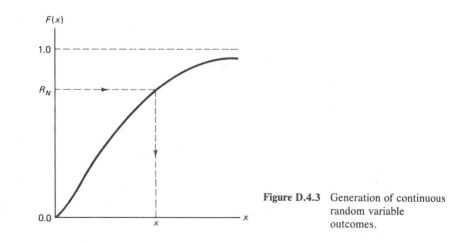

Figure D.4.3   Generation of continuous random variable outcomes.

Equating $F(x)$ to a random number in the range {0.0, 1.0} and solving for x,

$$x = -\frac{1}{a} \ln(1 - R_N) \qquad \text{(D.4.1)}$$

Since R_N is a uniformly distributed random number, its complement $(1 - R_N)$ is also a uniformly distributed random number. For this reason it is simpler to use the following equation:

$$x = -\frac{1}{a} \ln R_N \qquad \text{(D.4.2)}$$

Example D.14

Transform the first five of the random numbers given in Example D.13 to a sequence of vehicular headways, assuming that the average headway is 6.0 s.

Solution   In Section D.2.7, the parameter a of the negative exponential was shown to be the reciprocal of its mean value, in this case $a = \frac{1}{6}$. For the purpose of illustration, both Eqs. D.4.1 and D.4.2 are applied to this problem as follows:

Vehicle	R_N	Headway (s) (Eq. D.4.1)	Headway (s) (Eq. D.4.2)
1	0.5954	5.43	3.11
2	0.4501	3.59	4.79
3	0.2590	1.80	8.11
4	0.7081	7.39	2.07
5	0.1405	0.91	11.78

Discussion   These two sequences of headways conform to the same underlying distribution. Hence, they are two realizations of the same process. If needed, more or longer realizations may be produced by using different lists of random numbers.

D.4.4 Generation of Random Numbers

By definition, true random numbers are independent and uniformly distributed. The independence property means that a sequence of random numbers does not follow any systematic pattern. The fact that they are drawn from a uniform distribution implies that any number in the appropriate range is equally likely to be drawn. Theoretically, the uniform distribution of random numbers is continuous. However, in most practical applications, the numbers are limited to the number of significant figures required by the problem at hand. Many sophisticated methods of random-number generation have been devised. For example, the RAND Corporation has published, for use in scientific applications, a sequence of 1 million random digits that were generated by periodically sampling a random electronic noise [D.4].

A simple method for obtaining random digits is the *top hat method*: Ten cards, each bearing one of the ten numbers from 0 to 9, are thoroughly mixed in a receptacle. A card is drawn, its number is recorded, and the card is placed back in the receptacle; the cards are again mixed in preparation for the drawing of the next number. If random numbers within the range from 0 to 1 are desired with, say, five significant figures, the digits drawn from the hat are grouped in ordered sets of five and the decimal point is placed in front of each group.

Although the top hat method can produce a series of as many true random numbers as desired, it is a time-consuming and inefficient method, especially if the random numbers are required at the speed that a computer processes the instructions constituting a simulation program. For this reason, it is necessary to devise rapid generation methods based on carefully developed computer algorithms [D.5–D.8]. It should be noted that the numbers generated in this way are not truly random, since they obey the rules or pattern of the routine used in their generation. For this reason, they are referred to as *pseudorandom* numbers. Nevertheless, the better of the pseudorandom generators are considered to be adequate for most engineering applications.

The *middle-square method* suggested by von Newmann is one of the simplest pseudorandom number generators available. An initial number (the *seed*) is squared and the middle digits of the result are taken to represent the first pseudorandom number, which becomes the seed for the generation of the next number. The sequence of random numbers given in Example D.13 was generated by this method, using the number 3549 as the seed. Note that the square of the seed is equal to 12595401, of which the middle part constitutes the four digits given as the first random number. A problem with this method is that it eventually tends to degenerate to zeros.

D.4.5 The Simulation Model

The generation of random deviates by the Monte Carlo method is only a part of a larger simulation model. The heart of the model consists of a computer program that imitates the behavior of the system over time. For example, suppose that it is desired to simulate a signalized intersection. The intersection (system) involves (1) certain *entities* (e.g., arriving vehicles, the signal, or the traffic lanes provided), each having several essential *attributes* (e.g., the arrival time and movement desire of a vehicle, the cycle pattern of the signal, the permitted use of lanes); and (2) a set of rules that govern the *interactions* between entities (e.g., left-turning vehicles must use an exclusive lane, or left-turning vehicles must wait for adequate gaps in the opposing traffic). In this example, the headways between vehicular arrivals may be simulated by the method of Example D.14 for each intersection approach, and the turning desire of each arriving vehicle may be simulated by the method of Example D.13. The simulation program would then process these arrivals through the intersection according to the rules of interaction and collect data on the *measures of performance* (mop's) that are relevant to the problem at hand, such as vehicular delays or queue lengths. To simulate the passage of time, the model establishes a *simulation clock*, which is advanced periodically as the system changes from one *state* to another. The following two examples illustrate two ways by which the simulation clock may be advanced. The first (*interval-oriented simulation*) updates the clock by a constant time interval, and the second (*event-oriented simulation*) advances the clock to the next event that triggers a change in the system's state.

Example D.15: Interval-Oriented Simulation

Vehicles arrive at a parking garage at an average rate of 30 veh/h. Assuming that the arrival pattern is described by the Poisson distribution and that the arriving vehicles are served by a single attendant at a *constant* rate of one vehicle per 2.5 min, use the random numbers of Example D.13 and D.14 to simulate a sequence of ten 5-minute intervals. Assume that at the start (i.e., clock = 0) the system is empty.

Solution   The state of the system may be described as the number of vehicles in the queue awaiting to be served. The clock is advanced by 5-min intervals, and the model generates the number of arrivals during each interval according to the Poisson distribution (i.e., Eq. D.2.22). A maximum of two vehicles per interval are processed and the (nonnegative) difference between the number of vehicles that arrived and the number of vehicles processed represents the number of vehicles that join the queue at the end of each 5-min interval.

To generate vehicular arrivals, the cumulative Poisson distribution with a mean value of 2.5 vehicles per 5-min period is first calculated as follows:

x	$p(x) = P[X = x]$		$P(x) = P[X \leq x]$
0	0.08		0.08 } $p(0)$
1	0.21		0.29 } $p(1)$
2	0.26		0.55 } $p(2)$
3	0.21		0.76 } $p(3)$
4	0.13		0.89 } $p(4)$
5	0.07		0.96 } $p(5)$
6	0.03	$0.99 \approx$	1.00 } $p(6)$

An upper limit of six vehicles per period was placed on the distribution as a reasonable approximation, and the ranges in the values of the cumulative distribution corresponding to the seven possible outcomes are noted in the last column of the table.

The simulation entails the generation of the number of vehicular arrivals during each 5-min interval and the processing of up to two vehicles (if present) during the same interval to determine the queue length at the end of the interval. The first random number in the given sequence (i.e., 0.5954; Example D.13) translates to three arrivals during the first 5-min interval because

$$0.55 \leqslant 0.5954 \leqslant 0.76$$

Since two of these arrivals can be served during the interval, a queue consisting of one vehicle will remain at the end of the interval. The following table summarizes the results obtained for the ten consecutive 5-min intervals:

Interval	Arrivals	Departures	Queue length
1	3	2	1
2	2	2	1
3	1	2	0
4	3	2	1
5	1	2	0
6	6	2	4
7	4	2	6
8	1	2	5
9	2	2	5
10	0	2	3

Discussion This admittedly simple simulation illustrates the interval scanning method of advancing the clock. A total of 23 vehicular arrivals were simulated for the first 50 min. Twenty of these vehicles were served, leaving 3 vehicles in the waiting line at the end of the tenth period. In this particular example, the parking-lot attendant was busy all the time, since there were always vehicles awaiting service. For simplicity, the service time was assumed to be constant. A more realistic model would allow some variability in the number of vehicles that can be served during any 5-min interval. Moreover, the model can be further extended to allow for multiple service channels and service priorities. More complex models necessitate the preparation of a computer program describing the operation of the subject system. Many simulation models have been developed for use in specific contexts including traffic situations (e.g., [D.9, D.10]). Returning to Example D.15, it should be noted that a limitation of interval-oriented simulation models is the fact that they are oblivious to the detailed behavior of the system *within* each interval. For example, 3 vehicles were simulated to arrive during the first 5-min interval, but the precise arrival times of these vehicles within the interval are not known. Consequently, certain system characteristics (e.g., the average delay per vehicle) can only be approximated by this model.

Example D.16: Event-Oriented Simulation

Prepare an event-oriented model of the system described in the previous example and apply this model to simulate the first 11 vehicles that enter the system, assuming that the first vehicle arrives at time zero. The model should be able to calculate the time that each vehicle spends in the waiting line and the percent of time that the attendant is idle. If needed, use the same sequence of random numbers as before.

Solution The time that a vehicle spends in the queue is given by the time interval from the moment it arrives to the moment it begins to be served. The latter coincides with the moment when the servicing of the vehicle ahead has been completed. The arrival time of a vehicle can be computed by adding the headway between the previous arrival and the subject vehicle to the arrival time of the leader. Since the arrival pattern is described by the Poisson distribution, the interarrival times (i.e., headways) are described by the negative exponential (Eq. D.2.32). They can be generated by applying the procedure of Example D.14 to transform a sequence of random numbers to a sequence of headways. Since, in this case, the arrival rate is 30 veh/h, the average headway is 2 min.

The first vehicle is assumed to arrive at time zero. It will receive the attention of the attendant immediately. Hence, it will spend no time in the waiting line. Given a constant service time of 2.5 min, the first vehicle will be processed at clock time $0 + 2.5 = 2.5$ min and the attendant will be busy during this time. The headway between the first and the second vehicles can be generated by Eq. D.4.2 using the first random number (0.5954). Thus

$$x = -2.0 \ln(0.5954) = 1.04 \text{ min}$$

The second vehicle will arrive 1.04 min after the first, which arrived at time zero. But the servicing of the first vehicle will not be finished until clock time 2.5 min. Hence, the second vehicle must wait in line until then, for a total of $2.5 - 1.04 = 1.46$ min. The following table summarizes the results of the simulation for the first 11 vehicles to enter the system.

Vehicle number	Headway (min)	Arrival time	Service start	Delay (min)	Service finish	Idle time
1	—	0.00	0.00	0.00	2.50	0.00
2	1.04	1.04	2.50	1.46	5.00	0.00
3	1.60	2.64	5.00	2.36	7.50	0.00
4	2.70	5.34	7.50	2.16	10.00	0.00
5	0.69	6.03	10.00	3.97	12.50	0.00
6	3.93	9.96	12.50	2.54	15.00	0.00
7	0.05	10.01	15.00	4.99	17.50	0.00
8	0.28	10.29	17.50	7.21	20.00	0.00
9	2.60	12.89	20.00	7.11	22.50	0.00
10	1.61	14.50	22.50	8.00	25.00	0.00
11	8.20	22.70	25.00	2.30	27.50	0.00

Discussion   This simulation model differs from that of the previous example in that it advanced the clock to the next significant occurrence, that is, the arrival time, the start of servicing, or the finish of servicing of each vehicle. The clock began at time zero when the first vehicle arrived. The next event was the arrival of the second vehicle 1.04 min later. This was followed by the finish of the servicing of the first vehicle at clock = 2.50 min. The next event was the arrival of the third vehicle at clock = 2.70 min, and so forth. A total of 11 vehicles were examined after ten iterations of the model. By contrast, the first ten iterations of the alternative model of Example D.15 covered 23 vehicles. However, that model was not as detailed as the present model. This comparison stresses an important point: Often, the analyst has a choice between alternative models of the same system. The choice of model involves a balance between the degree of detail required and the available resources.

Consistent with the results of the interval-oriented model of Example D.15 are the results of the event-oriented model of the present example, which show that the attendant was continuously busy. The average time that each vehicle spent in the waiting line can be computed by dividing the sum of the delays shown in Column 5 of the given table by the total number of vehicles, to obtain $42.10/11 = 3.83$ min/ veh. A total of 11 vehicles arrived during the 22.70 min of simulated time. This translates to 29.07 veh/h, which is close to the stipulated 30 veh/h. Considering the limited number of vehicles simulated, such close agreement is surprising. Normally, larger deviations between the two values would be tolerated for such a small sample size.

D.5 SUMMARY

In this appendix we introduced the basic concepts and definitions of the theory of probability. The probability distributions associated with several discrete and continuous random variables were then presented, and the applications of these distributions to traffic phenomena were illustrated by some simple examples. Queuing, or waiting-line, models were presented next, and the analytical solutions to FIFO systems with Poisson arrivals and negative exponential service times were presented. Finally, the basic elements of the powerful numerical technique of computer simulation were presented. These included the generation of random and pseudorandom numbers, the transformation of these numbers to probable outcomes of underlying processes described by cumulative probability distributions, and the use of these realizations to follow the changes in the state of the simulated system to aid in assessing its likely behavior in terms of applicable measures of performance via simulation models.

D.6 EXERCISES

1. The outcome of an experiment is the sum obtained by casting two dice. Enumerate the simple outcomes of the experiment and calculate each probability.
   (a) Each simple outcome
   (b) An even outcome
   (c) An odd outcome greater than 6
   (d) An outcome that is either odd or greater than 4
   (e) An outcome that is less than 5 but greater than 2

2. For the experiment of Exercise 1, determine whether the following two events are (a) mutually exclusive and (b) independent.

   A: the outcome is less than 8

   B: the outcome is greater than 5

3. For the experiment of Exercise 1, determine if the following two events are (a) mutually exclusive and (b) independent:

   A: {2,3,4,5,6,10}

   B: {2,4,6,8,9,10,11,12}

4. Intersection A is located downstream of intersection B. A traffic engineer observed that during the morning peak period, the probability that intersection A is congested is 0.30. There is a 0.50 probability of A being congested given the knowledge that B is congested. On the other hand, the probability of B being congested given the knowledge that A is congested is 0.90. Calculate the probability that (a) B is congested during the peak period and (b) at least one of the two intersections is congested.

5. There are only two traffic-control signals in downtown Kahului, Maui. The *independent* probabilities that each of the signals will malfunction on a given day are 0.05 and 0.04, respectively. System failure is defined by the condition that at least one signal is out. Calculate the probability that the system will fail on any particular day.

6. A study has shown that in cars with a driver and a passenger, the probability that the driver wears a seat belt is 0.35 and the probability that the passenger buckles up is 0.50. If 80% of the passengers of drivers that buckle up do the same, calculate (a) the probability that both the driver *and* the passenger of a car are wearing seat belts and (b) the probability that a particular driver is wearing a seat belt given the knowledge that the passenger is buckled up.

7. The probability that downtown parking garage A is not full is 0.20 and the probability that garage B is full is 0.50. Knowing that at least one of the two garages is full 90% of the time, calculate the probability that a shopper will find parking in garage B given that garage A is full.

8. Prove Bayes' theorem, which states that

$$P[A \mid B] = \frac{P[B \mid A] \, P[A]}{P[B]}$$

9. Two alternative highway routes connect a suburb with a downtown area. Define event A: highway 1 is jammed during the peak period, and event B: highway 2 is jammed during the peak period. If $P[A]$ is 0.70, $P[B]$ is 0.60, and $P[B \mid A]$ is 0.50, calculate and interpret $P[A \cap B]$, $P[A \cup B]$, and $P[A \mid B]$.

10. Draw the probability mass function of the experiment described in Exercise 1 and compute its mean and its variance. Also, draw the cumulative distribution.

11. Decide which of the following functions can possibly be discrete probability distributions for the specified sample space.

(a)	X	1	2	3	4	5	6
	$p(x)$	0.2	0.3	0.2	0.2	0.1	0.1

(b)	X	1	2	3	4	5	6
	$p(x)$	0.5	0.4	0.3	0.1	-0.4	0.1
(c)	X	1	2	3	4	5	6
	$p(x)$	0.4	0.2	0.1	0.1	0.1	0.1

12. At a particular intersection approach, 30% of the left-turning vehicles fail to signal their intentions to turn. Assuming independence, calculate each probability.
   (a) Three vehicles in a row will fail to signal.
   (b) Three vehicles in a row will signal.
   (c) The second vehicle will not signal.
   (d) The second vehicle to signal will be the fifth vehicle observed.
   (e) Two vehicles in five will fail to signal.
   (f) The first vehicle to signal will be the fourth vehicle observed.
   (g) No more than two vehicles in five will signal.

13. Draw the probability function and the cumulative distribution for the Poisson case described in Example D.8.

14. Vehicles arrive at an isolated intersection according to the Poisson distribution. Given that the mean arrival rate is 500 veh/h, calculate (a) the probability that zero vehicles will arrive during a 10-s interval and (b) the probability that at least five vehicles will arrive during a 10-s interval.

15. Students arrive at a lecture room at the rate of 15 per minute according to the Poisson distribution. Calculate the probability of (a) *exactly* three arrivals in 20 s, (b) *no more than* three arrivals in 20 s, and (c) *at least* three arrivals in 20 s.

16. The average concentration of vehicles on a highway section is 70 veh/mi. Given that the concentration is Poisson distributed, calculate the probability of finding (a) exactly 10 vehicles and (b) five or more vehicles on any particular tenth of a mile.

17. Which of the following continuous functions can serve as probability distributions for the specified range of outcomes?
   (a) $f(x) = -1.0 + 0.2x, \ 0 \leqslant x \leqslant 10.0$
   (b) $f(x) = x(1.0 - 2.0x), \ 0 \leqslant x \leqslant 0.5$
   (c) $f(x) = 24.0x(1.0 - 2.0x), \ 0 \leqslant x \leqslant 0.5$

18. Prove that Eq. D.2.31 is correct.

19. Airplanes arrive at an airport area at an average rate of six per hour. Assuming that the arrival pattern is Poisson distributed, calculate the probability that the headway between two successive arrivals will be greater than 20 min.

20. The airport control tower (see Exercise 19) processes airplanes in their order of arrival. Assuming that the service time is negative exponential and that the service rate is 10 landings per hour, calculate (a) the average number of airplanes in the system (i.e., being served and stacked), (b) the average number of airplanes awaiting clearance to land, (c) the average time spent in the system, and (d) the average time an airplane is in the queue.

21. A turnpike toll area contains four toll booths arranged in parallel. The arriving vehicles conform to the Poisson distribution, with an average headway of 12 s. Assuming that the average service time is 5 s, that the service time is negative exponential, and that the queue discipline is FIFO, find the average queue length and the expected time in the system if (a) two of the booths are in operation and (b) only one booth is open.

22. Use the random numbers provided in Example D.13 to simulate, in two different ways, five tosses of two dice (see Exercise 1). Discuss your results.
23. A wheel of fortune is divided into 10 equal sectors numbered from 1 to 10. Devise a Monte Carlo simulation of this roulette and produce the result of (a) five spins for which each outcome is a digit from 1 to 10 and (b) 10 spins, assuming that the outcome is given by the following three events:

$$A: x < 3$$
$$B: 3 \leqslant x \leqslant 7$$
$$C: x > 7$$

24. Extend the simulation model of Example D.15 to allow for exponentially distributed service time with an *average* of 2.5 min.
25. Expand Example D.16 to allow for two service channels and a FIFO queue discipline.
26. Extend Example D.16 to allow for two service lines and a queue discipline stating that the next arrival chooses the shorter of the two lines 80% of the time. When the two queues are equal, the choice of line is made on a 50/50 basis.
27. Construct a simulation model of Exercise 20 incorporating the following modifications: (a) commercial flights constitute 30% of the arrivals and are given priority over general aviation flights, (b) the average service times for commercial and general aviation operations are 8 min and 6 min, respectively, and (c) your model should include as many measures of performance as practicable.
28. Computerize any of Exercises 22 through 27.

D.7 REFERENCES

D.1 BENJAMIN, JACK R., and C. ALLIN CORNELL, *Probability Statistics and Decision for Civil Engineers*, McGraw-Hill, New York, 1970.

D.2 MORSE, PHILIP M., *Queues, Inventory and Maintenance*, Wiley, New York, 1958.

D.3 GERLOUGH, DANIEL L., and MATTHEW J. HUBER, *Traffic Flow Theory: A Monograph*, Special Report 165, Transportation Research Board, National Research Council, Washington, D.C., 1975.

D.4 RAND CORPORATION, *A Million Random Digits with 100,000 Normal Deviates*, Free Press, New York, 1955.

D.5 GALLER, BERNARD A., *The Language of Computers*, McGraw-Hill, New York, 1962.

D.6 GORDON, GEOFFREY, *System Simulation*, 2nd ed., Prentice Hall, Englewood Cliffs, N.J., 1978.

D.7 GRAYBEAL, WAYNE, and UDO W. POOCH, *Simulation: Principles and Methods*, Winthrop Publishers, Cambridge, Mass., 1980.

D.8 JANNSON, BIRGER, *Random Number Generators*, Almqvist & Wiksell, Stockholm, 1966.

D.9 PAPACOSTAS, C. S., "Capacity Characteristics of Downtown Bus Streets," *Transportation Quarterly*, 36, 4 (1982): 617–630.

D.10 TRANSPORTATION RESEARCH BOARD, *The Application of Traffic Simulation Models*, Special Report 194, National Research Council, Washington, D.C., 1981.

Index

637